TAKING SIDES

Clashing Views in

Crime and Criminology

TENTH EDITION, EXPANDED

TAKING SIDES

Clashing Views in
Crime and Criminology

TENTH EDITION, EXPANDED

Selected, Edited, and with Introductions by

Thomas J. Hickey
State University of New York
(SUNY Cobleskill)

Thomas Devaney
Hartwick College

Mc Graw Hill

Connect
Learn
Succeed™

TAKING SIDES: CLASHING VIEWS IN CRIME AND CRIMINOLOGY, TENTH EDITION, EXPANDED

Published by McGraw-Hill, a business unit of The McGraw-Hill Companies, Inc., 1221 Avenue of the Americas, New York, NY 10020. Copyright © 2013 by The McGraw-Hill Companies, Inc. All rights reserved. Printed in the United States of America. Previous edition(s) © 2012, 2010, and 2008. No part of this publication may be reproduced or distributed in any form or by any means, or stored in a database or retrieval system, without the prior written consent of The McGraw-Hill Companies, Inc., including, but not limited to, in any network or other electronic storage or transmission, or broadcast for distance learning.

Some ancillaries, including electronic and print components, may not be available to customers outside the United States.

Taking Sides® is a registered trademark of the McGraw-Hill Companies, Inc.
Taking Sides is published by the **Contemporary Learning Series** group within the McGraw-Hill Higher Education division.

1 2 3 4 5 6 7 8 9 0 DOC/DOC 1 0 9 8 7 6 5 4 3 2

MHID: 0-07-805037-5
ISBN: 978-0-07-805037-4
ISSN: 1098-5379 (print)

Managing Editor: *Larry Loeppke*
Marketing Director: *Adam Kloza*
Marketing Manager: *Nathan Edwards*
Senior Developmental Editor: *Jade Benedict*
Lead Project Manager: *Jane Mohr*
Buyer: *Jennifer Pickel*
Cover Designer: *Studio Montage, St. Louis, MO.*
Cover Image: © *Digital Vision/Getty Images/RF*
Content Licensing Specialist: *Rita Hingtgen*
Media Project Manager: *Sridevi Palani*

Compositor: MPS Limited

www.mhhe.com

Editors/Academic Advisory Board

Members of the Academic Advisory Board are instrumental in the final selection of articles for each edition of TAKING SIDES. Their review of articles for content, level, and appropriateness provides critical direction to the editors and staff. We think that you will find their careful consideration well reflected in this volume.

TAKING SIDES: Clashing Views in CRIME AND CRIMINOLOGY

Tenth Edition, Expanded

EDITORS

Thomas J. Hickey
State University of New York (SUNY Cobleskill)

Thomas Devaney
Hartwick College

ACADEMIC ADVISORY BOARD MEMBERS

Preface

But the peculiar evil of silencing the expression of an opinion is that it is robbing the human race, posterity as well as the existing genera- tion—those who dissent from the opinion, still more than those who hold it. If the opinion is right, they are deprived of the opportunity of exchanging error for truth; if wrong, they lose, what is almost as great a benefit, the clearer perception and livelier impression of truth pro- duced by its collision with error.

(John Stuart Mill, On Liberty, 1859)

Discussion and debate are essential components of the learning process. To have confidence in our viewpoints, we must expose them to others and learn from their ideas in a constant process of reformulation and refinement. As J. S. Mill teaches, only rarely does any point of view present a complete version of the truth; however, we move closer to the truth when we are willing to exchange our opinions with others, defend our positions, and refine our ideas by what we learn from an intellectual opponent.

This book presents students and teachers with an opportunity to exchange viewpoints by focusing on a series of controversial issues in crime and criminology. Few issues in modern society generate more substantial disa- greement in our morning newspapers or around the dinner table. They focus on an important aspect of modern life and were selected in an effort to engage students. Hopefully, they will also generate classroom discussion and debate and provide a vehicle for interactive learning.

Many of the topics presented in this volume are hotly contested. Few reflective people will find themselves adopting truly neutral positions on these issues, and there may be a tendency to embrace one side of a debate without fully considering the opposing arguments. As you read these materials, try to resist that temptation and keep an open mind. For example, if you are a death penalty advocate, think about how you would develop an argument against capital punishment. Even though such an exercise may not change your views, it will provide you with greater insight into the capital punishment debate.

Organization of the book This book considers 20 issues in crime and crimi- nology and includes 40 articles presented in a pro and con format. The *Intro- duction* to each issue presents a synopsis and sets the stage for the *Yes* and *No* debate between the authors. All issues conclude with a *Postscript* that considers some of the more important points in the debate and includes up-to-date sug- gestions for further reading on the topics. In addition, the *Internet References* that accompanies each unit provides a list of Internet site addresses (URLs) that should prove informative. At the back of the book is a list of the *Contribu- tors to This Volume,* which provides a short biographical sketch of each contrib- uting author.

Changes to this edition This edition of *Taking Sides* continues the tradition of providing a detailed analysis of contemporary issues in Crime and Criminology. Because this field changes so rapidly, however, it is important to reevaluate prior editions to determine if there are issues that have taken on a greater importance. Thus, considerable changes have been made, including a new unit titled "The U.S. Supreme Court, Crime, and the Justice System." There are four new issues: *Does the U.S. Constitution Protect the Right to Possess a Firearm?* (Issue 17); *Is the Death Penalty an Unconstitutional Punishment for Juvenile Offenders?* (Issue 18); *Does Confining Sex Offenders Indefinitely in Mental Hospitals After They Have Served Their Prison Sentences Violate the Constitution?* (Issue 19); *Does an Imprisoned Individual Have a Constitutional Right to Access the State's Evidence for DNA Testing?* (Issue 20).

A word to the instructor An *Instructor's Manual with Test Questions* (multiple-choice and essay) is available from the publisher for instructors using *Taking Sides* in their courses. A guidebook, *Using Taking Sides in the Classroom,* which considers methods and techniques for integrating the pro-con format into a classroom setting, is available as well. An online version of *Using Taking Sides in the Classroom* and a correspondence service for adopters can be found at http://www.mhhe.com/takingsides.

Acknowledgments I would like to thank several of my friends and colleagues for their help and support: Sue Titus Reid, Rolando del Carmen, Richard Ayre, Alisa Smith, John Matthews, Trey Williams, Marilyn McShane, and Alex Thomas.

Thomas J. Hickey
SUNY

This book is dedicated to professor Richard Ayre, of the University of Maine, Presque Isle, a great friend and colleague and one of the finest educators I have ever met.

Contents In Brief

Contents

Attorney Andrew A. Moher argues that judicially sanctioned torture of terrorists is appropriate for the purpose of preventing a greater evil. He further contends a judicially monitored system in the United States would be far superior to the current policy of practicing torture "under the radar screen" in other countries. Elisa Massimino believes that the use of torture is immoral and counterproductive for the United States. She asserts that if the United States wishes to rely on the protections of the Geneva Conventions, then it must comply with its provisions prohibiting the torture of prisoners.

Jared Taylor, president of the New Century Foundation, and Glayde Whitney argue that the disparity in crimes committed by members of different races justifies racial profiling by the police. Professor Michael J. Lynch, however, argues that a proper analysis of the crime data does not support Taylor and Whitney's conclusions. He finds racial profiling to be objectionable from a legal and moral perspective as well.

Law professor Barry C. Feld contends that creating a separate juvenile court system has resulted in unanticipated negative consequences for America's children and for justice. Vincent Schiraldi, director of the Justice Policy Institute, and researcher Jason Ziedenberg maintain that moving thousands of kids into adult courts is unnecessary, harmful, and racist.

Wayne H. Calabrese, vice president of the Wackenhut Corporation, argues that the privatization of U.S. prisons saves money and provides quality services. Jeff Sinden, managing editor of *Human Rights Tribune*, contends that the private prison industry has failed to achieve substantial cost savings and that there have been systemic human rights abuses in for-profit correctional institutions.

David Von Drehle, a writer and the arts editor for *The Washington Post,* examines specific capital punishment cases and data and concludes that capital punishment is a bad social policy. Ernest van den Haag, a professor of jurisprudence and public policy (now retired), maintains that the death penalty is just retribution for heinous crime.

Attorney Lawrence Wright argues that while castration may not be an ideal solution, if we treat it as therapy rather than punishment, as help instead of revenge, and if we view offenders as troubled victims, not monsters, then perhaps castration will become an accepted and humane option for sex offender treatment. Attorney Kari A. Vanderzyl asserts that castration should be rejected as an unacceptable, ineffective, and unconstitutional alternative to imprisonment for sex offenders.

Professor Franklin E. Zimring argues that there is a strong relationship between gun use and the death rate from violent crime and that handgun use increases the death rate from violence by a factor of three to five. Professor Lance K. Stell asserts that strict gun control institutionalizes the natural predatory advantages of larger, stronger, violence-prone persons and increases the risks of violent victimization for less well-off, law-abiding citizens.

George L. Kelling, a professor in the School of Criminal Justice at Rutgers University, and William J. Bratton, former New York City Police Department commissioner, strongly defend Kelling's formulation of zero tolerance/broken windows theory and Bratton's implementation of Kelling's ideas. Judith A. Greene, senior fellow of the Institute on Criminal Justice of the University of Minnesota Law School, compares New York's policing style with San Diego's community policing model and argues that the latter is as effective and less costly.

Ethan A. Nadelmann, the founder and director of the Drug Policy Alliance, contends that contemporary marijuana laws are unique among American criminal laws because no other law is both enforced so widely and yet deemed unnecessary by such a substantial portion of the public. Enforcing marijuana laws also wastes tens of billions of taxpayer dollars annually. John P. Walters, director of the Office of National Drug Control Policy, argues that marijuana does the most social harm of any illegal drug.

Paul Butler, an associate professor at the George Washington University Law School, argues that black jurors should acquit black defendants of certain crimes to make up for inequities in the criminal justice system. Randall Kennedy, a professor at the Harvard Law School, finds it tragic that black jurors would pronounce a murderer "not guilty" just to send a message to white people.

Justice Antonin E. Scalia, writing for the U.S. Supreme Court in *District of Columbia v. Heller* (2008), held that a District of Columbia law making it a crime to carry an unregistered handgun and prohibiting the registration of handguns, but that authorizes the police chief to issue 1-year licenses, and requires residents to keep lawfully owned handguns unloaded and dissembled or bound by a trigger lock or similar device, violates the Second Amendment. Justice John Paul Stevens, dissenting in *District of Columbia v. Heller* (2008), asserted that neither the text of the Second Amendment nor the arguments advanced by its proponents evidenced the slightest interest in limiting any legislature's authority to regulate private civilian uses of firearms. Moreover, there is no indication that the Framers intended to enshrine the common-law right of self-defense in the Constitution.

Associate Justice Anthony M. Kennedy, writing for the Court, asserts that the death penalty is an unacceptable punishment for juveniles who commit murder because it constitutes cruel and unusual punishment in violation of the Eighth and Fourteenth Amendments. Associate Justice Antonin E. Scalia, dissenting in the same case, argues that there is no clear social consensus that would favor abolishing the death penalty in these cases and that in doing so, the Court's majority is usurping the powers of state legislatures.

Associate Justice Stephen Breyer asserts that if a state's law attempts to inflict additional punishment on an offender after he has served a prison sentence, it will violate the federal Constitution. Associate Justice Clarence Thomas, writing for the Court, contends that postimprisonment civil confinement laws do not violate the Constitution.

Justice John Paul Stevens, in a dissenting opinion in *District Attorney's Office for the Third Judicial District v. Osborne* (2009), contends that a fundamental responsibility to ensure that "justice" has been served requires a state to provide a defendant with postconviction access to DNA evidence. Because it could conclusively establish whether an accused had committed the crime in the first place, this right should be protected by the Fourteenth Amendment's Due Process Clause. Chief Justice John Roberts, writing for the majority, in *District Attorney's Office for the Third Judicial District v. Osborne* (2009), held that the U.S. Constitution's Due Process Clause provides no right to postconviction access to DNA evidence because it would take the development of rules and procedures in criminal cases out of the hands of state legislatures and courts.

Attorney Barry Shrum argues that downloading music illegally from the Internet is wrong morally and should be considered a crime because it fails to pay creative individuals for their intellectual property. Moreover, because approximately 95 percent of the music downloaded from the Internet is done so illegally, the problem is a very compelling one. Noted recording artist and songwriter Janis Ian, in contrast, believes that there is no evidence to support the proposition that material available for free online downloading is harming anyone, especially the artists who produce it. In fact, free downloading may actually benefit the majority of artists because it allows them potentially to reach millions of new listeners, who may later purchase CDs, and attend their live concerts.

U.S. Supreme Court Associate Justice Anthony M. Kennedy asserts that police officers and correctional officials must be permitted to develop reasonable search policies to detect and deter the possession of contraband within their facilities. Moreover, exempting people arrested for minor offenses from such searches may put the police at greater risk and result in more contraband being brought into jails. Associate Justice Stephen Breyer, in contrast, believes that because strip searches involve close observation of the private areas of the body, they constitute a serious invasion of personal privacy and may not be justified in cases involving minor offenses.

Correlation Guide

The Taking Sides series presents current issues in a debate-style format designed to stimulate student interest and develop critical thinking skills. Each issue is thoughtfully framed with an issue summary, an issue introduction, and a postscript. The pro and con essays—selected for their liveliness and substance—represent the arguments of leading scholars and commentators in their fields.

Taking Sides: Clashing Views in Crime and Criminology, 10/e, Expanded is an easy-to-use reader that presents issues on important topics such as *capital punishment, juvenile courts, DNA testing,* and *legalization of marijuana.* For more information on Taking Sides and other McGraw-Hill Contemporary Learning Series titles, visit www.mhhe.com/cls.

This convenient guide matches the issues in Taking Sides: Clashing Views in Crime and Criminology, 10/e, Expanded with the corresponding chapters in three of our best-selling McGraw-Hill Criminal Justice and Criminology textbooks by Adler et al., Masters et al., and Bohm/Haley.

Taking Sides: Clashing Views in Crime and Criminology, 10/e, Expanded	Criminal Justice: An Introduction 6/e, by Adler et al.	CJ: Realities and Challenges, 2/e, Masters et al.	Introduction to Criminal Justice 7/e, Bohm and Haley
Issue 1: Is Crime Beneficial to Society?	**Chapter 3:** Explaining Criminal Behavior	**Chapter 3:** Causes of Crime	**Chapter 3:** Explaining Crime
Issue 2: Is Criminal Behavior Determined Biologically?	**Chapter 3:** Explaining Criminal Behavior	**Chapter 3:** Causes of Crime	**Chapter 3:** Explaining Crime
Issue 3: Is a Person's Body Type Clearly Linked to Criminal Behavior?	**Chapter 3:** Explaining Criminal Behavior	**Chapter 3:** Causes of Crime	**Chapter 3:** Explaining Crime
Issue 4: Does the United States have a Right to Torture Suspected Terrorists?	**Chapter 7:** The Rule of Law in Law Enforcement	**Chapter 7:** Legal and Special Issues in Policing	**Chapter 7:** Policing America: Issues and Ethics
Issue 5: Is Racial Profiling an Acceptable Law Enforcement Strategy?	**Chapter 7:** The Rule of Law in Law Enforcement	**Chapter 7:** Legal and Special Issues in Policing	**Chapter 7:** Policing America: Issues and Ethics
Issue 6: Should Juvenile Courts Be Abolished?	**Chapter 15:** Justice for Juveniles and Victims	**Chapter 15:** Juvenile Justice	**Chapter 13:** Juvenile Justice
Issue 7: Is Exposure to Pornography Related to Increased Rates of Rape?	**Chapter 3:** Explaining Criminal Behavior	**Chapter 3:** Causes of Crime	**Chapter 3:** Explaining Crime
Issue 8: Are Supermax (Control Unit) Prisons an Appropriate Way to Punish Hardened Criminals?	**Chapter 13:** Institutional Corrections	**Chapter 12:** Jails and Prisons	**Chapter 10:** Institutional Corrections
Issue 9: Do Three Strikes Sentencing Laws and Other "Get Tough" Approaches Really Work?	**Chapter 11:** Sentencing	**Chapter 10:** Sentencing	**Chapter 9:** Sentencing, Appeals, and the Death Penalty

Taking Sides: Clashing Views in Crime and Criminology, 10/e, Expanded	Criminal Justice: An Introduction 6/e, by Adler et al.	CJ: Realities and Challenges, 2/e, Masters et al.	Introduction to Criminal Justice 7/e, Bohm and Haley
Issue 10: Should Private "For-Profit" Corporations Be Allowed to Run U.S. Prisons?	**Chapter 13:** Institutional Corrections	**Chapter 12:** Jails and Prisons	**Chapter 10:** Institutional Corrections
Issue 11: Is Capital Punishment a Bad Public Policy?	**Chapter 11:** Sentencing	**Chapter 10:** Sentencing	**Chapter 9:** Sentencing, Appeals, and the Death Penalty
Issue 12: Should Serious Sex Offenders Be Castrated?	**Chapter 11:** Sentencing	**Chapter 10:** Sentencing	**Chapter 9:** Sentencing, Appeals, and the Death Penalty
Issue 13: Do Strict Gun Control Laws Reduce the Number of Homicides in the United States?	**Chapter 3:** Explaining Criminal Behavior	**Chapter 3:** Causes of Crime	**Chapter 3:** Explaining Crime
Issue 14: Should the Police Enforce Zero-Tolerance Laws?	**Chapter 7:** The Rule of Law in Law Enforcement	**Chapter 7:** Legal and Special Issues in Policing	**Chapter 7:** Policing America: Issues and Ethics
Issue 15: Should Marijuana Be Legalized?	**Chapter 4:** The Criminal Law	**Chapter 4:** Criminal Law and Defenses	**Chapter 2:** Crime and Its Consequences **Chapter 4:** The Rule of Law
Issue 16: Should Juries Be Able to Disregard the Law and Free "Guilty" Persons in Racially Charged Cases?	**Chapter 10:** Criminal Prosecution and Adjudication	**Chapter 9:** Pretrial and Trial	**Chapter 8:** The Administration of Justice
Issue 17: Does the U.S. Constitution Protect the Right to Possess a Firearm?	**Chapter 4:** The Criminal Law	**Chapter 4:** Criminal Law and Defenses	**Chapter 4:** The Rule of Law
Issue 18: Is the Death Penalty an Unconstitutional Punishment for Juvenile Offenders?	**Chapter 15:** Justice for Juveniles and Victims	**Chapter 15:** Juvenile Justice	**Chapter 13:** Juvenile Justice
Issue 19: Does Confining Sex Offenders Indefinitely in Mental Hospitals After They Have Served Their Prison Sentences Violate the Constitution?	**Chapter 14:** Alternatives: Community Corrections	**Chapter 13:** Community Corrections **Chapter 16:** Contemporary Challenges	**Chapter 11:** Prison Life, Inmate Rights, Release, and Recidivism **Chapter 12:** Community Corrections
Issue 20: Does an Imprisoned Individual Have a Constitutional Right to Access the State's Evidence for DNA Testing?	**Chapter 4:** The Criminal Law	**Chapter 16:** Contemporary Challenges	**Chapter 11:** Prison Life, Inmate Rights, Release, and Recidivism
Issue 21: Should It Be a Crime to Download Copyrighted Music from the Internet?	**Chapter 3:** Explaining Criminal Behavior **Chapter 4:** The Criminal Law	**Chapter 16:** Contemporary Challenges	**Chapter 3:** Explaining Crime **Chapter 4:** The Rule of Law
Issue 22: Should It Be Lawful for the Police to Conduct Jailhouse Strip Searches of Persons Arrested for Minor Offenses?	**Chapter 7:** The Rule of Law in Law Enforcement	**Chapter 7:** Legal and Special Issues in Policing	**Chapter 7:** Policing America: Issues and Ethics

Introduction

The study of human behavior is a fascinating and complex enterprise. Throughout recorded history, people have speculated about the origins and causes of behavior. Early explanations focused on metaphysical forces, such as evil spirits or the devil, which were believed to somehow compel people to act. Later, the philosophers of the Enlightenment, including Jeremy Bentham and Jean Jacques Rosseau, who emphasized the rational nature of human behavior, believed that one's actions were freely chosen.

Based on this important idea, the early classical theorists maintained that crime could be controlled by making punishments associated with criminal behavior more painful than the pleasure that could be derived from the acts. Later, with the emergence of positivism, biological theories of human behavior became popular. Early biological positivists believed that a person's propensity for criminal behavior could be determined with simple measurements of physical features. For example, in the late nineteenth century, Cesare Lombroso, regarded by many as the father of modern criminology, believed that the length of a person's arms and the size of his teeth could indicate a criminal predisposition.

During the 1930s, sociological theories of criminal behavior became prominent in the United States. Theorists of the Chicago School of Sociology emphasized urban social conditions as the primary determinant of criminal behavior. The social policies that emerged from these theories became the driving force behind modern efforts to eradicate poverty, provide children with better educational opportunities, build stronger communities, and create better employment prospects for the poor. In fact, many of the crime control strategies that emerged from the Chicago School of Sociology have become cornerstones of American social policy in the twenty-first century. For example, even politically conservative social programs with attractive slogans such as "No child left behind" proceed directly from the assumption that adverse social conditions, such as those produced by bad schools, broken homes, single-parent families, a lack of parental attachment, and drug abuse, lead directly to antisocial behavior.

Although many U.S. social programs continued to assume a deterministic relationship between adverse social conditions and criminal behavior, a more conservative political climate began to emerge in the early 1970s. One influential criminologist, Robert Martinson, who had evaluated prison rehabilitation programs throughout the United States, concluded that they were largely ineffective. In the aftermath of these findings, as well as the realization that official measures of reported crime rates had increased during this period, conservative criminologists began to embrace a "new," more punitive approach to criminals and a return to the classical approach. This time, classical criminology was repackaged as rational choice theory.

James Q. Wilson, a UCLA political scientist, became one of the primary crusaders for the new classical movement. Wilson believed that regardless of the causes of criminal behavior, society must recognize the fact that "[w]icked people exist." Thus, the only solution is "to set them apart from innocent people."[1] The revised edition of his now-classic 1975 work, *Thinking About Crime,* outlined the foundations of the new classical philosophy:

> [T]he rate of crime is influenced by its costs. It is possible to lower the crime rate by increasing the certainty of sanctions . . . the wisest course of action for society is to try simultaneously to increase both the benefits of non-crime and the costs of crime.[2] . . .

Other prominent criminologists also embraced the new conservative approach to crime prevention. Economist Andrew Von Hirsh developed a model of punishment termed "just deserts," which emphasizes that criminals should be punished simply because they have earned it. Moreover, Von Hirsh believes that punishing criminals can have a utilitarian effect: It helps to return society to a condition of equilibrium that is disrupted by crime. In addition, imitating the philosophies of Cesare Beccaria and Jeremy Bentham of the late eighteenth century, Von Hirsh asserts that principles of social justice require that all criminals who commit a particular offense should be punished in the same way.

Rational Choices, Irrational Policies?

Has rational choice theory produced irrational social policies? After three decades, the weight of the evidence suggests that it may have. According to some criminologists, the ideas of the new rational choice advocates were converted into draconian and regressive social policies by politicians eager to find reductionist, "sound bite" solutions to criminal behavior. The problem is that some of these policies have had disastrous consequences for the U.S. justice system. For example, during the early part of his presidency, Ronald Reagan, who had embraced James Q. Wilson's new classical criminology, declared a "war on drugs." Since it began, this initiative has emphasized stringent law enforcement, interdiction efforts, and increasing sanctions for drug law violations, including mandatory minimum sentencing policies. The results of these initiatives have been striking: From 1980 to 1997, the number of persons incarcerated for drug offenses has risen by approximately 1040 percent, an 11-fold increase.[3]

More recently, even very conservative social critics such as William F. Buckley, Jr., have questioned the wisdom of this so-called "war on drugs." Stated Buckley:

> What are the relative costs, on the one hand, of medical and psychological treatment for addicts and, on the other incarceration for drug offenses? [T]reatment is seven times more cost-effective. By this is meant that one dollar spent on the treatment of an addict reduces the probability of continued addiction seven times more than one dollar spent on incarceration. . . . [T]he cost of the drug war is many times

more painful, in all its manifestations, than would be the licensing of drugs combined with intensive education of non-users and intensive education designed to warn those who experiment with drugs. . . . [I]t is outrageous to live in a society whose laws tolerate sending young people to life in prison because they grew, or distributed, a dozen ounces of marijuana.[4]

Data from a wide variety of sources, including the U.S. Department of Justice, appear to support Buckley's position. According to the Bureau of Justice Statistics, in 2000, 64.4 percent of the inmates confined in U.S. federal prisons and approximately 20.7 percent of those in state prisons were confined for drug law violations.[5] The costs of confining these individuals are a fiscal time bomb. At an average rate of $21,837.95 per inmate per year in the federal prison system, the annual cost to confine the 72,764 incarcerated drug offenders is approximately $1.6 billion.[6] At an average cost of $20,261.15, the price tag to the states for confining drug offenders exceeds $50 billion annually.[7]

A related policy trend has been the passage of "three strikes" sentencing laws, which provide generally that an offender will receive a mandatory life prison sentence upon conviction of a third felony. Such laws are rapidly turning U.S. prisons into expensive retirement homes for an aging inmate population. One study has projected that in 2010, U.S. prisons will confine approximately 200,000 elderly inmates, who will require special treatment and advanced medical care.[8] At an average cost of $75,000 for each elderly inmate, that amounts to a price tag in the neighborhood of $15 billion annually.[9]

Furthermore, the Bureau of Justice Statistics has found that in 2000, persons aged 45 years or older, who comprise approximately 33 percent of the U.S. population, accounted for less than 10 percent of the serious crime arrests.[10] This finding is consistent with virtually all of the credible research that points to a very strong inverse relationship between age and crime. Thus, it makes very little sense to confine elderly inmates in U.S. prisons. In view of these policies, perhaps the new mantra for U.S. corrections will become "Three strikes, we're out of money."

Moreover, the preceding discussion considered only the direct costs of imprisoning large numbers of nonviolent offenders. The indirect costs of confining these individuals may be substantially greater still. According to criminologist Todd Clear, "The removal of offenders who pose no risk to society can deplete valued resources, a particularly costly outcome for already disadvantaged neighborhoods." One must also question the wisdom of nonviolent offender confinement policies that produce single-parent households, financial instability, and social disorganization in many of our nation's poorest neighborhoods. As one of my students has cogently observed, "It's hard to coach your kid's basketball team from the inside of a prison."

Several important questions emerge logically from the preceding analysis: Are we utilizing justice system policies that simply do not work? Are governmental budgets so flush with cash that we can afford to fill our prisons with nonviolent inmates who present little genuine threat to society? Are we wasting our money on failed crime control policies when we could better spend it for providing shelter for homeless families, affordable health care for the poor, or a better education for our children? Are we as a society being sold a "bill of goods" by persons masquerading as experts who have a vested interest in keeping the current system the way it is?

Answers to the preceding questions must emerge from the systematic scientific study of crime and human behavior. Moreover, although there is much that we still have to learn, substantial progress has already been made.

Rational Justice System Policies That Work

Our thinking about crime has often been preoccupied with the idea of "causation." Voluminous research into crime and criminality demonstrates conclusively, however, that social scientists are on much more solid footing when they identify factors that correlate with higher crime rates. For example, while it would be inaccurate to state that "drinking alcohol causes crime" (because not all people who drink alcohol commit crimes), it would be quite accurate to suggest that alcohol consumption correlates with higher crime rates. Moreover, a great deal of solid research suggests that the relationship is a compelling one.

There are other things we know about crime as well, although once again, the relationships are best described as correlations, rather than causes. Although far from exhaustive, the following list of factors that appear to correlate with higher crime rates is instructive:

- Broken homes produce more criminals than two-parent families.
- People learn to commit crime; therefore, many children who are abused by their parents are more likely to become abusive adults.
- Children need a structured home environment in order to develop their full human potential.
- The ingestion of lead paint by children is strongly related to low intelligence and failure in school.
- Substance abuse (including alcohol and illegal drugs) is related to criminal behavior.
- Deteriorated urban areas have higher crime rates.
- African Americans and members of other minority groups are more often arrested and processed in our justice system.
- Women commit less crime than men, but the rate of female offending is increasing.
- Older people commit less crime than young persons.
- People tend to drift in and out of conventional and criminal behavior.
- Areas that have developed a sense of "community" have lower crime rates.
- Some human behavior may have a biological/genetic basis. Punishing such behaviors may be a waste of time and resources.

What we do know about crime and criminality should be used to develop effective social policies. For example, if poor nutrition is related to deficient school performance, policies that provide children from low-income homes with an adequate breakfast make a great deal of sense. Although spending on prisons skyrocketed under the Bush administration, nutritional programs have been gutted. It may be that such "liberal" policies are inconsistent with a conservative ideology stressing "just deserts" and social Darwinism. In the long run, however, providing children with a nutritious breakfast, better schools, and a stronger sense of community affiliation may be far cheaper than incarcerating them in prison for the rest of their lives.

Circularity in Our Study of Crime and Justice—Old Becomes New Once Again

To paraphrase George Santayana, "Those who cannot remember the lessons of history are condemned to repeat it." It is hard to study the history of crime and criminality and fail to notice a striking circularity in criminological theory. To illustrate, the Classical approach, which originated in the late eighteenth century, emphasized free will and a utilitarian approach to punishment. The early classicists also urged the elimination of judicial sentencing discretion, adoption of determinate sentencing laws, and the use of imprisonment as a form of punishment. Rational choice proponents also emphasize free will and a utilitarian approach to punishing criminals. Furthermore, the determinate sentencing laws that have been adopted by many states and the federal government virtually eliminate judicial sentencing discretion.

Just as classical criminology reemerged during the 1970s, biological positivism has reappeared more recently. Although the theories of the nineteenth- and twentieth-century positivists were interesting and novel in their time, their technical ability to measure and quantify their findings in a scientifically accurate way was very limited. As we begin the new millennium, we may be witnessing the development of a new biological positivism in criminology, one that emphasizes the interaction of genetic and environmental forces to produce human behavior. This time, however, our scientific measurement capabilities may actually have evolved to the point we will be able to draw meaningful conclusions about how biological factors interact with environmental forces to produce human behavior. In fact, we may be at the cutting edge of the emergence of a truly "new criminology," which emphasizes a synthesis of biological and social forces that produce human behavior.

In any case, it is an exciting time to be engaged in the study of criminal behavior. Criminology in the twenty-first century may provide us with the opportunity to learn to creatively manage human behavior in a way that is more consistent with human value and dignity. In the years ahead, criminologists will be called upon to provide honest answers to important policy questions that will have a substantial impact on the quality of life in the United States. We can only hope that those entrusted to develop enlightened social policies based on the answers we provide will learn history's lessons and resist the temptation to embrace politically expedient solutions that will eventually be exposed as expensive policy failures.

Notes

1. James Q. Wilson, *Thinking About Crime,* rev. ed. (Vintage Books, 1983, p. 128)

2. *Ibid.* (p. 143)

3. Center on Juvenile and Criminal Justice Executive Summary, "Poor Prescription: The Costs of Imprisoning Drug Offenders in the United States," (July 2000)

4. William F. Buckley, Jr., "The War on Drugs Is Lost," *The National Review* (July 1, 1996)

5. Bureau of Justice Statistics, *Sourcebook of Criminal Justice Statistics 2001* (U.S. Department of Justice, 2002)

6. George M. Camp and Camille Graham Camp, *The Corrections Yearbook, 1998* (Criminal Justice Institute, 1999)

7. *Ibid.*

8. Herbert J. Hoelter, "Proceedings: Technologies for Successful Aging—Institutional Issues," *Journal of Rehabilitation Research and Development* (vol. 38, no. 1, 2001, p. S38)

9. *Ibid.*

10. *Ibid.,* note 5, at p. 345

Internet References . . .

The Critical Criminology Division of the ASC

This site of the American Society of Criminology links to basic criminology sources and to resources developed within a critical sociology framework.

www.sociology.niu.edu

National Crime Victims Research and Treatment Center

This site, sponsored by the National Crime Victims Research and Treatment Center of the Medical University of South Carolina, describes the work of the center and provides an excellent list of related resources.

http://colleges.musc.edu/ncvc/

Explanations of Crime

*E*xactly *what is crime, who commits crime, and why, where, when, and how crimes are committed remain core questions for the public, criminal justice practitioners, and scholars alike. It would seem that defining crime, as well as explaining crime, is a straightforward matter. In reality, definitions, explanations, and even assessments of the harm that criminals do is problematic. Some experts, for instance, contend that crime is necessary and functional in all societies. Others say that society is concerned about the wrong kinds of crime. These questions are important for criminologists and policymakers.*

- Is Crime Beneficial to Society?
- Is Criminal Behavior Determined Biologically?
- Is a Person's Body Type Clearly Linked to Criminal Behavior?

ISSUE 1

Is Crime Beneficial to Society?

YES: Emile Durkheim, from *The Rules of Sociological Method* (The Free Press, 1938)

NO: Daniel Patrick Moynihan, from "Defining Deviancy Down," *The American Scholar* (Winter 1993)

ISSUE SUMMARY

YES: Classic sociologist Emile Durkheim (1858–1917) theorizes that crime reaffirms moral boundaries and helps bring about needed social changes.

NO: Former U.S. Senator Daniel Patrick Moynihan (D-New York) argues that modern crime has gone way beyond the point of being functional.

What is crime? Who commits it? And why? The importance given to these questions, and their answers, varies among different categories of people, although there is little certainty that any one group's meanings and interpretations are superior to those of another.

For example, younger and older people have different perceptions of crime (older people are more likely to fear crime, even though younger people are far more likely to be victims of crime). Public officials also disagree about crime. During election years many politicians have inflated the number of crimes committed and have attributed crime to forces and influences that only the politicians, if elected, can combat.

Criminological and criminal justice scholars, although generally slightly less shrill and self-serving than politicians in their definitions and explanations of crime, are also very likely to disagree among themselves about what crime is and what its causes are. Unlike politicians, they do not follow four-year cycles in their crime conceptualizations, but they do reflect trends. For example, 20 years ago most criminologists probably reflected a liberal ideology in their crime explanations and suggested treatments. Today some are more likely to reflect an ideologically conservative scholarly bias. Radical or Marxist criminologists continue to have a marginal position within the discipline.

The seminal essay by Emile Durkheim, excerpted in the first of the following selections, argues that deviancy, including crime, is functional and exists in all societies because it is needed to establish moral boundaries and to distinguish between those who obey and those who disobey society's rules. Although it was written almost 100 years ago, Durkheim's original structural or sociological approach continues to be relied on by criminological and criminal justice scholars.

There are, of course, many variants of the sociological approach to crime, its definitions, and its causes. However, Durkheim's approach is central for many criminologists and especially *structural functionalists*. Structural functionalists attempt to determine what patterns of interaction or structures exist in various groups. They investigate what these patterns contribute to the maintenance of a group and of the society to which the group belongs. In the United States, for example, dating patterns and their relation to marriage are studied. Marriage patterns and their relation to the economy, to religion, and so on are traced. In addition, structural functionalists want to know about the consequences of patterns of behavior for groups, for members of groups, and for society as a whole. Such consequences can be both positive and negative, intentional and unintentional.

Durkheim selects a pattern of behavior, in this case deviant acts, and attempts to determine what it contributes to the maintenance of society and what its consequences might be, including intended and unintended ones. Durkheim asserts that crime is functional (not necessarily good and certainly not to be encouraged) and helps to establish moral boundaries. Deviant acts also provide a sense of propriety and a feeling of righteousness for those who do not commit crimes, as they share sentiments of moral indignation about those who do violate society's norms. Durkheim says that crime also allows for a social change. It prevents a society from having too much rigidity and from becoming too slavish in its obedience to norms.

In the second selection, politician and sociologist Daniel Patrick Moynihan acknowledges his debt to Durkheim and to sociologist Kai T. Erikson, a follower of some of Durkheim's ideas. But he questions the soundness of Durkheim's contention that crime is functional for societies, especially in the context of violence-ridden 1990's America. Moynihan argues that on the one hand, certain classes of relatively harmless behavior are nowadays being defined as deviant, if not criminal (dysfunctional contraction of moral boundaries). On the other hand, and far more serious to Moynihan, moral boundaries are becoming too elastic as society expands its tolerance for serious crime. He asks, How can deviancy be said to be functional if citizens are no longer shocked by outrageous violence?

As you read the selections by Durkheim and Moynihan, consider examples from your life in which a type of deviancy might be functional or an act that might have been viewed as criminal a generation ago is no longer viewed that way. In addition, what types of acts do you tolerate today that would have been morally outrageous to your grandparents? Have society's legal and ethical boundaries become "too elastic"?

YES

Emile Durkheim

The Normal and the Pathological

Crime is present not only in the majority of societies of one particular species but in all societies of all types. There is no society that is not confronted with the problem of criminality. Its form changes; the acts thus characterized are not the same everywhere; but, everywhere and always, there have been men who have behaved in such a way as to draw upon themselves penal repression. If, in proportion as societies pass from the lower to the higher types, the rate of criminality, i.e., the relation between the yearly number of crimes and the population, tended to decline, it might be believed that crime, while still normal, is tending to lose this character of normality. But we have no reason to believe that such a regression is substantiated. Many facts would seem rather to indicate a movement in the opposite direction. From the beginning of the [nineteenth] century, statistics enable us to follow the course of criminality. It has everywhere increased. In France the increase is nearly 300 percent. There is, then, no phenomenon that presents more indisputably all the symptoms of normality, since it appears closely connected with the conditions of all collective life. To make of crime a form of social morbidity would be to admit that morbidity is not something accidental, but, on the contrary, that in certain cases it grows out of the fundamental constitution of the living organism; it would result in wiping out all distinction between the physiological and the pathological. No doubt it is possible that crime itself will have abnormal forms, as, for example, when its rate is unusually high. This excess is, indeed, undoubtedly morbid in nature. What is normal, simply, is the existence of criminality, provided that it attains and does not exceed, for each social type, a certain level, which it is perhaps not impossible to fix in conformity with the preceding rules.[1]

Here we are, then, in the presence of a conclusion in appearance quite paradoxical. Let us make no mistake. To classify crime among the phenomena of normal sociology is not to say merely that it is an inevitable, although regrettable phenomenon, due to the incorrigible wickedness of men; it is to affirm that it is a factor in public health, an integral part of all healthy societies. This result is, at first glance, surprising enough to have puzzled even ourselves for a long time. Once this first surprise has been overcome, however, it is not difficult to find reasons explaining this normality and at the same time confirming it.

In the first place crime is normal because a society exempt from it is utterly impossible. Crime, we have shown elsewhere, consists of an act that offends certain very strong collective sentiments. In a society in which criminal acts are no longer committed, the sentiments they offend would have to be found without exception in all individual consciousnesses, and they must be found to exist with the same degree as sentiments contrary to them. Assuming that this condition could actually be realized, crime would not thereby disappear; it would only change its form, for the very cause which would thus dry up the sources of criminality would immediately open up new ones.

Indeed, for the collective sentiments which are protected by the penal law of a people at a specified moment of its history to take possession of the public conscience or for them to acquire a stronger hold where they have an insufficient grip, they must acquire an intensity greater than that which they had hitherto had. The community as a whole must experience them more vividly, for it can acquire from no other source the greater force necessary to control these individuals who formerly were the most refractory. For murderers to disappear, the horror of bloodshed must become greater in those social strata from which murderers are recruited; but, first it must become greater throughout the entire society. Moreover, the very absence of crime would directly contribute to produce this horror; because any sentiment seems much more respectable when it is always and uniformly respected.

One easily overlooks the consideration that these strong states of the common consciousness cannot be thus reinforced without reinforcing at the same time the more feeble states, whose violation previously gave birth to mere infraction of convention—since the weaker ones are only the prolongation, the attenuated form, of the stronger. Thus robbery and simple bad taste injure the same single altruistic sentiment, the respect for that which is another's. However, this same sentiment is less grievously offended by bad taste than by robbery; and since, in addition, the average consciousness had not sufficient intensity to react keenly to the bad taste, it is treated with greater tolerance. That is why the person guilty of bad taste is merely blamed, whereas the thief is punished. But, if this sentiment grows stronger, to the point of silencing in all consciousnesses the inclination which disposes man to steal, he will become more sensitive to the offenses which, until then, touched him but lightly. He will react against them, then, with more energy; they will be the object of greater opprobrium, which will transform certain of them from the simple moral faults that they were and give them the quality of crimes. For example, improper contracts, or contracts improperly executed, which only incur public blame or civil damages, will become offenses in law.

Imagine a society of saints, a perfect cloister of exemplary individuals. Crimes, properly so called, will there be unknown; but faults which appear venial to the layman will create there the same scandal that the ordinary offense does in ordinary consciousnesses. If, then, this society has the power to judge and punish, it will define these acts as criminal and will treat them as such. For the same reason, the perfect and upright man judges his smallest failings with a severity that the majority reserve for acts more truly in the nature of an offense. Formerly, acts of violence against persons were more frequent than they are today, because respect for individual dignity was less strong. As this has increased, these crimes have become more rare; and also, many acts violating this sentiment have been introduced into the penal law which were not included there in primitive times.[2]

In order to exhaust all the hypotheses logically possible, it will perhaps be asked why this unanimity does not extend to all collective sentiments without exception. Why should not even the most feeble sentiment gather enough energy to prevent all dissent? The moral consciousness of the society would be present in its entirety in all the individuals, with a vitality sufficient to prevent all acts offending it—the purely conventional faults as well as the crimes. But a uniformity so universal and absolute is utterly impossible; for the immediate physical milieu in which each one of us is placed, the hereditary antecedents, and the social influences vary from one individual to the next, and consequently diversify consciousnesses. It is impossible for all to be alike, if only because each one has his own organism and that these organisms occupy different areas in space. That is why, even among the lower peoples, where individual originality is very little developed, it nevertheless does exist.

Thus, since there cannot be a society in which the individuals do not differ more or less from the collective type, it is also inevitable that, among these divergences, there are some with a criminal character. What confers this character upon them is not the intrinsic quality of a given act but that definition which the collective conscience lends them. If the collective conscience is stronger, if it has enough authority practically to suppress these divergences, it will also be more sensitive, more exacting; and, reacting against the slightest deviations with the energy it otherwise displays only against more considerable infractions, it will attribute to them the same gravity as formerly to crimes. In other words, it will designate them as criminal.

Crime is, then, necessary; it is bound up with fundamental conditions of all social life, and by that very fact it is useful, because these conditions of which it is a part are themselves indispensable to the normal evolution of morality and law.

Indeed, it is no longer possible today to dispute the fact that law and morality vary from one social type to the next, nor that they change within the same type if the conditions of life are modified. But, in order that these transformations may be possible, the collective sentiments at the basis of morality must not be hostile to change, and consequently must have but moderate energy. If they were too strong, they would no longer be plastic. Every pattern is an obstacle to new patterns, to the extent that the first pattern is inflexible. The better a structure is articulated, the more it offers a healthy resistance to all modification; and this is equally true of functional, as of anatomical, organization. If there were no crimes, this condition could not have been fulfilled; for such a hypothesis presupposes that collective sentiments have arrived at a degree of intensity unexampled in history. Nothing is good indefinitely and to an unlimited extent. The authority which the moral conscience enjoys must not be excessive; otherwise no one would dare criticize it, and it would too easily congeal into an immutable form. To make progress, individual originality must be able to express itself. In order that the originality of the idealist whose dreams transcend this century may find expression, it is necessary that the originality of the criminal, who is below the level of his time, shall also be possible. One does not occur without the other.

Nor is this all. Aside from this indirect utility, it happens that crime itself plays a useful role in this evolution. Crime implies not only that the way remains open to necessary changes but that in certain cases it directly prepares these changes. Where crime exists, collective sentiments are sufficiently flexible to take on a new form, and crime sometimes helps to determine the form they will take. How many times, indeed, it is only an anticipation of future morality—a step toward what will be! According to Athenian law, Socrates was a criminal, and his condemnation was no more than just. However, his crime, namely, the independence of this thought, rendered a service not only to humanity but to his country. It served to prepare a new morality and faith which the Athenians needed, since the traditions by which they had lived until then were no longer in harmony with the current conditions of life. Nor is the case of Socrates unique; it is reproduced periodically in history. It would never have been possible to establish the freedom of thought we now enjoy if the regulations prohibiting it had not been violated before being solemnly abrogated. At that time, however, the violation was a crime, since it was an offense against sentiments still very keen in the average conscience. And yet this crime was useful as a prelude to reforms which daily become more necessary. Liberal philosophy had as its precursors the heretics of all kinds who were justly punished by secular authorities during the entire course of the Middle Ages and until the eve of modern times.

From this point of view the fundamental facts of criminality present themselves to us in an entirely new light. Contrary to current ideas, the criminal no longer seems a totally unsociable being, a sort of parasitic element, a strange and unassimilable body, introduced into the midst of society.[3] On the contrary, he plays a definite role in social life. Crime, for its part, must no longer be conceived as an evil that cannot be too much suppressed. There is no occasion for self-congratulation when the crime rate drops noticeably below the average level, for we may be certain that this apparent progress is associated with some social disorder. Thus, the number of assault cases never falls so low as in times of want.[4] With the drop in the crime rate, and as a reaction to it, comes a revision, or the need of a revision in the theory of punishment. If, indeed, crime is a disease, its punishment is its remedy and cannot be otherwise conceived; thus, all the discussions it arouses bear on the point of determining what the punishment must be in order to fulfil this role of remedy. If crime is not pathological at all, the object of punishment cannot be to cure it, and its true function must be sought elsewhere.

Notes

1. From the fact that crime is a phenomenon of normal sociology, it does not follow that the criminal is an individual normally constituted from the biological and psychological points of view. The two questions are independent of each other. This independence will be better understood

when we have shown, later on, the difference between psychological and sociological facts.

2. Calumny, insults, slander, fraud, etc.

3. We have ourselves committed the error of speaking thus of the criminal, because of a failure to apply our rule (*Division du travail social*, pp. 395–96).

4. Although crime is a fact of normal sociology, it does not follow that we must not abhor it. Pain itself has nothing desirable about it; the individual dislikes it as society does crime, and yet it is a function of normal physiology. Not only is it necessarily derived from the very constitution of every living organism, but it plays a useful role in life, for which reason it cannot be replaced. It would, then, be a singular distortion of our thought to present it as an apology for crime. We would not even think of protesting against such an interpretation, did we not know to what strange accusations and misunderstandings one exposes oneself when one undertakes to study moral facts objectively and to speak of them in a different language from that of the layman.

Daniel Patrick Moynihan  **NO**

Defining Deviancy Down

In one of the founding texts of sociology, *The Rules of Sociological Method* (1895), Emile Durkheim set it down that "crime is normal." "It is," he wrote, "completely impossible for any society entirely free of it to exist." By defining what is deviant, we are enabled to know what is not, and hence to live by shared standards. . . . Durkheim writes:

> From this viewpoint the fundamental facts of criminology appear to us in an entirely new light. . . . [T]he criminal no longer appears as an utterly unsociable creature, a sort of parasitic element, a foreign, inassimilable body introduced into the bosom of society. He plays a normal role in social life. For its part, crime must no longer be conceived of as an evil which cannot be circumscribed closely enough. Far from there being cause for congratulation when it drops too noticeably below the normal level, this apparent progress assuredly coincides with and is linked to some social disturbance.

Durkheim suggests, for example, that "in times of scarcity" crimes of assault drop off. He does not imply that we ought to approve of crime—"[p]ain has likewise nothing desirable about it"—but we need to understand its function. He saw religion, in the sociologist Randall Collins's terms, as "fundamentally a set of ceremonial actions, assembling the group, heightening its emotions, and focusing its members on symbols of their common belongingness." In this context "a punishment ceremony creates social solidarity."

The matter was pretty much left at that until seventy years later when, in 1965, Kai T. Erikson published *Wayward Puritans,* a study of "crime rates" in the Massachusetts Bay Colony. The plan behind the book, as Erikson put it, was "to test [Durkheim's] notion that the number of deviant offenders a community can afford to recognize is likely to remain stable over time." The notion proved out very well indeed. Despite occasional crime waves, as when itinerant Quakers refused to take off their hats in the presence of magistrates, the amount of deviance in this corner of seventeenth-century New England fitted nicely with the supply of stocks and shipping posts. Erikson remarks:

> It is one of the arguments of the . . . study that the amount of deviation a community encounters is apt to remain fairly constant over time.

From *American Scholar,* vol. 62, no. 1, Winter 1993, pp. 17–30. Copyright © 1993 by Daniel Patrick Moynihan. Reprinted by permission of American Scholar, Phi Beta Kappa.

To start at the beginning, it is a simple logistic fact that the number of deviancies which come to a community's attention are limited by the kinds of equipment it uses to detect and handle them, and to that extent the rate of deviation found in a community is at least in part a function of the size and complexity of its social control apparatus. A community's capacity for handling deviance, let us say, can be roughly estimated by counting its prison cells and hospital beds, its policemen and psychiatrists, its courts and clinics. Most communities, it would seem, operate with the expectation that a relatively constant number of control agents is necessary to cope with a relatively constant number of offenders. The amount of men, money, and material assigned by society to "do something" about deviant behavior does not vary appreciably over time, and the implicit logic which governs the community's efforts to man a police force or maintain suitable facilities for the mentally ill seems to be that there is a fairly stable quota of trouble which should be anticipated.

In this sense, the agencies of control often seem to define their job as that of keeping deviance within bounds rather than that of obliterating it altogether. Many judges, for example, assume that severe punishments are a greater deterrent to crime than moderate ones, and so it is important to note that many of them are apt to impose harder penalties when crime seems to be on the increase and more lenient ones when it does not, almost as if the power of the bench were being used to keep the crime rate from getting out of hand.

Erikson was taking issue with what he described as "a dominant strain in sociological thinking" that took for granted that a well-structured society "is somehow designed to prevent deviant behavior from occurring." In both authors, Durkheim and Erikson, there is an undertone that suggests that, with deviancy, as with most social goods, there is the continuing problem of demand exceeding supply. Durkheim invites us to

imagine a society of saints, a perfect cloister of exemplary individuals. Crimes, properly so called, will there be unknown; but faults which appear venial to the layman will create there the same scandal that the ordinary offense does in ordinary consciousness. If, then, this society has the power to judge and punish, it will define these acts as criminal and will treat them as such.

Recall Durkheim's comment that there need be no cause for congratulations should the amount of crime drop "too noticeably below the normal level." It would not appear that Durkheim anywhere contemplates the possibility of too much crime. Clearly his theory would have required him to deplore such a development, but the possibility seems never to have occurred to him.

Erikson, writing much later in the twentieth century, contemplates both possibilities. "Deviant persons can be said to supply needed services to society." There is no doubt a tendency for the supply of any needed thing to run short. But he is consistent. There can, he believes, be *too much* of a good thing.

Hence "the number of deviant offenders a community can *afford* to recognize is likely to remain stable over time." [My emphasis]

Social scientists are said to be on the lookout for poor fellows getting a bum rap. But here is a theory that clearly implies that there are circumstances in which society will choose *not* to notice behavior that would be otherwise controlled, or disapproved, or even punished.

It appears to me that this is in fact what we in the United States have been doing of late. I proffer the thesis that, over the past generation, since the time Erikson wrote, the amount of deviant behavior in American society has increased beyond the levels the community can "afford to recognize" and that, accordingly, we have been re-defining deviancy so as to exempt much conduct previously stigmatized, and also quietly raising the "normal" level in categories where behavior is now abnormal by any earlier standard. This redefining has evoked fierce resistance from defenders of "old" standards, and accounts for much of the present "cultural war" such as proclaimed by many at the 1992 Republican National Convention.

Let me, then, offer three categories of redefinition in these regards: the *altruistic,* the *opportunistic,* and the *normalizing.*

The first category, the *altruistic,* may be illustrated by the deinstitution-alization movement within the mental health profession that appeared in the 1950s. The second category, the *opportunistic,* sees in the interest group rewards derived from the acceptance of "alternative" family structures. The third category, the *normalizing,* is to be observed in the growing acceptance of unprecedented levels of violent crime. . . .

Our *normalizing* category most directly corresponds to Erikson's proposition that "the number of deviant offenders a community can afford to recognize is likely to remain stable over time." Here we are dealing with the popular psychological notion of "denial." In 1965, having reached the conclusion that there would be a dramatic increase in single-parent families, I reached the further conclusion that this would in turn lead to a dramatic increase in crime. In an article in *America,* I wrote:

> From the wild Irish slums of the 19th century Eastern seaboard to the riot-torn suburbs of Los Angeles, there is one unmistakable lesson in American history: a community that allows a large number of young men to grow up in broken families, dominated by women, never acquiring any stable relationship to male authority, never acquiring any set of rational expectations about the future—that community asks for and gets chaos. Crime, violence, unrest, unrestrained lashing out at the whole social structure—that is not only to be expected; it is very near to inevitable.

The inevitable, as we now know, has come to pass, but here again our response is curiously passive. Crime is a more or less continuous subject of political pronouncement, and from time to time it will be at or near the top of opinion polls as a matter of public concern. But it never gets much further than that. In the words spoken from the bench, Judge Edwin Torres of the New York State Supreme Court, Twelfth Judicial District, described how "the slaughter of the innocent marches unabated: subway riders, bodega own-ers, cab drivers, babies; in laundromats, at cash machines, on elevators, in hallways." In personal communication, he writes: "This numbness, this near narcoleptic state can diminish the human condition to the level of combat infantrymen, who, in protracted campaigns, can eat their battlefield rations seated on the bodies of the fallen, friend and foe alike. A society that loses its sense of outrage is doomed to extinction." There is no expectation that this will change, nor any efficacious public insistence that it do so. The crime level has been *normalized*.

Consider the St. Valentine's Day Massacre. In 1929 in Chicago during Prohibition, four gangsters killed seven gangsters on February 14. The nation was shocked. The event became legend. It merits not one but two entries in the *World Book Encyclopedia*. I leave it to others to judge, but it would appear that the society in the 1920s was simply not willing to put up with this degree of deviancy. In the end, the Constitution was amended, and Prohibition, which lay behind so much gangster violence, ended.

In recent years, again in the context of illegal traffic in controlled sub-stances, this form of murder has returned. But it has done so at a level that induces denial. James Q. Wilson comments that Los Angeles has the equiva-lent of a St. Valentine's Day Massacre every weekend. Even the most ghastly reenactments of such human slaughter produce only moderate responses. On the morning after the close of the Democratic National Convention in New York City in July, there was such an account in the second section of the *New York Times*. It was not a big story; bottom of the page, but with a headline that got your attention. "3 Slain in Bronx Apartment, but a Baby is Saved." A subhead continued: "A mother's last act was to hide her little girl under the bed." The article described a drug execution; the now-routine blindfolds made from duct tape; a man and a woman and a teenager involved. "Each had been shot once in the head." The police had found them a day later. They also found, under a bed, a three-month-old baby, dehydrated but alive. A lieutenant remarked of the mother, "In her last dying act she protected her baby. She probably knew she was going to die, so she stuffed the baby where she knew it would be safe." But the matter was left there. The police would do their best. But the event passed quickly; forgotten by the next day, it will never make *World Book*.

Nor is it likely that any great heed will be paid to an uncanny reenact-ment of the Prohibition drama a few months later, also in the Bronx. The *Times* story, page B3, reported:

9 Men Posing as Police
Are Indicted in 3 Murders
Drug Dealers Were Kidnapped for Ransom

The *Daily News* story, same day, page 17, made it *four* murders, adding nice details about torture techniques. The gang members posed as federal Drug Enforcement Administration agents, real badges and all. The victims were drug dealers, whose families were uneasy about calling the police. Ransom seems generally to have been set in the $650,000 range. Some paid. Some got it in the back of the head. So it goes.

Yet, violent killings, often random, go on unabated. Peaks continue to attract some notice. But these are peaks above "average" levels that thirty years ago would have been thought epidemic.

> LOS ANGELES, AUG. 24. (Reuters) Twenty-two people were killed in Los Angeles over the weekend, the worst period of violence in the city since it was ravaged by riots earlier this year, the police said today.
>
> Twenty-four others were wounded by gunfire or stabbings, including a 19-year old woman in a wheelchair who was shot in the back when she failed to respond to a motorist who asked for directions in south Los Angeles.
>
> ["The guy stuck a gun out of the window and just fired at her," said a police spokesman, Lieut. David Rock. The woman was later described as being in stable condition.
>
> Among those who died was an off-duty officer, shot while investigating reports of a prowler in a neighbor's yard, and a Little League baseball coach who had argued with the father of a boy he was coaching.]
>
> The police said at least nine of the deaths were gang-related, including that of a 14-year old girl killed in a fight between rival gangs.
>
> Fifty-one people were killed in three days of rioting that started April 29 after the acquittal of four police officers in the beating of Rodney G. King.
>
> Los Angeles usually has above-average violence during August, but the police were at a loss to explain the sudden rise. On an average weekend in August, 14 fatalities occur.

Not to be outdone, two days later the poor Bronx came up with a near record, as reported in *New York Newsday:*

> Armed with 9-mm. pistols, shotguns and M-16 rifles, a group of masked men and women poured out of two vehicles in the South Bronx early yesterday and sprayed a stretch of Longwood Avenue with a fustillade of bullets, injuring 12 people.

A Kai Erikson of the future will surely need to know that the Department of Justice in 1990 found that Americans reported only about 38 percent of all crimes and 48 percent of violent crimes. This, too, can be seen as a means of *normalizing* crime. In much the same way, the vocabulary of crime reporting can be seen to move toward the normal-seeming. A teacher is shot on her way to class. The *Times* subhead reads: "Struck in the Shoulder in the Year's First Shooting Inside a School." First of the season.

It is too early, however, to know how to regard the arrival of the doctors on the scene declaring crime a "public health emergency." The June 10, 1992, issue of the *Journal of the American Medical Association* was devoted entirely to papers on the subject of violence, principally violence associated with fire-arms. An editorial in the issue signed by former Surgeon General C. Everett

Koop and Dr. George D. Lundberg is entitled: "Violence in America: A Public Health Emergency." Their proposition is admirably succinct.

> Regarding violence in our society as purely a sociological matter, or one of law enforcement, has led to unmitigated failure. It is time to test further whether violence can be amenable to medical/public health interventions.
>
> We believe violence in America to be a public health emergency, largely unresponsive to methods thus far used in its control. The solutions are very complex, but possible.

The authors cited the relative success of epidemiologists in gaining some jurisdiction in the area of motor vehicle casualties by re-defining what had been seen as a law enforcement issue into a public health issue. Again, this process began during the Harriman administration in New York in the 1950s. In the 1960s the morbidity and mortality associated with automobile crashes was, it could be argued, a major public health problem; the public health strategy, it could also be argued, brought the problem under a measure of control. Not in "the 1970s and 1980s," as the *Journal of the American Medical Association* would have us think: the federal legislation involved was signed in 1965. Such a strategy would surely produce insights into the control of violence that elude law enforcement professionals, but whether it would change anything is another question.

For some years now I have had legislation in the Senate that would prohibit the manufacture of .25 and .32 caliber bullets. These are the two calibers most typically used with the guns known as Saturday Night Specials. "Guns don't kill people," I argue, "bullets do."

Moreover, we have a two-century supply of handguns but only a four-year supply of ammunition. A public health official would immediately see the logic of trying to control the supply of bullets rather than of guns.

Even so, now that the doctor has come, it is important that criminal violence not be defined down by epidemiologists. Doctors Koop and Lundberg note that in 1990 in the state of Texas "deaths from firearms, for the first time in many decades, surpassed deaths from motor vehicles, by 3,443 to 3,309." A good comparison. And yet keep in mind that the number of motor vehicle deaths, having leveled off since the 1960s, is now pretty well accepted as normal at somewhat less than 50,000 a year, which is somewhat less than the level of the 1960s—the "carnage," as it once was thought to be, is now accepted as normal. This is the price we pay for high-speed transportation: there is a benefit associated with it. But there is no benefit associated with homicide, and no good in getting used to it. Epidemiologists have powerful insights that can contribute to lessening the medical trauma, but they must be wary of normalizing the social pathology that leads to such trauma.

The hope—if there be such—of this essay has been twofold. It is, first, to suggest that the Durkheim constant, as I put it, is maintained by a dynamic process which adjusts upwards and *downwards*. Liberals have traditionally been alert for upward redefining that does injustice to individuals.

Conservatives have been correspondingly sensitive to downward redefining that weakens societal standards. Might it not help if we could all agree that there is a dynamic at work here? It is not revealed truth, nor yet a scientifically derived formula. It is simply a pattern we observe in ourselves. Nor is it rigid. There may once have been an unchanging supply of jail cells which more or less determined the number of prisoners. No longer. We are building new prisons at a prodigious rate. Similarly, the executioner is back. There is something of a competition in Congress to think up new offenses for which the death penalty is deemed the only available deterrent. Possibly also modes of execution, as in "fry the kingpins." Even so, we are getting used to a lot of behavior that is not good for us.

As noted earlier, Durkheim states that there is "nothing desirable" about pain. Surely what he meant was that there is nothing pleasurable. Pain, even so, is an indispensable warning signal. But societies under stress, much like individuals, will turn to pain killers of various kinds that end up concealing real damage. There is surely nothing desirable about *this*. If our analysis wins general acceptance, if, for example, more of us came to share Judge Torres's genuine alarm at "the trivialization of the lunatic crime rate" in his city (and mine), we might surprise ourselves how well we respond to the manifest decline of the American civic order. Might.

POSTSCRIPT

Is Crime Beneficial to Society?

One of the first American sociologists to attempt to use the insights of Durkheim was Robert Merton in his classic article "Social Structure and Anomie," *American Sociological Review* (1938). Merton attempted to show the bearing that culturally established goals and legitimate means for achieving them or their absence has upon criminogenic behavior. A significant revision of Durkheim's and Merton's thinking is *Crime and the American Dream*, 2d ed., by S. Messner and R. Rosenfeld (Wadsworth, 1997). Also helpful is F. Hearn, *Moral Order and Social Disorder* (Aldine de Gruyter, 1998), especially Chapters 3 and 4 on anomie and Durkheim's sociology of morality. An analysis of communities' responses to crime in a culture outside of America is *Banana Justice: Field Notes on Philippine Crime and Customs* by W. T. Austin (Greenwood, 1999).

Note that Moynihan argues roughly from the same theoretic tradition as Durkheim: structural functionalism. Their disagreement centers around when deviancy becomes dysfunctional. A third argument would be that of some Marxists who see crime, including violent crime, as *functional* but only for the elite because it deflects society's concerns away from their own corporate crimes. For an outstanding presentation of this view, see J. Reiman's *The Rich Get Richer and the Poor Get Prison: Ideology, Class, and Criminal Justice*, 5th ed. (Allyn & Bacon, 1998). M. Lynch et al. identify linkages between economic cycles and criminal justice in "A Further Look at Long Cycles, Legislation and Crime," *Justice Quarterly* (June 1999).

Partial support of Moynihan's thinking can be found in *To Establish Justice, to Insure Domestic Tranquility* (Milton S. Eisenhower Foundation, 1999), a 30-year update of the 1969 violence report by the National Commission on the Causes and Prevention of Violence. A recent work by Moynihan is *Miles to Go: A Personal History of Social Policy* (Harvard University Press, 1997), and a discussion of Moynihan's ideas can be found in R. A. Katzmann, *Daniel Patrick Moynihan: The Intellectual in Public Life* (Johns Hopkins University Press, 1998).

There are many current analyses of crime and justice in terms of gender, including *Working With Women in the Criminal Justice System* by K. S. van Wormer and C. Bartollas (Allyn & Bacon, 1999) and part 1 of Sally Simpson, ed., *Of Crime and Criminality: The Use of Theory in Everyday Life* (Pine Forge Press, 2000). The neglected theoretical and research contributions of black criminologists are delineated by S. L. Gabbidon in "W. E. B. Du Bois on Crime," *The Criminologist* (January/February 1999). An interesting study on how U.S. scholars currently view crime is "Criminologists' Opinions About Causes and Theories of Crime," by L. Ellis and A. Walsh, *The Criminologist* (July/August 1999).

ISSUE 2

Is Criminal Behavior Determined Biologically?

YES: Adrian Raine, from "The Biological Basis of Crime," in James Q. Wilson and John Petersilia, eds., *Crime: Public Policies for Crime Control* (ICS Press, 2002)

NO: Jeffrey H. Reiman, from *The Rich Get Richer and the Poor Get Prison: Ideology, Class, and Criminal Justice* (Allyn & Bacon, 1998)

ISSUE SUMMARY

YES: Adrian Raine argues that one of the principal reasons why we have been so unsuccessful in preventing adult crime is because crime control policies have systematically ignored the biological side of human behavior.

NO: Professor Jeffrey Reiman asserts that social forces create the conditions that become sources of crime in American society.

Is human behavior a product of our biological makeup, or is it socially determined? This question has confronted those who have studied human behavior throughout history. It is an extremely important question, however, because the answer determines everything from the types of social policies used to control deviant behavior, to philosophical questions including the nature of human morality.

The classical legal reform movement, a product of the Enlightenment, originated during the late eighteenth century in Europe. In reaction to the idea that metaphysical forces controlled all aspects of human existence, Classical theorists, including Cesare Beccaria and Jeremy Bentham, believed that people were motivated by hedonism—the pursuit of pleasure and avoidance of pain. They also embraced the notion of rationality and free will as guiding principles in human affairs. The classicists believed that people, as rational beings, would choose to obey the law if punishments were slightly more severe than the pleasure they would derive from committing unlawful acts. In addition, they embraced the doctrine of utilitarianism, a principle that holds that the guiding principle of all social policy, including criminal punishment, must be "the greatest good for the greatest number."

Modern Western legal systems are predicated on these ideals. For example, criminal responsibility is based on the principle that a criminal has the capacity to formulate *mens rea,* or criminal intent based on an evil mind. Thus, at common law, children under the age of seven years were presumed incapable of committing a crime because they were unable to foster criminal intent. Likewise, those who are proved to be mentally insane at the time they committed a crime are not held responsible for their actions.

Our legal system assumes that punishment is justified because a criminal has freely chosen to violate the law and embraces the proposition that it serves a utilitarian purpose and will deter others from committing similar offenses.

What would happen to these assumptions, however, if it were to be demonstrated that internal biological forces compel people to act? Would it then be morally acceptable for society to "punish" criminals for committing antisocial acts? What if criminologists were able to completely eradicate an offender's desire to commit crime? Would such a treatment also eliminate the moral aspect of human conduct? Anthony Burgess, in the introduction to his classic work, *A Clockwork Orange,* considered this dilemma. Stated Burgess:

> [B]y definition, a human being is endowed with free will. He can use this to choose between good and evil. If he can only perform good or only perform evil, then he is a clockwork orange—meaning that he has the appearance of an organism lovely with colour and juice but is in fact only a clockwork toy to be wound up by God or the Devil or (since this is increasingly replacing both) the Almighty State. (ix)

The issues contemplated in this passage may have important consequences for the study of criminology as well as justice system policy in the twenty-first century. In the first reading, Adrian Raine details many compelling examples of the emerging vitality of the biological approach to the study of human behavior. His extensive review of twin studies, human cortical arousal, and brain abnormalities in criminals presents compelling evidence of a biological component of human behavior.

Jeffrey H. Reiman, however, asserts that social factors, including poverty, prisons, gun policies, and modern drug control efforts, generate circumstances in which people will violate the law. Reiman believes that a variety of social programs can work to reduce crime, including family therapy and parent training for delinquent and at-risk youths, teaching of social competency skills, vocational training, extra police patrols in high crime areas, and effective drug and rehabilitation programs for offenders.

What are the arguments on both sides of the "nature or nurture" controversy? Perhaps criminal behavior is a complex combination of both types of factors. When you read these articles, try to develop your own sense of whether criminality is primarily determined by biological or social forces as well as the implications of this controversy for our notions of criminal responsibility and justice system policy.

YES

Adrian Raine

The Biological Basis of Crime

Recognition is increasing that biological processes are at some level impli-cated in the development of criminal behavior. There is certainly debate about the precise contribution of such factors to crime outcome, and there is con-siderable debate about the precise mechanisms that these biological factors reflect. Yet few serious scientists in psychology and psychiatry would deny that biological factors are relevant to understanding crime, and public inter-est in and understanding of this perspective are increasing. The discipline of criminology, on the other hand, has been reluctant to embrace this new body of knowledge. Part of the reason may be interdisciplinary rivalries, part may simply be a lack of understanding, and part may be due to deep-seated his-torical and moral suspicions of a biological approach to crime causation. For whatever reason, these data have been largely ignored by criminologists and sociologists. . . .

Genetics

Twin Studies

The twin method for ascertaining whether a given trait is to any extent her-itable makes use of the fact that monozygotic (MZ) or "identical" twins are genetically identical, having 100 percent of their genes in common with one another. Conversely, dizygotic (DZ) or "fraternal" twins are less genetically alike than MZ twins, and are in fact no more alike genetically than non-twin siblings. . . .

Are identical twins more concordant for criminality than fraternal twins? The answer from many reviews conducted on this expanding field is undoubt-edly yes. As one example, a review of all the twin studies of crime conducted up to 1993 showed that although twin studies vary widely in terms of the age, sex, country of origin, sample size, determination of zygosity, and definition of crime, nevertheless all thirteen studies of crime show greater concordance rates for criminality in MZ as opposed to DZ twins. If one averages concord-ance rates across all studies (weighting for sample sizes), these thirteen studies result in concordances of 51.5 percent of MZ twins and 20.6 percent for DZ twins. Furthermore, the twin studies that have been conducted since 1993 have confirmed the hypothesis that there is greater concordance for antisocial and aggressive behavior in MZ relative to DZ twins. . . .

Adoption Studies

Adoption studies also overcome the problem with twin studies because they more cleanly separate out genetic and environmental influences. We can examine offspring who have been separated from their criminal, biological parents early in life and sent out to other families. If these offspring grow up to become criminal at greater rates than foster children whose biological parents were not criminal, this would indicate a genetic influence with its origin in the subject's biological parents. . . .

[A] review of fifteen other adoption studies conducted in Denmark, Sweden, and the United States shows that all but one find a genetic basis to criminal behavior. Importantly, evidence for this genetic predisposition has been found by several independent research groups in several different countries. . . .

Psychophysiology

Since the 1940s an extensive body of research has been built up on the psychophysiological basis of antisocial, delinquent, criminal, and psychopathic behavior. For example, there have been at least 150 studies on electrodermal (sweat rate) and cardiovascular (heart rate) activity in such populations, and in electroencephalographic (EEG) research alone there have been hundreds of studies on delinquency and crime. . . .

Definitions of psychophysiology vary, but one useful perspective outlined by Dawson is that it is "concerned with understanding the relationships between psychological states and processes on the one hand and physiological measures on the other hand." Psychophysiology is uniquely placed to provide important insights into criminal behavior because it rests at the interface between clinical science, cognitive science, and neuroscience. . . .

There are many psychophysiological correlates of antisocial, criminal, and psychopathic behavior. The focus here will lie with one particular psychophysiological construct, low arousal, because—as will become clear—it is the strongest psychophysiological finding in the field of antisocial and criminal behavior.

EEG Underarousal

One influential psychophysiological theory of antisocial behavior is that antisocial individuals are chronically underaroused. Traditional psychophysiological measures of arousal include heart rate, skin conductance activity, and electroencephalogram (EEG) measured during a "resting" state. Low heart rate and skin conductance activity, and more excessive slow-wave EEG . . . indicate underarousal, that is, less than average levels of physiological arousal. Most studies tend to employ single measures of arousal, although studies that employ multiple measures are in a stronger position to test an arousal theory of antisocial behavior.

EEG is recorded from scalp electrodes that measure the electrical activity of the brain. Literally hundreds of studies assessing EEG in criminals, delinquents, psychopaths, and violent offenders have been done over the past sixty years, and it is clear that a large number of them implicate EEG abnormalities in violent recidivistic offending behavior. . . . Murderers have more recently been shown to have more EEG deficits in the right than the left hemisphere of the brain, with multiple abnormalities being especially present in the right temporal cortex. On the other hand, Pillmann et al. showed greater abnormalities in the *left* temporal region of repeat violent offenders.

Generally speaking, the prevalence of EEG abnormalities in violent individuals in this large literature ranges from 25 percent to 50 percent, with the rate of abnormalities in normals estimated as ranging from 5 percent to 20 percent. The bulk of this research implicated the more frontal regions of the brain, areas that regulate executive functions such as planning and decision making. . . .

Cardiovascular Underarousal

Data on resting heart rate provides striking support for underarousal in antisocials. Indeed, the findings for heart rate level (HRL) on non-institutionalized antisocials are believed to represent the strongest and best replicated biological correlate of antisocial behavior.

A low resting heart rate is the best-replicated biological marker of antisocial and aggressive behavior in childhood and adolescent community samples. Resting HRL was measured in a wide variety of ways, including polygraphs, pulse meters, and stopwatches. A wide number of definitions of antisocial behavior are used, ranging from legal criminality and delinquency to teacher ratings of antisocial behavior in school, self-report socialization measures, diagnostic criteria for conduct disorder, and genetically inferred law breaking (i.e. offspring of criminals). Subjects were also assessed in a wide variety of settings, including medical interview, study office, school, university laboratory, and hospital. In the light of such variability, it is surprising that consistency in findings have been obtained, attesting to the robustness of the observed effects. Importantly, there has also been good cross-laboratory replication of the finding, and it has also been found in six different countries—England, Germany, New Zealand, the United States, Mauritius, and Canada—illustrating invariance to cultural context.

The link between low heart rate and crime is not the result of such things as height, weight, body bulk, physical development, and muscle tone; scholastic ability and IQ; excess motor activity and inattention; drug and alcohol use; engagement in physical exercise and sports; or low social class, divorce, family size, teenage pregnancy, and other psychosocial adversity. Intriguingly, an unusual and important feature of the relationship is its diagnostic specificity. No other psychiatric condition has been linked to low resting heart rate. Other psychiatric conditions, including alcoholism, depression, schizophrenia, and anxiety disorder, have, if anything, been linked to *higher* (not lower) resting heart rate.

Low heart rate has been found to be an independent predictor of violence. . . . Indeed, low heart rate was more strongly related to both self-report and teacher measures of violence than having a criminal parent. These findings led Farrington to conclude that low heart rate may be one of the most important explanatory factors for violence. . . . Low heart rate characterizes female as well as male antisocial individuals. Several studies, including two that are prospective, have now established that, *within* females, low heart rate is linked to antisocial behavior. . . .

Interpretations of Low Arousal: Fearlessness and Stimulation-Seeking Theories

Why should low arousal and low heart rate predispose to antisocial and criminal behavior? There are two main theoretical interpretations. Fearlessness theory indicates that low levels of arousal are markers of low levels of fear. For example, particularly fearless individuals such as bomb disposal experts who have been decorated for their bravery have particularly low HRLs and reactivity, as do British paratroopers decorated in the Falklands War. A fearlessness interpretation of low arousal levels assumes that subjects are not actually at "rest," but that instead the rest periods of psychophysiological testing represent a mildly stressful paradigm and that low arousal during this period indicates lack of anxiety and fear. Lack of fear would predispose to antisocial and violent behavior because such behavior (for example, fights and assaults) requires a degree of fearlessness to execute, while lack of fear, especially in childhood, would help explain poor socialization since low fear of punishment would reduce the effectiveness of conditioning. Fearlessness theory receives support from the fact that autonomic underarousal also provides the underpinning for a fearless or uninhibited temperament in infancy and childhood.

A second theory explaining reduced arousal is stimulation-seeking theory. This theory argues that low arousal represents an unpleasant physiological state; antisocials seek stimulation in order to increase their arousal levels back to an optimal or normal level: Antisocial behavior is thus viewed as a form of stimulation-seeking, in that committing a burglary, assault, or robbery could be stimulating for some individuals. . . .

Psychophysiological Protective Factors against Crime Development

Until recently, there had been no research on biological factors that *protect* against crime development, but that is changing. We are discovering that *higher* autonomic activity during adolescence may act as a protective factor against crime development. . . . Findings suggest that boys who are antisocial during adolescence but who do not go on to adult criminal offending may be protected from such an outcome by their high arousal levels.

Overall, the initial profile that is being built up on the psychophysiological characteristics of the Desistor is one of heightened information processing (better orienting), greater responsivity to environmental stimuli in general (fast recovery), greater sensitivity to cues predicting punishment in particular (better classical conditioning), and higher fearfulness (high

HRLs). The importance of research on psychophysiological protective factors such as these is that they offer suggestions for possible intervention and prevention strategies.

Brain Imaging

Advances in brain imaging techniques in the past fifteen years have provided the opportunity to gain dramatic new insights into the brain mechanisms that may be dysfunctional in violent, psychopathic offenders. In the past, the idea of peering into the mind of a murderer to gain insights into his or her acts was the province of pulp fiction or space-age movies. Yet now we can literally look at, and into, the brains of murderers using functional and structural imaging techniques that are currently revolutionizing our understanding of the causes of clinical disorders.

Brain imaging studies of violent and psychopathic populations . . . concur in indicating that violent offenders have structural and functional deficits to the frontal lobe (behind the forehead) and the temporal lobe (near the ears). . . . Despite some discrepancies, the first generation of brain imaging studies supports earlier contentions from animal and neurological studies implicating the frontal (and to some extent temporal) brain regions in the regulation and expression of aggression.

Prefrontal Dysfunction in Murderers

In the first published brain imaging study of murderers, we scanned the brains of twenty-two murderers pleading not guilty by reason of insanity (or otherwise found incompetent to stand trial) and compared them to the brains of twenty-two normal controls who were matched with the murderers on sex and age. The technique we used was positron emission tomography (PET), which allowed us to measure the metabolic activity of many different regions of the brain including the prefrontal cortex, the frontalmost part of the brain. We had subjects perform a task that required them to maintain focused attention and be vigilant for a continuous period of time, and it is the prefrontal region of the brain that in part subserves this vigilance function.

The key finding was that the murderers showed significantly poorer functioning of the prefrontal cortex, that part of the brain lying above the eyes and behind the forehead. . . . Prefrontal damage also encourages risk-taking, irresponsibility, rule breaking, emotional and aggressive outbursts, and argumentative behavior that can also predispose to violent criminal acts. Loss of self-control, immaturity, lack of tact, inability to modify and inhibit behavior appropriately, and poor social judgment could predispose to violence as well. This loss of intellectual flexibility and problem-solving skills, and reduced ability to use information provided by verbal cues can impair social skills essential for formulating nonaggressive solutions to fractious encounters. Poor reasoning ability and divergent thinking that results from prefrontal damage can lead to school failure, unemployment, and economic deprivation, thereby predisposing to a criminal and violent way of life. . . .

Other Biological Processes: Birth Complications, Minor Physical Anomalies, Nutrition, and Neurochemistry

Birth Complications

Several studies have shown that babies who suffer birth complications are more likely to develop conduct disorder, delinquency, and impulsive crime and violence in adulthood. Birth complications such as anoxia (getting too little oxygen), forceps delivery, and preeclampsia (hypertension leading to anoxia) are thought to contribute to brain damage, and this damage in turn may predispose to antisocial and criminal behavior. On the other hand, birth complications may not by themselves predispose to crime, but may require the presence of negative environmental circumstance to trigger later adult crime and violence.

One example of this "biosocial interaction" is a study of birth complications and maternal rejection in all 4,269 live male births that took place in one hospital in Copenhagen, Denmark. A highly significant interaction was found between birth complications and maternal rejection. Babies who only suffered birth complications or who only suffered maternal rejection were no more likely than normal controls to become violent in adulthood. On the other hand, those who had both risk factors were much more likely to become violent. . . .

Nutrition

Although deficiency in nutrition itself has been rarely studied in relation to childhood aggression, several studies have demonstrated the effects of related processes including food additives, hypoglycemia, and more recently cholesterol on human behavior. In addition, some studies have shown associations between overaggressive behavior and vitamin and mineral deficiency. Furthermore, one study claimed that nearly a third of a population of juvenile delinquents (mostly males) showed evidence of iron deficiency. Nevertheless, these findings remain both conflicting and controversial.

One intriguing study illustrates the potentially causal role of malnutrition as early as pregnancy in predisposing to antisocial behavior. Toward the end of World War II when Germany was withdrawing from Holland, they placed a food blockade on the country that led to major food shortages and near starvation in the cities and towns for several months. Women who were pregnant at this time were exposed to severe malnutrition at different stages of pregnancy. The male offspring of these women were followed up into adulthood to ascertain rates of Antisocial Personality Disorder and were compared to controls who were not exposed to malnutrition. Pregnant women starved during the blockade had 2.5 times the rates of Antisocial Personality Disorder in their adult offspring compared to controls.

Initial evidence also shows relationships between both protein and zinc deficiency and aggression in animals. Recent studies of humans support these animal findings. Protein and zinc deficiency may lead to aggression by negatively impacting brain functioning. . . . In humans, zinc deficiency in pregnancy has been linked to impaired DNA, RNA, and protein synthesis during brain development, and congenital brain abnormalities. . . . The amygdala, which also shows abnormal functioning in PET imaging of violent offenders, is densely innervated by zinc-containing neurons, and males with a history of assaultive behavior were found to have lower zinc relative to copper ratios in their blood compared to nonassaultive controls. Consequently, protein and zinc deficiency may contribute to the brain impairments shown in violent offenders which in turn are thought to predispose to violence.

Environmental Pollutants and Neurotoxicity

It has long been suspected that exposure to pollutants, particularly heavy metals that have neurotoxic effects, can lead to mild degrees of brain impairment which in turn predisposes to antisocial and aggressive behavior. One of the best studies to date is that of Needleman et al. who assessed lead levels in the bones of 301 eleven-year-old schoolboys. Boys with higher lead levels were found to have significantly higher teacher ratings of delinquent and aggressive behavior, higher parent ratings of delinquent and aggressive behavior, and higher self-report delinquency scores. These findings do not occur in isolation: Similar links between lead levels and antisocial, delinquent behavior and aggression have been found in at least six other studies in several different countries. . . .

Less strong to date, but nevertheless provocative, are findings with respect to manganese. At high levels, manganese has toxic effects on the brain and can damage the brain so much that it can even lead to Parkinson-like symptoms. Furthermore, it reduces levels of serotonin and dopamine, neurotransmitters that play a key role in brain communication. . . .

Hormones

Testosterone. Excellent reviews and discussions of the potential role played by testosterone in both animals and man can be found in Olweus, Brain, Archer, and Susman and Ponirakis. Animal research suggests that the steroid hormone testosterone plays an important role in the genesis and maintenance of some forms of aggressive behavior in rodents, and early exposure to testosterone had been found to increase aggression in a wide range of animal species. . . .

The critical question in this literature concerns whether testosterone-violence relationships are causal. Little doubt exists that castration decreases aggression in animals and administration of testosterone increases aggression. Few experimental studies have been conducted in humans, but there is nevertheless evidence of a causal relationship. Olweus et al. assessed their finding of higher testosterone in male adolescents with high levels of self-reported aggression using path analysis and concluded that testosterone had causal effects on both provoked and unprovoked aggressive behavior. One study that comes close to such an ideal experiment is that of Wille and Beier, who showed that ninety-nine castrated German sex offenders had a significantly lower recidivism rate eleven years postrelease (3 percent) compared to thirty-five noncastrated sex offenders (46 percent). . . .

Clearly, links between testosterone and aggression are complex, and simplistic explanations of this link are probably incorrect. By the same token, it would be equally erroneous to discount the evidence for the role of hormones in influencing aggression merely because hormones are influenced by the environment. . . .

Policy Implications

One of the biggest and widely held myths in criminology research is that biology is destiny. Instead, the reality is that the biological bases of crime and violence are amenable to change through benign interventions. In the past fifty years, intervention programs have not been as successful in reducing crime and violence as had been hoped, and it is possible that part of their failure has been due to the fact that they have systematically ignored the biological component of the biosocial equation.

Brain damage and poor brain functioning have been shown to predispose to violence, and one possible source of this brain damage could be birth complications. The implication is that providing better pre- and postbirth health care to poor mothers may help reduce birth complications and thus reduce violence. . . .

Another source of brain damage could be poor nutrition; and as has been seen earlier, there is evidence for a link between poor nutrition during pregnancy and later crime. Furthermore, cigarette and alcohol usage during pregnancy have been linked to later antisocial behavior. . . . These studies provide more support to the notion that nutrition plays a causal role in the development of childhood aggression, but future prevention trials that focus explicitly on the specific role of nutrition are required to further support the specific role of malnutrition.

It has been shown that low physiological arousal is the best-replicated biological correlate of antisocial behavior in child and adolescent samples. An important question from a prevention perspective concerns whether low arousal is amenable to change using noninvasive procedures. Recent findings from Mauritius suggest that it is. A nutritional, physical exercise, and educational enrichment from ages three to five resulted in increased psychophysiological arousal and orienting at age eleven compared to a matched control group. . . .

The policy implications of biological research on crime also extend to the criminal justice system. One question raised by these and other studies is whether any of us have freedom of will in the strict sense of the term. If brain deficits make it more likely that a person will commit violence, and if the cause of the brain deficits was not under the control of the individual, then the question becomes whether or not that person should be held fully responsible for the crimes. Of course we have to protect society, and unless we can treat this brain dysfunction, we may need to keep violent offenders in secure conditions for the rest of their lives; but do they deserve to be executed given the early constraints on their free will? It could be argued that if an individual possesses risk factors that make him disproportionately more likely to commit violence, then he has to take responsibility for these predispositions. Just like an alcoholic who knows he suffers from the disease of alcoholism, the person at risk for violence needs to recognize his risk factors and take preventive steps to ensure that he does not harm others. These persons have risk factors, but they still have responsibility and they have free will. . . .

Biological research is beginning to give us new insights into what makes a violent criminal offender. It is hoped that these early findings may lead us to rethink our approach to violence and goad us into obtaining new answers to the causes and cures of crime while we continue to protect society.

 **NO**

Crime Control in America

Known Sources of Crime

There are many things that we do know about the sources of crime. Note that I have said *sources* rather than *causes* because the kind of knowledge we have is far from the precise knowledge that a physicist has about how some event *causes* another. We know that poverty, slums, and unemployment are *sources* of street crime. We do not fully understand how they *cause* crime, because we know as well that many, if not most, poor, unemployed slum dwellers do not engage in street crime. Yet, to say that this means we do not know that such conditions are sources of violent crime is like saying that we do not know that a bullet in the head is deadly because some people survive or because we do not fully understand the physiological process that links the wound with the termination of life.

Poverty

Those youngsters who figure so prominently in arrest statistics are not drawn equally from all economic strata. Although there is much reported and even more unreported crime among middle-class youngsters, the street crime attributed to this age group that makes our city streets a perpetual war zone is largely the work of poor inner-city youth. This is the group at the lowest end of the economic spectrum. This is a group among whom unemployment approaches 50 percent, with underemployment (the percentage of persons either jobless or with part-time, low-wage jobs) still higher. This is a group with no realistic chance (for any but a rare individual) to enter college or amass sufficient capital (legally) to start a business or to get into the high-wage, skilled job markets. We know that poverty is a *source* of crime, even if we do not know how it *causes* crime, and yet we do virtually nothing to improve the life chances of the vast majority of the inner-city poor. They are as poor as ever and are facing cuts in welfare and other services.

That poverty is a source of crime is not refuted by the large and growing amount of white-collar crime that I shall document later. In fact, poverty contributes to crime by creating need, while, at the other end of the spectrum, wealth can contribute to crime by unleashing greed. Some criminologists have argued that economic inequality itself worsens crimes of the poor and of the well-off by increasing the opportunities for the well-off and increasing the humiliation of the poor. And inequality has worsened in recent years.

The gap between rich and poor worsened during the 1980s and 1990s. In 1970, the poorest fifth of the nation's families received 5.4 percent of the aggregate income, and the richest fifth received 40.9 percent. In 1980, the share of the poorest fifth was 5.1 percent of aggregate income, and that of the richest fifth was 41.6 percent. By 1999, the share of the poorest fifth had declined to 4.3 percent, while that of the richest fifth had risen to 47.2 percent. In this period from 1980 to 1999, the share of the top 5 percent rose from 14.6 to 20.3 percent. By 1999, the number of poor Americans was 32.3 million (almost 1 in 9 Americans), up from 30.1 million in 1990, and from 25.2 million in 1980. And, due to cuts in welfare,

> From 1995 to 1997, despite continued economic growth, the average incomes of the poorest 20 percent of female-headed households fell . . . an average of $580 per family. Among the poorest 10 percent of female-headed families with children, income fell an average of $810 between 1995 and 1997.

An analysis of data issued by the Congressional Budget Office indicates that "Among the bottom fifth of households, average after-tax income is anticipated to *fall* nine percent from 1977 to 1999." The same report concludes that:

> Income disparities have widened to such a degree that in 1999, the richest one percent of the population is projected to receive as much after-tax income as the bottom 38 percent combined. That is, the 2.7 million Americans with the largest incomes are expected to receive as much after-tax income as the 100 million Americans with the lowest incomes.

By 2001, the share of the richest fifth grew to over half of the nation's before-tax income.

Moreover, these developments were the predictable outcome of the Reagan administration's strategy of fighting inflation by cutting services to the poor while reducing the taxes of the wealthy. In September 1982, a group of 34 prominent economists sharply criticized Reagan's economic policy as "extremely regressive in its impact on our society, redistributing wealth and power from the middle class and the poor to the rich, and shifting more of the tax burden away from business and onto low- and middle-income consumers." In that same month, a study released by the Urban Institute concluded that "the Reagan administration's policies are not only aiding upper-income families at the expense of the working poor, but also are widening the gulf between affluent and poorer regions of the country." The study maintained that Reagan's tax cuts required sacrifices of low-income families, while yielding small gains for middle-income families and large gains for upper-income families; and that the combined effect of the administration's tax and social service spending cuts was "to penalize working families near the poverty line who receive some federal benefits . . . creating 'major work disincentives.'"

Edward Wolff writes that the "Equalizing trends of the 1930s–1970s reversed sharply in the 1980s. The gap between the haves and have-nots is greater now than at any time since 1929. The sharp increase in inequality since the late 1970s has made wealth distribution in the United States more unequal than in what used to be perceived as the class-ridden societies of northwestern Europe. An article in *Business Week* notes "the extraordinarily high level of child poverty in America today. One in five children under the age of 15 lives in poverty, and a staggering 50% of all black children under the age of six live in poverty."

Furthermore, as unemployment has gone up and down over the past decades, unemployment at the bottom of society remains strikingly worse than the national average. For example, over the past 35 years black unemployment has remained slightly more than twice the rate of white unemployment. In 1967, when 3.4 percent of white workers were unemployed, 7.4 percent of black workers were jobless. By 2000, when overall unemployment was about 4 percent, 3.5 percent of white workers were unemployed and 7.6 percent of blacks were. Among those in the crime-prone ages of 16 to 19, 11.4 percent of white youngsters and 24.7 percent (almost one in every four) black youngsters were jobless. Now, when the economy is in a slump, overall unemployment rose to 6 percent in December 2002, but for whites the jobless rate is 5.2 percent, while for blacks it is 11 percent.

Writes Todd Clear, professor of criminal justice at Rutgers University, "Let's start investing in things that really reduce crime: good schools, jobs and a future for young parents and their children." Why don't we?

Prison

We know that prison produces more criminals than it cures. We know that more than 70 percent of the inmates in the nation's prisons or jails are not there for the first time. A study from the Bureau of Justice Statistics indicates that, of inmates released in 1994, 67.5 percent were rearrested within three years, "almost exclusively for a felony or serious misdemeanor." We know that prison inmates are denied autonomy and privacy and subjected to indignities and acts of violence as regular features of their confinement, all of which is heightened by overcrowding. As of the last day of 1998, state prison systems were operating at between 13 percent and 22 percent over their reported capacity; the federal prison system was operating at 27 percent above capacity. A later report from the Bureau of Justice Statistics confirms that this pattern continues through 2001. A study of prisons in four Midwestern states found that about one-fifth of male inmates reported "a pressured or forced sex incident while incarcerated. About nine percent of male inmates reported that they had been raped." It is perhaps needless to add that prison rapes are almost never prosecuted.

The predictable result, as delineated by Robert Johnson and Hans Toch in *The Pains of Imprisonment*, "is that the prison's survivors become tougher, more pugnacious, and less able to feel for themselves and others, while its nonsurvivors become weaker, more susceptible, and less able to control their lives." Prisoners are thus bereft of both training and capacity to handle daily problems in competent and socially constructive ways, inside or outside of prison. The organization Stop Prison Rape reports that, "Upon release, male prisoner rape survivors may bring with them emotional scars and learned violent behavior that continue the cycle of harm. Feelings of rage can be suppressed until release, when survivors may engage in violent, antisocial behavior." According to a Human Rights Watch report entitled "No Escape: Male Rape in U.S. Prisons," "the only way to avoid the repetition of sexual abuse, many prisoners assert, is to strike back violently." The report quotes a victim of prison rape saying: "People start to treat you right, once you become deadly." In this way, prison makes inmates a greater harm to society than they were when they entered.

Once on the outside, burdened with the stigma of a prison record and rarely trained in a marketable skill, they find few opportunities for noncriminal employment open to them. Nor does this affect all groups in America alike. According to Professor Michael Tonry, author of *Malign Neglect: Race, Crime and Punishment in America,* "By affecting so many young black men, American criminal laws have further undermined the black family and made it harder for black men to get an education and find good jobs." A recent study by the Sentencing Project indicates that the enormous number of African American men who have been convicted of felonies, and therefore deprived of their right to vote, is "having a profound [negative!] impact on the black community's ability to participate in the political process."

What's more, because so much of the recent increase in imprisonment has been of inner-city black men who were involved in families and who had at least part-time legitimate employment at the time of their arrest and incarceration, social scientists are beginning to study the ways in which massive imprisonment is undermining the family and other community institutions, depriving children of male role models, and depriving women of potential husbands and support. Though this research is still in its infancy, the limited evidence collected so far suggests that massive imprisonment may weaken inner-city institutions of social control *and thus lead to more crime in the long run.*

Can we honestly act as if we do not know that both our imprisonment policies and our prison system (combined with our failure to ensure a meaningful postrelease noncriminal alternative for the ex-con) is a *source* of crime? Should we really pretend, then, that we do not *know* why ex-cons turn to crime? Recidivism does not happen because ex-cons miss their alma mater. In fact, if prisons are built to deter people from crime, one would expect that ex-prisoners would be the most deterred, because the deprivations of prison are more real to them than to the rest of us. Recidivism is thus a doubly poignant testimony to the job that prison does in preparing its graduates for crime, yet we do little to change the nature of prisons or to provide real services to ex-convicts.

Guns

Since 1965 more than *one million* Americans have been shot to death. Our firearm death rate is higher by far than that of any other modern nation. And, because the fatality rate for robberies using a gun is three times higher than for robberies with knives and ten times higher for robberies with other weapons, countries like Italy and Australia that have robbery rates comparable to the U.S.'s have far fewer robberies that end up as homicides.

Speaking about the extraordinary spate of deadly violence that we had in the late 1980s and early 1990s, Garen Wintemute puts it bluntly: "the entire increase in homicide in the United States through 1993 was attributable to firearm homicide." Increasingly this was due to highly lethal semiautomatic pistols (during the same period, the percentage of homicides with regular revolvers declined significantly). Hospitals reported an increase in gunshot wounds per victim, and in the size of bullets removed. This phenomenon is closely linked to trends in handgun production. Starting in the late 1980s, American gun manufacturers started producing "high capacity, medium-caliber semiautomatic pistols that were also very inexpensive." Almost all were produced "by a small group of manufacturers in Southern California."

We have long known that it is about as difficult to obtain a handgun in the United States as a candy bar. "Sixty-two percent of urban middle and high school students in 1993 reported that they could get a firearm with little difficulty. One in six reported that they had actually carried a firearm in the prior month."

Gary Kleck estimates that, by 1990, the civilian stock of guns in the United States had passed the 200 million mark. This estimate is corroborated by a 1993 report from the Bureau of Alcohol, Tobacco, and Firearms, which estimated 200 million guns, about 1 percent of which were assault rifles. They also note that the "number of large caliber pistols produced annually increased substantially after 1986." Nearly one-half of U.S. households have at least one gun, and about a quarter have at least one handgun. Half of handgun owners surveyed said that their guns were currently loaded.

The President's Crime Commission reported that, in 1965, "5,600 murders, 34,700 aggravated assaults and the vast majority of the 68,400 armed robberies were committed by means of firearms. All but 10 of 278 law enforcement officers murdered during the period 1960–65 were killed with firearms." The commission concluded almost 30 years ago that

> more than one-half of all willful homicides and armed robberies, and almost one-fifth of all aggravated assaults, involve use of firearms. As long as there is no effective gun-control legislation, violent crimes and the injuries they inflict will be harder to reduce than they might otherwise be.

The situation has worsened since the commission's warning. The FBI reported that the "proportion of violent crimes committed with firearms has increased in recent years," from being employed in the commission of 26 percent of violent offenses in 1987 to 32 percent in 1993. The FBI writes: "In 1975, 66 percent of murders of persons (aged 15 to 19) were attributable to guns, while in 1992 the figure rose to 85 percent. This increase supports the theory that today's high-school-aged youths are exposed to an environment that includes guns." The Office of Juvenile Justice reports that, "By 1997, the homicide rate for 15- to 24-year-olds was 15.2 per 100,000, which is higher than the combined total homicide rate of eleven industrialized nations," and goes on to point out that "Firearms were the weapons of choice in nearly two-third[s] of all murders."

Furthermore, guns kill and maim outside of crime as well. "Every 14 minutes someone in America dies from a gunshot wound. Slightly more than half of those deaths are suicides, about 44 percent are homicides and 4 percent are unintentional shootings." The Centers for Disease Control report that there were 143,000 nonfatal shootings in 1994. A study published in the *New England Journal of Medicine* in October 1993 found that people in households with guns were almost three times more likely to experience a homicide than people in homes without guns. Guns also take a grave and worsening toll among our children. According to a report from the Children's Defense Fund, nearly 50,000 children were killed by guns between 1979 and 1991.

In the face of facts like these—indeed, in the face of his own nearly fatal shooting by a would-be assassin—President Reagan refused to support any legislative attempts to control the sale of handguns. His successor, President George Bush, followed suit. On Thanksgiving Day, 1993, Bush's successor, Bill Clinton, signed into law the so-called Brady Bill, which goes only so far as imposing a five-day waiting period for gun purchases, to enable checks to see whether would-be gun purchasers have criminal records. The Brady Bill leaves it to the states to enforce the waiting period and to get their police to make a "reasonable effort" to conduct the background checks. However, the bill provides no sanctions for states that do not comply, and it leaves it effectively up to the states to provide funding for the checks and to determine what is a "reasonable effort." Since the Brady Bill went into effect, writes Blumstein, "over 400,000 attempted handgun purchases have been denied, but it is not known how many of those customers eventually bought guns from an unregulated source."

Can we believe that our leaders sincerely want to cut down on violent crime and the injuries it produces when they oppose even as much as *registering* guns or *licensing* gun owners, much less actually restricting the sale and movement of guns as a matter of national policy? Can we really believe that if guns were less readily available, violent criminals would simply switch to other weapons to commit the same number of crimes and do the same amount of damage? Is there a weapon other than the handgun that works as quickly, that allows its user so safe a distance, or that makes the criminal's physical strength (or speed or courage for that matter) irrelevant? Could a bank robber hold a row of tellers at bay with a switchblade? Studies indicate that, if gun users switched to the next deadliest weapon—the knife—and attempted the same number of crimes, we could still expect *two-thirds fewer fatalities* because the fatality rate of the knife is roughly one-third that of the gun. In other words, even if guns were eliminated and the number of crimes held steady, we could expect to save as many as two out of every three persons who are now the victims of firearm homicide.

Drugs

Finally, the United States has an enormous drug abuse and addiction problem. There is considerable evidence, however, that our attempts to cure it are worse than the disease itself. Consider first heroin. Some people think this drug is out of fashion and no longer widely used. Far from it! Its use is widespread and persistent. The number of heroin users is hard to estimate because we only know about the ones who get caught and because there is a large but unknown number of individuals who (contrary to popular mythology) shoot up occasionally without becoming addicts, a practice known as "chipping." In his book, *The Heroin Solution,* Arnold Trebach suggests that this number may be as high as 3.5 million. For 1994, a U.S. government report states that "[g]rowing evidence indicated that domestic heroin consumption was on the rise." And further, that "[e]stimates suggested that there may be 600,000 hard-core drug users who report heroin as their principal drug of abuse," and that "heroin was readily available to addicts in all major metropolitan areas. Stable wholesale prices per kilogram and high retail-level purities indicated increasing supplies—a development consistent with nationwide trends over the past several years."

As shocking as these numbers may be, it must be at least as shocking to discover that there is little evidence proving that heroin is a *dangerous* drug. There is no evidence conclusively establishing a link between heroin and disease or tissue degeneration such as that established for tobacco and alcohol. James Q. Wilson, a defender of the prohibition on heroin and other drugs, admits that "there are apparently no specific pathologies—serious illnesses or physiological deterioration—that are known to result from heroin use per se." On the basis of available scientific evidence, there is every reason to suspect that we do our bodies more damage, more *irreversible* damage, by smoking cigarettes and drinking liquor than by using heroin. Most of the physical damage associated with heroin use is probably attributable to the trauma of withdrawal, a product not so much of heroin as of its occasional unobtainability.

It remains the case that most drug arrests are for marijuana use or possession, and that marijuana is a relatively safe drug. The 1988 surgeon general's report lists tobacco as a more dangerous drug than marijuana. According to the findings and conclusions of Francis Young, administrative law judge for the Drug Enforcement Administration, there are no documented marijuana user fatalities ("despite [its 5,000 year-] long history of use and the extraordinarily high numbers of social smokers, there are simply no credible medical reports to suggest that consuming marijuana has caused a single death"!), and no amount of marijuana that a person could possibly eat or smoke would constitute a lethal dose. By contrast, even aspirin overdose causes hundreds of deaths a year.

Regarding the drugs that can cause death from overdose, the dangers have been blown wildly out of proportion. Trebach points out that, although federal authorities documented 2,177 deaths from the most popular illicit drugs in 1985, between 400,000 and 500,000 people died from alcohol and tobacco during that same year. He adds that 50 children aged 17 and under died from drug overdoses in 1987, while "408 American children (from infants through the age of 14) were murdered by their parents in 1983"!

It might be said that the evil of drugs such as heroin is that they are *addicting*, because this is a bad thing even if the addicting substance is not itself harmful. It is hard to deny that the image of a person enslaved to a chemical is rather ugly and is repugnant to our sense that the dignity of human beings lies in their capacity to control their destinies. More questionable, however, is whether this is, in the case of adults, anybody's business but their own. Even so, suppose we agree that addiction is an evil worthy of prevention. Doesn't that make us hypocrites? What about all our other addictions? What about cigarette smoking, which, unlike heroin, contributes to cancer and heart disease? Nicotine's addictiveness—according to former Surgeon General C. Everett Koop—is similar to that of heroin. (By the way, cigarettes appear to be *more addicting than cocaine,* more likely to addict the new user, and more difficult to quit once addicted.) What about the roughly 15 million alcoholics in the nation working their way through their livers and into their graves? What about the people who cannot get started without a caffeine fix in the morning and those who, once started, cannot slow down without their alcohol fix in the evening? What of the folks who can't face daily life without their Valium? Are they not all addicts?

Suffice it to say, then, at the very least, our attitudes about heroin are inconsistent and irrational, and there is reason to believe they are outrageous and hypocritical. Even if this were not so, even if we could be much more certain that heroin addiction is a disease worth preventing, the fact would remain that the "cure" we have chosen is worse than the disease. We *know* that treating the possession of heroin as a criminal offense produces more crime than it prevents.

Alfred Blumstein provides a useful categorization of the relationship between drugs and crime:

- Pharmacological/psychological consequences. The drug itself causes criminal activity.
- Economic/compulsive crimes. Drug users commit crimes to get money to support their habit.
- Systemic crime. Crimes are committed as part of the regular means of doing business in the drug industry.

About the pharmacological effects of drugs, says Blumstein, the drug "that has the strongest pharmacological effect is alcohol. . . . Heroin is a downer, so heroin doesn't do much. And there hasn't been shown to be much pharmacological effect of the other serious drugs on crime, not anything comparable to that of alcohol, which has been shown to be a strong stimulator of violence." PCP tends to be one of the only other drugs to have a pharmacological link to violence. High doses of cocaine and methamphetamine can lead to some psychoses that include paranoia and delusion, which can lead to violence, but most of the violence associated with drugs falls under the second and third of Blumstein's categories. As for systemic crime, we have already seen the link between the crack trade and the murder epidemic of the late 1980s and early 1990s. Both these crimes and the economic/compulsive crimes that are engaged in by drug users to support their habits are due to the fact that drugs are so costly, and that is due to the fact that the drugs are illegal.

Prior to 1914, when anyone could go into a drugstore and purchase heroin and other opiates the way we buy aspirin today, hundreds of thousands of upstanding, law-abiding citizens were hooked. Opiate addiction is not in itself a *cause* of crime. If anything, it is a pacifier. There is, writes Trebach, "nothing in the pharmacology, or physical and psychological impact, of the drug that would propel a user to crime." Nor is there anything about heroin itself that makes it extremely costly. The heroin for which an addict pays $100 or more a day could be produced legally at a cost of a few cents for a day's supply. However, once sale or possession of heroin is made a serious criminal offense, a number of consequences follow. First, the prices go up because those who supply it face grave penalties, and those who want it want it bad. Second, because the supply (and the quality) of the drug fluctuates, depending on how vigorously the agents of the law try to prevent it, the addict's life is continuously unstable. Addicts live in constant uncertainty about the next fix and must devote much of their wit and energy to getting it and to getting enough money to pay for it. They do not, then, fit easily into the routines of a nine-to-five job, even if they could get one that would pay enough to support their habits. Finally, all the difficulties of securing the drug add up to an incentive to be not merely a user of heroin but a dealer as well, because this both earns money and makes one's own supply more certain. Addicts thus have an incentive to find and encourage new addicts, which they would not have if heroin were legally and cheaply available. If we add to this the fact that heroin addiction has remained widespread, and possibly even increased in spite of all our law enforcement efforts, can we doubt that the cure is worse than the disease? Can we doubt that the cure is a *source* of crime?

Says former Washington, D.C., Police Chief Maurice Turner, "If you see an addict going through withdrawal, he's in some kind of damn pain. . . . When they get pretty well strung out, they have about a $100- to $120-a-day habit. When they get that type of habit, they're going to have to steal approximately six times that much," because fences don't pay list price. Professor Blumstein agrees, "you need money to buy drugs, so the higher the price of the drug, the greater the incentive to commit the crime." The result is a recipe for large-scale and continual robbery and burglary, which would not exist if the drug were available legally. A recent study by Anglin and Speckart of the relationship between narcotics use and crime concludes that there is "strong evidence that there is a strong causal relationship, at least in the United States, between addiction to narcotics and property crime levels."

Do a little arithmetic. Suppose that there are half a million addicts with $100-a-day habits. And let's make some conservative assumptions about these addicts. Suppose that they fill their habits only 250 days a year (sometimes they're in jail or in the hospital). Suppose that they have to steal for half their drug needs, and that they must steal three times the dollar value of what they need because they must convert their booty into cash through a fence. (These conservative assumptions are similar to those made in a report of the U.S. Department of Health, Education, and Welfare, entitled *Social Cost of Drug Abuse*, estimating the amount of theft in which heroin addicts had to engage to support their habits in 1974.) If you've done your arithmetic, you have seen that our half-million addicts need to steal $18,750,000,000 a year to support their habits. This is more than the $16.6 billion that the FBI estimates as the loss due to property crimes during 2001, and it doesn't even take into consideration theft by those addicted to other drugs, such as crack.

Even if you think that this $18.75 billion in theft is an improbable figure, and even if you also assume that the FBI's estimate of the value of stolen property would increase dramatically if we knew the value of unreported theft, you cannot escape the conclusion that theft by drug addicts—who have few other means of supporting their habit—accounts for an astounding amount of property crime. The Bureau of Justice Statistics reports that, in 1997, roughly one of every six prisoners—19 percent of state inmates, 15 percent of federal inmates—said that they had committed their current offense in order to get money for drugs. Because heroin doesn't produce crime through its pharmacological effects, and because it is so costly only because it's illegal, it is not the "disease" of heroin addiction but its "cure" that leads to property crime. *It is our steadfast refusal to provide heroin through legal sources that, for approximately a half a million individuals on the streets, translates a physical need for a drug into a physical need to steal billions of dollars worth of property a year.*

Against this conclusion, it is sometimes countered that studies show that a large proportion of criminal heroin addicts were criminals before they were addicts. Such studies would only refute the claim that the illegality of heroin is a source of crime if the claim was that heroin addiction turns otherwise law-abiding citizens into thieves. Rather, the claim is that the illegality of heroin (and, thus, its limited availability and almost unlimited price) places addicts in situations in which they *must* engage in theft, continually and at a high level, to keep a step ahead of the pains of withdrawal. Anglin and Speckart affirm that "while involvement in property crime activities generally precedes the addiction career, after addiction occurs the highly elevated property crime levels demonstrated by addicts appear to be regulated by similarly high narcotics use levels." Thus, even for addicts who already were criminals, heroin addiction increases the amount they need to steal and works to make them virtually immune to attempts to wean them from a life of crime. Consequently, even if all heroin addicts were criminals before they were addicts, the illegality of heroin would still be a source of crime because of the increased pressure it places on the addict to steal a lot and to steal often. Much the same reasoning applies to other illegal addictive drugs.

Recently, attention has shifted from heroin to "crack," a highly addictive derivative of cocaine. The Office of National Drug Control Policy reports that there were nearly 2 million hardcore cocaine users in 1993. Having learned nothing from our experience with heroin, we have applied to cocaine and crack the same policy that failed with heroin, with predictable results: First of all, our large-scale attempts to reduce the flow of cocaine into the country have failed. Says Trebach:

> After seven years of a multi-billion dollar drug war, our prisons are filled to record levels, violent drug traffickers pollute our cities, and drug abuse is rampant. Despite the most aggressive drug war campaign in history, so much cocaine has been imported since 1981 that the price has dropped to one-third its former level. While some of our children now find it more difficult to buy marijuana, many find it much easier to buy crack and cocaine.

A report from the Office of National Drug Control Policy (ONDCP) indicates that "[i]n 1995, Americans spent $57 billion on these illegal drugs: $38 billion on cocaine, $10 billion on heroin, $7 billion on marijuana, and $3 billion on other illegal drugs and legal drugs used illicitly." A more recent report indicates that "Americans spent approximately $64 billion for illegal drugs in 2000." Because the price per pure gram of cocaine and of heroin has gone down between 1995 and 2000, we can only conclude that, for all the hoopla of the war on drugs, not to mention the enormous increase in the number of persons sent to prison on drug offenses, people are buying more and more.

According to the ONDCP, "About 287 to 340 metric tons of cocaine were available for domestic consumption in 1995." According to a United Nations estimate, illicit drugs account for some $400 billion worldwide, nearly one-tenth of world trade in all products! The General Accounting Office reports that U.S. efforts to reduce cultivation of drug crops in Bolivia and Colombia "have been almost entirely ineffective and the cultivation of drug crops has increased dramatically in both countries." This caps a long history of failure, starting with President Nixon's (successful) attempt to pressure Turkey into eradicating local cultivation of poppies (source of opium and thus of heroin) in 1971 and continuing with both Reagan's and Bush's attempts to pressure foreign countries to reduce domestic production of narcotic substances.

Though Nixon was successful with Turkey, the result was just to move production elsewhere. In spite of three U.S.-led international drug wars since then, worldwide illicit opium production rose from 990 tons in 1971 to 4,200 tons in 1989, and Andean coca leaf (source of cocaine and thus of crack) production grew from 291,100 tons in 1987 to 337,100 tons in 1991. (Total world opium production in 1991 was up 8 percent from the year prior, and nearly double the level of the mid-1980s.) Likewise, attempts to use the coast guard and navy to interdict cocaine coming into the United States by sea have failed to put a dent in the traffic. After all, America has over 88,000 miles of coastline. *The Wall Street Journal* reports that a kilogram of cocaine that cost between $55,000 and $65,000 in 1981 cost between $20,000 and $40,000 in 1987. They even report a "rock-bottom" price in Miami of $14,000 for a kilo. The National Narcotics Intelligence Consumers' Committee reports cocaine prices as low as $10,500 per kilogram in 1994, and an April 1999 report from the ONDCP shows steadily declining prices for both cocaine and heroin from 1981 to 1998, and steady if not rising levels of purity, all of which testifies to the general failure of our costly "war on drugs" to make these drugs harder to obtain.

In 1988, the *National Law Journal* surveyed 181 chief prosecutors or their top drug deputies throughout the United States and reported that "nearly two-thirds of the country's top state and local prosecutors say they are having little to no impact in the fight against illegal narcotics." This failing drug war is now costing federal, state, and local governments approximately $33 billion in 1999, up nearly $5 billion from 1994. The National Drug Control Budget alone is $18.8 billion for fiscal year 2002.

To that must be added the *nonfinancial* costs, such as increased violence among competing drug traffickers and increased corruption among law enforcement officials on the front line in the drug war. The year 1988 saw the nation's capital reach and overtake its annual homicide record, with all experts attributing the surge in murders to the struggle to capture the lucrative drug market. *The New York Times* reports that "researchers say there are now more than 100 cases each year in state and Federal courts in which law enforcement officials are charged or implicated in drug corruption." Says William Green, assistant commissioner for internal affairs at the U.S. Customs Service, "The money that's being offered by the drug dealers is so big it is just hard to visualize." The Mollen Commission report on police corruption in New York City found "willful blindness" to corruption throughout the police department, resulting in networks of rogue officers who dealt in drugs and preyed on black and Hispanic neighborhoods.

In sum, we have an antidrug policy that is failing at its own goals and succeeding only in adding to crime. First, there are the heroin and crack addicts, who must steal to support their habits. Then, there are the drug merchants who are offered fabulous incentives to provide illicit substances to a willing body of consumers. This in turn contributes to the high rate of inner-city murders and other violence as drug gangs battle for the enormous sums of money available. Next, there are the law enforcement officials who, after risking their lives for low salaries, are corrupted by nearly irresistible amounts of money. Finally, there are the otherwise law-abiding citizens who are made criminals because they use cocaine, a drug less harmful than tobacco, and those who are made criminals because they use marijuana, a drug that is safer than alcohol and less deadly than aspirin.

Much of the recent dramatic growth in our prison population (documented above) is the result of the hardening of drug enforcement policy starting in the Reagan years and continuing into the present: In 1968 there were 162,000 drug arrests nationwide, in 1977 there were 569,000, and in 1989 there were 1,150,000 drug arrests. In 1997 there were 1.6 million drug arrests, 200,000 more than in 1995, and the Bureau of Justice Statistics reports that 57 percent of federal inmates were serving sentences for drug violations in 2000. The absolute numbers are even more striking. In 2000, federal prisons held 73,389 drug offenders, compared to 30,470 in 1990. Because numerous studies show that arrested drug dealers in inner-city neighborhoods are quickly replaced, it was apparent from the start that this policy would have little success in reducing the availability of illicit drugs.

All this is occurring at a time when there is increasing evidence that what does work to reduce substance abuse is public education. Because this has succeeded in reducing alcohol and tobacco consumption and, in some cases, marijuana and cocaine consumption as well, it's time that we take the money we are wasting in the "war on drugs" and spend it on public education instead. Because that would be far less costly than the "war," this would leave over money to fight a more effective war against muggers and rapists rather than recreational drug users. Evidence from the 11 states that decriminalized marijuana possession in the 1970s suggests that decriminalization does not lead to increased use. And President Clinton's former surgeon general, Joycelyn Elders, recommended that we study seriously the possibility of decriminalizing drugs as a means to reducing violence, noting that "other countries had decriminalized drug use and had reduced their crime rates without increasing the use of narcotics." Baltimore Mayor Kurt Schmoke has called for consideration of decriminalization, and so has Jerry Wilson, former Chief of Police of Washington, D.C. (where 42 percent of murders were drug-related in 1990). A draft of a report commissioned by the American Medical Association recommended legalization of marijuana and decriminalization of other illicit drugs. The report was shelved when some doctors "expressed outrage at its recommendation." Some form of decriminalization of marijuana, heroin, and cocaine would reduce the criminalization of otherwise law-abiding users; it would drive down the price of drugs, which would reduce the need for addicts to steal, and reduce as well the incentives to drug traffickers and smugglers to ply their trades and to find new users; and it would free up personnel and resources for a more effective war against the crimes that people fear most.

In the face of all this, it is hard to believe that we do not know how to reduce crime at all. It is hard not to share the frustration expressed by Norval Morris, former dean of the University of Chicago Law School: "It is trite but it remains true that the main causes of crime are social and economic. The question arises whether people really care. The solutions are so obvious. *It's almost as if America wished for a high crime rate.*" If this is so, then *the system's failure is only in the eye of the victim: For those in control, it is a roaring success!*

What Works to Reduce Crime

Surveying the programs that might contribute to reducing crime, criminologist Elliot Currie concludes that "four priorities seem especially critical: preventing child abuse and neglect, enhancing children's intellectual and social development, providing support and guidance to vulnerable adolescents, and working extensively with juvenile offenders." About these programs, Currie observes, "the best of them work, and they work remarkably well given how limited and underfunded they usually are." A study entitled *Diverting Children from a Life of Crime: Measuring Costs and Benefits,* issued in June 1996 by the Rand Corporation, concluded:

> Programs that try to steer the young from wrongdoing—the training of parents whose children often misbehave, for example, or incentives to graduate from high school—are far more cost-effective in preventing crime over the long term than are mandatory sentences that imprison repeat adult offenders for long periods.

A more recent report from the Rand Corporation, entitled *Investing in Our Children: What We Know and Don't Know about the Costs and Benefits of Early Childhood Interventions,* reached a similar conclusion. Evaluating nine programs in which early interventions were targeted at disadvantaged children, the study concludes that such programs lead to decreased criminal activity and save taxpayer dollars at the same time. Similar results were found for Head Start programs. "At age 27, those who participated [in Head Start programs as children] had lower arrest rates, higher education rates, earned more money, were more likely to be homeowners and less likely to receive social services."

The National Treatment Improvement Study, "the largest study of its kind, which followed more than 5,300 clients in programs funded by the federal Center for Substance Abuse Treatment," concludes that "drug and alcohol treatment programs significantly reduced substance use, crime, and homelessness. . . . Use of most illicit substances in the year after treatment entry declined about 50 percent compared with the year before. . . . Arrest rates fell substantially in the sample—from 48 percent to 17 percent." And a study by the Rand Corporation Drug Policy Research Center, entitled *Controlling Cocaine: Supply versus Demand Programs,* found that "[t]reatment is seven times more cost-effective than domestic drug enforcement in reducing cocaine use and 15 times more cost-effective in reducing the social costs of crime and lost productivity." The study also concluded that "treatment is the most effective way to reduce violent crime."

A recent review of more than 500 crime-prevention program evaluations yielded a list of what works. Among the programs that appear effective in reducing crime the report lists: family therapy and parent training for delinquent and at-risk adolescents; teaching of social competency skills in schools and coaching of high-risk youth in "thinking skills"; vocational training for older male ex-offenders; extra police patrols in high-crime hot spots; monitoring of high-risk repeat offenders by specialized police forces as well as incarceration; rehabilitation programs with risk-focused treatments for convicted offenders; and therapeutic community treatment for drug-using offenders in prisons.

In short, there is a growing body of knowledge showing that early childhood intervention and drug treatment and numerous other programs can work to reduce crime. As Professor Blumstein observed, "If you intervene early, you not only save the costs of incarceration, you also save the costs of crime and gain the benefits of an individual who is a taxpaying contributor to the economy." But, as Peter Greenwood, author of the Rand Corporation Study, *Diverting Children from a Life of Crime,* says, "The big policy question is, Who will act on this?"

POSTSCRIPT

Is Criminal Behavior Determined Biologically?

For much of the twentieth century the biological perspective in criminology was regarded as an anachronism that conjured images of Cesare Lombroso slicing open cadavers and the early phrenologists measuring the contours of criminals' heads. As Adrian Raine demonstrates, however, the biological approach to the study of criminal behavior is making a strong comeback. For example, it is hard for modern criminologists to ignore identical twin studies, which indicate a significant amount of behavioral concordance, even when the individuals are separated shortly after birth and raised apart. In fact, as technology advances and our ability to identify the biological correlates of human behavior further improves, we may reach a point when behavioral scientists are more prepared to assign hard percentages to the nature-nurture controversy.

On the other hand, as Jeffrey H. Reiman demonstrates, there is also a significant social component to human behavior. People are social beings. Just examine the interaction dynamics in your classroom and think about how we influence the behavior of others in virtually every social situation.

Moreover, Reiman's theory has a great deal of intuitive appeal. Most people would agree about a number of the sources of crime in U.S. society. For example, we know that contemporary drug control policies have been largely ineffective; however, we appear to lack the political will to make the changes to our social policies that will have a lasting impact on drug crimes.

It appears likely that the definitive answer to the mystery of human behavior may eventually determine that both biological factors and social forces combine in a complex interactive web. Thus, for future behavioral scientists it is quite possible that the "nature OR nurture" controversy will become the "nature AND nurture" issue.

Fortunately, there are many outstanding resources that shed additional light on the issues presented in this section. For example, an excellent article that discusses potential strategies to reduce violent crime that considers environmental and biological correlates of human behavior is Robert M. Sade's "Introduction: Evolution, Prevention, and Responses to Aggressive Behavior and Violence," *The Journal of Law, Medicine & Ethics* (vol. 32, no. 1, 2004). Insightful discussions of the interplay among conscious choice, environmental factors, and basic human biology are presented as well by Michael Edmund O'Neill in "Stalking the Mark of Cain," *Harvard Journal of Law and Public Policy* (vol. 25, no. 1, Fall 2001); Gene E. Robinson, "Beyond Nature and Nurture," *Science* (Apr. 16, 2004); and Christiane Charlemaine, "What Might MZ Twin

Research Teach Us about Race, Gender & Class Issues," *Race, Gender & Class* (Oct. 31, 2002). Julie Horney considers the relationship between menstruation and crime in "Menstrual Cycles and Criminal Responsibility," *Law and Human Nature* (vol. 2, 1978).

Additional resources that consider the role of genetic and environmental factors in human behavior include: Edmund O. Wilson, *Sociobiology* (Harvard University Press, 1975); Lee Ellis, *Theories of Rape* (Hemisphere Publications, 1989); and Deborah Denno, *Biology, Crime and Violence* (Cambridge University Press, 1989).

ISSUE 3

Is a Person's Body Type Clearly Linked to Criminal Behavior?

YES: Sean Maddan, Jeffery T. Walker, and J. Mitchell Miller, from "Physiques, Somatotypes and Crime." An essay. (2009)

NO: Chris L. Gibson and Kevin M. Beaver, from "Does Body Type Really Have an Effect on Criminal Behavior?" An essay. (2009)

ISSUE SUMMARY

YES: Professors Maddan, Walker, and Miller argue that body type is related to criminal behavior because more criminals have muscular body builds. In other words, there is a strong correlation between a person's body build and criminal behavior.

NO: Professors Gibson and Beaver argue, in contrast, that both biological and social factors lead to criminal behavior and that no single variable, such as body build, can explain crime. Moreover, they assert that while body type may be a predisposing factor for crime, that predisposition will surface only under certain environmental conditions.

There has been a long debate over the relationship between body type and crime. Some of the earliest studies of this relationship were conducted by Professor Ernest Sheldon at the University of Chicago. In 1940, Sheldon published *The Varieties of Human Physique* and used a classification process termed "somatyping," to categorize three different body types based on their dominant characteristics. Endomorphs were characterized by a soft roundness to the body. Mesomorphs were stronger looking and had a more muscular appearance. Ectomorphs were taller, thinner, and more fragile looking. Sheldon later concluded that juvenile delinquents were much more likely to have mesomorphic body types.

On an intuitive level it seems to make sense that there could be a clear relationship between body type and criminal behavior. Compared to most sedentary individuals, athletic persons may be generally stronger and more active, and may engage in more aggressive activities. Doesn't it seem to make sense that young people who can run faster are more likely to become involved in mischief, vandalism, and related incidents that would lead to conflict with the criminal justice system?

Moreover, think about the kinds of people you see when you view a movie or television special on U.S. prisons. Scenes of convicts "pumping iron," or engaging in other types of physical exercise, are commonplace. Speaking generally, a significant number of these inmates are physically imposing individuals who have very athletic body types.

Problems develop, however, when we try to posit a direct causal link between body type and the likelihood of being a criminal. Remember the last time you observed the swimmers or gymnasts who compete in high-level competitions, such as the Olympic Games. Almost without exception, they are lean, strong, athletic-looking individuals, who would excel in almost any type of physical activity.

Why, then, do some people with athletic body types become criminals, whereas others become champion swimmers, gymnasts, or even sometimes college professors? The renowned criminologist Dr. Sue Titus Reid has described this type of problem as a "dualistic fallacy." This is essentially an error in reasoning that points to the existence of exceptions that cast doubt on a particular theory. In other words, while some persons with athletic body types do commit crimes, many do not, and others become highly successful in a wide variety of different endeavors. There is no easy answer to the question posed above. As the authors of the essays in this section note, there may well be additional factors or variables that influence the relationship between body type and crime.

To summarize, biological explanations of criminal behavior such as body-type theories have considerable appeal. The implications of these explanations may, however, lead to difficult, or even Orwellian, social policy choices. Does our current state of knowledge permit us to state conclusively that there is a clear link between a person's body type and criminal behavior? The authors of the essays in this section provide different answers to this question.

Professors Maddan, Walker, and Miller argue that there is a strong correlation between a person's body build and criminal behavior. Utilizing a more modern method of assessing a person's body type termed a body mass index (BMI), these authors assert that "mesomorphic" (athletic body type) offenders "were more likely to be in prison for a violent offense" than persons with other types of body builds.

Professors Gibson and Beaver, in contrast, believe that "the jury is still out" on the question and that the relationship between a person's body type and criminal behavior is highly inconclusive.

Do you agree initially with Professors Maddan, Walker, and Miller, or with Professors Gibson and Beaver? Do you feel that a person's body type influences his or her likelihood of becoming involved in criminal behavior, or is the relationship between body type and crime simply too speculative? The answers to these questions may have a significant impact on future social and corrections policies in this country.

YES    Sean Maddan, Jeffery T. Walker, and J. Mitchell Miller

Physique, Somatotypes and Crime

Introduction

From the earliest days of criminological thought, researchers have sought bio-logical causes of criminality. Because some of the earlier biological studies were disproved due to methodological shortcomings or antiquated statistical tech-niques, a majority of criminologists today dismiss the biological research of criminality with relative ease. As Wilson and Herrnstein (1985, p. 80) wrote, "many criminologists . . . are simply uneasy with biological and psychologi-cal concepts" involved with the causes of criminality due to their sociological training. In fact, "physical correlates of crime are often dismissed by most criminologists, for whom these are at best historical stages in the development of their subject" (Wilson & Herrnstein, 1985, p. 72). The last decade has seen a massive resurgence in the study of the links between biology and crime (Raine, 1993; Walsh, 2002).

Under the mantle of the biological theories of criminality, the debate of whether or not criminals are characterized by a certain type of body build has long been debated in the field of criminology. Eysenck and Gudjonsson (1989, p. 22) wrote that the study of physique "is a complex subject, with many differ-ent typologies and methods of measurement." In the 1940s, William Sheldon attempted to study the relationship between human physique and criminality. Although Sheldon was not the first to attempt this line of research, his method of doing so was more advanced than his predecessors. Sheldon put forth the idea of the somatotype; this is a personal score that is determined by differ-ent measurements taken from a human body. Sheldon posited three types of extreme somatotypes: Mesomorphs which are athletically built, endomorphs which are overweight, and ectomorphs which are underweight. Sheldon sug-gested that these somatotypes corresponded directly to psychological states, i.e., mesomorphs are active, dynamic, assertive, aggressive, etc., endomorphs are relaxed, comfortable, extroverted, etc., and ectomorphs are introverted, thoughtful, inhibited, sensitive, etc.

While many studies have been conducted on somatotyping and crimi-nality over the last 50 years, overall interest in the subject has waned. This is due primarily to the stigma that has been associated with conducting research on the link between biological causes of crime in the past. Even though this is the case, it is hard to discard some of the findings from the somatotype literature; research has consistently shown that mesomorphic physiques are more associated with criminal groups than with non-criminal control groups (Sheldon, 1949; Glueck & Glueck, 1956; Hartl et al., 1982). This makes it difficult to simply dismiss the relevance of somatotypes as correlates to criminal behavior.

This [essay] examines Sheldon's body of work and the research linking somatotypes to criminality. First, [we] explore Sheldon's classification system and the research that resulted from initial studies on somatotypes. Second, [we] examine alternative somatotypic classification methods produced to advance the work of Sheldon.

Somatotyping

There have been numerous attempts to study the links between physique and criminality that have yielded different measurements. These measurements have ranged from the simplistic to the complex. For instance, Hooten (1968) separated height and weight into a three by three matrix, or nine subgroups, to see if there was a relationship between physique and crime; height was identified as short, medium, and tall, and weight was identified as slender, medium, and heavy. While a host of physique studies were completed in Europe in the 1800s, one of the preeminent studies of physique was completed by Kretschmer. Kretschmer (1970) studied 400 patients of every age and occupation in a hospital in an effort to link physique and character. Kretschmer's key contribution to Sheldon's research was the three types of physique he identified: the asthenic, athletic, and pyknic forms.

The extreme asthenic type of physique has a "deficiency in thickness combined with an average unlessened length" (Kretschmer, 1970, p. 22); this type is characterized as weak and frail. The extreme athletic type of physique is "recognized by the strong development of the skeleton, the musculature and also the skin" (Kretschmer, 1970, p. 25). The extreme pyknic type of physique "is characterized by the pronounced peripheral development of the body cavities, and a tendency to a distribution of fat about the trunk, with a more graceful construction of the motor apparatus" (Kretschmer, 1970, p. 30). Sheldon's somatotypes would greatly resemble Kretschmer's physical types.

Sheldon (1940) outlined the study of physique and the measurement of somatotypes in *The Varieties of Human Physique*. His theory was founded on the "assumption that it is possible to discriminate differences among human beings" (1940, p. 108). Sheldon decided on three extreme physical types, adapted from embryology, which correspond approximately to Kretschmer's: Endomorphs (pycknic), mesomorphs (athletic), and ectomorphs (asthenic). Sheldon (1940, p. 5) defined endomorphy as the "relative predominance of soft roundness throughout the various regions of the body." Mesomorphy means the "relative predominance of muscle, bone, and connective tissue" (1940, p. 5). Ectomorphy means the "relative predominance of linearity and fragility" (1940, p. 5); Sheldon noted that this form had the largest brain and central nervous system.

To refine his method, Sheldon examined 400 male undergraduate students at the University of Chicago. In an effort of standardization, naked subjects were photographed from three angles (1940, p. 4): A front view, a side view, and a back view. The subject stood on a pedestal a certain distance away from the camera. From the 400 subjects, over 4000 photographs were amassed and examined. From these photographs, 17 measurements (dependent on the height to convert into ratio form) were taken from a body, and from this a three number scale was derived to conclude a person's somatotype. The first number in the score reflects the amount of endomorphy in an individual, the second number represents the amount of mesomorphy in an individual, and the third number represents the amount of ectomorphy present in an individual; thus, an extreme endomorph would receive a score of 7-1-1, an extreme mesomorph would receive a score of 1-7-1, and an extreme ectomorph would receive a score of 1-1-7. There are potentially 343 different identifiable somatotypes when using Sheldon's classification procedure.

In 1949, Sheldon put his method of somatotyping to the test in studying crime for the first time. Sheldon followed the lives of a sample of 200 juveniles from the Hayden Goodwill Inn; because it was a social service agency, the sample consisted of youth with antisocial personalities as well as delinquent histories. This gave Sheldon's study a comparison group of non-criminals on which to base his results. Although Sheldon examined many different sociological variables as well as biological variables, Sheldon's key finding was that delinquents were more likely to be mesomorphically built. In essence, criminals tended to be more athletic. With the exception of a thirty-year follow up study, this would also mark the last time that Sheldon's method of somatotyping would be used in the study of the link between physique and crime.

In the thirty-year follow-up of Sheldon's research, Hartl et al. (1982) reexamined the 200 men whose biographies were presented by Sheldon in 1949. Hartl et al.'s major finding was that future adult criminals differed from non-criminal subjects in the sample in terms of mesomorphy. As in Sheldon's original study, criminals were more likely to have a mesomorphic build. In their analysis on all of the data, Hartl et al. found mesomorphy to be the strongest discriminating variable. When conducting a multiple regression on criminal behavior, however, Hartl et al. indicated that none of the variables relating to morphology, mesomorphy, endomorphy, or ectomorphy, were statistically significant. In other words, physique did a poor job in predicting future criminality.

Alternate Somatotype Classifications

Sheldon's somatotyping approach was inevitably eclipsed by the work of Parnell in 1958. Parnell's method of somatotyping was considered to be more objective than Sheldon's. This method of somatotyping emphasized the phenotype, not the somatotype. The phenotype is the body as it appears at a particular point in time (Parnell, 1958, p. 4). Because of this, Parnell indicated that his method for somatotyping was not a good variable for prediction purposes because it could change, i.e., a person could go from being overweight to athletic over time. Unlike Sheldon, Parnell labeled his physical types on the chart as Fat, Muscularity, and Linearity which correspond to the endomorph, mesomorph, and ectomorph, respectively.

Inspired by the somatotyping work of Sheldon and Parnell, the Gluecks conducted an analysis on the relationship between physique and crime. The Gluecks (1951) compared the physiques between a sample of delinquents and a sample of non-delinquents. It was Parnell's method of somatotyping that was used to study the physique of subjects in the Gluecks' study. Based on their work, the Gluecks concluded that mesomorphy was more predominant among the delinquents, while the control group of non-delinquents contained no predominance of any single somatotype.

The Gluecks (1956) examined this data source further by examining the physique of criminals in relation to other sociological variables and traits they had found. The Gluecks looked at the relationship between physique and several categories of variables that included neurological traits, intelligence, character, family, environment, and personality. While some of the variables in each category were found to be correlated with the different body types, the Gluecks concluded that there is no combination of physical traits and sociological traits which could predict delinquency in an individual. This is true even for the mesomorphs, who comprised the majority of the criminal sample.

Besides the Gluecks' study, two other studies utilized Parnell's somatotyping procedure. Cortes and Gatti (1966) examined the relationship between a person's physique and the need for achievement, or motivation. They examined 100 delinquent youths and a comparison group of 100 non-delinquents in a high school. In both groups, a significant and positive relationship was found between mesomorphy and motivation; they also found that a significant, but negative, relationship existed between ectomorphy and motivation. Cortes and Gatti (1966, p. 412) concluded that a relationship existed between athletic individuals and the desire to achieve.

McCandless, Persons, and Roberts (1972) examined perceived criminal opportunity and body build among delinquent youth. McCandless et al. examined 500 adjudicated delinquent youth by both somatotyping the youth and administering a questionnaire to measure opportunity. McCandless et al. hypothesized that mesomorphs would be more likely to have committed more delinquent acts than either ectomorphs or endomorphs; however, their data analysis lent no credence to this. Race was the only variable to have a significant relationship with perceived criminal opportunity.

After the McCandless et al. study in 1972, research utilizing somatotypes was discontinued predicated on the sociological move away from criminological-biological theories. It was not until 2008 that a new method of somatotyping emerged. In an effort to utilize a newer, more refined method of somatotyping, Maddan, Walker, and Miller (2008) utilized the body mass index as a measure of an individual's somatotype.

The body mass index (BMI), often referred to as the Quetelet Index, utilizes a person's height and weight to gauge the total body fat in adults; it is an indicator of optimal weight for health and different from lean mass or percent body fat calculations because it only considers height and weight (National Heart, Lung, and Blood Institute, 1998). This measure correlates primarily to body fat and can be used on either males or females. The BMI is a "heterogeneous phenotype" (Feitosa et al., 2002, p. 72) or how the person's physique is at a given point in time. In this sense it is a measure of somatotyping more similar to Parsons' method, which was based on physical phenotype as well.

A person's BMI is calculated by dividing weight (in kilograms) by height (in meters) squared. Thus, the BMI equation relies heavily upon the subject's height. The relationship between the physique and height of an individual was mentioned time and time again in the literature. Even Sheldon (1940) foreshadowed the importance of height and weight in measuring somatotypes noting that with height-weight norms, it will be possible to create a scale of height-weight measures for each different somatotype. BMI values can range from one and up, making it a continuous, interval level variable. According to the BMI, a person who is an endomorph receives a BMI score of 26 and above, a person who is a mesomorph will receive a BMI score of between 19 and 25, and a person who is an ectomorph will receive a score of less than 19.

To test the reliability of the BMI measure, Maddan, Walker, and Miller (2008) took Sheldon's original data from *Varieties of Delinquent Youth* and compared the results of his somatotyping technique with the same sample using the BMI scale to determine the individual's somatotype. The correlation analyses that were completed to measure the relationship between the two types of somatotype metrics showed a strong relationship between Sheldon's method of somatotyping and the BMI measure. These analyses indicated that the BMI is a reliable measure of somatotyping.

The most important finding of the Maddan et al. (2008) research was that somatotypes still accounted for some of the variation in violent and non-violent prison sentences in a sample of male prisoners (N=5,000) taken in Arkansas from 1975 to 2000. While the somatotype showed effects, the impact was minor across the somatotype measures. The analysis illustrated that the somatotypes had a statistically significant effect, albeit weak, and added to the overall model. More importantly, the direction of the effects was in line with previous research on physique and criminality. Mesomorphic offenders were more likely to be in prison for a violent offense than their endomorphic counterparts; the direction was the same for ectomorphs, but this variable failed to gain statistical significance.

Conclusion

The biological approach to studying criminality has been much maligned. These studies have suffered from methodological issues, ranging from measurement to sampling, and conceptual issues, ranging from un-testability to logic. One of the key problems with biological studies has been with regards to the types of variables included in analyses; most of the biological research, not including the work in this area today, has focused primarily on strictly biological variables. Raine (1993, p. 204) asserted that "no factor linked to crime should be viewed in the anachronistic terms of genetics versus environment." To do this is both divisive and overly simplistic. Criminologists should move toward an integration of genetic and social factors for crime in an effort to examine how these two factors relate to one another. This chapter has focused on a biological approach that has largely fallen to the wayside of criminological history: Somatotypes.

The somatotype is now an antiquated concept in the field of criminology. Sheldon's original methodology for collecting somatotypes would not make it through an institutional review board today due to the collection of naked pictures of subjects. In addition to the impracticality of taking photographs of the naked subjects, the original somatotype measure was also marred by a high degree of subjectivity. The somatotype was also plagued by poor conceptualization, operationalization, and the resulting metrics that delivered non-mutually exclusive measurements. With these problems, the measure of Sheldon's somatotype has no real empirical utility.

Because of the inherent problems associated with Sheldon's somatotyping technique, Maddan et al. (2008) attempted to promulgate a hybrid somatotype procedure that took from the works of Sheldon and Parnell. The Body Mass Index overcomes the problems associated with the mutual exclusivity pervasive in Sheldon's work while utilizing the phenotypic quality of Parnell's method. The BMI also solves the problems associated with subjectivity by researchers conducting the study.

Physique is not the cause of crime. This much is known from all of the studies related to somatotyping. But while it is not the cause of criminality or particular types of criminal offending, the research illustrates that there is a correlation between the two. Until criminologists have determined what it is about mesomorphy that is linked to criminality and how, criminologists in this area will continue the work of Sheldon on somatotypes.

References

Eysenck, H.J., & Gudjonsson, G.H. (1989). *The causes and cures of criminality.* New York: Plenum Press.

Cortes, J.B., & Gatti, F.M. (1966). Physique and motivation. *Journal of consulting psychology, 30*(5), 408–414.

Feitosa, M.F., Borecki, I.B., Rich, S.S., Arnett, D.K., Sholinsky, P., Myers, R.H., Leppert, M, & Province, M.A. (2002). Quantitative-trait loci influencing body-mass index reside on chromosomes 7 and 13: The National Heart, Lung, and Blood Institute family heart study. *American Journal of Human Genetics 70*(1), 72–82.

Glueck, S., & Glueck, E. (1951). *Unraveling juvenile delinquency.* Cambridge: Harvard University Press.

Glueck, S., & Glueck, E. (1956). *Physique and delinquency.* New York: Harper and Brothers Publishers.

Hartl, E.M., Monnelly, E.P., & Elderkin, R.D. (1982). *Physique and delinquent behavior: A thirty-year follow-up of William H. Sheldon's varieties of delinquent youth.* New York: Academic Press.

Hooten, E.A. (1968). *Crime and the man.* New York: Greenwood Press, Publishers.

Kretschmer, E. (1970). *Physique and character: An investigation of the nature of constitution and of the theory of temperment.* New York: Cooper Square Publishers, Inc.

Maddan, S., Walker, J.T., & Miller, J.M. (2008). Does size really matter?: A reexamination of Sheldon's somatotypes and criminal behavior. *Social Science Journal 45*(2), 330–344.

McCandless, B.R., Persons III, W.S., & Roberts, A. (1972). Perceived opportunity, delinquency, race, and body build among delinquent youth. *Journal of Consulting and Clinical Psychology 38*(2), 281–287.

National Heart, Lung, and Blood Institute. (1998). *Clinical guidelines on the identification, evaluation, and treatment of overweight, and obesity in adults: The evidence report.* Washington D.C.: National Institute of Health.

Raine, A. (1993). *The psychopathology of crime: Criminal behavior as a clinical disorder.* New York: Academic Press.

Sheldon, W., Stevens, S.S., & Tucker, W.B. (1940). *The varieties of human physique: An introduction to constitutional psychology.* New York: Harper and Brothers Publishers.

Sheldon, W., Hartl, W.M., & McDermott, E. (1949). *Varieties of delinquent youth: An introduction to constitutional psychiatry.* New York: Harper and Brothers Publishers.

Walsh, A. (2002). *Biosocial criminology: Introduction and integration.* Cincinnati: Anderson Publishing Co.

Wilson, J.Q., & Herrnstein, R.J. (1985). *Crime and human nature.* New York: Simon and Schuster, Inc.

Chris L. Gibson and
Kevin M. Beaver

 **NO**

Does Body Type Really Have an Effect on Criminal Behavior?

Imagine that your research methods professor came to class one day and told you that he has found consistent evidence in his research that the amount of ice cream sales has an effect on the number of deaths by drowning after studying this pattern for several years in many different settings, across various countries, and using different measures of ice cream sales. He then quantified the effect by telling you that overwhelming evidence suggests that as ice cream sales increase so does the number of deaths by drowning. Imagine that another professor told you that she has found tremendous evidence indicating that the number of medical doctors in a region has an effect on the number of people in that region dying from disease. That is, when a geographical area has increasingly more medical doctors it also has more people dying from disease. She says that this effect has held true across the United States and other westernized countries for the last century.

Why would increases in ice cream sales influence the number of deaths by drowning? Why would increases in the number of medical doctors in a geographical region increase the number of people dying from disease? Is it possible to think that ice cream makes people want to swim and then they drown due to ice cream overload? Is it possible to think that doctors are killing people by injecting them with diseases? In other words, is there a reason to believe that a direct link exists in these scenarios? While most people would think these relationships are absurd, others may conjure up weird or even bizarre theoretical reasons to expect such direct links.

It is probably safe to say that these so-called effects are merely relationships due to some other driving force(s). In other words, these relationships are spurious in that they can be explained by some third variable that makes them appear to be directly linked when in fact they are not. For instance, it is highly probable that the reason ice cream sales and deaths by drowning are linked over time is because they tend to both occur at higher rates in warmer months where both are less likely to occur in colder months. When it is hot outside people are more likely to go swimming and more likely to eat ice cream to cool down; thus a greater chance of people drowning. It is also highly probable that the reason why the number of doctors in a region is linked to the number of people dying from disease is because in regions where there is greater population density there are also more doctors as well as people dying from disease.

This brings us to the question of this essay: Does body type really have an effect on criminal behavior? Dating back several decades, it has been argued that a person's body type may determine whether he will engage in criminal and violent behaviors (Sheldon, Hartl, McDermott, 1949). In fact some have argued (Hooten, 1968, p. 281) that "variation in physique and body build [was] causally related to the nature of [the criminal] offense." Sheldon and colleagues (1949) proposed a theory on physiques and criminal involvement that suggests individuals having particular body types are more inclined to engage in such behaviors compared to their counterparts that have other body types. Specifically, he identified three body types: ectomorph (thin, linear, and fragile), mesomorph (athletic/muscle build), and endomorph (soft roundness or overweight). He argued and found support for the notion that mesomorphs are more inclined to be criminally involved than the others. Specifically, in a sample of 200 young men he found that the mesomorphic physique was the most common somatotype of those who were labeled criminal in his sample. Since the early work of Sheldon, other researchers have made similar observations using different samples of individuals (including prison inmates), different measures to classify body type (e.g., Body Mass Index to classify subjects by somatotypes), and various statistical techniques that take into account some characteristics of persons that may be related to criminal behavior and physique (race, education, age, etc.) (Maddan, Walker, & Miller, 2008). In the face of this evidence, can we really conclude that an individual's body type leads him to commit crime?

As with the examples on ice cream and drowning and the number of doctors and death by disease, we argue in this chapter that there is no direct causal effect of body type on one's involvement in criminal behavior. Further, if there is an effect of body type on criminal behavior we argue that it is interacting with environmental variables, leading us to endorse a biosocial explanation of the link between body type and criminal involvement. As we proceed, we will first debunk the myth that body type is directly related to criminal behavior by assessing what it would require of a study to show this and how studies to date do not meet these standards. Additionally, we will make an argument that a more plausible explanation for the link between body type and criminal offending is how one's size interacts with one's environment to predict behaviors, rather than body type having a direct impact on behavior.

What Would It Take to Show a Direct Effect of Body Type on Criminal Behavior?

When most research methods textbooks discuss direct effects they often refer to causation. That is, when "A" happens then "B" follows. For instance, when an adolescent becomes a member of a criminal gang does his involvement in violence begin to skyrocket, beyond his previous involvement in violence that was prior to joining a gang? It is quite common to observe a correlation between being a member of a criminal gang and involvement in violence, but what we really would like to know is whether one directly causes the other. This question is a lot more difficult to answer. Establishing a correlation is not enough to say that gang membership has a direct effect on violence. Other conditions generally need to be met. First, joining a gang has to be observed before increases in violence occur; thus temporal order must be established. If not then it is really unknown what came first, the "chicken or the egg," or in this case gang membership or increases in violence. Second, one must rule out alternative explanations. For instance, are being a criminal gang member and being involved in violence related due to some third unobserved, unmeasured factor such as impulsivity, lack of parental involvement, or differential association with friends who engage in delinquency? The goal would be to have pairs of adolescents who are similar on all characteristics, but differ in that one of each pair belongs to a gang and the other does not so that the only thing that could be causing increases in future violence, measured at a later date, would be joining a gang. This is a difficult research task to accomplish!

Now we will apply the basic criteria discussed above to research on body type and criminal behavior. First, the majority of studies that have been conducted on this topic have certainly found a correlation between body type and criminal behavior. In fact, this relationship holds for different samples, various methods of measuring body type, and across decades (see Maddan et al., 2008). Importantly though, this relationship is merely a correlation. Some studies have ruled out other characteristics that may be related to body type and criminal offending (e.g., age), but no study to date has been able to measure all important characteristics that could be related to both body type and criminal offending (e.g., genetics). Without such evidence it is hard to determine if a direct effect of body type on criminal behavior exists. One might argue that the best way to control or overcome this is through random assignment so that any difference between people with different body types is only due to chance. While random assignment is the "golden standard" for experimental designs that attempt to assess causality, it would be near impossible to randomly assign individuals to be mesomorphs, endomorphs, or ectomorphs. Thus, it would be hard to establish groups of these body types that are equal on all other characteristics so that the direct effect of body type on future criminal behavior could be assessed.

Second, some studies that have assessed body type and criminal behavior may potentially have the temporal ordering issue incorrect. For instance, what about studies that measure body type but then assess criminal involvement that occurred years before body type was measured? It would certainly be difficult to say that body type leads to involvement in crime because you would not know the body type of an individual before he engaged in crime. The temporal order issue as mentioned above becomes apparent. Further, if body type is directly related to criminal involvement then one might expect that as criminal behavior changes so too will the body type of an individual. To date, no research that we are aware of has measured body type and criminal behavior as it waxes and wanes over time for individuals. In sum, and given the ideas and information presented above, we believe it is safe to say that body type, at least given the research to date, shows no signs of a direct effect on crime. However, this does not mean that an effect of body type is absent. We believe if body type does have an effect on crime then it is through interactions with social environments.

A Biosocial Explanation for the Link Between Body Type and Criminal Behavior

Although we argue that body type does not have a direct effect on criminal behavior, we do recognize that body type may work in combination with social factors to produce a variety of antisocial outcomes, including crime. To understand what we mean by this, first it is important to realize that there is an emerging perspective within criminology known as biosocial criminology. Biosocial criminology seeks to integrate biological variables with social variables to create an interdisciplinary study of crime and delinquency (Beaver, 2009; Walsh, 2002). This perspective has generated a growing body of research in recent years revealing the very real likelihood that biological risk factors (e.g., body type) and social variables (e.g., delinquent friends) are both involved in the development of misbehavior, such as violence and aggression. Unfortunately, the extant research on the nexus between body type and criminal involvement has failed to examine the effects of social factors. This is a serious oversight, one that seriously biases the results of these studies. Below we outline the possible ways in which body type and the environment have effects on crime.

The biosocial criminological literature has revealed that certain biological risk factors (in this case, the biological risk factor would be body type) only have effects when they are paired to certain environments. To see what we mean by this, let us take a look at a health-related example. Suppose there were two genetically identical people (e.g., two identical twins). Imagine that they were both born with the genetic predisposition to develop heart disease (i.e., a biological risk factor). Now pretend that one of the people exercised regularly, ate a healthy diet, and had annual physical examinations, while the other person never exercised, ate a diet that was high in fats, and never went to the doctor for a check-up. Which of the two people will most likely develop heart disease? The answer is obvious: the person who never exercises, eats an unhealthy diet, and is not monitored by a doctor. In this example, it is easy to see that the biological effect (i.e., the genetic predisposition for heart disease) is contingent on the presence of the environment (i.e., an unhealthy lifestyle). Of course, heart disease could emerge for people who only have a genetic predisposition or who only live an unhealthy lifestyle, but the key point is that heart disease is most likely to surface for people who have both of these risk factors.

This exact same logic can easily be applied to the study of body type and crime. In this context, body type would most likely lead to criminal involvement in certain social contexts. Precisely what these social contexts are remains unknown because no research has examined this issue. Environments that provide crime opportunities, however, are the most likely suspects. For example, let us suppose that there are two mesomorphs that we were interested in studying. According to the existing literature, these two people would be at-risk for committing crime because their body type is a predisposing factor. Pretend that one mesomorph is from an adequate neighborhood and the other is from a disadvantaged, crime-ridden neighborhood. In the crime-ridden neighborhood, there are likely to be high amounts of crime and criminal opportunities. In this case, the mesomorph may use their body type to take advantage of the crime opportunities (e.g., assaulting someone, joining a gang, etc.), while the mesomorph from the adequate neighborhood may not engage in crime because the opportunities are lacking. Seen from this viewpoint, it is apparent that if body type is associated with crime, it would likely be contingent on the presence of a criminogenic environment.

There are other ways that body type and environmental conditions might interlock to produce crime. Again, an example may help to make this point clear. Suppose that two adolescents were confronted with a situation where they could steal a substantial amount of money. The catch, however, is that they would have to steal it from a relatively large man walking down the street. One adolescent, who would be considered a mesomorph, had learned from his past experiences that his body size could be used to intimidate people. The other adolescent, who would be considered an ectomorph, had learned from his past experiences that he was weak and that he would not be able to intimidate people based on his physique. The likely outcome in this situation would be that the mesomorph would use his muscular stature as a means to steal the money, while the ectomorph, lacking physical endowment, would be left with no other choice than to let the opportunity pass. From a biosocial perspective, the important point is that while body type might be a predisposing factor for crime, that predisposition will only surface under certain environmental conditions.

Conclusion

Many outcomes of interest to criminologists, including criminal behavior, can only be understood by using a lens that captures the dynamic interactions between a person and the multiple environments in which he or she is exposed to through the life-course. We believe this is no different for research on somatotypes. If body size does have an effect on criminal behavior it is probably not direct.

Several ways exist to advance knowledge on how body type may influence antisocial and criminal behaviors. For instance, some researchers have begun to advance more objective measures of somatotypes using the Body Mass Index score (Maddan et al., 2008), as opposed to more subjective measures used in the past. However, to truly understand the complex ways in which physique influences behavior we believe that researchers must start asking research questions that will allow for a more complete understanding of the environments that people with different physiques find themselves in and how these environments interact with their physique. It is not only important to understand how people with various physiques select particular environments they enjoy being in and avoiding ones they dislike, but it will also be important to understand how people with different physiques will respond to the same environments, situations, and opportunities when exposed to them.

References

Beaver, K. (2009). *Biosocial criminology: A primer.* Dubuque, Iowa: Kendall/Hunt Publishing Co.

Hooten, E.A. (1969). *The American criminal: An anthropological study.* Greenwood Press, Publishers.

Maddan, S., Walker, J.T., & Miller, J.M. (2008). Does size really matter? A reexamination of Sheldon's somatotypes and criminal behavior. *The Social Science Journal,* 45, 330–344.

Sheldon, W., Hartl, W.M., & McDermott, E. (1949). *Varieties of delinquent youth: An introduction to constitutional psychiatry.* New York: Harper and Brothers Publishers.

Walsh, A. (2002). *Biosocial criminology: Introduction and integration.* Cincinnati: Anderson Publishing Co.

POSTSCRIPT

Is a Person's Body Type Clearly Linked to Criminal Behavior?

The issue of whether a person's body type may be linked to the likelihood of criminal behavior is a longstanding debate. On one hand, Professors Maddan, Walker, and Miller's contention that body type is correlated strongly to criminal behavior has a measure of intuitive appeal and empirical support. On the other side, as Professors Gibson and Beaver suggest, the "jury may still be out" on this important question. The key to finding the cause(s) of criminal behavior may well involve a complex of biological and social factors. For example, it may be imperative to consider environmental factors to provide an answer to the question of why one person with a mesomorphic body build becomes a criminal, whereas another becomes a linebacker in the National Football League (NFL).

In addition, it is very important to consider that crime is a social construct. In his now classic work, *The Social Reality of Crime* (1970), sociologist Richard P. Quinney, a Marxist criminologist, developed six propositions that comprise the social reality of crime:

> PROPOSITION 1 (DEFINITION OF CRIME): Crime is a definition of human conduct that is created by authorized agents in a politically organized society.
> PROPOSITION 2 (FORMULATION OF CRIMINAL DEFINITIONS): Criminal definitions describe behaviors that conflict with the interests of the segments of society that have the power to shape public policy.
> PROPOSITION 3 (APPLICATION OF CRIMINAL DEFINITIONS): Criminal definitions are applied by the segments of society that have the power to shape the enforcement and administration of criminal law.
> PROPOSITION 4 (DEVELOPMENT OF BEHAVIOR PATTERNS IN RELATION TO CRIMINAL DEFINITIONS): Behavior patterns are structured in segmentally organized society in relation to criminal definitions and within this context persons engage in actions that have relative probabilities of being defined as criminal.
> PROPOSITION 5 (CONSTRUCTION OF CRIMINAL CONCEPTIONS): Conceptions of crime are constructed and diffused in the segments of society by various means of communication.
> PROPOSITION 6 (THE SOCIAL REALITY OF CRIME): The social reality of crime is constructed by the formulation and application of criminal definitions, the development of behavior patterns related to criminal definitions, and the construction of criminal conceptions.

Although a detailed discussion of Quinney's ideas are beyond the scope of this initiative, his point is that crime can only be considered in its social context.

In addition, one must also consider how the definitions of crimes are developed and applied. To illustrate, while behaviors commonly associated with individuals of lower social status are defined as crimes, the acts of higher social status individuals, which may cause greater social harm, are often ignored by the criminal justice system. For example, why is it a crime for a hungry person to steal a loaf of bread from a local convenience store, but not a crime for a congressperson to take campaign contributions from individuals seeking to influence the formation of a law for personal gain? A "critical" criminologist (a term used to describe criminologists who embrace a Marxist perspective on society and crime) would be likely to point to the imbalance of power between the hungry person and the congressperson. Clearly, the congressperson has the power to ensure that his/her acts that are harmful to society never come to be defined as "crimes," whereas the hungry person does not.

Significantly, many biological theories of crime fail to address such important questions.

Another related issue concerns the question of what should be done if we ever actually do find a conclusive answer to the question: "What causes crime?" One professor uses the following provocative assignment in her criminology class: "Suppose you were to find what you are certain is the solution to crime that has washed up on a beach in a small glass vial. Tell me what you would do with it, how you would do it, and why." The easy answer is that you would use it to change society and develop a perfect world. Is this the best solution, however? What problems might occur if this approach were to be adopted? Do you believe that finding the solution to crime could have Orwellian implications for society?

To summarize, body type theories of crime have considerable potential to expand our understanding of criminal behavior. As with many of the other issues we have considered in this volume, however, it is important to recognize that the ultimate explanation for crime is very likely to involve a complex interaction of both organic and social factors that work together to produce criminal behavior.

There are compelling additional resources that discuss the issues considered in this section. See Richard P. Quinney, *The Social Reality of Crime* (Little, Brown, 1970); Hans J. Eysenck & G.H. Gudjonsson, *The Causes and Cures of Criminality* (Plenum Press, 1989); Sheldon Glueck & Eleanor Glueck, *Unraveling Juvenile Delinquency* (Harvard University Press, 1951); E.A. Hooten, *Crime and the Man* (Greenwood Press, 1968); E.A. Hooten, *The American Criminal: An Anthropological Study* (Greenwood Press, 1969); Adrian Raine, *The Psychopathology of Crime: Criminal Behavior as a Clinical Disorder* (Academic Press, 1993); E. Kretschmer, *Physique and Character: An Investigation of the Nature of Constitution and of the Theory of Temperment* (Cooper Square Publishers, 1970); Kevin Beaver, *Biosocial Criminology: A Primer* (Kendall/Hunt Publishing, 2009); Sean Maddan, Jeffery Walker, & J. Mitchell Miller, "Does Size Really Matter?: A Reexamination of Sheldon's Somatotypes and Criminal Behavior," *Social Science Journal* (vol. 45, no. 2, 2008); B.R. McCandless, W.S. Persons III, & A. Roberts, "Perceived Opportunity, Delinquency, Race, and Body Build Among Delinquent Youth," *Journal of Consulting and Clinical Psychology* (vol. 38, no. 2, 1972).

Internet References . . .

American Society of Criminology

An excellent starting point for a study of all aspects of criminology and criminal justice, this page provides links to sites on criminal justice in general, international criminal justice, juvenile justice, courts, the police, and the government.

http://www.americansocietyofcriminology.org

Basics of Juvenile Justice

A list of similarities and differences between juvenile and adult justice systems is available at this site. Also listed are changes in the philosophy of juvenile justice by time periods.

http://justice.uaa.alaska.edu

National Institute of Justice

The National Institute of Justice (NIJ) sponsors projects and conveys research to practitioners in the field. From the institute's home page, you can link to NIJ programs, publications, and related sites.

http://www.ojp.usdoj.gov/nij/

Office for Victims of Crime

The Office for Victims of Crime (OVC) was established by the 1984 Victims of Crime Act to oversee diverse programs that benefit victims of crime. From this Web site of the OVC, you can download a great deal of pertinent information.

http://www.ojp.usdoj.gov/ovc/

Contemporary Public Policy Issues in Criminology and Criminal Justice

*U*nderstanding *society's reactions to crime—such as investigating, arresting, and incarcerating criminals, as well as providing alternatives to incarceration—is often complicated. Scholars and practitioners also have to reckon with the unanticipated negative outcomes of that system. The criminal justice system has been accused of ignoring crimes and injustices committed against women, racial and ethnic minorities, and children. Some say that policies and procedures adopted in fighting the war on crime may very well be more harmful than helpful. In addition, people have questioned efforts to protect children against predators, both on the streets and on the Internet; the effects of the war on drugs on the black, inner-city community; and whether or not juvenile courts should be abolished. These issues are explored in this section.*

- Does the United States Have a Right to Torture Suspected Terrorists?
- Is Racial Profiling an Acceptable Law Enforcement Strategy?
- Should Juvenile Courts Be Abolished?
- Is Exposure to Pornography Related to Increased Rates of Rape?

ISSUE 4

Does the United States Have a Right to Torture Suspected Terrorists?

YES: Andrew A. Moher, from "The Lesser of Two Evils? An Argument for Judicially Sanctioned Torture in a Post–9/11 World," *Thomas Jefferson Law Review* (Spring 2004)

NO: Elisa Massimino, from "Leading by Example? U.S. Interrogation of Prisoners in the War on Terror," *Criminal Justice Ethics* (Winter 2004)

ISSUE SUMMARY

YES: Attorney Andrew A. Moher argues that judicially sanctioned torture of terrorists is appropriate for the purpose of preventing a greater evil. He further contends a judicially monitored system in the United States would be far superior to the current policy of practicing torture "under the radar screen" in other countries.

NO: Elisa Massimino believes that the use of torture is immoral and counterproductive for the United States. She asserts that if the United States wishes to rely on the protections of the Geneva Conventions, then it must comply with its provisions prohibiting the torture of prisoners.

Torture is an insidious practice, which conjures sadistic images of medieval dungeons, the rack, and thumbscrews. Consider the following hypothetical situation: A suspected terrorist has planted a nuclear bomb somewhere in a large U.S. city of 2 million people. Based on information from an informant, who has proven to be completely reliable on many past occasions, government authorities have reason to believe that it is set to explode in three hours. It would be impossible to evacuate the city within this time frame. Moreover, the informant has given the authorities the name and description of the suspected terrorist and he is taken into custody. If the suspect refuses to talk, is torture justified?

The Introduction of this book discussed the doctrine of utilitarianism, which asserts that a social policy should be assessed according to whether it produces the greatest benefit for public good. In our hypothetical situation, the greatest public benefit would be served by locating the bomb and defusing it. Do you believe that the greatest public good would be served by using whatever means were necessary to extract the information from the suspect? This situation illustrates a potential deficiency in the doctrine of utilitarianism—perhaps there are absolute principles that should never be compromised, regardless of whether an action will serve the greatest public good. The use of torture to extract information *may* be one of these principles.

U.S. courts have consistently condemned the use of torture by government authorities to gain information from criminal suspects because it violates due process of law, a "principle of justice so rooted in the traditions and conscience of our people as to be ranked as fundamental." For example, in *Brown v. Mississippi,* 297 U.S. 278 (1936), sheriff's deputies obtained the confessions of three African American suspects in a murder case by whipping and hanging them. And they were convicted of murder in state court. The U.S. Supreme Court held, however: "[T]he freedom of the State in establishing its policy is the freedom of constitutional government. . . . The rack and torture chamber may not be substituted for the witness stand. . . ."

The authors of the articles in this section have different viewpoints on the use of torture to extract information from suspected terrorists. Andrew Moher argues that judicially sanctioned torture of terrorists is appropriate for the purpose of preventing a greater evil. He further contends a judicially monitored system in the United States would be far superior to the current policy of practicing torture "under the radar screen" in other countries. Moher's position is fundamentally a statement of a utilitarian approach to the use of torture to extract information from terrorists.

Elisa Massimino, in contrast, believes that the use of torture is immoral and counterproductive for the United States. She asserts that if the United States wishes to rely on the protections of the Geneva Conventions, then it must comply with its provisions regarding torture of prisoners. Massimino's position is consistent with an absolutist position regarding the use of torture— it is contrary to human dignity and always wrong.

What is your position regarding the use of torture to extract information from suspected terrorists? Are your views influenced by the bombing of the World Trade Center in New York City on 9/11/2001? As you read the articles in this section, try to develop a sense of whether you support the utilitarian or absolutist positions regarding the use of torture.

YES

Andrew A. Moher

The Lesser of Two Evils? An Argument for Judicially Sanctioned Torture in a Post–9/11 World

I. Introduction

Torture is illegal under both United States and international law. It is considered among the most heinous practices in human history, and its use is publicly condemned by nearly every government in existence today. However, it is also considered an effective method of gathering information, and to that end it is habitually employed "under the radar screen" in desperate situations by these same governments. Since the catastrophic attacks of September 11, 2001, several noted scholars and politicians have advocated the use of torture in extreme scenarios, while others have expressed fear that legitimizing torture would spawn a dangerous slippery-slope of morally reprehensible state actions. Specifically, the use of torture to extract information from terrorists with knowledge of impending attacks has been the subject of intense debate.

Before surveying the landscape of state sponsored torture, it is essential to distinguish between two categories of torture. The more notorious form of torture is punishment-based. It is inextricably intertwined with medieval images of diabolical torture devices found in movies and museums around the world. Such methods have historically been used in violent tyrannies and dictatorships, and exist in "rogue" states today. This type of torture is morally indefensible and is not at issue here. Rather, this discussion deals with torture for the purpose of preventing a greater evil, as part of the interrogation process. Such methods have been used in the past, with some success.

An interesting dialogue might be fashioned on whether the United States should adhere to international restrictions on torture under the shadow of post-9/11 threats of terrorism. After all, many potential subjects of torture are "part of the conspiracy [to destroy] . . . innocent Americans." Conversely, there is a danger that condoning torture of suspects might harm innocents unnecessarily, or that American captives would be subjected to inhumane treatment in response to United States policy. These contentions are largely beyond the scope of this discussion, and serve as background to the present debate.

From *Thomas Jefferson Law Review*, vol. 26, issue 2, Spring 2004, pp. 469–489. Copyright © 2004 by Thomas Jefferson Law Review. Reprinted by permission.

This Note will argue that judicially sanctioned torture is appropriate, but only under certain, well-defined circumstances. Part II will discuss the current status of domestic and international law as it applies to torture. Part III will analyze the pattern of United States noncompliance with these laws, and the general ineffectiveness of the current policy on torture. Finally, Part IV will illustrate why a balanced approach allowing judicially sanctioned torture would be a more effective and humane alternative to the current practice of using torture "under the radar screen."

II. The Legality of Torture Under Current United States Law

The United States is compelled by both domestic and international law not to practice torture. Torture is banned by several amendments to the Constitution, and implicitly barred by the sentiment of the Constitution itself. Furthermore, the practice of torture conflicts with United States obligations under international law, including signed and ratified treaties. Over the years, the prohibition against torture has become a fixture of international law, and has been routinely condemned by the vast plurality of nations. Today, the torturer is considered "hostis humani generis," an enemy of all mankind.

A. Constitutional Prohibitions on Torture

The practice of torture runs directly counter to the Fifth, Eighth and Fourteenth Amendments of the Constitution. Some advocates of legalizing torture have argued that loopholes exist in each of these amendments, and suggest torture could be rationalized under existing law. Upon closer examination, it is clear the use of torture is wholly incompatible with the Constitution. This contention is further borne out by important court decisions emphasizing the protections of personal liberty from governmental intrusion.

The Eighth Amendment bans all cruel and unusual punishment. This prohibition would ostensibly include torture, as the drafters of the amendment were "primarily concerned . . . with proscribing 'tortures' and other barbarous forms of punishment." On the other hand, the Eighth Amendment has been construed by the Supreme Court to protect only those convicted of crimes. Thus, it stands to reason that although convicted criminals are protected under the Eighth Amendment, others (such as prisoners of war, or so-called "enemy combatants") are not protected. Through this loophole created under the guise of the Supreme Court's interpretation, the Eighth Amendment would most likely be deemed ineffectual in cases involving suspected terrorists that have not yet been convicted in the criminal justice system.

Even if the practice of torture were to effectively circumvent the Eighth Amendment, it would almost certainly be found unconstitutional under the due process protections of the Fifth and Fourteenth Amendments. These protections grant all persons the substantive rights not to be deprived of life, liberty, and property, without due process of law. Although substantive due process is admittedly a very subjective and malleable standard, it has been utilized in the past to overturn practices less odious than torture. In recent years, the Supreme Court has adopted the rationale that state conduct that "shocks the conscience" will violate due process protections.

In *Brown v. Mississippi,* the police severely whipped a subject while hanging him from a tree to coerce a confession. The Supreme Court of the United States declared, "[I]t would be difficult to conceive of methods more revolting to the sense of justice than those taken to procure [these] confessions." The Court later lowered the bar when it found less violent conduct to meet the "shock the conscience" benchmark. In *Rochin v. United States,* the Supreme Court found a violation of due process when authorities pumped the stomach of a man suspected of swallowing morphine capsules. Speaking for the court in *Rochin,* Justice Frankfurter defined the objective of substantive due process as "respect for those personal immunities which . . . are 'so rooted in the traditions and conscience of our people as to be ranked as fundamental.'"

Brown and its progeny illustrate the scope of substantive due process, and its incompatibility with the practice of torture. Indeed, the atrocious whipping in *Brown* could easily be analogized to torture, and that conduct was found to violate due process. The broader standard put forth in *Rochin* further strengthens the case against torture. If the right to be free from torture was not egregious enough to meet Justice Frankfurter's standard of fundamental rights, it would be hard to imagine what conduct would be. Based on these cases, and the Court's obvious desire to protect bodily integrity, the intentional infliction of pain by torture would sufficiently "shock the conscience" to violate due process.

B. International Prohibitions Against Torture

The United States is further bound by several international treaties that prohibit the practice of torture. International treaties have authority so long as they do not offend the Constitution. The United States is obligated to provide humane treatment to prisoners of war under the 1949 incarnation of the Geneva Convention. The United States is also bound by the International Covenant on Civil and Political Rights, or ICCPR, which contains express prohibitions against torture. Article 7 of the ICCPR states, inter alia, "No one shall be subjected to torture or to cruel, inhuman, or degrading treatment or punishment." Under the Convention, the right to be protected from torture is non-derogable, meaning that it applies at all times, including wartime. The ICCPR, like the Geneva Convention, bars torture under any and all circumstances.

The United States is also party to the Convention against Torture (CAT), a subsidiary to the ICCPR that was ratified by the United States in 1994. Under UUU Article 4, the CAT demands that "each state party . . . ensure that all acts of torture are offences under its criminal law," and that the offences are "punishable by appropriate penalties which take into account their grave nature." The State Department recently confirmed the full implementation of the CAT into United States law, averring, "every act constituting torture under the [CAT] constitutes a criminal offense under the law of the United States."

Finally, the United States must adhere to jus cogens. According to the Vienna Convention on the Law of Treaties, jus cogens are international legal standards that are "accepted and recognized by the international community of States as a whole as a norm from which no derogation is permitted and which can be modified only by a subsequent norm of general international law having the same character." In other words, universally abhorred practices such as genocide, slavery, and summary executions qualify as jus cogens and are illegal at all times and all places, regardless of existing laws. Torture has long been considered an immutable violation of jus cogens, and declared as such in Federal court. The United States is therefore bound by jus cogens not to practice torture under any conceivable scenario.

III. The Reality of Torture Under Current United States Law

Few writers would be naive enough to suggest torture has been completely eradicated from all societies today. Yet many would underestimate its prevalence as a tool of interrogation, particularly in "civilized" countries such as the United States. There has been a plethora of evidence since the September 11 attacks suggesting United States complicity in interrogational torture and yet no tangible ramifications have been encountered to date. Often, a nation can avoid responsibility by exploiting the amorphous definition of torture under various laws. It has become evident that the implementation mechanisms of the international system are not compatible with the security concerns of the post 9/11 world.

A. United States Evasion of International Law

As arguably the world's lone remaining superpower, the United States is in a unique position with regards to its participation in international law, most notably in its ability to avoid repercussions for its legal offenses. International law has long been criticized as ineffective because of its weak enforcement mechanisms. For example, Iraq has been a party to the ICCPR since before the United States' ratification, yet has managed to avoid responsibility for its government's blatantly illegal mass murder of the Kurds in the north of the country. Indeed, the most damaging punishment for a nation's violation of international law is often the so-called "mobilization of shame," whereby the publication of the offending nation's transgressions can damage its perception among the other nations of the world. The sheer power and influence of the United States at the present time renders it all but immune from this attempt at deterrence, and in this light the consequences of offending the international law system appear obsolete.

To that end, the United States has acted evasively in carrying out its obligations under international treaties. For example, the United States recently rebuffed claims that it was in violation of the Geneva Convention regarding its treatment of suspected former Taliban fighters at Camp X-Ray in Guantanamo Bay, Cuba. The United States government escaped liability under the provisions of the Convention by refusing to label the captives 'prisoners of war.' By repudiating any classification of the Guantanamo inmates, the government was successful in employing an obvious labeling loophole in the Geneva Convention, thereby allowing the United States to interrogate the prisoners in a manner unrestricted by the Convention. The United States Supreme Court will decide this year whether the Guantanamo inmates can appeal their detentions to the Government, or whether they will continue to be held in a prison that operates entirely outside of the law. In the interim, the United States and similarly situated nations continue to exploit the inefficacies of the international law system.

B. Torture Under a Different Name

The Convention Against Torture (CAT) defines torture as:

> [A]ny act by which severe pain or suffering, whether physical or mental, is intentionally inflicted on a person for such purposes as obtaining from him or a third person information or a confession, punishing him for an act he or a third person has committed or is suspected of having committed, or for any reason based on discrimination of any kind, when such pain or suffering is inflicted by or at the instigation of, or with the consent or acquiescence of a public official or other person acting in an official capacity.

This definition, while not dispositive, is certainly illustrative of the general conception of torture and its legal boundaries. Many nations, however, sidestep admissions of the practice of torture simply by redefining the word. Recently, academics and politicians have analyzed the distinction between "torture" and "torture lite." The latter, it is reasoned, is tantamount to aggressive but legal interrogation and is distinguishable from the traditional concept of torture in several important ways.

Torture is intended, it would seem, to encompass activities that bring about severe pain and suffering. Understandably, the question of what is severe has never been definitively resolved. Traditional methods of torture, such as mutilation, amputation, mock executions, rape, and stoning are presumably intended to cause severe pain. By contrast, torture lite is commonly understood as referring to interrogation methods such as sleep deprivation, exposure to extreme temperatures, mild physical abuse, use of drugs to cause confusion, or psychological coercion. Arguably, these types of methods do not cause severe pain, and are therefore beyond the dominion of torture, at least as defined by the CAT.

The result of this exercise in semantics is increased confusion about what exactly is allowed under international law and what is prohibited. The Geneva Convention, for instance, bans all mistreatment of prisoners during wartime, which probably prohibits both torture and torture lite. In contrast, the International Covenant on Civil and Political Rights may leave the door open to torture lite practices with its subjective "cruel, inhuman, or degrading standard." Under this paradigm, a nation acting from purely selfish interests would likely argue that practices such as mind games and sleep deprivation do not meet the threshold of cruel, inhuman, or degrading punishment. Similarly, the CAT definition of torture presents the aforementioned uncertainty of what is severe. A ruling by the United Nations High Commissioner for Human Rights under the CAT underscores the ambiguity of the law: "[W]hen employed for the purpose of breaking a prisoner's will, sleep deprivation may in some cases constitute torture." Such deviation in the definition of torture leads to a classic slippery slope scenario, where the lines may be loosely drawn to serve the interests of the interrogating nation.

Not surprisingly, there remains a lack of consensus among international courts regarding the point at which interrogation becomes torture. In 1976, the European Commission of Human Rights found that a British combination of five tactics used against Northern Irish prisoners collectively constituted torture under the European Convention of Human Rights. The tactics used included subjecting the prisoners to hooding, extended wall standing in painful postures, loud noises, sleep deprivation, and deprivation of food and drink. Two years later, the European Court for Human Rights reversed this ruling, declaring the conduct had risen to the level of "inhuman and degrading treatment," but not torture. This TT decision influenced one official inquiry by the state of Israel, defining moderate physical pressure against a suspected Palestinian terrorist as compatible with international laws on interrogation. The Israeli High Court of justice later declared this treatment illegal. These inconsistent interpretations of the law allow countries to practice torture under a different name, which cannot be an acceptable solution to the problem of torture.

C. Evidence of United States Practice of Torture

Whether the United States uses torture as a method of interrogation is an open question, subject to both the interpretation of testimony and the definition of torture itself. It would not be inaccurate to conclude the questioning methods of the United States often transcend the lines of humane interrogation. Representatives of the United States have repeatedly implied that torture-like methods are utilized to prevent future terrorist attacks. Cofer Black, then-head of the CIA Counterterrorist Center joint hearing of the House and Senate Intelligence Committees, acknowledged, "[T]here was a before 9/11, and there was an after 9/11. After 9/11 the gloves come off." An unnamed official, interviewed by the *Washington Post,* added: "[I]f you don't violate someone's human rights some of the time, you probably aren't doing your job."

Third party accounts by respected non-governmental organizations also tend to support the notion that the United States uses torturous techniques in its interrogations. Amnesty International reported that prisoners under United States control at the Bagram Air Base in Afghanistan were deprived of sleep with a 24-hour bombardment of lights, held in awkward, painful positions, and constantly subjected to stress and duress techniques. Indeed, many prisoners have attempted suicide at Camp X-Ray in Guantanamo Bay. Human Rights Watch added in their report that prisoners were "subjected to electric shocks . . .

and beaten throughout the night." In an open letter to President George W. Bush, Human Rights Watch Executive Director Kenneth Roth relayed his concern that the United States might be "in violation of some of the most fundamental prohibitions of international human rights law."

The Central Intelligence Agency ("CIA"), though understandably reluctant to admit such practices, is fully cognizant of the effectiveness of torture in investigation. CIA officials sometimes refer to the Kubark Manual, a journal of interrogative techniques, which includes physical and psychological tactics that could easily be classified as torture. A representative from the CIA described the questioning methods used against a typical high-level terrorist suspect:

> He would most likely have been locked naked in a cell with no trace of daylight. The space would be filled day and night with light and noise, and would be so small that he would be unable to stand upright, to sit comfortably, or to recline fully. He would be kept awake, cold, and probably wet. If he managed to doze, he would be roughly awakened. He would be fed infrequently and irregularly, and then only with thin, tasteless meals. . . . On occasion he might be given a drug to elevate his mood prior to interrogation; marijuana, heroin, and sodium pentothal have been shown to overcome a reluctance to speak, and methamphetamine can unleash a torrent of talk in even the most stubborn subjects.

It is interesting to note that all of these techniques, individually, might be classified as torture lite. Taken together, however, they seem to epitomize a routine of torture so devious that it cannot reasonably be described any other way. It becomes impractical to make legal exceptions for torture lite practices when they will add up to extreme torture in the aggregate.

D. The Question of Rendition

The most obvious example of United States complicity in torture is the practice of irregular rendition. Rendition, a system of sending captives to other countries with less progressive human rights standards in order to interrogate them more aggressively, often results in torture. Since September 11, the United States has sent prisoners to Pakistan, Saudi Arabia, Egypt, Morocco, and Uzbekistan, as well as other countries with documented histories of torturing suspects. Through this process, the United States can gain valuable information with impunity, while claiming that they have "no direct knowledge" of the host country's interrogation methods. Fred Hitz, the former CIA Inspector General, commented on the practice of rendition: "We don't do torture, and we can't countenance torture in terms of we can't know of it. But if a country offers information gleaned from interrogations, we can use the fruits of it."

There is no accountability in rendition, and some nations have accused the United States of rendering suspects for immoral or political reasons. The case of Maher Arar is illustrative. Arar, a longtime Canadian citizen, was captured by United States authorities and rendered to Syria. He was tortured at the hands of Syrian and Jordanian authorities, which ceased the treatment only when he "confessed" to being associated with another Canadian citizen who had been arrested. The rendition of Mr. Arar has sparked criticism from various human rights groups.

Renditions are also considered dangerous because the interrogation methods of the receiving countries are often ghastly in nature. The case of Abdul Hakim Murad sheds light on the procedures used during some renditions. Murad was rendered to the Philippines in 1995. According to the *Washington Post*, Philippine authority agents beat Murad, "with a chair and a long piece of wood [breaking most of his ribs], forced water into his mouth, and crushed lighted cigarettes into his private parts." After 63 days of this "tactical interrogation," Murad disclosed a plan to assassinate the pope, and to crash eleven commercial airliners carrying approximately four thousand passengers into the Pacific Ocean, as well as to fly a private plane packed with explosives into CIA headquarters. Although the veracity of Murad's confessions has recently come into dispute, his experience remains an informative example of the techniques utilized during rendition.

The consequence of rendition is the manipulation of the international law system, as well as the circumnavigation of domestic law prohibitions against torture. Again, mobilization of shame appears the most effective international remedy against nations suspected of irregular rendition, and again, some nations are influenced far more than others. Human Rights Watch utilized a mobilization of shame tactic when they publicly announced: "The United States . . . has a duty to refrain from sending persons to countries with a history of torture without explicit, verifiable guarantees that they will not be tortured or otherwise mistreated." The United States' response was evasive, insisting that the renditions occur for the purpose of cultural affinities, as opposed to illegal interrogations. Although this might conceivably be a factor in the renditions, the totality of the evidence yields the conclusion that torture has become a frequent by-product of these renditions.

E. The Two Choices

The stark reality that torture is practiced today leaves a responsible society with two choices. The first is the implementation of an effective international body to regulate torture. In order to address the many problems of today's system, the body would first need a controlling definition of torture. This would effectively limit a nation's ability to practice torture under the guise of torture lite. An effective body would also have implementation powers beyond that of the current mobilization of shame. Without such "teeth," the system would not be effective against powerful nations. Finally, the body would have to make rendition explicitly illegal, and punish countries accordingly. Unfortunately, without drastic and unprecedented cooperation among the myriad nations of the world, this model is not realistic under today's international system.

The other choice is to legalize torture.

IV. Should Torture Be Legalized?

In his farewell address from the presidency, Ronald Reagan spoke of America as a "shining city upon the hill." Reagan's Utopian vision included a principled commitment to human rights and freedoms, similar to that espoused by the current United States administration. In the 2002 State of the Union Address, President George W. Bush proclaimed, "America will always stand firm for the non-negotiable rights of human dignity." This self-imposed higher standard of morality may prove to be both a blessing and a curse. On one hand, this approach has traditionally given the United States a powerful and respected voice in the world community. On the other, the legalization of torture might be considered irreconcilable with President Reagan's "shining city." Although it may be difficult to conceive of a moral society practicing torture, there is an argument to be made that legalizing torture would actually enhance the moral stature of the United States when juxtaposed against the current policy of underground torture.

A. History of State-Sponsored Torture

The concept of state-sponsored torture is not without precedent. The English overtly incorporated torture into their legal system in the seventeenth century. The English employed torture warrants against people that were thought to have information necessary to prevent attacks on the state. The torture warrant served several beneficial purposes, such as making the practice more visible and thus "more subject to public accountability." However, the English torture policy was conducted at a time quite different than our own, and by a government structured quite different than our own.

Perhaps a more germane comparison to this debate is the Israeli experience. Few, if any, countries in the history of the world have been under the constant shadow of terrorism as much as modern-day Israel. The Israelis face threats from both hostile neighboring countries and international terrorist organizations such as Hamas, Hizbollah, and Islamic Jihad. In order to cope with the threat of homicide bombings, the Israelis have traditionally employed torture lite tactics. In 1987, a commission led by former Israeli Supreme Court President Moshe Landau investigated the interrogation practices of the Israeli General Security Service. The commission found that, under the rule of necessity, the use of force in interrogation was authorized if the interrogator reasonably believed the lesser evil of force was necessary to get information that would prevent the greater evil of loss of innocent lives. This ruling temporarily established the foundation for legalized torture in Israel.

Predictably, there were both significant benefits and significant problems associated with the Israeli legalization of torture. Like the English model, the use of torture was publicized and became more visible. However, witnesses claim that Israeli interrogators were loathe to stop at the proscribed limits of questioning. In fact, some authors suggest that up to 85% of Palestinian inmates were tortured by Israeli authorities. Moreover, at least 10 Palestinians died as a result of torture prior to 1994. The publication of these abuses alarmed the United Nations, and their involvement led to a landmark 1999 decision in which the High Court of justice in Israel found the use of moderate physical pressure in interrogation to "[infringe] on both the suspect's dignity and his privacy." The Israeli government subsequently scaled back physical force during interrogations, although some suggest the ruling merely moved the torture movement underground.

B. The Dershowitz Torture Warrant

In his book *Why Terrorism Works: Understanding the Threat, Responding to the Challenge,* Professor Alan Dershowitz analyzes the applicability of judicially sanctioned torture to modernday American jurisprudence. Specifically, Professor Dershowitz addresses the problem of the ticking-bomb terrorist, who possesses crucial information of an imminent disastrous attack, but refuses to give information to his captors. In this situation, one writer emphasizes, society "pay[s] for his silence in blood."

To obtain this critical information, Professor Dershowitz introduces the concept of a torture warrant: a process whereby a neutral magistrate would decide whether there was sufficient evidence to compel a suspect to be subjected to torture. Unlike the current policy, the torture would be medically supervised and designed not to cause any permanent physical damage. One possibility anticipated in the book is the insertion of a long needle under the fingernail, intended to cause excruciating pain but no lasting damage. Professor Dershowitz's proposal is largely based on a cost-benefit framework, reminiscent of philosopher Jeremy Bentham's moral calculus of utility. In the end, Professor Dershowitz theorizes, "absolute opposition to torture—even nonlethal torture in the ticking bomb case—may rest more on historical and aesthetic considerations than on moral or logical ones."

Professor Dershowitz's support of torture is not without its critics. Theorists have unleashed a parade of horribles that could result from the legalization of torture. Foremost among these events are the violation of human dignity, the potential for abusing the law, and the fear of instigating a domino effect and creating a world of legalized torture. Although these arguments are meritorious in their own respects, they are all easily answered from Professor Dershowitz's perspective. With regards to human dignity, the legalization of torture would promote respect for human dignity, insofar as torture would be changed from an inhumane tool of oppression to a last-resort tool for saving lives. The potential for abusing the law is another legitimate concern, but this can be addressed by instituting the necessary and appropriate safeguards. Finally, worldwide legalization of torture is not a negative event in Professor Dershowitz's eyes, if it can be regulated effectively. The legalization of torture is not a perfect solution, and it doubtless would have its downfalls. As Professor Dershowitz observes, "[S]uch is the nature of tragic choices in a complex world."

C. "Degrees" of Torture and the Balancing Test

When weighing the benefits of legalizing torture against preserving the status quo, it is essential to understand the difference in "degrees" of torture. Torture in a legalized system would consist of a nonpermanent act meant to maximize the possibility of gaining crucial information, while minimizing necessary pain. By contrast, torture in rendition might utilize the mind-numbing tactics used against Abdul Hakim Murad in the Philippines, if not worse. The torturers in these situations are not accountable to any authority, and seemingly would not hesitate to take the lives of uncooperative subjects. The degree of torture used in the legalization proposal is, therefore, inherently more humane than the degree of torture practiced today.

Courts often use balancing tests to influence the direction of the law. For instance, in a classic decision on due process, the Supreme Court explained that whether an individual's constitutional rights have been violated "must be determined by balancing [the individual's] liberty interest against the relevant state interests." Here, this logic would probably support the use of torture in a dire situation. Assume, for example, that a known terrorist announced the presence of a nuclear bomb in a major U.S. city that would kill thousands of people. The terrorist further stated that he knew the location and time assigned for the detonation of the bomb, but refused to disclose these crucial details. The terrorist's liberty interest in not being tortured is, no doubt, significant. However, the state interest in saving thousands of lives is far more compelling. Applying Constitutional due process analysis, the use of torture would seemingly be upheld.

There are additional benefits that may be gained from the system without resorting to torture. According to the Kubark Manual, "the threat of coercion usually weakens or destroys resistance more effectively than coercion itself." For example, it is an effective practice to stage mock executions in neighboring cells while a prisoner is interrogated. The CIA's finding that the threat of coercion often leads to compliance, without the actual use of coercion (i.e. torture), is promising. If such a system were implemented, it is possible that important information might be gleaned from a suspect without having to ever resort to torture. Similarly, a transparent regulation of torture practice would encourage dialogue among prisoners such as Maher Arar, without fear of deportation or forced confessions. Both of these factors weigh heavily in favor of a regulated torture system.

There are negative factors that must be considered as well. Legalizing torture would set a dangerous precedent for other countries who might abuse their newfound ability to practice torture. United States officials might abuse their discretion in validating torture warrants. The truth of the statements made under duress of torture might be questioned. Furthermore, some writers have made the argument that legalizing torture would do little to curb the existence of underground torture. For instance, writer Jean Maria Arrigo hypothesized, "[A] regulated program cannot eliminate use of rogue torture interrogation services, because they still serve to circumvent moral and procedural constraints on the official program." Although there is undoubtedly some truth in this theory, there is still hope that a regulated system would curb underground torture to a very significant degree.

Furthermore, these dangers pale in comparison to the dangers in today's system. Currently, the United States participates in underground rendition, which leads to undocumented torture and manipulation. This practice involves a more severe and brutal form of torture, and likely contributes to many undocumented fatalities. Moreover, the information gained from this process is probably less reliable than information extrapolated from a judicially monitored system. The documentation of rendition activities is sparse, and the penalties for offending international laws on torture are virtually nonexistent. On balance, there is much more to lose by embracing the status quo. The balancing test in this analysis yields the conclusion that legalizing torture provides an overall benefit for humankind.

D. Towards a More Humane System

Assuming the requisite support in principle for legalizing torture, the creation and implementation of the torture policy would be both complicated and controversial. Every ambit of these new laws would be duly scrutinized on such an unstable world stage. Who would make the decision of granting or denying the torture warrant? Would there be an adequate appeals system? How would the safety of the torture subjects be ensured? How could the United States condone a policy that offends its Constitution and flagrantly violates the peremptory norms of international law?

Many of these questions are directed towards the intricacies of the torture system itself, and are thus beyond the scope of this Note. However, there are some policy concerns worth discussing. Time constraints would likely pose the biggest roadblock to an effective policy. If a terrorist threatens a bomb strike within hours, it becomes a formidable task to employ a traditional appeals process before initiating torture. The protocol would necessarily be more elaborate than the search warrant process, which demands only an objectively reasonable action by a police officer to obtain a search warrant. The former Israeli standard (reasonable belief that force is necessary to prevent a greater evil) is probably not exacting enough to justify torture. Perhaps the standard should mirror that of the public necessity defense under American tort law, which is limited to actions necessary to avert an impending public disaster. Whatever the solution, it is of the utmost importance that torture be used as a last resort in only the most desperate of scenarios.

An interesting blueprint for a torture warrant procedure might be drawn from the Foreign Intelligence Surveillance Act (FISA) and its implementation. "FISA was created by the United States government as a corollary to the public legal system in order to discreetly process search warrants against suspected terrorists and spies. As initially enacted, FISA allowed specially designated judges to authorize surveillance to acquire foreign intelligence information under certain circumstances, on a court known as the Foreign Intelligence Surveillance Committee (FISC). The seven-judge FISC court was expanded to eleven judges under the 2001 USA Patriot Act. This model is adaptable to the torture warrant proposal, insofar as an eleven-judge panel might be effective at quickly expediting decisions on torture warrants, and making tough decisions regarding ticking-bomb terrorists.

Unfortunately, the FISC model (as amended by the Patriot Act and other legislation) has also proved an embodiment of the critics' worst fears. The records and files of cases involving FISC search warrants are sealed and may only be revealed to an extremely limited degree. Furthermore, the annual reports to Congress for the calendar year 2002 showed that 1,226 of 1,228 applications for search warrants had been approved by the FISC. The remaining two were approved by the supplementary appeals council to the FISC, the FISCR. A system that always approves torture warrant applications would bluntly defeat the purpose of the system. Moreover, the sealing of the documents would defeat the goals of transparency and accountability. Only an arrangement that accounted for these inherent flaws in government-run judgment panels would be able to legitimize torture and bring an appropriate warrant system to fruition.

V. Conclusion

It is incumbent upon us to engage in an open and truthful debate about the state of torture in the world today. Even if there is no perfect solution, the creation of a transparent and judicially monitored system on torture would mark a dramatic improvement over the current policy of ignorance. The dangers for abuse in the current system are truly boundless, and the practice of rendition often leaves the fate of suspects in the dangerous hands of acknowledged torturers. The practice of torture should not be denied simply because it is concealed and hidden half a world away. Legalizing torture certainly presents imposing obstacles, both in its challenging implementation and in its visceral dissonance. Compared to the current policy of practicing torture "under the radar screen," however, it may indeed be the lesser of two evils.

Elisa Massimino

 **NO**

Leading by Example? U.S. Interrogation of Prisoners in the War on Terror

When "trophy photos" taken by soldiers involved in the abuse of Iraqi prisoners at Abu Ghraib prison—one of the most notorious under Saddam Hussein's regime—were made public in late April 2004, the Pentagon had already completed two investigations into allegations of abuse at the prison. The graphic and disturbing photographs, some aired on prime-time American television, show naked Iraqi prisoners in humiliating poses, many with smiling uniformed soldiers looking on and pointing or giving a "thumbs up" sign. In one of the photographs, two naked prisoners are posed to make it look as though one is performing oral sex on another. Another shows a hooded prisoner standing on a box with wires attached to his wrists; the army says the prisoner was told that if he fell off the box, he would be electrocuted. Two pictures show dead prisoners—one with a battered and bruised face, the other whose bloodied body was wrapped in cellophane and packed in ice. One shows an empty room, splattered with blood. Reportedly, there is video as well.

These gruesome photographs were splashed across the front pages of newspapers in the Middle East and around the world, the headlines screaming "TORTURE." But the abuse was not news to the Pentagon. According to news accounts, a scathing 53-page report by Major General Antonio M. Taguba, completed in February, concluded that there was ongoing systematic and criminal abuse of detainees at the Abu Ghraib prison. As Seymour Hersh reported in the *New Yorker* magazine in May, General Taguba's report confirmed that abuses were taking place at the prison, including: threatening male detainees with rape, sodomizing a male detainee with a broomstick or chemical light, threatening detainees with dogs, and pouring chemicals from broken light bulbs onto detainees. As a result of this investigation, six soldiers are facing court-martial on charges that include cruelty toward prisoners, dereliction of duty, and indecent acts.

Are the soldiers who engaged in these acts just "sick bastards," as their commanding officer recently said, or is there something more profoundly

Reprinted by permission from *Criminal Justice Ethics*, vol. 23, no. 1, Winter 2004, pp. 2–5. Copyright © 2004 by Institute for Criminal Justice Ethics, 555 W 57 Street, Suite 601, New York, NY 10019-1029.

disturbing going on here? Why did the soldiers feel free to document their crimes on camera? Some answers to these questions will likely emerge in the prosecution of the soldiers involved. But it appears from the information already available that this was abuse with a particular purpose—to "create conditions favorable for successful interrogation"—that is, to break down a prisoner's will.

The Descent to Lawlessness

As shocking as these abuses are, to anyone who has followed closely the Bush Administration's descent into lawlessness in its prosecution of the "war on terrorism," they are not surprising. Three factors contribute to an environment in which such torture and cruelty can proliferate.

First is the Administration's persistent degradation of the Geneva Conventions and other international standards governing its conduct toward prisoners. Beginning with the initial transfer of prisoners from Afghanistan to Guantanamo, White House officials argued that the Geneva Conventions were not relevant to the war on terrorism. Later, under pressure from secretary of State Colin Powell and other current and former military officers who revere the Geneva Conventions as a source of protection in case of capture, the Administration announced that it "believes in the principles" of the Geneva Conventions, but neither Taliban fighters nor al Qaeda suspects were eligible for their protections. Thus, as we continue to learn from Guantanamo, Bagram, and now Abu Ghraib, believing in the principles of the Geneva Conventions and actually complying with them are two different things—and there is no in-between. Complying with the Geneva Conventions requires that all of the detainees on Guantanamo and elsewhere have a recognized legal status. This, the Administration has steadfastly refused to do. But if the United States wants to be able to rely on the protections in the Geneva Conventions, then it must comply with them—not just in word, but in deed. Failing to do so not only places U.S. soldiers at greater risk, but contributes to a situation in which the details and importance of the Geneva Conventions are completely unrecognized by soldiers, like those at Abu Ghraib, charged with guarding and interrogating prisoners.

Second is the way in which the United States has played fast and loose with the prohibition on torture and cruel, inhuman, or degrading treatment. For example, one government official described the interrogation of an alleged high-ranking al Qaeda operative as "not quite torture, but about as close as you can get." Various administration officials—as well as some detainees who have been released—report that prisoners in U.S. custody have been beaten; thrown into walls; subjected to loud noises and extreme heat and cold; deprived of sleep, light, food, and water; bound or forced to stand in painful positions for long periods of time; kept naked; hooded; and shackled to the ceiling. Euphemistically called "stress and duress" techniques, U.S. officials who admit to these practices seem to think they are permissible so long as they don't cross the line into "outright torture." They are mistaken. When President Bush's father pushed the Convention

Against Torture through the Senate, he committed to interpret the phrase "cruel, inhuman or degrading treatment or punishment" in ways consistent with the Eighth Amendment's prohibition on cruel and unusual punishment. To put these "stress and duress" techniques into constitutional context, the U.S. Supreme Court ruled in 2002 that handcuffing a prisoner to a hitching post in a painful position for eight hours clearly violated the protection against cruel and unusual punishment. While there are certainly some interrogation methods that are unpleasant but not illegal, "stress and duress" interrogation techniques are clearly illegal. Pentagon General Counsel William J. Haynes III asserts that U.S. policy is "to treat all detainees and conduct all interrogations wherever they may occur, in a manner consistent with" the prohibition on cruel treatment. But because many detainees are interrogated without the presence of lawyers or even the confidentiality-bound International Committee of the Red Cross (ICRC), it is difficult to know if that policy is known to interrogators, let alone whether they comply with it.

The third factor contributing to the kinds of interrogation abuses that are now coming to light is the Administration's focus on using interrogation almost exclusively for the purpose of obtaining information, rather than to obtain a confession or other evidence admissible in court. When the goal of interrogation is prosecution, the rules are familiar: Miranda, lawyers, a day in court. But what are the rules when there is no day in court in a detainee's future? Almost immediately after September 11, 2001, Attorney General Ashcroft and other senior officials at the Justice Department began talking about a fundamental shift in approach when dealing with terrorist suspects, from prosecution to prevention. Facilitated by an "enemy combatant" policy that so far has allowed the government to keep even U.S. citizens in incommunicado detention for prolonged periods, the Administration argues that detainees have no rights—to counsel, to appear before a judge, to speak to anyone at all—that might interfere with the sense of dependency and lack of control designed to make a detainee "lose hope."

Justifying Torture

Most discussions of interrogation and torture begin with the so-called "ticking time bomb" scenario, which posits a situation in which a detainee has information that, if revealed, could spare those about to be slaughtered. Is torture permissible if it would save those lives? People who focus on this hypothetical often do so in order to expose as "soft" those wide-eyed moralists unwilling to "do what is necessary" for the greater good. Since September 11, some lawyers and even judges have argued that if the taboo against torture has not already been broken, it should be now. Harvard law professor Alan Dershowitz proposed "torture warrants" for the ticking time bomb scenario, so that the abuses could be undertaken with judicial and societal sanction. Federal Judge Richard Posner has said that anyone who doubts torture is permissible when the stakes are high enough should not be in a position of responsibility. The end—saving innocent lives—justifies the means.

This is tough talk. But those who advocate for torture in these circumstances are the ones who are out of touch with reality. Many experienced interrogators have pointed out that the "ticking time bomb" scenario, with its factual (if not moral) clarity, is a fantasy, a situation that simply never presents itself in the real world. Abu Ghraib prison, on the other hand, is reality, and it is a reality where the means—torture and humiliation—quite likely will help to undermine the ends that the U.S. government is pursuing—Iraqi acceptance of a U.S. military presence in a free and democratic Iraq.

Outlawing Torture

Just before the beating deaths of two Afghan prisoners who died under interrogation at Bagram Air Force Base were made public, I told a friend of mine—a senior military officer at the Pentagon—how disturbed I was by the fact that so many Americans with whom I talked casually believed, without distress or the slightest bit of cognitive dissonance, that the United States was torturing suspects for information. I asked my friend whether he believed that prisoners being held by the United States were being tortured. "I can't believe that," he said. "I could never be involved in a mission that relied on torture and abuse. It's a betrayal of everything we stand for."

Not only that, it's also illegal. When the U.S. Senate gave its advice and consent to ratification of the United Nations Convention Against Torture and Other Cruel, Inhuman or Degrading Treatment or Punishment, it recognized that ratification would have to await the passage and implementation of legislation, required by the treaty, making torture a crime. Congress did so in 1994. Title 18, Section 2340 of the United States Code defines torture as "an act committed by a person acting under the color of law specifically intended to inflict severe physical or mental pain or suffering (other than pain or suffering incidental to lawful sanctions) upon another person within his custody or physical control." Section 2340A makes torture, attempted torture, and conspiracy to commit torture a federal crime, punishable by up to 20 years in prison; if the victim dies as a result of torture, the punishment could be death. The law applies only to torture committed outside the United States, but includes acts by U.S. citizens. While the conduct of U.S. soldiers is governed by the Uniform Code of Military Justice (hence the charges of "cruelty" and "indecent acts" in the Abu Ghraib prison abuse case), it appears that other U.S. personnel—private contractors and intelligence officials—may also have been involved in the abuse. In the 10 years that the anti-torture law has been on the books, not a single person has been charged under its provisions. That may now change.

No Exceptions

Regardless of the words used to prohibit it, the ban on the use of torture is absolute. Unlike other provisions of international human rights law—such as the right to be free from arbitrary arrest or detention—that can be suspended during a declared emergency that "threatens the life of the nation," no exigency can justify torture.

This prohibition applies to the outsourcing option as well. International law prohibits the United States, as a signatory of the Convention Against Torture, from sending a person to a country where there is a substantial likelihood that he will be tortured. Congress reiterated this obligation in legislation in 1998, requiring regulations from all relevant executive agencies detailing how this obligation would be implemented. The Departments of Justice and State both issued regulations; the Pentagon and the CIA never complied. Over the last 18 months, a number of Administration officials have confirmed that the United States is handing some al Qaeda suspects in military or CIA custody over to other governments for interrogation. These transfers are known as "extraordinary rendition"—a highly legalistic term for a completely extra-legal arrangement. Some of the countries where the detainees are sent—Egypt, Syria, Morocco—are places where, according to the State Department's annual country reports on human rights practices, torture and other prisoner abuse is routine. Some detainees have been transferred with a list of questions that their American interrogators want answered; in other cases, U.S. officials maintain more of a distance, simply receiving the fruits of the interrogation. It is unclear whether U.S. officials are ever present at these sessions. But even if they are not, it is a fiction that "extraordinary rendition" allows the United States to preserve clean hands, despite one U.S. official's claim that "We don't kick the [expletive] out of them. We send them to other countries so they can kick the [expletive] out of them." Interestingly, when those countries comply, they may get a free pass from the State Department. In 2002, new instructions were issued to U.S. embassy personnel who draft the human rights reports: "Actions by governments taken at the request of the United States or with the expressed support of the United States should not be included in the report."

When pressed to explain how its policy of "extraordinary rendition" to countries known to practice torture comports with its obligations under both the Convention Against Torture and domestic law, the Administration's response is either disingenuous or rather naïve. In a letter to Senator Patrick Leahy responding to just this question, Pentagon General Counsel Haynes said that when it transfers a detainee to a third country, U.S. policy is "to obtain specific assurances from the receiving country that it will not torture the individual being transferred to that country." In other words, we just take Syria's word for it. As Senator Leahy responded, "mere assurances from countries that are known to practice torture systematically are not sufficient." Though Haynes has said that the United States will follow up on any evidence that these "diplomatic assurances" were not being honored, it seems that it would be awfully rare that such evidence would ever emerge, since the detention is likely to be incommunicado.

However, though rare, such evidence is not impossible. In September of 2002, U.S. officials arrested Maher Arar, a dual citizen of Canada and Syria, as he was changing planes at JFK airport in New York, en route home to Canada. Although he was traveling on his Canadian passport, U.S. officials—apparently CIA and Justice Department working together—secretly transferred Arar first to Jordan then to Syria, a move that evoked strong protest in Canada. Arar arrived in Syria after being interrogated for 11 days at a CIA interrogation center in

Jordan. He then spent 10 months in a Syrian jail, during which time he alleges he was repeatedly tortured. Under increasing public pressure from Canadians and human rights groups, Syria finally released Arar, claiming they never had any interest in him anyway, but had only jailed and interrogated him to curry favor with the United States. This case provides an opportunity to test whether the United States is serious about the safeguards it says it employs when it transfers detainees to the custody of other governments. Did the United States government seek "diplomatic assurances" from Syria before handing Arar over? It hasn't said. If it did, has it complained to Syria that its treatment of Arar violates those assurances? It appears not. Perhaps that is because, as Arar alleges, the transfer to Syria was for the purpose of interrogation under torture. While in Syrian custody, Arar confessed to being a terrorist and having trained in an al Qaeda camp, all of which he now denies. With the Syrian government's later dismissal of Arar's importance, it appears even the Syrians did not believe his confessions.

Credibility

If another country is willing to torture a prisoner in whom it has no independent interest just to appease the United States, imagine what effect we are having on repressive governments anxious to legitimize their own abusive conduct towards political dissidents and others they wish to silence. As the world stares in horror at pictures of grinning American soldiers engaging in war crimes, it is becoming increasingly deaf to the President's proclamation that "America will always stand firm for the non-negotiable demands of human dignity." Last summer, the President issued a clear and forceful statement reaffirming the "inalienable human right" to be free from torture. "The United States is committed to the world-wide elimination of torture and we are leading this fight by example," President Bush said in a statement commemorating the U.N. International Day in Support of Victims of Torture. Now, nearly a year later, the world has good reason to doubt the integrity of the President's pledge.

POSTSCRIPT

Does the United States Have a Right to Torture Suspected Terrorists?

U.S. Supreme Court Associate Justice Hugo Black once stated that in times of social crisis "the fog of public excitement obscures the ancient landmarks set up in our Bill of Rights. Yet then, of all times, should this Court adhere more closely to the course they mark." The Bill of Rights, the first ten amendments to the U.S. Constitution, establishes the framework for protection of basic liberties by our government. The rights provided therein include some of the most fundamental values of American society: Freedom of the Press, Speech, and Religion, the right to be free from unreasonable searches and seizures, the right to be free from double jeopardy, the privilege against self-incrimination, the right to counsel, the right to a trial by jury, the right not to be subjected to cruel and unusual punishment, and the right to due process of law.

Do you agree with Justice Black's statement that at times of social crisis public sentiment may tempt us to compromise our most important social values? What are the implications of Justice Black's position for the development of laws in the wake of the war on terrorism?

In the articles presented in this section, attorney Andrew A. Moher argues for laws permitting judicially sanctioned torture of terrorists when it is necessary to prevent a greater evil. Moreover, Moher asserts that a judicially monitored system in the United States is far preferable to the Bush administration's current policy of practicing torture "under the radar screen." Elisa Massimino, in contrast, believes that the use of torture is immoral and counterproductive. She asserts that if the United States wishes to rely on the protections of the Geneva Conventions, then it must comply with its provisions prohibiting the torture of prisoners.

After reading the articles in this section and considering Justice Black's statement, what is your position on the use of torture of suspected terrorists? Is there any middle ground in this debate?

There is a good deal of compelling and recent literature relevant to the issue considered in this section. For an excellent analysis of the philosophical problems associated with using torture, see David Sussman, "What's Wrong with Torture?" *Philosophy and Public Affairs* (vol. 33, no. 1, 2005). Anthony Lewis, the author of *Gideon's Trumpet*, has also written a very interesting article discussing the state of civil liberties in the aftermath of the war on terrorism, "One Liberty at a Time," *Mother Jones* (vol. 29, no. 3, 2004); see also, Harvey Silverglate, "Civil Liberties and Enemy Combatants," *Reason* (vol. 36, no. 8, 2005); Mark Bowden, "The Dark Art of Interrogation," *The Atlantic Monthly* (vol. 292, no. 3, 2003);

Christopher Tindale, "The Logic of Torture: A Critical Examination," *Social Theory and Practice* (vol. 22, no. 3, 1996); George J. Annas, "Unspeakably Cruel—Torture, Medical Ethics, and the Law," *The New England Journal of Medicine* (May 19, 2005); Stuart Taylor, "The Perils of Torturing Suspected Terrorists," *National Journal* (May 8, 2004); and Laura M. Kelly, "Big Brother Inc: Surveillance, Security and the U.S. Citizen," *Analog Science Fiction & Fact* (vol. 125, no. 5, 2005).

ISSUE 5

Is Racial Profiling an Acceptable Law Enforcement Strategy?

YES: Jared Taylor and Glayde Whitney, from "Racial Profiling: Is There an Empirical Basis?" *Mankind Quarterly* (Spring 2002)

NO: Michael J. Lynch, from "Misleading 'Evidence' and the Misguided Attempt to Generate Racial Profiles of Criminals; Correcting Fallacies and Calculations Concerning Race and Crime in Taylor and Whitney's Analysis of Racial Profiling," *Mankind Quarterly* (Spring 2002)

ISSUE SUMMARY

YES: Jared Taylor, president of the New Century Foundation, and Glayde Whitney argue that the disparity in crimes committed by members of different races justifies racial profiling by the police.

NO: Professor Michael J. Lynch, however, argues that a proper analysis of the crime data does not support Taylor and Whitney's conclusions. He finds racial profiling to be objectionable from a legal and moral perspective as well.

One of the more controversial issues in American society is race relations. It has now been more than 50 years since the U.S. Supreme Court's seminal decision in *Brown v. Board of Education,* 347 U.S. 483 (1954), which ended the doctrine of "separate but equal" treatment of the races. This decision was grounded on the principle that separate treatment based on race can never truly be equal. Stated Chief Justice Earl Warren:

> To separate [school children] from others of similar age and qualifications solely because of their race generates a feeling of inferiority as to their status in the community that may affect their hearts and minds in a way unlikely ever to be undone. . . (494).

Feelings of inferiority as to one's status in the community could be caused by many different things. Most of us have been stopped by the police for a traffic violation at one time or another. How did it make you feel? Did your heart rate increase? Did you begin to perspire slightly? Were you nervous, or did you become tongue-tied when you began to talk with the officer? Now, put yourself in the place of a 21-year-old African-American male who is stopped by the police. Would the experience be any different? Would you be suspicious that the only reason you were stopped was because of your race? If you were a young Hispanic-American male driving in an upscale neighborhood and were stopped by the police and were told "you don't belong here," would it produce the same feelings of inferiority Chief Justice Warren had described in *Brown v. Board of Education?*

In contrast, suppose that criminologists could show statistically that a disproportionate number of young minority group members were responsible for committing crimes such as burglary in the upscale neighborhood. Would the police be justified in questioning any young minority group member found in the area? Likewise, suppose it could be demonstrated that the individuals who carried out the September 11 bombings of the World Trade Center buildings were exclusively young males of Middle-eastern descent. Would TSA officials at our nation's airports be justified in targeting such individuals for intensive pre-flight searches?

Jared Taylor and Glayde Whitney assert that the police are justified in using racial profiling strategies based on their analysis of macro-level crime data. These authors contend that African-Americans commit violent crimes at four to eight times the white rate. Hispanics, they believe, commit violent crimes at approximately three times the white rate, and Asians at one-half to three-quarters of the white rate. Taylor and Whitney assert that criminologists, in a spirit of political correctness, have succumbed to media and political pressure to avoid acknowledgment of the differences and their implications for public policy.

Criminologist Michael J. Lynch maintains that Taylor and Whitney have made errors in their analysis that produce misleading conclusions about racial profiling. While he agrees that African-Americans are overrepresented in the crime data, he contends that this may be a measure of a bias that selects them more often for official processing within the justice system. Moreover, Lynch believes that Taylor and Whitney's views on the propriety of racial profiling by law enforcement officials either are purposely misleading or are completely naïve analyses of crime and victimization data.

Suppose you accept Taylor and Whitney's view that the members of racial minorities do commit more crime in the United States. Does that mean that racial profiling by law enforcement officials is justified? Or, might there be a moral component to this debate, which says that it is wrong to target persons based on their race, no matter how effective the practice may potentially be? When you read these articles, try to develop your own sense of whether racial profiling is a legitimate law enforcement practice as well as its implications in a pluralistic nation.

YES

Jared Taylor and
Glayde Whitney

Racial Profiling: Is There an Empirical Basis?

The disparity between public sensibilities and empirical data has become so extreme that certain topics can no longer be investigated without bringing down cries of "racism." Nevertheless, blacks commit violent crimes at four to eight times the white rate. Hispanics commit violent crimes at about three times the white rate, and Asians at one half to three quarters the white rate. Blacks are as much more criminally violent than whites, as men are more violent than women. Therefore, just as police stop and question men more often than women, they should stop blacks more often than whites. Of the approximately 1,700,000 interracial crimes of violence involving blacks and whites, 90 percent are committed by blacks against whites. Blacks are 50 times more likely than whites to commit individual acts of interracial violence. They are up to 250 times more likely than whites to engage in multiple-offender or group interracial violence. There is more black-on-white than black-on-black violent crime. Fifty-six percent of violent crimes committed by blacks have white victims. Only two to three percent of violent crimes committed by whites have black victims. Violent crime and interracial violence are important, agonizing concerns in this country, and we cannot begin to formulate solutions until we understand the problems.

One of the strangest phenomena in contemporary criminology is the treatment of race and ethnicity. On the one hand there is a long history of academic attention to differences among racial and ethnic groups in involvement in various sorts of criminality (Hooton, 1939; Wilson & Herrnstein, 1985). On the other hand there appears to be media and political pressure to avoid acknowledgement of the differences and possible consequences of the differences. Recently the New Jersey State Police Superintendent Col. Carl Williams was fired by Gov. Christie Whitman after he said in an interview that some minority groups were more likely to be involved in certain crimes (AP, 1999). The Governor is quoted as having said that Williams' comments were "inconsistent with our efforts to enhance public confidence in the State Police." The same article reports that Williams said he did not condone racial profiling, and has never condoned racial profiling, but at the same time he said "it is naive to think race is not an issue" in some sorts of crime (AP, 1999). While Col. Williams claims not to condone racial profiling, the American Civil

From *Mankind Quarterly*, vol. 42, no. 3, Spring 2002, pp. 285–312 (excerpts). Copyright © 2002 by Council for Social and Economic Studies. Reprinted by permission.

Liberties Union (ACLU) reported in June, 1999, that it was a widespread practice: "Citing police statistics, case studies from 23 states and media reports, the organization asserts that law-enforcement agencies have systematically targeted minority travelers for search . . . based on the belief that they are more likely than whites to commit crimes" (Drummond, 1999).

Although reports such as that of the ACLU which criticize the practice of racial profiling and criticize the "belief" that there may be race differences in criminality get wide media coverage, even being featured in national news magazines such as *Time*, (Drummond, 1999), other reports that deal with the actual incidence of crimes as related to race get short shrift. The nationally syndicated columnist Samuel Francis recently wrote:

> Black Americans commit 90 percent of the 1.7 million interracial crimes that occur in the United States every year and are more than 50 times more likely to commit violent crimes against whites than whites are against blacks. These facts were the main findings of a study released earlier this month by the New Century Foundation, but they're not the really big news.
>
> The big news is that the report, despite having been made available to virtually all newspapers and news outlets in the United States as well as to most major columnists and opinion writers, has been almost totally ignored by the national news media. The study was released on June 2 of this year. To date, all of one single news story about it has appeared. (Francis, 1999)

It does indeed seem strange for there to be a great disparity between media reports and the subsequent public apperception, and the actual data concerning one of the more important issues in criminology today.

The inconsistency between media reports and criminological data concerning race is not a new phenomenon. About a decade ago we reviewed the literature dealing with race differences in criminal behavior. Taylor (1992) largely reviewed media reports, while Whitney (1990) reviewed the scientific literature. A main finding of the review of media accounts of race and crime was the existence of a double standard with regard to reports of crime that mentioned race of perpetrator or race of victim, with white victimization of blacks receiving considerably more prominent coverage than black victimization of whites (Taylor, 1992). The review of scientific literature was remarkable for both the quantity and consistency of prior literature (Whitney, 1990). Furthermore, the racial differences were accentuated when one considered more serious offenses and offenses that were variously described as victimful or predatory crimes. In a major review Ellis (1988) had reported that for serious victimful crimes, whenever comparisons had been made, blacks had always had higher rates than whites. Whenever blacks or whites had been compared with Orientals in roughly the same geographical areas, Orientals had always had the lowest serious victimful crime rates. The results were much less consistent for minor and/ or victimless offenses. Overall, an order of blacks > whites > Orientals prevailed, with racial differences being larger the more serious and clearly victimful the offenses (Whitney, 1990).

In their classic *Crime and Human Nature,* Wilson and Herrnstein (1985:461) reviewed some literature on race and crime. They mentioned that blacks then constituted about one-eighth of the population of the United States and about one-half of arrestees for murder, rape, and robbery, and from one-fourth to one-third of arrestees for burglary, larceny, auto theft, and aggravated assault. Even with adjustments for other demographic variables, such as age and urban residence, in comparison to whites, blacks were overrepresented about four to one with regard to violent crimes and about three to one with regard to property crimes. Rushton (1985) pointed out that experience in England was consistent with that in the United States: blacks then constituted about 13 percent of the population of London and accounted for 50 percent of the crime. Indeed, violent crime by blacks had been mentioned as a factor contributing to the rearming of London's Metropolitan Police (Could & Waldren, 1986). Blacks were similarly overrepresented with regard to white-collar crimes such as fraud and embezzlement. Blacks were underrepresented only with regard to offenses, such as securities violations, that usually required access to high-status occupations in which they were at that time underrepresented (Wilson & Herrnstein, 1985:462).

Whitney (1990) analyzed the race-specific arrest rates for various offenses that had been compiled for the years 1965 to 1986 (UCRP, 1988). For 19 categories listed in each of 22 years (418 comparisons), the rate for nonwhites always exceeded the rate for whites in the same year, typically by a factor of four to ten. For example, averaged across years, the nonwhite murder rate was nine times the white rate. Considerations of rate of crime combine prevalence (individuals who participate in crime) and incidence (recidivism, number of crimes by individuals who participate). Prevalence has been estimated through accumulation of first arrests across age (Blumstein & Graddy, 1981–1982; Blumstein & Cohen, 1987). Blumstein's results suggest that incidence is not strongly different among participants of different races. Rather, the race differences in crime rates are largely attributable to differences in the proportion of individuals of various races that participate in crime (Blumstein & Cohen, 1987). Among urban males the probability that by age 55 a black had been arrested for an FBI index crime was about 0.51; for whites it was 0.14 (Blumstein & Graddy, 1981–1982). Comparable age accumulated participation rates are not available for Orientals due primarily to their very low overall participation rates. Conversion of percentages to areas under a normal curve can be useful for comparing populations. These individual participation rates suggest about a one-standard-deviation difference between male urban blacks and whites for criminal liability (Whitney, 1990). The apologist argument that arrest data are inappropriate for documentation of race differences in crime rates due to bias in arrests was thoroughly considered, and essentially debunked in Wilbank's 1987 book *The Myth of a Racist Criminal Justice System.* More recently Dilulio (1996) has also presented data concerning crime disparities among races, and the suggestion that the disparities are real in that they do not reflect differential law enforcement.

For regions within the United States, Whitney (1995) pointed out that the best predictor of local murder rate was simply the percent of the population that was black. Across all of the 170 cities in the United States that had a 1980 population of at least 100,000, the correlation between murder rate and percent of the population that was black was $r = +0.69$. With data from 1980 aggregated for the 50 states of the United States, the simple correlation between murder rate and percent of the population that was black was $r = +0.77$. More recently Hama (1999) used data from 1995 to calculate the correlation across the 50 states between percent of the population that is black and violent crime rate, where violent crime rate was an aggregate of murder, non-negligent manslaughter, rape, robbery, and aggravated assault. Hama (1999) reported the correlation to be $r = +0.76$.

Clearly the existing data briefly reviewed above are quite consistent. They are also somewhat limited in scope. There are two areas of criminality related to race that are not considered above, but which have become of interest in recent years. One is the question of hate crime categorization, and the other is that of interracial crime. In crimes where the perpetrator and the victim are of different races, are there any patterns in incidence, and what amount of interracial crime gets included in hate crime statistics? The analyses reported in the present paper were conducted to obtain information concerning the questions of interracial crime and hate crimes, as well as to update the investigation of incidence of crime as related to race in the United States.

Sources and Methods

The primary sources of data for consideration were governmental compilations of statistical information having to do with crime. The major sources are described here. One of the most important sources is the National Crime Victimization Survey (NCVS). Every year since 1972, the U.S. Department of Justice has carried out what is called the NCVS to ascertain the frequency of certain kinds of crimes. The NCVS sample is large, upwards of 80,000 people from about 50,000 households, and carefully stratified on the basis of census data to be representative of the nation as a whole. The NCVS is unique as a record of criminal victimization as reported directly by Americans, not filtered through police reports. It is the only significant nationwide measure of interracial crime. The NCVS is carried out annually, but the Department of Justice does not issue full reports every year; 1994 is the most recent year for complete data.

Ever since passage of the Hate Crime Statistics act of 1990, the FBI has been charged with collecting national statistics on criminal acts "motivated, in whole or in part, by bias." The law does not compel local law enforcement agencies to supply the FBI with this information, but many do. In 1997, the most recent year for which data are available, the FBI received hate crime information from 11,211 local agencies serving more than 83 percent of the United States population.

Uniform Crime Reports (UCR), published annually by the FBI, is the standard reference work for crime and crime rates in the United States. The UCR is a nationwide compilation of criminal offenses and arrest data, reported voluntarily by local law enforcement agencies. In the most recent

UCR, which covers 1997, the FBI included reports from 17,000 law enforcement agencies, covering 95 percent of the country's population. The UCR is unquestionably the most comprehensive and authoritative report on crimes brought to the attention of the police. News stories about rising or falling crime rates are almost always based on the UCR.

Our primary methodology throughout this study is to calculate rates of various offenses as a function of victim and offender characteristics. Such calculations are straightforward, but can appear arcane to investigators experienced with other analytical approaches. Therefore we here provide a detailed example.

The most recent complete NCVS data are for the year 1994 (USDJ, 1997). In that report Table 42 lists categories of single-offender interracial violent crimes. The various numbers at the top of the table represent totals calculated for single-offender violent crimes reported for that year. They are extrapolated from the actual crimes reported by the survey sample. We find that in 1994 6,830,360 whites were victims of violent crimes, and that 16.7 percent (1,140,670) reported that the perpetrator was black. Blacks were victims of 1,100,490 violent crimes, of which 12.3 percent (135,360) were committed by whites. Summing these figures for interracial crime (1,140,670 plus 135,360) we get a total of 1,276,030 interracial crimes, of which 1,140,670 or 89 percent were committed by blacks.

To get the rates at which blacks and whites commit interracial crime we divide the number of crimes by the population to get crimes per 100,000 population. The Census Bureau reports that the 1994 white and black populations were 216,413,000 and 32,653,000 respectively. Whites therefore committed acts of interracial violence at a rate of 62.55 per 100,000 while the black rate was 3,493.63 per 100,000, a figure that is 55.85 times the white rate. Put in the most straightforward terms, the average black was 56 times more likely to commit criminal violence against a white than was a white to commit criminal violence against a black. The multiple of 56 does not mean that blacks commit 56 times as much interracial violence as whites. What it means is that if whites commit interracial violence at a rate of 10 crimes per 100,000 whites, the rate for blacks is 560 per 100,000, or 56 times the white rate. This is the kind of calculation that is represented in most of the analyses in this report.

Results and Discussion

Calculations from the NCVS similar to those detailed above indicate that the black rate for interracial robbery, or "mugging", was 103 times the white rate. . . .

Again using the NCVS (USDJ, 1997), we calculate the total number of crimes committed by perpetrators of each race, and the percentage that is committed against the other race. The 1,140,670 acts of violence committed by blacks against whites constitute 56.3 percent of all violent crimes committed by blacks. That is to say that when blacks commit violent crimes they target whites more than half the time or, put differently, there is more black-on-white crime than black-on-black crime. Similar calculations for whites show that of the 5,114,696 acts of criminal violence committed by whites, only 2.6 percent were directed at blacks. Although homicide is a violent crime, the NCVS does not include it because victims cannot be interviewed. The number of interracial homicides is rather small and does not substantially affect the percentages and ratios presented here.

It may be suggested that blacks commit violence against whites because whites are more likely to have money and are therefore more promising robbery targets. However, of the 1,140,670 black-on-white acts of single-perpetrator violence reported in 1994, only 173,374 were robberies. The remaining 84.8 percent were aggravated assaults, rapes, and simple assaults, which presumably were not motivated by profit. Rape, in particular, has nothing to do with the presumed wealth of the victim. More than 30,000 white women were raped by black men in 1994, while about 5,400 black women were raped by white men. The black interracial rape rate was thus 38 times the white rate.

The NCVS (USDJ, 1997) Table 48 contains interracial crime data for acts of violence committed by multiple offenders. By doing calculations as before, we determine how much group or "gang" violence (not in the sense of organized gangs) is interracial and how much is committed by blacks and by whites. Of the total of 490,266 acts of multiple-offender interracial violence, no fewer than 93.9 percent were committed by blacks against whites. Robbery, for which there is a monetary motive, accounted for fewer than one-third of these crimes. The rest were gang assaults, including rapes, presumably for motives other than profit.

Rates of group violence for each race can be calculated as before, and the difference between the races is stark. The black rate of overall interracial gang violence is 101.75 times the white rate; for robbery it is 277.31 times the white rate. . . .

Race and Crime

Different racial groups in the United States commit crimes at different rates. Most Americans have a sense that non-white neighborhoods are more dangerous than white neighborhoods—and they are correct. However, it is very unusual to find reliable information on just how much more dangerous some groups are than others.

The Uniform Crime Reports (UCR) from the FBI is the standard reference for crime and crime rates in the United States. In trying to determine crime rates for different racial groups, it is important to be aware of the differences between the UCR and the NCVS referenced above. The NCVS contains only one kind of information: crimes Americans say they have suffered. The UCR includes two different kinds of data: crimes reported to the police and arrests of perpetrators. Even for the same year and for the same crime, these three sets of numbers are different. The largest numbers are in the NCVS, because they include crimes not reported to the police. Somewhat smaller are the UCR figures on offenses reported to authorities, and smaller still are arrest figures, which represent offenses for which a suspect is arrested.

For example, in the 1997 NCVS Americans say they suffered a total of 1,883,000 cases of aggravated assault (USDJ, 1998a), but according to the UCR, only 1,022,000 were reported to the police. During that same year, there were only 535,000 arrests for aggravated assault (UCR, 1998). Racial data enter the UCR numbers only when an arrest is made, so it can be argued that racial comparisons should not be based on UCR data. Different racial groups may report crime to the police at different rates, some groups may be more successful at escaping arrest, and the police may discriminate between racial groups in their arrest efforts. However, although racial bias in arrests is frequently discussed, when investigated the data suggest that arrest rates actually track perpetrator rates (Dilulio, 1996; Wilbanks, 1987). Furthermore, there is an advantage to using UCR data because its racial categories are more detailed. Unlike the NCVS, which reports only "black", "white", and "other", the UCR compiles arrest data on "black", "white", "American Indian/Eskimo", and "Asian/Pacific Islander." These are the only national crime data that make these distinctions. Also, as will be explicated below, UCR arrest data can be compared to other data sources in ways that make it possible to treat Hispanics as a separate ethnic category.

Another good reason to use UCR arrest data (race of persons arrested) is that the racial proportions are actually quite close to those from NCVS survey data (race of perpetrator as reported by victims). For example, according to the UCR, 57 percent of people arrested for robbery in 1997 were black, as were 37 percent of those arrested for aggravated assault (UCR, 1998). According to NCVS data on single-offender crimes, 51 percent of robbers were reported by their victims to be black as were 30 percent of those who committed aggravated assault (USDJ, 1997). Since there is a greater overrepresentation by blacks in NCVS-reported multiple-offender crimes, combining the two sets of figures brings the racial proportions in the NCVS figures extremely close to the racial proportions in UCR arrest numbers. Put differently, police are arresting criminals of different races in very close to the same proportions as Americans say they are victimized by people of those races.

By this measure, who is committing crime in America? . . .

The white rate is always set to one, so if the black rate is three, for example, it means that blacks are arrested at three times the white rate. Once again, it does not mean that three times as many blacks as whites were arrested; it means that if 100 of every 100,000 whites were arrested for a crime, 300 of every 100,000 blacks were arrested for the same crime. The data show a consistent pattern: Blacks are arrested at dramatically higher rates than other racial groups. American Indians and Eskimos (hereinafter "Indians") are arrested at slightly higher rates than whites, and Asians/Pacific Islanders (hereinafter "Asians") are arrested at consistently lower rates. The popular conception of crime in America is correct: rates are much higher among blacks than among whites or other groups.

To return to the view that arrest data reflect police bias rather than genuine group differences in crime rates, police actually have very little discretion in whom they arrest for violent crimes. Except for murder victims, most people can tell the police the race of an assailant. If a victim says she was mugged by a white man, the police cannot very well arrest a black man even if they want to. For this reason, many people accept that police have little discretion in whom they arrest for violent crime, but still believe drug laws are enforced unfairly against minorities. Drug offenses are beyond the scope of this investigation, but here, too, there is independent evidence that arrest rates reflect differences in criminal behavior, not selective law enforcement. The U.S. Department of Health and Human Services keeps records by race of drug-related emergency room admissions. It reports that blacks are admitted at 6.67 times the non-Hispanic white rate for heroin and morphine, and no less than 10.49 times the non-Hispanic white rate for cocaine (Rates for Hispanics are 2.82 and 2.35 times the white rates; information is not reported for American Indians or Asians) (USDJ, 1998b). There is only one plausible explanation for these rates: Blacks are much more likely to be using drugs in the first place. Finally, if racist white police were unfairly arresting non-whites we would expect arrest rates for Asians to be higher than those for whites. Instead, they are lower for almost every kind of crime.

Measuring Hispanic Crime Rates

Any study of crime rates in America is complicated by the inconsistent treatment of Hispanics by different government agencies. For example, the Census Bureau's official estimate for the 1997 population of the United States divides all 268 million Americans into four racial groups: white, black, Indian and Eskimo, and Asian and Pacific Islander. The bureau then explains that among these 268 million people there are 29 million Hispanics who "can be of any race." However, it also counts non-Hispanic whites, non-Hispanic blacks, Indians, etc. Thus we find that although according to the strictly racial classification, there are 221 million whites in the United States, there are only 195 million non-Hispanic whites. When American Hispanics, approximately half of whom are Mexican, are apportioned to the four racial categories, the Census Bureau considers 91 percent to be white, six percent black, one percent American Indian, and two percent Asian.

The treatment of Hispanics can make for odd results. For example, according to the 1990 census, the 3,485,000 people of Los Angeles were 52.9 percent white, 13.9 percent black, 0.4 percent American Indian, and 22.9 percent Asian—which adds up to 100 percent. This makes the city appear to be majority white. However, Los Angeles was also 39.3 percent Hispanic, and if we subtract the 91 percent of them who are classified as whites, the non-Hispanic white population drops to only 16.6 percent.

What does this mean for crime statistics? Because the UCR figures do not treat Hispanics as a separate category, almost all the Hispanics arrested in the United States go into official records as "white." This is contrary to the usual cultural understanding of the term, which is not normally thought to include most Mexicans and Latinos.

If violent crime rates for Hispanics are different from those of non-Hispanic whites, putting Hispanics in the "white" category distorts the results. This is not as serious as in the case of hate crimes, in which the crime itself has to do with the very personal characteristics that are being omitted from the records, but there is no legitimate reason not to make ethnic and racial comparisons as accurate as possible. The UCR tabulates separate data on American Indians and Eskimos—who are less than one percent of the population—but it ignores Hispanics, who are 12 percent of the population.

Some data-gathering agencies do treat Hispanic and non-Hispanic whites separately. The California Department of Justice, which records all arrests within the state, consistently makes this distinction (although it lumps Asians and American Indians into the "other" category) (Calif, 1998). In conjunction with Census Bureau population figures for Hispanics, non-Hispanic whites, and non-Hispanic blacks living in California in 1997, we can calculate the arrest rates for the different groups for various crimes. . . . As is the case with national UCR data, blacks are arrested at much higher rates than whites, but Hispanics are also arrested at considerably higher rates.

The different rates at which Hispanics and non-Hispanic whites are held in prisons and jails are another indicator of the differences in crime rates between the two groups. Although the UCR does not treat Hispanics as a separate category for arrest purposes, some government reports on the prison population do consider them separately. For example, the Department of Justice has calculated incarceration rates per 100,000 population for non-Hispanic whites (193), Hispanics (688), and non-Hispanic blacks (1,571) (USDJ, 1998b). Expressed as multiples of the white rate, the Hispanic rate is 3.56 and black rate is 8.14.

These multiples are close to those from the California arrest data, and justify the conclusion that Hispanics are roughly three times more likely than non-Hispanic whites to be arrested for various crimes. By accepting this assumption, we can use the following formula to incorporate this differential into the UCR racial data on white arrests so as to calculate more accurate arrest rates for non-Hispanic whites:

R(Number of non-Hispanic whites) + 3R(Number of white Hispanics) = Actual Number of Arrests.

Here, R is the arrest rate for non-Hispanic whites and 3R is the arrest rate for Hispanics who are categorized as white when they are arrested. Calculations of this sort show that if Hispanics are broken out as a separate ethnic category with an arrest rate three times the non-Hispanic rate, the rate for non-Hispanic whites decreases by 19.5 percent. . . . Due to lack of precise information, the multiple for Hispanics is set to three times the white rate for all crimes even though there is certain to be some variation in the multiples for different types of crimes. . . .

It should be noted here that the NCVS survey data on interracial crime also includes most Hispanics in the "white" category. It is therefore impossible to know how many of the "whites" who committed violent crimes against blacks were actually Hispanic or how many of the "whites" against whom blacks committed violent crimes were Hispanic. If Hispanics commit violent crimes against blacks at a higher rate than whites—and judging from their higher arrest and incarceration rates for violent offenses this seems likely—the NCVS report also inflates the crime rates of non-Hispanic whites.

Men vs. Women, Blacks vs. Whites

Many people resist the idea that different racial groups have substantially different rates of violent crime. However, there are several group differences in crime rates that virtually everyone accepts and, indeed, takes for granted. Men in their late teens and 20s, for example, are much more prone to violence than men beyond their 50s. When young men are arrested more frequently for violent offenses, no one doubts that it is because they commit more violent crime. Likewise, virtually no one disputes the reason for higher arrest rates for men than for women: Men commit more violent crime than women (Wilson & Herrnstein, 1985). This is the case for racial groups as well: Asians are arrested at lower rates than whites because they commit fewer crimes; blacks and Hispanics are arrested at higher rates because they commit more crimes (Levin, 1997; Rushton, 1995; Whitney, 1990).

When it comes to violent crime, blacks are approximately as much more likely to be arrested than whites, as men are more likely to be arrested than women. The multiples of black vs. white arrest rates are very close to the multiples of male vs. female arrest rates, suggesting that blacks are as much more dangerous than whites as men are more dangerous than women.

What does this mean? Although most people have no idea what the arrest rate multiples may be, they have an intuitive understanding that men are more violent and dangerous than women. If someone in unfamiliar circumstances is approached by a group of strange men she feels more uneasy than if she is approached by an otherwise similar group of strange women. No one would suggest that this differential uneasiness is "prejudice." It is common sense, born out by the objective reality that men are more dangerous than women.

In fact, it is just as reasonable to feel more uneasy when approached by blacks than by otherwise similar whites; the difference in danger as reflected by arrest rates is virtually the same. It is rational to fear blacks more than whites, just as it is rational to fear men more than women. Whatever additional precautions a person would take are justified because a potential assailant was male rather than female are, from a statistical point of view, equally justified if a potential assailant is black rather than white. . . .

Likewise, there is now much controversy about so-called "racial profiling" by the police, that is, the practice of questioning blacks in disproportionate numbers in the expectation that they are more likely than people of other races to be criminals. The philosophical, legal and rational case for racial profiling has been elaborated by the philosopher Michael Levin (Levin, 1997). "Racial" profiling is just as rational and productive as "age" or "sex" profiling. Police would be wasting their time if they stopped and questioned as many little old ladies as they do young black men. It is the job of the police to catch criminals, and they know from experience who is likely to be an offender. Americans who do not question the wisdom of police officers who notice a possible suspect's age and sex should not be surprised to learn those officers also notice race.

Conclusions

Two things can be said about most of the information in this investigation: It is easily discovered but little known. Every year, the FBI issues its report on hate crimes, and distributes thousands of copies to scholars and the media. Why does no one find it odd that hundreds of whites are reportedly committing hate crimes against whites? And why does no one question the wisdom of calling someone white when he is a perpetrator but Hispanic when he is a victim?

For some years there has been an extended national discussion about the prevalence of black-on-black crime—and for good reason. Blacks suffer from considerably more violent crime than do Americans of other races. And yet, amid this national outcry over the extent of black-on-black crime, there appears to be little concern about the fact that there is actually more black-on-white crime. Nor does there seem to be much interest in the fact that blacks are 50 to 200 times more likely than whites to commit interracial crimes of violence. Differences as great as this are seldom found in comparative studies of group behavior, and they cry out for causal investigation and explanation. It is probably safe to say that if the races were reversed, and gangs of whites were attacking blacks at merely four or five times the rate at which blacks were attacking whites the country would consider this a national crisis that required urgent attention.

Everyone knows that young people are more dangerous than old people, and that men are more dangerous than women. We adjust our behavior accordingly and do not apologize for doing so. Why then must we pretend that blacks are no more dangerous than whites or Asians? But of course it is no more than pretense. Everyone knows that blacks are dangerous, and everyone—black and white—takes greater precautions in black neighborhoods or even avoids such neighborhoods entirely.

The answers to these questions lie in the current intellectual climate. Americans are extremely hesitant to "perpetuate stereotypes", and generally take care not to draw or publicize conclusions that may reflect badly on racial minorities. This is understandable, but has reached the point that certain subjects can no longer be investigated without bringing down cries of "racism." Needless to say, research that reflects badly on the majority population is not constrained by the same fears. However, our willingness to ignore sensibilities should not be selective. Violent crime and interracial violence are important, agonizing concerns in this country, and we cannot begin to formulate solutions unless we understand the problems.

References

AP, 1999, Whitman fires State Police superintendent over remarks to newspaper. Trenton NJ: Associated Press, March 1, 1999.

Blumstein, A., and J. Cohen, 1987, Characterizing criminal careers. *Science*, 237: 985–991.

Blumstein, A., and E. Graddy, 1981–82, Prevalence and recidivism in index arrests: A feedback model. *Law and Society Review*, 16: 265–290.

Calif, 1998, Adult and juvenile arrests reported, 1997. Race/ethnic group by specific offense statewide, January through December 1997. California Department of Justice Division of Criminal Justice, Criminal Justice Statistics Center: p. 5939, printed 04/15/98 (unpublished).

Could, R.W., and M.J. Waldren, 1986, *London's Armed Police: 1829 to the present.* London: Arms and Armour Press.

Dilulio, John J., Jr., 1996, My black crime problem and ours. *City Journal,* Spring: 14ff.

Drummond, Tammerlin, 1999, It's not just in New Jersey. *Time* 153 (23), June 14, 1999:61.

Ellis, Lee, 1987, The victimful–victimless crime distinction, and seven universal demographic correlates of victimful criminal behavior. *Personality and Individual Differences,* 91: 525–548.

Francis, Samuel, 1999, Media blackout on black-on-white crime. *Conservative Chronicle,* June 30, 1999: 23.

Hama, Aldric, 1999, Demographic changes and social breakdown: The role of intelligence. (manuscript under review).

Hooton, Earnest Albert, 1939, *Crime and the Man.* Cambridge MA: Harvard University Press.

Levin, Michael, 1997, *Why Race Matters: Race differences and what they mean.* Westport CT: Praeger.

Rushton, J. Philippe, 1985, Differential K theory: The sociobiology of individual and group differences. *Personality and Individual Differences,* 6: 441–452.

Rushton, J. Philippe, 1995, *Race, Evolution, and Behavior. A life history perspective.* New Brunswick, NJ: Transaction.

Taylor, Jared, 1992, *Paved with Good Intentions: The failure of race relations in contemporary America.* New York: Carroll & Graf.

UCR, 1998, Crime in the United States, 1997. Washington DC: U.S. Department of Justice, Federal Bureau of Investigation, USGPO.

USDJ, 1997, Criminal Victimization in the United States, 1994. Washington DC: U.S. Department of Justice, Bureau of Justice Statistics, USGPO.

USDJ, 1998a, Criminal Victimization in the United States, 1997. Washington DC: U.S. Department of Justice, Bureau of Justice Statistics, USGPO.

USDJ, 1998b, Sourcebook of Criminal Justice Statistics, 1997. Washington DC: U.S. Department of Justice, Bureau of Justice Statistics, USGPO.

Whitney, Glayde, 1990, On possible genetic bases of race differences in criminality. In: Ellis, Lee and Harry Hoffman (Eds.), *Crime in Biological, Social, and Moral Contexts.* Westport CT: Praeger. 134–149.

Whitney, Glayde, 1995, Ideology and censorship in behavior genetics. *The Mankind Quarterly,* 35: 327–342.

Wilbanks, William, 1986, *The Myth of a Racist Criminal Justice System.* Monterey CA: Brooks/Cole.

Wilson, James Q., and Richard J. Herrnstein, 1985, *Crime and Human Nature.* New York: Simon & Schuster.

Michael J. Lynch  **NO**

Misleading "Evidence" and the Misguided Attempt to Generate Racial Profiles of Criminals; Correcting Fallacies and Calculations Concerning Race and Crime in Taylor and Whitney's Analysis of Racial Profiling

In 1999, *The Journal of Social, Political and Economic Studies* published an article written by Taylor and Whitney that endeavored to demonstrate the efficacy of racial profiling of criminals. In that article, Taylor and Whitney made two significant general errors that influenced their conclusions concerning the utility of racial profiling. Their first error threatens the validity of their theoretical position. The second invalidates their statistical results and conclusions. Taken together, these general errors invalidate their position on race and crime.

To be more specific about these errors, Taylor and Whitney ground their argument concerning race and crime on a rather restricted review of extant literature. Excluding their own prior research from considerations, Taylor and Whitney refer approvingly to studies by Hooton, Wilson and Herrnstein, Wilbanks and Rushton, and appear to hold them out as exposing sound criminological explanations of the relationship between race and crime. In truth, the views on race and crime expressed by these authors have been refuted and rejected by the majority of criminologists (for criticism of these researchers and their general views on race see: Cernovsky and Litman, 1993; Gabor and Roberts, 1990; Lynch, 1990, 2000; Neopolitan, 1998; Shipman, 1994; Yee et al., 1993; Zuckerman, 1990).

Taylor and Whitney also make several methodological errors in their analyses of criminological data sources that generate misleading results and conclusions concerning the appropriateness of racial profiling. Specifically, these errors include: the use of prevalence rates rather than incidence rates; the failure to use race-based population-adjusted comparisons for offender and victimization data; focusing on rare forms of inter-racial crime and generalizing

From *Mankind Quarterly*, vol. 42, no. 3, Spring 2002, pp. 313–329. Copyright © 2002 by Michael J. Lynch. Reprinted by permission of the author.

to the entire populations of criminals; and using data useful for addressing racial biases in criminal justice processes (Uniform Crime Report and imprisonment data) to calculate racial differences in offending.

To be sure, Blacks are over-represented in criminal justice data. But, Black over-representation in the criminal justice system (measured against the size of the Black population) cannot be employed as evidence that Blacks are responsible for more crime than Whites because over-representation may be a measure of processing biases (Mann, 1993). In short, observations concerning Black over-representation in criminal justice data do not directly translate into claims related to racial differences in offending. Taylor and Whitney, however, use criminal justice data as evidence of differences in offending by race. They are not the first to make this error and the researchers they site approvingly (Rushton, Wilbanks, Wilson and Herrnstein) have also misinterpreted criminal justice data as indicating race differences in offending.[1] Taylor and Whitney's argument begins with literature based on a misinterpretation of criminal justice data, and justifies this view with what can be described either as purposefully misleading or completely naive analyses of crime and victimization data. In either case, their conclusions are incorrect.

Taylor and Whitney's specific focus centers on the fact that "society" seems to express greater concern over Black-on-Black crime when, in fact, Taylor and Whitney believe that Black-on-White crime is the larger social problem. Had their argument been limited to this minor issue, their point would have some validity (though, as we demonstrate, even this contention turns out to be incorrect). But, this turns out not to be their point at all. Rather, as they conclude "it is certainly understandable that police should take these statistics into account when searching for suspects, and that they may wish to take more precautions when entering some neighborhoods than others."[2] This conclusion, as we demonstrate below, is the result of the inappropriate use, analysis of and generalizations made from criminal justice data.

Taylor and Whitney make numerous errors in their analysis and use of criminal justice data. It is not our intention to review each of these errors here because these errors are repeated across different sources of data and our comments would become unnecessarily lengthy. Thus, to simplify our analysis, we focus only on one aspect of Taylor and Whitney's analysis: their use of National Crime Victimization Survey (NCVS). To further reduce unnecessary repetition, we have restricted this reanalysis of NCVS data to violent crimes where victims report a single offender.

The NCVS

According to the Bureau of Justice Statistics, The National Crime Victimization Survey is the Nation's primary source of information on criminal victimization. Each year, data are obtained from a nationally representative sample of roughly 50,000 households comprising nearly 100,000 persons on the frequency, characteristics and consequences of criminal victimization in the United States. The survey enables BJS to estimate the likelihood of victimization by rape, sexual assault, robbery, assault, theft, household burglary, and motor vehicle theft for the population as a whole as well as for segments of the population such as women, the elderly, members of various racial groups, city dwellers, or other groups. The NCVS provides the largest national forum for victims to describe the impact of crime and characteristics of violent offenders. . . .

Taylor and Whitney report on data from the 1994 NCVS, while this reanalysis reports on 1999 NCVS data. Employing a different year for NCVS should not be problematic or invalidate our reanalysis. NCVS data do not change dramatically from year to year, and are especially consistent with respect to reports of offender's race. Further, since Taylor and Whitney's goal is to validate racial profiling of criminals, evidence that this profile is stable across time would need to be produced. Consequently, it makes sense to repeat their analysis with several different years of NCVS data.

For the present discussion, we employ 1999 victim reports of offender's race for three violent or personal offenses where victims reported a single or lone offender: rape, robbery and assault. These three crimes are the only ones for which victim reports of offender race are available. . . . The next section provides an overview of these data.

Overview of the 1999 NCVS

In 1999, the NCVS indicated 5,620,080 lone offender victimizations for the crimes of rape, robbery and assault reported by Black and White victims.[3] Approximately eighty-five percent of these victimizations were reported by White victims (N = 4,760,930). The remaining 867,150 victimizations were reported by Blacks.

Taylor and Whitney direct our attention to the inter-racial offenses reported in these data—that is, cases involving Black offenders and White victims, and cases involving White offenders and Black victims. In 1999, there were 748,058 inter-racial victimizations (91,050 + 657,008). This figure, which appears to indicate an abundance of Black-on-White crime is misleading on two accounts. First, inter-racial violent crimes are rare events with respect to all crimes, comprising less than 2 percent of all reported criminal victimizations in any given year. Second, inter-racial violence is only one dimension of crime and thus generalizations from these data alone may lead to invalid conclusions.

Of these 748,058 inter-racial acts of violence, 657,008 involved a Black offender-White victim, while 91,050 involved a White offender-Black victim pairing. Taylor and Whitney make much of this finding, claiming that these data illustrate the extensively disproportionate nature of interracial victimizations involving White victims-Black offenders. That fact that nearly 88 percent of violent interracial victimizations involve Black offender-White victim dyads is interesting, but, as we demonstrate below, not unexpected given the claims of opportunity theory, which would predict this outcome based upon knowing the racial distribution of the U.S. population.

Employing less than 2 percent of crimes—that is, by focusing on data depicting the extent of inter-racial crimes of violence—Taylor and Whitney conclude that Black-on-White crimes are serious enough to justify the use of racial profiling. As we have already noted, this conclusion is likely to be misleading because it is generalized from a non-representative sub-sample of all crimes. To get a better understanding of the relationship between race and violent criminal victimizations, it is necessary to analyze a broader portion of NCVS cases for which offender race is reported. The next section begins to address the basis for a reanalysis of NCVS data that presents the "big picture" of crime.

The Bigger Picture of Crime

In 1999, White victims of personal violence reported that 74.5 percent of lone attackers in rape, robbery and assault cases were White (N = 3,546,893), while only 13.3 percent were Black. In other words, the majority of crimes committed against Whites were by White offenders. This is not the conclusion drawn from reading Taylor and Whitney's research.

A similar picture of crime and victimization emerges when we examine Black responses to the NCVS: Blacks report that 80 percent of lone attackers are Black, while 10.5 percent are White. Taken together, these data clearly indicate that for the majority of offenses, crime is an intra-racial phenomenon, involving a victim and offender of the same race. From a crime profiling perspective, these data indicate that racial profiling, if we accept this idea as legitimate, should be performed on the basis of the victim's race because of the high correlation between race of victim and offender. It should be noted, however, that this form of profiling, while legitimate statistically, is hardly practical, since it fails in its mission of reducing the pool of potential suspects sufficiently.

The basic data provided by the NCVS makes it clear that the "crime problem" for each racial group consists of other members of the racial group to which one belongs. This conclusion is not apparent in Taylor and Whitney's research, which consistently points to the threat Black offenders present to Whites. How is it that Taylor and Whitney derive and justify this result? Answering this question requires investigating the proper use of rate standardized crime data that focuses on racial comparisons.

Misleading with Rate Comparisons

Taylor and Whitney mislead readers when they engage in a common criminological practice by using rate standardized data as a basis for comparing crime across racial groups. While it is commonplace for criminologists to standardize crime data and transform them into rates per 100,000 for comparison, racial comparisons based on rate standardization lead to erroneous conclusions. Rate standardization is useful for specific kinds of comparisons. One appropriate use would be to compare the prevalence of crime across locations known to have different sized populations. Doing so, we might address questions of relative safety. Second, we can use a rate comparison when we are able to assume that the populations in question may be present in equal proportions. In the United States, this latter assumption is violated when race is the basis of the comparison. Black-White racial compositions vary from place to place. Whites, however, comprise a higher percentage of the US population than Blacks. Locations where the population is represented by an equal number of Blacks and Whites would be rare or unusual (Massey and Denton, 1993). Thus, there would be relatively few places to which racially-specific standardized rates of victimization (or offending) would be applicable.[4]

Taylor and Whitney further compound the prediction error they make by relying on rate standardized race comparisons when they transform these standardized rates into ratios or odds of victimization and offending. For example, Taylor and Whitney calculate the ratio of Black to White rates of inter-racial offending by dividing the rate of White victim-Black offenders per 100,000 population by the Black victim-White offender rate per 100,000 population. Constructing ratios from standardized rates that depict unequal populations as existing in equal proportions inflates the level of crime attributable to one group, while deflating the level of crime attributed to the other. This procedure, in other words, contains two opposing errors that compound the original error and inflate the ratio substantially. In this case, the ratio is inflated in a way that favors the interpretation that Black-on-White crime is more serious than White-on-Black crime.

Rate standardized data cannot be directly employed to reach conclusions concerning levels of offending by race. Rather, rate data need to be adjusted properly before comparisons across races are made, and before we can draw conclusions concerning the contribution of each race to crime. To do so, race specific rates need to be adjusted to reflect race-based population compositions. A corrected example of how race specific rates of offending should be used is provided below.

Turning Race-Specific Rates into Meaningful Data: An Example

The U.S. population is approximately 12 percent Black and 80 percent White. These figures have been rounded to make the calculations which follow simpler. Each calculation is an approximation, and the results reported are valid though not exact.

In 1999, 4,760,930 single offender violent crime victimizations were reported by Whites. Translated into a rate per 100,000, Whites report approximately 2204 victimizations per 100,000 Whites in the populations (Number of victimizations reported by Whites/White Population for the U.S. $\times$ 100,000). The comparable victimization rate for Blacks is 2710 victimizations per 100,000 Blacks in the population. These figures tell us that in a population composed of an equal number of Black and Whites (100,000), Blacks are more likely to be the victim of crimes than Whites (2710/2204 = 1.23).

The problem with this comparison is that in most locales the population is not composed of an equal number of Blacks and Whites, and the practice of standardization misrepresents the real victimization ratio. To address this problem of unequivalent populations, we could either rely on raw numbers of victims if available, or adjust the standardized race specific victimization (or offering) rate by the population's racial composition. We will illustrate this procedure by applying victimization data to a fictitious city (City X) with a population of 100,000 and a racial composition that reflects the national average for the US: 80 percent White and 12 percent Black. In City X there will be 80,000 Whites and 12,000 Blacks.

Our first step is to calculate the number of White victims from the race-specific standardized victimization rate data and City X population data cited above. We know that the standardized White victimization rate was 2204/100,000. Thus, we can multiply the victimization rate by the White population parameter in City X—80% or .80—to derive the number of White victims (2204 × .80). Doing so, we discover that there are 1763 White victims of interpersonal violence in City X. We then follow the same procedure to calculate the number of Black victims of interpersonal crime in City X. Thus, we take the Black rate of interpersonal victimization (2710/100,000) and multiply this figure by the Black population parameter, 12% or .12, yielding 325. Black victims of interpersonal violence in City X is 325.

Before going any further, let us be clear about the meaning of the figures that were just derived. In City X there are 2088 Black and White victims of violent, interpersonal crimes. Eighty-four percent of these victims are White. The ratio of White to Black victims in City X is 5.4; that is, there are 5.4 White victims for every 1 Black victim of interpersonal violence.

Now that we have derived the total number of victims of each race from population and victimization rate data, we can employ the number of victims we have derived to calculate the number of offenders by race. We do so by multiplying NCVS perceived race of offender data by City X victimization figures. . . .

In total, there are 1850 interpersonal victimizations involving only Black and White victims-offenders (while Black and Whites report a total of 2088 victimizations, 238 of these are committed by members of a racial group other than Black or White). Seventy-one percent of these victimizations were committed against Whites by White offenders (1313/1850). In contrast, 14.5 percent of victimizations (260/1850) are committed by Blacks against Blacks; 13.3 percent are committed by Blacks versus Whites (243/1850); and 1.8 percent are by Whites versus Blacks (34/1850). Overall, Whites commit 73 percent of interpersonal crimes of violence in City X (1313 + 34/1850), which represents an average American city in terms of racial composition and interpersonal victimization and perceived offending by race as described in the NCVS.

What implications do these population adjusted victimization and offending data have for efforts at criminal profiling? They indicate that the offender is White in nearly three out of four crimes of interpersonal violence involving Black or White crime victims. Further, they illustrate that numerically, Black-on-White crimes of interpersonal violence (N = 243) are less likely than Black-on-Black crimes of interpersonal violence (N = 260). This finding from population adjusted rates is important because it directly disproves one of Taylor and Whitney's contentions; namely, that Black-on-White crime is more frequent than Black-on-Black crime. As we argued earlier, Taylor and Whitney's conclusion was generated by making inappropriate use of criminological data. The use of standardized rates of victimization and offending makes it appear that Whites are more likely to be victimized by violent Black offenders than Blacks are when, in reality, the situation is reversed. This occurs because the standardized rate comparison assumes equivalent sized Black and White populations. When we adjust these rates to reflect the real world, the conclusion is reversed.

Taylor and Whitney also employed the use of odds or ratio calculations to reach conclusions concerning Black-on-White and White-on-Black crime. The odds they present are inaccurate and invalid because they are derived from rate standardized data and are not adjusted for real racial population proportions. Below we describe a more valid approach to deriving the ratio of White-on-Black to Black-on-White crimes of violence.

Calculating the Odds of Victimization

Throughout their article, Taylor and Whitney assert that the odds of Black-on-White crime are between 50–200 times greater than the odds of White-on-Black crimes. As Taylor and Whitney admit early on, the figures they represent as odds are not actually odds because of the manner in which they are calculated. Consistent with our earlier argument, we contend that the odds they calculated provide inaccurate estimates because they are based on prevalence rates (rates per 100,000) rather than incidence data.

Taylor and Whitney hinge their argument here on the statement that the odds of a White being victimized by a Black is disproportionate. But, disproportionate to what? Taylor and Whitney fail to define what they mean by the word disproportionate, and we are left to ponder the significance of this idea.

As we have already shown using population adjusted victimization rates, Black-on-White crime is not disproportionate to Black-on-Black crime. This finding fails to support an essential aspect of Taylor and Whitney's argument. Thus, the only remaining means for interpreting this idea of disproportionate racial offending is to compare real victim-offender ratios to expected victim-offender ratios. The justification for doing so is easily derived from the popular criminological position called "opportunity theory" (Cohen and Felson, 1980a, 1980b; Felson and Cohen). Recent evidence supports the utility of opportunity theory for making predictions concerning violent victimizations (Lee, 2000).

Opportunity theory predicts that crime results from an intersection of motivated offenders with suitable targets. The opportunities for crime vary by numerous situational characteristics, but are defined or limited in the absolute sense by the availability of potential targets. The nature of targets varies by the type of crime. For crimes of violence, this opportunity is measured by the availability of potential victims. The first parameter of opportunity, in this case, is defined by the size of a population.

In the specific case under examination, the opportunity dimension for crime is being defined by racial composition of the population. In other words, if opportunity arguments are correct, and there are no other forces in operation, the opportunity for inter-racial violent crime ought to be a product of the White/Black population ratio. This is easily calculated. In our hypothetical city—City X—we can divide the White population by the Black population. Doing so, we derive a White/Black population ratio of 6.7 (80,000/12,000). This figure indicates that we would expect Whites to be the victims of more crime more often than Blacks solely on the basis of opportunity for violence. This assumption can be easily assessed as follows.

First, we derive the ratio of victimization by race by creating a ratio of White to Black victimizations. We use the population data derived for our hypothetical city for these calculations which represented an average US city of 100,000 in terms of racial composition, crime and victimization patterns. Total White victimizations in City X was 1556 (1313 + 243); total Black victimization was 294 (260 + 34). The overall race victimization ratio is 1556/294, or 5.3—much lower—20 percent lower—than the expected ratio of 6.7. This figure indicates that in general, White victimizations are below the level predicted simply on the basis of opportunity or availability.

As noted, Taylor and Whitney's arguments specifically and consistently focused only on interracial crimes. The same opportunity ratios can be calculated for interracial crimes of violence. Though these ratios may be misleading because of the relative rare nature of the behavior in question, we estimate these ratios to illustrate the extent to which Taylor and Whitney's odds calculations are inflated by relying on prevalence (rate per 100,000) rather than incidence data.

To calculate the interracial opportunity ratio, we simply take the number of cases involving White victims and Black offenders (243) and dividing by the number of cases where there are Black victims and White offenders (34). The opportunity ratio in this case is 7.2, slightly higher (7%) than the interracial ratio predicted by opportunity theory alone (6.7).[5]

In sum, the disproportionate ratio or odds of Black-on-White violent crime victimization that appear to "shock" Taylor and Whitney are actually a function of their method for calculating odds. Using incidence data and appropriate populations for comparison, we estimated that Black victimizations of Whites are not disproportionate to Black/White population ratios. Indeed, our calculations confirmed the idea that victimization ratios could be explained by opportunity theory as a function of the US population's racial composition.

Conclusion

Taylor and Whitney conclude their article with the following:

> Everyone knows that young people are more dangerous than old people, and that men are more dangerous than women. We adjust our behavior accordingly and do not apologize for doing so. Why then must we pretend that statistics regarding race differences in violent crime are to be ignored?

If Taylor and Whitney's analysis was valid, used appropriate methods for comparing racially-linked criminal justice data, and did not mislead readers by generalizing from a fraction of violent crime to either all violent crimes or all crimes, then we might have to take their question seriously. However, because they either purposefully or unintentionally deceived readers due to their ignorance of the proper use of criminal justice data and specific issues that emerge when making comparisons of standardized race-based crime data, their question can be dismissed as nonsense. Their conclusion, in other words, is as misleading as their analysis and interpretation of victimization, crime, and criminal justice data.

As I have shown, proper use of NCVS data does not support Taylor and Whitney's contentions. Using NCVS data appropriately—focusing on all crimes of violence as the appropriate basis for generalization rather than Taylor and Whitney's focus on a fraction of violent crime—we can clearly see that the majority of victims of violent crime report that their offender was White. This is not a statistical fallacy; there are more White than Black victims of crimes; the majority of Whites—nearly three-quarters—report that their offenders are White, not Black. Further, when we use the NCVS appropriately, one of the lessons we learn is that crime is primarily an intra-racial phenomenon. Whites are more likely to victimize Whites; Blacks are more likely to victimize Blacks. Further, the incidence of inter-racial crime is a function of opportunities for victimization as determined by the racial composition of the US population.

One of Taylor and Whitney's primary concerns is that society concentrates too much attention on Black-on-Black crime while neglecting Black-on-White crime. Their argument seems, then, to express concern for the safety of Whites. Their focus on Black-on-White crimes, however, creates a misleading conclusion concerning the threat Whites face. As we have demonstrated employing NCVS data, the majority of White crime victims are victimized by White offenders. In short, the safety of Whites is more greatly threatened by Whites rather than by Blacks.

Further, if Taylor and Whitney had actually been concerned that society concentrates too strongly on Black-on-Black crime, the correct comparison group for analysis should be White-on-White crime. By using this comparison group we could indeed argue that society's emphasis on Black-on-Black crime is misdirected, and that, instead, society's focus ought to be on White-on-White crimes, which are much more numerous. But, pointing out that the majority of crimes are committed by Whites, and that White victimization frequently comes at the hands of a White offender would not fit the broader research agenda established by these investigators.

Taylor and Whitney's claim that Black-on-White crime is extensive enough to justify racial profiling is based on the misuse of data and inappropriate comparisons and generalizations. As we have argued, the conclusion that racial profiling is acceptable is based on generalizing from less than 2 percent of crime—this 2 percent being the approximate percent of crime that is comprised of inter-racial crimes of violence. No criminologists would find such a procedure legitimate.

Taylor and Whitney also legitimize racial profiling by using prevalence rather than incidence data. Incidence data indicates that most crimes are committed by Whites; indeed the ratio of White-to-Black crimes of violence in the NCVS is 2.69 White offenders per every Black offender. Thus, despite the prevalence of crime among Black communities and populations, and despite the fact that Blacks are over-represented in criminal justice data, Whites are the problematic crime population. Consequently, if we favored the use of racial profiling—and we do not—correct calculations of offender incidence indicate that police ought to concentrate their efforts on Whites: as potential offenders Whites far outnumber Blacks. Further, if the police were to use racial profiling, it should be based on the race of the victim. NCVS data makes it clear that the race of the victim and offender are the same more than seventy-five percent of the time. Thus, if a Black victim reports a crime, the police would do well to look for a Black offender based upon odds alone. Likewise, if a White victim reports a crime to police, the police would do well to look for a White offender, based on odds alone.

When people speak of racial profiling, what they mean is the creation of criminal profiles that target Black offenders. As our analysis indicates, the legitimacy of racial profiling—of targeting Black offenders over White offenders—is misleading at best, and at worst, a form of institutionalized racism. Our data indicate that it is high time that the notion of racial profiling be put to rest.

Throughout this article, we have demonstrated that racial profiling is objectionable from a statistical perspective. In closing, it should also be noted that racial profiling is objectionable to criminologists from both a legal and philosophical perspective. Our nation's criminal laws are based on the premise that guilt is determined on a case by case basis as a result of specific evidence. The inquiry that examines this evidence should be carried out without prejudice. Further, crime suspects are to be assumed innocent until proven guilty. Our Constitution, Courts and legal scholars speak to principles including: probable cause, which requires direct evidence rather than a suspicion or hunch based on someone's race or other status; due process of law and the rule of law; and the right to be judged by a juror of peers rather than by police or other actors in the criminal justice system. The idea of racial profiling reverses the important legal and philosophical ideas upon which the American system of democratic justice rests. Taylor and Whitney's support of racial profiling is not only misleading and inaccurate, it strikes at the heart of the American justice system and American democracy.

Notes

1. It bears mention that among Rushton, Wilbanks, Wilson and Herrnstein, only Wilbanks was trained as a criminologist.

2. What police may want to take into account when deciding the dangerousness of a situation is the data on police killings and assaults. Taylor and Whitney's conclusions concerning police safety and race would be considered misleading and inaccurate based on even a cursory reading of these data. For example, between 1988 and 1997, the Sourcebook of Criminal Justice Statistics notes that White offenders (49%) are responsible for

killing more police officers than Black offenders (42%). While Black kill-ings may be disproportionate to their population composition, this does not eliminate the fact that police are more likely to be killed by Whites than by Blacks. Further, these data do not take into account the differen-tial treatment Blacks receive that may escalate their reactions to police such as heightened use of force and a greater likelihood of being killed by police than White suspects (Mann 1993).

3. We have excluded other racial groups from consideration to simplify the results and discussion. Including other races would not significantly alter the results reported here.

4. While it may sometimes be useful to employ rate standardized data to compare the prevalence of a behavior among race-groups, a reliance on rate standardized data would still produce misleading results when we employ them to make generalizations concerning the amount of crime each racial group produced. An example of this situation is illustrated in the text of this article.

5. This minor difference in estimation could be due in part to the exclu-sion of other races from the analysis, and to rounding of population figures used to generate these outcomes. It is also possible that White-on-Black and Black-on-White crime are the product of factors other than opportunity.

References

Cernovsky, Z., and L. Litman. 1993. Reanalysis of Rushton's Crime Data. *Cana-dian Journal of Criminology.* 35, 1: 31–36.

Cohen, Lawrence, and Marcus Felson, 1980a. The Property Crime Rate in the United States: A Macro-Dynamic Analysis, 1947–1977, With Ex-Ante Fore-casts for the Mid-1980s. *American Journal of Sociology.* 86, 1: 90–118.

Gabor, T., and J. Roberts. 1990 Rushton on Race and Crime: The Evidence Remains Unconvincing. *Canadian Journal of Criminology.* 32: 335–343.

Lee, Matthew. 2000. Community cohesion and violent predatory victimization: A theoretical extension and cross-national test of opportunity theory. *Social Forces.* 79, 2: 683–706.

Lynch, M.J. 2000. J. Phillippe Rushton on Crime: An Examination and Critique of the Explanation of Crime and Race. *Social Pathology.* 6, 3: 228–244.

Lynch, M.J. 1990. "Racial Bias and Criminal Justice: Methodological and Defini-tional Issues." In B. MacLean and D. Milovanovic's (eds.), *Racism, Empiricism and Criminal Justice.* Vancouver: Collective Press.

Mann, Coramae Richey. 1993. *Unequal Justice.* Bloomington, IN: University of Indiana Press.

Massey, Douglas, and Nancy Nenton. 1993. *American Apartheid.* Cambridge, MA: Harvard University Press.

Neopolitan, J. 1998. Cross-National Variation in Homicide: Is Race a Factor? *Criminology.* 36, 1: 139–155.

Shipman, Pat. 1994. *The Evolution of Racism: Human Differences and the Use and Abuse of Science.* NY: Simon and Schuster.

Taylor, Jared, and Glayde Whitney. 1999. Crime and Racial Profiling by U.S. Police: Is There any Empirical Evidence? *The Journal of Social, Political and Economic Studies.* 24, 4: 485–510.

Yee, A., H. Fairchild, F. Weizmann, and G. Wyatt. 1993. Addressing Psychology's Problems with Race. *The American Psychologist.* 48: 1132–1140.

Zuckerman, M. 1990. Some Dubious Premises in Research and Theory on Racial Differences. *The American Psychologist.* 45: 1297–1303.

POSTSCRIPT

Is Racial Profiling an Acceptable Law Enforcement Strategy?

$\mathbf{R}$acial issues have a way of generating substantial controversy. One of the more contentious issues in the U.S. justice system in recent years has been whether members of minority groups commit more crime, or if the disparity in official crime statistics among different races reflects a systemic selection bias. In other words, are the members of minority groups selected for arrest and official processing in the U.S. justice system more often than whites?

Taylor and Whitney assert that there is a true difference in the number of crimes committed by different races. In fact, these authors believe that racial profiling is just as rational and productive as age or gender profiling. Because "it is the job of the police to catch criminals, and they know from experience who is likely to be an offender," they are justified in following policies that emphasize race as a predictor of criminal behavior.

Michael J. Lynch believes that racial profiling is not justified by the crime data. Moreover, he contends that racial profiling may be a thinly veiled form of institutional racism and that it is objectionable from a legal and philosophical perspective as well.

The legal problems with racial profiling by law enforcement officials are indeed compelling. In *United States v. Brignoni-Ponce,* 422 U.S. 873 (1975), the U.S. Supreme Court held that stopping subjects because they "appear[ed] to be of Mexican ancestry," violated the Fourth Amendment to the U.S. Constitution. Following this principle, law enforcement practices that target minority group members for investigation due solely to their appearance seem likely to be held unconstitutional by reviewing courts.

Moreover, as Professor Lynch observes, racial profiling by law enforcement officials may be challenged from a philosophical and moral perspective as well. Is it morally permissible to stereotype people based on a group characteristic such as their race or religion? We must remember too that when law enforcement personnel as agents of our government use racial profiling strategies, it lends an official stamp of approval to the practices. Does this not conjure images of governmentally enforced school segregation and institutionalized racism during the Civil Rights era?

The question posed in this section is a challenging one. After reading these articles, which author presents the most compelling arguments? Remember that to justify racial profiling, the government must be able to support these practices on an empirical, legal, and moral basis as well. Based on the available evidence, it would seem that supporters of these practices will face an uphill battle on all levels.

There is a wealth of additional information available on this topic. Please see: David A. Harris, *Profiles in Injustice: Why Racial Profiling Cannot Work* (The New Press, 2002); Avram Bornstein, "Antiterrorist Policing in New York City after 9/11: Comparing Perspectives on a Complex Process," *Human Organization* (Spring 2005); P.A.J. Waddington, Kevin Stenson, and David Don, "In Proportion: Race and Police Stop and Search," *The British Journal of Criminology* (November 2004); Bernard E. Harcourt, "Rethinking Racial Profiling: A Critique of the Economics, Civil Liberties, and Constitutional Literature, and of Criminal Profiling More Generally," *The University of Chicago Law Review* (Fall 2004); Thomas Gabor, "Inflammatory Rhetoric on Racial Profiling Can Undermine Police Services," *Canadian Journal of Criminology and Criminal Justice* (July 2004); and Bernard E. Harcourt, "Unconstitutional Police Searches and Collective Responsibility," *Criminology & Public Policy* (July 2004).

ISSUE 6

Should Juvenile Courts
Be Abolished?

YES: Barry C. Feld, from *Bad Kids: Race and the Transformation of the Juvenile Court* (Oxford University Press, 1999)

NO: Vincent Schiraldi and Jason Ziedenberg, from *The Florida Experiment: An Analysis of the Impact of Granting Prosecutors Discretion to Try Juveniles as Adults* (July 1999)

ISSUE SUMMARY

YES: Law professor Barry C. Feld contends that creating a separate juvenile court system has resulted in unanticipated negative consequences for America's children and for justice.

NO: Vincent Schiraldi, director of the Justice Policy Institute, and researcher Jason Ziedenberg maintain that moving thousands of kids into adult courts is unnecessary, harmful, and racist.

In the 1890s Judge Ben Lindsey, with the help of socially prominent and active citizens and their wives, helped to establish the juvenile court movement. His work was hailed as innovative and compassionate. Horror tales and news exposes of the dreadful treatment of America's youngsters in adult prisons, as well as in the adult courts, that often processed them as if they were common criminals, were well-known. Something had to be done, progressive elements among the rich and the intellectuals maintained. They felt that child criminals and criminal children needed help, guidance, love, an opportunity for a second chance, and education, not punishment, humiliation, degradation, additional undeserved pain, and torment.

Soon states around the country had separate facilities for treating juvenile offenders as well as separate facilities for incarcerating them. In some areas judges were called "Masters" and were encouraged to be kind and sympathetic, not gruff, procedural, and legalistic. *Parens patriae* (state as parents) became the role of the juvenile court procedures. Guilt or innocence was not the issue, nor was "punishment." The goal was to determine through case studies what the needs of referred youngsters were, and then, if necessary, to provide for these needs through a juvenile facility. Such needs could include food, shelter, education, separation from terrible families or neighborhoods, separation from peers who smoked, and so on.

Since the function of the proceedings was to ascertain and provide needs, legalities such as determining guilt or innocence or even a specific sentence were ignored. Often youngsters who were not initially charged with criminal offenses but were status offenders were sentenced to juvenile facilities. Status offenses included truancy, running away from home, hanging out on the street, and sassing teachers or social workers. Some more progressive states had a classification system distinguishing such offenders. These terms included *CINS* (children in need of supervision) and *PINS* (persons in need of supervision). However, often they were housed under the same administrative roof as youngsters who were charged with more serious offenses.

The age range for juveniles varied from state to state; some classified juveniles as anyone who is 19 or younger, and most demarcated children from adults at age 18 or 16. Many juvenile facilities, though, would keep offenders until they were 21 "for their own good." Since the purpose of the juvenile system was to "help" youngsters, a 12-year-old who had been truant could be held in custody until he was 18 or even 21. Until Supreme Court decisions in the 1960s provided some basic constitutional rights, children were not entitled to an attorney, could not appeal their sentences, and could be held incommunicado indefinitely.

Yet the juvenile courts were almost universally considered progressive. Eventually, some had second thoughts. It was theorized that the real function of the courts and juvenile system was to "Americanize" the children of immigrants and to more smoothly pipe marginal American children (poor white ethnics and blacks) into mainstream industrial society. According to this perspective, the juvenile court system, along with required public school education, functioned as socializing agencies more than as helping ones. Meanwhile, word slowly leaked out that many juvenile reformatories were quite different from what many people thought. Treatment was often nonexistent, and a variety of cruelties were typical.

As we enter the twenty-first century still carrying the weight of a very conservative, get-tough-with-all-delinquent-kids mode, to some the question becomes, which is the lesser of two evils, juvenile courts or adult courts for criminal children? The issue is in many ways a very sad one for the protagonists. Barry C. Feld, who has worked to help troubled youth for many years, reluctantly advocates abolishing juvenile courts. He is convinced that trying to salvage the existing system will only enable the get-tough side to do even worse things to delinquents. Vincent Schiraldi, who is arguably America's top advocate for the compassionate treatment of children, is convinced that additional transfers of juveniles into adult courts will be a disaster. He and coauthor Jason Ziedenberg draw from empirical research to document their concerns.

YES

Barry C. Feld

Abolish the Juvenile Court

In the three decades since *Gault*,[1] judicial decisions, legislative amendments, and administrative changes have transformed the juvenile court from a nominally rehabilitative welfare agency into a scaled-down, second-class criminal court for young people. These revisions have converted the historical ideal of the juvenile court as a social welfare institution into a penal system that provides young offenders with neither therapy nor justice. Even as legal reforms foster increased punitiveness and convergence with criminal court, juvenile courts deflect, co-opt, ignore, or accommodate constitutional procedural mandates with minimal institutional change. They use courtroom procedures under which no adult would consent to be tried if she faced the prospect of confinement and then incarcerate youths in prisonlike settings for substantial terms.

Popular concerns about youth crime, especially drugs, guns and violence, bolster policies to repress rather than to rehabilitate young offenders. . . . Indeed, public unwillingness to provide for the welfare of all children, much less for those who commit crimes, forces us to question whether the juvenile court can or should be rehabilitated.

. . . [Y]ouths whom judges remove from home or incarcerate in institutions for terms of months or years receive substantially fewer procedural safeguards than do adults convicted of comparable crimes. As a result, juvenile courts punish delinquents in the name of treatment but deny to them protections available to criminals. In view of this convergence with criminal courts, do we need a separate, procedurally deficient justice system simply to punish middle-level younger offenders?

Most juvenile justice scholars and practitioners recognize juvenile courts' functional convergence with criminal courts but recoil at the prospect of abolishing them and trying and sentencing all offenders in criminal court. They argue that significant developmental differences exist between young people and adults or that rehabilitation still differs from punishment and urge policymakers to maintain the distinctions between delinquents and criminals. . . . [P]roponents of a separate juvenile justice system invoke the Progressives' fallback position—despite juvenile courts' procedural deficiencies and substantive bankruptcy, criminal courts constitute even worse places to try and sentence younger offenders.

From *Bad Kids: Race and the Transformation of the Juvenile Court* by Barry C. Feld, pp. 287–330 (excerpts). Copyright © 1999 by Oxford University Press. Reprinted by permission.

. . . Because we do not regard young people as the moral equals of adults, then why and how do we blame, punish, protect, or treat young offenders differently?

This [selection] explores three possible resolutions to the dilemma posed when the child is a criminal and the criminal is a child: a "rehabilitative" juvenile court, a juvenile version of a criminal court, and an integrated criminal court. Proponents of a welfare-oriented juvenile court urge that we "reinvent juvenile justice" and restructure juvenile courts to pursue their original rehabilitative purposes. Advocates of a juvenile version of a criminal court propose that we honestly acknowledge juvenile courts' criminal social control functions, incorporate punishment as a legitimate component of delinquency sanctions, and provide all criminal procedural safeguards but in judicially separate delinquency proceedings. Advocates of an integrated criminal court recommend that we abolish juvenile court jurisdiction over criminal conduct, try all offenders in criminal courts, and introduce certain procedural and substantive modifications to accommodate the youthfulness of younger offenders.

In this [selection], I endorse an integrated criminal court as a better solution to the conundrum posed when a child is a criminal. I will first explain why neither a rehabilitative juvenile court nor a juvenile version of criminal court can "work" as their proponents envision. I argue that traditional juvenile courts' deficiencies reflect a fundamental flaw in their conception rather than *simply* a century-long failure of implementation. Juvenile courts attempt to combine social welfare and criminal social control in one agency and inevitably do both badly because of the inherent contradiction in those two missions. On the other hand, a juvenile version of a criminal court is an institution without a rationale. Because we already have criminal courts, without some other social welfare rationale, a juvenile version of a criminal court simply would be redundant and a temporary way station on the road to full integration.

If we uncouple social welfare from criminal social control, then we can abolish juvenile courts and formally recognize youthfulness as a mitigating factor in criminal sentencing to accommodate the reduced culpability of younger offenders. Young people differ from adults in their breadth of experience, temporal perspective, willingness to take risks, maturity of judgment, and susceptibility to peer influences. These generic and developmental characteristics of adolescents affect their opportunity to learn to be responsible, to develop fully a capacity for self-control, and provide compelling policy rationale to mitigate their criminal sentences. I propose an age-based "youth discount" of sentences— a sliding scale of developmental and criminal responsibility—to implement the lesser culpability of young offenders in the legal system. Only an integrated justice system can avoid the legal dichotomies and contradictory policies inherent in all current binary formulations—either adult or child, either punishment or treatment. . . . [A]dvantages include enhanced protection for the many young offenders whom criminal courts already sentence as adults; affirmation of individual responsibility; . . . elimination of the sentencing disparities associated with waiver decision making; rejection of the ideology of individualized justice that fosters racial, gender, and geographic disparities;

and, ultimately, simple honesty about the reality of criminal social control in the juvenile court.

Rehabilitate the "Rehabilitative" Juvenile Court?

The *parens patriae* juvenile court rests on the dual ideas of "treatment" and "children." It provided a mechanism to protect, reform, and treat "innocent" children and rejected the criminal law's jurisprudence of guilt, blameworthiness, and punishment. It affirmed deterministic models of behavior and adopted paternalistic policies to treat the child as an object for adults to shape and manipulate in her "best interests," rather than as an autonomous and responsible person. . . . [H]owever, ideological and jurisprudential changes have blurred both the "treatment-punishment" and "child-adult" dichotomies. Increasingly the juvenile court functions as a system of criminal social control to protect society from young offenders, rather than as a welfare agency to nurture and protect vulnerable children from a wrathful community. In this revised formulation of adolescence, the justice systems more often emphasize young people's "almost adult" status rather than their "childlike" qualities. When these agencies encounter "other people's children," especially poor and minority youths, the ambivalence and conflict experienced when the child is a criminal "[are] easily converted to hostility and take institutional form in social policies to control and incarcerate youth rather than to enhance their development."

Inadequate Social Welfare

. . . State agencies, rather than juvenile courts, control the institutions and programs to which judges send delinquents. From their inception, these correctional facilities have had more in common with prisons than with hospitals or clinics. By the time of *Gault,* the juvenile courts' failures of implementation were readily apparent.

Juvenile courts lack necessary resources because providing for child welfare is a societal responsibility, not simply a judicial one. Historically and currently, public officials deny juvenile courts adequate resources because of pervasive public antipathy to their clients, those who are poor, disadvantaged, and minority offenders. Thus, any proposal to reinvigorate the juvenile court as a social welfare agency first must address why political leaders who have failed to provide minimally adequate resources and personnel for the past century now will do so. The ideological shift from treatment to punishment and the accompanying "criminalizing" of the juvenile court may portend a more fundamental shift from public responsibility for citizens' welfare to private individual responsibility.

Proponents of a rehabilitative juvenile court also must account for and avoid the failures of earlier generations of juvenile court reforms. Many reforms reflect organizational responses to crises of legitimacy and serve primarily to deflect or neutralize critics. For example, . . . the escalation in youth homicide fostered extensive policy debate about only the relative merits of different ways to "crack down" and transfer more youths to criminal court and thereby to preserve the juvenile court for the "less bad" remaining delinquents. Juvenile justice specialists frame policy options within a "scientific paradigm" of expertise and professional competence to assert a veneer of legitimacy. The ensuing technical tinkering narrows the range of debate, produces symbolic rather than substantive reforms, and fails to address issues of discretion and penal social control or the relationships between social structure and crime, gun, or social welfare policies. . . .

Others attribute the failures of child welfare policies to contradictions embedded in *parens patriae* ideology and divisions between public and private obligations toward young people. Because parents bear primary responsibility to raise their own children, public programs to assist other people's children stipulate that parents demonstrably must fail at the task as a prerequisite of receiving public assistance. But, stigmatizing the clients and social programs by making failure a requirement of eligibility undermines public support for those programs and ensures their inadequacy. . . .

If we formulated a child social welfare policy *ab initio,* would we select a juvenile court as the most appropriate agency through which to deliver social services and make criminality a condition precedent to the receipt of services? If we would not create a court to deliver social services, then does the fact of a youth's criminality confer on it any special competency as a welfare agency? Many young people who do not commit crimes desperately need social services, and many youths who commit crimes do not require or will not respond to the meager services available. Because our society chooses to deny adequate social welfare services to meet the "real needs" of all young people, juvenile courts' treatment ideology serves primarily to legitimate the exercise of judicial coercion of some *because of their criminality.* In short, little commends the *idea* of a juvenile court as a social welfare delivery system except bureaucratic inertia.

Individualized Justice and the Rule of Law

Quite apart from its unsuitability as a social welfare agency, the individualized justice of a rehabilitative juvenile court fosters lawlessness and thus detracts from its role as a court of law. Despite statutes and procedural rules, juvenile court judges purport to decide each case to achieve a child's best interests. But a treatment ideology without a scientific foundation breeds lawlessness. . . . Unlike punishment, which implies limits, treatment may continue "for the duration of minority." Thus, juvenile courts in theory and in practice sentence or treat minor offenders severely and sanction serious offenders mildly. . . .

If judges possess neither practical scientific bases by which to classify youths for treatment nor demonstrably effective programs to prescribe for them, then the exercise of "sound discretion" simply constitutes a euphemism for idiosyncratic subjectivity. Racial, gender, geographic, and socioeconomic disparities constitute almost inevitable corollaries of an individualized treatment ideology. At the least, judges will sentence youths differently based on extraneous personal characteristics for which they bear no responsibility.

If juvenile courts provided exclusively benign and effective services, then perhaps differential processing of male and female, urban and rural, or black and white juveniles might be tolerable. At the worst, however, judges impose haphazard, unequal, and discriminatory punishment on similarly situated offenders without any effective procedural or appellate checks.

Is the discretion that judges exercise to classify for treatment warranted? Do the successes of rehabilitation justify its concomitant lawlessness? Do the incremental benefits of juvenile court intervention for some youths outweigh the inevitable inequalities and racial disparities that result from the exercise of individualized discretion for others? . . . Although some treatment does "work" for some youths, states do not routinely provide . . . model demonstration services universally for ordinary, run-of-the-mill delinquents. . . . [I]n the face of unproven efficacy and uncertain resources, the possibility that rehabilitation may occur does not justify incarcerating young offenders with fewer procedural safeguards than we provide to adults charged, convicted, and confined for crimes.

Procedural informality constitutes an essential adjunct of a "welfare" court's substantive discretion; juvenile courts predicate their informal process on the promise of benign and effective treatment. . . . The informal and confidential nature of delinquency proceedings reduces the visibility and accountability of the process and precludes external checks on coercive interventions. As long as the mythology prevails that juvenile court intervention constitutes only benign coercion and that, in any event, children should not expect more, youths will continue to receive the "worst of both worlds."

Failure of Implementation Versus Conception

The fundamental shortcoming of the juvenile court's welfare *idea* reflects a failure of conception rather than *simply* a failure of implementation. The juvenile court's creators envisioned a social service agency in a judicial setting and attempted to fuse its social welfare mission with the power of state coercion. The juvenile court *idea* that judicial clinicians successfully can combine social welfare and penal social control in one agency represents an inherent conceptual flaw and an innate contradiction. Combining social welfare and penal social control functions only ensures that the court performs both functions badly. Providing for child welfare is a societal responsibility, not a judicial one, and the polity declines to provide those necessary resources because juvenile courts' clients are poor, disproportionately minorities, *and* criminal offenders. As a result, juvenile courts subordinate social welfare concerns to crime control considerations.

The conflicted impulses engendered between concern for child welfare and punitive responses to criminal violations form the root of the ambivalence embedded in the juvenile court. The hostile reactions that people experience toward other people's children whom they regard as a threat to themselves and their own children undermine benevolent aspirations and elevate concerns for their control. Juvenile justice personnel simultaneously profess child-saving aspirations but more often function as agents of criminal social control. Because they possess few resources besides the power to incarcerate for crimes, juvenile courts function as agencies of social control. . . .

Because juvenile courts operate in a societal context that does not provide adequate social services for children in general, juvenile justice intervenes in the lives of those who commit crimes for purposes of social control rather than of social welfare. This in-built contradiction places the juvenile court in an untenable position. . . .

Neither juvenile court judges nor any other criminal justice agencies realistically can ameliorate the social ills that afflict young people or significantly reduce youth crime.

A Juvenile Version of a Criminal Court: Due Process and Reduced Punishment

. . . [I]f we acknowledge that juvenile courts punish young offenders, then we assume an obligation to provide them with all criminal procedural safeguards. . . . [T]o punish juveniles in the name of treatment, and to deny them basic safeguards foster a sense of injustice that thwarts any reform efforts.

The current juvenile court provides neither therapy nor justice *and* cannot be rehabilitated. The alternative policy options are either to make juvenile courts more like criminal courts or to make criminal courts more like juvenile courts. Whether we try young offenders in a separate juvenile court or in a unified criminal court, we must reconsider basic premises and address issues of substance and procedure. Issues of substantive justice include developing and implementing a doctrinal rationale—diminished responsibility, reduced capacity, immaturity of judgment, or truncated self-control—to sentence young offenders differently, and more leniently, than older defendants. Issues of procedural justice include providing youths with *all* the procedural safeguards adults receive *and* additional protections that recognize their immaturity and vulnerability in the justice process.

Many analysts acknowledge that "the assumptions underlying the juvenile court show it to be a bankrupt legal institution" that functions as an extension of criminal courts and requires a new rationale to justify its continued existence. Rather than abolishing the juvenile court, however, they propose to transform it into an explicitly penal juvenile justice system that provides enhanced procedural protections and imposes less-severe punishment than do criminal courts because of youths' reduced culpability. . . .

Proponents of a juvenile version of a criminal court point to the manifold deficiencies of criminal courts. . . . However, . . . charges of excessive caseloads, ineffective defense counsel, inadequate sentencing options, inattention to children's real needs, and assembly-line justice apply equally to juvenile courts. An unsentimental comparison of the relative quality of juvenile and criminal "justice" leaves little basis on which to decide whether either system treats young people or adult defendants justly and fairly. If the state charged you with a crime, under which system of procedures would you rather be tried? . . .

Young Offenders in Criminal Courts: Youthfulness as a Mitigating Factor

. . . If the child is a criminal and the "real" reason he appears in court is for formal social control, then states could abolish juvenile courts' delinquency jurisdiction and try youths in criminal courts alongside their adult counterparts. But if the criminal is a child, then states must modify their sentencing provisions to accommodate the youthfulness of some defendants. Politically popular sound bites—"old enough to do the crime, old enough to do the time" or "adult crime, adult time"—do not analyze adequately the complexities of a youth sentencing policy. My proposal to abolish the juvenile court constitutes neither a mindless endorsement of punishment nor a primitive throwback to earlier centuries' views of young people as miniature adults. Rather, it honestly acknowledges that juvenile courts currently exercise criminal social control, asserts that young offenders in a criminal justice system *deserve* less-severe consequences for their misdeeds than do more mature offenders simply because they are young and addresses the many problems created by trying to maintain binary, dichotomous, and contradictory criminal justice systems based on an arbitrary age classification of a youth as a child or an adult.

Formulating a youth sentencing policy entails two tasks. First, . . . a rationale to sentence young offenders differently, and *more leniently,* than older defendants. Explicitly punishing young offenders rests on the premise that adolescents possess sufficient cognitive capacity and volitional controls to be responsible for their behavior, albeit not to the same extent as adults. . . . Second, I . . . propose a "youth discount" as a practical administrative mechanism to institutionalize the principle of youthfulness in sentencing. A sentencing policy that recognizes youthfulness as a mitigating factor and provides a youth discount fosters greater honesty about the role of the justice system and greater realism about young people's developmental capacity and criminal responsibility. . . .

Juveniles' Criminal Responsibility

. . . Quite apart from decisions about guilt or innocence, individual capacity and criminal responsibility also affect appropriate sentences. . . .

A formal mitigation of punishment based on youthfulness constitutes a necessary component of a criminal justice system in order to avoid the equally undersirable alternatives of either excessively harsh penalties disproportionate to culpability on the one hand or of nullification and excessive leniency on the other. Youthfulness provides a rationale to mitigate sentences to some degree without excusing criminal conduct.

Shorter sentences for young people do not require a separate justice system in which to try them. Both juvenile and criminal courts separate determinations of guilt or innocence from sentencing and restrict consideration of individual circumstances largely to the latter phase. Criminal courts may impose lenient sentences on young offenders when appropriate. . . .

Sentencing policies can and should protect young people from the adverse consequences of their developmentally less competent decisions. . . .

Reduced Culpability

. . . [I]n *Thompson v. Oklahoma* (487 U.S. 815 [1988]), the Supreme Court analyzed the criminal responsibility of young offenders and provided some additional support for shorter sentences for reduced culpability for youths older than the common-law infancy threshold of age fourteen. The *Thompson* plurality vacated Thompson's capital sentence because the Court concluded that a fifteen-year-old offender could not act "with the degree of culpability that can justify the ultimate penalty" (486 U.S. at 834). Although the Court provided several rationales for its decision, it explicitly decided that juveniles are less culpable for the same crimes than are their adult counterparts. Also, *Thompson* reaffirmed several earlier decisions that also emphasized that youthfulness constitutes an important mitigating factor when judges sentence young defendants. . . .

Administering Youthfulness As a Mitigating Factor at Sentencing: The "Youth Discount"

. . . A statutory sentencing policy that integrates youthfulness and limited opportunities to learn self-control with principles of proportionality and reduced culpability would provide younger offenders with categorical fractional reductions of adult sentences. . . .

This categorical approach would take the form of an explicit "youth discount" at sentencing. A fourteen-year-old offender might receive, for example, 25 to 33 percent of the adult penalty; a 16-year-old defendant, 50 to 66 percent; and an eighteen-year-old adult, the full penalty, as is presently the case. The "deeper discounts" for younger offenders correspond to the developmental continuum and their more limited opportunities to learn self-control and to exercise responsibility.

. . . [Y]oung offenders commit their crimes in groups to a much greater extent than do adults. Although the law treats all participants in a crime as equally responsible and may sentence them alike, young people's susceptibility to peer group influences requires a more nuanced assessment of their degree of participation, personal responsibility, and culpability. . . . The group nature of youth crime affects sentencing policy in several ways. Because of susceptibility to peer influences, the presence of a social audience may induce youths to participate in criminal behavior in which they would not engage if alone. Even though the criminal law treats all accomplices as equally guilty, they may not all bear equal responsibility for the actual harm inflicted and may *deserve* different sentences. . . . Thus, the group nature of adolescent criminality requires some formal mechanism to distinguish between active participants and passive accomplices with even greater "discounts" for the latter.

Virtue of Affirming Partial Responsibility for Youth

. . . The juvenile court's rehabilitative ideal elevated determinism over free will, characterized delinquent offenders as victims rather than perpetrators, and envisioned a therapeutic institution that resembled more closely a preventive, forward-looking civil commitment process rather than a criminal court. By denying youth's personal responsibility, juvenile court's treatment ideology reduces offenders' duty to exercise self-control, erodes their obligation to change, and sustains a self-fulfilling prophecy that delinquency occurs inevitably for youths from certain backgrounds.

Affirming responsibility encourages people to learn the virtues of moderation, self-discipline, and personal accountability. Acknowledging that we *punish* young offenders for their misconduct "becomes part of a complex of cultural forces that keep alive the moral lessons, and the myths, which are essential to the continued order of society. . . . A culture that values autonomous individuals must emphasize both freedom and responsibility."

While the paternalistic stance of the traditional juvenile courts rests on the humane desire to protect young people from the adverse consequences of their bad decisions, protectionism disables young people from the opportunity to learn to make choices and to be responsible for their natural consequences. . . .

Age-Segregated Dispositional Facilities and "Room to Reform"

Questions about young offenders' criminal liability or their degree of accountability differ from issues about the appropriate place of confinement or the services or resources the state should provide to them. Even explicitly punitive sentences do not require judges or correctional authorities to confine young people with adults in jails and prisons, as is the current practice for waived youths, or to consign them to custodial warehouses or "punk prisons." States should maintain separate, age-segregated youth correctional facilities to protect both younger offenders and older inmates. . . . Insisting on humane conditions of confinement can do as much to improve the lives of incarcerated youths as the "right to treatment" or the rehabilitative ideal. Some research indicates that youths sentenced to juvenile correctional facilities may reoffend somewhat less often, seriously, or rapidly than comparable youths sentenced to adult facilities. If consistently replicated, these findings provide modest support for a separate youth correctional system, rather than for an entire separate juvenile justice system. . . .

Eliminate Civil Disabilities

. . . [Y]oung first- or second-time offenders need not suffer all the disabilities and losses of rights associated with a conviction. A legislature can provide young offenders with relief from collateral consequence, restore civil rights, or nullify the effects of felony convictions upon the conclusion of a sentence and supervision.

Conclusion

. . . Even far-reaching justice system changes can have only a modest effect on social problems as complex as crime and violence. . . .

A proposal to abolish the juvenile court and to try all young offenders in an integrated justice system makes no utilitarian claims but represents a commitment to honesty about state coercion. States bring young offenders who break the law to juvenile court for social control and to punish them. Juvenile courts' rehabilitative claims fly in the face of their penal reality, undermine their legitimacy, and impair their ability to function as judicial agencies. . . .

[C]haracterizing penal coercion as "social welfare" seems both dangerous and dishonest. The *idea* of rehabilitation inherently and seductively expands, widens nets of social control, and promotes abuse through self-delusion. . . . [U]ltimately, youths incarcerated in the name of treatment recognize that the justice system had deceived them.

The shortcomings of the rehabilitative juvenile court run far deeper than inadequate resources or unproven treatment techniques. Rather, the flaw lies in the very *idea* that the juvenile court can combine successfully criminal social control and social welfare in one system. . . .

I propose to abolish the juvenile court with considerable trepidation. On the one hand, combining enhanced procedural safeguards with a youth discount in an integrated criminal court provides young offenders with greater protections and justice than they currently receive in the rehabilitative juvenile system and more proportional and humane consequences than judges presently inflict on them as adults in the criminal justice system. Integration may foster a more consistent crime control response than the current dual system permits to violent and chronic young offenders at various stages of the developmental and criminal career continuum. On the other hand, politicians may ignore the significance of youthfulness as a mitigating factor and instead use these proposals to escalate the punishment of young people. Although abolition of the juvenile court, enhanced procedural protections, and a youth discount constitute essential components of a youth sentencing policy package, nothing can prevent get-tough legislators from selectively choosing only those elements that serve their punitive agenda, even though doing so unravels the threads that make coherent a proposal for an integrated court.

In either event, the ensuing debate about a youth sentencing policy would require public officials to consider whether to focus primarily on the fact that young offenders are *young* or *offenders*. A public policy debate when the child is a criminal and the criminal is a child forces a long overdue and critical reassessment of the entire social construction of "childhood." . . .

Most people tolerate an intolerable juvenile justice because they believe that it will affect only other people's children—children of other colors, classes, and cultures—and not their own. Juvenile courts tap a resonant legitimating theme because they invoke *parens patriae* and child welfare ideals even as they impose penal controls on young offenders.

Note

1. In *In re Gault*, Gerald Gault, a juvenile, challenged the constitutionality of the Arizona Juvenile Code, which led to his being sentenced to six years in an industrial school after he was found guilty of making obscene phone calls. As an adult, he would have been entitled to representation by a lawyer and would have had the opportunity to be confronted by the person who charged him. However, since he was a juvenile, he was not entitled to these rights. In a 7–2 decision, the Supreme Court granted children some but not all of these rights.

**Vincent Schiraldi and
Jason Ziedenberg**

 **NO**

The Florida Experiment

"Anthony Laster is the kind of kid who has never been a danger to anyone. A 15-year-old, eighth grader with an IQ of 58, Anthony is described by relatives as having the mind of a five-year-old. Late last year, a few days after his mother died, Anthony asked another boy in his class at a Florida middle school to give him lunch money, claiming he was hungry. When the boy refused, Anthony reached into his pocket and took $2. That's when Anthony ran smack into Palm Beach County prosecutor Barry Kirscher's brand of compassionless conservatism. Rather than handling the case in the principal's office, where it belonged, Mr. Kirscher decided to prosecute Anthony as an adult for this, his first arrest. Anthony spent the next seven weeks—including his first Christmas since his mother died—in custody, much of it in an adult jail."[1]

Introduction

Anthony Laster was one of 4,660 youth who Florida prosecutors sent to adult court last year under the wide ranging powers they enjoy with the state's direct file provisions. Florida is one of 15 states that allow prosecutors—not a judge—to decide whether children arrested for crimes ranging from shoplifting to robbery should be dealt with in the juvenile justice or criminal justice system.[2] While 43 states have changed their laws to make it easier for judges to send children into the adult criminal system since 1993, Florida is leading the nation in using prosecutors to make the decision to try children as adults. In 1995 alone (Figure 1), Florida prosecutors sent 7,000 cases to adult court nearly matching the number of cases judges sent to the criminal justice system nationwide that year.[3]

A juvenile crime bill currently being considered by the U.S. Congress (House-Senate Conference Committee) would give U.S. Attorneys even greater powers than those enjoyed by prosecutors in Florida.

The change in federal law would remove judges from the process of deciding which justice system would serve young people, and transfer that power to the sole discretion of prosecutors. The Justice Department also appears to support giving prosecutors expanded powers to try youth as adults in federal court.[4] Given the current legislative drive, it is worthwhile to examine the Florida experience to see what the future will hold for the nation.

From *The Florida Experiment: An Analysis of the Impact of Granting Prosecutors Discretion to Try Juveniles as Adults* by Vincent Schiraldi and Jason Ziedenberg, July 1999, pp. 2–12. Copyright © 1999 by Justice Policy Institute. Reprinted by permission.

Figure 1

In 1995, Florida Prosecutors Rival Judges in the Rest of
U.S. in Sending Youth to Adult Court

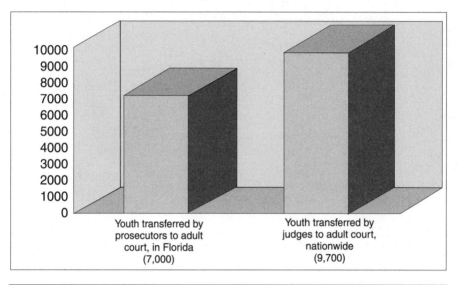

Source: The Urban Institute, 1998.

Profile: Who Are Prosecutors Sending to Adult Court in Florida?

I. Offense Category

When prosecutorial waiver was introduced in 1981, the percentage of delinquency cases transferred to adult court in Florida soared from 1.2% to nearly 9% by 1987.[5] In fiscal year 1997–98, 6,425 of the 94,693 cases disposed of by judicial processing in Florida resulted in transfer to adult court. While these waiver provisions were originally designed to ensure that violent juvenile offenders were being detained, a 1991 study of two representative Florida counties showed that only 28% of the youths prosecutors waived to adult court were for violent crimes.[6] More than half (55%) of the youths prosecutors sent to adult court were charged with property offenses that involved no violence, and fully 5% were tried as adults for misdemeanors (Figure 2). Almost a quarter of the cases waived were first time, low level offenders.[7]

II. Disproportionate Minority Confinement

The most striking feature of Florida's transferred youth population profile is the extent to which minority youth are overrepresented in the ranks of

Figure 2

Most Youth Transferred by Prosecutors in Florida Were Charged With Non-Violent Offenses

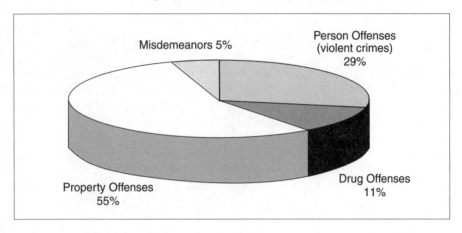

Source: Notre Dame Journal of Law, Ethics, and Public Policy (1996).

the youth being referred to adult court. One study conducted by the Florida Department of Juvenile Justice found that black youths were 2.3 times more likely than white youth to be transferred in Florida.[8] Even though non-whites account for 24% of the 10–17 age bracket in Florida, they currently represent 74% of those 10–17 held in the Florida prison system.[9] "I think the way the system sets up programs shows some institutional bias," is the way one candid Florida prosecutor describes it.[10]

Policy Impact in Florida

I. Sentencing: Longer Terms for Youths in Adult Court?

While some have suggested that huge numbers of children are being held in adult facilities across the state, it is not clear that youth going to adult court via prosecutorial waiver are serving long sentences. A study published in the *Notre Dame Journal of Law, Ethics and Public Policy* found that, of the youth who were incarcerated after disposition, half received short sentences, some shorter than they would have received in the juvenile justice system. The majority (54%) of those sentenced to prison were released within three years.[11] A 1998 survey of the Florida transferred population shows that a majority of youth prosecutors sent to adult court for property, drug and weapons offenses received jail sentences or probation terms well within the range of what could have been prescribed to them in the juvenile court.[12] The same study showed that in

1995, 61% of the youth found guilty in adult court were incarcerated, but only 31% were served prison terms.[13]

II. More Youths to Adult Jail and to Juvenile Detention

While it might be expected that prosecutorial waiver would reduce the number of youths being funneled into Florida's juvenile justice system, the opposite has been true. Between 1993 and 1998, the number of annual commitments to Florida's juvenile justice system increased by 85% despite its liberal use of waiver to adult court. Florida has the sixth highest incarceration rate for youth per 100,000 in the nation, and detains young people at a rate 25% greater than the national average.[14] This happened during a time when the number of waiver cases was increasing, and the number of felony referrals to the juvenile justice system was decreasing. This is happening, despite the fact that youths waived to adult court are held before trial in adult jails, further slackening the numbers that would need to be held in juvenile detention. Rather than the happy prospect of devoting more resources in the juvenile justice system to fewer youths, the system has widened its "net of control" by committing youth for lower level offenses.[15]

Crime Control Impact

I. Recidivism: Adult Court Prosecution Increases Propensity for Crime

Quantitative: Studies and Data

A number of studies have shown that youth sent to adult court generally recidivate at a higher rate than they do if they are sent to the juvenile justice system. A series of studies in Florida have analyzed what happens to youth referred to adult court—90% of whom are referred there directly by a prosecutor. A study published in the journal *Crime and Delinquency* showed that youth transferred to adult court in Florida were a third more likely to reoffend than those sent to the juvenile justice system.[16] The transferred youths reoffended almost twice as fast as those who were sent to juvenile detention.[17] Of those who committed new crimes, the youth who had previously been tried as adults committed serious crimes at double the rate of those sent to juvenile court.[18] While a 1997 study by the same authors showed that property offenders were slightly less likely to recidivate when transferred to adult court, the authors note: "Once the effect of offense type was controlled, the logistic regression analysis indicated that transfer led to more recidivism. Moreover, the transferred youths who subsequently reoffended were rearrested more times and more quickly than were the non-transferee youth who reoffended regardless of the offense for which they were prosecuted . . . although property felons who were transferred may have been less likely to reoffend, when they did reoffend they reoffended more often and more quickly."[19]

JUVENILE OFFENDERS GENERALLY FOLLOW ONE OF THREE PATHS TO ADULT COURT

Judicial Waiver: A juvenile court judge waives jurisdiction over the case after considering the merits of transfer for the individual youth.

Legislative Exclusion: A state legislature determines that an entire class of juvenile crimes should be sent to adult court automatically, usually serious and violent offenses.

Prosecutorial Discretion: A state or local prosecutor has the authority to file charges against some juveniles directly in adult court.

Source: The Urban Institute, 1998

Qualitative: Interviews With Youths in Deep End Juvenile Programs
The same authors recently conducted in-depth interviews with fifty youths sent to prison by Florida prosecutors, versus fifty who were sent to a state "maximum risk" juvenile detention facility.[20] This study found that the youth themselves recognized the rehabilitative strengths of the juvenile justice system in contrast to the adult prison system.

Sixty percent of the sample sent to juvenile detention said they expect they would not reoffend, 30% said they were uncertain whether they would reoffend, while 3% said they would likely reoffend. Of those expected not to reoffend, 90% said good juvenile justice programming and services were the reason for their rehabilitation. Only one of the youths in juvenile detention said they were learning new ways to commit crimes. Most reported at least one favorable contact with a staff person that helped them. As such, the juvenile justice system responses were overwhelmingly positive:

A: "This place is all about rehabilitation and counseling. . . . This place here, we have people to listen to when you have something on your mind . . . and need to talk. They understand you and help you."

B: "They helped me know how to act. I never knew any of this stuff. That really helped me, cause I ain't had too good a life."[21]

By contrast, 40% of the transferred youth said they were learning new ways to commit crimes in prison. Most reported that the guards and staff in prisons were indifferent, hostile, and showed little care for them. Only 1/3 of the youths in prison said they expected not to reoffend. Not surprisingly, the youths sent to prison by prosecutors responded in an overwhelmingly despondent and negative way:

C: "When I was in juvenile programs, they were telling me that I am somebody and that I can change my ways, and get back on the right tracks. In here, they tell me I am nobody and I never will be anybody."

D: "In the juvenile systems, the staff and I were real close. They wanted to help me. They were hopeful for me here. They think I am nothing but a convict now."

Figure 3

Florida Has the Second Highest Violent Crime Rate in the Country,
48% Higher Than the National Average

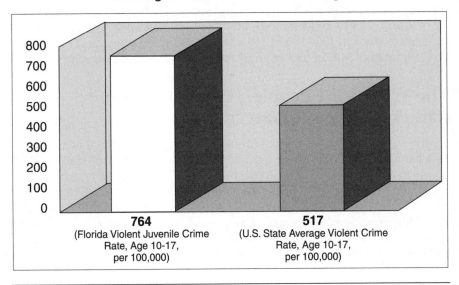

764
(Florida Violent Juvenile Crime
Rate, Age 10-17,
per 100,000)

517
(U.S. State Average Violent Crime
Rate, Age 10-17,
per 100,000)

Source: Office of Juvenile Justice and Delinquency Prevention, 1997.

II. Crime Control Impact: Crime Rate

Despite having prosecutorial waiver on the books since 1981, Florida has the second highest overall violent crime rate of any state in the country, and that status has remained virtually unchanged throughout the 1990s.[22] Florida's violent juvenile crime rate is fully 48% higher than the national average (Figure 3).[23]

Though Florida leads the nation in using prosecutorial waiver, the other 14 states which allow states attorneys discretion to send youth to criminal court do not fare much better. Of the 15 states that currently employ prosecutorial waiver provisions, five (Florida, Arizona, Massachusetts, the District of Columbia and Louisiana) are among the ten states with the highest violent crime arrest rate (age 10–17). While the rest of the nation enjoyed a decline in juvenile crime between 1992 and 1996, five states that employ prosecutorial waiver—Arkansas, Nebraska, Arizona, Virginia and New Hampshire—actually experienced an increase in their violent juvenile crime rates.[24]

The Risks Youth Face in Adult Jails

The children who prosecutors are sending to adult court in Florida face greater threats to their life, limb and future when they enter Florida's adult jail and prison systems. These well-documented risks affect both the youth who are convicted in adult court, and those (like Anthony Laster) who are merely being held in pre-trial detention in jail, on crimes of which they may be exonerated.

One study has shown that youths are five times more likely to report being a victim of rape when they are held in an adult facility versus juvenile detention.[25] Youth in adult jails are also twice as likely to report being beaten by staff and 50% more likely to be attacked with a weapon. A Justice Department study done in 1981 showed that the suicide rate of juveniles in adult jails is 7.7 times higher than that of youth in juvenile detention centers.[26]

The Will of the People?: Public Opinion and Prosecutorial Waiver

A survey published in the journal *Crime and Delinquency* found that a majority of Americans oppose changing federal law to allow for prosecutorial waiver of youth to adult court.[27] When asked, "Would you agree strongly, agree somewhat, disagree somewhat, or disagree strongly that federal prosecutors should have total discretion to try juveniles as adults for all felonies?," 56% of a nationally representative sample of Americans disagreed or disagreed strongly with the idea (41% agreed, and 3% said they had no opinion). Nearly twice as many respondents were strongly opposed to the idea compared to those who strongly supported it (29% vs. 16%).[28]

Conclusion

As the United States Congress and states around the country weigh various approaches to curbing juvenile crime, the "Florida Experiment" of giving prosecutors broad discretion to decide whether juveniles should be tried as adults has come under serious consideration.[29] On almost every measure examined in this report—statewide crime control, individual recidivism, racial equity and the youth's own perception of future offense behavior—the Florida system of prosecutorial discretion waiver was found wanting.

Notes

1. Schiraldi, Vincent. "Prosecutorial Zeal vs. America's Kids." *The Christian Science Monitor,* March 22, 1999.
2. The 15 states or jurisdictions which employ Direct File (prosecutorial discretion waiver) include Arkansas, Colorado, Florida, Georgia, Louisiana, Michigan, Nebraska, New Hampshire, Vermont, Arizona, Massachusetts, Montana, Oklahoma, Virginia, and the District of Columbia. Griffin, P., Torbet, P., and Szymanski, L. 1998. "Trying Juveniles as Adults in Criminal Court: Analysis of State Transfer Provisions." Washington, D.C.: U.S. Department of Justice, Office of Justice Programs, Office of Juvenile Justice and Delinquency Prevention.
3. Butts, Jeffrey A. and Adele V. Harrell. "Delinquents or Criminals: Policy Options for Young Offenders." Washington, D.C.: The Urban Institute, 1998, p. 6.

4. "In our view, the system should be fundamentally altered so that, in appropriate circumstances, the prosecutor alone determines whether to prosecute the juvenile as an adult." Gregory, Kevin V., Deputy Assistant Attorney General, in Testimony before the Subcommittee on Crime, Committee on the Judiciary, U.S. House of Representatives, March 10, 1999.

5. 1999 Annual Report and Juvenile Justice Fact Book, Florida Juvenile Justice Accountability Board, February, 1999.

6. Bishop, Donna M. and Charles E. Frazier. "Transfer of Juveniles to Criminal Court: A Case Study and Analysis of Prosecutorial Discretion." *The Notre Dame Journal of Law, Ethics and Public Policy,* Vol. 5: pp. 281–302, 1991.

7. Ibid.

8. Department of Juvenile Justice-Management Report, No. 42. March 24, 1996.

9. Inmate Population: Current Inmate Age. Agency Annual Report, Department of Corrections, 1998.

10. Bishop, Donna M. and Charles E. Frazier, "Race Effects in Juvenile Justice Decision Making: Findings of a Statewide Analysis." *The Journal of Criminal Law and Criminology,* Vol. 86, 1996.

11. Bishop, et al., 1991.

12. Bishop, Donna M. and Charles E. Frazier, "The Consequences of Transfer" in *The Changing Borders of Juvenile Justice: Transfer of Adolescents to the Criminal Court.* Chicago: University of Chicago Press [in press].

13. Bishop, Donna M., Charles E. Frazier, Lonn Lanza-Kaduce and Henry George White. "Juvenile Transfers to Criminal Court Study: Phase I Final Report." Washington, D.C.: Office of Juvenile Justice and Delinquency Prevention, 1998.

14. Snyder, Howard N. and Melissa Sickmund. "Juvenile Offenders and Victims: Update on Violence." Washington, DC: Office of Juvenile Justice and Delinquency Prevention, 1998.

15. Bishop and Frazier [in press].

16. Bishop, Donna M. et al. "The Transfer of Juveniles to Criminal Court: Does It Make a Difference?" *Crime & Delinquency,* Vol. 42, No. 2, April 1996.

17. Ibid.

18. Ibid.

19. Bishop, Donna M., Charles E. Frazier, Lonn Lanza-Kaduce and Lawrence Winner. "The Transfer of Juveniles to Criminal Court: Reexamining Recidivism Over the Long Term." *Crime and Delinquency,* Vol. 43, No. 4, October 1997.

20. Bishop and Frazier, Office of Juvenile Justice and Delinquency Prevention, 1998.

21. Ibid, and keynote address, National Association of Sentencing Advocates Conference, Miami, Florida, April 15, 1999.

22. Snyder, p. 22.

23. Ibid.

24. Kathleen Maguire and Ann L. Pastore, eds., *Sourcebook of Criminal Justice Statistics 1997*. U.S. Department of Justice, Bureau of Justice Statistics, 1997; (1996); (1995). U.S. Department of Justice, Bureau of Justice Statistics. Washington, D.C., USGPO, 1998 (1997); (1996).

25. Fagan, Jeffrey, Martin Forst, and T. Scott Vivona. "Youth in Prisons and Training Schools: Perceptions and the Consequences of the Treatment Custody Dichotomy." *Juvenile and Family Court*, No. 2, 1989, p. 10.

26. Flaherty, Michael G. "An Assessment of the National Incidences of Juvenile Suicides in Adult Jails, Lockups and Juvenile Detention Centers." The University of Illinois, Urbana, Champaign, 1980.

27. Schiraldi, Vincent and Mark Soler. "The Will of the People: The Public's Opinion of the Violent and Repeat Juvenile Offender Act of 1997." *Crime and Delinquency*, Vol. 44., No. 4, October, 1998.

28. Ibid.

29. For example, in March, 2000, Californians will be voting on the "Gang Violence and Juvenile Crime Prevention Act of 1998" initiative, which will give prosecutors discretion to try certain juveniles as adults at the age of 14.

POSTSCRIPT

Should Juvenile Courts
Be Abolished?

$\mathbf{A}$s the public and politicians increasingly reflect intolerance toward criminals, especially violent ones, might Feld's proposal be viewed as an extreme one rising from desperation? That is, if we lived in different times, needed monies and staffing for juvenile courts, facilities, and services in the community would be provided. Is Feld's "sliding scale" fair for youngsters in adult courts? Can it be argued that because it is impossible to tell precisely how emotionally "developed" a youth is, it is ethically and legally unacceptable to sentence one youngster to a longer term than another youngster who did the same crime? Is Feld correct when he asserts that the juvenile court concept itself is untenable because it is impossible to have both the goal of crime control and treatment simultaneously? For instance, Schiraldi and Ziedenberg could argue that if courts were sympathetic toward and knowledgeable of youth, programs could be developed to treat children and consequently to reduce their involvement in crime.

For the most part, Schiraldi and Ziedenberg base their arguments on a Florida study. Is that a good basis for suggesting national policy, especially since Florida is an extreme case? Are the authors confusing the issues of waivering kids to adult courts and incarcerating kids in adult jails and prisons? Does their drawing from tear-jerking testimonies of selected child cases really serve to clarify the issue? For instance, might one just as easily juxtapose their reports with sad statements from victims of juvenile violence?

Can the two positions be synthesized? If federal monies were provided for randomly selected states to experiment with abolishing juvenile courts for, say, 20 years, would that be a better basis for deciding what is best for society and for child criminals? Meanwhile, should juvenile courts be abolished, as Feld says, or should the traditional system be maintained, as Schiraldi and Ziedenberg suggest?

Among the many works by Feld pertaining to the issue is his *Readings in Juvenile Justice Administration* (Oxford University Press, 1999). Among the many publications of the Justice Policy Institute, which is directed by Schiraldi, is *Second Chances: One Hundred Years of the Children's Court* (1999).

A positive though balanced overview is "Juvenile Justice: A Century of Experience," by S. Drizin, *Current* (November 1999). Several highly favorable articles on juvenile courts can be found in the special issue of *Juvenile Justice* entitled "100th Anniversary of the Juvenile Court, 1899–1999" (December 1999), published by the Office of Juvenile Justice and Delinquency Prevention (OJJDP). Several other relevant reports are available from the OJJDP, including

From the Courthouse to the Schoolhouse: Making Successful Transitions (March 2000), *Focus on Accountability: Best Practices for Juvenile Court and Probation* (1999), and *Offenders in Juvenile Court, 1996* (1999). Two helpful overviews of female offenders and the system are *Women Offenders* by L. Greenfeld and T. Snell (December 1999), published by the Bureau of Justice Statistics, and *Juvenile Justice Journal Volume VI, Number 1 (Investing in Girls: A Twenty-First Century Strategy)* (October 1999), published by the OJJDP. An alternative system that neither of the protaganists address is teen courts, which are explored in J. Butts, D. Hoffman, and J. Buck, *Teen Courts in the United States: A Profile of Current Programs* (1999), also available from the OJJDP.

An excellent source from the federal level is S. G. Mezey's *Children in Court: Public Policymaking and Federal Court Decisions* (State University of New York Press, 1996). A brief discussion of a judge's analysis is "Judge Recommends Overhaul of Juvenile Supervision System," *Criminal Justice Weekly* (August 3, 1999). Two news articles that outline problems and prospects of the juvenile court system are "Regrettable Regression in the Way We Treat Young Criminals," by L. Dodge, *The Washington Post* (August 29, 1999) and "Juvenile Court Comes of Age," by C. Wetzstein, *The Washington Times* (August 29, 1999). An analysis of gender differences can be found in "Explaining the Gender Difference in Adolescent Delinquent Behavior: A Longitudinal Test of Mediating Mechanisms," by X. Liu and H. B. Kaplan, *Criminology* (February 1999).

ISSUE 7

Is Exposure to Pornography Related to Increased Rates of Rape?

YES: Diana E. H. Russell, from *Dangerous Relationships: Pornography, Misogyny, and Rape* (Sage, 1998)

NO: Anthony D'Amato, from "Porn Up, Rape Down," *Northwestern Public Law Research Paper No. 913013* (2006)

ISSUE SUMMARY

YES: Diana E. H. Russell argues that the evidence is overwhelming that exposure to pornography is a major causal factor of rape. She utilizes the concept of "multiple causation" to explain the relationship between pornography and rape.

NO: Anthony D'Amato contends that the incidence of rape has declined 85% in the last 25 years while access to pornography via the Internet has become more widely available to teenagers and adults.

The role of pornography in rape and sexual assault cases is a highly controversial issue. While many persons believe that the availability of pornography is directly or indirectly related to increasing rates of aberrant forms of sexual behavior, others believe that access to pornographic materials may be a healthy form of sexual expression. In some countries, pornography is readily available to virtually everyone. In the United States, serious efforts have been made through the legal system to control its distribution and availability, although there appears to be an ambivalent attitude toward pornography throughout society. This ambivalence is reflected in the decisions of U.S. court systems as they have struggled to define precisely what constitutes pornography.

For example, one of the U.S. Supreme Court's most important decisions on pornography was *Miller v. California*, 413 U.S. 15 (1972). The Court had previously held that pornography, as a form of expression, is not protected by the First Amendment. In reaffirming that principle, the Court developed the contemporary legal standard for lower courts to use to determine whether a specific depiction of sexual behavior is pornographic. Chief Justice Warren Burger described this standard as whether:

> (a) the average person, 'applying contemporary community standards' would find that the work, taken as a whole, appeals to the prurient

interest (b) whether the work depicts or describes, in a patently offensive way, sexual conduct specifically defined by the applicable state law, and (c) whether the work, taken as a whole, lacks serious literary, artistic, political, or scientific value. (24).

As a practical matter, the *Miller* standard has led to very few restrictions on the publication of sexually explicit materials in the United States. Attorneys arguing that state pornography laws should be upheld have often struggled to convince the courts that particular depictions lack serious literary, artistic, political, or scientific value. The result has been that even representations that most people would find to be highly offensive are protected by the First Amendment.

But what is the impact of exposure to pornography on the Internet, and elsewhere, on increased rates of rape? Diana E. H. Russell argues that the evidence is overwhelming: Exposure to pornography is a major causal factor in rape cases. She takes issue with the idea that pornography should not be viewed as a "cause" of rape because there are a number of other factors that are also contributing factors in rape cases. States Russell:

> Because all viewers of pornography are not equally affected by it, many people conclude that pornography cannot be playing a causative role in rape and other forms of violence against women. This is similar to the tobacco industry's defense of cigarette smoking. They maintain that because many smokers do not die of lung cancer, and because some nonsmokers *do* die of this disease, it is incorrect to believe that smoking causes lung cancer. But the tobacco industry's reasoning here is faulty. They have no grounds for assuming that the proponents of smoking as a cause of lung cancer believe that smoking is the *only* cause. (118–119).

Anthony D'Amato, in contrast, argues that the incidence of rape has actually declined 85% in the last 25 years while access to pornography via the Internet has become more freely available to teenagers and adults. States D'Amato:

> From data compiled by the National Telecommunications and Information Administration in 2001, the four states with the *lowest* per capita access to the internet were Arkansas, Kentucky, Minnesota, and West Virginia. The four states with the *highest* internet access were Alaska, Colorado, New Jersey, and Washington. . . . While the nationwide incidence of rape was showing a drastic decline, the incidence of rape in the four states having the *least* access to the internet showed an actual *increase* in rape over the same time period.

Moreover, in the states with the *most* access to the Internet, three of the four states showed declines in the incidence of rape during the same time period. D'Amato concludes that "[I]nternet porn has thoroughly demystified sex," and has resulted in substantial decreases in rape and sexual assault.

Before reading these articles in their entirety, which of the positions embraced by these authors appears to be the more intuitively compelling one? Do you believe that exposure to pornography is directly related to increased or decreased rates of rape and other forms of sexual violence? The answer to this question has very significant implications for the future development of law and social policy in this country and will have a profound impact on our cultural conversation about appropriate sexual behavior in the twenty-first century.

140

YES    Diana E. H. Russell

Pornography Is No Fantasy

I don't need studies and statistics to tell me that there is a relationship between pornography and real violence against women. My body
remembers.

Woman's testimony, Public Hearings, 1983[1]

Before pornography became the pornographer's speech it was somebody's life.

Catharine MacKinnon, 1987, p. 179

When addressing the question of whether or not pornography causes
rape, as well as other forms of sexual assault and violence, many people fail to
acknowledge that the actual *making* of pornography sometimes involves, or even
requires, violence and sexual assault. Testimony by women and men involved
in such activity provides numerous examples of this *(Attorney General's Commission, 1986; Public Hearings, 1983)*.

In one case, a man who said he had participated in over a hundred pornographic movies testified at the Commission (1986) hearings in Los Angeles as
follows:

> I, myself, have been on a couple of sets where the young ladies have
> been forced to do even anal sex scenes with a guy which [*sic*] is rather
> large and I have seen them crying in pain. (p. 773)

Another witness gave the following testimony at the same hearings in
Los Angeles:

> Women and young girls were tortured and suffered permanent physi-
> cal injuries to answer publisher demands for photographs depicting
> sadomasochistic abuse. When the torturer/photographer inquired of
> the publisher as to the types of depictions that would sell, the torturer/
> photographer was instructed to get similar existing publications and
> use the depiction therein for instruction. The torturer/photographer
> followed the publisher's instructions, tortured women and girls accord-
> ingly, and then sold the photographs to the publisher. The photographs

From *Dangerous Relationships: Pornography, Mysogyny, and Rape* by Diana E. H. Russell, (Sage
1998), pp. 113–132 (excerpts). Copyright © 1998 by Sage Publications, Inc. Reprinted by permission via Copyright Clearance Center.

were included in magazines sold nationally in pornographic outlets. (Attorney General's Commission, 1986, pp. 787–788)

Peter Bogdanovich (1984) writes of *Playboy* "Playmate of the Year" Dorothy Stratten's response to her participation in a pornographic movie:

> A key sequence in "Galaxina" called for Dorothy to be spread-eagled against a cold water tower. The producers insisted she remain bound there for several hours, day and night. In one shot of the completed film, the tears she cries are real. (p. 59)

Although *Galaxina* was not made for the so-called adult movie houses, I consider it pornography because of its sexist and degrading combination of sexuality and bondage.

It should not be assumed that violence occurs only in the making of violent pornography. For example, although many people would classify the movie *Deep Throat* as nonviolent pornography because it does not portray rape or other violence, we now know from Linda (Lovelace) Marchiano's two books (*Ordeal* and *Out of Bondage; Lovelace*, 1981,1986), as well as from her public testimony (e.g., *Public Hearings*, 1983), that this film is, in fact, a documentary of her rape from beginning to end.

Most people, including some of the foremost researchers on pornography in the United States, ignore the violence used by pornographers in the manufacturing of these misogynist materials (e.g., see Malamuth & Donnerstein, 1984). As Catharine MacKinnon (1987) points out in one of the opening epigraphs to this section, pornography is somebody's life before it becomes the pornographer's free speech (p. 179). Testimony presented at the hearings held on the anti-pornography civil rights ordinance in Minneapolis, Minnesota, in 1983 provides powerful evidence for the truth of her statement (*Public Hearings*, 1983; Russell, 1993b).

Before we can address the issue of pornography as a cause of rape, it is important to know the proclivities of those who read and view pornography. Hence, data on males' propensity to rape will be presented next.

Males' Propensity to Rape[2]

Why do I want to rape women? Because I am basically, as a male, a predator and all women look to men like prey. I fantasize about the expression on a woman's face when I "capture" her and she realizes she cannot escape. It's like I won, I own her.

Male respondent, quoted in Shere Hite, 1981, p. 718

Research indicates that 25% to 30% of male college students in the United States and Canada admit that there is some likelihood they would rape a woman if they could get away with it.[3] In the first study of males' self-reported likelihood to rape that was conducted at the University of California at Los Angeles, the word *rape* was not used; instead, an account of rape (described

below) was read to the male subjects, of whom 53% said there was some likelihood that they would behave in the same fashion as the man described in
the story *if* they could be sure of getting away with it (Malamuth, Haber, &
Feshbach, 1980). Without this assurance, only 17% said they might emulate
the rapist's behavior. It is pertinent to know exactly what behavior these
students said they might emulate:

> Bill soon caught up with Susan and offered to escort her to her car.
> Susan politely refused him. Bill was enraged by the rejection. "Who the
> hell does this bitch think she is, turning me down," Bill thought to
> himself as he reached into his pocket and took out a Swiss army knife.
> With his left hand he placed the knife at her throat. "If you try to get
> away, I'll cut you," said Bill. Susan nodded her head, her eyes wild with
> terror.
>   The story then depicted the rape. There was a description of sex-
> ual acts with the victim continuously portrayed as clearly opposing the
> assault. (Malamuth et al., 1980, p. 124)

In another study, 356 male students were asked:

> If you could be assured that no one would know and that you could in
> no way be punished for engaging in the following acts, how likely, if at
> all, would you be to commit such acts? (Briere & Malamuth, 1983)

Among the sexual acts listed were the two of interest to these researchers:
"forcing a female to do something she really didn't want to do" and "rape"
(Briere & Malamuth, 1983). *Sixty percent of the sample indicated that under the
right circumstances, there was some likelihood that they would rape, use force, or
do both.*

Jacqueline Goodchilds and Gail Zellman (1984) conducted personal
interviews with high school males and females between 14 and 18 years of age
to find out under what circumstances they believed it to be "OK for a guy to
hold a girl down and force her to have sexual intercourse" (p. 241). Seventy-
nine percent of the study subjects thought it was acceptable to rape a girl in
at least one of nine circumstances. The high school students rank ordered the
different circumstances that justified the assaultive male behavior from the
least justifying to the most justifying:

1. He spends a lot of money on her;
2. He's so turned on he can't stop;
3. She is stoned or drunk;
4. She has had sexual intercourse with other guys;
5. She lets him touch her above the waist;
6. She says she's going to have sex with him and then changes her
   mind;
7. They have dated a long time;
8. She's led him on;
9. She gets him sexually excited. (Goodchilds & Zellman, 1984, pp. 241–242)

Goodchilds and Zellman conclude that their experiment shows that their adolescent subjects

> accept as the norm an essentially adversarial cross-gender relationship by the man against the woman as an ever-present and sometimes acceptable possibility in the context of intimate cross-gender encounters, (p. 242)

To put it in plainer language: Both male and female adolescents see rape of females by males as an "ever-present and sometimes acceptable possibility" in women's lives.

Some people dismiss the findings from these studies as "merely attitudinal." However, this conclusion is incorrect. Malamuth has found that male subjects' self-reported likelihood of raping is correlated with physiological measures of sexual arousal to rape depictions. Clearly, erections cannot be considered attitudes.

More specifically, the male students who say they might rape a woman if they could get away with it are significantly more likely than other male students to be sexually aroused by portrayals of rape. Indeed, these males were more sexually aroused by depictions of rape than by mutually consenting depictions. In addition, when asked if they would find committing a rape sexually arousing, they said yes (Donnerstein, 1983, p. 7). They were also more likely than the other male subjects to admit to having used actual physical force to obtain sex with a woman. These latter data were self-reported, but because they refer to actual behavior, they too cannot be dismissed as merely attitudinal.

Looking at the sexual arousal data alone (as measured by penile tumescence) rather than its correlation with self-reported likelihood to rape, Malamuth reports that:

- About 10% of the population of male students is sexually aroused by "very extreme violence" with "a great deal of blood and gore" that "has very little of the sexual element" (Malamuth, 1985, p. 95).
- About 20% to 30% show substantial sexual arousal by depictions of rape in which the woman never shows signs of arousal, only abhorrence (p. 95).
- About 50% to 60% show some degree of sexual arousal by a rape depiction in which the victim is portrayed as becoming sexually aroused at the end (Malamuth, personal communication, August 18,1986).

Given these findings, it is hardly surprising that after reviewing a whole series of related experiments, Neil Malamuth (1981b) concluded that "the overall pattern of the data is . . . consistent with contentions that many men have a proclivity to rape" (p. 139).

Unlike Malamuth's student-based studies, the men who completed Shere Hite's (1981) questionnaires about their self-reported desire to rape women came from all walks of life (p. 1123). Distinguishing between the men who revealed their identities and those who concealed them, Hite reports the following answers by the anonymous group to her question "Have you ever wanted to rape a woman?": 46% answered "yes" or "sometimes," 47% answered "no," and 7% said they had fantasies of rape (p. 1123). Presumably, the latter group had not acted them out—yet.

Surprisingly, the non-anonymous group of men reported slightly more interest in rape: 52% answered "yes" or "sometimes," 36% answered "no," and 11% reported having rape fantasies. (Could it be that many men don't think there is anything wrong with wanting to rape women?) Although Hite's survey was not based on a random sample, and therefore, like the experimental work cited above, cannot be generalized to the population at large, her finding that *roughly half of the more than 7,000 men she surveyed admitted to having wanted to rape a woman* on one or more occasions suggests that men's propensity to rape is probably very widespread indeed. It is interesting to note that the high percentages of men in Hite's study who admitted to wanting to rape a woman are comparable to the high percentage—44%—of women in my San Francisco probability sample of 930 women who reported having been the victim of one or more rapes or attempted rapes by men over the course of their lives (Russell, 1984). . . .

Pornography as a Cause of Rape: Theory and Research

. . . Smoking is not the only cause of lung cancer; nor is pornography the only cause of rape. I believe there are many factors that play a causal role in this crime.[4] I will not attempt to evaluate the relative importance of different causal factors . . ., but merely to show the overwhelming evidence that pornography is a major one of them.

Because all viewers of pornography are not equally affected by it, many people conclude that pornography cannot be playing a causative role in rape and other forms of violence against women. This is similar to the tobacco industry's defense of cigarette smoking. They maintain that because many smokers do not die of lung cancer, and because some nonsmokers *do* die of this disease, it is incorrect to believe that smoking causes lung cancer. But the tobacco industry's reasoning here is faulty. They have no grounds for assuming that the proponents of smoking as a cause of lung cancer believe that smoking is the *only* cause. In addition, the tobacco industry focuses on explaining individual rather than group differences, whereas the proponents of smoking as a cause of cancer focus on the higher number of lung cancer cases found in smokers as a group compared with nonsmokers as a group. . . .

The Meaning of "Cause"

Given the intense debate about whether or not pornography plays a causal role in rape, it is surprising that so few of those engaged in it ever state what they mean by "cause." A definition of the concept of *simple causation* follows:

An event (or events) that precedes and results in the occurrence of another event. Whenever the first event (the cause) occurs, the second event (the effect) necessarily or inevitably follows. Moreover, in simple causation the second event does not occur unless the first event has occurred. Thus the cause is both the SUFFICIENT CONDITION and the NECESSARY CONDITION for the occurrence of the effect. (Theodorson & Theodorson, 1979, p. 40)

By this definition, pornography clearly does not cause rape, as it seems safe to assume that some pornography consumers do not rape women and that many rapes are unrelated to pornography. However, the concept of *multiple causation* (defined below) *is* applicable to the relationship between pornography and rape.

With the conception of MULTIPLE CAUSATION, various possible causes may be seen for a given event, any one of which may be a sufficient but not necessary condition for the occurrence of the effect, or a necessary but not sufficient condition. In the case of multiple causation, then, the given effect may occur in the absence of all but one of the possible sufficient but not necessary causes; and, conversely, the given effect would not follow the occurrence of some but not all of the various necessary but not sufficient causes. (Theodorson & Theodorson, 1979, p. 40) . . .

I. The Role of Pornography in Predisposing Some Males to Want to Rape

. . . This section will provide the evidence for the four different ways in which pornography can induce [a predisposition to rape].

1. Predisposes by Pairing of Sexually Arousing Stimuli With Portrayals of Rape. The laws of social learning (e.g., classical conditioning, instrumental conditioning, and social modeling), about which there is now considerable consensus among psychologists, apply to all the mass media, including pornography. As Donnerstein (1983) testified at the hearings in Minneapolis: "If you assume that your child can learn from Sesame Street how to count one, two, three, four, five, believe me, they can learn how to pick up a gun" (p. 11). Presumably, males can learn equally well how to rape, beat, sexually abuse, and degrade females.

A simple application of the laws of social learning suggests that viewers of pornography can develop arousal responses to depictions of rape, murder, child sexual abuse, or other assaultive behavior. Researcher S. Rachman of the Institute of Psychiatry, Maudsley Hospital, London, has demonstrated that male subjects can learn to become sexually aroused by seeing a picture of a woman's boot after repeatedly seeing women's boots in association with sexually arousing slides of nude females (Rachman & Hodgson, 1968). The laws of learning that operated in the acquisition of the boot fetish can also teach males who were not previously aroused by depictions of rape to become so. All it may take is the repeated association of rape with arousing portrayals of female nudity (or clothed females in provocative poses).

Even for males who are not sexually excited during movie portrayals of rape, masturbation following the movie reinforces the association between rape and sexual gratification. This constitutes what R. J. McGuire, J. M. Carlisle, and B. G. Young refer to as "masturbatory conditioning" (Cline, 1974, p. 210). The pleasurable experience of orgasm—an expected and planned-for activity in many pornography parlors—is an exceptionally potent reinforcer. The fact that pornography is widely used by males as ejaculation material is a major factor that differentiates it from other mass media, intensifying the lessons that male consumers learn from it.

2. Predisposes by Generating Rape Fantasies. Further evidence that exposure to pornography can create in males a predisposition to rape where none existed before is provided by an experiment conducted by Malamuth. Malamuth (1981a) classified 29 male students as sexually force-oriented or non-force-oriented on the basis of their responses to a questionnaire. These students were then randomly assigned to view either a rape version of a slide-audio presentation or a mutually consenting version. . . .

After the 29 male students had been exposed to the rape audio tape, they were asked to try to reach as high a level of sexual arousal as possible by fantasizing about whatever they wanted but without any direct stimulation of the penis (Malamuth, 1981a, p. 40). Self-reported sexual arousal during the fantasy period indicated that those students who had been exposed to the rape version of the first slide-audio presentation created more violent sexual fantasies than those exposed to the mutually consenting version *irrespective of whether they had been* [*previously*] *classified as force-oriented or non-force-oriented* (p. 33).

As the rape version of the slide-audio presentation is typical of what is seen in pornography, the results of this experiment suggest that similar pornographic depictions are likely to generate rape fantasies even in previously non-force-oriented male consumers. . . .

3. Predisposes by Sexualizing Dominance and Submission. The first two ways in which pornography can predispose some males to desire rape, or intensify this desire . . . both relate to the viewing of *violent* pornography. However, both violent *and* nonviolent pornography sexualizes dominance and submission. Hence, nonviolent pornography can also predispose some males to want to rape women.

James Check and Ted Guloien's (1989) distinctions among sexually violent pornography, nonviolent dehumanizing pornography, and erotica, and the contents of the videotapes they constructed to exemplify these three types of sexual materials, were described earlier. James Check and Ted Guloien (1989) conducted an experiment in which they exposed 436 male Toronto residents and college students to one of the three types of sexual material over three viewing sessions, or to no sexual material. Subjects in the no-exposure condition (the control group) participated in only one session in which they viewed and evaluated a videotape that was devoid of sexual material.

Following are some of the significant findings that Check and Guloien (1989) reported:

- "More than twice as many men who had been exposed to sexually violent or to nonviolent dehumanizing pornography reported that there was at least some likelihood that they would rape, compared to the men in the no-exposure condition."[5]
- "High-frequency consumers who had been exposed to the nonviolent, dehumanizing pornography subsequently reported a greater likelihood of raping, [and] were more sexually callous . . . than high-frequency pornography consumers in the no-exposure condition."
- "Exposure to the nonviolent, erotica materials did not have any demonstrated antisocial impact."

I pointed out earlier that men's self-reported likelihood of raping is not the best measure of *desire* to rape because this variable combines desire with the self-reported probability of acting out that desire. Nevertheless, since rape is clearly an act of dominance that forces submission, as are other coerced sex acts, Check and Guloien's finding that exposure to pornography increases men's self-reported likelihood of rape does offer tentative support for my theoretical model's claim that pornography predisposes some males to desire rape or intensifies this desire by sexualizing dominance and submission. Furthermore, this effect is not confined to violent pornography. It also makes sense theoretically that the sexualizing of dominance and submission would include the eroticization of rape and/or other abusive sexual behavior for some males. . . .

4. Predisposes by Creating an Appetite for Increasingly Stronger Material. Dolf Zillmann and Jennings Bryant (1984) have studied the effects of what they refer to as "massive exposure" to pornography. (In fact, it was not particularly massive: 4 hours and 48 minutes per week over a period of 6 weeks. In later publications, Zillmann and Bryant use the term "prolonged exposure" instead of "massive" exposure.) These researchers, unlike Malamuth and Donnerstein, are interested in ascertaining the effects of nonviolent pornography and, in the study to be described, their sample was drawn from an adult nonstudent population.

Male subjects in the so-called *massive exposure* condition saw 36 nonviolent pornographic films, six per session per week; male subjects in the *intermediate* condition saw 18 such movies, three per session per week. Male subjects in the control group saw 36 nonpornographic movies. Various measures were taken after 1 week, 2 weeks, and 3 weeks of exposure. Information was also obtained about the kind of materials that the subjects were most interested in viewing.

Zillmann and Bryant (1984) report that as a result of massive exposure to pornography, "consumers graduate from common to less common forms," including pornography portraying "some degree of pseudoviolence or violence." These researchers suggest that this change may be "because familiar material becomes unexciting as a result of habituation."

According to Zillmann and Bryant's research, then, pornography can transform a male who was not previously interested in the more abusive types of pornography into one who *is* turned on by such material. This is consistent with findings that males who did not previously find rape sexually arousing generate such fantasies after being exposed to a typical example of violent pornography. [Notes omitted]

Anthony D'Amato  **NO**

Porn Up, Rape Down

T he headlines are shouting RAPE IN DECLINE![1]
Official figures just released show a plunge in the number of rapes per capita in the United States since the 1970s. Even when measured in different ways, including police reports and survey interviews, the results are in agreement: there has been an 85% reduction in sexual violence in the past 25 years. The decline, steeper than the stock market crash that led to the Great Depression, is depicted in this chart prepared by the United States Department of Justice:

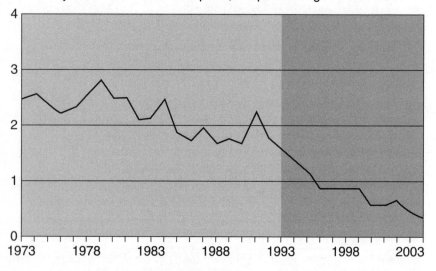

Rape Rates
Adjusted victimization rate per 1,000 persons age 12 and over

Source: U.S. Department of Justice • Office of Justice Programs, Bureau of Justice Statistics, National Crime Victimization Survey. The National Crime Victimization Survey. Includes both attempted and completed rapes.

As the chart shows, there were 2.7 rapes for every 1,000 people in 1980; by 2004, the same survey found the rate had decreased to 0.4 per 1000 people, a decline of 85%.

D'Amato, Anthony, "Porn Up, Rape Down" (June 23, 2006). *Northwestern Public Law Research Paper* No. 913013. Available at SSRN: http://ssrn.com/abstract=913013. Reprinted by permission.

Official explanations for the unexpected decline include:

- less lawlessness associated with crack cocaine;
- women have been taught to avoid unsafe situations;
- more would-be rapists already in prison for other crimes;
- sex education classes telling boys that "no means no."

But these minor factors cannot begin to explain such a sharp decline in the incidence of rape.

There is, however, one social factor that correlates almost exactly with the rape statistics. The American public is probably not ready to believe it. My theory is that the sharp rise in access to pornography accounts for the decline in rape. The correlation is inverse: the more pornography, the less rape. It is like the inverse correlation: the more police officers on the street, the less crime.

The pornographic movie *Deep Throat* which started the flood of X-rated VHS and later DVD films, was released in 1972. Movie rental shops at first catered primarily to the adult film trade. Pornographic magazines also sharply increased in numbers in the 1970s and 1980s. Then came a seismic change: pornography became available on the new internet. Today, purveyors of inter-net porn earn a combined annual income exceeding the total of the major networks ABC, CBS, and NBC.

Deep Throat has moved from the adult theatre to a laptop near you.

National trends are one thing; what do the figures for the states show? From data compiled by the National Telecommunications and Information Administration in 2001, the four states with the *lowest* per capita access to the internet were Arkansas, Kentucky, Minnesota, and West Virginia. The four states with the *highest* internet access were Alaska, Colorado, New Jersey, and Washington. (I would not have guessed this.)

Next I took the figures for forcible rape compiled by police reports by the Disaster Center for the years 1980 and 2000. The following two charts display the results:

Table 1

States with Lowest Internet Access[2]

STATE	Internet 2001	Rape 1980	Rape 2000
Arkansas	36.9	26.7	31.7
Kentucky	40.2	19.2	27.4
Minnesota	36.1	23.2	45.5
W. Virginia	40.7	15.8	18.3

All figures are per capita.

Table 2

States with Highest Internet Access[3]

STATE	Internet 2001	Rape 1980	Rape 2000
Alaska	64.1	56.8	70.3
Colorado	58.5	52.5	41.2
New Jersey	61.6	30.7	16.1
Washington	60.4	52.7	46.4

All figures are per capita.

While the nationwide incidence of rape was showing a drastic decline, the incidence of rape in the four states having the *least* access to the internet showed an actual *increase* in rape over the same time period. This result was almost too clear and convincing, so to check it I compiled figures for the four states having the *most* access to the internet. Three out of four of these states showed declines (in New Jersey, an almost 50% decline). Alaska was an anomaly: it increased both in internet access and incidence of rape. However, the population of Alaska is less than one-tenth that of the other three states in its category. To adjust for the disparity in population, I took the combined population of the four states in each table and calculated the percentage change in the rape statistics:

Table 3

Combined Per Capita Percentage Change in Incidence of Rape

Aggregate per capita increase or decline in rape

Four states with lowest internet access	Increase in rape of 53%
Four states with highest internet access	Decrease in rape of 27%

I find these results to be statistically significant beyond the .95 confidence interval.

Yet proof of correlation is not the same thing as causation. If autumn regularly precedes winter, that doesn't mean that autumn causes winter. When six years ago my former Northwestern colleague John Donohue, together with Steven Levitt,[4] found that legalized abortion correlated with a reduction in crime, theirs would have only been an academically curious thesis if they had not identified a causal factor. But they did identify one: that prior to legalization there were many unwanted babies born due to the lack of a legal abortion alternative. Those unwanted children became the most likely group to turn to crime.

My own interest in the rape-pornography question began in 1970 when I served as a consultant to President Nixon's Commission on Obscenity and Pornography. The Commission concluded that there was no causal relationship between exposure to sexually explicit materials and delinquent or criminal behavior. The President was furious when he learned of the conclusion.

Later President Reagan tried the same thing, except unlike his predecessor he packed the Commission with persons who passed his ideological litmus test. (Small wonder that I was not asked to participate.) This time, Reagan's Commission on Pornography reached the approved result: that there does exist a causal relationship between pornography and violent sex crimes.

The drafter of the Commission's report was Frederich Schauer, a prominent law professor. In a separate statement, he assured readers that neither he nor the other Commissioners were at all influenced by their personal moral values.[5]

Professor Schauer's disclaimer aroused my skepticism. If the commissioners were unbiased, how could the social facts have changed so drastically in the decade between the Nixon and Reagan reports as to turn non-causality into causality? My examination of the Commission's evidence resulted in an article published by the *William and Mary Law Review*.[6]

Although the Reagan Commission had at its disposal all the evidence gathered by psychology and social-science departments throughout the world on the question whether a student's exposure to pornography increased his tendency to commit antisocial acts, I found that the Commission was unable to adduce a shred of evidence to support its affirmative conclusion. No scientist had ever found that pornography raised the probability of rape. However, the Commission was not seeking truth; rather, as I said in the title to my article, it sought political truth.

Neither Professor Schauer nor the other Commissioners ever responded to my *William & Mary* article. Now they can forget it. For if they had been right that exposure to pornography leads to an increase in social violence, then the vast exposure to pornography furnished by the internet would by now have resulted in scores of rapes per day on university campuses, hundreds of rapes daily in every town, and thousands of rapes per day in every city. Instead, the Commissioners were so incredibly wrong that the incidence of rape has actually declined by the astounding rate of 85%.

Correlations aside, could access to pornography actually cause a decline in rape? In my article I mentioned one possibility: that some people watching pornography may "get it out of their system" and thus have no further desire to go out and actually try it. Another possibility might be labeled the "Victorian effect": the more that people covered up their bodies with clothes in those days, the greater the mystery of what they looked like in the nude. The sight of a woman's ankle was considered shocking and erotic. But today, internet porn has thoroughly de-mystified sex. Times have changed so much that some high school teachers of sex education are beginning to show triple-X porn movies to their students in order to depict techniques of satisfactory intercourse.

I am sure there will be other explanations forthcoming as to why access to pornography is the most important causal factor in the decline of rape. Once one accepts the observation that there is a precise negative correlation between the two, the rest can safely be left to the imagination.

Notes

1. E.G., *Washington Post,* June 19, 2006; *Chicago Tribune,* June 21, 2006.

2. Statistics on Internet Access compiled from National Telecommunications and Information Administration, at . . .

3. Statistics on forcible rape compiled from . . .

4. Author of *Freakonomics* (2005).

5. U.S. Dept. of Justice, *Final Report: Attorney General's Commission on Pornography* 176–79 (1986) (personal statement of Commissioner Schauer).

6. Anthony D'Amato, "A New Political Truth: Exposure to Sexually Violent Materials Causes Sexual Violence," 31 *Wm. & Mary L. Rev.* 575 (1990), downloadable at . . .

POSTSCRIPT

Is Exposure to Pornography Related to Increased Rates of Rape?

This very interesting question has intrigued researchers for years. On an intuitive level, it may seem more likely that exposure to pornography would lead some susceptible individuals to commit rape and sexual assault. As the articles in this section illustrate, however, arguments that seem to make sense on an intuitive level may lead to conclusions that are not accurate when tested empirically and legally. Moreover, while it may be difficult legally to prevent depictions of sexual relations between consenting adults, there seems to be little debate that states may prohibit depictions of sexual behavior involving children. U.S. courts have adopted a much less tolerant stance in these cases and have held consistently that depictions of sexual activity involving children is not a form of expression protected by the First Amendment.

In New York v. Ferber, 458 U.S. 747 (1982), a New York law prohibited knowingly promoting a sexual performance by a child under the age of 16 by distributing materials that illustrated such acts. The law defined "sexual performance" as any one that included sexual conduct by a child, which was described as actual or simulated sexual intercourse, deviant sexual intercourse, sexual bestiality, masturbation, sado-masochistic abuse, or lewd exhibition of the genitals. A New York City bookstore operator was convicted under the law for selling films of young boys masturbating. The N.Y. Court of Appeals reversed the conviction, holding that the law violated the First Amendment. The State of New York appealed the case to the U.S. Supreme Court.

Writing for a unanimous Supreme Court, Associate Justice Byron White upheld the N.Y. law. Stated Justice White:

> It is evident beyond the need for elaboration that a State's interest in 'safeguarding the physical and psychological well-being of a minor' is compelling. 'A democratic society rests, for its continuance, upon the healthy, well-rounded growth of young people into full maturity as citizens.' Accordingly, we have sustained legislation aimed at protecting the physical and emotional well-being of youth even when the laws have operated in the sensitive area of constitutionally protected rights. . . . The prevention of sexual exploitation and abuse of children constitutes a government objective of surpassing importance. . . .We shall not second-guess this legislative judgment. (757–758) [Citations omitted].

In addition to state laws prohibiting child pornography, the U.S. Congress has made it a felony to possess or distribute pornographic depictions of sexual activities involving children. In the Internet age, given the ease with which virtually any material may be "forwarded" to others, this is an important law. Title 18, U.S.C. Section 2252, is titled "Certain activities relating to material involving the sexual exploitation of minors." This statute prohibits the possession or distribution of materials or a visual depiction that "involves the use of a minor engaging in sexually explicit conduct." The law further provides that persons violating these provisions may be fined and imprisoned for "not less than 5 years and not more than 20 years." If, however, a defendant has a prior conviction for a sexual offense under applicable state or federal law, he or she may be fined and imprisoned "for not less than 15 years or more than 40 years."

It is important to know as well that the law states that it is a defense to these charges if a recipient "promptly and in good faith," and without providing access to the materials to others, "took reasonable steps to destroy each such visual depiction, or reported the matter to a law enforcement agency and afforded that agency access to each such visual depiction." The rule that emerges from this law is an easy and important one to remember: If you receive an email message or other material that you believe may depict children engaging in sexually explicit conduct, take immediate steps to destroy it or report it to law enforcement authorities. Under no circumstances should you print or convey it to anyone other than law enforcement authorities.

The preceding discussion has focused on the legal issues regarding pornographic materials. The authors of the articles in this section focused more closely on what is perhaps the most compelling empirical question in the pornography debate: What is the impact of exposure to pornography on rape and sexual assault?

Diana E. H. Russell argues that the evidence is overwhelming that exposure to pornography is a major causal factor of rape and sexual assault. Russell's position is compelling intuitively. Excessive exposure to pornographic materials has long been associated with aberrant sexual behavior. Moreover, her contention that exposure to pornographic materials may exert a desensitization effect on susceptible males seems to be an accurate one. Further, as Russell suggests, the actors and actresses involved in the production of pornography should be considered victims as well.

Russell's contention that exposure to pornography is a central "cause" of rape is more problematic, however. Like the relationship between body type and crime, perhaps it may be more accurate to describe the relationship between exposure to pornography and rape as one that demonstrates a correlation, rather than a causal one.

It is also difficult to dismiss Anthony D'Amato's analysis of the relationship between exposure to pornography on the Internet and declining rates of rape and sexual assault. If, in fact, the incidence of rape has declined 85% in the last 25 years while access to pornography via the Internet has become more freely available to teenagers and adults, it may suggest that exposure to this medium is a healthy and positive thing. While this data does not constitute conclusive proof of a cause-and-effect inverse relationship between Internet usage and the incidence of rape, it is certainly compelling evidence.

156

After reading the articles in this section, which position do you find to be the more compelling one? If you remain undecided, there is a wealth of information on these topics in the academic literature. See, Catherine A. MacKinnon and Andrea Dworkin, *In Harm's Way: The Pornography Civil Rights Hearings* (Harvard University Press, 1997); Andrea Dworkin, *Pornography—Men Possessing Women* (Plume, 1991); Catherine A. MacKinnon, *Women's Lives, Men's Laws* (Belknap Press, 2005); Philipe Bensimon, "The Role of Pornography in Sexual Offending," *Sexual Addiction & Compulsivity* (vol. 14, no. 2, 2007); Chiara Sabina, Janis Wolak and David Finkelhor, "The Nature and Dynamics of Pornography Exposure for Youth," *CyberPsychology & Behavior* (vol. 11, no. 6, 2008); LeeAnn Kahlor and Dan Morrison, "Television Viewing and Rape Myth Acceptance Among College Women," *Sex Roles* (vol. 56, no. 11/12, 2007); Janis Wolak, Kimberly Mitchell, and David Finkelhor, "Unwanted and Wanted Exposure to Online Pornography in a National Sample of Youth Internet Users," *Pediatrics* (vol. 119, no. 2, 2007); Dominique A. Simons, Sandy K. Wurtele, and Robert L. Durham, "Developmental Experiences of Child Sexual Abusers and Rapists," *Child Abuse & Neglect* (vol. 32, no. 5, 2008); Alan McKee, "The Relationship Between Attitudes Towards Women, Consumption of Pornography, and Other Demographic Variables in a Survey of 1,023 Consumers of Pornography," *International Journal of Sexual Health*, (vol. 19, no. 1, 2007); Juliann Petley, "Web Control," *Index on Censorship*, (vol. 38, no. 1, 2009); Jochen Peter and Patti M. Valkenburg, "Adolescents' Exposure to Sexually Explicit Internet Material, Sexual Uncertainty, and Attitudes Toward Uncommitted Sexual Exploration: Is There a Link?" *Communication Research*, (vol. 35, no. 5, 2008).

Internet References . . .

Correctional Service of Canada

The Correctional Service of Canada (CSC), as part of the criminal justice system and respecting the rule of law, contributes to the protection of society by actively encouraging and assisting offenders to become law-abiding citizens, while exercising reasonable, safe, secure, and humane control. Learn how the CSC operates, obtain facts and statistics about corrections in Canada, and find out about Canada's federal penetentiaries.

http://www.csc-scc.gc.ca

Criminal Offenders Statistics

At this site, the U.S. Department of Justice's Bureau of Justice Statistics (BJS) provides a variety of statistics of criminal offenders, including characteristics of state prison inmates, recidivism rates, and statistics on women offenders. This site also links to BJS reports.

http://www.ojp.usdoj.gov/bjs/crimoff.htm

HIV InSite

This HIV InSite page provides numerous categorized links to statistics, news reports, legal cases, and organizations related to HIV and prisons. Categories include epidemiology, sexual assault, policy and legal materials, compassionate release, women in prisons, global dimensions, and more.

http://hivinsite.ucsf.edu

Punishment

*S*ince *the 1950s, scholars have supported the idea that imprisonment, especially for the young, should be avoided. If incarceration is required, according to this viewpoint, then it should be for the purpose of rehabilitation, not punishment, deterrence, or incapacitation. Yet today America's fear of crime is extremely high, and U.S. incarceration rates are greater than they have ever been. As a result, the penal issues have shifted dramatically. The presence of AIDS, the notorious recidivism rates, and other factors have changed the rules, if not the incarceration game itself. What should be done to imprisoned offenders, particularly those who will probably assault again or worse upon release?*

- Are Supermax (Control Unit) Prisons an Appropriate Way to Punish Hardened Criminals?

- Do Three Strikes Sentencing Laws and Other "Get Tough" Approaches Really Work?

- Should Private "For-Profit" Corporations Be Allowed to Run U.S. Prisons?

- Is Capital Punishment a Bad Public Policy?

ISSUE 8

Are Supermax (Control Unit) Prisons an Appropriate Way to Punish Hardened Criminals?

YES: Gregory L. Hershberger, from "To the Max," *Corrections Today* (February 1998)

NO: Rodney J. Henningsen, W. Wesley Johnson, and Terry Wells, from "Supermax Prisons: Panacea or Desperation?" *Corrections Management Quarterly* (Spring 1999)

ISSUE SUMMARY

YES: Federal Bureau of Prisons regional director Gregory L. Hershberger contends that the challenges posed by hardened prison inmates support confining dangerous offenders in a supermax prison facility.

NO: Professors Rodney J. Henningsen, W. Wesley Johnson, and Terry Wells argue that supermax prisons are symbolic of the desperation Americans face in trying to reduce crime using traditional crime control methods.

Supermax security prisons often house the worst criminals in our nation's prison systems. Strict regulations and policies in these prisons regulate virtually every aspect of an inmate's life. It is not uncommon to discover that inmates in supermax prisons spend 23 hours of every day locked in a small cell. Their communication with other inmates is highly restricted and reading materials and other "privileges" must be earned by the inmates through good behavior. It should not be surprising then that the regimentation and sensory deprivation used in these facilities appears to produce a substantially higher rate of mental illness among inmates.

As corrections scholar Hans Toch has observed, such penal techniques are nothing new. Prison conditions resembling those in supermax prisons have been adopted on several different occasions in the past but were abandoned because they produced high rates of mental illness among inmates. Sasha Abramsky states that supermax prisons may have become the high-tech equivalent of the nineteenth-century snake pit.

In general, U.S. courts have accorded great deference to prison authorities' decisions regarding the conditions of confinement in our prison systems. This approach to corrections law, which the courts followed carefully until the 1960s, has been termed the "hands-off" doctrine. It assumed that because correctional administrators were the "experts," courts should defer to their judgment.

You may recall a now classic movie starring Paul Newman and George Kennedy titled *Cool Hand Luke*, which illustrated just how bad the conditions were in some 1950s-era correctional facilities. Due in large part to the inhumane conditions existing in some prison systems, the courts gradually started to scrutinize the decisions of correctional administrators. In fact, during the 1960s, the conditions of confinement in several state prison systems were held to violate the Eighth Amendment's prohibition on cruel and unusual punishment and significant correctional reforms were instituted.

The decade of the 1970s witnessed an increasing conservatism in the United States. At least partially in response to rising crime rates and the widely held belief that prison rehabilitation programs were ineffective, some scholars and politicians began to advocate a "get tough" approach to crime control. The justice system policies that resulted from this approach included mandatory sentencing laws and a correctional philosophy that emphasized incapacitation and punishment, rather than rehabilitation. The development of supermax prison facilities in the 1980s was the logical extension of this new philosophy.

In the Introduction to this volume we considered the doctrine of social utility. Basically, this concept asserts that the guiding principle for all social policies should be the well-being of the majority of people. Does the use of supermax prison facilities satisfy this principle? Are they an appropriate way to punish hardened criminals? The authors of the articles in this section would answer these questions in very different ways.

Federal Bureau of Prisons regional director Gregory L. Hershberger contends that the challenges posed by hardened prison inmates support confining the worst offenders in a supermax prison facility. This approach may increase the safety of staff and inmates at other locations in the system and allow it to operate in a more effective manner.

Professors Rodney J. Henningsen, W. Wesley Johnson, and Terry Wells would take issue with director Hershberger's view of supermax prisons. They believe that as the cost of incarceration continues to increase, correctional officials will be forced to adopt a more balanced approach to punishing criminals.

Do you agree initially with director Hershberger, or with professors Henningsen, Johnson, and Wells? Do you believe that supermax prisons are an effective and justified approach to punishing hardened criminals, or are they inconsistent with human value and dignity? These are intriguing questions that will have a highly significant impact on corrections policy in the new millennium.

YES

Gregory L. Hershberger

To the Max

Over the past decade, correctional systems around the nation have activated several high security prisons, which are popularly known as "supermax" institutions. These facilities are designed to hold the most violent, disruptive or escape-prone offenders. By isolating the "worst of the worst," these facilities increase the safety of staff, other inmates and the general public. They also allow inmates in other institutions to live in a more normalized prison environment, with greater freedom of movement and access to educational, vocational and other correctional programs.

In some correctional systems, offenders may be sent to supermax facilities as direct commitments from the courts, but most inmates are sent to them because of their behavior in prison. Among the roughly 400 inmates in the Federal Bureau of Prisons' (BOP) most secure facility, the U.S. Penitentiary Administrative Maximum (ADX) in Florence, Colo., approximately 20 percent are there for the murder or attempted murder of a fellow inmate, 18 percent for assaulting another inmate with a weapon, 16 percent for serious assault on a staff member, 10 percent for a serious escape attempt and 5 percent for rioting. Other reasons for placement in this facility include attempted murder of a staff member, taking a staff member hostage, leading a work or food strike, introducing narcotics into an institution and having a leadership role in a prison gang. Only about 3 percent of the inmates were sent there directly from court. About 6 percent are state boarders, inmates who were involved in the murder of state correctional staff, or inmates who are too disruptive or dangerous for state officials to house safely.

Dispersion vs. Consolidation

For years, correctional administrators have used various strategies for handling especially dangerous inmates and minimizing the disruption they cause to the rest of the system. Historically, they have used two basic models—dispersion and consolidation.

The dispersion model scatters offenders with unusually dangerous histories or disruptive behavioral patterns throughout the correctional system, thus avoiding a concentration of such offenders in any one location. Staff in each institution share the burden and dangers of supervising and controlling these

From *Corrections Today*, vol. 60, no. 1, February 1998, pp. 54–57. Copyright © 1998 by American Correctional Association. Reprinted with permission of the American Correctional Association, Alexandria, Va.

inmates. In smaller prison systems, the aggressive conduct of these inmates often results in their placement in long-term segregation or detention status. In larger systems, administrators transfer inmates from one institution to another, if only to disrupt their alliances and give staff relief from the stress of dealing with them. In the past, entire institutions often were managed in a more rigid, highly controlled manner in order to reduce the threat posed by this relatively small number of inmates.

Among the benefits of the dispersion model is the fact that no single institution is required to deal with a large number of problem inmates. In addition, some prison administrators believe that it is easier to manage small groups of inmates of this caliber. Finally, it was once thought that a number of institutions holding a few such individuals each would require the allocation of fewer security-related resources overall.

In contrast, the consolidation model involves placing all highly dangerous inmates at one location and controlling them through reliance on heightened security procedures. The potential drawback of adopting a consolidation model is that the institution holding this group is necessarily subjected to a dramatically different routine and will, in all likelihood, require additional staff and expensive security modifications.

Alcatraz was the prototypical consolidation-model institution at the federal level. From 1934 to 1963, it operated as the prime federal prison resource, housing many of the more notorious or dangerous offenders in the federal system. Alcatraz was closed in 1963—not because of flaws in the consolidation model, but because the island prison was very expensive to operate and maintain, and because there was a shift in correctional philosophy during the so-called "medical model" or rehabilitation era.

When the BOP closed Alcatraz, it decided to disperse its hard-core offenders throughout the various federal prisons, rather than move them as a group to another single location. During most of the 1960s and the early 1970s, the BOP managed its most dangerous offenders by using the dispersion model. However, in the late '70s, the BOP began moving toward the consolidation model once again, concentrating its most troublesome inmates at the U.S. Penitentiary in Marion, Ill.

Consolidation Pros and Cons

Focusing extra security resources on a single location is thought by many corrections practitioners to be far more efficient and effective. Under the consolidation model, staff training for managing this more homogeneous group is simplified, and operational procedures are much more refined. But more important, staff and inmates in other institutions throughout the prison system see their safety enhanced, and rigid controls lessened, once the most dangerous individuals are removed to a single, more highly controlled location.

The BOP recognized that the consolidation strategy for reducing violence in its mainline institutions had its risks. While the benefits in terms of overall system safety and order clearly were worthwhile, the dimensions of those risks soon became evident. In 1979, a series of serious assaults, inmate murders and the attempted murders of two staff in Marion's dining room demonstrated the volatility and potential danger of the new population mixture. A special task force, convened to deal with the increasing violence at Marion, recommended that the institution be converted to a tightly controlled, unitized operation that would permit the continued consolidation of the most violent, assaultive and disruptive inmates at one institution and would better protect staff and inmates from violence. However, implementation of that recommendation was deferred, and Marion's daily routines continued to resemble those of a traditional institution.

By 1980, Marion's operation began to show clear signs of the underlying stresses of using this quasi-normal system to deal with such aggressive offenders. Assaults on inmates and staff continued; there were major incidents in the administrative detention unit; and inmates staged three major work stoppages, the last of which lasted for four months. The BOP decided to remove industrial operations from Marion altogether, and convert the institution into the more highly structured operation envisioned several years earlier. This was done by expanding the restricted movement and program procedures which were initiated during the strike.

Management Challenges

Prison administrators recognize better than most the difficulty of operating a minimum privilege, maximum control facility. As a result, even though numerous serious incidents underscored the difficult and dangerous nature of the inmate group at Marion, various attempts were made to return the institution to some semblance of normalcy throughout 1982 and most of 1983. Unfortunately, each step toward normalization was met by additional assaults and other serious incidents, generating increased concern for the safety of staff and inmates. In October 1983, two staff members who were working in the most secure area of Marion were murdered in separate incidents on the same day, and two other staff were seriously injured. Just days later, an inmate was murdered and several staff were assaulted during a group disturbance. These events culminated in the final realization that the type of inmates confined at Marion could not be managed in the same manner as typical penitentiary inmates. Thus, the decision was made to convert the institution into a longterm, highly controlled operation—a "supermax" facility.

While this management program seemed to control the inmate population, the BOP found that Marion's design and layout was not particularly well-suited for its mission. For example, because education, recreation, health services and other vital program areas were centrally located, inmates often had to be moved from one location to another. For security reasons, each move had to be escorted. Consequently, the high volume of inmate movement consumed an enormous number of staff hours and significantly threatened staff safety. Accordingly, in the mid-'80s, BOP administrators began thinking about a new high-security facility, one that was designed specifically for high-security operations and that took advantage of the many advances in inmate management and correctional technology that occurred between 1960 and 1980.

After years of careful planning, the BOP opened ADX Florence—one of the most sophisticated supermax prisons in the nation. Since its activation in 1994, ADX Florence has been extremely effective in housing the federal prison system's most dangerous offenders in a safe, secure and humane manner.

ADX Operations

Supermax facilities have been incorrectly characterized as "lockdown" institutions. This is misleading. Lockdowns are relatively short periods of time when all inmates in an institution are confined to their cells because of an institutional emergency, or for some other overriding reason such as a facilitywide shakedown. During a lockdown, all but the most basic services are suspended. True supermax facilities operate quite differently. A supermax facility is not simply a segregation unit in a maximum security penitentiary. It is a full institution, with unique security elements and programmatic features.

The main purpose of a supermax facility is to control the inmates' behavior until they demonstrate that they can be moved back to a traditional, open-population penitentiary. As they demonstrate increasingly responsible behavior, ADX inmates move incrementally from more to less restrictive housing units. Each successive unit allows more privileges and more interaction with staff and other inmates.

Administrative maximum security operations differ from typical penitentiary operations in several ways. Inmates are handcuffed whenever they come in contact with staff; this prevents violent offenders from assaulting staff and other inmates, and eliminates the possibility that escape-prone inmates will attempt to take a hostage or access an area of the institution that will facilitate an escape. Inmates eat and recreate individually, or in small, carefully screened and supervised groups; this differs from procedures in a typical prison, where inmates have largely unrestrained contact with each other and staff throughout the day. Inmates are confined in their cells for larger portions of the day; in a typical prison, an inmate would have 12 to 16 hours of out-of-cell time, while an inmate in an administrative maximum security institution would be much more restricted.

Programs in an administrative maximum security setting rely primarily upon individual inmate-based delivery systems (self-study courses, closed circuit television, staff visits to the housing unit) as opposed to having inmates go in groups to a central program area. Visiting in such an institution is generally noncontact, in contrast to the contact visiting that is permitted in most institutions. Staff/inmate ratios are higher, to provide increased supervision and capability for searching inmates, cells and other areas of the institution in order to prevent assaults and disruptive incidents.

Unique Confinement Conditions

While conditions of confinement for inmates in an administrative maximum security setting are highly restrictive relative to the general population of most typical penitentiaries, these facilities are an improvement on conditions in a typical detention or segregation unit at a regular penitentiary, because they provide increased movement, more contact with staff and more opportunities to participate in programs. Institutions such as ADX Florence are intended to control disruptive and dangerous behavior, yet also permit a reasonable amount of access to necessary programs and offer inmates the means to progress to a more typical penitentiary setting.

Rather than being housed in traditional lockdown conditions, inmates at ADX Florence, for example, are offered a range of programs and services. Most are delivered at the inmate's cell or in the individual unit, eliminating the danger and expense associated with frequent escorted moves. Inmates do start their time at Florence under relatively close controls; they spend the majority of their time in their cells or in the cellhouse. On- and off-unit recreation, visiting, medical care, in-cell television, religious activities, education and other self-improvement programs are available from the day of arrival at Florence. The federal courts have consistently found that the BOP's administrative maximum operations are consistent with constitutional requirements related to conditions of confinement.

ADX inmates are offered an opportunity to demonstrate nondangerous behavior through compliance with institutional rules. As they do, they progress through a graduated system of housing units, with each unit providing increased freedom and work opportunities, all contingent on the inmate avoiding misconduct. Proper conduct in this program results in eventual transfer to other, less controlled institutions.

The ADX program is based on the assumption that every inmate will be given the opportunity to demonstrate that he or she doesn't need to be at the ADX. Most progress through the program in a little more than three years (42 months, on average) and then are returned to open population prisons. Once in regular penitentiaries, more than 80 percent of former administrative maximum inmates behave well enough that a return to the program is unnecessary.

Conclusion

The essential challenge of operating a supermax facility is to properly balance staff and inmate safety needs against important constitutional and correctional management principles that govern prison life. It is critical to remember that with this type of offender, good treatment starts with vital safety considerations—for both staff and inmates.

The challenges posed by these inmates are very real, as are the dangers they present to staff, other inmates and the public. If a prison system confines all of its dangerous offenders in one institution, it can increase the safety of staff and inmates at other locations in the system and operate these facilities in a more open, normalized fashion. Highly refined security procedures and appropriate programming within the supermax facility allow for safe and secure operations while providing even the most dangerous offenders with reasonable opportunities to demonstrate pro-social behavior and earn their way back into an open population institution.

Rodney J. Henningsen, W. Wesley
Johnson, and Terry Wells

 **NO**

Supermax Prisons:
Panacea or Desperation?

For over a century Americans have sought to find the silver bullet to solve its crime problems. Fads and experiments in corrections have included public humiliation, singleceiling, silent systems, 12-step recovery programs, boot camps, electronic surveillance, and now, supermax. Supermax prisons have evolved out of America's love-hate relationship with crime and punishment. A supermax prison has been defined as:

> A free-standing facility, or distinct unit within a facility, that provides for the management and secure control of inmates who have been officially designated as exhibiting violent or seriously disruptive behavior while incarcerated. Such inmates have been determined to be a threat to safety and security in traditional high-security facilities, and their behavior can be controlled by separation, restricted movement, and limited access to staff and other inmates.

At least in theory, this type of prison unit can and should be distinguished from administrative segregation (ad-seg). While most every prison has administrative segregation cells used for holding prisoners in short-term disciplinary or protective custody, supermax units are designed to house prisoners for a much longer period of time. Proponents of supermax prisons contend that they warehouse the worst of the worst, the most violent prisoners who threaten the security of guards and other prisoners while undermining the moral fabric of American society.

While the American public has increasingly turned to government for solutions to its social problems in the last 30 years, its perceptions of the criminal justice system have remained jaundiced. Over 75 percent of respondents in a recent national survey reported only "some" or "very little" confidence in state prison systems. Similarly, over 80 percent of people surveyed each year since 1980 have indicated that the courts are too soft on crime.

The American judiciary has responded to public concerns that they are soft on crime and cries for vengeance by placing more people under correctional supervision than ever before. To accommodate the increases in new prison admissions and increases in time served by prisoners, some 168 state and

From *Corrections Management Quarterly*, vol. 3, no. 2, Spring 1999, pp. 53–59 (refs. omitted).
Copyright © 1999 by Wolters Kluwer Law & Business/Aspen Publishers. Reprinted by permission.

45 federal prisons have been built since 1990. Today, there are a total of approximately 1,500 state and federal prisons. Between 1990 and 1995, the number of prison beds increased by 41 percent. Despite this tremendous fiscal investment, there are both state and federal prisons that operate in excess of their design capacity, state prisons by 3 percent and federal prisons by 24 percent.

While there are more prisons and prisoners than ever before, there is sustained interest in making prisons even "tougher." This interest may be based on the notion, not strongly supported in the criminological research on recidivism that prisons deter. Another reason may be simply that victims of crime, and those that see themselves as potential victims, want prisoners to suffer. While harm is a critical component of punishment, its generic application to prison life creates unique challenges for correctional officers, staff, and correctional executives.

Political Popularity of Supermax Prisons

Getting tough on crime has become an increasingly popular campaign platform among elected officials, and support of supermax institutions is a politically popular position in many areas across the country. The American judiciary has also supported the need for supermax prison environments. In *Bruscino v Carlson,* federal prisoners at Marion, Illinois, sought compensation for the attacks on them by correctional officers during the October 1983 shakedown and relief from the ongoing conditions created by the subsequent lockdown. A 1985 U.S. Magistrate's Report approved by the U.S. District Court for Southern Illinois in 1987 indicated that 50 prisoners who testified to beatings and other brutalities were not credible witnesses, and that only the single prisoner who testified that there were no beatings was believable. When the prisoners appealed the decision, the ruling of the Fifth Circuit Court of Appeals described conditions at Marion as "ghastly," "sordid and horrible," and "depressing in extreme," but the court maintained that they were necessary for security reasons and did not violate prisoners' constitutional rights.

The New Controversial Control Models

Today, control units go by many different names. They have been referred to as adjustment centers, security housing units, maximum control complexes, administrative maximum (Ad-Max), special housing units, violence control units, special management units, intensive management units, management control units, or "supermax" prisons. These new units are designed to subdue any and all resistance to order. A survey by the Federal Bureau of Prisons conducted in 1990 found that 36 states operated some form of supermax security prison or unit within a prison. At that time, another six states were planning to build supermax prisons. By 1993, 25 states had specialized control units and control unit prisons were in operation in every part of the country.

The new model for high-security prisons is the security housing unit (SITU) at Pelican Bay Prison in California. Pelican Bay opened in December 1989. Prisoners in such units are kept in solitary confinement in relatively small cells between 22 and 23 hours a day. There is no congregate dining or congregate exercise, and there are no work opportunities or congregate religious services. Prisoners are denied standard vocational, educational, and recreational activities.

The conditions are officially justified not as punishment for prisoners, but as an administrative measure. Prisoners are placed in control units as a result of an administrative decision. Because such moves are a result of an administrative decision, prisoners' ability to challenge such changes in imprisonment is severely limited. Today, throughout the country, conditions in "new" supermax prisons closely resemble those set forth at Pelican Bay.

Since their inception, supermax prison units have had their opponents. Typically, opponents have focused upon conditions that allegedly are illegal or inhumane. In some reports, prison guards have testified to shackling prisoners to their beds and spraying them with high-pressure fire hoses. Other criticisms have centered on issues surrounding arbitrary placement/assignment to control unit, the long-term psychological effects from years of isolation from both prison and outside communities while being housed in solitary or small group isolation (celled 22.5 hours/day), denial of access to educational, religious, or work programs, physical torture, such as forced cell extractions, four-point restraint and hog-tying, caging, beating after restraint, back-room beatings, and staged fights for officer entertainment. . . .

Arbitrary Placement

Prisoners are placed in high-security units for administrative and/or disciplinary reasons. Such decisions are based on results during (re-) classification hearings. Critics have called the hearings a kangaroo court claiming prisoners are being denied due process. What is called misbehavior is (arbitrarily) decided by the guard on duty and has been known to include refusing to make beds or complaining about clogged and overflowing toilets.

Violations of Human Rights and Abuses

There are many claims of human rights violations and abuses in control units, including denial of medical care to injured and/or sick prisoners (including diabetics and epileptics), extremely cold cells during winter months and extremely hot cells during summer months, arbitrary beatings, psychological abuse of mentally unstable prisoners, illegal censorship of mail, extended isolation and indoor confinement, denial of access to educational programs, and administrative rather than judicial decisions about punishment for misbehaved prisoners.

Ability to Reduce Violence in Prisons and Society

Prison officials claim that Marion, Pelican Bay, and the other supermax-type control units reduce violence in the rest of the prison system. All the evidence points to the opposite being true. The creation of control units and increased use of administrative segregation have not reduced the level of violence within general prison populations. In fact, assaults on prison staff nationwide rose from 175 in 1991 to 906 to 1993. The number of inmate assaults on prison employees reached 14,000 in 1995. That was up 32 percent from 1990. The number of assaults per 1,000 employees remained stable at 15. It may also be that the potential of supermax prisons to reduce overall prison violence has yet to be realized. As more disruptive inmates are placed in supermax prison cells, assaults in prisons may decline.

While supermax prisons provide correctional executives with another weapon to facilitate order in prison, most supermax prisoners are released back into the general prison population or into society. Conditions in control units produce feelings of resentment and rage and exacerbate mental deterioration. It is anticipated that control unit prisoners who re-enter the general prison population or society will have even greater difficulty coping with social situations than in the past.

The Texas Experience

Overcrowding and the control of violence are critical issues in correctional management, especially in states like Texas where the federal government, in *Ruiz v Texas,* declared the entire department of corrections unconstitutional. As a result of the Ruiz decision, the federal government actively monitored virtually every facet of the Texas Department of Corrections–Institutional Division for over 20 years. In attempts to shed federal control over Texas prisons, relieve massive prison overcrowding, and avoid future lawsuits, an unprecedented number of new prisons were built in a relatively short period of time. In August 1993, the Texas Department of Criminal Justice, one of the largest correctional systems in the world, operated 54 inmate facilities. By August 1998, the number of correctional facilities in Texas doubled, housing prisoners in 107 correctional facilities.

According to David Stanley, of the Executive Services, Texas Department of Criminal Justice-Institutional Division, Texas prisons will soon be at maximum capacity again. In August 1997, Texas's men's prisons were at 98 percent of their capacity, while women's prisons approached 85 percent of their design capacity. Currently, there are about 126,000 men and 10,000 women incarcerated in Texas prisons. Estimates are that maximum design capacity for housing male inmates will be reached in little more than a year. If current inmate population trends continue, many institutions across the country will be operating above design capacity. These factors, combined with the fact that more violent offenders are now entering prisons at an earlier age for longer periods of time than just a decade ago, affect correctional administrators' ability to maintain order and protect their own staff from assaults.

In attempts to keep the lid on a more volatile prison population, Texas has been one of the first states to make a commitment to new prison construction and new state-of-the-art high-security, supermax correctional facilities. This commitment has required an investment of substantial tax revenues. The new high-security prisons, according to a spokesman for the Texas Department of Criminal Justice—Institutional Division, Larry Fitzgerald, are being built and designed with efficiency and economy in mind. The estimated cost of the some 1,300 beds (double-celled) in the new control units will be a mere $19,000 compared to the current national average of $79,770 per maximum-security bed. Costs are being reduced by using inmate labor for nonsecurity tasks, such as masonry, painting, and welding.

Currently, one high-security unit has been completed near Huntsville, Texas and construction on two other similar units has already begun. Officials estimated that inmate labor saved Texas taxpayers over 2 million dollars in the construction of the new control unit near Huntsville, Texas. Currently, high-security inmates are housed in single-cells.

On August 4, 1997, inmates began arriving at the new $25 million high-security unit of the Texas prison system. The high-security unit is located on the grounds of the Estelle Unit near Huntsville. Similar to high-security units in other states, Texas inmates who are placed in the new high-security unit are put there for one of three reasons: (1) they have tried to escape; (2) they pose a physical threat to staff or inmates; or (3) they are members of disruptive groups, such as an organized gang. Approximately 50 percent to 60 percent of the current residents have been officially classified as belonging to a particular gang.

The Gilbane Corporation, with the help of inmates, began construction on the 65,780 square foot facility in October 1995. Outside, two motion detector fences surround the prison. The exterior of the new unit, although secured by electronic surveillance of the outer fence and certain portions of the building and a patrol vehicle, ironically gives less of the appearance of a traditional fortress prison in that there is no guard tower. Some have likened its appearance to that of a modern high school gym.

Despite its relative benign external appearance, its overall design seeks to provide an alternative for the most recalcitrant inmates. Although two beds per cell are still found in accordance with the original plan, a change from the original purpose of the facility now calls for one inmate per cell. While it would be possible to house 1,300 inmates, the current plan is to house only 650 inmates.

The building has a central corridor with two-story wings on the east and west sides. The east wings contain 63 cells with two beds per cell. The east side recreation yard is 22,451 square feet with 42 individual yards. The west wings have 67 cells with two beds per cell. The west side recreation yard is 24,857 square feet and contains 40 individual yards.

The concern for security prompted the design to establish 8 × 10-foot cells. Unlike the traditional cell with barred doors, all doors on this unit consist of a solid sheet of steel. A slot in the door allows officers to pass items to inmates. An inmate can contact an officer by using an intercom system in his cell. The unit's supporters champion these new doors, convinced that officers will no longer need to fear being assaulted by inmates or their waste products as they walk the unit.

The computerized high-tech design is used to monitor staff as well as inmates. All of the projected 246 employees are required to go through extensive security checks upon entering the building. They are required to place their right hands into a palm print recognition station and then enter their four-digit code. Their name and time of entrance into the unit are recorded and stored digitally.

Once access is authorized, a steel door is opened and shut electronically. The computer keeps a log of all times the door was opened and closed. This feature serves as a source of information for administrators to monitor employee traffic and as an additional source of information when prisoners file allegations of abuse or neglect. All incoming on-duty officers then proceed to a central room near the facility's entrance where monitors with split screens transmit views from the many cameras providing surveillance everywhere both inside and outside the unit.

The central control room, which contains several split-screen monitors, is the hub for internal surveillance. Smaller versions of these computerized nerve centers are found in all prison wings and in the hallways. The setup makes it possible for one officer to monitor each wing.

Operational Conditions in the Texas High Security Unit

Most of the conditions found in other control units are also found in the new unit in Texas as well. As in other such units the main objective is to minimize/eliminate an inmates' contact with staff and other prisoners. Such isolation is routine and can be up to 24 hours a day. The inmates in the new Texas control unit will spend most of their time alone in cells. Virtually all their activities both day and night take place in their cells. They eat, shower, and use the restroom in their own cells. The ability to shower the entire unit within a few hours is a major cost- and time-savings procedure, especially compared to showering individual ad-seg inmates under double and sometimes triple custody.

Each cell contains a steel toilet, sink, and showerhead. These are all bolted into the wall. Inmates have the opportunity to shower daily; at other times showers are turned off. Water for the sink and toilet is made available at all times. However, like other "amenities," they can be shut off by the central control system should the cell occupant try to flood his cell block. Inmates receive daily meals in their cells. The food is prepared within the unit by inmates from another institution and is delivered to the inmates by officers.

The high-security unit has no day rooms or television sets other than computer monitors. It does have a visitation room, however, where inmates and their visitors are separated by a thick, impact-resistant glass wall. A steel stool bolted to the floor and a two-way telephone are the only items in the room. No physical contact is possible between inmates and visitors. Likewise, inmates approved for legally prescribed visits may visit other inmates under similar conditions. Such visits are generally conducted in holding cells. Here a wall with a small window, crisscrossed by bars for communication, separates the two inmates who are seated on either side of the wall on a single steel stool bolted to the floor.

Inmates, depending on their level of classification, receive from one hour, three days a week to one hour, seven days a week outdoor recreation time. Oftentimes the only real reprieve from their nearly total isolation takes place at these times. During this time, inmates are moved to individual "cages" where they are separated physically from other inmates by (only) fences. There they are able to see and talk to other inmates. The 18' × 20' enclosed recreation yards include a basketball court, a chin-up bar, and a hard wall on which inmates can play handball. Each "cage" is secured by a floor-to-ceiling 35-foot-high mesh steel fence. If other inmates are nearby, they can converse.

While out-of-cell programming is available to supermax inmates in 13 states, in Texas, the intense physical limitations are compounded by the absence of educational, training, or recreational programs. Thus far, supermax imprisonment in Texas has not attempted to include formal rehabilitation programs as part of its daily routine.

Consequences of Total Control

As a result, control unit inmates live in a psychologically assaultive environment that destabilizes personal and social identities. While the same can be said of the prison system as a whole, in control units mind control is a primary weapon, implemented through architectural design and a day-to-day regimen that produces isolation, inwardness, and self-containment. Within this severely limited space, inmates are under constant scrutiny and observation. In the unit, cameras and listening devices ensure constant surveillance and control of not only the inmate but also every movement of the staff.

The rural location of control units increases (or supplements) isolation and makes contact with family and community difficult for many. The difficulty for inmates in maintaining contacts with the outside world is exacerbated by the unit's isolation from major urban centers. This alienation heightens inmate frustration, deprivation, and despair. Over long periods of time, the inevitable result is the creation of dysfunctional individuals who are completely self-involved, socially neutered, unable to participate in organized social activities, and unprepared for eventual reintegration into either the general prison population, or life on the outside. Those inmates who resist less, demand less, and see each other as fierce competitors for the few privileges allowed will fare best in the system. Programs that normally exist in other prisons to rehabilitate are deemed frivolous here.

Discussion

The present system of mass incarceration accompanied by the specter of more and more control units can only be maintained with at least the tacit approval of society as a whole. In times of relative economic prosperity, America has had the luxury of focusing its resources on crime reduction. As the new millennium approaches, crime and its control has become a major industry. Despite the lack of valid scientific evidence that massive imprisonment reduces crime, billions of dollars have been spent to build new prisons and satisfy the American public's growing desire for vengeance. While there is some scientific evidence that there is a (weak) negative correlation between imprisonment and crime rates, the vast majority of studies indicate that imprisonment is not causally related to the variability in crime. Critics of current imprisonment trends have argued that imprisoning large numbers of people in order to stop crime has been a spectacular and massively expensive failure. Even prison officials sometimes admit to the reality of the situation.

Supermax prisons, perhaps our most costly prison experiment ever, have been promoted as the new panacea for correctional management problems, a form of deterrence that is guaranteed to work. On the other hand, supermax prisons are symbolic of the desperation Americans face in trying to take out crime using traditional formal control methods. The efficacy of such approaches is generally limited by their reactive nature. As the cost of incarceration continues to increase, public officials may be forced to consider a more balanced approach incorporating a more holistic view of crime control; one which focuses more on community and restoration and less on imprisonment. The challenge of the future lies in the creation of a society and a criminal justice system that is able to thwart violence with less violent means.

What we need, in all seriousness, is a better class of inmates. Such change will take time and substantial resources. As we approach the next century, we have the luxury of a relatively strong economy. While many planners have their eye on the future of the global market, failure to learn from our mistakes of the past and strategically invest in proactive crime control strategies in local communities, will eventually limit our ability to compete with other countries and life in America will become, in the words of Hobbes, even more "short, brutish, and nasty."

POSTSCRIPT

Are Supermax (Control Unit) Prisons an Appropriate Way to Punish Hardened Criminals?

The use of supermax security prisons is a controversial practice in the U.S. justice system. On one hand, Regional Director Hershberger's perspective on this issue is a compelling one: It may make sense to confine the "worst of the worst" inmates in one supermax facility where every facet of their lives can be regulated and we can minimize the dangers they pose to the prison staff and other inmates. On the other side, however, if supermax security prisons are simply another "quick fix" for America's crime problems, we are likely to be sorely disappointed in these costly corrections experiments.

Moreover, control unit prison facilities are nothing new. As Hans Toch has observed, correctional policymakers have used the types of control techniques employed in supermax prisons at different times in the past. For example, the "Pennsylvania" system of prison discipline was developed in the late 1700s at the Walnut Street Jail in Philadelphia. The basic assumption of this system, based on the ideas of prison reformers including Benjamin Franklin and Benjamin Rush, was that prisoners should be placed in solitary confinement and not permitted to work. The assumption was that they would reflect on their crimes and become reformed. Eventually, the system's administrators realized that the prisoners had to be given activities such as work to occupy their time. Without meaningful activity, many inmates experience various forms of mental illness. Based on your knowledge of the history of our justice system, do you find it ironic that, as in the case of supermax prisons, we appear to be forever destined to repeat the past?

Another interesting aspect of the supermax prison debate is the role of the courts in assessing the conditions of confinement in these total institutions. As noted in the Introduction to this issue, since the late 1970s, U.S. courts have been highly deferential to the decisions of correctional administrators regarding the appropriate conditions of confinement in our nation's prisons. However, when a U.S. district court considered the conditions in the Pelican Bay State Prison, a supermax facility operated by the State of California, it found some of the conditions there to be intolerable constitutionally. In *Madrid v. Gomez*, 889 F. Supp. 1146 (1995), inmates confined at the Pelican Bay State Prison, a supermax facility operated by the State of California, filed a class action lawsuit challenging a broad range of conditions and practices that impacted almost every facet of their prison life. The inmates sought to have the conditions of confinement at Pelican Bay declared to be a violation of their civil rights and the U.S. Constitution. One portion of this huge lawsuit asserted that prison authorities had engaged in a pattern of using excessive force against the inmates. On this issue, the Court concluded:

> [T]he Court is compelled to conclude that the Eighth Amendment's restraint on using excessive force has been repeatedly violated at Pelican Bay, leading to a conspicuous pattern of excessive force. In many instances, there was either no justification for the use of force, or alternately, the use of force was appropriate, but the amount of force applied was so strikingly disproportionate to the circumstances that it was imposed, more likely than not for the very purpose of causing harm, rather than in a good faith effort to restore or maintain order.

Inmates in this case were not so successful with a number of their other claims, however. But, *Madrid v. Gomez* does appear to indicate that there is some reason to believe that the federal courts will intervene in state supermax conditions cases where there is a significant reason to believe that prison authorities are not acting in good faith.

Fortunately, there are additional resources that discuss the issues considered in this section. See, Lorna A. Rhodes, *Total Confinement: Madness and Reason in the Maximum Security Prison* (University of California Press, 2004); Michael Tonry (Ed.), *The Future of Imprisonment* (Oxford University Press, 2004); Harry L. Allen and Clifford E. Simonsen, *Corrections in America: An Introduction* (8th Ed.) (Prentice Hall, 1998); Lorna A. Rhodes, "Changing the Subject: Conversation in Supermax," *Cultural Anthropology* (vol. 20, no. 3, 2005); "United States: Hell on Earth; The Delights of Supermax Prisons," *The Economist* (April 2, 2005); Jesenia Pizarro and Vanja M. K. Stenius, "Supermax Prisons: Their Rise, Current Practices, and Effect on Inmates," *The Prison Journal* (vol. 84, no. 2, 2004); Mikel-Meredith Weidman, "The Culture of Judicial Deference and the Problem of Supermax Prisons," *UCLA Law Review* (vol. 51, no. 5, 2004); Chad S. Briggs, Jody L. Sundt, and Thomas C. Castellano, "The Effect of Supermax Security Prisons on Aggregate Levels of Institutional Violence," *Criminology* (vol. 41, no. 4, 2003); Hans Toch, "The Contemporary Relevance of Early Experiments with Supermax Reform," *The Prison Journal* (vol. 83, no. 2, 2003); Craig Haney, "Mental Health Issues in Long-Term Solitary and 'Supermax' Confinement," *Crime & Delinquency* (vol. 49, no. 1, 2003); Sasha Abramsky, "Return of the Madhouse," *The American Prospect* (vol. 13, no. 3, 2002); and Hans Toch, "The Future of Supermax Confinement," *The Prison Journal* (vol. 81, no. 3, 2001).

ISSUE 9

Do Three Strikes Sentencing Laws and Other "Get Tough" Approaches Really Work?

YES: Eugene H. Methvin, from "Mugged by Reality," *Policy Review* (July/August 1997)

NO: David Shichor, from "Three Strikes as a Public Policy," *Crime & Delinquency* (October 1997)

ISSUE SUMMARY

YES: Eugene H. Methvin, senior editor for *Reader's Digest*, contends that a very small number of juveniles and adults commit the majority of serious crimes. The main solution to the crime problem, then, is to identify them as early as possible and increase the punishments each time they offend, eventually incarcerating the repeat offenders.

NO: Professor of criminal justice David Shichor argues that "three strikes" laws are costly, inefficient, unfair, and do little to reduce crime.

The traditional approaches to crime are retribution (sometimes conceptually couched as vengeance or justice), deterrence, and incapacitation. Many criminologists and liberal politicians called for rehabilitation during the twentieth century. For a variety of reasons, including increasing fear of crime, significant increases in violent crimes in many areas, a shrinking economy, and the election in 1980 of a conservative president, there has been a decisive paradigmatic shift. Current constructions of the crime problem and responses to crime policies seem to ignore rehabilitation as a goal of incarceration.

"Criminals need to be locked up," many say these days, because they deserve to be punished, to deter others from doing the same thing, and to get bad people off the streets. Structural or environmental factors, with their concomitant theoretical response modalities, are forgotten by many. That is, racism, blocked opportunities, lack of education, poverty, and the like as theorized causes of crime implying a need for rehabilitation (such as job training, education, and improved opportunities) are seemingly receding rapidly into distant criminological memory.

Initially framed as federal law, now being replicated in different variants in 24 states, three-strikes criminal justice ideologically "makes sense" within the current *weltanschauungen* (world view). If an individual has already committed two serious felonies and now commits a third one, defenders argue, what can be more rational than making sure that he gets a very long sentence for his third crime? Studies show that a hard core of offenders, if taken off the streets, would save taxpayers hundreds of thousands of dollars a year. A life prison sentence would clearly incapacitate them. Individuals, then, would be deterred from committing their third crime, and general deterrence would result from others being afraid of being imprisoned for the remainder of their lives.

Supporters of tough sentencing laws also say, if criminals have already done terrible things and are obviously still doing them, justice would be served better by separating them from you and me. After all, what good has "rehabilitation" done them if they are still committing crimes?

In the second selection, David Shichor attempts to counter much of this by applying to penology four key concepts—efficiency, calculability, prediction, and control—derived from social theorist George Ritzer's "McDonaldization of society" theory. What distinguishes modern, industrial societies from all others is the bureaucratization of social and economic life. According to classic theorist Max Weber (1864–1920), whom both Shichor and Ritzer draw from, modernity necessitates increased rational behavior that is oriented to economic values over family and personal ones. Both market and social life are increasingly routinized, controlled, planned, and calculated. This enables increased productivity and industrial survival. However, as Weber warned with his prophecy of the "iron cage of the future" consequence, there is a tremendous cost: Life becomes more routinized and regimented. People and policies run the risk of becoming robot-like. Ritzer extends this argument to suggest that with increased technological efficiency comes a curvilinear relationship (a U-shaped curve). That is, after certain points, the "efficiency" and "savings" backfire, or become counterproductive and irrational.

As you wrestle with this important debate, notice Eugene H. Methvin's classifications of the types of offenders in the first selection. Which does he seem to be addressing? What does he see as the causes of crime? Are they sometimes contradictory? How often does Shichor actually prove that three strikes does not work as opposed to speculating that it *could* be a problem?

YES

Eugene H. Methvin

Mugged by Reality

The most serious offenders against people and property in this country generally hit their criminal peak between 16 and 18 years of age. The hard-core young thug-to-be starts stealing from mama's purse before he's 10. By the fourth and fifth grades, he is skipping school. As he enters his teens, he's gangbanging—and on the track to prison or an early violent death. Typically he is committing burglaries at about 15, armed robberies at 16, and often killing by 18—and sometimes much younger. After years of effort to contain the crime committed by these hoodlums, we know what works and what doesn't. At long last, we have all the knowledge we need to design an effective strategy for the prevention of crime.

1. Most serious crime is committed by a violent minority of predatory recidivists.

Criminologist Marvin Wolfgang compiled records of all of the 9,945 males born in 1945 and attending school in Philadelphia between the ages of 10 and 18. A mere 627—just under 7 percent—were chronic offenders, with five or more arrests by age 18. These so-called Dirty Seven Percenters committed more than half of all offenses and two-thirds of the violent crimes, including all the murders, that were committed by the entire cohort.

Wolfgang followed his "Class of '45" through its 30th year in 1975. Shockingly few offenders were incarcerated. Even the 14 murderers among them spent an average of only four years behind bars for these crimes. Worse, these hard-core criminals admitted in interviews that, for each arrest, they typically got away with 8 to 11 other serious crimes. Wolfgang found that 70 percent of juveniles arrested three times committed a fourth offense; of those, 80 percent not only committed a fifth offense, but kept at it through 20 or more. If the city's judges had sent each Dirty Seven Percenter to prison for just a year after his *third* offense, Wolfgang calculated, Philadelphians would have suffered 7,200 fewer serious crimes while they [were] off the streets.

Wolfgang's findings electrified the law-enforcement world. At the request of U.S. Attorney General Edward Levi, Wolfgang repeated the study on the 13,160 Philadelphian males born in 1958. The proportion of chronic offenders was virtually the same: 982 young men (7.5 percent) collected five or more arrests before age 18. But the crimes committed by the "Class of '58" were

From *Policy Review,* no. 84, July/August 1997, pp. 32–38. Copyright © 1997 by Heritage Foundation. Reprinted by permission.

bloodier and far more frequent. Compared with the Class of '45, these youths were twice as likely to commit rape and aggravated assault, three times more likely to murder, and five times more likely to commit robbery. They were, concluded Wolfgang, "a very violent criminal population of a small number of nasty, brutal offenders. They begin early in life and should be controlled equally early."

Other studies with different methodologies corroborated Wolfgang's approximate finding of 7 percent in places as different as London; Copenhagen; Orange County, California; Racine, Wisconsin; Columbus, Ohio; Phoenix, Arizona; and Salt Lake City, Utah.

2. *A minority of this minority is extraordinarily violent, persistent, or both.*

They are "Super Predators," far more dangerous than the rest. Researchers for Rand questioned 2,190 prisoners convicted of robbery in California, Texas, and Michigan. Nearly all admitted to many more crimes than those for which they were jailed. But a tiny fraction of these career criminals proved to be *extraordinarily* frequent offenders. The least active 50 percent of burglars averaged a little under six burglaries a year, while the most prolific 10 percent averaged more than 230. The least active 50 percent of the robbers committed five robberies a year on average, but the top 10 percent averaged 87. The distribution of drug-dealing offenses was even more skewed: Half of these convicts did 100 deals a year on average, while the highest tenth averaged 3,251.

Sociologist Delbert S. Elliott of the University of Colorado has tracked a nationally representative sample of 1,725 boys and girls who were between 11 and 17 years old in 1976. By 1989, 369 of them had committed one or more serious, violent offenses. But only 32 were high-rate offenders. Year after year, those in this small group committed an average of 30 violent crimes each and hundreds of lesser crimes. Just under 2 percent of the whole, they accounted for half the serious crimes committed by the entire group. These Super Predators distinguish themselves by their arrest records, by the early age at which they first tangle with the law, and by the seriousness of their early offenses. Nationally, we can crudely estimate the current crop of young "super felons" at about 500,000 of our 26.7 million 11- to 17-year-olds.

3. *Most of these persistent predators are criminal psychopaths, and we now have a scientifically valid instrument to identify them with reasonable accuracy.*

Psychopaths are responsible for more than half of all serious crimes. The normal criminal has an internalized set of values, however warped, and he feels guilt whenever he violates his standards. The psychopath doesn't even know what guilt is, because he has never experienced it. But he is good at *faking* it.

Even within prison populations, psychopaths stand out because their antisocial and illegal behavior is more varied and frequent than that of ordinary criminals. In prisons and mental hospitals, they are generally the nastiest inmates. They are more resistant to treatment, more likely to try to escape, and more violent with other inmates and the staff. After they are released, they re-offend at four to five times the rate of other criminals. Psychopaths constitute an estimated 1 to 2 percent of the population—and 20 to 25 percent of our prison population. This means the United States has at least *2 million* psychopaths.

After 25 years of research, psychologist Robert D. Hare of the University of British Columbia developed a reliable instrument for diagnosing psychopathy: the Hare Psychopathy Check List [PCL]. After interviewing relatives and associates and studying criminal and other records, a trained clinician interviews the subject and scores him on 20 personality traits and behaviors characteristic of this personality disorder. Is the person glib, manipulative, a liar, sexually promiscuous, grandiose in his sense of self-worth, impulsive, averse to boredom, incapable of remorse? Was he trouble from an early age? Does he have a juvenile and adult arrest record? Has he had many short-term marital relationships? And so on.

Hare, in his 1993 book *Without Conscience: The Disturbing World of Psychopaths Among Us,* says: "Psychopaths are social predators who charm, manipulate, and ruthlessly plow their way through life, leaving a broad trail of broken hearts, shattered expectations, and empty wallets. Completely lacking in conscience and feelings for others, they selfishly take what they want and do as they please, violating social norms and expectations without the slightest sense of guilt or regret."

Studies of Canadian and American convicts released from prison show that only about 20 percent of the low scorers on the PCL are re-arrested within three years, but 80 percent of the high scorers end up back behind bars.

The PCL can be a powerful tool for prison administrators, parole boards, judges, and others who must cope with this extraordinarily destructive population. High scorers are poor risks for probation or parole and good candidates for maximum sentences in higher security institutions. Maryland prison officials have used the PCL to assess some 10,000 inmates. It has enabled them to divert low scorers from costly maximum-security facilities into lower-cost units or parole, freeing up 1,100 prison beds a day, which yields $19.8 million in savings a year. Moreover, the state has avoided an estimated $55 million in new prison construction. Canada, New Zealand, the United Kingdom, and most American states are now using the PCL in their prison systems.

4. *Savvy police, prosecutors, and judges can identify and isolate high-rate violent predators.*

In Miami, sociologist James A. Inciardi used a "snowballing" interview technique to find them. He sent researchers into high-crime neighborhoods to talk to youngsters about "who's doing drugs" and "who's into crime." They found 611 youngsters ages 12 to 17 who admitted to multiple crimes and repeated drug use. Ninety percent of them had been arrested, an equal proportion had been thrown out of school, and almost half had been incarcerated. Typically they began to use alcohol at age seven and turned to crime and drugs at 11; almost two-thirds had participated in a robbery by the age of 13. The interviewees confessed to a total of 429,136 criminal acts during the year prior to their interviews—more than 700 each, or nearly two a day. Of these acts,

18,477, or 30 apiece, were major felonies, including 6,269 robberies and 721 assaults. Nearly 18 percent had committed armed robberies, as young as 14, and 90 percent carried weapons most of the time. Among this violent crowd, 361 committed the 6,269 robberies—an average of 17 each—and two-thirds of them robbed before the age of 13.

If sociologists can find the Super Predators, police can, too. William Bratton proved it, first in New York City's subway system in 1990, then citywide after Mayor Rudolph Giuliani named him police commissioner in 1994. By 1990, the New York subway had become a lawless jungle. Riders were deserting by the tens of thousands. An estimated 180,000 fare evaders jumped the turnstiles every day, costing the system $65 million a year. Vandals jammed coin slots and opened exit doors; aggressive panhandlers threatened riders on the cars; muggers stole their tokens and money. Violent teenagers prowled the subways in "wolfpacks."

As the chief of New York's 4,000 transit police offices, Bratton created strategies for winnowing out the criminal minority. He ordered uniformed officers to enforce all subway rules. He planted plainclothes teams to arrest fare evaders. Each of them was searched; one in 14 was arrested for packing illegal guns, and one out of seven was wanted on previous criminal warrants. Whenever detectives caught one mugger, they extracted information about other wolfpack members. They also tracked down a group of about 75 hardcore graffiti vandals. Bratton insisted that his officers act on bench warrants for subway crimes within 24 hours. Their apprehension rate rose sharply to more than 60 percent. The hunters became the hunted. Bratton's strategies cut subway crime by two-thirds—and robberies by three-fourths. Fare evaders were reduced by two-thirds, too. Riders returned by the ten of thousands. By 1994 New York's subways were the scene of fewer than 20 felonies a day, down 64 percent in five years.

Named in 1994 to head the whole police department, Bratton and his deputy commissioner, Jack Maple, implemented a strategy of "relentless pursuit." Bratton personally urged officers to cite citizens for "quality of life" offenses such as drinking beer in public, smoking marijuana, or urinating in the street, and to frisk offenders for illegal weapons at the slightest suspicion. Maple launched a campaign to remind officers to interrogate every arrestee. Talented interrogators created a three-day "verbal judo" course at the police academy to teach officers how to extract information from suspects. New York's cops responded enthusiastically, and with dramatic results. A topless dancer arrested for prostitution fingered the bouncer at her Brooklyn club in an unsolved murder. A car thief turned in a fence, who then turned in a father-son gun-dealing team. A parolee arrested for failing to report turned out to have been the only eyewitness to a drug-related murder.

This campaign produced "a miracle happening before our eyes," says Jeffrey Fagan, the director of Columbia University's Center for Violence Research and Prevention. From 1994 to 1996, New York City's murders declined by 49 percent, robberies 43 percent, burglaries 39 percent, and grand larcenies 32 percent. In 1995, the city accounted for 70 percent of the heralded national decline in serious crimes.

5. The rehabilitation ideal of the juvenile-court system leads to costly coddling of serious and persistent offenders.

Studies show that youths who land in juvenile court a second time will likely become chronic offenders. Howard N. Snyder, a researcher with the National Council of Family and Juvenile Court Judges, analyzed the records of 48,311 boys who went through juvenile courts in Utah and Arizona. More than half never returned after the first trip. But most of those who landed in court a second time before their 16th birthdays became persistent repeaters, and the earlier their first prosecution, the more likely they were to be violent chronics.

It is important to note that a troublesome youngster typically has 10 to 12 contacts with the criminal-justice system and many more undiscovered offenses before he ever receives any formal "adjudication," or finding of guilt, from a judge. He quickly concludes that he will never face any serious consequences for his delinquency. For each young chronic offender who comes before him, a juvenile-court judge typically moves toward more severe punishments and costly interventions in five or more small steps. Snyder recommends that judges impose upon second-time convicts stiffer penalties and the more intense (and costly) rehabilitation programs. Waiting until the fourth or fifth offense to do so only wastes court time and money—and looses serious crime upon the public.

In Richmond, Virginia, a juvenile-court psychologist estimated that court costs, rehabilitation efforts, and incarceration for just 14 defendants who cycled through her court regularly totaled more than $2 million. Welfare, food stamps, court-appointed lawyers, and other services over the years swelled their cost to taxpayers to more than $5 million. She tracked 56 young men locked in the youth-detention center over one five-day period. On average, they were 15 years old and had compiled 12 arrests apiece for crimes of escalating severity. Social-service agencies had intervened in their lives at an average age of nine, and their criminal activity began four years later, on average, though some started as early as age seven. Their offenses ranged from curfew violation to rape and murder. A year later, one-third had graduated to adult prisons. Three-fourths were still incarcerated or faced new charges or warrants. Almost all those older than 15 who had been released faced new charges.

6. Punishment works—and the United States has barely tried it.

Psychologist Sarnoff A. Mednick of the University of Southern California studied the records of thousands of Danish criminals and discovered that punishment is very effective in deterring crime. He compared the criminal histories of thousands of offenders in Copenhagen and Philadelphia who had exactly four or five arrests. Those who received four punishments in a row for their crimes were unlikely to have a fifth arrest. But those who had been punished irregularly after the earlier arrests were more likely to be arrested again.

Mednick studied 28,879 males born in Copenhagen between 1944 and 1947 who lived there through age 26. He found that 6,579 had at least one arrest. The third of arrestees who were not punished went on to commit far more crimes. Mednick found 3,809 offenders were punished after every single arrest, while 2,793 were not. Those who escaped punishment committed three times as many crimes as those consistently punished. Punishment delivered after every offense significantly reduced later offenses. But an offender who was punished for early crimes and received none for later offenses resumed criminal activity at the higher rates.

It made little difference whether the punishment was fines, probation, or incarceration. Consistent delivery of sanctions was more effective than intermittent sanctions, and criminal recidivism recovered when punishment was discontinued. Severity of sanction also made little difference: Longer jail terms, higher fines, and longer probations did not decrease subsequent offenses more than lighter sanctions did.

"Punishment is very effective in suppressing crime, and it does not have to be severe if you get on them early enough," says Mednick. "The way to reduce prison populations is to punish offenders from their first offense with graduated, increasingly severe and certain sanctions. But the records show we do not do that in America." Mednick compared the Danish criminals to those in Marvin Wolfgang's Philadelphia cohort studies. The Philadelphia figures confirmed the effectiveness of punishment, but he also found that only 14 percent of the four- and five-time offenders in the Philadelphia cohorts were punished, compared with 60 percent of those in Denmark.

"The big problem with our handling of criminals in America is that they're not punished," he wrote. "People are usually surprised to hear that, because of all our prisons. But the fact is by the time a guy makes his way to jail, that's very often his first punishment. And he usually has committed 15 offenses by then. He might have been arrested 10 times. In Philadelphia, the kids committed huge numbers of offenses, and serious ones, and nothing happened. They just laughed. Our laws provide severe punishments, but . . . they deter not the criminals but the judges. They don't want to throw a kid who's done some little thing in jail, so they just let him go."

7. *Prisons work, and they are a relative bargain.*

Critics of incarceration claim it has failed because about two-thirds of those released soon land back behind bars. But these studies begin with a batch of released convicts, and each batch contains a high proportion of repeaters who cycle through the revolving doors of justice. Moreover, criminologists have found that these hard-core repeaters get away with a dozen or more serious crimes for every arrest. But two-thirds to three-fourths of criminals sent to prison for the first time never return.

One study that tracked the careers of 6,310 California prisoners released in 1962–63 revealed a shocking picture. These were hard-core criminals: 56 percent had been in prison before, and 44 percent served time for violent crimes, burglary, or robbery. Over the next 26 years, these convicts were arrested 30,464 times, and were probably responsible for more than a quarter-million unsolved crimes. More than half the arrests were nuisance offenses such as parole violations, drunk driving, and disorderly conduct. But the ex-cons were also arrested for about 10,000 serious crimes, including 184 homicides, 2,084 assaults, 126 kidnappings, 144 rapes, 2,756 burglaries, 655 auto thefts, and 1,193 robberies. California could have kept all 5,192 second-termers locked away for an estimated cost of only $2.1 billion—a real bargain in public safety.

Patrick A. Langan, a statistician at the U.S. Department of Justice, calculates that, by doubling the number of criminals in prison from 1973 to 1982, the United States reduced reported crime by 10 to 20 percent. This amounted to 66,000 to 190,000 fewer robberies and 350,000 to 900,000 fewer burglaries in 1982 alone. By tripling the prison population from 1975 to 1989, Langan estimates, we prevented 390,000 murders, rapes, robberies, and aggravated assaults just in 1989.

California tripled its prison population in the decade after 1984—and achieved a significant drop in the rates of reported crime from its peak in 1980–81. Bucking nationwide trends, by 1993 California had reduced murders by 10.4 percent, rapes by 36 percent, and burglaries by a whopping 43 percent. By the 1990s, that meant nearly 1,000 fewer murders, 16,000 fewer robberies, and a quarter of a million fewer burglaries yearly. The overall serious crime rate fell 14 percent.

The American public is catching on. In 1990, Oregon voters passed, by a margin of three to one, an anti-crime initiative that requires a criminal convicted of a second violent offense to serve his entire sentence with no parole. In November 1993, voters in Washington state passed by a similar margin a "three strikes and you're out" law, which imposes automatic life sentences for three-time felony convicts. Within two years, 14 states altogether and Congress had adopted such laws.

California has been a leader in the "three strikes" movement. The state automatically doubles the sentence for a felon with a prior conviction for a serious or violent felony. A third felony of any sort can trigger a life sentence, with eligibility for parole after 25 years. Philip J. Romero, Governor Pete Wilson's chief economist, estimates that the new law will add an extra 8,300 convicts a year to the state's prison population and will cost $6.5 billion for new prisons in the first five years—but will save society $23 billion net in crime prevented. A Rand study concluded that the new California law, if fully implemented, will cut serious felonies committed by adults between 22 and 34 percent.

In 1994, the American Legislative Exchange Council, the largest bipartisan association of state legislators, published a stunning analysis of prison populations and crime rates in all 50 states. The 10 states that increased their prison populations the most in relation to serious crimes between 1980 and 1992 cut their crime rates by an average of 19 percent. Meanwhile, the 10 states with the smallest increases in incarceration rates saw their crime rates go up by 9 percent on average.

In the 1980s, New Hampshire's legislature executed one of the sharpest policy reversals in the nation. For 20 years, legislators had added little new prison capacity, and the imprisonment rate—the number of prisoners per 1,000 crimes—declined by more than 80 percent, the third sharpest decline of any state. Meanwhile crime had soared by 579 percent, the highest increase in the nation.

All that changed after convicted killer Edward Coolidge, while serving a prison sentence of 25 to 40 years, was released after 18 years with "time off for good behavior." Coolidge had murdered Pamela Mason, a teenaged baby-sitter, and left her abused body in a snow bank. Outraged at his early release, Mason's family started a statewide petition drive for a "truth in sentencing" law to require convicts to serve their minimum sentences in full. Legislators passed the law in 1984 and appropriated $65 million for new prison construction. As a result, New Hampshire increased its incarceration rate between 1980 and 1992 more than any state. In the meantime, crime declined by 34 percent, the steepest drop in the nation.

> 8. *Families are the first line of defense, and we now know how to target and help children raised in our "cradles of crime."*

Experts agree that criminal behavior patterns crystallize by the age of eight, and sometimes much sooner. After age eight, youngsters are less likely to respond to correctional treatment as they gravitate toward truancy, street gangs, violent crime, and prison or early death. In Bellingham, Washington, Detective Steve Lance, who directs a police unit that targets serious habitual offenders who are juveniles, echoes: "If we wait until they're eight, it's too late. We've got to get them when they're *two.*"

Dozens of scientific studies back up the cop's street wisdom. For 60 years, criminologists and psychologists have tracked thousands of youngsters from early childhood into their adult years, identifying the risk factors and early warning signs of delinquency and persistent crime. In recent decades, they have carefully evaluated various early interventions and correctional treatments, comparing treated youngsters to matched groups of untreated ones, winnowing what works and what doesn't. Today we know that the typical "cradles of crime" are households headed by poor unwed mothers who bore their first children as teenagers and live on welfare, usually in public housing with others like them, with few law-abiding, employed male role models among them. Seventy percent of the juvenile offenders in our state reform institutions grew up in a household with only one parent or no parent at all. Children whose mothers are teenagers when they are born have a 10.3 percent chance of landing in jail as juveniles, triple that of children whose mothers bore them between the ages of 20 and 23.

A number of early-childhood intervention programs have been shown to knock many high-risk youngsters off the track to crime, prison, and possible early violent death:

New York Syracuse University's Family Development Research Program experimented with a concentrated five-year child-care program for the group at highest risk for child-abuse and neglect complaints: poor, mostly single, pregnant teen-agers who had not completed high school. Sixty-five of the women received prenatal health care and two years of weekly home visits by specialists who taught parenting skills, provided counseling in employment and education, and encouraged friends and family to help. Until their children entered public school, they received free day care at the University Children's Center, which aims to develop children's intellectual abilities.

At age 15, the delinquency rate of these kids was 89 percent lower than that of a control group. Moreover, the few who had tangled with the law committed less serious and fewer offenses than their counterparts. The untreated youngsters had cost the criminal-justice system alone—excluding injuries or property losses to victims—$1,985 apiece, compared with $186 per treated child.

Michigan   David Weikart, a University of Michigan doctoral candidate, randomly chose for a two-year enrichment program 58 three- and four-year-old black children from a poor Ypsilanti neighborhood with a terrible school failure rate. The program kids attended daily two-hour classes in small groups with a specialist in the teaching of language through play. Counselors visited their homes weekly to reinforce class activities and to teach the mothers parenting skills.

By the time they turned 27, the pre-schooled group earned higher grades and were more likely to have graduated, found well-paying jobs, and formed stable families than those in a control group. Even more sensational, the preschooled group averaged half the arrests of the control group, and only a fifth as many had been arrested five or more times. For every $1 spent on early enrichment, taxpayers realized $7.16 in benefits, mostly in savings from crimes prevented.

Quebec   Richard Trembley, a psychologist from the University of Montreal, tracked 104 of the most disruptive boys from 53 kindergartens. He gave 46 of the boys and their families two years of special training. Parents on average took part in 20 one-hour sessions in how to monitor their children's behavior, praise and punish effectively, and handle family crises. Their boys got 19 sessions in how to make friends, invite others to play, handle anger, respond to rejection and teasing, and follow rules. Five years later, when the boys were 12, the proportion of those who had been involved in gang mischief, a precursor of serious delinquency, was one-tenth that of the untreated youths.

The popular "Head Start" program was also modeled on the Ypsilanti experiment's successes. But, says James Q. Wilson, a political scientist at UCLA, bureaucrats and policymakers "stripped it down to the part that was the most popular, least expensive, and easiest to run, namely, preschool education. Absent from much of Head Start are the high teacher-to-child caseloads, the extensive home visits, and the elaborate parent training—the very things that probably account for much of the success of these programs."

A National Strategy

In outline, a strategy for reducing crime through prevention and punishment would look like this: We should identify the families—mostly households started by unwed teenage mothers—that are likely to be "cradles of crime." For a modest investment, we can sharply reduce the likelihood that their children will engage in persistent criminality by providing educational enrichment, parenting advice, and training in disciplined behavior. In pre-school or first or second grades, we can apply screening techniques at school to find those youngsters with a high risk of troubled futures. At the first contact with police, we should begin keeping permanent records. At the second offense, at the latest, we should bring to bear our best efforts at intensive supervision and family intervention, and impose the first of a series of unequivocal and escalating sanctions. Jailing serious three-time offenders would be a prudent alternative to suffering the millions of crimes habitual criminals perpetrate each year. We should insist that police and prosecutors learn to identify and pursue repeat offenders aggressively. We should hold judges and parole boards accountable for sentencing and incarcerating those felons for whom intervention has come too late, and we should not shrink from investing in the prison space needed to keep recidivists off the streets for good.

It is both humane and smart to turn delinquent youngsters away from a path of crime early, but in cases where all these efforts ultimately fail, in the words of the late sociologist Robert Martinson, "Lock 'em up and weld the door shut!" Our crime rates will plummet.

David Shichor  **NO**

Three Strikes as a Public Policy

Introduction

Street crime has become one of the major public concerns in the United States during the past two decades. In response to it, several "war on crime" campaigns have been waged since the 1970s, and there is a growing public demand to get "tough on crime" and to get even tougher on violent and repeating criminals. . . . In the spring of 1994, the U.S. prison population passed the 1 million mark and the nation gained the dubious honor of having the highest incarceration rate in the world. By 1996, the U.S. jail and prison population was around the 1.5 million mark.

. . . [T]he Violent Crime Control and Law Enforcement Act, also known as the Federal Crime Bill, was enacted by Congress [in 1994]. Among other things, this law "mandates life in prison for criminals convicted of three violent felonies or drug offenses if the third conviction is a federal crime." It became labeled, using the popular baseball lingo, as the "three strikes and you're out" law. Several states followed suit and enacted similar measures. One of those mentioned most often was the California mandatory sentencing law, which came into effect in March 1994 and prescribes that "felons found guilty of a third serious crime be locked up for 25 years to life." . . .

This article focuses on the "three-strikes" laws in general with particular emphasis on the California measure because that law has been the most scrutinized and quoted in the professional literature so far. Although there are differences in some of the details among the various three-strikes laws, their main aims and principles are similar.

Several scholars maintain that recent penal thinking and the ensuing policies have gone through a major paradigm change. According to them, a "new penology" has emerged shifting the traditional penological concern that focused on the individual offender to an actuarial model focusing on the management of aggregates. . . .

The analysis to follow examines three-strikes laws in relation to the new penology and in relation to their connections to a more general sociocultural orientation, identified by Ritzer (1993) as the "McDonaldization" of society, based on the rationalization process suggested by Max Weber (one of the pioneers of sociological thought), that is embodied in the model of fast-food restaurants. . . .

From *Crime & Delinquency*, vol. 43, no.4, October 1997, pp. 470–476, 480–487. Copyright © 1997 by Sage Publications. Reprinted by permission via Rightslink.

Three Strikes and the New Penology

. . . The change from penal policies aimed at punishment and rehabilitation of individuals to the management and control of certain categories of people has followed the pessimism expressed about the criminal justice system's ability to change offenders, making them into law-abiding citizens. In this vein, Bottoms noted that "the abandonment of the rehabilitative ethic has led to a widespread abandonment of hope" because the idea of rehabilitation was an expression of optimism about human nature and about the ability of social organizations to bring out the positive in people. The new penology takes for granted that a high level of criminal behavior will continue to occur, and its concern is how to manage the criminal justice system efficiently rather than to effect major changes in crime rates or to bring about rehabilitation of a significant number of offenders.

The new penology has rekindled the historical notion of "dangerous classes" that traditionally has been linked to the urban poor. Feeley and Simon (1992) claimed that the new penology is oriented toward the management of a "permanently dangerous population." Their description of this population parallels Wilson's (1987) depiction of the "underclass," which, because of the social realities of capitalist industrial societies in which production is based on a high level of technology and a reduction of manual labor, became a marginal population, unemployable, lacking in adequate education and marketable skills, and without any real prospects or hope to change its situation. . . .

The new penal approach, focusing on the control and management of specific aggregates, has made increasing use of actuarial methods that rely heavily on statistical decision theory, operations research techniques, and system analysis to devise and implement penal policies. These reflect the positivist orientation in criminology that concentrates on "methods, techniques, or rules of procedure" rather than on "substantive theory or perspectives." . . .

Three-strikes laws have historical roots in American penology. . . . They are based on the penal principle of incapacitation. . . . In theory, three-strikes laws were meant to target repeating violent and dangerous felons, similar to "selective incapacitation" strategies. . . .

Simon and Feeley (1994) criticized the three-strikes measures, stating, "This spate of three-strikes laws as well as other types of mandatory sentences can easily be characterized as mindless 'spending sprees' or 'throwing money at a problem' without likelihood of benefit." . . .

The McDonaldization of Punishment

In a recent book, Ritzer (1993) used the analogy of fast-food establishments to characterize and analyze the social and cultural ethos of modern technological societies, particularly that of the United States. He defined McDonaldization as "the process by which the principles of the fast-food restaurant are coming to dominate more and more sectors of American society as well as the rest of the world." This process also has a major impact on the social control policies of these societies. The theoretical underpinnings of the three-strikes measures, their definitions of strikeable offenses, and the wide-scale public support of these types of legislation are closely related to, and are influenced by, McDonaldization.

In this model, which is based on the Weberian concept of "formal rationality" (Weber 1968), there are four basic dimensions of the fast-food industry: efficiency, calculability, predictability, and control. Efficiency refers to the tendency to choose the optimum means to a given end, calculability is identified as the tendency to quantify and calculate every product and to use quantity as a measure of quality, predictability has to do with the preference to know what to expect in all situations at all times, and control involves the replacement of human technology with nonhuman technology in a way that goods, services, products, and workers are better controlled. Ritzer (1993) suggested that there are various degrees of McDonaldization and that some phenomena are more McDonaldized than others. As mentioned previously, the contention of this article is that three-strikes laws are promoting punishment policies in accordance with this model. . . .

The Irrational Consequences of McDonaldization in Penology

Three-strikes laws and McDonaldization are phenomena of modernization that put a high value on rationality. However, although McDonaldization represents rationalism (i.e., scientific approach, positivism, modernity), it also leads to irrational consequences. Borrowing from Weber's concept of the "iron cage of rationality," Ritzer referred to these consequences as the "irrationality of rationality." In the case of McDonaldization, irrationalities may result in inefficiency, incalculability, unpredictability, and lack of control, which may have serious effects on penal policies and practices.

Inefficiency

One of the inefficiencies of fast-food sites is that although they are meant to be "fast," often long lines of people have to wait to be served (Ritzer 1993). In the criminal justice system, three-strikes laws contribute to the clogging up of courts and the overcrowding of confinement facilities. The measure also seems to have had a major impact on the number of cases that go to trial. In California before the new law came into effect in March 1994, about 90% to 94% of all criminal cases were settled through plea bargaining. But in the summer of that year, Santa Clara County projected a 160% increase in the number of criminal trials. In an assessment of the preliminary impacts of the three-strikes implementation for the first eight months, the California Legislative Analyst's Office (1995b) found a 144% increase in jury trials in Los Angeles County. In San Diego County, it is expected that there will be a 300% increase in jury trials. The decline in plea bargaining is the result of the mandatory aspect of the three-strikes law. Many offenders feel that they cannot gain much from a negotiated settlement under the new law and that it is preferable to exercise their constitutional right to jury trials without increasing their risks of substantially more severe sentences. The increase in the number of trials not only has affected the three-strikes cases but also has caused delays in nonstrike criminal and civil cases. For example, Los Angeles district attorney transferred a large number of attorneys who previously were handling white-collar cases to work on three-strikes offenses.

The growing backlog in the courts also has had an impact on county jails because more suspects are detained for longer periods of time prior to their trials. . . .

Another efficiency issue is concerned with the type of offenders handled by the three-strikes law. This law was enacted to curb violent crime, or at least "serious" crime, through the incapacitation of "dangerous" and violent criminals. However, early findings in California indicate that most offenders prosecuted and convicted under this measure have been brought into the system for nonviolent offenses. Furthermore, this measure inevitably will increase the numbers of elderly inmates in prisons because of the long terms mandated in this legislation. In 1994, inmates age 50 years or older represented about 4% of the California prison population, but it was estimated that by 2005 they will constitute around 12% of the inmates. . . .

According to all indications, the three-strikes law will increase considerably the cost of criminal justice operations because (a) more people will be detained in jails, (b) the increase in the number of trials will necessitate the building of more courts and the hiring of more judges and other court personnel, (c) the number of long-term prisoners will grow and so more prisons will have to be built, (d) the growing number of elderly prisoners will need additional (and more expensive) health care than prisons usually provide, and (e) welfare agencies will have to support a larger number of dependents of incarcerated felons for longer periods of time than ever before.

. . . Greenwood et al. (1994) projected that, in California, "to support the implementation of the law, total spending for higher education and other services would have to fall by more than 40 percent over the next 8 years."

Incalculability

The outcomes of three-strikes cases, which were supposedly easily calculable, often are not so. . . .

For example, because of overcrowding of jails by detainees who were reluctant to plea bargain, many minor offenders have been released early from jail, and a large number of misdemeanants have not even been prosecuted. Thus, the calculability of punishment for minor offenders has been neglected and even sacrificed for that of three-strikes offenders. In other instances, some arrests that could have been qualified as three-strikes cases have been processed as parole violations rather than new offenses and, thus, were not considered as felonies.

In other cases, prosecutors and judges have ignored some previous felonies or redefined them as nonstrike offenses. . . .

[L]ittle concern has been paid to the concept of justice that requires a balance between the seriousness of the crime and the severity of punishment. In 1994, a California offender was sentenced to prison for 25 years to life for grabbing a slice of pepperoni pizza from a youngster (this sentence was reduced in January 1997, and he will be released by 1999). Another offender received 30 years to life for stealing a video recorder and a coin collection. Still another three-striker got 25 years to life for stealing a package of meat worth $5.62, apparently to feed his family. More recently, a heroin addict with a record of previous theft-related offenses was sentenced to 25 years to life for stealing two pair of jeans worth $80 from a store. . . . Similarly, another aspect of justice, equal treatment, is being neglected because three-strikes measures focus almost exclusively on street crimes that usually are committed by poor offenders. Meanwhile, crimes of the middle and upper classes either are not affected or will be handled even more leniently than before because the criminal justice system that is overoccupied by predatory street crimes will have diminishing resources to deal with them. . . . Thus, the implementation of this measure will increase perceptions, which already are pervasive among many, that the criminal justice system is biased, discriminatory, and unjust.

Another factor that adds to the incalculability of this measure is that it is not applied uniformly. Data pertaining to the first six months of implementation compiled by the Los Angeles Public Defender's Office indicate that minorities with criminal histories comparable to those of White offenders were being charged under the three-strikes law at 17 times the rate of Whites. . . .

Unpredictability

Several of the issues concerning predictability resemble those that emerged in relation to efficiency and calculability. For various reasons, the outcomes of three-strikes cases are not as clearly predictable as they were intended to be, based on this law's mandatory and determinate nature. For example, in some instances victims refuse to testify when the convictions would carry sentences of long-term incarceration under the three-strikes law. In other cases, juries may fail to convict for the same reason. . . .

[B]ecause of jail overcrowding caused by the growing numbers of detainees waiting for trials, many sheriff departments release minor offenders early to ease the situation. Sometimes this is done because of court orders that limit facility crowding. According to court sources, in Los Angeles County, misdemeanor offenders sentenced to one year in jail are serving on the average only 19 days. Thus, the implementation of the three-strikes law, instead of increasing the predictability of punishment, may have an opposite impact in nonstrike cases. Moreover, . . . the outcome of a case under this law may be entirely different from what was foreseen because juries may refuse to convict, authorities may refuse to press a felony charge, or the courts may not count previous felonies. Also, by decreasing considerably the number of plea bargains and by increasing the number of jury trials, a larger number of outcomes may become unpredictable. Although plea bargaining should not be considered as the best method of dispensing justice, it does provide a certain level of predictability. . . .

[T]hree-strikes laws cannot predict, and are not interested in predicting, the effects of the punishment on individual convicts, and they may waste a great deal of money, time, and effort on false positives by keeping those who would not cause further harm to society incarcerated for long periods of time. . . . Three-strikes legislation was based on the assumption that the high rate of criminal behavior of "dangerous" offenders already has been proven; however, many times it is dependent on how the offenders' criminal records are being used by the prosecution and the courts. . . .

Lack of Control

Rational systems often can spin out of the control of those who devise and use them (Ritzer 1993). Sentencing based on an almost automatic decision-making system drastically reduces the court's authority to consider particular circumstances of offenses and individual differences among offenders. However, there are experts who maintain that to render a high quality of justice, a certain degree of judicial discretion is essential. . . .

There also is the issue of "hidden discretion"; that is, whereas the court's decision-making power in the imposition of punishment is severely curtailed, the discretion of law enforcement, and especially that of the prosecution, increases greatly. The charges brought against a suspect will be determined by these agencies. The major discretionary decision in many instances will be whether a case should be filed as a misdemeanor or a felony, which bears directly on the application of three-strikes laws. . . . [T]he ability of the judicial system to control the imposition and administration of the law will be affected. In many instances, the lack of control will stem not from the latitude in sentencing but rather from the growing discretionary powers given to agencies in the pretrial stages of the criminal justice process. Because of the reduced visibility of decision making in the determination of charges, in many cases sentencing disparities among jurisdictions may become even greater in spite of the promise of increased control over such differences under three-strikes laws.

. . . Many three-strikes cases involve property offenders and drug abusers rather than vicious, violent criminals. . . .

Conclusion

The three-strikes laws that have spread recently in the United States are a reaction to a moral panic that has swept the country since the late 1970s. On the public policy level, these measures can be viewed as being related to the new penology trend. They are based on the concern for managing aggregates of "dangerous" people rather than being concerned with rendering justice, protecting the community, or attempting to rehabilitate individual offenders. The emphasis is on rational criminal justice operations that apply management methods based on statistical estimates of patterns of crimes and future inmate populations, risk indicators of future criminal behavior, operations research, and system analysis.

Three-strikes laws also are in line with the modern sociocultural ethos of McDonaldization (Ritzer 1993), a model built on the principles of rationality embodying an attitude that "it is possible to calculate and purposively manipulate the environment." However, the quest for extreme rationality can lead to irrationalities in the practical workings of this model. Often, the application of three-strikes laws results in inefficiency of the criminal justice process, punishments are not always clearly calculable, predictability of outcomes may be negatively affected by rational procedures, and the system may lose control over the nature of punishment. In short, as is the case with many other public policies, three-strikes laws could lead to a host of unintended consequences that may defeat the purposes for which they were intended. Probably, the greatest irrationality of the penal policy represented by three-strikes laws is their tremendous economic cost. . . . In sum, it seems that, as Ritzer claimed, modern contemporary society is locked into the "iron cage of rationality," which is characterized by policies made on a rational basis that lead to irrational consequences. This is demonstrated in current penal policies.

References

Greenwood, Peter W., C. Peter Rydell, Allan F. Abrahamse, Jonathan P. Caulkins, James Chiesa, Karyn E. Model, and Stephen P. Klein. 1994. *Three Strikes and You're Out: Estimated Benefits and Costs of California's New Mandatory Sentencing Law*. Santa Monica, CA: RAND.

Irwin, John and James Austin. 1994. *It Is About Time: America's Imprisonment Binge*. Belmont, CA: Wadsworth.

Kramer, John H. and Jeffery T. Ulmer. 1996. "Sentencing Disparity and Departures From Guidelines." *Justice Quarterly* 13: 81–105.

McCarthy, Nancy. 1995. "A Year Later, '3 Strikes' Clogs Jails, Slows Trials." *California Bar Journal*, March: 1, 6–7.

Ritzer, George. 1993. *The McDonaldization of Society*. Newbury Park, CA: Pine Forge.

Saint-Germain, Michelle A. and Robert A. Calamia. 1996. "Three Strikes and You're In: A Streams and Windows Model Incremental Policy Change." *Journal of Criminal Justice* 24: 57–70.

Shichor, David and Dale K. Sechrest. 1996. "Three Strikes as Public Policy: Future Implications." pp. 265–77 in *Three Strikes and You're Out: Vengeance as Public Policy*, edited by D. Shichor and D. K. Sechrest. Thousand Oaks, CA: Sage.

Turner, Michael G., Jody L. Sundt, Brandon K. Applegate, and Francis T. Cullen. 1995. " 'Three Strikes and You're Out' Legislation: A National Assessment." *Federal Probation* 59 (3): 16–35.

Weber, Max. 1968. *Economy and Society*. Totowa, NJ: Bedminster.

POSTSCRIPT

Do Three Strikes Sentencing Laws and Other "Get Tough" Approaches Really Work?

Before three strikes, most states already had provisions for enhancing sentences for those with prior serious convictions. However, with the passage of three strikes, life or lengthy sentences after a third violent felony conviction became mandatory. However, exactly which felonies are "third strikeable"; the number of inmates incarcerated under this mandate; negative consequences such as jail overcrowding due to offenders opting to go to trial instead of plea bargaining, which would automatically result in life or lengthy sentences with no hope of parole; and the reluctance of prosecutors to charge offenders who might face life after committing a relatively minor felony are remarkably inconsistent from state to state.

The two states that initially passed three strikes, Washington and California, have had radically different experiences. For example, Washington has had only 86 inmates incarcerated under this provision, while California has had over 26,000. The issue of fairness of law is self-evident from these statistics as well as racial, economic, and other disparities identified by Shichor. Yet defenders of three strikes point out that in a democracy, citizens have a right to pass legislation that they feel will protect them. Even if there are extreme cases, such as receiving a life sentence for stealing a slice of pizza, people still have that right.

Some suggest that criminologists who ridicule the severity of assaults are being arrogant by trivializing possible harms experienced by those whose personal space was invaded. Moreover, the examples that Methvin cites of horrible crimes committed by individuals with several prior, equally terrible felonies—who, if three strikes had been applied, could not have done additional harm—can easily be multiplied. They would probably far exceed the examples that Shichor gives of life sentences resulting from "minor" acts of violence.

Two striking cases involving repeat offenders include the 1994 murder of 7-year-old Megan Kanga by two-time convicted offender Jesse Timmendequas and the 1978 case in which violent felon Lawrence Singleton chopped off a 15-year-old California girl's arms after raping her. He served less than 10 years and was recently convicted of first-degree murder in Florida. These cases are troubling. What may be equally troubling, however, as Shichor illustrates, is that a significant number of "striked" criminals (at least in California) were not convicted on their third offense of *violent* felonies. Moreover, thus far it is unclear whether or not the policy has resulted in a net lowering of crime rates. Most studies indicate that the law, its applications, and its consequences are uneven.

Recent studies by Shichor include "Private Prisons, Criminological Research, and Conflict of Interest: A Case Study," coauthored by G. Geis and A. Mobley, *Crime and Delinquency* (July 1999) and *Privatization in Criminal Justice: Past, Present, and Future* coedited by M. J. Gilbert (Anderson, 2000). For a current debate on the effectiveness of incarceration and the allegation that nonviolent offenders are being sentenced to longer terms than violent ones, see "Alternative Sanctions: Diverting Nonviolent Prisoners to Intermediate Sanctions," by J. Petersilia, as well as comments by J. J. DiIulio, Jr., and N. Morris, in E. L. Rubin, ed., *Minimizing Harm: A New Crime Policy for Modern America* (Westview Press, 1999). In an apparent modification of his support of three strikes and other get-tough approaches, DiIulio has commented that locking offenders up is reaching a point of "diminishing returns." See W. Raspberry, "Conveyor-Belt Justice," *The Washington Post* (April 5, 1999).

An outstanding book that is already being widely discussed and that supports the view that getting tough on criminals has backfired is J. May, ed., *Building Violence: How America's Rush to Incarcerate Creates More Violence* (Sage Publications, 2000). An excellent work that examines the unanticipated negative consequences of current crime policies for women and children is S. L. Miller, ed., *Crime Control and Women: Feminist Implications of Criminal Justice Policy* (Sage Publications, 1998).

Excellent overviews of three-strikes laws are "Three Strikes and You're Out: A Review of State Legislation," by J. Clark et al., *National Institute of Justice* (September 1997); "Striking Out: The Crime Control Impact of 'Three-Strikes' Laws," by V. Schiraldi and T. Ambrosio, *The Justice Policy Institute* (March 1997); *Three Strikes and You're Out: Vengeance as Public Policy* edited by D. Shichor and E. K. Sechrest (Sage Publications, 1996); and *The Tough-On-Crime Myth* by P. Elikann (Plenum, 1996).

Another helpful study is "Assessing Public Support for Three-Strikes-and-You're-Out Laws," by F. Cullen et al., *Crime and Delinquency* (October 1996). Sources agreeing with Methvin are B. Jones, "California's Three-Strikes Law Has Made Big Cuts in Crime," *The New York Times* (April 20, 1995) and *Body Count* by J. J. DiIulio, Jr., et al. (Simon & Schuster, 1996). For a critique of the get-tough movement, see "Science and the Punishment/Control Movement," by T. Clear, *Social Pathology* (Spring 1996). For an update of his thesis, see G. Ritzer's *The McDonaldization Thesis: Explorations and Extensions* (Sage Publications, 1998). For charges that the National Institute of Justice (NIJ) censored a critical study of the three-strikes policy, see S. Glass, "Anatomy of a Policy Fraud," *The New Republic* (November 17, 1997).

ISSUE 10

Should Private "For-Profit" Corporations Be Allowed to Run U.S. Prisons?

YES: **Wayne H. Calabrese**, from "Low Cost, High Quality, Good Fit: Why Not Privatization?" *Privatizing Correctional Institutions* (1996)

NO: **Jeff Sinden**, from "The Problem of Prison Privatization: The U.S. Experience," *Capitalist Punishment: Prison Privatization & Human Rights* (2003)

ISSUE SUMMARY

YES: Wayne H. Calabrese, vice president of the Wackenhut Corporation, argues that the privatization of U.S. prisons saves money and provides quality services.

NO: Jeff Sinden, managing editor of *Human Rights Tribune*, contends that the private prison industry has failed to achieve substantial cost savings and that there have been systemic human rights abuses in for-profit correctional institutions.

Should private corporations be allowed to profit from the punishment of prison inmates? Is there something wrong morally with allowing a corporation's stockholders to make a profit from human misery? These are difficult questions that will become increasingly relevant as governmental administrators try to squeeze limited financial resources from tight state budgets. Moreover, the movement to privatize corrections in the United States appears to be consistent with conservative political principles sweeping our nation that emphasize a more restrictive view of government services. For example, in the last several years the federal government has privatized some services at our national parks. Local privatization initiatives have included basic social services, educational programs, water treatment, and trash collection.

Private prisons are not a new development. As Jeff Sinden observes, privately run jails operated in England centuries ago. In the United States, early prisons in California and Texas were privately owned. The operation of U.S. prisons became a governmental responsibility during the twentieth century as a direct result of the squalid conditions existing in the privately owned penal facilities.

The contemporary privatization movement in American corrections has focused on providing a number of different types of services: inmate health care, psychological services, food services, educational programs, maintenance, as well as traditional confinement and security. It is also noteworthy that many college students may have something in common with some of our nation's prison inmates: Sodexho Marriott Services provides food services for a number of state correctional systems as well as many colleges and universities.

On a theoretical level, an offender is sentenced to prison for committing an act that has somehow harmed society. Most persons would have little trouble with the proposition that society has a right to punish the person and that the government, as society's representative, should administer the appropriate sanctions. Privatization of correctional facilities, however, appears to be somewhat inconsistent with this basic proposition.

The Introduction to this edition discussed the contemporary state of American corrections. According to recent studies the United States has the highest imprisonment rates in the world. The total number of people housed in American prisons has reached 2.1 million and is continuing to grow at an alarming rate. This has occurred at a time when the crime rate in this country is actually falling! A large number of these individuals are confined to prisons for nonviolent offenses, such as possession of illegal drugs, and the cost to house them is staggering—perhaps as much as $15 billion for drug offenders alone.

Given the amount of money involved, is it surprising that private industry would become interested in providing correctional services? Is it an accident that conservative politicians, who receive campaign contributions from the private corrections corporations, would develop ever more draconian laws that will result in the incarceration of increasing numbers of nonviolent offenders? These are interesting questions that the authors of the articles in this section would be likely to answer in a very different way.

Wayne H. Calabrese, of the Wackenhut Corporation, asserts that in a time of dwindling public sector budgets, privatizing corrections services has one great advantage over governmental programs: highly significant cost savings. He believes that money is saved because "no one has yet developed a better pencil sharpener than free market competition."

Jeff Sinden, in contrast, maintains that the promised cost savings have not materialized. He cites a 2001 U.S. Department of Justice study concluding that "rather than the projected 20% savings, the average savings from privatization was only about one percent, and most of that was achieved through lower labor costs."

What are the arguments on both sides of the private prison debate? Do you believe that saving money is a good enough reason to privatize U.S. prisons? Moreover, does the move toward the privatization of our correctional institutions distract us from addressing more fundamental questions about the morality of our contemporary penal system? Should American corrections focus on alternatives to incarceration, such as drug rehabilitation and job training programs for nonviolent offenders? As you read the articles in this section, try to develop a sense of whether privatization is likely to become the dominant model for U.S. corrections in the twenty-first century.

YES

Wayne H. Calabrese

Low Cost, High Quality, Good Fit: Why Not Privatization?

As the privatization of corrections has taken root and grown, initial questions of propriety—"Should this be done?"—have given way to secondary questions of efficacy—"Does this work?" Perhaps inevitably in a time of dwindling public sector budgets and rising public service demands, those who seek a definitive answer to the question of privatization's value look to cost comparisons between public and private corrections. While the evidence thus far clearly establishes the economic advantages of privatized corrections, a careful analysis of the reasons for such advantages reveals a number of complex and subtle factors which contribute to cost savings. . . .

Of course, the inquiry into the relative worth of privatized corrections does not end with a chart of purported cost savings. Indeed, those who are critical of privatized corrections often cite reluctantly admitted cost savings as direct evidence of failed service delivery. To these critics, a dollar saved is a service shorted. The record indicates otherwise. The quality of services delivered by privatized corrections has, in the main, been equal or superior to the quality of correctional services delivered by the public sector. The second part of this chapter explores the ways public sector administrators can ensure adherence to quality standards by private providers of correctional services.

Finally, the third part of this chapter addresses a proper role for privatization in our criminal justice system, a role which can complement existing prison systems without unduly threatening the continued central role of public sector corrections departments.

Cost Comparisons

Add to the list of life's great imponderables the question of how much we are paying for our prisons. Political and religious discourse appear deliberate and calm compared to the sparks raised by those who grind their axes on the stone of public/private corrections cost comparisons. The pitfalls are legion: aging public facilities compared to newly designed and constructed private facilities; security level, average length of stay, and offense category of compared incarcerated populations; required offender programming for public vs. private

From *Privatizing Correctional Institutions* by Gary W. Bowman et al., eds. (Transaction, 1996), pp. 175–182, 189–191 (excerpts). Copyright © 1996 by Transaction Publishers. Reprinted by permission via Copyright Clearance Center.

providers and degree of adherence to required standards; indirect and hidden public sector costs; to name only a few. . . .

Nevertheless, cost comparisons have been made that clearly indicate that privatization of correctional facilities leads to significant cost savings. In an article first published in the September/October 1989 issue of *NIJ Reports*, Charles Logan and Bill W. McGriff (1989) exhaustively examined the cost savings that Hamilton County, Tennessee realized through the privatization of its 350-bed Hamilton County Penal Farm. The authors state,

> Hamilton County found that contracting out prison management generated annual savings of at least 4 to 8 percent—and more likely in the range of 5 to 15 percent—compared to the estimated cost of direct county management. (Logan and McGriff 1989, 2)

In a report of the University of Florida at Gainesville, Center for Studies in Criminology and Law, Charles W. Thomas (1990) examined available data on forty-five privately managed correctional facilities. Of the ten facilities readily capable of cost comparison with a public counterpart, all ten evidenced cost savings ranging from 10.71 percent to 52.23 percent. . . .

Construction Costs

While design-build and construction management models of new construction have made some inroads into public sector construction, the traditional three-party "pyramid" format, with the government/owner independently contracting with an architect-engineer firm to design the facility and with a general contractor to construct the facility, still prevails in most jurisdictions. The reasons for this continuing adherence to the traditional format include statutory/regulatory impediments or prohibitions, lack of public sector expertise or experience with relatively newer models, comfort with established methods, and so on.

The traditional public sector approach to constructing a new correctional facility has within its seemingly elegant three-sided design a built-in paradigm for cost overruns and missed schedules. First, the design phase must generally be completed before the construction begins. This lineal format adds months and consequential costs to the construction process. Second, the general contractor is generally selected through competitive bidding which requires an award to the "lowest and best bid." While the low bidder is not always selected, experienced contractors know that the "bottom line" receives significantly more scrutiny than the experience and credit-worthiness of the subcontractors contributing to the total. Accordingly, subcontractors are frequently selected for the wrong reason—low cost—without regard to the level of experience or expertise they may bring to the project.

Third, the contractor may intentionally underbid the project, relying upon anticipated change-orders to regain the temporarily lost profit margin. No construction contract yet devised can eliminate all "gray areas." The traditional public sector construction model requires the architect-engineer firm to approve and certify all change orders and then pays the architect-engineer firm a percentage of the cost of any such changes. This feature alone virtually guarantees cost overruns. . . .

This system has many advantages. First, the design and construction processes are begun in coordinated tandem, saving months in the construction timetable. These time savings result in substantial cost savings based upon reduced project capitalized interest. Second, the general contractor is selected, as in turn are his subcontractors, based upon demonstrated expertise, experience and reliability. The experienced private provider is therefore confident that the general contractor's bottom line is not a bottomless well. A bond of trust in this essential relationship can develop due, in part, to the contractor's desire to become part of the private provider's established team for future projects. . . .

Inasmuch as the project is delivered to the public sector client on a "turnkey" basis, the need for public sector participation in the day-to-day construction process is greatly reduced. Construction is monitored, rather than managed by the client. Only projects completed in accordance with project specifications and standards are accepted and paid for; incentive enough to generally guarantee completion of private design-build projects on time and within budget.

Operational Costs

Many of those who readily accept and agree with the premise that private providers can construct the same correctional facility in less time and at lower cost than the public sector, nevertheless have difficulty accepting the premise that the same private provider can manage and operate the facility at less cost with equivalent quality of service. Again, an examination of the factors contributing to operating costs reveals an almost inevitable cost advantage in privatizing corrections without any sacrifice of service quality.

Operational costs may be understood as consisting of three main categories: direct, indirect, and hidden. Direct costs, in turn, include costs associated with labor, supplies and services. Labor costs are comprised of wages and benefits. Private providers can, and generally will, pay wages equivalent to their public sector counterparts. Contrary to what some critics suggest, non-competitive wages result in disproportionately higher costs due to unacceptable levels of employee attrition. This results in increased employee training costs and other losses generally attributable to organizational upheaval.

The provision of employee benefits does, in fact, differ substantially between the public sector and the private provider. Public sector benefits include a retirement benefit known as a defined benefit plan which essentially guarantees the covered employee a specified benefit level upon retirement. This is generally expressed as a percentage of highest earnings formula. Private providers tend to either eliminate direct employer contribution retirement benefits, or if provided, the benefit is of the type known as a defined contribution plan. The defined contribution plan guarantees a level of contribution to a tax-deferred employee retirement account. . . .

The savings resulting from this single benefit are enormous. Public employee retirement contributions currently hover between 20 percent to

25 percent of the employee's wages in most public sector systems. Privatization offers the public sector client the flexibility to eliminate or modify the cost of such benefits without demonstrably affecting the quality of provided service.

Private providers also save money with respect to the procurement of facility supplies. Bulk purchasing through established national accounts, together with less bureaucratic purchasing systems, reduces costs through competitive pricing and reduced administrative overhead. The procurement of facility services such as medical, food, program instructors, counselors, and so on also benefit from competitive private sector pricing and lower administrative overhead. In short, the direct costs of operating a facility will almost always be lower for the private provider than the public sector, for reasons inherent in the respective systems of each. To recognize this advantage of the private provider is not to indict the public sector employee as less capable or motivated; rather, it is a recognition that public sector protections and systemic redundancies are purchased at a cost and eliminated or modified at a savings. . . .

No discussion of private/public cost comparisons would be complete without mention of the "hidden costs" of public sector corrections. These hidden costs are endemic to the public sector system. Private providers are sometimes criticized for operating on a for-profit basis, almost as though profitability is incompatible with the public good. The private providers have shareholder investors; the public sector has taxpayer investors. Both sets of investors expect a reasonable return on their investments. It is the means by which these expectations are measured that distinguish the private and public sectors from one another. The private sector marketplace regulates cost efficiency and quality of service by rewarding success and punishing failure. The public sector is not subject to the same rigors of the marketplace, and therefore is insulated in its "investor accountability." Public "profits" are seldom, if ever, returned to the investor. Budgets are exceeded and expanded, service quality suffers, and the hidden costs skyrocket until, as now, new and creative private market solutions are demanded by taxpayer investors in search of accountability. . . .

Resource Allocation

. . . [Public] sector corrections departments often perceive privatization as a threat or potential embarrassment. Yet, properly viewed, privatization can be presented as an integral part of a comprehensive correctional system with potential benefits to taxpayers and public sector departments alike.

Nearly every level of government responsible for incarcerating arrested or sentenced individuals is experiencing dramatic overcrowding and underfunding. Incarceration rates in the United States are at an all time high and continue to spiral upward in response to social pressures to remove offenders from our streets, neighborhoods and communities. From Willie Horton presidential politics to worried local elected officials scanning the morning headlines for news of heinous crimes committed by felons released after serving as little as one-fifth of their sentence, prisons and prison costs remain the number one domestic issue facing America today.

There are hardened criminals in our society who require hard time behind bars. Maximum security prison beds are expensive to build and costly to operate. Too often, however, these maximum security beds are home to medium and minimum security inmates, inmates who require neither the level of security nor the allocation of cost attendant to the level of security built into the design of their cells.

Rather than spend scarce tax dollars on the construction and operation of more maximum security prisons, the public sector should, whenever possible, reallocate its resources to the construction and operation of lower security diversionary or pre-release detention facilities designed to concentrate on the specific security, programmatic, and rehabilitative needs of the intended incarcerated population.

When viewed as a continuum, the correctional system offers many opportunities for maximizing limited public resources. First-time offenders, nonviolent offenders, parole violators, sentenced offenders within one or two years of release, geriatric offenders, offenders suffering from mental illness, and so on, all represent "niche" populations capable of being incarcerated in facilities that cost less to build, and operate than the maximum security prisons in which they are currently housed. Privatization is perfectly suited to meet the needs of such populations. Private providers can design, finance, build and operate efficient facilities dedicated to the specific correctional needs of a specified population group. Based upon consistent average-lengths-of-stay, type of offense, security level, and so on, appropriate programmatic and rehabilitative services can be tailored to meet the needs of the incarcerated population.

By removing and allocating minimum/medium security inmates from maximum security beds, at least two important goals are met. First, the number of available maximum security beds within a system is increased at a lower cost than through the construction of new high security prisons; and second, targeted offender populations can be dealt with in a manner consistent with their level of security and classification, hopefully with better rehabilitative results. Public sector corrections officials should therefore regard privatized corrections as less threatening to their continued core function as keeper of our most hardened cases.

This is not to say that private providers cannot effectively manage and operate maximum security facilities. Obviously, nothing in the nature of maximum security prisons, in and of itself, mitigates against the use of private providers. The suggestion to concentrate on the privatization of the many "niche" offender populations is merely a recognition of deeply felt institutional resistance and acknowledgment of a cost-effective, less threatening, direction for embracing privatization as a meaningful part of a larger whole.

Conclusion

While advocates and opponents continue to make their closing arguments with respect to the advantages and disadvantages of privatized corrections, the jury has returned its verdict: privatization saves money, provides quality services and fulfills a need. Money is saved because no one has yet developed a better pencil sharpener than free market competition. Quality services can be ensured through careful attention to sound drafting of competitive procurement solicitations and resulting operating contracts. When properly utilized, privatization can become a cost-effective tool for fashioning specific correctional solutions within the context of the larger correctional system continuum.

References

Logan, Charles H. and Bill McGriff. (1989) *Comparing Costs of Public and Private Prisons: A Case Study.* NU Reports (September/October).

Thomas, Charles W. (1990) *Private Corrections Adult Secure Facility Census.* Correction Studies in Criminology and Law. Gainesville, Florida: University of Florida, May.

 **NO**

The Problem of Prison Privatization: The U.S. Experience

The past two decades have witnessed a disturbing trend in the American criminal justice system. From immigration detention centers and work farms to county jails and state prisons, private corporations have entered the incarceration 'business' en masse. In fact, there are currently more than 100,000 people incarcerated in private prisons in the United States.[1] Privatization of the criminal justice system has been driven largely by the currently dominant ethos of a neoliberal agenda in which a wide variety of traditionally public goods have been transferred to the supposedly more efficient and less corrupt private sector. However, correctional services are fundamentally different from other goods, such as garbage collection, which have been transferred into private hands. Providing correctional services is a vastly complex and difficult task. Institutions are charged with the task not only of protecting society but also caring for the physical, psychological and emotional needs of inmates so that they may one day successfully return to the community. Unfortunately, private corrections firms have failed miserably in the task they were so eager to take on, as systematic human rights abuses have become the rule and not the exception.

Various forms of private sector involvement in the corrections industry exist in the United States, some more problematic than others. The most common and least controversial involves the private delivery of goods and services in publicly run prisons. According to a report by the US Bureau of Justice Assistance, during the past twenty years, "the practice of state and local correctional agencies contracting with private entities for medical, mental health, educational, food services, maintenance, and administrative office security functions has risen sharply."[2] For example, Sodexho Marriott Services provides food services for public correctional institutions (and college and university campuses) across North America.[3] Generally, this practice is not incompatible with a healthy respect for prisoners' rights.

. . . [H]owever, many aspects of privatization have been much more problematic. For example, the private delivery of medical services in

From *Capitalist Punishment: Prison Privatization & Human Rights* by Jeff Sinden, (Clarity Press, 2003), pp. 39–47. Copyright © 2003 by Jeff Sinden. Reprinted by permission of Clarity Press and the author.

correctional institutions, both public and private, has caused significant problems as every dollar of a fixed annual stipend not spent on health services for prisoners benefits the company's bottom line, encouraging an unacceptable incentive to skimp on critical care.[4] In fact, a 1998 independent prison health care audit found that "more than twenty inmates died as a result of negligence, indifference, under-staffing, inadequate training or overzealous cost-cutting."[5]

The use of prisoner labor by the private sector to produce goods and services has also been controversial. There has been a long tradition of exploiting prison labor in the United States and throughout the world by governments and corporations alike.[6] For example, during the 19th century, inmates at the Kingston, Ontario penitentiary in Canada "were either leased out to farmers, or their work was contracted to provide industry with cheap labor."[7] While this practice was largely abolished during the early twentieth century, it has returned as of late. In 1986, former US Supreme Court Justice Warren Burger called for prisons in the United States to be transformed into "factories with fences" in order to reduce the costs of incarceration.[8] Prison administrators have taken his advice to heart as many states have allowed corporations to purchase convict labor at cut-rate prices. For example, in California, prisoners who make clothing for export make between 35 cents and $1 an hour.[9] Similarly, in Ohio, prisoners are paid approximately 50 cents an hour for data entry work.[10]

The most controversial form of private sector involvement in correctional services is the management and operation of entire correctional facilities by for-profit corporations. In some cases, private firms have taken over the operation of public facilities; in others, corporations have constructed and then managed entire sites. This type of involvement has fostered situations in which a myriad of human rights abuses have occurred.

In many cases, the corporation's desire for cost-effectiveness has led to simple corner-cutting, which in turn fosters abuses. For example, low pay and a subsequently high turnover rate has led to a grossly underqualified and inexperienced staff at many institutions.[11] Far too often, this has resulted in the flagrant abuse of prisoners. In 1997, a videotape surfaced in the media that showed guards at a private facility in Texas shooting unresisting prisoners with stun guns and kicking them to the ground. One of the guards involved had recently been fired from a government-run prison for similar conduct.[12]

Rehabilitation costs have also been systematically slashed by the prison firms. In many of the institutions, opportunities for meaningful education, exercise and rehabilitation are virtually non-existent. For example, in 1995 a private jail in Texas was investigated for diverting $700,000 intended for drug treatment when it was found that inmates with dependency problems were receiving absolutely no treatment.[13] This type of flagrant neglect amounts to abuse and almost certain recidivism as job training and education programs, drug and alcohol rehabilitation services, as well as social and psychological counseling, are absolutely critical if the transition back into society is to be successful.

Neoliberalism, Increased Criminalization and the Drive to Privatize

Privately operated prisons are not a new phenomenon in the United States or in the Western world. In fact, privately run jails were in operation centuries ago in medieval England.[14] In the US, the seventeenth and eighteenth centuries witnessed the private ownership and operation of prisons in several states.[15] During this period, the Texas state penitentiary was leased out to a private business, which in turn subleased inmate labor to farms and industry. Similarly, the California state penitentiary at San Quentin was constructed and operated by private business.[16] "Conditions were so horrid" in these facilities, states John Dilulio "that some inmates were driven to suicide while others maimed themselves to get out of work or as a pathetic form of protest."[17]

Partly as a result of poor conditions and systematic abuse, the ownership and operation of private correctional facilities were transferred to the state in the early 20th century and thereafter "the operations and administrative functions in correctional facilitates were delegated to governmental agencies, authorized by statute, staffed by government employees, and funded solely by the government."[18] During the ensuing period, there was virtually no private sector involvement in correctional services. This changed rapidly in the 1980s.

The 1980s saw the return of neoliberal, market-driven policies championed by President Reagan in the United States and Prime Minister Thatcher in the United Kingdom. In 1980, Ronald Reagan roared into the White House, riding a wave of popular anti-government sentiment and Cold War fear. His promise to get the government "off the backs" of the American people was welcomed by many in the US who were tired of the deep economic recession and growing public debt. Reagan's neoliberal mantra included deregulation, free trade, a hostility towards taxes and the labor unions and an almost maniacal desire for defense spending.[19] However, the central value of Reagan's doctrine and of neoliberalism itself is the notion of free-market competition. . . .

The American criminal justice system was seen as ripe for privatization by Reagan's supporters largely as a result of the rapid and steady increase in the cost of correctional services over the previous several years. According to the US General Accounting Office (GAO), total prison operating costs (for both federal and state) grew from about US $3.1 billion in 1980 to more than $17 billion in 1994, an increase of nearly 550 percent based on inflation-adjusted dollars.[20]

These increasing costs were a direct result of a similar rise in the prison population as the past twenty years has seen an explosion in the number of individuals incarcerated in America. The number of prisoners—with 2 million currently behind bars—has increased three fold since 1980.[21] This scale of imprisonment is unmatched throughout the world (with the possible exception of Russia); in 1998, the US incarcerated 690 residents per 100,000, compared with 123 per 100,000 in Canada and 60 per 100,000 in Sweden.[22]

How can this huge increase in the prison population be explained? Rising crime and arrests are clearly not the cause. Douglas McDonald documents that "the annual number of arrests nationwide rose only slightly during this period."[23] The increase is due mainly to sentencing policies. According to a 1996 report by the US GAO, "inmate population growth in recent years can be traced in large part to major legislation intended to get tough on criminals, particularly drug offenders. Examples of this new "get tough" policy include mandatory minimum sentences and repeat offender provisions."[24]

The War on Drugs, Mandatory Minimums, and Three Strikes Legislation

In the early 1980s, President Reagan began a concerted 'war on drugs', which he and First Lady Nancy Reagan pursued with enthusiasm throughout their tenure in the White House. Anyone involved with the drug trade—producers, traffickers, dealers and users—was to be identified, criminalized and harshly punished. To this end, Reagan significantly increased the budget of law enforcement agencies, doubling the FBI's funding and increasing the resources of the Drug Enforcement Administration.[25] Additionally, he oversaw the creation of new institutions such as the Organized Crime Drug Enforcement Task Force (OCDETF), whose mandate is to coordinate the efforts of the multitude of agencies that fight the war on drugs.[26] Federal legislators also embraced the drug war, enacting comprehensive laws to deal with convicted offenders.

In 1984 the US Congress enacted both the Comprehensive Crime Control Act and the Sentencing Reform Act. These laws eliminated federal parole and established mandatory minimums for many drug-related offences.[27] Mandatory minimum sentences impose a strict lower limit on the number of years an individual convicted of a particular crime must serve in prison. Regardless of their assessment of the appropriateness of the punishment, judges must sentence convicted defendants to the minimum prison term. . . .

The war on drugs continues unabated to this day. According to the Office of National Drug Control Policy, the US federal government will spend over $19.2 billion on the war on drugs in 2001.[28] This massive amount of funds is not without result. It is estimated that more than 1.5 million people were arrested for drug-related charges in 2001 alone.[29]

The war on drugs and its cohort, mandatory minimum sentencing, are together part of a broader trend which, during the past two decades, has seen politicians across the US clamoring to 'get tough on crime'. One of the most dramatic illustrations of this has been the so-called 'Three Strikes' legislation, first passed by the state of California in 1994. Under this law, individuals convicted of a third felony offense are automatically sentenced to twenty-five years to life in prison. Since 1994, half of the states in the US have enacted similar laws.[30]

While the three strikes law was ostensibly designed to isolate and punish the most serious, habitual offenders, far too often this has not been the case as "an ever increasing number of 'three strikes' prosecutions are for crimes as menial as petty theft of a can of beer or a few packs of batteries."[31] For example, one California man is currently serving a sentence of 25 years to life after being convicted of stealing a pair of sneakers (he was previously convicted twice for theft).[32] In 2000, another man's appeal of a three strikes sentence for the theft of $20 worth of instant coffee was denied.[33] . . .

The 'war on drugs', featuring mandatory minimums and other 'tough on crime' legislation such as the three strikes law, has been largely responsible for the explosive scale of incarceration in the US since the 1980s. The public corrections system was overwhelmed by the huge influx of inmates during this period. The system, it was argued, simply could not accommodate the sheer number of prisoners as prisons were consistently overflowing. This overcrowded system, coupled with ballooning costs and the rise of neoliberalism, set the stage for private sector involvement in American corrections in the early 1980s. The market was quick to react, and a number of firms emerged to fill the newly found niche. These corporations promised to provide the same level of correctional services for substantially less money—predicting savings to be between 5 and 15 percent.[34]

It was argued that privately operated facilities could perform more efficiently than their public counterparts for several reasons. Firstly, public agencies are believed to have few incentives to reduce costs. In fact, many public administration experts argue that public bureaucracies have a natural tendency to seek to increase their own budgets.[35] Conversely, in the private sector, competition in the marketplace and the possibility of loss and bankruptcy require managers to minimize costs. According to privatization advocates, pressure from shareholders to provide dividends will lead to more cost-effective operations.[36]

Another major advantage of the private sector often cited by prison privatization advocates is the speed and efficiency with which the market can finance and construct new prison facilities. The rapidly increasing prison population has necessitated the construction of countless new facilities throughout the US. In fact, the annual cost of building new penitentiaries in the past decade has been approximately $7 billion per year.[37] While state governments have generally taken five to six years to construct each new facility, private companies claimed to be able to do the same job in half the time.[38]

The Re-emergence of Private Prisons in the US

Privately owned and operated prisons first re-emerged in the US in the early 1980s in response to an acute overcrowding problem in Immigration and Naturalization Service (INS) facilities in Texas and California. State governments transferred some of their detainees to institutions run by Behavioral Systems Southwest (BSS), a for-profit firm, for a daily fee of $2 per prisoner plus costs.[39] While the lifespan of BSS was relatively short, the practice of detaining undocumented people in private institutions quickly became commonplace. By 1986, 25 percent of all INS detention facilities were operated by private firms.[40]

State governments soon followed suit. By 1989 private correctional firms were operating approximately two dozen major facilitates, including three medium or maximum adult correctional institutions.[41] Today there are approximately 102 private facilities, holding more than 100,000 prisoners across the US.[42] Texas currently has the most facilities (43), followed by California (24), Florida (10), and Colorado (9).[43] In 1999, a corporate plan to take control of the entire Tennessee prison system was narrowly averted, as anti-privatization advocates succeeded in having the enacting legislation quashed in the state legislature.[44]

A few major players have emerged in the private prison industry, the oldest and largest of which is the Tennessee-based Corrections Corporation of America (CCA) established by the same entrepreneurs as was the Kentucky Fried Chicken fast-food chain. CCA currently controls approximately half of the private prison beds in the United States and has operations in the United Kingdom and until recently Australia.[45] The next largest prison corporation, controlling about a quarter of the private prison beds in the US, is Wackenhut Corrections, a subsidiary of the well-established Wackenhut private security service.[46] In addition to CCA and Wackenhut, there are about a dozen other for-profit prison firms currently operating in the US.[47]

Most private institutions are located in small towns in the southern and western United States. Politicians offer tax breaks and low, non-union wages in order to attract investment and jobs to their often poverty-stricken jurisdictions. A prison can literally 'make' a small town, providing hundreds of jobs and millions of tax dollars.[48] In order to fill the facilities, prisoners are often shipped in from out of state. Private prisons in Arizona, for example, have been stocked with Native Americans from as far away as Alaska.[49]

The private corrections industry quickly became a favorite on Wall Street. From an initial public offering price of $8 per share in 1995, the price of CCA stocks quadrupled in less than a year and hit highs of more than $100 in 1998 as investors rushed to secure their place in the booming industry.[50] Similarly, Wackenhut investors were treated to skyrocketing share prices in the mid 1990s.[51] While both have come down from their dizzying heights (CCA shares are currently at approximately $13 while Wackenhut's are at about $16), they are still seen by experts as secure investments[52] with excellent fundamentals: a recent report by the US Department of Justice estimates that annual total revenues for the industry are approximately $1 billion.[53]

Legal and Human Rights Issues

The emergence of the private prison industry in the US has fostered a tense legal debate. Many have questioned whether it is legal for federal and state governments to source out correctional services. One of the major features of the modern nation state is its monopoly on the legitimate use of violence and coercion in society. Only the state can detain, arrest and punish criminals. Many argue that "to continue to be legitimate and morally significant, the authority to govern those behind bars, to deprive citizens of their liberty, to coerce (and even kill) them, must remain in the hands of government authorities."[54] The American Bar Association has pointed out that "incarceration is an inherent function of the government and that the government should not abdicate this responsibility by turning over prison operations to private industry.[55] However, most legal scholars have suggested that private prisons are in fact legal in the US, unless specifically prohibited within a jurisdiction: "the question of whether a state can delegate the task of imprisonment has been raised occasionally, but thus far no authoritative court ruling or constitutional provision has been cited to prevent such delegation."[56] . . .

Conclusion

An exploding prison population in the US and the rising costs accompanying it, coupled with a neoliberal reliance on the market for the provision of traditionally public goods and services, provided an impetus for prison privatization in the early 1980s. State and federal legislatures were lured by the promise of substantial savings made by for-profit jailers. Interestingly, the cost savings that were promised by the industry have not materialized. In 1996, the US GAO "could not conclude whether privatization saved money."[57] Similarly, a 2001 study commissioned by the US Department of Justice concluded that "rather than the projected 20 percent savings, the average saving from privatization was only about 1 percent, and most of that was achieved though lower labor costs."[58]

The private prison industry has clearly not achieved the substantial cost savings that were billed as a major feature in the drive to privatize. Nevertheless, free-market advocates may be inclined to argue that the services provided by private facilities are more efficient and of a higher quality than that provided by government-run operations. However, as subsequent chapters will clearly show, human rights abuses in for-profit correctional institutions have been systemic.

Notes

1. J. Austin and G. Coventry, *Emerging Issues on Privatized Prisons* (2001): x.
2. *Id.,* 2.
3. [. . .]
4. W. Allen and K. Bell, "Death, Neglect and the Bottom Line: Push to Cut Costs Poses Risks," *St. Louis Post-Dispatch,* 27 September 1998.
5. *Id.*
6. D. Shicor, *Punishment for Profit: Private Prisons/Public Concerns* (1995): 31.
7. J. Gandy and L. Hurl, "Private sector involvement in prison industries" (1987): 186.
8. P. Wright, "Slaves of the State," *Prison Legal News,* May 1994.
9. *Id.*
10. D. Cahill, "The Global Economy Behind Ohio Prison Walls," *Prison Legal News,* March 1995 / April 1996.
11. J. Greene, "Prison Privatization: Recent Developments in the United States," Presented at the International Conference on Penal Abolition, 12 May 2000.
12. S. Smalley, "For-profit prisons offer privatization lessons," *National Journal,* 3 May 1999.

13. K. Silverstein, "America's Private Gulag," *Prison Legal News,* June 1997.

14. R. Pugh, *Imprisonment in Medieval England* (1968).

15. J. Dilulio, "The duty to govern" (1990): 158.

16. J. Austin and G. Coventry, *Emerging Issues on Privatized Prisons, supra* note 1 at 10.

17. J. Dilulio, "The duty to govern," *supra* note 15 at 159.

18. J. Austin and G. Coventry, *Emerging Issues on Privatized Prisons, supra* note 1 at 11.

19. J. Karaagac, *Between promise and policy* (2000).

20. *Id.,* 1.

21. "US Jails Two Millionth Inmate," *Manchester Guardian Weekly,* 17 February 2000: 1.

22. R. Walmsley, *World Prison Population List* (2000).

23. D. McDonald, ed., *Private Prisons and the Public Interest* (1990): 5.

24. United States General Accounting Office, "Private and public prisons—studies comparing operational costs and/or quality of service," (1996).

25. C. Parenti (1999): 17.

26. *Id.*

27. *Id.,* 50.

28. Office of National Drug Control Policy [. . .]

29. Federal Bureau of Investigation, Uniform Crime Reports . . .

30. Sentencing Project, *supra* note 31.

31. *Id.*

32. *Id.*

33. *Id.*

34. J. Austin and G. Coventry, *Emerging Issues on Privatized Prisons, supra* note 1 at 22.

35. Public choice theorists argue that the self-interest of public bureaucrats leads them to maximize their bureau's budget because larger budgets are a source of power, prestige and higher salaries. Please see Iain McLean, *Public Choice: An Introduction* (Oxford: Basil Blackwell, 1987).

36. C. Thomas, *Corrections in America* (1987).

37. C. Parenti, *supra* note 27 at 213.

38. J. Austin and G. Coventry, *Emerging Issues on Privatized Prisons, supra* note at 15.

39. A. Press, "The Good, the Bad and the Ugly" (1990): 25.

40. *Id.,* 25.

41. D. McDonald, *Private Prisons and the Public Interest, supra* note 25 at 1.

42. J. Austin and G. Coventry, *Emerging Issues on Privatized Prisons, supra* note 1.

43. *Id.,* ix.

44. A. Press, "The Good, the Bad and the Ugly," *supra* note 46 at 28.

45. C. Parenti, *supra* note 27 at 218.

46. *Id.*
47. *Id.*
48. *Id.,* 212.
49. *Id.*
50. S. Smalley, "For-profit prisons offer privatization lessons"; *supra* note 12.
51. *Id.*
52. C. Parenti, *supra* note 27 at 219.
53. J. Austin and G. Coventry, *Emerging Issues on Privatized Prisons, supra* note 1 at ix.
54. J. Dilulio, "The duty to govern," *supra* note 15 at 159.
55. D. Shicor, *Punishment for Profit, supra* note 6 at 52.
56. A. Press, "The Good, the Bad and the Ugly," *supra* note 46 at 25.
57. J. Austin and G. Coventry, *Emerging Issues on Privatized Prisons, supra* note 1 at iii.
58. *Id.*

POSTSCRIPT

Should Private "For-Profit" Corporations Be Allowed to Run U.S. Prisons?

The Introduction to this edition discussed George Santayana's often-repeated observation that those who fail to learn from history are doomed to repeat it. It is interesting to consider whether this principle applies compellingly to the contemporary privatization movement in U.S. corrections.

Privatized correctional institutions are nothing new. As Jeff Sinden observes, privately owned jails operated in England centuries ago. In the United States, early prisons in California and Texas were privately owned. Corrections emerged as a governmental responsibility as a direct consequence of the problems with these privately owned facilities.

Privately held corporations have one basic responsibility: to generate a profit for their investors. Suppose you were the director of a privately owned prison or jail that houses 2,000 detainees per year. Your contract with the corporation provides that you are to receive an annual performance bonus based on the profit generated at your facility. Assume further that it costs $12 per day to feed each inmate. If you could reduce the cost to $10 per day, your institution would save $1,460,000 in the following year. Would you be tempted to do so to improve the facility's bottom line and the prospects for your annual bonus? The same principle would apply to reducing the costs of medical care, clothing, security, education, drug and alcohol treatment, and job training.

The point is that the philosophy of correctional privatization may be fundamentally incompatible with what the ultimate goal of "corrections" should be: rehabilitating a person and enabling him or her to return to the community as a productive member of society. Privatizing corrections may distract us as well from attempting to find more effective alternatives to confinement for nonviolent offenders. In addition, if private industry has invested huge sums of money in corrections facilities, is it likely that unscrupulous politicians, who have been known to benefit from corporate campaign contributions, will simply continue to pass draconian measures that will generate more unwilling "clients"?

There are many additional resources that will shed additional light on the issues presented in this section. See Martha Minow, "Public and Private Partnerships: Accounting for the New Religion," *Harvard Law Review* (vol. 116, no. 5, March 2003); Gerald G. Gaes, "Prison Privatization in Florida: Promise, Premise, and Performance," *Criminology & Public Policy* (vol. 4, no. 1, Feb. 2005); William D. Bales, Laura E. Beddard, Susan T. Quinn, David Ensley, and Glen P. Holley, "Recidivism of Public and Private State Prison Inmates in Florida," *Criminology &*

Public Policy (Vol. 4, Iss. 1, Feb. 2005); Colin Fenwick, "Private Use of Prisoners' Labor: Paradoxes of International Human Rights Law," *Human Rights Quarterly* (Vol. 27, Iss. 1, Feb. 2005); Sasha Abramsky, "Incarceration, Inc.," *The Nation* (Vol. 279, Iss. 3, July 19–26, 2004); Mark Wilson, "Capitalist Punishment: Prison Privatization & Human Rights," *Prison Legal News* (Vol. 15, Iss. 6, June 2004); Sean Nicholson-Crotty, "The Politics of Privatization: Contracting Out for Corrections Management in the United States," *Policy Studies Journal* (Vol. 32, Iss. 1, Feb. 2004); Patricia Lefevere, "Mixing Prisons and the Profit Motive," *National Catholic Reporter* (Vol. 39, Iss. 38, Sept. 5, 2003); Gilbert Geis, Alan Mobeley, and David Shichor, "Private Prisons, Criminological Research, and Conflict of Interest: A Case Study," *Crime and Delinquency* (Vol. 45, Iss. 3, 1999); Lanza-Kaduce, L., K. F. Parker, and C. W. Thomas, "Comparative Recidivism Analysis of Releasees from Private and Public Prisons," *Crime and Delinquency* (Vol. 45, Iss. 1, 1999); Charles H. Logan, "Well Kept: Comparing Quality of Confinement in Private and Public Prisons," *Journal of Criminal Law and Criminology* (Vol. 83, Iss. 3, 1992).

Additional resources that provide competing viewpoints on these issues include: Gary W. Bowman, Simon Hakim, and Paul Seidenstat (eds.), *Privatizing Correctional Institutions* (Transaction Publishers, 1993); Andrew Coyle, Allison Campbell, and Rodney Neufeld (eds.), *Capitalist Punishment: Prison Privatization & Human Rights* (Clarity Press, Inc., 2003); C. W. Thomas, M. A. Frank, and S. L. Martin, *Privatization of American Corrections: A Selected Bibliography* (University of Florida Center for Studies in Criminology and Law, 1994).

ISSUE 11

Is Capital Punishment a Bad Public Policy?

YES: David Von Drehle, from "Miscarriage of Justice: Why the Death Penalty Doesn't Work," *The Washington Post Magazine* (February 5, 1995)

NO: Ernest van den Haag, from "The Ultimate Punishment: A Defense," *Harvard Law Review* (May 1986)

ISSUE SUMMARY

YES: David Von Drehle, a writer and the arts editor for *The Washington Post,* examines specific capital punishment cases and data and concludes that capital punishment is a bad social policy.

NO: Ernest van den Haag, a professor of jurisprudence and public policy (now retired), maintains that the death penalty is just retribution for heinous crime.

In 1968 only 38 percent of all Americans supported the death penalty for certain crimes. In 1972, when the U.S. Supreme Court handed down its decision in *Furman v. Georgia* stating that capital punishment violated the Eighth Amendment, which prohibits cruel and unusual punishment, many Americans were convinced that capital punishment was permanently abolished. After all, even though there were 500 inmates on death row at the time, there had been a steady decline in the number of executions in the United States: In the 1930s there were on average 152 executions per year; in 1962 there were 47 executions; and in 1966 there was 1. Polls in the late 1960s showed that most Americans opposed the death penalty, and virtually every other Western industrial nation had long since eliminated the death sentence or severely modified its use.

Polls taken in the 1990s showed that 75–80 percent of all Americans support capital punishment. In 1990, 23 people were executed, but in 1999, this number increased to 98. Since 1976, when capital punishment was restored, over 600 people have been executed. Currently, there are approximately 3500 people on death row. Eighteen states allow executions of defendants who are as young as 16, and there are currently over 60 juveniles on death row. Texas leads the nation in executions: 36 percent of all executions in 1999 were held in that state. Of the 1999 executions, 94 were by lethal injection, and 3 were by electrocution.

What has happened since the 1960s? We will probably never know the full answer to this question, but there are some clues. To begin with, in *Furman v. Georgia*, the Supreme Court did not really ban capital punishment because it was cruel and unusual in itself. It simply argued that it was unconstitutional for juries to be given the right to decide arbitrarily and discriminatorily on capital punishment. Thus, if states can show that capital punishment is not arbitrary or discriminatory and that the sentencing process is performed in two separate stages—first guilt or innocence is established, and *then* the determination of the sentence occurs—then some offenses are legally punishable by death. This was the Supreme Court's ruling in 1976 in *Gregg v. Georgia,* which effectively restored the death penalty.

Since the late 1960s Americans have become more conservative. Fear of crime has greatly increased, although the number of crimes may not have changed. Moreover, many of the measures taken under the Omnibus Safe Streets Act to reduce crime, speed up judicial processes, and rehabilitate criminals are now viewed by professionals and laypeople alike as failures. The national mood is now solidly behind "getting tough" on criminals, especially drug dealers and murderers. Support and utilization of capital punishment make sense within the logic of the present cultural and political situation.

There is a movement among criminologists to reassess studies done before the 1960s that indicated that states in which capital punishment prevailed had homicide rates that were just as high as those in which it was not a penalty and that executions did not deter others from committing crimes. Isaac Ehrlich, for instance, in an extensive statistical analysis of executions between 1933 and 1967, reached very different conclusions. He contends not only that the executions reduced the murder rate but also that one additional execution per year between 1933 and 1967 would have resulted in seven or eight fewer murders per year!

Many scholars have bitterly attacked Ehrlich's empirical findings. Most attempt to fault his methods, but others assert that even if he is empirically correct, the trade-off is not worth it. The state should not have the right to extract such a primitive "justice" as the murder of a human being, even a convicted killer. Other scholars emphasize the fact that there have been a disproportionate number of blacks executed (between 1930 and 1967, 2066 blacks were executed as opposed to 1751 whites, even though blacks constituted only 10 percent of the total population then). Some counter that this simply indicates that more whites need to be executed as well!

Is capital punishment bad policy? If not, what crimes should it be reserved for? Murder? Rape? Espionage? Drug dealing? Kidnapping? How should it be carried out?

YES

David Von Drehle

Miscarriage of Justice: Why the Death Penalty Doesn't Work

As a boy of 8, the son of good, poor parents, James Curtis "Doug" McCray had limitless dreams; he told everyone he met that someday he would be president of the United States. Soon enough, he realized that poor black children did not grow up to be president, but still he was a striver. At Dunbar High School in Fort Myers, Fla., he was an all-state receiver on the football team, an all-conference guard in basketball and the state champion in the 440-yard dash. He made the honor roll, and became the first and only of the eight McCray kids to attend college.

His was a success story, but for one flaw. McCray had a drinking problem. He washed out of college and joined the Army. A year and a half later, the Army gave him a medical discharge because he had been found to suffer from epilepsy. McCray married, fathered a son, tried college again; nothing took. He wound up back home, a tarnished golden boy.

On an October evening in 1973, an elderly woman named Margaret Mears was at home in her apartment, picking no trouble, harming no one, when someone burst in, stripped and raped her, then beat her to death. A bloody handprint was matched to Doug McCray's. He insisted that he had no memory of the night in question, and his jury unanimously recommended a life sentence. But McCray had the bad fortune to be tried by Judge William Lamar Rose.

. . . To him, the murder of Margaret Mears was precisely the type of savagery the law was intended to punish: committed in the course of another felony, and surely heinous, surely atrocious, surely cruel. Rose overruled the jury and banged the gavel on death.

When McCray arrived at Florida State Prison in 1974, nine men awaited execution and he made 10. His case entered the appeals process, and as the years went by, McCray wept for his best friend on death row, John Spenkelink, who became the first man in America executed against his will under modern death penalty laws. He watched as a young man named Bob Graham became governor of Florida and led the nation in executing criminals. Eight years later, he

From *The Washington Post Magazine,* February 5, 1995, pp. 8–13, 20–21, 23–24. Copyright © 1995 by Washington Post Writers Group. Reprinted by permission via PARS International Corp.

watched Gov. Bob Martinez take Graham's place and sign 139 death warrants in four years. McCray saw the infamous serial killer Ted Bundy come to the row, and almost 10 years later saw him go quietly to Old Sparky.

Living on death row, McCray saw men cut, saw men burned, even saw a man killed. He saw inmates carried from their cells after committing suicide, and others taken away after going insane. He saw wardens and presidents come and go. Death row got bigger and bigger. By the time Spenkelink was executed in May 1979, Jacksonville police officers printed T-shirts proclaiming "One down, 133 to go!" . . .

Doug McCray watched as death row doubled in size, and grew still more until it was not a row but a small town, Death Town, home to more than 300 killers. Nationwide, the condemned population climbed toward 3,000. The seasons passed through a sliver of dirty glass beyond two sets of bars outside McCray's tiny cell on the row, which was very cold in the winter and very hot in the summer, noisy at all times and stinking with the odor of smoking, sweating, dirty, defecating men. Four seasons made a year, and the years piled up: 5, 10, 15, 16, 17 . . .

All this time, Doug McCray was sentenced to death but he did not die. Which makes him the perfect symbol of the modern death penalty.

People talk a great deal these days about getting rid of government programs that cost too much and produce scant results. So it's curious that one of the least efficient government programs in America is also among the most popular. Capital punishment is favored by more than three-quarters of American voters. And yet, in 1994, the death row population nationwide exceeded 3,000 for the first time ever; out of all those condemned prisoners, only 31 were executed. There are hundreds of prisoners in America who have been on death row more than a decade, and at least one—Thomas Knight of Florida—has been awaiting execution for 20 years. Every cost study undertaken has found that it is far more expensive, because of added legal safeguards, to carry out a death sentence than it is to jail a killer for life. Capital punishment is the principal burden on the state and federal appellate courts in every jurisdiction where it is routinely practiced. The most efficient death penalty state, Texas, has a backlog of more than 300 people on its death row. It manages to execute only about one killer for every four newly sentenced to die—and the number of executions may drop now that the U.S. Supreme Court has ordered Texas to provide lawyers for death row inmate appeals. Overall, America has executed approximately one in every 20 inmates sentenced to die under modern death penalty laws.

This poor record of delivering the punishments authorized by legislatures and imposed by courts has persisted despite a broad shift to the right in the federal courts. It has resisted legislative and judicial efforts to streamline the process. It has outlasted William J. Brennan Jr. and Thurgood Marshall, the Supreme Court's strongest anti-death penalty justices. It has endured countless campaigns by state legislators and governors and U.S. representatives and senators and even presidents who have promised to get things moving. If New York reinstates the death penalty this year, as Gov. George Pataki has promised, there is no reason to believe things will change; New York is unlikely to see another execution in this century. Congress extended the death penalty to cover more than 50 new crimes last year, but that bill will be long forgotten before Uncle Sam executes more than a handful of prisoners.

Most people like the death penalty in theory; virtually no one familiar with it likes the slow, costly and inefficient reality. But after 20 years of trying to make the death penalty work, it is becoming clear that we are stuck with the reality, and not the ideal.

❧

To understand why this is, you have to understand the basic mechanics of the modern death penalty. The story begins in 1972.

For most of American history, capital punishment was a state or even a local issue. Criminals were tried, convicted and sentenced according to local rules and customs, and their executions were generally carried out by town sheriffs in courthouse squares. Federal judges took almost no interest in the death penalty, and even state appeals courts tended to give the matter little consideration.

Not surprisingly, a disproportionate number of the people executed under these customs were black, and the execution rate was most dramatically skewed for the crime of rape. As sensibilities became more refined, however, decent folks began to object to the spectacle of local executions. In Florida in the 1920s, for example, a coalition of women's clubs lobbied the legislature to ban the practice, arguing that the sight of bodies swinging in town squares had a brutalizing effect on their communities. Similar efforts around the country led to the centralizing of executions at state prisons, where they took place outside the public view, often at midnight or dawn.

Still, the death penalty remained a state matter, with the federal government extremely reluctant to exert its authority. Washington kept its nose out of the death chambers, just as it steered clear of the schools, courtrooms, prisons and voting booths. All that changed, and changed dramatically, in the 1950s and '60s, when the Supreme Court, in the era of Chief Justice Earl Warren, asserted more vigorously than ever that the protections of the U.S. Constitution applied to actions in the states. For the first time, federal standards of equality were used to strike down such state and local practices as school segregation, segregation of buses and trains, poll taxes and voter tests. The lengthened arm of the federal government reached into police stations: For example, in *Miranda v. Arizona,* the Supreme Court required that suspects be advised to their constitutional rights when arrested. The long arm reached into the courtrooms: In *Gideon v. Wainwright,* the high court declared that the federal guarantee of due process required that felony defendants in state trials be provided with lawyers.

Opponents of capital punishment urged the courts to reach into death rows as well. Anthony Amsterdam, at the time a Stanford University law professor, crafted arguments to convince the federal courts that the death penalty violated the Eighth Amendment (which bars "cruel and unusual punishments") and the 14th Amendment (which guarantees "equal protection of the laws").

Amsterdam's arguments won serious consideration in the newly aggressive federal courts, and on January 17, 1972, the greatest of Amsterdam's lawsuits, *Furman v. Georgia,* was heard in the Supreme Court.

Amsterdam delivered a brilliant four-pronged attack on capital punishment. He began by presenting statistical proof that the death penalty in America was overwhelmingly used against the poor and minorities. Next, Amsterdam argued that the death penalty was imposed arbitrarily, almost randomly. Judges and juries meted out their sentences without clear standards to guide them, and as a result men were on death row for armed robbery, while nearby, murderers served life, or less. Discretion in death sentencing was virtually unfettered. Amsterdam's third point was his most audacious, but it turned out to be crucial: The death penalty was so rarely carried out in contemporary America that it could no longer be justified as a deterrent to crime. In the years leading up to Amsterdam's argument, use of the death penalty had steeply declined. What made this argument so daring was that the sharp drop in executions was partly a result of Amsterdam's own legal campaign to abolish the death penalty. He was, in effect, challenging a state of affairs he had helped to create.

In closing, Amsterdam argued that the death penalty had become "unacceptable in contemporary society," that the "evolving standards" of decent behavior had moved beyond the point of legal killing. This was the weakest of his arguments, because nearly 40 states still had death penalty laws on the books, but previous Supreme Court decisions suggested that the shortest route to abolishing the death penalty would be to convince a majority of the justices that "standards of decency" had changed. Amsterdam had to try.

Behind closed doors, the nine justices of the court revealed a wide range of reactions to Amsterdam's case—from Brennan and Marshall, the court's liberal stalwarts, who voted to abolish capital punishment outright, to Justice William H. Rehnquist, the new conservative beacon, who rejected all of the arguments. Justice William O. Douglas was unpersuaded by the notion that standards of decency had evolved to the point that capital punishment was cruel and unusual punishment, but he agreed the death penalty was unconstitutionally arbitrary. Chief Justice Warren E. Burger and Justice Harry A. Blackmun both expressed personal opposition to capital punishment—if they were legislators, they would vote against it—but they believed that the language of the Constitution clearly left the matter to the states. That made three votes to strike down the death penalty, and three to sustain it.

Justice Lewis F. Powell Jr. also strongly objected to the court taking the question of the death penalty out of the hands of elected legislatures. This would be an egregious example of the sort of judicial activism he had always opposed. Though moved by Amsterdam's showing of racial discrimination, Powell believed this was a vestige of the past, and could be rectified without a sweeping decision in Furman. Powell's vote made four to sustain the death penalty. Justice Potter Stewart, painfully aware of the more than 600 prisoners whose lives were dangling on his vote, moved toward Douglas's view that the death penalty had become unconstitutionally arbitrary. Stewart's vote made four to strike down the death penalty as it existed.

That left Justice Byron R. White, known to observers of the court as a strict law-and-order man. In his brusque opinions, White backed prosecutors and police at almost every turn. But he was deeply impressed by Amsterdam's presentation; he told his law clerks that it was "possibly the best" oral argument he had ever heard. The point that had won White was Amsterdam's boldest: that the death penalty was applied too infrequently to serve any purpose. White cast the deciding vote to strike down the death penalty not because he wanted to see an end to capital punishment, but because he wanted to see more of it.

The product of these deliberations was one of the most difficult decisions in the history of the U.S. Supreme Court. The broad impact of *Furman v. Georgia*, striking down hundreds of separate laws in nearly 40 separate jurisdictions, was unprecedented. Rambling and inchoate—nine separate opinions totaling some 50,000 words—it remains easily the longest decision ever published by the court. But for all its wordy impact, Furman was almost useless as a precedent for future cases. It set out no clear legal standards. As Powell noted in his stinging dissent:

"Mr. Justice Douglas concludes that capital punishment is incompatible with notions of 'equal protection' that he finds 'implicit' in the Eighth Amendment . . . Mr. Justice Brennan bases his judgment primarily on the thesis that the penalty 'does not comport with human dignity' . . . Mr. Justice Stewart concludes that the penalty is applied in a 'wanton' and 'freakish' manner . . . For Mr. Justice White it is the 'infrequency' with which the penalty is imposed that renders its use unconstitutional . . . Mr. Justice Marshall finds that capital punishment is an impermissible form of punishment because it is 'morally unacceptable' and 'excessive' . . .

"I [will not] attempt to predict what forms of capital statutes, if any, may avoid condemnation in the future under the variety of views expressed by the collective majority today."

In other words, totally missing from the longest Supreme Court decision in history was any clear notion of how the death penalty might be fixed.

◆

That painfully splintered 5-to-4 vote turned out to be a high-water mark of the Supreme Court's willingness to intervene in the business of the states. In Furman, the justices were willing to abolish the death penalty as it existed. But the justices were not willing to forbid executions forever. They kicked the question of whether the death penalty was "cruel and unusual" back to the state legislatures. For nearly 20 years, the states—especially the Southern states—had felt pounded by the Supreme Court. Rarely did they get the chance to answer. The court did not ask what they thought about school desegregation, or voting rights, or the right to counsel. But *Furman v. Georgia* invited the states to respond to a hostile Supreme Court decision.

Florida was the first state to craft an answer, after calling its legislature into special session. Blue-ribbon panels appointed by the governor and legislature struggled to make sense of Furman—but how? On the governor's commission, legal advisers unanimously predicted that no capital punishment law would ever satisfy the high court, but the membership turned instead to a nugget from Justice Douglas's opinion. Douglas wrote that the problem with the pre-Furman laws was that "under these laws no standards govern the selection of the penalty." Douglas seemed to be saying that judges and juries needed rules to guide their sentencing.

The legislative commission reached a different conclusion, simply by seizing on a different snippet from the Furman ruling. Figuring that Byron White was the most likely justice to change his position, commission members combed his opinion for clues. White had complained that "the legislature authorizes [but] does not mandate the penalty in any particular class or kind of case . . ." That phrase seemed crucial: "Authorizes but does not mandate." Apparently, White would prefer to see death made mandatory for certain crimes.

Furman was as cryptic as the Gnostic gospels. Robert Shevin, Florida's attorney general at the time, was just as confused. He summoned George Georgieff and Ray Marky, his two top death penalty aides, to explain the ruling. "I've been reading it since it came out," Marky told his boss, "and I still have no idea what it means."

Gov. Reubin Askew refused to go along with mandatory sentences—he considered them barbaric. And so it was that while rank-and-file lawmakers made interminable tough-on-crime speeches, in the last month of 1972 Florida's power brokers hashed out a deal behind closed doors. Their new law spelled out "aggravating" circumstances—such as a defendant's criminal record and the degree of violence involved in the crime—which, if proven, would make a guilty man eligible for the death penalty. The law also spelled out "mitigating" circumstances, such as a defendant's age or mental state, that might suggest a life sentence instead. After a defendant was found guilty of a capital offense, the jury would hear evidence of aggravating and mitigating factors. By majority vote, the jurors would recommend either life in prison or the death penalty. Then the judge would be required to reweigh the aggravating and mitigating factors and impose the sentence, justifying it in writing. As a final safeguard, the sentence would be reviewed by the state's highest court. In this way, perhaps, they could thread the Furman needle: setting standards, limiting discretion, erasing caprice—all while avoiding mandatory sentences.

They were a few men in a back room, trading power and guessing over an incoherent Supreme Court document. It was not a particularly promising effort. Nevertheless, their compromise passed overwhelmingly, giving America its first legislative answer to Furman. Immediately, officials from states across the country began calling Florida for advice and guidance. And very soon, lawyers and judges began to discover that the law drafted in confusion and passed in haste was going to be hell to administer.

❧◈❧

The problem was that underneath the tidy, legalistic, polysyllabic, etched-in-marble tone of the new law was a lot of slippery mishmash. The aggravating and mitigating factors sounded specific and empirical, but many of them were matters of judgment rather than fact. A murderer was more deserving of the death penalty, for example, if his actions involved "a great risk of death to many persons"—but where one judge might feel that phrase applied to a drive-by killer who sprays a whole street with gunfire, another might apply it to a burglar who stabs a man to death while the victim's wife slumbers nearby. How much risk makes a "great" risk, and what number of persons constitutes "many"?

Another aggravating circumstance was even harder to interpret— "especially heinous, atrocious or cruel." The idea was to identify only the worst of the hundreds of murders each year in Florida. But wasn't the act of murder itself "heinous, atrocious or cruel"? Again, this aggravating circumstance was very much in the eye of the beholder: To one judge, stabbing might seem more cruel than shooting, because it involved such close contact between killer and victim. Another judge, however, might think it crueler to place a cold gun barrel to a victim's head before squeezing the trigger. One jury might find it especially heinous for a victim to be killed by a stranger, while the next set of jurors might find it more atrocious for a victim to die at the hands of a trusted friend. And so forth. It was an attempt to define the undefinable.

The imprecision was even more obvious on the side of mitigation, where it weighed in a defendant's favor if he had no "significant history" of past criminal behavior. How much history was that? "The age of the defendant" was supposed to be considered under the new law—but where one jury might think 15 was old enough to face the death penalty, another might have qualms about executing a man who was "only" 20. What about elderly criminals? Was there an age beyond which a man should qualify for mercy—and if so, what was it?

Clearly, a lot of discretion was left to the judge and jury. Even more discretion was allowed in tallying the aggravating versus the mitigating circumstances, and still more in deciding what weight to give each factor. The jury was supposed to render an "advisory" opinion on the proper sentence, death or life in prison, but how much deference did the judge have to pay to that advice? The law said nothing. After the judge imposed a death sentence, the state supreme court was required to review it. But what standards was the court supposed to apply? The law said nothing.

These questions might have seemed tendentious and picayune, except for the fact that Doug McCray and dozens of others were quickly sent to death row, and these seemingly trivial questions became the cruxes of life-and-death litigation. The law, shot through with question marks, became a lawyer's playground. After all, laws were supposed to be clear and fixed; they were supposed to mean the same thing from day to day, courtroom to courtroom, town to town. And given that their clients were going to be killed for breaking the law, it seemed only fair for defense lawyers to demand that simple degree of reliability.

In 1976, when the U.S. Supreme Court returned to the question of capital punishment, the justices agreed that the laws must be reliable. By then some 35 states had passed new death penalty laws, many of them modeled on Florida's. In a string of rulings the high court outlawed mandatory death sentences and affirmed the complex systems for weighing specified factors in favor of and against a death sentence.

But in striking down mandatory sentences, the court made consistency a constitutional requirement for the death penalty; the law must treat "same" cases the same and "different" cases differently. The thousands of capital crimes committed each year in America raised a mountain of peculiarities—each criminal and crime was subtly unique. Somehow the law must penetrate this mountain to discern some conceptual key that would consistently identify cases that were the "same" and cull ones that were "different." Furthermore, the court decided, the Constitution requires extraordinary consistency from capital punishment laws. "The penalty of death is qualitatively different from a sentence of imprisonment, however long," Justice Potter Stewart wrote. "Because of that qualitative difference, there is a corresponding difference in the need for reliability . . ."

Each year, some 20,000 homicides are committed in America, and the swing justices expected the death penalty laws to steer precisely and consistently through this carnage to find the relatively few criminals deserving execution. Somehow, using the black-and-white of the criminal code, the system must determine the very nature of evil. King Solomon himself might demur.

"The main legal battle is over," declared the *New York Times* in an editorial following the 1976 decisions. In fact, the battles were only beginning.

ஐ

After Doug McCray was sentenced to die in 1974, his case went to the Florida Supreme Court for the required review. . . . In October 1980, the Florida Supreme Court agreed that Doug McCray should die. The following year the U.S. Supreme Court declined to review the state court's decision.

Through all this, McCray continued to insist that he had no memory of murdering Margaret Mears. He passed a lie detector test, and though such tests are not admissible in court, there was another reason to believe what he said. It was possible that McCray's epilepsy, which had first emerged in several powerful seizures during his Army basic training, was the type known as "temporal lobe seizure disorder." This disease often emerges in late adolescence; it is known to cause violent blackouts; and it can be triggered by alcohol. The possibility had not come out at McCray's trial, nor was it properly researched in preparation for his hearing on executive clemency. The hearing, held on December 16, 1981, went badly for McCray. An attorney, Jesse James Wolbert, had been appointed to represent him, but Wolbert did not bother to read the trial record, let alone prepare a compelling case for mercy. Perhaps he had other things on his mind: By the time McCray's death warrant was signed three months later, Wolbert had drained another client's trust fund and become a federal fugitive.

Wolbert's disappearance turned out to be a blessing for McCray, because an anti-death penalty activist named Scharlette Holdman persuaded Bob Dillinger of St. Petersburg to take the case, and Dillinger was a damn good lawyer. He filed a hasty appeal in the Florida Supreme Court asking for a stay of execution. The result was amazing: Having affirmed McCray's death sentence 18 months earlier, the justices now ordered a new trial. The sentence, they ruled, had been based on the theory that the murder had been committed in conjunction with a rape. "Felony murder," this is called—murder coupled with another felony. In 1982, the Florida Supreme Court, by a vote of 4 to 3, declared that the underlying felony, rape, had not been proven beyond a reasonable doubt. Eight years after the original sentence, Doug McCray was going back to trial.

Except that something even more amazing happened a few weeks later. The state supreme court granted the prosecution's request for a rehearing, and Justice Ray Ehrlich abruptly changed his mind. His vote made it 4 to 3 in favor of upholding McCray's death sentence. In the course of six months, Ehrlich had gone from believing McCray's sentence was so flawed that he should have a new trial to believing that his sentence was sound enough to warrant his death. The court contacted the company that publishes all its decisions and asked that the first half of this flip-flop—the order for a new trial—be erased from history.

Gov. Bob Graham signed a second death warrant on May 27, 1983. By this time, Bob Dillinger had located his client's ex-wife in California, where she lived with her son by Doug McCray. The son was what his father had once been: bright as a whip, interested in current events, a devourer of books, good at games. The ex-wife, Myra Starks, was mystified by the course her husband's life had taken. They had been high school sweethearts, and she had married him certain that he was upward bound. When McCray had left school to join the Army, Starks had clung to that vision, picturing a steady string of promotions leading to a comfortable pension. Then came the seizures and the medical discharge, and her husband's behavior changed horribly. He drank heavily, and sometimes when he was drunk he struck out at her violently—though after each of these outbursts, he insisted he remembered nothing. Myra Starks did not make a connection between the medical discharge and the change in her man; instead, she packed up their baby boy and moved out. Within a year, McCray was on trial for murder.

In addition to locating Starks, Bob Dillinger also arranged for a full-scale medical evaluation of his client, and the doctor concluded that McCray indeed suffered from temporal lobe seizure disorder. It all came together: the violent blackouts, triggered by drink. In prison, after a number of seizures, McCray was put on a drug regimen to control his disease: Dilantin, a standard epilepsy treatment, in the mornings, and phenobarbital, a sedative, at night. When Dillinger arranged for Myra Starks to see her ex-husband, after a decade apart, she exclaimed, "He's just like the old Doug!"

But he was scheduled to die. Following established procedure, Dillinger returned to the Florida Supreme Court. It was the fifth time the court had considered McCray's case. This time, the justices concluded that the new medical evidence might be important in weighing whether death was the appropriate sentence. They ordered the trial court to hold a hearing and stayed the execution while this was done.

Doug McCray had lived on death row nine years. . . .

In all that time, though, his case had not moved past the first level of appeals. The Florida Supreme Court had weighed and reweighed his case, and with each weighing the justices had reached a different conclusion.

McCray's case was far from unusual. Every death penalty case winds up on spongy ground, even the most outrageous. It took nearly a decade for Florida to execute serial killer Ted Bundy, and even longer for John Wayne Gacy to reach the end in Illinois. The courts routinely reverse themselves, then double back again. The same case can look different with each fresh examination or new group of judges. Defenders have learned to exploit every possible advantage from the tiniest detail to the loftiest constitutional principle. A conscientious defense attorney has no choice—especially if any question remains as to whether the condemned man actually committed the crime for which he was sentenced. The effort involves huge expenditures of time and resources, and results are notoriously uncertain. . . .

By the time Doug McCray's case returned to the trial court for a new sentence in 1986, the hanging judge, William Lamar Rose, was gone. So many years had passed. But in his place was another stern man who was no less outraged at the enormity of McCray's crime. . . .

McCray had, over the years, become a favorite of death penalty opponents, because he seemed so gentle and redeemable. Frequently, they argued that not all death row prisoners are "like Ted Bundy," and McCray was the sort of prisoner they were talking about. The harshest word in his vocabulary was "shucks." He read every book he could get his hands on. There was a poignant vulnerability to him.

But the new judge focused, as the old one had done, on the crime: A defenseless, innocent, helpless woman alone, terrorized, apparently raped, then killed. He sentenced McCray to death once more. And the case returned to the Florida Supreme Court for a sixth time. In June 1987, after a U.S. Supreme Court decision in favor of another Florida inmate, the justices sent McCray's case back because the judge had overruled the jury's advisory sentence. What was his justification? The judge's justification was an elderly woman savagely murdered. Once again, he imposed the death sentence.

So the case of Doug McCray returned for the seventh time to the Florida Supreme Court. Did he deserve to die? Four times, a trial judge insisted that he did. Twice, the state's high court agreed. And four times, the same court expressed doubts. A single case, considered and reconsidered, strained and restrained, weighed and reweighed. A prism, a kaleidoscope, a rune of unknown meaning. The life of a man, viewed through the lens of a complex, uncertain, demanding law. Should he live or die?

In May 1991, after weighing his case for the seventh time in 17 years, the Florida Supreme Court reversed McCray's death sentence and imposed a sentence of life in prison. For 17 years, two courts had debated—the trial court and the state supreme court. No liberal outsiders stalled the process, no bleeding hearts intervened. Even the lawyers added little to the essential conundrum, which was in the beginning as it was in the end: Doug McCray, bad guy, versus Doug McCray, not-quite-so-bad guy. The case was far from aberrant. It was one of hundreds of such cases.

⋅✦⋅

Some politicians and pundits still talk as if the confusion over the death penalty can be eliminated by a healthy dose of conservative toughness, but among the people who know the system best that explanation is losing steam. More than 20 years have passed since *Furman v. Georgia;* courts and legislatures have gotten tougher and tougher on the issue—but the results have remained negligible. The execution rate hovers at around 25 or 30 per year, while America's death row population has swelled past 3,000. It makes no real difference who controls the courts, as California voters learned after they dumped their liberal chief justice in 1986. The court turned rightward, but 7½ years later, California had executed just two of the more than 300 prisoners on its death row. (One of the two had voluntarily surrendered his appeals.) No matter how strongly judges and politicians favor capital punishment, the law has remained a mishmash.

It is hard to see a way out. The idea that the death penalty should not be imposed arbitrarily—that each case should be analyzed by a rational set of standards—has been so deeply woven into so many federal and state court rulings that there is little chance of it being reversed. Courts have softened that requirement, but softening has not solved the problem. Proposals to limit access to appeals for death row inmates have become staples of America's political campaigns, and many limits have been set. But it can take up to a decade for a prisoner to complete just one trip through the courts, and no one has proposed denying condemned inmates one trip.

. . . [E]ven the most vicious killers . . . cannot be executed quickly. Gerald Stano, who in the early 1980s confessed to killing more than two dozen women, is alive. Thomas Knight, who in 1980 murdered a prison guard while awaiting execution for two other murders, is alive. Jesus Scull, who in 1983 robbed and murdered two victims and burned their house around them, is alive. Howard Douglas, who in 1973 forced his wife to have sex with her boyfriend as he watched, then smashed the man's head in, is alive. Robert Buford, who in 1977 raped and beat a 7-year-old girl to death, is alive. Eddie Lee Freeman, who in 1976 strangled a former nun and dumped her in a river to drown, is alive. Jesse Hall, who in 1975 raped and murdered a teenage girl and killed her boyfriend, is alive. James Rose, who in 1976 raped and murdered an 8-year-old girl in Fort Lauderdale, is alive. Larry Mann, who in 1980 cut a little girl's throat and clubbed her to death as she crawled away, is alive.

And that's just in Florida. The story is the same across the country.

In 1972, Justice Harry Blackmun cast one of the four votes in favor of preserving the death penalty in *Furman v. Georgia,* and he voted with the majority to approve the new laws four years later. For two decades, he stuck to the belief that the death penalty could meet the constitutional test of reliability. But last year Blackmun threw up his hands. "Twenty years have passed since this Court declared that the death penalty must be imposed fairly and with reasonable consistency or not all," he wrote. ". . . In the years following Furman, serious efforts were made to comply with its mandate. State legislatures and appellate courts struggled to provide judges and juries with sensible and objective guidelines for determining who should live and who should die . . . Unfortunately, all this experimentation and ingenuity yielded little of what Furman demanded . . . It seems that the decision whether a human being should live or die is so inherently subjective, rife with all of life's understandings, experiences, prejudices and passions, that it inevitably defies the rationality and consistency required by the Constitution . . . I feel morally and intellectually obligated simply to concede that the death penalty experiment has failed."

Also last year, an admiring biography of retired Justice Lewis Powell was published. Powell was one of the architects of the modern death penalty. As a swing vote in 1976, he had helped to define the intricate weighing system that restored capital punishment in America. Later, as the deciding vote in a 1987 case, *McCleskey v. Kemp*, Powell had saved the death penalty from the assertion that racial disparities proved the system was still arbitrary. Now Powell was quoted as telling his biographer, "I have come to think that capital punishment should be abolished." The death penalty "brings discredit on the whole legal system," Powell said, because the vast majority of death sentences are never carried out. Biographer John C. Jeffries Jr. had asked Powell if he would like to undo any decisions from his long career. "Yes," the justice answered. "McCleskey v. Kemp."

No one has done more than Ray Marky to make a success of the death penalty. As a top aide in the Florida attorney general's office, he worked himself into an early heart attack prosecuting capital appeals. Eventually, he took a less stressful job at the local prosecutor's office, where he watched, dispirited, as the modern death penalty—the law he had helped write and had struggled to enforce—reached its convoluted maturity. One day a potential death penalty case came across his new desk, and instead of pushing as he had in the old days, he advised the victim's mother to accept a life sentence for her son's killer. "Ma'am, bury your son and get on with your life, or over the next dozen years, this defendant will destroy you, as well as your son," Marky told her. Why put the woman through all the waiting, the hearings and the stays, when the odds were heavy that the death sentence would never be carried out? "I never would have said that 15 years ago," Marky reflected. "But now I will, because I'm not going to put someone through the nightmare. If we had deliberately set out to create a chaotic system, we couldn't have come up with anything worse. It's a merry-go-round, it's ridiculous; it's so clogged up only an arbitrary few ever get it.

"I don't get any damn pleasure out of the death penalty and I never have," the prosecutor said. "And frankly, if they abolished it tomorrow, I'd go get drunk in celebration."

Ernest van den Haag  **NO**

The Ultimate Punishment: A Defense

In an average year about 20,000 homicides occur in the United States. Fewer than 300 convicted murderers are sentenced to death. But because no more than thirty murderers have been executed in any recent year, most convicts sentenced to death are likely to die of old age.[1] Nonetheless, the death penalty looms large in discussions: it raises important moral questions independent of the number of executions.

The death penalty is our harshest punishment. It is irrevocable: it ends the existence of those punished, instead of temporarily imprisoning them. Further, although not intended to cause physical pain, execution is the only corporal punishment still applied to adults. These singular characteristics contribute to the perennial, impassioned controversy about capital punishment.

I. Distribution

Consideration of the justice, morality, or usefulness, of capital punishment is often conflated with objections to its alleged discriminatory or capricious distribution among the guilty. Wrongly so. If capital punishment is immoral *in se,* no distribution among the guilty could make it moral. If capital punishment is moral, no distribution would make it immoral. Improper distribution cannot affect the quality of what is distributed, be it punishments or rewards. Discriminatory or capricious distribution thus could not justify abolition of the death penalty. Further, maldistribution inheres no more in capital punishment than in any other punishment.

Maldistribution between the guilty and the innocent is, by definition, unjust. But the injustice does not lie in the nature of the punishment. Because of the finality of the death penalty, the most grievous maldistribution occurs when it is imposed upon the innocent. However, the frequent allegations of discrimination and capriciousness refer to maldistribution among the guilty and not to the punishment of the innocent.

Maldistribution of any punishment among those who deserve it is irrelevant to its justice or morality. Even if poor or black convicts guilty of capital offenses suffer capital punishment, and other convicts equally guilty of the same crimes do not, a more equal distribution, however desirable, would merely be more equal. It would not be more just to the convicts under sentence of death.

From *Harvard Law Review,* vol. 99, no. 7, May 1986. Copyright © 1986 by Harvard Law Review. Reprinted by permission.

Punishments are imposed on persons, not on racial or economic groups. Guilt is personal. The only relevant question is: does the person to be executed deserve the punishment? Whether or not others who deserved the same punishment, whatever their economic or racial group, have avoided execution is irrelevant. If they have, the guilt of the executed convicts would not be diminished, nor would their punishment be less deserved. To put the issue starkly, if the death penalty were imposed on guilty blacks, but not on guilty whites, or, if it were imposed by a lottery among the guilty, this irrationally discriminatory or capricious distribution would neither make the penalty unjust, nor cause anyone to be unjustly punished, despite the undue impunity bestowed on others.

Equality, in short, seems morally less important than justice. And justice is independent of distributional inequalities. The ideal of equal justice demands that justice be equally distributed, not that it be replaced by equality. Justice requires that as many of the guilty as possible be punished, regardless of whether others have avoided punishment. To let these others escape the deserved punishment does not do justice to them, or to society. But it is not unjust to those who could not escape.

These moral considerations are not meant to deny that irrational discrimination, or capriciousness, would be inconsistent with constitutional requirements. But I am satisfied that the Supreme Court has in fact provided for adherence to the constitutional requirement of equality as much as possible. Some inequality is indeed unavoidable as a practical matter in any system.[2] But, *ultra posse neo obligatur.* (Nobody is bound beyond ability.)

Recent data reveal little direct racial discrimination in the sentencing of those arrested and convicted of murder. The abrogation of the death penalty for rape has eliminated a major source of racial discrimination. Concededly, some discrimination based on the race of murder victims may exist; yet, this discrimination affects criminal victimizers in an unexpected way. Murderers of whites are thought more likely to be executed than murderers of blacks. Black victims, then, are less fully vindicated than white ones. However, because most black murderers kill blacks, black murderers are spared the death penalty more often than are white murderers. They fare better than most white murderers. The motivation behind unequal distribution of the death penalty may well have been to discriminate against blacks, but the result has favored them. Maldistribution is thus a straw man for empirical as well as analytical reasons.

II. Miscarriages of Justice

In a recent survey Professors Hugo Adam Bedau and Michael Radelet found that 7000 persons were executed in the United States between 1900 and 1985 and that 25 were innocent of capital crimes. Among the innocents they list Sacco and Vanzetti as well as Ethel and Julius Rosenberg. Although their data may be questionable, I do not doubt that, over a long enough period, miscarriages of justice will occur even in capital cases.

Despite precautions, nearly all human activities, such as trucking, lighting, or construction, cost the lives of some innocent bystanders. We do not give up these activities, because the advantages, moral or material, outweigh the unintended losses. Analogously, for those who think the death penalty just, miscarriages of justice are offset by the moral benefits and the usefulness of doing justice. For those who think the death penalty unjust even when it does not miscarry, miscarriages can hardly be decisive.

III. Deterrence

Despite much recent work, there has been no conclusive statistical demonstration that the death penalty is a better deterrent than are alternative punishments. However, deterrence is less than decisive for either side. Most abolitionists acknowledge that they would continue to favor abolition even if the death penalty were shown to deter more murders than alternatives could deter. Abolitionists appear to value the life of a convicted murderer or, at least, his nonexecution, more highly than they value the lives of the innocent victims who might be spared by deterring prospective murderers.

Deterrence is not altogether decisive for me either. I would favor retention of the death penalty as retribution even if it were shown that the threat of execution could not deter prospective murderers not already deterred by the threat of imprisonment.[3] Still, I believe the death penalty, because of its finality, is more feared than imprisonment, and deters some prospective murderers not deterred by the threat of imprisonment. Sparing the lives of even a few prospective victims by deterring their murderers is more important than preserving the lives of convicted murderers because of the possibility, or even the probability, that executing them would not deter others. Whereas the lives of the victims who might be saved are valuable, that of the murderer has only negative value, because of his crime. Surely the criminal law is meant to protect the lives of potential victims in preference to those of actual murderers.

Murder rates are determined by many factors; neither the severity nor the probability of the threatened sanction is always decisive. However, for the long run, I share the view of Sir James Fitzjames Stephen: "Some men, probably, abstain from murder because they fear that if they committed murder they would be hanged. Hundreds of thousands abstain from it because they regard it with horror. One great reason why they regard it with horror is that murderers are hanged." Penal sanctions are useful in the long run for the formation of the internal restraints so necessary to control crime. The severity and finality of the death penalty is appropriate to the seriousness and the finality of murder.

IV. Incidental Issues: Cost, Relative Suffering, Brutalization

Many nondecisive issues are associated with capital punishment. Some believe that the monetary cost of appealing a capital sentence is excessive. Yet most comparisons of the cost of life imprisonment with the cost of execution, apart from their dubious relevance, are flawed at least by the implied assumption that life prisoners will generate no judicial costs during their imprisonment.

At any rate, the actual monetary costs are trumped by the importance of doing justice.

Others insist that a person sentenced to death suffers more than his victim suffered, and that this (excess) suffering is undue according to the *lex talionis* (rule of retaliation). We cannot know whether the murderer on death row suffers more than his victim suffered; however, unlike the murderer, the victim deserved none of the suffering inflicted. Further, the limitations of the *lex talionis* were meant to restrain private vengeance, not the social retribution that has taken its place. Punishment—regardless of the motivation—is not intended to revenge, offset, or compensate for the victim's suffering, or to be measured by it. Punishment is to vindicate the law and the social order undermined by the crime. This is why a kidnapper's penal confinement is not limited to the period for which he imprisoned his victim; nor is a burglar's confinement meant merely to offset the suffering or the harm he caused his victim; nor is it meant only to offset the advantage he gained.[4]

Another argument heard at least since Beccaria is that, by killing a murderer, we encourage, endorse, or legitimize unlawful killing. Yet, although all punishments are meant to be unpleasant, it is seldom argued that they legitimize the unlawful imposition of identical unpleasantness. Imprisonment is not thought to legitimize kidnapping; neither are fines thought to legitimize robbery. The difference between murder and execution, or between kidnapping and imprisonment, is that the first is unlawful and undeserved, the second a lawful and deserved punishment for an unlawful act. The physical similarities of the punishment to the crime are irrelevant. The relevant difference is not physical, but social.[5]

V. Justice, Excess, Degradation

We threaten punishments in order to deter crime. We impose them not only to make the threats credible but also as retribution (justice) for the crimes that were not deterred. Threats and punishments are necessary to deter and deterrence is a sufficient practical justification for them. Retribution is an independent moral justification. Although penalties can be unwise, repulsive, or inappropriate, and those punished can be pitiable, in a sense the infliction of legal punishment on a guilty person cannot be unjust. By committing the crime, the criminal volunteered to assume the risk of receiving a legal punishment that he could have avoided by not committing the crime. The punishment he suffers is the punishment he voluntarily risked suffering and, therefore, it is no more unjust to him than any other event for which one knowingly volunteers to assume the risk. Thus, the death penalty cannot be unjust to the guilty criminal.

There remain, however, two moral objections. The penalty may be regarded as always excessive as retribution and always morally degrading. To regard the death penalty as always excessive, one must believe that no crime—no matter how heinous—could possibly justify capital punishment. Such a belief can be neither corroborated nor refuted; it is an article of faith.

Alternatively, or concurrently, one may believe that everybody, the murderer no less than the victim, has an imprescriptible (natural?) right to life. The law therefore should not deprive anyone of life. I share Jeremy Bentham's view that any such "natural and imprescriptible rights" are "nonsense upon stilts."

Justice Brennan has insisted that the death penalty is "uncivilized," "inhuman," inconsistent with "human dignity" and with "the sanctity of life," that it "treats members of the human race as nonhumans, as objects to be toyed with and discarded," that it is "uniquely degrading to human dignity" and "by its very nature, [involves] a denial of the executed person's humanity." Justice Brennan does not say why he thinks execution "uncivilized." Hitherto most civilizations have had the death penalty, although it has been discarded in Western Europe, where it is currently unfashionable probably because of its abuse by totalitarian regimes.

By "degrading," Justice Brennan seems to mean that execution degrades the executed convicts. Yet philosophers, such as Immanuel Kant and G. F. W. Hegel, have insisted that, when deserved, execution, far from degrading the executed convict, affirms his humanity by affirming his rationality and his responsibility for his actions. They thought that execution, when deserved, is required for the sake of the convict's dignity. (Does not life imprisonment violate human dignity more than execution, by keeping alive a prisoner deprived of all autonomy?)

Common sense indicates that it cannot be death—or common fate—that is inhuman. Therefore, Justice Brennan must mean that death degrades when it comes not as a natural or accidental event, but as a deliberate social imposition. The murderer learns through his punishment that his fellow men have found him unworthy of living; that because he has murdered, he is being expelled from the community of the living. This degradation is self-inflicted. By murdering, the murderer has so dehumanized himself that he cannot remain among the living. The social recognition of his self-degradation is the punitive essence of execution. To believe, as Justice Brennan appears to, that the degradation is inflicted by the execution reverses the direction of causality.

Execution of those who have committed heinous murders may deter only one murder per year. If it does, it seems quite warranted. It is also the only fitting retribution for murder I can think of.

Notes

1. Death row as a semipermanent residence is cruel, because convicts are denied the normal amenities of prison life. Thus, unless death row residents are integrated into the prison population, the continuing accumulation of convicts on death row should lead us to accelerate either the rate of executions or the rate of commutations. I find little objection to integration.

2. The ideal of equality, unlike the ideal of retributive justice (which can be approximated separately in each instance), is clearly unattainable unless all guilty persons are apprehended, and thereafter tried, convicted and sentenced by the same court, at the same time. Unequal justice is the best

we can do; it is still better than the injustice, equal or unequal, which occurs if, for the sake of equality, we deliberately allow some who could be punished to escape.

3. If executions were shown to increase the murder rate in the long run, I would favor abolition. Sparing the innocent victims who would be spared, *ex hypothesi*, by the nonexecution of murderers would be more important to me than the execution, however just, of murderers. But although there is a lively discussion of the subject, no serious evidence exists to support the hypothesis that executions produce a higher murder rate. *Cf.* Phillips, *The Deterrent Effect of Capital Punishment: New Evidence on an Old Controversy,* 86 AM. J. Soc. 139 (1980) (arguing that murder rates drop immediately after executions of criminals).

4. Thus restitution (a civil liability) cannot satisfy the punitive purpose of penal sanctions, whether the purpose be retributive or deterrent.

5. Some abolitionists challenge: if the death penalty is just and serves as a deterrent, why not televise executions? The answer is simple. The death even of a murderer, however well-deserved, should not serve as public entertainment. It so served in earlier centuries. But in this respect our sensibility has changed for the better, I believe. Further, television unavoidably would trivialize executions, wedged in, as they would be, between game shows, situation comedies and the like. Finally, because televised executions would focus on the physical aspects of the punishment, rather than the nature of the crime and the suffering of the victim, a televised execution would present the murderer as the victim of the state. Far from communicating the moral significance of the execution, television would shift the focus to the pitiable fear of the murderer. We no longer place in cages those sentenced to imprisonment to expose them to public view. Why should we so expose those sentenced to execution?

POSTSCRIPT

Is Capital Punishment a Bad Public Policy?

One of the most striking elements about the issue of capital punishment is that most of the public, the politicians, and even many criminological scholars do not seem to be fazed by empirical evidence. Each side marshalls empirical evidence to support its respective position. Opponents of capital punishment often draw from Thorsten Sellin's classic study *The Penalty of Death* (Sage Publications) to "prove" that the number of capital offenses is no lower in states that have the death penalty as compared to states that have abolished executions.

Almost all of the major presidential candidates in early 2000 supported the death penalty. In fact, most political candidates seem to support capital punishment nowadays. Supporters of capital punishment draw from numerous studies, including I. Ehrlich's "The Deterrent Effect of Capital Punishment," *American Economic Review* (vol. 65, 1975), pp. 397–417, and his "Capital Punishment and Deterrence: Some Further Thoughts and Additional Evidence," *Journal of Political Economy* (vol. 85, 1977), pp. 741–788. They also draw from W. Berns's *For Capital Punishment: Crime and the Morality of the Death Penalty* (Basic Books, 1979).

Generally, the empirical research indicates that the death penalty cannot conclusively be proven to deter others from committing homicides and other serious crimes. Entire scientific commissions have been charged with the responsibility of determining the deterrent effects of the death penalty (for example, the National Academy of Sciences in 1975). The gist of their conclusions was that the value of the death penalty as a deterrent "is not a settled matter."

As is typical with most aspects of human behavior, including crime and crime control, the issue is filled with much irony, paradox, and contradiction. First, clashing views over capital punishment rely largely on emotion. The public's attitudes, politicians' attitudes, and even scholarly attitudes are frequently shaped more by sentiment and preconceived notions than by rational discourse. As F. Zimring and G. Hawkins indicate in *Capital Punishment and the American Agenda* (Cambridge University Press, 1986), very few scholars have ever changed their opinions about capital punishment.

However, a remarkable transformation occurred in February 2000: Governor George Ryan (R-Illinois) stopped executions in his state after 13 condemned criminals were exonerated while on death row. Twelve inmates had been executed in Illinois since 1976. Ryan and others now wonder if perhaps some of them had been innocent as well.

As we enter the twenty-first century, capital punishment remains a divisive issue. And despite dramatic opposition, such as Governor Ryan's, it probably has growing support. One useful, recent work in strong opposition to the practice is A. Sarat, ed., *The Killing State: Capital Punishment in Law, Politics, and Culture* (Oxford University Press, 1998). Also see "The Cruel and Ever More Unusual Punishment," *The Economist* (May 15, 1999).

An interesting book that looks at both sides of the issue is *The Death Penalty: For and Against* (Rowman & Littlefield, 1997), with J. Reiman attacking and coauthor L. Pojman defending executions as retribution. An empirical study of a neglected aspect of the issue is "An Empirical Examination of Commutations and Executions in Post-*Furman* Capital Cases," by W. Pridemore, *Justice Quarterly* (March 2000). Another series of research articles can be found in the issue of *Criminal Justice Policy Review* entitled "Special Issue on the Death Penalty" (vol. 10, no. 1, 1999). A recent work by a longtime critic of capital punishment is R. M. Bohn's *Deathquest: An Introduction to the Theory and Practice of Capital Punishment in the United States* (Anderson, 1999).

For a take on Hollywood's many films on executions, see "Death Row, Aisle Seat," by A. Sarat, *The American Prospect* (February 14, 2000). A good overview dealing with women and the death penalty is K. A. O'Shea's *Women and the Death Penalty in the United States, 1900–1998* (Greenwood, 1999). In addition to the many studies by Victor Streib on executing children, see *A Review of Juvenile Executions in America* by R. L. Hale (Edwin Mellen Press, 1997). A concise overview of relevant statistics through December 1999 is *Capital Punishment 1998*, a Bureau of Justice Statistics Bulletin (December 1999).

Two studies of the deterrence issue are "Capital Punishment and the Deterrence of Violent Crime in Comparable Countries," by D. Cheatwood, *Criminal Justice Review* (August 1993) and "Deterrence or Brutalization?" by J. Cochran et al., *Criminology* (February 1994). For a survey of the attitudes toward capital punishment among politicians, see M. Sandys and E. McGarrell, "Attitudes Toward Capital Punishment Among Indiana Legislators," *Justice Quarterly* (December 1994). A popular media account of a death penalty sentence given to a mentally impaired individual is "Untrue Confessions," by J. Smolowe, *Time* (May 22, 1995). An interesting comparison of the effects of publicized executions on whites and blacks is "The Impact of Publicized Executions on Homicide," by S. Stack, *Criminal Justice and Behavior* (June 1995). The *Bureau of Justice Statistics Bulletin* routinely updates death penalty statistics. For an outstanding description of death row, see Von Drehle's *Among the Lowest of the Dead: The Culture of Death Row* (Times Books, 1995).

L. K. Gillespie's *Dancehall Ladies: The Crimes and Executions of America's Condemned Women* (University Press of America, 1997) is a solid historical discussion. D. A. Cabana's *Death at Midnight: The Confessions of an Executioner* (Northeast University Press, 1996) is an insightful insider's account. A helpful legal overview is *Death Penalty Cases: Leading U.S. Supreme Court Cases on Capital Punishment* by B. Latzer (Butterworth-Heinemann, 1998). Finally, two outstanding articles that provide both historical and theoretical background for understanding violence and capital punishment as an extension of inequalities maintenance are Roberta Senechal de la Roche, "Collective Violence As Social Control," *Sociological Forum* (March 1996) and "The Sociogenesis of Lynching," in W. F. Brundae, ed., *Under Penalty of Death: Essays on Lynching in the South* (University of North Carolina Press, 1997).

Internet References . . .

Federal Bureau of Investigation

The home page of the FBI leads to the 10 most wanted criminals, uniform crime reports, FBI case reports, major investigations, and more.

http://www.fbi.gov

Sourcebook of Criminal Justice Statistics Online

Data about all aspects of criminal justice in the United States is available at this site, which includes over 655 tables and figures from more than 100 sources.

http://www.albany.edu/sourcebook/

Gun Owners of America

Gun Owners of America is a gun lobby organization based in Springfield, Virginia. Their site links to current national alerts and statewide alerts about gun owners' rights, proposed gun-control legislation, and other gun-related information.

http://www.gunowners.org

Brady Campaign to Prevent Gun Violence

The Brady Campaign to Prevent Gun Violence is a nonpartisan, not-for-profit organization that lobbies in favor of commonsense gun regulations at both state and national levels. This site offers action alerts, information on gun laws and legislation, and advice on how to avoid becoming a victim of handgun violence.

http://www.handguncontrol.org

NYPD Crime Strategies

This site from the chief of the New York Police Department details several crime strategies adopted by the department, including "Reclaiming the Public Spaces of New York City," which is based on the broken windows theory.

http://www.nyc.gov/html/nypd/home.html

Modern Trends in Criminology and Criminal Justice

*A*lthough research—in particular, its interpretations and applications—can be highly problematic, it remains a core task for criminologists and criminal justice scholars. Among the most important criminological research findings of the past 25 years is that a relatively small core of criminals commit a disproportionate amount of crime. Also important to criminal justice is the development and utilization of technology, such as DNA technology, computer units in police cars, and innovations in investigation techniques. Yet just how helpful is this research?

Questions addressed in this selection ask, Why haven't increased executions reduced violent crime? Is it possible that more guns in the hands of Americans could actually lead to less crime? And, lastly, will zero tolerance policing solve much of America's cities' crime problems? Perhaps researching crime, and then deciding how to use the results, is one of criminology's biggest problems.

- Should Serious Sex Offenders Be Castrated?

- Do Strict Gun Control Laws Reduce the Number of Homicides in the United States?

- Should the Police Enforce Zero-Tolerance Laws?

- Should Marijuana Be Legalized?

- Should Juries Be Able to Disregard the Law and Free "Guilty" Persons in Racially Charged Cases?

ISSUE 12

Should Serious Sex Offenders Be Castrated?

YES: Lawrence Wright, from "The Case for Castration," *Texas Monthly* (May 1992)

NO: Kari A. Vanderzyl, from "Castration as an Alternative to Incarceration: An Impotent Approach to the Punishment of Sex Offenders," *Northern Illinois University Law Review* (Fall 1994)

ISSUE SUMMARY

YES: Attorney Lawrence Wright argues that while castration may not be an ideal solution, if we treat it as therapy rather than punishment, as help instead of revenge, and if we view offenders as troubled victims, not monsters, then perhaps castration will become an accepted and humane option for sex offender treatment.

NO: Attorney Kari A. Vanderzyl asserts that castration should be rejected as an unacceptable, ineffective, and unconstitutional alternative to imprisonment for sex offenders.

Castration of sex offenders is a frightening issue that for some will conjure images of Joseph Mengele, the Nazi physician who performed horrible experiments on human subjects in concentration camps during World War II. Is it possible to view castration, however, as a voluntary and humane therapeutic solution for serious sex offenders? Moreover, does castration work? If serious offenders are castrated, will they cease committing sex offenses? The articles in this section demonstrate that at least three different issues must be examined before considering castration as a routine form of treatment for sex offenders: the empirical evidence, its constitutionality, and the moral propriety of castrating sex offenders.

The available evidence on castrating sex offenders is interesting indeed. A German study conducted between 1970 and 1980 analyzed 104 individuals who had undergone voluntary castration as a form of treatment. Seventy percent of these individuals were categorized as pedophiles, 25 percent were aggressive sex offenders, 3 percent were exhibitionists, and 2 percent were classified as homosexuals. The control group consisted of individuals who had applied for castration during the same period but did not have the surgery. The researchers found that sexual interest, sex drive, erection, and ejaculation had generally decreased in 75 percent of the cases within six months of the operation. Moreover, the postoperative recidivism rate for sex crimes was 3 percent at most, compared to 46 percent for non-castrated subjects. The authors of the study also concluded that the social adjustment of the castrated subjects appeared to be more favorable than that of the non-castrated individuals. Among the castrated subjects, 70 percent were satisfied with the treatment, 20 percent were ambivalent, and 10 percent were not satisfied.

The U.S. Supreme Court has not expressly considered the issue of the constitutionality of castration as a form of treatment for sex offenders. In *Buck v. Bell*, 274 U.S. 200 (1927), however, a Virginia law was upheld that provided for the involuntary sterilization of persons confined to a state mental institution who were found to be afflicted with a hereditary form of insanity or imbecility. Justice Oliver Wendell Holmes, widely regarded as one of the greatest Supreme Court justices in U.S. history, stated: "It is better for all the world, if instead of waiting to execute degenerate offspring for crime, or to let them starve for their imbecility, society can prevent those who are manifestly unfit from continuing their kind. . . . Three generations of imbeciles is enough."

Fifteen years later, in *Skinner v. Oklahoma*, 316 U.S. 535 (1942), the Court considered a related issue—the constitutionality of an Oklahoma law that provided for the forced sterilization of habitual criminals for committing a third felony involving "moral turpitude." Stated Justice William O. Douglas:

> We are dealing here with legislation which involves one of the basic civil rights of man. Marriage and procreations are fundamental to the very existence and survival of the race. The power to sterilize, if exercised, may have subtle, far-reaching and devastating effects. In evil or reckless hands it can cause races or types which are inimical to the dominant group to wither and disappear. (541)

So, where are we regarding the Supreme Court's likely handling of mandatory sex offender castration laws? Although *Buck v. Bell* has been strongly criticized, more recent state court decisions have upheld compulsory sterilization laws in the context of mentally incompetent individuals. In addition, four states, including Texas, Florida, California, and Montana, have enacted laws to require involuntary chemical or surgical castration of certain convicted sex offenders. It will be very interesting to see whether U.S. courts will uphold *mandatory* castration laws.

What are your views on the issue of castrating serious sex offenders? Should it become a routine form of treatment for all those who cannot control their sexual urges? Or, should it be reserved for particular types of egregious sex offenders, such as pedophiles and serial rapists? Moreover, how should society draw the line between the types of sex offenders who are castrated and those who receive other forms of "treatment"? Is there a moral principle that should limit the use of this form of treatment, regardless of its utility? These are difficult questions. When you read these articles, try to develop a sense of whether this form of treatment is consistent with principles of basic fairness that are the foundation of our justice system.

YES

Lawrence Wright

The Case for Castration

Everybody from Jesse Jackson to feminist leaders told child molester Steve Butler he shouldn't be able to trade his manhood for his freedom. Everybody was wrong.

⁍❀⁌

There is a lesson in every disaster. Now that the hysteria has quieted in Houston, we can survey the ruins left by the Great Castration Fiasco. When a young black man named Steve Allen Butler offered to place his testicles on the scales of justice, he began a debate that spread through Texas and soon across the entire country, illuminating the divisions between classes, races, and genders. Concerns were raised about the Constitution and medical ethics. Charges were hurled and mud was slung. The image of the state of Texas was damaged by the sneering of the national press. And yet the question that no one in this broad argument seemed willing to address was exactly what we should do with our sex offenders.

If one thing is clear in this whole messy episode, it's that what we're doing now is a failure. Again and again, critics have said that castration is not an effective answer to sexual offense. So far no one has asked, "Compared with what?" Today there are nearly eight thousand sex offenders in Texas prisons. Their crimes include indecent exposure, sex with minors, incest, aggravated sexual assault, and rape. Yet only two hundred are receiving counseling—an indication of how little faith we place in therapeutic solutions. Given the turnover in our prisons, most of those offenders will be out on the streets after serving a small portion of their sentences. More than half will be arrested for another sex crime in fewer than three years.

We may despise the people who commit such acts, but we should realize that most of them are victims themselves, not just of childhood sexual abuse but of their own overwhelming sexual impulses. As was evident in the Butler case, some of the offenders are crying out for another form of treatment. They want to be castrated. Until we find a better solution, perhaps voluntary castration of sex offenders is a good idea.

From *Texas Monthly*, vol. 20, no. 5, May 1992, pp. 108–122. Copyright © 1992 by Texas Monthly. Reprinted by permission.

و☙و

The debate began last fall at a dinner party in Tanglewood. "Like every gathering I've been to in Houston recently, the subject of crime captured the whole conversation," recalls state district judge Michael McSpadden. . . .

It was at that dinner party that Dr. Louis J. Girard mentioned his then-unpublished paper on castration. . . . Being a scientist, Girard decided to examine what factors influence criminal behavior. "A lot of crime is based on high levels of testosterone," he concluded. This powerful hormone determines a man's body shape, his hair patterns, the pitch of his voice. "It also produces aggressiveness in the males," Girard told the judge. "It is the reason that stallions are high-strung and impossible to train, the reason male dogs become vicious and start to bite people. It's why boys take chances and chase girls, why they drive too fast and deliberately start fights. In violent criminals, these tendencies are exaggerated and carried to extremes." In Girard's opinion, castration would reduce and possibly eliminate such aggressive impulses. The castrated criminal would be more docile and have a better opportunity to be rehabilitated, educated, and to become a worthwhile citizen," Girard contended.

Girard's idea rang a bell with McSpadden. If there was a painless, inexpensive procedure that would reduce the overflowing prison population, allow criminals to gain control over their violent natures, make them more susceptible to rehabilitation, and also act as a powerful deterrent to other offenders, what could be wrong with that? . . .

The controversy might have died out soon after that except for 27-year-old Steve Butler, who read about it in the paper in October. At the time, Butler was sitting on the fifth floor of the Harris County jail, accused of having had sex with a 13-year-old girl. Butler was already on probation in McSpadden's court for fondling a 7-year-old girl in 1989. The new charge could result in a lengthy prison term. Butler might get life, plus 10 years for violating his probation. He had already rejected the plea bargain offered by the assistant district attorney handling the case, Bill Hawkins, in which Butler would plead guilty to aggravated sexual assault and receive 35 years. Because it was an aggravated charge (meaning that the victim was under 14), Butler would have to serve at least one fourth of his time before he would be eligible for parole. He would spend the next 8 years and 9 months in prison as a convicted child molester, the lowest rung on the criminal hierarchy. . . .

Butler's problem, as he later admitted to psychologists who examined him, was that he had no control over his sexual impulses. Dr. Michael Cox, a well-respected therapist at Baylor College of Medicine who counsels sex offenders, examined Butler at Judge McSpadden's request. After administering a battery of standard psychological tests, Cox found Butler to be mildly depressed but otherwise sane and competent. Butler "didn't look any different from the garden-variety child molesters I see in the program," says Cox. "He had been abused when he was young. He seemed to be more of a situational offender—in other words, his sexual preference is for adult women. But he does have a drinking problem, and if there is a female child available and he's been drinking, one thing can lead to another." . . .

As for Butler, his motives were varied. "I just think it would help me a whole lot," he admits. "I could be a better person. I could go on with my life and take care of my family." He is also frightened by the idea of going to prison, especially as a child molester. "I've heard stories about it," he says in a near whisper. "Some say it's hard. You have to fight."

* * *

"Frankly, I think the judge is titillated by the idea of cutting the balls off a black man," says the Reverend Jew Don Boney, the chairman of the Houston chapter of the Black United Front. "This is McSpadden playing God. It's unprecedented; it's outside of normal legal bounds; and it introduces a whole new level of inhumanity into the criminal justice system." . . .

Castration is a profound symbol of the historic oppression of black men. In 1855 the Territory of Kansas introduced judicial castration of Negroes and mulattoes who raped or attempted to rape white women. In the South, blacks were sometimes castrated before being lynched. "It's a reminder of what I read about in the days of slavery and in the late eighteen-hundreds and early nineteen-hundreds," says Burns. "If this is the best we can come up with in terms of punishing or trying to deal with people guilty of that type of crime, then I'm wondering what changes we have made between 1892 and 1992." "It's just too close to an ugly part of our history," says Robert Newberry. "You would have to have gone through that type of history to really feel the emotional impact of how our forefathers were treated." Newberry recalls seeing a photo of a lynched black man with a bloody gash where his sex organs had been. "This castration issue brings it all back. It stirs up the pain."

For many black people, the contrast between the white judge—maverick Republican who plays tennis at the Houston Racquet Club—and the shine man sitting in the jailhouse seemed to characterize the imbalance of power between the races. One had privilege and the respect of society; the other was a high school dropout with no prospects, the sort of castoff that society notices only when he becomes a statistic in the criminal justice system. What was there left to take away from Steve Butler—except his manliness?

That Butler himself sought castration was rarely commented upon, except to say that he was a victim of judicial coercion. In fact, McSpadden had been elaborately cautious in making sure that Butler's choice was free and informed. He instructed Butler to talk to four psychiatrists and therapists, including Michael Cox, who was outspokenly opposed to the castration option. No one was able to change Butler's mind. He still preferred castration to prison, a choice denounced as "a very dangerous precedent" by Frank Burns. And yet when I asked Burns what he would do if he were in Butler's place, having to choose between a lengthy spell in prison or castration, he said he "may very well" make the same choice: castration and freedom. . . .

"People hear the word 'castration' and it scares them," McSpadden told me one afternoon in his chambers. "They don't realize it is a simple surgical procedure that can be done on an outpatient basis. It's not cutting off the penis. It's far less intrusive than a hysterectomy. What's more, the crime we see in Texas is a direct result of the failure of present punishments to serve their intended purposes of retribution, rehabilitation, and deterrence. If castration does work, then we not only let that person live a normal life because of a simple medical treatment, but we also protect society from that same person for years to come." . . .

༺◉༻

It was clear from the hundreds of calls and letters that the castration issue strikes a deep chord of fear and anger and a longing for revenge. That is exactly what worries Cassandra Thomas, the director of the rape program at the Houston Area Women's Center. "I don't think castration should be used as punishment," she says. "It only buys into the myth that sexual assault is about sex, and so therefore if you get rid of sexual desires you get rid of rape. The reality is that sexual assault is about violence; it's about a need for power and control. It has nothing to do with the genital organs." Castration, she says, is "an empty symbolic gesture." . . .

Many women see rape as a political act, evidence of the male need to control the female. Viewed through that lens, treating the problem by removing the sex organs will only frustrate men and make them, as Thomas argues, "more likely to use violence as a way of dealing with their issues of inadequacy and powerlessness and helplessness that perpetuate sexual assaults in the first place." . . .

༺◉༻

Nearly everyone involved in the Butler case—like nearly everyone in Texas— has had some experience with castrated animals. The district attorney of Harris County, Johnny Holmes, keeps a herd of Longhorns, and he has personally castrated many of them. "My experience is that they get a lot bigger and a lot gentler," says Holmes. Girard castrated bulls when he was young; he also played polo at the Bayou Club. "Believe me, there's a tremendous difference in the amount of control you have between a gelding and a stallion." Recently one of his German shepherds became cantankerous and nipped Girard's daughter and his niece. "So I just castrated him, and he stopped." Michael Cox, the Baylor sex therapist, had his cat castrated. "He doesn't get into fights about female cats, but he still fights over territory." . . .

Voluntary castration became legally permissible in Denmark through the Access to Sterilization law of 1929, which permitted the operation on a "person whose sexual drive is abnormal in power or tendency, thus making him liable to commit crimes." Although the Danish law did permit forced castrations, that provision was never put into practice and was subsequently eliminated. Other European countries implemented similar voluntary programs. In this country, Oklahoma allowed forced castration of repeated felons convicted of crimes involving "moral turpitude"—a larger category than sex offenses—until the U.S. Supreme Court declared its law unconstitutional in 1942. Recently bills were knocked down in Washington, Alabama, and Indiana that would have permitted sex offenders to be castrated in exchange for a reduction in their sentences. The historical associations make it difficult to talk about castration without the specter of government-imposed sterilization becoming a part of the argument. Unfortunately, that is exactly the way Girard and McSpadden have framed their proposal.

Dr. John Bradford of the Royal Ottawa Hospital in Canada says that as a rule, the recidivism rate of sex offenders (that is, their likelihood to offend again) averages 80 percent before castration, dropping to less than 5 percent afterwards. In Europe, many studies on the consequences of therapeutic castration show essentially the same thing—that it is profoundly effective in lowering the rates of repeated sex offenses. A 1973 Swiss study of 121 castrated offenders found that their recidivism rate dropped to 4.3 percent, compared with 76.8 percent for the control group. In Germany, a similar report showed a post-operative recidivism rate of 2.3 percent for sex offenses, compared with 84 percent for non-castrates. Various Danish studies have followed as many as 900 castrated sex offenders for several decades; they show that recidivism rates drop to 2.2 percent. What is also important is that 90 percent of the castrated men reported that they themselves are satisfied with the outcome. "The main conclusion to be derived from all this material on castrated men," wrote Dr. Georg K. Sturup, chief psychiatrist of Denmark's Herstedvester Detention Center, in 1968, "is that a person who has suffered acutely as a result of his sexual drive will, after castration, feel a great sense of relief at being freed from these urges." . . .

Many people who oppose castration believe that the main problem sex offenders have is psychological, not physical. Therefore, they assume, diligent treatment involving therapy and the latest behavior modification techniques should make a difference. In fact, when counseling succeeds, it is only with a very limited group. It's an inside joke among sex counselors that if you want to have a successful program, you fill it with incest perpetrators, whose reoffense rate is about 3 percent, and keep out all the difficult cases, especially the rapists. . . .

No doubt there is progress in the field of sex offender treatment. No doubt some offenders are susceptible to treatment and others are not. But the stark fact is that none of these programs compares in effectiveness with castration.

The cost of our failure to treat sex offenders can't be known or measured, only guessed at. The tendency to sexually offend is usually lifelong. The chances of ever being arrested for a sex crime are very small—2 percent by some measures. "I went twelve years without being arrested, but I never went more than three days without acting out," an exhibitionist told me. The sheer number of offenses buried in the term "recidivate" can be imagined by a ten-year study of 550 sex offenders (many of whom had never been arrested), which asked each perpetrator how many victims he could specifically identify. The tally was 190,000 victims. . . .

⊷◉⊶

The pressure was building on Steve Butler. The Reverend Jesse Jackson came to Houston and was allowed to see Butler, even against Butler's request not to see any visitors. Butler still wouldn't talk about his case. "This is not just a Houston matter, just as Selma was not just for Alabama," Jackson proclaimed outside the jailhouse, thus putting the matter of Butler's voluntary castration on a par with the civil rights movement. "We shall make a broad public appeal here and around the country, because such a precedent would be an ugly and dangerous precedent. Rape is sickness. Castration is sickness. The judge's complicity is sickness. We must break this cycle of sickness." . . .

Meanwhile, in Dallas, a man accused of sexually assaulting two girls seven months after being released from prison, said he would prefer castration to prison. "If you cut off man's desire to have sex whatsoever, that should solve the problem," Andrew Jackson, a 52-year-old white man, told a reporter. The prosecutor refused his offer, but it is clear that the castration issue in Texas isn't going to go away with the Butler case. It is also clear that Butler himself is not going to be castrated, despite his own wishes. The surgeon who had volunteered to perform the operation backed out when the publicity became too intense. Another doctor called the judge's office and left word that he'd be happy to perform the procedure for free, but on investigation the man turned out to be a dentist.

It was, finally, the lack of a surgeon that caused McSpadden to resign from the case. The weekend before he did so, he agreed to meet with Butler's five sisters and their attorney. "I told them step by step what had happened, but they were convinced it was a white conspiracy to railroad their younger brother," says McSpadden. The sisters were demanding that Butler be granted probation, which the prosecution had no interest in offering.

Now Butler's case will go to another court. If the victim's mother agrees to let her testify, Butler may be convicted and sent to prison for a long time. He may decide to reconsider the state's offer of 35 years and expect to be out in about a decade. If the victim doesn't testify, Butler will be a free man—free, but probably unchanged. The likelihood that he will reoffend is high even if he does join the eight thousand sex offenders we are currently incarcerating. Because eventually Butler will be back in society, as will the rest of them. Nothing that we are doing with the offender population has made any real difference in their lives; on the other hand, what sex offenders are doing to us, the rest of society, is seen every day in the courts and hospitals and rape crisis centers and child treatment programs—the circle of tragedy touches us all, somehow, if only in the financial burden of caring for the victims and jailing the perpetrators. We do a sorry job even of that.

❦

Now that the Butler case is out of the news, perhaps it's time to think about whether voluntary castration has a place in the treatment of sex offenders. It is a mistake to make castration a punishment, as Girard and McSpadden have proposed; the Supreme Court would probably rule it unconstitutional, and in any case it is simply too offensive to too many people. Moreover, it should be limited to sex offenders. Castration does lower testosterone, which influences aggressive and violent behavior, but taking away the sex drive won't make a bad man good. It should be reserved for those men with uncontrollable sexual urges. In the case of pedophiles, when they exercise their sexuality they violate the law, not to mention the damage they do to the children. What good is their sexuality to them? If they want to be relieved of it, why can't they be?

Most sex offenders are white; this is a crime where blacks are not overly represented in the prison system. There is no reason for this to be a race issue or even a class issue, since sex offenses cut across economic lines as well. "If I saw some semblance of evidence that this would work, I'd be for it," Robert Newberry admitted after the Butler case cooled off, "but let it start with a white man." Given the history of castration in this country, that may be a fair request.

Finally, it is a foolish consistency to castrate women for sexual or other crimes. There can be a change in behavior after such an operation, but so far it has never been correlated with sex crimes. That said, the fact is that women can have their Fallopian tubes tied as a contraceptive measure or their entire uterus removed as treatment for premenstrual syndrome, while men who rape or molest children or expose themselves up to thirty times a day can't be castrated because that would be barbarous.

"Why can't it be like abortion, available on demand?" one offender asks. That seems a reasonable question. As it stands now, the only way Butler could be castrated is if he gets a sex-change operation. Society poses no objection to that.

We should acknowledge that men who seek castration are making a sacrifice. The way we can do so is by reducing their prison time and giving them adequate adjustment counseling. The critics may be right that some men may reoffend, but everything we know about the subjects suggests that castration works better than any other approach. Why can't we honor the plea of Steve Butler and many other men and give them the help they are begging for? Castration may not be an ideal solution, but if we treat it as therapy rather than punishment, as help instead of revenge, and if we view offenders as troubled victims, not monsters, then perhaps the castration option will be seen as evidence of our wisdom and humanity, not of our backwardness and cruelty.

Kari A. Vanderzyl  **NO**

Castration as an Alternative to Incarceration: An Impotent Approach to the Punishment of Sex Offenders

The use of castration as a punitive measure, practiced for centuries by other cultures, has enjoyed newfound prominence in this country's criminal justice system as a potential remedy for the proliferation of sex offenses. Not surprisingly, the implementation of castration as an alternative to incarceration has generated considerable debate, including questions regarding its constitutionality and desirability from a public policy standpoint. Fueling the controversy, several recently convicted sex offenders have requested that they be castrated rather than receive lengthy prison sentences.

In March of 1992, Steven Allen Butler, a convicted rapist, stood before Texas District Court Judge Michael McSpadden and requested that the judge order surgical castration rather than sentencing him to prison. Judge McSpadden initially assented to the request, but ultimately withdrew approval in the wake of national publicity and protests by civil libertarians. Physicians in the area refused to perform the operation, and even Butler found himself reconsidering his unusual request.

In Great Britain, a man with a forty-year history of child sex abuse privately arranged for his own surgical castration after prison authorities ignored his repeated pleas for the operation. The subject, a sixty year old former coal miner, has served numerous prison terms for sex offenses against children and has threatened suicide, gone on hunger strikes and even attempted to castrate himself. Although officials at a psychiatric hospital offered to administer chemical castration, the offender refused such treatment, considering chemical castration a temporary, and therefore inadequate, solution to his deviant behavior.

Sharing this desire for sterilization, a thirty-eight year old convicted rapist sentenced in McLean County, Illinois, expressed a preference for castration rather than a prison sentence. Despite the offender's request for sterilization, the sentencing judge concluded that castration was not a viable alternative to incarceration and sentenced the repeat offender to a thirty-seven year term of imprisonment.

From *Northern Illinois University Law Review,* 15 N. III University Law Review 107 (Fall 1994). Copyright © 1994 by Kari A. Vanderzyl. Reprinted by permission. All notes and citations in the original have been omitted. Ellipses in the article reflect material that has been omitted from the original text.

This [article] addresses the legal implications of castration as a punitive measure, tracing the development of compulsory sterilization from its origins in the eugenics movement in the early twentieth century to its present status as an alternative to imprisonment. In particular, the first section explores the rise of eugenics legislation in the United States, the Supreme Court's legitimization of compulsory sterilization and the current practice among the courts of upholding sterilization legislation for the mentally retarded. Within the second section, the use of castration as a punitive measure both in the United States and abroad is discussed. In addition, the second section describes methods of male sterilization, including surgical castration, vasectomy and the non-surgical alternative, chemical castration. The third section analyzes common constitutional challenges to compulsory castration and asserts that the use of castration as an alternative to incarceration violates the rights of privacy and procreation, and may also violate the Eighth Amendment protection against cruel and unusual punishment. In the fourth section, the reasonable relationship test is applied to castration as a term of probation, yielding mixed results. The informed consent objection presented in the fifth section suggests that castration as an alternative to a prison sentence violates the voluntariness requirement of the informed consent doctrine. Finally, section six explores the economic and social policy considerations implicated by sterilization in the punitive context, focusing on the financial burdens to society and the failure of castration to address the uncontrollable hostility manifesting itself in acts of sexual violence. The article concludes by asserting that castration in any form constitutes an ineffective, unconstitutional alternative to incarceration.

Background

Historical Framework: Eugenics and the Socially Unfit

Compulsory sterilization is not a novel concept. The controversy over a court's or state agency's authority to destroy an individual's ability to procreate has persisted for over a century, since the notion of involuntary sterilization originated with the eugenics movement. Defined by its creator, Sir Francis Galton, as "the science which deals with all influences that improve the unborn qualities of the race . . . [and] develop them to the utmost advantage," eugenics seeks to achieve the elimination of social ills through biological reformation. American eugenicists relied upon Darwin's theory of evolution and Mendel's genetics experimentation to provide scientific support for their movement. Borrowing from the research of Darwin and Mendel, eugenicists theorized that feeble-mindedness and other negative qualities resulted from inferior genes. Operating on this premise, proponents of eugenics linked every existing social problem to heredity and concluded that the solution to the country's social ills required control over human reproduction. Through lecture tours and written propaganda, positive eugenics encouraged individuals with superior genes to select mates from within their own ranks and to maximize family size.

Negative eugenics utilized a different approach, calling for the implementation of a program of sterilization to eliminate procreation of the unfit. Before 1900, compulsory sterilization of the unfit enjoyed limited popular support. Surgical castration, that era's prevailing method of sterilization, produced hormonal imbalance and psychological and physiological effects. With the emergence of two less severe methods, vasectomy and salpingectomy, compulsory eugenics sterilization grew in popularity.

Compulsory Sterilization Legislation

Inspired by the eugenics rationale that played on the pervasive fear of a growing mentally retarded citizenry, in the early 1900s, a number of states enacted compulsory sterilization legislation. State laws mandated sterilization for punitive and therapeutic purposes, with surgical procedures such as castration, vasectomies and salpingectomies performed to punish convicted felons and rehabilitate mentally retarded individuals in state institutions. State officials invoked the doctrine of *parens patriae* to justify the involuntary sterilization of the mentally retarded, claiming to act in the best interests of the institutionalized individuals. Under the doctrine of *parens patriae,* the state bears the responsibility of caring for citizens incapable of protecting their own interests. Despite legislators' efforts to legitimize the practice of involuntary sterilization through reliance on the *parens patriae* justification, the courts nevertheless established a pattern of invalidating compulsory sterilization laws as violations of equal protection or due process.

"Three Generations of Imbeciles. . .":
Buck V. Bell and the Aftermath

At the height of the United States eugenics movement, proponents found an unlikely ally in the nation's highest court. In the now famous case of an institutionalized sixteen year old girl facing compulsory sterilization pursuant to a Virginia statute, the Court upheld the legislation as a valid exercise of the state's police power. Writing for the majority, Justice Holmes reasoned that it would be "better for all the world, if instead of waiting to execute degenerate offspring for crime, or to let them starve for their imbecility, society can prevent those who are manifestly unfit from continuing their kind. . . . Three generations of imbeciles are enough." . . .

Castration as a Punitive Measure

While the involuntary sterilization of mentally retarded persons remains a prominent issue, the greatest and most recent controversy regarding procreative rights has arisen in the punitive context. As an alternative to imprisonment, male sex offenders may elect to undergo castration as punishment for their crimes, raising a number of legal, social and moral issues. . . .

Constitutional Challenges to Sterilization in the Punitive Context

The sterilization of individuals for punitive purposes raises a number of constitutional issues. Government interference with an individual's ability to reproduce implicates constitutional rights to privacy and procreation and the guarantee against cruel and unusual punishment. To achieve recognition as a legitimate, viable alternative to incarceration, male sterilization must pass constitutional muster in each of the areas implicated. . . .

Castration and the Right to Privacy

Although the Constitution contains no explicit mention of a privacy right, the Supreme Court has acknowledged an implied right to privacy under the Fourteenth Amendment protecting an individual's autonomy in making decisions concerning childbearing and contraception. In *Griswold v. Connecticut,* the Court held that a state statute barring married persons' use of contraceptives violated the Fourteenth Amendment's Due Process Clause, reasoning that the penumbras of the Bill of Rights' enumerated protections created a "zone of privacy." The Court in *Griswold* characterized an individual's privacy interest as a fundamental right upon which the state cannot intrude in the absence of a compelling governmental interest. The Supreme Court further articulated the protected realm of privacy in *Eisenstadt v. Baird,* concluding that to have any meaning at all, the right of privacy must include the "right of any individual, married or single, to be free from unwarranted governmental intrusion" into his or her decision of whether or not to have children. . . .

An interference with an individual's ability to reproduce, whether permanent or temporary, clearly implicates the constitutional right of privacy. By offering castration to convicted sex offenders as an alternative to imprisonment, legislatures and courts intrude upon an offender's decision whether or not to have children, a decision the (U.S. Supreme) Court . . . deemed protected from unwarranted governmental invasion under the Fourteenth Amendment. Just as a state may not prohibit married and single persons from using contraception, so it should not be allowed to compel individuals to practice contraception. Proponents of the use of castration as a form of punishment for sex offenders may argue that because the offender has the opportunity to reject sterilization and choose incarceration instead, no intrusion of protected privacy rights occurs. However, the inherently coercive nature of the choice between freedom through castration and an extended prison sentence renders voluntary consent to sterilization an impossibility. The privacy right primarily implicated by castration in the punitive context is the fundamental right of procreation, a privacy interest meriting a separate discussion that includes analysis under the strict scrutiny standard.

The Fundamental Right of Procreation

Castration as an alternative to incarceration, whether surgical or chemical, violates the right of procreative freedom. To render a convicted sex offender sterile is to deprive him of his right to procreate, a right characterized by Justice Douglas in *Skinner* as "one of the basic civil rights of man." Castration, like a vasectomy, eliminates the offender's capacity for procreation. However, castration by surgery or injections represents a more intrusive procedure than the vasectomy at issue in *Skinner* because it results in the cessation of the sexual drive. . . .

Castration as Cruel and Unusual Punishment

Another objection to male sterilization as an alternative to incarceration may be premised on the prohibition against cruel and unusual punishment provided by the Eighth Amendment. An Eighth Amendment analysis of castration as punishment for convicted sex offenders requires an examination of . . . whether the procedure constitutes cruel and unusual punishment. . . .

While the Eighth Amendment may have been originally intended to protect against punishment deemed inhuman and barbarous, the Supreme Court has construed the provision more broadly. In *Weems v. United States,* for example, the Court focused on the disproportionality between the penalty and offense to determine whether the defendant's sentence constituted cruel and unusual punishment. Not merely a static concept, the Eighth Amendment "must draw its meaning from the evolving standards of decency that mark the progress of a maturing society." Despite its seeming reluctance to explicitly define the limits of the provision prohibiting cruel and unusual punishment, the Court has established some guidelines for determining Eighth Amendment violations. The Court has incorporated three interrelated tests to identify cruel and unusual punishment: (1) whether the punishment is inherently cruel; (2) whether the punishment is disproportionate to the offense; and (3) whether the punishment exceeds the extent necessary to achieve the legitimate governmental objectives. . . .

[T]he Supreme Court of South Carolina voided the suspended sentence of a sex offender where the suspension and probation were conditioned on the offender's submission to surgical castration. According to the court in *State v. Brown,* because castration constitutes physical mutilation, it satisfies the cruelty requirement of the prohibition against cruel and unusual punishment. While the *Brown* decision seems to focus on the physical suffering associated with castration, "mutilation" as used by the court also suggests an element of degradation, consistent with earlier courts' analysis of cruelty. . . .

The preceding analysis of constitutional objections to castration demonstrates that sex offenders possess the fundamental right to be free from unwarranted governmental intrusion into their decision-making concerning procreation. Because castration is not the least restrictive means available to effectuate the governmental interest of protecting society, sterilization as a punitive measure violates offenders' Fourteenth Amendment privacy rights. Additionally, offenders enjoy a constitutionally protected liberty interest to refuse unwanted medical treatment in the form of surgical or pharmacological castration, or vasectomy. Finally, castration implicates the Eighth Amendment prohibition against cruel and unusual punishment. Failing to qualify as treatment, when subjected to scrutiny under any of the established tests, castration would most likely be found to constitute cruel and unusual punishment violative of the Eighth Amendment. . . .

Policy Considerations

In addition to its constitutional and common law implications, castration raises several significant policy considerations. Most important to a determination of its viability as an alternative to incarceration is its effectiveness as a punitive measure. According to recent studies, approximately forty percent of rapists and pedophiles will repeat their crimes. A primary criticism of castration as a form of punishment for sex offenders is that it fails to address the anger and hatred motivating sex offenses against women and children. To take away an offender's ability to procreate is merely to eliminate one channel of aggression. While advocates of chemical castration hail its five percent recidivism rate as evidence of the program's success, that statistic may be misleading. A high percentage of sex crimes go unreported, and further, most treatment programs track participants' progress for only a short time after the termination of treatment, when the risk of relapse is the lowest.

Critics also attack castration as a sanctioning alternative for its seeming lenience. Instead of serving thirty years in prison, a convicted sex offender may elect to undergo surgical castration, vasectomy, or chemical castration and retain his freedom. Victims of serious sex offenses would most likely not be reassured knowing that the violent offender who injured them will escape incarceration upon completion of a sterilization procedure. Moreover, castration merely validates the offender's distorted self-portrait, that he is a victim who cannot help himself. The source of the violence, the uncontrollable anger and hostility, will remain long after the scalpel or injection removes the offender's capability to procreate.

Finally, the cost to society of practicing compulsory castration may also undermine its viability. Admittedly, the state would incur minimal expense in surgically castrating sex offenders in relation to the money spent keeping those same offenders in prison. However, castrated offenders may very well vent their aggression in other criminal ways and therefore ultimately require incarceration. Similarly, those offenders undergoing chemical castration and counseling present a financial burden. Not only must the state cover the cost of the drug for those offenders unable to pay for their own treatment, but financial resources must also be used to provide counseling services. A counseling staff must be funded in order to treat and monitor the progress of chemically castrated offenders. Such a program requires a great deal of both time and money to operate effectively. Viewed in terms of the above social and economic considerations, sterilization does not appear to be a viable alternative to incarceration.

Conclusion

Castration should be rejected as an unacceptable, ineffective and unconstitutional alternative to imprisonment. A lingering spectre from the American eugenics movement at the turn of the century, the sterilization of criminals has enjoyed limited legislative and judicial support in contemporary society. However, relatively recent technological developments resulting in the marketing of hormone suppressers has added a new dimension to the issue of sterilization of sex offenders and has received support for its non-surgical method of temporarily reducing the sexual drives of paraphiliac offenders. Despite the procedural differences, however, chemical castration and its surgical equivalents share constitutional flaws which render them inappropriate substitutes for incarceration.

The prevailing forms of male sterilization interfere with an offender's ability to produce offspring, and, as a consequence, violate the offender's constitutionally protected privacy rights, including the fundamental right of procreation. Moreover, the offender maintains a liberty interest in exercising his right to refuse unwanted medical treatment. A state is therefore precluded from forcing an offender to undergo sterilization unless it demonstrates a legitimate interest overriding the offender's right of self-determination. Subjected to Eighth Amendment analysis, castration in any form fails to qualify as treatment and instead constitutes cruel and unusual punishment. . . .

Finally, policy considerations mandate the elimination of punitive sterilization practices for sex offenders. The seemingly low recidivism rate hailed by proponents as evidence of chemical castration's success fails to reflect the high number of sex crimes that go unreported each year. Proponents additionally ignore the substantial administrative costs associated with implementing a treatment program of chemical castration for criminals who cannot pay for it themselves and who may likely have to continue treatment for long periods of time. Not only does this procedure drain valuable public resources, but at the same time, it subjects the offenders to potentially dangerous side effects, the full extent of which remains unknown. In a society besieged by crime and the fear it begets, where prison overcrowding has grown to massive proportions and society is desperate for a cure, castration may seem to be the definitive remedy. Nevertheless, a remedy which necessitates the deprivation of fundamental rights and personal liberties and which fails to address the source of the problem must be rejected as an unacceptable solution.

POSTSCRIPT

Should Serious Sex Offenders Be Castrated?

At first glance, castrating serious sex offenders seems to be a radical and somewhat Orwellian solution to a difficult social problem. But, what if it works? If we can significantly reduce serious sex offender recidivism by castrating them and eliminating their sexual urges, is it a good social policy?

Kari A. Vanderzyl asserts that a primary criticism of castration is that it fails to address the anger and hatred motivating sex offenses against women and children. Thus, castration merely eliminates one channel of an offender's aggression. Vanderzyl asserts that the source of the violence, anger, and hostility will remain. She believes as well that the low recidivism rates reported in castration studies may be misleading. A high number of sex offenses go unreported, and most treatment programs track offender progress for only a short time. Moreover, Vanderzyl believes that castration as a form of treatment conjures an image of eugenics movements and is a deprivation of fundamental rights and personal liberties.

Lawrence Wright argues, however, that even though castrating sex offenders is not an ideal solution, it works better than any other approach. In addition, it may be a more humane form of sex offender treatment because it will help offenders control their behavior and reduce prison time.

Castration as a form of sex offender treatment does appear to be gaining some momentum in the United States. It will be interesting to see whether the public and the courts are receptive to this form of treatment, or if it will be rejected as an approach that is barbaric and unacceptable in society.

There are a number of additional resources that may shed light on the issues discussed in this section. See, for example, J. Michael Bailey and Aaron S. Greenberg, "The Science and Ethics of Castration: Lessons from the *Morse* Case," *Northwestern University Law Review* (Summer 1998); William Winslade, "Castrating Pedophiles Convicted of Sex Offenses Against Children: New Treatment or Old Punishment?" *Southern Methodist University Law Review* (vol. 51, p. 349, 1998); Douglas J. Besharov and Andrew Fachhs, "Sex Offenders: Is Castration an Acceptable Punishment?" *American Bar Association Journal* (July 1992); Nickolaus Heim and Carolyn J. Hursch, "Castration for Sex Offenders: Treatment or Punishment? A Review of Recent European Literature," *Archives of Sexual Behavior* (vol. 8, 1979); and Christopher Meisenkothen, "Chemical Castration—Breaking the Cycle of Paraphiliac Recidivism," *Social Justice* (Spring 1999).

Additional resources include: Reinhard Wille and Klaus M. Beier, "Castration in Germany," *Annals of Sex Research* (vol. 2, pp. 103–133, 1989), which examined the results of a treatment program for a sample of 104 men who underwent voluntary castration over a 10-year period. This study found a postoperative recidivism rate of approximately 3 percent. Other resources are Marjorie A. Fonza, "A Review of Sex Offender Treatment Programs," *ABNF Journal* (Mar/Apr 2001); Catherine A. Gallagher, David B. Wilson, Paul Hirshfield, Mark B. Coggeshall, and Doris L. MacKenzie, "A Quantitative Review of the Effects of Sex Offfender Treatment on Sexual Reoffending," *Corrections Management Quarterly* (Fall 1999); Craig Turk, "Kinder Cut," *The New Republic* (Aug. 25, 1997); and J. Paul Federoff and Beverly Moran, "Myths and Misconceptions About Sex Offenders," *The Canadian Journal of Human Sexuality* (vol. 6, issue 4, 1997).

ISSUE 13

Do Strict Gun Control Laws Reduce the Number of Homicides in the United States?

YES: Franklin E. Zimring, from "Firearms, Violence, and the Potential Impact of Firearms Control," *Journal of Law, Medicine and Ethics* (Spring 2004)

NO: Lance K. Stell, from "The Production of Criminal Violence in America: Is Strict Gun Control the Solution?" *Journal of Law, Medicine and Ethics* (Spring 2004)

ISSUE SUMMARY

YES: Professor Franklin E. Zimring argues that there is a strong relationship between gun use and the death rate from violent crime and that handgun use increases the death rate from violence by a factor of three to five.

NO: Professor Lance K. Stell asserts that strict gun control institutionalizes the natural predatory advantages of larger, stronger, violence-prone persons and increases the risks of violent victimization for less well-off, law-abiding citizens.

Do strict gun control laws help to reduce violent crime? Or, do gun control laws fail to stem violent behavior and help social predators to victimize law-abiding citizens? Does the Second Amendment to the U.S. Constitution give people an absolute right to bear arms? These are interesting questions that have important implications for violence control in U.S. society.

Because the issue of a constitutional right to bear arms has been so controversial, perhaps it is best to begin our analysis here. The Second Amendment states: "A well regulated Militia being necessary to the security of a free State, the right of the people to keep and bear Arms shall not be infringed." While the U.S. Supreme Court has held that most of the protections in the U.S. Constitution's Bill of Rights—"fundamental rights"—apply to state proceedings, it has never held that the Second Amendment's "right to bear arms" is fundamental. The Supreme Court's main decision interpreting the Second Amendment, *United States v. Miller,* 307 U.S. 174 (1939), upheld the National Firearms Act of 1934, which required the registration of sawed-off shotguns. The Court stated:

[Without] any evidence tending to show that possession or use of a "shotgun having a barrel of less than 18 inches in length" at this time has some reasonable relationship to the preservation or efficiency of a well regulated militia, we cannot say that the Second Amendment guarantees the right to keep and bear such an instrument.

As *Miller* illustrates, the Supreme Court and most lower courts have tied the right to bear arms to the maintenance of a "well regulated militia." They have not construed the Second Amendment to convey a more generalized right of the citizenry to own all types of firearms.

In 2007, however, the U.S. Court of Appeals for the District of Columbia struck down portions of Washington, D.C.'s rather stringent gun control ordinance and recognized a personal right to own firearms based on the Second Amendment to the U.S. Constitution, independent of an individual's participation in a state militia. In *Parker v. District of Columbia*, 478 F.3d 370 (D.C. Cir. 2007), the Court stated:

[T]he Second Amendment protects an individual right to keep and bear arms. That right existed prior to the formation of the new government [of the United States] under the Constitution and was premised on the private use of arms for activities such as hunting and self-defense, the latter being understood as resistance to either private lawlessness or the depredations of a tyrannical government (or a threat from abroad).

It will be interesting, indeed, to see if the U.S. Supreme Court will agree to consider *Parker* and, if so, whether it will recognize a personal right to bear arms based on the Second Amendment. If the Court decides to uphold *Parker*, it would seem inevitable that many state and local gun control laws throughout the United States will be invalidated.

Another important issue, however, is the impact of strict gun control laws on the homicide rate in the United States. The authors of the articles in this section have very different views on this controversy. Professor Franklin E. Zimring argues that there is a strong relationship between gun use and the death rate from violent crime. In addition, handgun use increases the death rate from violence by a factor of three to five.

Professor Lance K. Stell contends, however, that strict gun control laws institutionalize the natural predatory advantages of larger, stronger, violence-prone persons and increase the risks of violent victimization for less well-off, law-abiding citizens. In response to the arguments posed by Dr. Zimring, Professor Stell states: "[P]ursuing any gun control measure designed to impose (hand)gun scarcity on the general population is both needless and useless."

What is your position regarding the ownership of firearms? Should the right to own a firearm be a fundamental right of citizenship in the United States? Should states and their municipal subdivisions have the authority to regulate gun ownership? Would taking guns from the population effectively reduce homicide rates in the United States? These are important questions that directly impact our quality of life. As you read the articles in this section, try to develop a sense of whether gun ownership should be freely permitted, restricted, or banned altogether.

YES

Franklin E. Zimring

Firearms, Violence, and the Potential Impact of Firearms Control

T his paper organizes the question of gun controls as violence policy under two quite different headings. The first issue to be discussed is the relationship between gun use and the death rate from violent crime. The second question is whether and how firearms control strategies might reduce the death rate from violence. When we review the evidence on the relationship between guns and violence, it seems clear that gun use, usually handgun use, increases the death rate from violence by a factor of three to five. Nobody in mainstream social science or criminology argues against such weapon effects these days, although some are more skeptical of the magnitude estimated than others (one example is Lance Stell).[1] Thus the problem is both genuine and important. When we review the extent to which particular approaches to controlling firearms might reduce the death rate from violence, the evidence for modern attempts at gun control saving lives is much weaker than the evidence that gun use causes death. So gun control is a potential life-saving tool but only if the use of guns in attack can be reduced, and achieving that in our city streets will neither be easy or cheap.

Gun Use and Violence

It is not true that guns are used in most criminal events, nor can we say that guns are employed in most violent crimes. . . .

Guns are only used in 4% of all crimes, and only 20% of all violent crimes, but about 70% of all criminal killings. This tells us immediately what the special problem of gun use is in violent crime—an increase in the death rate per 100 violent attacks. If the problem you worry about is crime, guns are involved in 4% of the acts. If the problem is lethal violence, the market share for firearms is 70%. Guns alone account for twice as many criminal deaths as all other means of killing combined. Why is that?

Most criminal homicides result from violent assaults without any other criminal motive such as robbery or rape. Gun assaults are seven times as likely to kill as all other kinds of criminal assault,[2] and about five times as likely to kill as are knives, the next most deadly weapon that is frequently used in criminal

From *Journal of Law, Medicine and Ethics*, vol. 32, no. 1, Spring 2004, pp. 34–37. Copyright © 2004 by American Society of Law, Medicine & Ethics. Reprinted by permission.

attacks. Firearms robbery is about four times as likely to produce a victim death as a non-firearms robbery.

In this section, I discuss what elements of gun use might increase the lethality of gun assaults and then briefly discuss the situation with gun versus non-gun robbery.

The Causes of Differential Lethality

Guns may cause increases in the death rate from assault in a variety of different ways. The use of guns as opposed to other weapons in assault may be associated with both mechanical and social changes in violent assault that can increase its death rate. Among the mechanical or instrumentality aspects of gun use that can increase death rates are: the greater injurious impact of bullets; the longer range of firearms; and the greater capacity of firearms for executing multiple attacks. Among the features in social setting related to gun use are: the need to use more lethal instruments of assault in situations where an attacker fears that his adversary may have a gun, the need to sustain or intensify a deadly assault because an opponent possesses or is using firearms, and the increased willingness to use guns and other lethal weapons in personal conflict because such weapons are used generally. All of these aspects may increase the lethality of assaults committed with guns, but by no means to the same degree. There are also two social impacts of gun possession and use that can lower death rates: the deterrence of assaults because of fear of gun-owning victims and the prevention of attempted assaults by an armed victim.

In this paper, I will stress the most important of the mechanisms that increase death rates when guns are used, so-called instrumentality effects. For a summary of all these other potential causes and their assessment, see Zimring and Hawkins.[3]

Instrumentality Effects

Of all the possible ways that gun use increases the deadliness of attacks, the theory that gunshot wounds inflict more damage than other methods of personal attacks is considered the most important and has been the subject of the most research. The early debate about the dangerousness of guns on deaths from assault involved different theories of the types of intention that produced assaults that lead to death. Marvin Wolfgang in his study of homicide doubted that the weapon used in an attack made much difference in the chance that a death would result since so many different weapons could produce death if an attacker tried hard enough.[4] I responded to this assertion with a study of knife and gun assaults in Chicago.[5]

My data suggested that many homicides were the result of attacks apparently conducted with less than a single-minded intent to kill. Unlike the Wolfgang study where only fatal attacks were examined, the Zimring studies compared fatal and nonfatal gun and knife assaults in Chicago over four police periods in 1968 and gun assaults in 1972. The studies found that 70 percent of all gun killings in Chicago were the result of attacks that resulted in only one wound to the victim,[6] and that most attacks with guns or knives that killed a victim looked quite similar to the knife and gun attacks that did not kill.[7] From this data, I argued that most homicides were the result of ambiguously motivated assaults, so that the offender would risk his victim's death, but usually did not press on until death was assured.

Under such circumstances, the capacity of a weapon to inflict life-threatening injury would have an important influence on the death rate from assault. The 1908 Chicago study found that gun attacks were about five times as likely to kill as knife attacks, and this ratio held when the comparison was controlled for the number of wounds inflicted and the specific location of the most serious wound.[8] Since knives were the next most deadly frequently used method of inflicting injury in attacks, the large difference in death rate suggested that substituting knives or other less dangerous instruments for guns would reduce the death rate from assault.

This weapon dangerousness comparison was first reported for Chicago in 1908 and has been replicated in other sites.[9] The follow-up study demonstrated that a difference in weapon as subtle as firearm caliber can double the death rate from gun assaults.[10] The summary conclusion from this line of research can be simply stated: the objective dangerousness of a weapon used in violent assaults appears to be a major influence on the number of victims who will die from attacks. This "instrumentality effect" is the major documented influence of guns on death rate.[11]

The use of guns in robbery is different from their use in woundings since the weapon is not necessarily used to inflict harm. Because robberies with guns frighten their victims into complying with the robbers' demands more often than other robberies, a smaller number of gun robberies result in woundings than personal force robberies and robberies with knives. Still, the greater dangerousness of guns when they are fired more than compensates for the lower number of wounds. For street robberies and those that take place in commercial establishments, the death rate for every 1,000 gun robberies is about three times that generated by robberies at knife point, and about ten times the death rate from robberies involving personal force.[12]

Firearms as a Contributing Cause of Lethal Violence

The use of firearms in assault and robbery is the single environmental feature of American society that is most clearly linked to the extraordinary death rate from interpersonal violence in the United States. But the strength of this relationship does not mean that firearms ownership and use has a simple, invariable, or independent influence on homicide rates. In this section, I consider the question of the causal connection between gun use and lethality. I do this not only because it is an important issue in relation to firearms and lethal violence, but also because reflecting on the questions of causation that arise in connection with firearms teaches us an important lesson about the role of many other environmental influences on the incidence of lethal violence.

The American debate about guns has produced one of the few causal critiques ever to appear on a bumper sticker: the famous slogan "Guns don't kill people, people kill people." Behind the strong sentiment that inspired this and a multitude of related appeals lies an important logical point. Firearms ownership and use is neither a necessary nor a sufficient cause of violent death in the United States. Firearms are not a necessary cause of killings because of the wide army of alternative methods of killing that are available ranging from the strangler's hands to car bombs. Even in the United States at the turn of the 21st century, nearly 30 percent of all killings did not involve guns. Moreover, the widespread availability of firearms is not a sufficient condition for intentional homicide by a wide margin. Almost one-half of all American households own some kind of guns and it is estimated that one-quarter of all households own a handgun—the weapon used in more than three-quarters of all gun homicides. Yet only a small fraction of all gun owners become gun attackers. The logical point here is that guns do not become dangerous instruments of attack if they are not used in an attack.

If gun use is neither a necessary nor a sufficient cause of violent death, what is the proper descriptive label for the role gun use plays in deaths due to intentional injury? The most accurate label for the role of firearms in those cases of death and injury from intentional attacks in which they are used is contributing cause. Even where the availability of a gun plays no important role in the decision to commit an assault, the use of a gun can be an important contributing cause in the death and injury that results for gun attacks. When guns are used in a high proportion of such attacks, the death rate from violent attack will be high. Current evidence suggests that a combination of the ready availability of guns and the willingness to use maximum force in interpersonal conflict is the most important single contribution to the high U.S. death rate from violence. Our rate of assault is not exceptional; our death rate from assault is exceptional.[13]

The role of gun use as a contributing cause means that the net effect of firearms on violence will depend on the interaction of gun availability with other factors which influence the rate of violent assaults in a society and the willingness of people to use guns in such assaults. So the precise contribution of firearms to the death toll from violence is contingent on many other factors that may influence the number and character of violent attacks.

Some implications of this contingency deserve emphasis. Introducing 10,000 loaded handguns into a social environment where violent assault is a rare occurrence will not produce a large number of additional homicide deaths unless it also increases the rate of assault. The percentage increase in homicide might be considerable if guns become substitutes for less lethal weapons. But the additional number of killings would be small because of the low rate of attack. Introducing 10,000 handguns into an environment where rates of attack and willingness to use handguns in attack are both high is a change that would produce many more additional deaths. The net effect of guns depends on how they are likely to be used.

One corollary of viewing guns as an interactive and contributing cause to intentional homicide is that societies with low rates of violent assault will pay a lower price if they allow guns to be widely available than will societies with higher rates of violence. The sanguine sound bite encountered in American debates about guns is: "An armed society is a polite society."[14] As stated on the bumper sticker, this does not seem particularly plausible, but it does seem likely that only a very polite society can be heavily armed without paying a high price.

The United States of 2004 is far from that polite society, although things are better now than they were as recently as 1994. Our considerable propensity for violent conflict would be a serious societal problem even if gun availability and use were low. But the very fact that the United States is a high-violence environment makes the contribution of gun use to the death toll from violence very much greater. When viewed in the light of the concept of contributing causation, the United States has both a violence problem and a gun problem, and each makes the other more deadly.

Varieties of Firearms Control

The objective of almost all forms of firearms control is to reduce the use of loaded guns in attacks and robberies and thus to reduce the death rate from crime. There turns out to be several different strategies of control, many different intensities of gun regulation, and many different contexts in which controls can be attempted. One common strategy is to prohibit dangerous uses of guns—so that hundreds if not thousands of statutes prohibit concealed handguns from being carried at all, and from being taken into airports, churches, schools, and courthouses. Other "time, place and manner laws" prohibit shooting in city streets. The idea is that some settings are so dangerous that otherwise allowable weapons and uses should be prohibited.

One dispute about a "time, place and manner" regulation generated its own considerable literature in the late 1990s. John Lott provided an econometric study which argued that expanding the criteria for concealed weapons permits was associated with lower crime rates.[15] Several published criticisms have undermined Lott's findings either by criticizing the quality of his multi-variate regression evidence[16] or by counter-demonstrations using similar methodology.[17] Because the impact of such laws on citizen gun carrying behavior and the use of guns in self defense has not been measured, the evidence that "shall issue" permit-to-carry laws has impact on crime rates is thin.

A second class of controls attempt to restrict dangerous users from obtaining and using guns. In federal law, convicted felons, youth, and certain diagnosed and previously institutionalized persons with emotional illnesses are excluded from being eligible to obtain weapons. This is the primary type of firearms control strategy in federal law and in most states.

A third approach is to try to exclude from general ownership particular types of guns that are too easily misused. Federal law has all but banned automatic weapons and sawed-off shotguns since 1934, and the Federal Gun Control Act of 1908 added "destructive devices" such as bazookas and hand grenades to the list of classes of weapon thought too dangerous for general ownership.[18] In the late 1980s, a controversy arose over semi-automatic weapons with large ammunition magazines—so-called assault weapons—which have been restricted in a variety of ways under different laws with different definitions.[19] And special restrictions also exist in a few states and cities for handguns.

A "dangerous uses" approach tries to govern the use of guns without reference to the people who can possess them or the kind of guns that can be owned. A "dangerous user" strategy tries to segregate higher risk users without making any guns unavailable for the rest of the population. A "dangerous guns" strategy tries to restrict the general availability of certain types of guns. Every state and city has a mix of different laws—there are no examples in the United States of jurisdictions that rely on only one general approach and not any I know of with only one set of regulations.

Can Gun Control Work?

The answer to this general question is a highly qualified "yes, but." If and to the extent that regulation reduces the use of loaded guns in crimes it will save American lives. But reducing the share of violence with guns is not an easy task to achieve in urban environments with large inventories of available handguns. Most gun control efforts do not make measurable impacts on gun use, particularly low budget symbolic legislation. If Congress when creating what it called a "gun-free school zone" by legislation did reduce firearms violence, the result would be on a par with that of the miracle of loaves and the fishes. But New York City's effort to tightly enforce one of the nation's most restrictive handgun laws did apparently have a substantial payoff in reduced shootings that saved many lives.[20]

What I would emphasize here is the fallacy of categorical generalizations. We have no business asking whether broad classes of laws—criminal prohibitions, anti-theft statutes or gun control strategies—work or don't. That is an aggregation error as long as guns are a contributing cause to the death rate from violent crime in the United States. The serious work is in identifying the specific strategies and contexts in which regulation can reduce the use of firearms in violent assault and attempting to achieve these results at tolerable public and personal cost.

References

1. J. B. Jacobs, *Can Gun Control Work?* (New York: Oxford University Press, 2002).

2. F. E. Zimring and G. Hawkins, *Crime Is Not the Problem: Lethal Violence in America* (New York: Oxford University Press, 1997): at 108.

3. See Zimring and Hawkins, supra note 2: 113–122.

4. M. Wolfgang, *Patterns in Criminal Homicide* (Philadelphia: University of Pennsylvania Press, 1958).

5. F. E. Zimring, "Is Gun Control Likely to Reduce Violent Killings?" *University of Chicago Law Review* 35 (1968): 721–737.

6. F. E. Zimring, "The Medium is the Message: Firearms Caliber as a Determinant of the Death Rate from Assault," *Journal of Legal Studies* 1 (1972): 97–123.

7. See Zimring, supra note 5.

8. Zimring, supra note 5.

9. T. Vinson, "Gun and Knife Attacks," *Australian Journal of Forensic Sciences* 7 (1974): 76; R. Sarvesvaran and C. H. S. Jayewarclene, "The Role of the Weapon in the Homicide Drama," *Medicine and Law* 4 (1985): 315–326.

10. Zimring, supra note 6.

11. P. J. Cook, "The Technology of Personal Violence," in M. Tonry, ed., *Crime and Justice: A Review of Research* (Chicago: Chicago University Press, 1991).

12. F. E. Zimring and J. Zuehl, "Victim Injury and Death in Urban Robbery: A Chicago Study," *Journal of Legal Studies* 15 (1986): 1–40; Cook supra note 11: 17.

13. Zimring and Hawkins, supra note 2: 34–50.

14. Handgun Control Inc., *Carrying Concealed Weapons: Questions and Answers* (Washington, D.C.: Handgun Control Inc., 1995).

15. J. R. Lott, *More Guns, Less Crime* (second edition) (Chicago: University of Chicago Press, 2000).

16. D. Black and D. Nagin, "Do 'Right-to-Carry' Laws Deter Violent Crime?" *Journal of Legal Studies* 27 (1998): 209–219; F. E. Zimring and G. Hawkins, "Concealed Handguns: The Counterfeit Deterrent," *The Responsive Community* 1 (1997): 46–60.

17. J. Donohue and I. Ayers, "Shooting Down the More Guns, Less Crime Hypothesis," National Bureau of Economic Research (working paper no. w9336, 2002); J. Donohue and I. Ayers, "The Latest Misfires in Support of the More Guns, Less Crime Hypothesis," *Stanford Law Review* 55 (2003): 1371–1398.

18. F. E. Zimring, "Firearms and Federal Law: The Gun Control Act of 1968," *Journal of Legal Studies* 4 (1975): 133–198.

19. F. E. Zimring, "The Problem of Assault Firearms," *Crime and Delinquency* 35 (1989): 538–545.

20. J. Fagan, F. E. Zimring, and J. Kim, "Declining Homicide in New York City: A Tale of Two Trends," *Journal of Criminal Law and Criminology* 88 (1998): 1277–1323.

Lance K. Stell  **NO**

The Production of Criminal Violence in America: Is Strict Gun Control the Solution?

"**S**trict gun control" (SGC) has no clear meaning, so it is necessary to clarify it. I define SGC as an array of legally sanctioned restrictions designed to impose firearm scarcity on the general population. SGC's public policy goal, gun scarcity, commonly rests on the predicates that "dangerous criminal control" is not the central problem for reducing the problem of criminal gun violence but rather that it is the social prevalence of the distinctively-lethal instruments (guns) by which both supposedly "good citizens" as well as violent criminals inflict a staggeringly high percentage of injury and death.

Professor Zimring is one SGC's most distinguished, prolific and comprehensive theorists. He has advocated for handgun scarcity among the general population since at least 1969.[1] Recognizing that Americans have had a long love affair with their guns and are loathe to give them up, Zimring has been candid that stigmatizing guns must be a component of a violence-reduction strategy that seeks ultimately to impose gun scarcity on the general population.[2] He has been candid too in acknowledging that none of this will be accomplished quickly, easily, or cheaply. Thus, in 1989, he predicted a grim, culture-rending and violent future for America over the near term, even if the policies he favors were enacted. He wrote "The most marked reduction in firearms violence cannot be expected until well past the introduction of legislation designed to achieve handgun scarcity and long after the period of most intense social and political detriment or cost."[3]

Professor Zimring argues that even the most cursory review of American gun-homicide data show that reducing guns' "market share" of homicide must be a key ingredient of an enlightened firearms policy. This supposedly follows from the fact that gun assaults are 5–7 times more likely to result in death than non-gun assaults and from the fact that 70% of American homicides are committed with guns. Other countries with assault rates similar to America's but with lower gun prevalence and with a commensurately lower percentage of homicide committed with guns enjoy homicide rates 50%+ lower than America. He concludes that it only stands to reason that were a smaller percentage of America's assaults committed with guns, its homicide rate must marginally decline, if the overall assault rate stayed the same.

From *Journal of Law, Medicine and Ethics*, vol. 32, no. 1, Spring 2004, pp. 38–46. Copyright © 2004 by American Society of Law, Medicine & Ethics. Reprinted by permission.

Points of Convergence

Professor Zimring and I agree that carefully-crafted, well-enforced firearms control policies can contribute to marginal reductions in criminal violence. We agree that what matters from the standpoint of enlightened gun policy making is the question of who has guns, how they use their guns and the incentive effects that gun policy can have on both "who" and "how" at the margin. I also agree with Professor Zimring's speculative hypothetical claim that putting an additional 10,000 guns on the street will not automatically result in a proportional increase in the homicide rate. Finally, we agree that while no firearms policy by itself can usher in a Utopian, violence-free social order, even marginal reductions in criminal violence are worth pursing when the benefits exceed the costs and the method pursued is cost-effective. Changes in gun policy that reasonably hold out such promise deserve thoughtful consideration.[4]

Overview

In this paper, I will demonstrate the speciousness of Professor Zimring's argument that reducing the percentage of homicides committed with guns is the key to reducing America's homicide rate. I will further argue that pursuing any gun control measure designed to impose (hand)gun scarcity on the general population is both needless and useless. Whether it is ethically enlightened to fuel America's culture wars by encouraging gun-stigmatization and blatant displays of intolerance directed at private gun ownership per se is a topic for another day.[5]

Zimring's Argument for Changing Course with America's Firearm Policy

Professor Zimring thinks that gun control laws can marginally reduce the homicide rate by making guns progressively scarcer in the social environment. How large a marginal reduction might such policies win over time? Zimring has relied on a single FBI statistic to tell the tale.[6] Guns are used in approximately 70% of all criminal killings. He writes "this tells us immediately what the special problem of gun use is in violent crime—an increase in the death rate . . ." Because he subscribes to (and can fairly claim to be have originated) the "instrumentality hypothesis," according to which the (supposed) greater inherent lethality of guns makes assaults committed with them 5–7 times more deadly, independent of perpetrator-factors, Professor Zimring intimates that the potential marginal reduction in the homicide rate resulting from supply-side restrictions might be quite large.

Professor Zimring claims that all mainstream criminologists now recognize that guns are an independent "contributing cause" to society's homicide rate and that the terms of their intramural debates now concern how large a homicide rate reduction might result were guns' "market share" of assaults reduced.

Although suicide is not a crime and so, by definition, does not qualify as a criminal assault, it is common to count a suicide as a violent death. If so, Zimring's "instrumentality hypothesis" should also extend to a lethality reduction analysis of "self-assaults" (suicide attempts). America's suicide rate is approximately twice as high as its current homicide rate (roughly 11 versus roughly 6). More than 30,000 Americans commit suicide each year, putting suicide in the top ten causes of death. Guns' "market share" in suicide is 50%—not as large as their market share in homicide, percentage-wise, but the body count is nearly twice as high.

Assuming that guns are 5–7 times inherently more lethal than other mechanisms of injury, and with guns' market share of suicide at 50%, the instrumentality thesis says that America's suicide rate should fall if fewer self-assaults were committed with guns, if the overall number of self-assaults (suicide attempts) were to remain the same. And the instrumentality hypothesis predicts finding lower suicide rates in countries where comparative gun scarcity results in a smaller percentage of suicides committed with guns.

Unfortunately, the hypothesis generated by the suicide corollary of the instrumentality thesis is false. Countries known for having very restrictive gun policies and for having much lower gun prevalence than the United States (for examples, Hungary, Denmark, Austria, Norway, and France) nevertheless have persistently higher suicide rates, notwithstanding that a comparatively low percentage are committed with guns.[7]

The Seventy Percent Solution?

The statistic that Zimring finds so telling in favor of his instrumentality thesis does not tell the tale he thinks it does. America's estimated homicide rate fluctuated by an order of magnitude—from a reported low of 1.1 per 100,000 in 1903 to a high of 10.7 in 1980.[8]

In summary:

- At the beginning of the century, there were 1.2 homicides per 100,000 population.
- Rates rose significantly after 1904 reaching a peak of 9.7 in 1933.
- From 1934 to 1944 (encompassing the years of the Great Depression) rates fell to 5.0 in 1944.
- After a slight increase from 1945 and 1946 when rates reached 6.1, rates declined, falling to 4.5 in 1955.
- After 1955 rates increased slightly each year until the mid 1960s when there was a steep increase reaching a peak of 10.1 in 1974.
- Rates fell slightly in 1975 and 1976 but began rising thereafter, reaching an all time high of 10.7 in 1980.
- From 1981 to 1984, rates declined, falling to 8.4 in 1984.
- After 1985, rates increased again peaking in 1991 at 10.5.
- After 1991 rates declined slightly but remained at around 10 through 1993.
- Starting in 1994, rates declined each year, reaching 6.1 in 2000, the lowest rate since 1967.

However, unlike the nation's homicide rate, a random sampling indicates that the percentage of homicides committed with firearms remained comparatively constant. For example, in the period 1920–26, 71% of homicides were by gun.[9] According to the FBI, the percentage of homicides committed with guns dropped to 62% in 1989[10] but was back up to 70% in 1993, as Professor Zimring has noted. Most recently, the FBI estimated that, of the 16,204 homicides committed in 2002, 67% were committed with firearms.[11]

Since the homicide rate varied remarkably over the last 100 years but the percentage of homicides committed with guns did not, the latter figure cannot provide an explanation for the former. Instead of giving us insight, a century's worth of data say that America's homicide rate is virtually independent of the percentage of homicides committed with guns.

This is not a subtle point, so I reiterate its importance for Professor Zimring's argument. The data do not support that America's homicide rate is strongly and independently determined by the percentage of homicides committed with guns. Therefore, we should not infer "immediately" that reducing guns' 70% "market share" of criminal killings must be sine qua non in a comprehensive strategy to reduce the nation's homicide rate.[12]

Professor Zimring may be correct to say that the debate amongst mainstream contemporary criminologists has shifted from perpetrator-focused theories to their arguing the magnitude of the instrumentality effect on the homicide rate, but the data support only those criminologists who estimate its effect as very small or negligible.[13]

It is not clear what might explain a shift Zimring claims to have occurred amongst "mainstream" criminologists. Kleck's comprehensive review of the data and of the criminological literature found no empirical basis for it.[14] For example, Kleck notes that in 1972 Zimring acknowledged "differential intention or personality may play some role in gross intercaliber differences in death rates."

Kleck further notes that in 1982 Philip Cook, another strong proponent of SGC, seemed to share Zimring's view that perpetrator factors cannot be ignored when he postulated that "the task determines the tool." And again in 1987, Cook opined that "the choice of weapon may also be associated with . . . the assailant's intent. If the robber plans to kill the victim, then presumably he will try to equip himself with the most appropriate tool for the task." However, by 1991, both Cook and Zimring apparently had abandoned acknowledging that perpetrator factors (such as his intent and his ability to sustain murderous motivation during the few seconds it takes to inflict lethal injuries) are important lethality-enhancers that make a difference in both weapon selection and use. If we infer the comparative importance a criminologist attributes to various lethality-enhancing factors in the production of criminal violence from the emphasis he gives it, it seems that Zimring now discounts a perpetrator's lethality-enhancing factors in favor of the instrumentality effect. Thus he says, "fatality seem[s] to be an almost accidental outcome of a large number of assaults committed with guns or knives."[15] And in his article, he says his data "suggested that many homicides were the result of attacks apparently conducted with less than a single-minded intent to kill."

Zimring does not further define "large number," or "many," nor does he say how one might reliably discern whether a killer was single-minded or ambivalent or acting inadvertently during the seconds or minutes it took him/her to inflict a mortal wound on a victim. Why does it matter that we have such clarifications and accounts? Because we should demand, at a minimum, clear and convincing evidence to rebut our presumptions that competent adults, including perpetrators of criminal gun assaults, intend the reasonably foreseeable consequences of what they do and that they perform acts intentionally (such as, carry a loaded gun rather than a pack of chewing gum in anticipation of their criminal encounters, pull the trigger while the gun is pointed at the victim, or thrust the blade when the victim's abdomen is within arm's length) precisely because they intend to produce or are willing to risk producing the reasonably expectable results. Absent a compelling account for comparatively neglecting perpetrator-factors, Zimring seems to be claiming that in "a large number of assaults," the killer is as much a victim of circumstance as the person he kills—just luckier, because of where the gun was pointed when the trigger pulled his finger.

Inherent Lethality?

On cursory review, this graph might seem to confirm Professor Zimring's "market share" hypothesis about homicide. Beginning approximately in 1993, there commenced a remarkable decline in firearm use in crime. Associated with the declining use of guns in crime was a 40% decline in the homicide rate. So far so good for the market-share corollary of the instrumentality thesis.

However, the 40% decline in the homicide rate was not associated with a remarkable reduction in the percentage of homicides committed with guns (which at 67% in 2002, remained close to the 70% level found in 1993). And, it should not be necessary to add that the homicide rate decline was not associated with any documented, progressive gun-scarcity among the general population nor among criminals.

In 2002, incidents involving a firearm constituted 7% of the 4.9 million violent crimes of rape, sexual assault, robbery, and aggravated and simple assault. Over the period 1993–2002, the non-fatal, firearm-related violent victimization rate fell to the lowest level ever recorded.

So what do these data tell us about the truth of the instrumentality thesis?

- Firearms have not become scarce among the general population.
- As far as we know, the percentage of criminals who own guns has not declined.
- There has been a dramatic decline in criminal gun use.
- The rate of non-fatal firearm assaults has declined to the lowest level ever recorded.
- The homicide rate has declined to a level last seen in the mid-1960s.
- Yet, the percentage of homicides committed with firearms remains within a narrow range that has held constant for 100 years.

These data suggest that the instrumentality thesis is almost certainly false.

Perpetrators and Their Tools

It is a truism that gun assaults are perpetrated by gun-armed perpetrators. But in this case, the truism is not too true to be good. The data on fatal outcome frequency do not permit our distinguishing a weapon's inherent lethal properties from the closely related effects of a perpetrator's dangerousness.

It is obvious and unarguable that some killings occur that wouldn't have occurred had the perpetrator possessed some other weapon type or none at all. However, we must not be too hasty to map gun/non-gun onto this point. Substituting some other gun, different from the one actually used to kill, one unfamiliar to the perpetrator, heavier, more awkward, and with a very stiff grip safety (as some 1911s have) might have made the outcome non-fatal. The perpetrator may not have been able to make the imaginary-substitute firearm fire at all, or while fiddling with it, trying to figure out why it wouldn't fire, the victim might have taken the opportunity to escape, or frustration resulting from an inability to make the gun fire might have cooled our would-be killer's murderous motivation. But there is no free lunch. A clunky, hard-to-use firearm may interfere with an otherwise comparatively helpless person's lawful use of deadly force in self-defense such that she dies in the assault she might otherwise have forestalled.

That injuries inflicted with firearms are 5–7 times more likely to result in death does not prove that guns are inherently "more lethal" mechanisms for inflicting injury than others, such as bombs, bludgeons or butcher knives. The lethality of a suicide bomber, for example, importantly involves "personality factors," appearance factors, facts about his/her intent and willingness to "push the button" when the time comes, not merely the contents of the belt s/he wears, concealed from view. (Would suicide bombers become more lethal by substituting firearms for their explosive under-garments? Palestinian terrorists used to use firearms in their attacks, but the scope of their planned carnage was too often truncated by armed victim/bystander intervention.)

The limitations of our criminological data notwithstanding, the trauma literature enables a clearer focus on comparative inherent lethality by mechanism of injury. However, this evidence source seems not to support that gunshot wounds, as a class, are remarkably more life-threatening than wounds inflicted by other mechanisms, such as butcher knives or ice-picks. For example, a study published in the Annals of Surgery investigated the mortality associated with 430 cases involving penetrating wounds to the abdomen. In 266 cases the mechanism of injury was known. Shotguns proved the most lethal with a mortality of 20.4%. Pistol-inflicted abdominal wounds had a mortality of 16.8%. Ice picks wounds and butcher knife wounds ranked next with 14.3% and 13.3% mortality respectively. These findings support that gun shot wounds (GSWs) to the abdomen are somewhat more life-threatening than penetrating wounds inflicted with other weapons, but not 5–7 times more life-threatening.[16]

It is plausible to suppose that perpetrators of assault who are generally more willing to inflict lethal injuries and who desire to be thus perceived by others (and who, unlike suicide-bombers, want to survive the assault themselves), are also more likely to choose guns rather than other mechanisms. Whether guns have 5–7 times greater intimidation value than other weapons in a criminal assault is unknown, but in so far as guns have marginally greater intimidation value than some other weapons, it is partially because of the estimated increased seriousness of purpose that gun possession tends to convey to others.

Behavior modification theory also suggests that a criminal may index his own intimidation level to the weapon he carries. Thus he may select a gun type widely regarded among fellow gang members as more intimidating and he may actually become more intimidating when he has it in his possession. ("I must be a pretty tough guy, after all I'm carrying a .45 caliber model 1911 just like the toughest of my drug-dealer buddies, not some wussy, nickel-plated .25 caliber 'pimp gun.'")

It is well-appreciated that gun-underwritten intimidation deters victim resistance and increases victim compliance and submission. That gun-armed robbers are less likely to inflict injury on their victims than unarmed robbers or robbers armed with other weapons is consistent with their preferring submission to inflicting injury. The type of victim on whom the perpetrator typically preys will also play a role in his choice of weapon. Robbing children of their lunch money requires a different calculus of intimidation than robbing convenience stores, banks or fellow drug dealers. Robbing drug dealers is risky because they enjoy a reputation for violence and will almost certainly be armed. But bank robber Willie Sutton's principle still recommends considering them because drug dealers are known to carry large amounts of unmarked cash and will likely not report victimization to the police. (Sutton was once asked "Why do you rob banks?" He replied, "Because, that's where the money is.")

A preference for victim submission does not rule out a criminal's contingent willingness to inflict injury, nor does it exclude his having a comparatively high susceptibility to preference inversions regarding violence that may be triggered by seemingly trivial situational factors such as his victim's having an "attitude" (or even having a contemptible lack of it). The criminological dynamics of labile preferences amongst opportunistic criminals has been well described by James Q. Wilson and Richard J. Herrnstein.[17]

Who Shoots People, Who Gets Shot?

The romantic stereotype of gun-shot-wound-inflicting-criminal perpetrators as ordinary folk, like you and me, who just happen to have a gun ready when momentarily provoked to anger by friends or family members does not square with the facts. In so far as the data permits stereotyping, neither killers nor their victims are just plain folks.[18] It has long been appreciated that killers are significantly more likely than the general population to suffer from below-average cognitive ability, brain dysfunction, brain injury or mental illness, alcoholism or other substance abuse or all or several of these in combination. Violent offenders also tend to have histories of personal violence from childhood, initially as a victim and eventually as victimizers of other children, siblings and non-human animals.[19] Data gathered from 1960 to date indicate that most homicide perpetrators are male, younger than 30, 70–80% have criminal records and average four arrests for major felonies. By contrast, 85% of the general population has never once been arrested. None of these statistics permit inferring that any individual captured by this demographic profile who has not yet murdered anyone, to a high degree of certainty, will do so eventually. Most will not.

The demographic profile of homicide victims tends to mirror that of their killers. A study of GSWs reported to the police in Charlotte, NC, found that 71% of adult victims had criminal records. The Bureau of Justice Statistics reports that young African American males are 6 times more likely to murder someone and 6 times more likely to be a murder victim than their white counterparts. As Professor Zimring documents in *Crime Is Not the Problem*, America's lethal violence problem is overwhelmingly and disproportionately a problem among its young, poor, African American population. Blacks are more than seven times as likely as whites to be arrested for violent offenses and more than eight times as likely to be arrested for homicide. Assaults by black offenders are more than twice as likely to result in a death than assaults committed by white offenders. Zimring notes that the concentration of serious violence among blacks is so much greater than the concentration of other criminal offenses that if robbery and homicide were not so concentrated among black offenders, the United States would be a much safer country,[20] and most especially for African-Americans.[21] But again, these relative-risk statistics must be balanced by the facts that most young African-American males whether poor or not poor, do not commit robbery or homicide and that homicide statistics have improved for African-Americans just as they have for every other demographic category.

10,000 Guns

Professor Zimring claims that introducing 10,000 guns into an environment where violent assault is rare will not produce a large number of additional deaths unless doing so somehow were to increase the assault rate. On the other hand, were 10,000 guns added to an environment where rates of criminal attack are already high the contribution made to the expectable increase in the death toll from violence must be high.

This thought experiment (taken from his book *Crime Is Not the Problem*) captures Zimring's sociological theory of lethal violence in a nutshell. Note that, in the hypotheticals he considers, Zimring limits speculating to whether a bolus of 10,000 (of not further specified types of) guns added to an imaginary society would result in a small or large number of additional deaths. He does not even consider that adding 10,000 guns to a social environment might have no net-effect on the number of deaths. Nor does he consider that an additional 10,000 guns might actually be associated with an overall decline in the violent death total or rate. That adding 10,000 guns might have net-positive social effects is not even among the remote possibilities.

But we needn't limit ourselves to subjectively speculating along with Professor Zimring about the more or less likely consequences of adding 10,000 guns in a simulated social experiment. Instead we can analyze data from a real-world experiment that enables less speculative answers. We have Bureau for Alcohol, Tobacco and Firearms (BATF) firearms production/import/export data that enables an objective estimate of how large a bolus of guns America has actually received over the past 20 years. We also have the perspective provided by a century's worth of year-by-year homicide data. And we have a huge, county-by-county data-set from the entire United

States that enables a judgment whether the nation's 34 CCW states' putting approximately 3+ million non-police carriers of concealed handguns on the streets has transformed them into the bloodiest jurisdictions.

According to BATF's data,[22] from 1982–2001 American gun manufacturers produced 77,361,013 firearms, including 34,484,470 handguns. All were sold in the American retail market except for 64,813 handguns and 96,861 long guns (rifles and shotguns) that were exported. What was happening in the homicide market over that period?

. . . The number of homicides committed with "other guns" (which would include shotguns that the trauma data say are inherently more lethal than handguns), knives, blunt objects and "other methods" held remarkably constant. By contrast, the number of homicides committed with handguns is much higher and more highly variable.

In 1980, when America's homicide rate hit its all time high (10.7), there were 23,040 homicides, with slightly fewer than 50% committed with handguns. By 1992, the homicide rate was 9.3 but the homicide total hit an all-time high, 24,700. In 1993, while the number of homicides committed with handguns soared to more than 14,000 (with homicide from all mechanisms totaling 24,530), the homicide rate actually had declined (albeit not much) from its 1980 all-time high to 9.5.

Beginning in 1993, the homicide rate began a steep decline to its current level of 6/100,000, the lowest since the mid 1960s. Handgun homicides also declined sharply. However, the handgun infusion continued, albeit also declining from a peak of 2.6 million in 1993 to 943,213 in 2001. Handgun killings declined, handgun production declined and the homicide rate declined. But I reiterate, the percentage of killings committed with firearms, to which Professor Zimring's lethality hypothesis attaches such great importance, did not change remarkably (namely, 67% in 2002) from what it had been in 1993 (namely, 70%).

Beginning in Florida in 1987 and now including 34 CCW-issuing states, more than 3 million so-called "shall issue" licenses to carry a concealed handgun have been obtained by qualified persons. Typically, these laws prohibit the carrying of concealed handguns to anyone who has not satisfied statutory requirements but mandate issuing a permit to every person who satisfies them. Requirements include age restrictions; a personal history free of felony convictions or arrests for violence and a medical history free from documented mental illness as verified by an applicant-authorized investigation of his/her medical records; enrollment in a state-approved course on gun safety, legally permissible gun use in personal protection, and demonstrated minimum proficiency in actual gun use, finger-printing and FBI background check. Associated application fees, course-tuition fees, etc vary the costs associated with obtaining a (renewable) license from $150–$500.

The most important and rigorous work on the criminological consequences of CCW laws has been done by John Lott who claims to have found a substantial reduction in criminal violence in CCW-issuing jurisdictions, with the apparent deterrent effects being proportionally greater in counties that issue licenses in proportionally greater numbers.[23] Lott has freely shared his data set with anyone who requests it. Several scholars have replicated Lott's findings, others have been highly critical on methodological grounds and many harshly so, on political grounds.

Irrespective the details of the Lott-related controversy, it is unarguable that jurisdictions that have adopted CCW laws have not paid a heavy price in blood and gore, as was first predicted for Florida in 1987 and predicted again and again in every subsequent political battle over their adoption elsewhere. Criminological theories rarely enjoy such a direct verifying/falsifying reality check. Some theories have been rescued from refutation by contrary appearances by making the logically-available claim that CCW laws did not change social reality, they only made legal what was widely done when illegal. This might make all Lott's "discoveries" investigation-relative artifacts, absorbed into nothingness by properly-done regressions. If so, logic provides a refuge for proponents of Zimring's instrumentality thesis and the nation's experience with CCW does not necessarily "slam dunk" over the theoretical obstacle interposed by it after all.

Why Zimring Ignores the Apparent Benefits of Armed Self-Defense

Professor Zimring has always opposed the use of force in self-defense. Initially, his arguments against resisting criminal attack were pragmatic. Early analysis of the data on victim-resistance showed that victims who were criminally attacked and resisted were also more likely to be injured or killed than victims who put up no resistance at all. However, the early analysis only found a statistically significant association between victims who did worse and victims who resisted. The data were not recorded in such a way as to permit inferring that resisters did worse because their resistance provoked an injury-causing attack that might have not have occurred otherwise. And the early analysis did not distinguish between gun-backed resistance and non-gun resistance.

However, further analysis of the data did distinguish between types of resistance. It was found that victims who used a gun to resist criminal attack not only did better than victims who resisted by other means, they also did better than victims who offered no resistance whatsoever. Where once we had no data on the efficacy and frequency of defensive gun use (DGU), we now have at least 15 such studies. The most statistically sophisticated of these supports that DGU occurs more frequently than criminal gun-assaults, probably not significantly less than 2.5 million times per year and perhaps more frequently.[24]

These findings have apparently prompted Zimring to shift his ground. With apparent benefit and frequency of civilian defensive gun use now established, Zimring now denies that there is a valid difference between criminal lethal violence and lawful use of force in self-defense. He lumps these together under the general rubric "lethal violence." Indeed, Zimring thinks that the American tradition that attaches ethical importance to the distinction between criminal violence and lawful use of force in self-defense contributes to perpetuating America's violence problem. This explains why Professor Zimring thinks that America's "violence problem" is not merely criminological, but comprehensively societal.

Since Zimring regards all uses of deadly force as malignant, irrespective whether it is perpetrated by criminals or used by (allegedly) "good citizens" in self-defense, his social calculus refuses to count as beneficial any use of deadly force by private citizens. Theoretically, this makes the now-substantial literature on defensive gun use irrelevant to an ethical inquiry whether the net-effect of firearms violence is beneficial, or malignant. It's all malignant per se.

It is also noteworthy that Zimring ignores lethal violence perpetrated by government officials, irrespective whether clearly lawful, e.g., when a law enforcement officer justifiably shoots a violent felon in the line of duty or outrageously violates individual rights under the color of law, e.g., as when the attorney general of the United States authorized use of tanks, incendiaries and automatic weapons to kill indiscriminately men, women and 19 children, as she did in Waco, Texas in 1994.

Conclusion

The fundamental ethical problem posed by imposing gun scarcity on the general population has nothing to do with the comparatively trivial "sporting interests" of the public. Nor does gun control implicate merely idiosyncratic, outmoded notions of personal liberty. On the contrary, the fundamental ethical problems posed for proponents of SGC arise when they subscribe simultaneously to the following propositions:

1. An ethically legitimate state must recognize and respect equally the fundamental, individual right to bodily integrity, which includes a fundamental, serious right to self-defense, and;

2. the state has no general duty to provide minimally adequate protection from criminal violence to any individual, nor does it incur a special obligation to anyone by expressly promising an individual that it will provide her a reasonable, minimum of protection from criminal violence, and;

3. the State's inherent police powers include the authority to threaten competent, non-felon adults with criminal penalties for having arms for self-preservation and defense.[25]

4. A state whose laws seriously impair the right of a competent, trustworthy citizen to defend herself from violence, owes her compensating protection from bodily injury.

Affirming 1-3 is incoherent. 2 & 3 rule out 1.[26] Prohibitory gun laws directly implicate the state's duty to respect equally each person's interest in bodily integrity. If the state bans civilian possession of "equalizers" by invoking a monopoly power under prospect 3, it forbids those who are, as a result, made vulnerable to offset the criminological effects of natural inequalities (of being frailer, smaller and weaker). Machiavelli put it crisply: "There simply is no equality between a man who is armed and one who is not."[27]

Strict gun control, by effect if not intent, institutionalizes the natural predatory advantages of larger, stronger, violence-prone persons or gangs of such persons, and yet its proponents incur no liability to offset resulting risks unless they renounce proposition 2 above.

Prohibiting competent, adult, non-felons to possess "equalizers" also has distributional wealth effects not only between criminals and the law-abiding, but also among the law-abiding. Strict gun control disproportionately increases the risks of violent victimization for less well-off law-abiding citizens who cannot take advantage of the privileged connections to officials that wealthier citizens take for granted. Less well-off citizens cannot afford the services of professional body guards who guard our social elites. They cannot afford alarm systems or the enhanced physical security that comes with living in exclusive, gated communities. Strict gun control institutionalizes unequal respect for each citizen's fundamental interest in bodily integrity.

Similarly, banning "cheap" so-called Saturday Night Specials effectively discounts the equal bodily integrity interests of poorer citizens, and not merely the interests of predatory criminals, who tend generally to be poorer than average. Outlawing "cheap" guns threatens to transform poor but law-abiding citizens into lawbreakers solely for choosing a product on the basis of its affordability. Too, eliminating a class of "cheap" guns necessarily demotes what were formerly "marginally non-cheap" guns to "cheap" gun status, eligible for banning as "cheap guns," step by step.

Since supply-side restricting gun control laws that target the general population mitigate the citizen's fundamental interest in bodily integrity and as well as his/her interest in being a political equal, while also materially affect the balance of advantage between criminals and the law-abiding in favor of criminals, and have distributional wealth effects among the law-abiding, effectively pricing lives differentially, every rational, liberal-minded person has reason to get the data necessary for responsible reflection on supply-side restrictive gun control.

We should also consider the associated administrative and enforcement costs secondary to enacting gun laws aimed at the general population and predicate all discussions about the costs/benefits of gun control on an assumption of imperfect compliance. Prohibiting murder has not eliminated it; nor has punishing its perpetrators with death. Banning handguns cannot make them disappear, nor even make them scarce. Despite decades prosecuting our socially and economically ruinous "war on drugs," cocaine, crack and other banned substances remain readily available.

Finally, we should never forget that officially authorized violence, whether inflicted in war against aliens or inflicted in genocidal, domestic exterminations perpetrated under the color of law, has a grim, stubbornly enduring history. When compared with the officially-sanctioned killing fields in Cambodia or Rwanda or Kosovo or Iraq, or Hitler's massive extermination apparatus, or Stalin's mass killings, or Mao's various "Campaigns" against "Bad Elements," private violence, mere criminality, pales in comparison Enthusiasm for a state monopoly over firearms must be tempered by these memories.

References

1. See F. E. Zimring, "Is Gun Control Likely to Reduce Violent Killings?" *University of Chicago Law Review* 35 (1968): 721–37.

2. See F. E. Zimring and G. Hawkins, *Crime Is Not the Problem: Lethal Violence in America* (New York: Oxford University Press, 1997). "Putting social stigma on the instruments of lethal violence [irrespective who uses them, is key because] The rhetorical high ground in violence prevention may leave little room for distinguishing between types of violence," p. 208. By "distinguishing between types of violence," Zimring means the currently made distinction between unlawful offensive violence and lawful defensive violence.

3. See F. E. Zimring and G. Hawkins, *The Citizen's Guide to Gun Control* (New York: Macmillan Press, 1989): 205.

4. Urging "thoughtful consideration" of gun policy changes may be as oxymoronic politically as commending "thoughtful consideration" of changes in abortion policy.

5. A "back of the envelope," county-based calculation indicates that, in the 2000 Presidential Election, counties going for Al Gore had a homicide rate of 13.2, while counties going for Bush had a homicide rate of 1.2. Our current fascination with red v. blue states and or counties underwrites effective political strategy but is potentially very harmful to the country as a whole.

6. In *Crime Is Not the Problem,* he additionally supports it by noting that the homicide rates in the G7 countries are markedly lower than that in the United States despite their having assault rates similar to the United States'. See especially Chapter 7, 106–110.

7. See D. H. Kates, H. E. Schaffer, J. K. Lattimer, G. H. Murray, and E. H. Cassem, "Guns and Public Health: Epidemic of Violence or Pandemic of Propaganda?" *Tennessee Law Review* 62 (1995): 513–596 at 563. The problem of differential suicide-attempt rates remains. Since many developed countries have suicide rates higher than the United States', it would seem that their attempt-rates must be higher too, since every suicide presupposes a (successful) attempt. The number of failed attempts is largely unknowable, for a host of obvious reasons.

8. The graph of the nation's homicide rate is available at the Bureau of Justice Statistics Website. It should be noted that at the beginning of the 20th Century, several states known or suspected of having comparatively high homicide rates did not report their homicide data to the federal government. This suggests that the nation's homicide rate must have been higher than the reported national estimate during those years.

   Professor Kleck has pointed out to me in a personal communication that "The data for 1903–1932 are not actually national data, but rather merely cover the changing subsets of the U.S. that were included in the 'Death Registration Area' (DRA), which consisted of those states that have achieved relatively complete coverage of deaths in their vital statistics systems. Most of the apparently enormous increase in homicide rates from 1903–1920, and part of the 1921–1933 increase, is a statistical mirage, attributable to new, mostly high homicide, states being added to the DRA. Only a minority of the U.S. was covered by the 1903 DRA, predominantly low-homicide Northeast states, while all of it was covered by 1933. Unfortunately, there was a systematic pattern to which states got added to the DRA latest—generally the states that were the last to get their statistical systems up to speed and join the DRA also tended to be the homicide states, mostly from the South and Southwest. E.g., the very last state to join was Texas, a huge contributor to the national homicide rate both because of its high rate and its large population. In reality, the increase in the U.S. homicide rate was much milder than your chart indicates, up until Prohibition went into effect in 1920, at which point homicide really did jump up, though not as much as the DRA-based data seems to indicate."

9. See Brearley, cited in G. Kleck, *Point Blank: Guns and Violence in America* (New York: Aldine deGruyter,1991): 20.

10. FBI data cited in Kleck, supra note 9:20.

11. Firearms and Crime Statistics, at http://www.ojp.usdoj.gov/bjs/guns.htm (last checked February 29, 2004).

12. Supra note 2: 199–202.

13. For a further, critical discussion of the comparative merits of perpetrator theories and instrumentality theories, see D. D. Palsy and D. B. Kats, "American Homicide Exceptionalism," *University of Colorado Law Review* 69, no. 4 (1998): 969–1008.

14. See G. Kleck, *Targeting Guns: Firearms and Their Control* (New York: Aldine de Gruyter,1997): 227–230.

15. F.E. Zimring, "Firearms, Violence and Public Policy," *Scientific American* 265 (1991): 48–58, at 49.

16. See H. Wilson and R. Shaman, "Civilian Penetrating Wounds of the Abdomen," *Annals of Surgery* 153, no. 5 (1961): 639–649.

17. See J. Q. Wilson and R. J. Herrnstein, *Crime and Human Nature: The Definitive Study of the Causes of Crime* (New York: Simon & Schuster, 1985), especially chapter 2.

18. Supra note 13, esp. 992–999.

19. See L. H. Athens, *The Creation of Dangerous Violent Criminals* (Urbana and Chicago: University of Illinois Press, 1992). Also see R. Rhodes, *Why They Kill: The Discoveries of a Maverick Criminologist.* (New York: Knopf Publishers, 1999).

20. See, esp. Supra note 2: 75ff.

21. By federal law, every firearm produced by American gun manufacturers must bear a serial number. Each firearm imported must also bear a serial number. Domestic production totals, imports and exports must be reported annually to the Bureau of Alcohol, Firearms and Tobacco. The trade publication *Shooting Industry* also publishes annually, based on BATF-provided data, the number of firearms produced over a running 20 year period. These data include BATF totals by handgun type (revolvers and pistols) and by

caliber. They enable an objective basis for evaluating market trends and for estimating and updating the number of civilian-owned guns.

Using BATF figures to establish a 1945 baseline, Gary Kleck has developed a production-based model that cumulates annual domestic production, adds imports and subtracts exports. From 1945–1994, the American civilian gun total rose from an estimated 46,909,183 guns to an estimated 235,604,001 guns, an increase of 502.25%. Over that period, the number of privately-owned handguns increased from an estimated 12,657,618 to an estimated 84,665,690, a gain of 668.9%. From 1945–1994, Americans bought handguns at a higher rate than they bought long guns. The whole-period handgun growth rate was 151% of the whole period long gun growth rate (a total handgun increase of 668.9% vs. a total long gun increase of 440.7%).

Between 1993–1999 the industry produced approximately 28.6 million firearms, including 12.5 million handguns. Allowing for imports and subtracting for exports, we may reasonably estimate that the current gun total approximates the size of the U.S. population, including approximately 95–100 million handguns. Figured on a per capita basis, American civilians probably own guns at a rate between 969 and 1016 per 1,000 adults, including a rate between 365 and 388 handguns per 1000 adults.

22. See J. R. Lott, *More Guns, Less Crime: Understanding Crime and Gun Control Laws* (2d Edition) (Chicago: University of Chicago Press, 2000).

23. See supra note 14, ch. 5 for a comprehensive review.

24. See H. Lafollette, "Gun Control," *Ethics* 266 (2000): 110 for an otherwise sophisticated discussion that ignores the ethical implications of the "public service" doctrine of State immunity.

25. See S. Wheeler, "Self-Defense and Coerced Risk-Acceptance," *Public Affairs Quarterly* 11 (1997): 431.

26. N. Machiavelli, *The Prince* (New York: Penguin Books, 1981): 88.

27. See, S. Wheeler, "Arms as Insurance," *Public Affairs Quarterly* 13 (1999): 111.

POSTSCRIPT

Do Strict Gun Control Laws Reduce the Number of Homicides in the United States?

$\mathbf{V}$iolent crime is an unfortunate fact of life in the United States. According to a study published in June 2005 by the U.S. Bureau of Justice Statistics (BJS), 16,204 murders were committed in the United States in 2002.[1] The study also included information about the types of weapons used in these crimes. For all murders in 2002 in which the type of weapon used was known, 64.0% were committed with firearms. Interestingly, 51.7% of the murders were committed with handguns, 4.3% with rifles, 4.3% with shotguns, and 3.6% were not specified. Moreover, knives were used in 16.5% of the cases and blunt objects were used 5.7% of the time.

Similar patterns were observed in family violence cases. In the 1,958 murder cases involving family members, 50.1% used firearms: 36.8% involved handguns, 4.4% used rifles, 6.1% used shotguns, and 2.9% were not specified.

What then, do these statistics tell us about murder in the United States? First, a majority of murders are committed with firearms. Moreover, a large percentage of all murder cases involved handguns. In 2002, murder cases involving family members were somewhat less likely to involve firearms; however, a large number of these murders involved guns as well.

Based on these findings, do you believe that states should pass laws to remove firearms from the population? The authors of the articles in this section would be likely to answer this question in very different ways. Professor Franklin E. Zimring would be likely to assert that the number of murders committed with firearms would support gun ownership restrictions. Conversely, Professor Lance K. Stell would contend that restricting gun ownership would harm law-abiding citizens.

After reading the articles in this section are you more or less likely to support restrictions on firearms ownership in the United States? Is there a middle ground in this debate that you would support, such as a ban on assault weapons or handguns?

In any case, gun control is an issue that generates heated debate. Fortunately, there are many compelling resources that shed additional light on this topic. For example, see Robert J. Spitzer, *The Politics of Gun Control* (Chatham

---

[1]Bureau of Justice Statistics, "Family Violence Statistics." Washington, DC: United States Department of Justice (June 2005).

House Pub, 1995); Lisa D. Brush, "Blown Away: American Women and Guns," *Violence Against Women* (vol. 11, no. 9, September 2005); Linda A. Teplin, Gary M. McClelland, Karen M. Abram, and Darinka Miluesnic, "Early Violent Death Among Delinquent Youth: A Prospective Longitudinal Study," *Pediatrics* (vol. 115, no. 6, June 2005); Jeffrey B. Bingenheimer, Robert T. Brennan, and Felton J. Earls, "Firearm Violence Exposure and Serious Violent Behavior," *Science* (vol. 308, no. 5726, May 27, 2005); Janice Hopkins Tanne, "U.S. Workers Who Carry Guns Are More Likely to Be Killed on the Job," *British Medical Journal* (International Edition) (vol. 330, no. 7499, May 7, 2005); Amie L. Neilsen, Ramiro Martinez, Jr., and Richard Rosenfeld, "Firearm Use, Injury, and Lethality in Assaultive Violence: An Examination of Ethnic Differences," *Homicide Studies* (vol. 9, no. 2, May 2005).

See as well, Abigail A. Kohn, Don B. Kates, Wendy Faminer, and Michael I. Krauss, "Straight Shooting on Gun Control," *Reason* (vol. 37, no. 1, May 2005); Ik-Whan G. Kwon and Daniel W. Baack, "The Effectiveness of Legislation Controlling Gun Usage: A Holistic Measure of Gun Control Legislation," *The American Journal of Economics and Sociology* (vol. 64, no. 2, April 2005); James O. E. Norell, "The Great Debate," *American Rifleman* (vol. 153, no. 1, January 2005); Linda L. Dahlberg, Robin M. Ikeda, and Marcie-jo Kresnow, "Guns in the Home and Risk of a Violent Death in the Home: Findings from a National Study," *American Journal of Epidemiology* (vol. 160, no. 10, November 15, 2004); and John Casteen, "Ditching the Rubric on Gun Control: Notes from an American Moderate," *The Virginia Quarterly Review* (vol. 80, no. 4, Fall 2004).

ISSUE 14

Should the Police Enforce Zero-Tolerance Laws?

YES: George L. Kelling and William J. Bratton, from "Declining Crime Rates: Insiders' Views of the New York City Story," *The Journal of Criminal Law & Criminology* (Summer 1998)

NO: Judith A. Greene, from "Zero Tolerance: A Case Study of Police Policies and Practices in New York City," *Crime & Delinquency* (April 1999)

ISSUE SUMMARY

YES: George L. Kelling, a professor in the School of Criminal Justice at Rutgers University, and William J. Bratton, former New York City Police Department commissioner, strongly defend Kelling's formulation of zero tolerance/broken windows theory and Bratton's implementation of Kelling's ideas.

NO: Judith A. Greene, senior fellow of the Institute on Criminal Justice of the University of Minnesota Law School, compares New York's policing style with San Diego's community policing model and argues that the latter is as effective and less costly.

$\mathbf{M}$any ironies, paradoxes, and contradictions permeate this issue in terms of both criminal justice and policing. First, the theory of crime control put forth in March 1982 by George L. Kelling and James Q. Wilson in their article "Broken Windows," *Atlantic Monthly,* is one of the few examples of specific ideas clearly formulated by scholars that have been directly drawn from to guide crime control practices in the real world. Part of the reason for its application is that Kelling was on hand as a consultant to encourage its development.

Second, it is rare to see immediate results from any criminal justice policy shift. Although critics contend that former police commissioner William J. Bratton or current commissioner Howard Safir's zero-tolerance mode of policing did not cause New York's rapid crime drop, there is little doubt that a miracle somehow occurred in New York City.

Third, while any innovations or program changes in criminal justice (especially in agencies as close-knit as the police) will generate misunderstanding and strains, this is a calculated part of the costs. The trade-off for an improved technology or mode of police interaction is often hurt feelings, bruised egos for those whose old way of doing things are modified or discarded, and diffuse resentments fueled at times by overt envy. In addition, with virtually any new crime control practice, mistakes will happen. These also should be factored into the costs for improvements. However, the incredible backlash from the New York City model of policing was unexpected. Moreover, unlike the vast majority of new police innovations, the backlash is not internal. Instead, the backlash has been primarily external. First, many scholars indignantly attacked zero tolerance as racist, retrograde, and a violation of the narrowly framed "depolicing" perception since the 1960s of what police work is supposed to be about (the less policing the better). Next came the predictable bitterness of political and community interest groups who sometimes feel threatened by any neighborhood success that they do not control or can claim for their own. The tragic mistakes that may or may not have been a result of zero tolerance—such as the killing of minority citizens mistakenly thought to be threatening criminals—more than provide proof for skeptics of zero tolerance that the experiment is racist, misguided, and contemptible. In some states, political candidates have leaped into office or been thrown out based on their positions on zero-tolerance policing.

A last irony is that while the definition of many criminal justice and criminological terms are ambiguous (including crime itself!), the meaning of *zero tolerance* is highly problematic. Many scholars and politicians have distanced themselves from the term, substituting phrases that sound more politically correct. As you read the following selections, consider the different components of zero tolerance/broken windows policing. What is the role of the cop on the beat? The administrators? Technologies? Compare and contrast community policing with Kelling and Bratton's approach. Notice that most consider zero tolerance a polar opposite of community policing. Yet defenders such as Kelling and Bratton seem to suggest that community policing can be subsumed under zero tolerance. How can that be?

In her selection, Judith A. Greene cites several criticisms of the New York approach, and then compares and contrasts its crime reduction statistics with that of San Diego, California. That city has the allegedly opposite policing style, community policing, to New York's. As you read Greene's selection, consider the basis for her comparison and the importance and value of doing comparative analysis in criminology. Note also the many favorable aspects of Bratton's administration as commissioner that she identifies. How would you separate the alleged good from the alleged bad in zero tolerance? Should this style of policing be encouraged?

YES

George L. Kelling and
William J. Bratton

Declining Crime Rates

Introduction

Something dramatic happened in New York City in 1994: a lot of people stopped committing crimes, especially violent ones. The reduction in the number of persons committing murders, for example, while not unprecedented, was extraordinary. Since 1994, a debate has raged about why this happened. Putting our position up front, we believe the police played an important, even central, role in getting people to stop committing crime in New York City. Despite arguments to the contrary,[1] no evidence exists that the substantial drops in crime in New York City, especially the initial ones when one of the authors of this paper, William Bratton, was commissioner, were the result of economic change, changes in drug use patterns, or demographic changes. Arguably, New York City's economy, drug use patterns, and demography might be different now in 1998. Unemployment was at 10% the month Bratton took over the New York City Police Department (NYPD) (January 1994) and at 8.7% when he resigned (April 1996)—hardly a booming economy. And remember as well, the initial reductions in crime were so steep that by August of 1995—three years ago, but only twenty months after Bratton took office—*New York* magazine declared in a cover story, "The End of Crime As We Know It."

Readers should understand that this debate about the origins of crime reductions in the United States, especially in New York City, are not just academic in the sense that detached scholars are searching objectively for some "truth" lurking out there somewhere in the data. In fact, criminological and political ideologies have shaped a good portion of this debate and are barely beneath the surface of even the most "detached" presentations. We do not pretend to be free from strong points of view about what happened in New York City. We were there and our presence belies any "detached objectivity." Yet, we are not alone in having important vested interests in the outcome of the debate. Aside from the lack of any competing explanations, our confidence that the police played an important role in New York City has three origins:

1. We had a guiding "idea" about how to prevent crime; put another way, we had a theory of action;

From *Journal of Criminal Law & Criminology*, vol. 88, no. 4, Summer 1998, pp. 1217–1231. Copyright © 1998 by Northwestern University School of Law. Reprinted by permission.

2. We applied this idea in New York City's subway and, without anticipating it, the subway experiences became the "pretest" for what was to happen later citywide;

3. Bratton, most importantly, but Kelling as well, had been struggling with issues of how to improve policing through police leadership, management, and administration for over two decades—principles developed in the context of organizational and policy literature and experience.

In the three sections that follow, we will be brief. We have written elsewhere about these issues and will not repeat our arguments here in detail.

The "Idea"—Broken Windows

The "broken windows" metaphor had its origin in an *Atlantic Monthly* article by James Q. Wilson and Kelling. It argued that, just as a broken window left untended was a sign that nobody cares and leads to more and severe property damage, so disorderly conditions and behaviors left untended send a signal that nobody cares and results in citizen fear of crime, serious crime, and the "downward spiral of urban decay." The article also argued that whenever crime and communities verged on being out of control in the past, residents and authorities in neighborhoods moved to reassert controls over youth and over disorderly behavior.

The implications of this point of view are that minor offenses have serious consequences for the life of neighborhoods and communities. Citizens, city officials, and police ignore them at their peril. This point of view is at odds with the reigning crime control policy view that had been developing throughout the 1950s and 1960s and made explicit by President Johnson's Crime Control Commission. Police, in this view, are "law enforcement officers," the front end of the criminal justice system whose business is serious crime—arresting offenders. For a variety of reasons police got out of the business of minor offenses. These reasons went beyond the utilitarian view that scarce police resources should best be concentrated on "serious" crimes. They included an understanding of how police abused loitering and vagrancy ordinances in the past; a desire for less intrusive policing and a more judicious use of police authority in a democracy; and, a view that many of the offenses, like prostitution, are victimless.

Nonetheless, we argued that the links between disorder, fear, and crime went something like the following:

Disorder → Citizen Fear → Withdrawal (Physical & Social) → Increased Predatory Behavior → Increased Crime → Spiral of Decline

According to this model, waiting until serious crimes occur to intervene is too late: dealing with disorderly behavior early, like successful communities have in the past, prevented the cycle from accelerating and perpetuating itself.

Moreover, experiences in the subway taught us that many chronic, serious offenders also behave in a disorderly fashion and commit minor offenses like farebeating. Police order maintenance activities also give police the opportunity to make contact with and arrest serious offenders for minor offenses.

We never claimed that order maintenance alone is the sole means of preventing crime. Solving crimes, incarceration, social change, deterrence by other means, police presence and persuasion, citizen vigilance, reduction of opportunities, environmental design, and other factors play a role as well. In New York City's subway, however, we argue that order maintenance was an especially significant part of reclaiming the subway and reducing crime.

The Subway

In April of 1989, Robert Kiley, Chairman of New York State's Metropolitan Transportation Authority (MTA) asked Kelling to assist the MTA in solving a problem in the New York City Transit Authority's subway (NYCTA). Kiley believed that the subway was in deep trouble—passenger usage of the subway was in rapid decline. New York City's late 1980s economic slump partially explained this decline. But marketing surveys suggested a more complicated problem: "homelessness" was frightening passengers and causing them to abandon the subway in droves. This was after 8 billion dollars had been poured into the subway to upgrade trains and tracks during the early and mid-1980s.

The NYCTA had already largely solved the problem of subway graffiti—a problem considered so intractable that its eradication was considered by some to be one of the most successful urban policy "wins" on record. Yet, despite this achievement, the frightening and intimidating behavior of a large group of miscreants overmatched whatever advantages accrued from graffiti elimination.

For those who have not experienced New York's subway during the late 1980s, its nightmarish circumstances are hard to describe. "In your face" panhandlers confronted riders throughout the system, from station entrances to trains. A quarter of a million passengers a day were "farebeaters," going over, under, and around turnstiles. Youths deliberately blocked turnstiles, held open emergency gates, and extorted fares from passengers. Platforms, trains, and passageways reeked from public urination and defecation. Young men stalked tollbooths planning to rob them if by any chance their doors were opened. These same tollbooths—literally under siege—had already been firmly secured, including being equipped with special automatic fire extinguishers that would be activated if youths poured gasoline into the money window and lit it to force toll-takers to open booth doors. Drug and alcohol abusers and the emotionally disturbed, often one and the same, sprawled throughout the entire system—at times taking over entire cars on a train. Robberies of passengers were increasing.

For the Transit Police Department (TPD), at this time an independent police department of some 4,000 officers, it was business as usual. They shared the common view held by everyone from homeless advocates, to the New York City Civil Liberties Union, to the *New York Times*. The problem was "homelessness" and homelessness was not the TPD's problem. Robberies consumed its attention. For example, the TPD was eager to restart an earlier discredited decoy unit. When confronted by Kiley about the subway's "homelessness" problems,

TPD's administration at first balked. Later, under pressure, it proposed massive cleaning crews armed with high-powered hoses supported by a special police unit that would eject the "homeless" as they "interfered" with or got in the way of cleaning.

The story of reclaiming the subway by the police has been told elsewhere and need not be repeated here. Summarizing, a large scale problem-solving exercise was conducted, the problem in the subway was properly understood as illegal disorderly behavior, policies were developed and officers trained to deal with disorder. The legal battles over police activities to rein in panhandling were fought and ultimately won; TPD leadership, however, was recalcitrant and the effort flagged. Bratton was recruited as Chief of the TPD in April of 1990; he provided leadership and implemented a large-scale effort to restore order. Following these actions, serious crime began an immediate and steep decline.

Disorder and crime are no longer serious problems in New York's subway—it is among the safest in the world. It feels, smells, and "tastes" different. Indeed, the culture was so different that by the mid-1990s the Transit Authority initiated a civility campaign, encouraging citizens to queue before boarding trains—a campaign that would have been a joke in the late 1980s. Returning ex-New Yorkers are stunned by the changes.

We highlight the subway experience because it has been lost in the bigger New York City disorder and crime story, especially since the TPD was absorbed by the New York City Police Department (NYPD) in 1995. Yet, it is an important story. It is probably one of the largest problem-solving exercises on record. The police tactics, organizational change, and administrative processes implemented in the TPD foreshadowed changes in the New York City Police Department. Still and all the reclamation of the subway stands as a major event in public policy—certainly on a par with graffiti eradication—that raised and managed complex policy, constitutional, legal, and moral issues.

From our point of view and within the context of this discussion, it is especially important because it is hard to attribute the changes in the subway to anything other than police action. To be sure, the NYCTA implemented major efforts to deal with the genuinely homeless who were attempting to use the subway as a surrogate shelter. Graffiti had been eliminated and trains and tracks upgraded. Attempts had been made to target-harden the tollbooths and token-boxes (youths had been able to "spring" their doors with large screwdrivers and steal hundreds of tokens at a time), and some areas had been blocked off to the public. Moreover, subway officials were implementing a "station manager" program that focused on restoring a sense of station "ownership" and concern for passengers. But the subway environment was spinning out of control despite subway improvements and attempts at target hardening. Moreover, post-hoc explanations used to explain the later citywide reductions in crime—changes in drug use patterns, improved economy, declines in the number of youths, etc.—simply do not apply. Drug selling was not a major issue in the subway; unemployment was increasing during the time in question; and there was no evidence of a decline in the youth population.

The question is raised, "But isn't the subway a simpler system and easier to reclaim than city streets and public spaces?" This is the point of the subway story. It is a simpler system. People pay to enter it. There are few private spaces—only trains, platforms, passageways, and entrances and exits. One would expect that if police action, in this case to restore order, were to have an impact in any setting, it would be in such a restricted environment. From our standpoint it was an ideal place to test the broken windows hypothesis: that is, one way to reduce fear of crime and prevent serious crime is to restore order. The subway is a system in which the potentially confounding variables cited by social scientists are controlled.

Certainly, we cannot aver with scientific certainty that the crime reductions in the subway are the result of the police intervention. We put forward the following, however:

1. In response to a growing problem, the TPD developed a specific set of interventions that included police tactics and changes in organizational structure and administrative processes;
2. The TPD "called its shots," predicting that order could be restored and that crime would be reduced;[2]
3. Immediately following the intervention, crime began a steep decline.

The "after, therefore because of" fallacy? Perhaps. We doubt it. No other explanation seems plausible. Did graffiti elimination play a role? Target hardening? Social services for the genuinely homeless? Other factors? Of course. But action by the TPD achieved a "tipping point." We will return to the idea of "tipping point."

A final point in this introduction: no explanation of what happened in New York City can ignore the subway experience. While originally not conceived of as such, it became the pretest to what happened in the city.

Leadership and Management

The New York City story is more complicated than the subway story. New York City is an intricate political, social, economic, and cultural entity in its own right. It has elaborate linkages to state, national, and international institutions and forces. Crime is more complicated in the city than in the subway. For example, the serious crime problem in the subway is largely robbery, with most of them being "grab and run"—crimes that, while not trivial, are less ominous than many of the confrontational robberies on city streets. Crime varies in other respects as well.

Moreover, more complex control systems operate in the city—from the "small change" of neighborhood life, to schools, churches, family, workplace, business improvement districts, community groups, and others. Potentially confounding influences are not naturally controlled.

The NYPD is more complicated than the TPD was, and, frankly, it was in deep trouble when Bratton assumed control in 1994. Its troubles with abuse and corruption during the early 1990s were well known, largely as a result of newspaper revelations and the subsequent work of the Mollen Commission. But there was another story in the NYPD, at least as dark as the abuse and corruption accounts, but far less well known—the lack of quality policing. Since the

1970s Knapp Commission, the NYPD has been preoccupied with corruption. So much so that it was widely understood, but only partially true, that the "business" of the NYPD had become "staying out of trouble." And, of course, the most certain way to stay out of trouble was "to do nothing." Surely this is an overstatement, but nonetheless, it had considerable basis in fact. Most symptomatic of this "stay out of trouble by doing nothing" orientation was that line patrol officers were restrained by policy from making drug arrests, even if dealing was conducted right in front of their noses. In respects it was the worst of all possible scenarios: too much abuse and corruption, too much corruption control, and not enough quality policing. Bratton described the NYPD administrative world in *Turnaround:*

> [T]he New York City Police department was dysfunctional.
>
> First, it was divided into little fiefdoms, and some bureau chiefs didn't even talk to each other. OCCP didn't talk to patrol, patrol didn't get along with the Detective Bureau, and nobody talked to internal affairs. . . .
>
> . . . Each bureau was like a silo: Information entered at the bottom and had to be delivered up the chain of command from one level to another until it reached the chief's office. . .
>
> . . . .
>
> When Maple [a key Bratton advisor who had been a lieutenant in the TPD and who was a deputy commissioner under Bratton] analyzed the bureaus, the news got worse. How was the NYPD deployed? The Narcotics Bureau, he discovered, worked largely nine to five or five to one, Monday through Friday. The warrant squad was off weekends. Auto-crimes squad, off weekends. Robbery squads? Off weekends. The community-policing officers—those six thousand baby-faced twenty-two-year-olds who were going to solve all the neighborhoods' problems—off weekends. Essentially, except for the detectives, patrol officers, and some other operations going round the clock, the whole place took Saturdays and Sundays off.

Leading and managing such troubled organizations had become Bratton's stock-in-trade. The NYPD had been the fifth police organization he had headed that was in organizational trouble. His conviction that leading, inspiring, and directing middle-management was the key to improving police organizations was evident in a paper he published with Kelling and was apparent in his work with the TPD. His closest organizational advisors, Robert Wasserman (a police leader and consultant for over 30 years) and Robert Johnson (President of First Security—a Boston-based private security firm) had struggled with management issues for decades. Wasserman, who had been an advisor to previous NYPD Commissioner Lee Brown, knew where the strengths of the NYPD were buried. Johnson had struggled to find leadership and management methods in the private sector to maintain core values and technologies in highly decentralized and geographically dispersed organizations. Other key advisors included John Linder, who had developed methods to do quick scans on organizational problems and opportunities, and Jack Maple, who is perhaps one of the savviest, street wise, and creative cops around. The ideas for Compstat—an organizational method both for holding precinct commanders accountable and for developing anti-crime tactics—grew directly out of the private sector management experiences of Johnson and the street sense of Maples.

This, too has all been discussed previously. We summarize it here to make the following point: Bratton approached his commissionership in New York City with a clear plan. He had an idea about how to prevent crime; he had an organizational strategy he wanted to implement; and he had pretested both with great success in New York City's subways. Again as in the subway, he called his shots—both by demanding that mid-level managers be held accountable for crime reduction and by producing plans for dealing with specific problems such as guns, youth violence, domestic violence, quality of life, auto crimes, and others. One of the hallmarks in social science is that research should be guided by theory. Bratton's strategy was, in effect, management guided by theory. Innovations were implemented and crime dropped. A lot.

Conclusion

What happened in New York City? We, of course, will never know with scientific certainty. No credible alternatives, however, have been put forward to contradict our belief that police action played a pivotal role. In the final analysis, we believe that we have seen New York City do what cities and communities have traditionally done when confronted by disorder, crime, and mayhem: it has moved to reassert control over disorderly behavior, fear, and crime.

The move to reassert control has been discernible in New York City since the late 1970s. Communities organized, business improvement districts organized, graffiti was eliminated from the subway, additional police were recruited and hired, prosecutors turned to communities for guidance (especially in Brooklyn), order was restored in the subway, and Mayor Rudolph Giuliani was given a political mandate to restore order and help bring crime under control. But, there were limits to what could be accomplished without an active police presence. Things had been allowed to deteriorate for so long, aggressive youths had been so emboldened—indeed in the absence of an active police presence, they virtually dominated public spaces in many communities— that traditional control measures were simply not robust enough to restrain their predatory behavior. And, in the midst of the "crack" epidemic, their violence spun out of control. Thus, the pattern described in Fagan et al.'s "Tale of Two Trends" comes as no surprise to us. They compare non-gun homicides with gun homicides. That non-gun homicides should be declining over an extended period of time is consistent with our view of how New Yorkers have been reclaiming their city over the long haul. Fagan et al.'s assertion that "The rate of lethal violence broke important new ground only after 1995 or 1996" is consistent with our interpretation as well. This was the *exact* period during which police were reinvigorated and their impact started to be felt. Likewise, we have no quarrel with Curtis' basic thesis,[3] that poor people are capable of helping themselves. We have never asserted otherwise: it has been basic to

Bratton's practice and it is explicit in both the original "Broken Windows" and "Fixing Broken Windows."

Our basic premise is this: the restoration of assertive policing in 1994 and 1995 interacted with community forces to achieve an unprecedented "tipping point" in violent and other forms of crime. Community forces, although formidable, could not do it alone. History and research gives us evidence that police cannot do it alone. To assert that both the community and police played significant roles demeans neither. Can we ever be more specific in attributing causality? We doubt it.

The interesting question is, however, why things got so out of control. What happened that communities throughout the country either lacked the will or capacity to maintain order and keep its miscreants under control during the past three decades? Certainly macroeconomic and demographic forces were at play. More specifically the forces that have been aligned against neighborhoods and communities over the last three decades have been staggering. As Kelling wrote elsewhere:

> Aside from the seemingly inevitable growth of the suburbs, consider what was done to our cities during the 1950s, 1960s, and 1970s. In the name of urban renewal, entire inner-city neighborhoods were torn apart. No provisions were made for displaced residents, so naturally they moved into adjacent neighborhoods. Because many of those displaced were African Americans, real estate blockbusters followed them, undercutting property values and scaring other residents into moving. In the renewal areas, concrete blocks of multi-story public housing was built, often, as in Chicago with external unsecured elevators. This was the housing of the last resort for the most troubled and troublesome families. Expanded tenant "rights," however, made it virtually impossible to evict troublemakers regardless of their behavior or capacity for mayhem. Expressway construction followed and cut wide swaths through communities, displacing entire neighborhoods and dividing others. Neighborhood schools were abandoned and students were bussed throughout the city. Mental hospitals emptied patients onto city streets and drunkenness was decriminalized. The mentally ill and alcohol and drug abusers drifted into urban centers. In the name of their "liberty interests" and to forestall family and governmental abuse, parental and governmental authority over youths was reduced. To ensure that . . . children would not be stigmatized, we abandoned the idea of early identification of predelinquents.[4]

Intermingling with these urban policies, were equally disastrous police and criminal justice policies that grew out of the 1960's Presidential Commission on Law Enforcement and the Administration of Justice. Its position was explicit: poverty, racism, and economic injustices caused crime. To prevent crime one had to eliminate these "root causes." The business of the police and other criminal justice agencies became arresting and processing offenders. This view became so pervasive that many early defenders of community policing asserted that because police could not deal with poverty, racism, etc., they could do little about crime. Thus the crime problem was "de-policed" for many police leaders—a view that most line officers found absolutely unacceptable, complicating the implementation of community policing. Police tactics grew out of these assumptions and police became "law enforcement officers" responding to serious crimes and calls for service—their isolation in cars virtually "de-policing" city streets. The political far right came in with their variation: crime was caused by breakdown of family values associated with welfare. Consequently, crime prevention was held hostage by both the ideologies of the far left and right: economic redistribution or elimination of welfare. Aside from community policing, criminal justice innovations were limited to more certain and longer incarceration.

Happily, police, criminal justice practitioners, and urban officials are breaking new ground. Most criminal justice professionals have no quarrel with the idea that disorder and crime are somehow linked to poverty, racism, and breakdown of values. But, they also understand that these linkages interact in an extraordinarily complex way. Meantime, they have rediscovered policing, as opposed to law enforcement, and prevention, as opposed to case processing. The changes that are taking place in the basic modalities of many public housing agencies, schools, zoning agencies, city attorneys' offices, and other agencies are equally as impressive. The interesting thing, as both of us travel around the country, is that different cities are doing it in different ways. The starting points are different. Powerful collaborations are forming among citizen groups, business, city agencies, prosecutors, correctional officials, and others. They take different configurations in different cities and deal with different problems in different ways. But this, of course, is the lesson. Each city is singular. Within cities, communities are unique. They are asserting control over themselves in unique ways as well.

In sum, neither of us would back away from a concluding statement in Bratton's *Turnaround:*

> In terms of importance and potential and commitment, police in America are probably the most misunderstood entity in public life today. Old images exist, and, in truth, old-guard departments exist as well. But, as we approach the millennium, there is a new breed of police leader and a new breed of police officer. We need more of them.
>
> I was privileged during my last half-dozen years in policing to work on the national and international stage, and I feel there is still more the police can do. The turnaround of the NYPD was the catalyst for the turnaround of New York City itself and offers a potential blueprint for the turnaround of the crime situation in the entire country. We clearly showed that when properly led, properly managed, and in effective partnership with the neighborhoods and the political leaders, police can effect great change. We have clearly shown that police can take back streets that were given up as lost for decades. The continuing challenge for American police leaders is to take them back in a lawful and respectful manner so that the behavior of the police reflects the civil behavior society expects of its citizens.

Notes

1. *See generally,* Alfred Blumstein & Richard Rosenfeld, *Explaining Recent Trends in U.S. Homicide Rates,* 88 J. Crim. L. & Criminology 1175 (1998).

2. The TPD's slogan under Bratton was "Disorder, farebeating, and robbery are one problem—deal with one and you deal with all."

3. Richard Curtis, *The Improbable Transformation of Inner-City Neighborhoods: Crime, Violence, Drugs and Youth in the 1990s,* 88 J. Crim. L. & Criminology 1233, 1263 (1998).

4. George L. Kelling, National Institute of Justice, *Crime Control, The Police, and Culture Wars: Broken Windows and Cultural Pluralism, in* II Perspectives on Crime & Justice: 1997–1998 Lecture Series 1, 13–14 (1998).

Judith A. Greene  **NO**

Zero Tolerance

The police reforms introduced in New York City by William Bratton are now hailed by Mayor Rudy Giuliani as the epitome of "zero-tolerance" policing, and he credits them for winning dramatic reductions in the city's crime rate. But the number of citizen complaints filed before the Civilian Complaint Review Board has jumped skyward, as has the number of lawsuits alleging police misconduct and abuse of force. Comparison of crime rates, arrest statistics, and citizen complaints in New York with those in San Diego—where a more problem-oriented community policing strategy has been implemented—gives strong evidence that effective crime control can be achieved while producing fewer negative impacts on urban neighborhoods.

The 1998 New York City Mayor's Management Report lists many concrete improvements in the quality of life in New York City, which Mayor Rudy Giuliani believes have been won directly through the New York Police Department's targeted approach to crime control—now held up by many observers as the epitome of "zero-tolerance" policing. . . .

The Mayor's office reports that from 1993 to 1997 the number of felony complaints in New York City dropped by 44.3 percent: a 60.2 percent drop in murders and nonnegligent homicides, a 12.4 percent drop in forcible rape, a 48.4 percent drop in robbery, and a 45.7 drop in burglary. Mayor Giuliani points out that New York City is responsible for a large share of the overall crime reduction for the country as a whole. Comparing data from cities of more than 100,000 population for the first half of 1997 with data from these cities in the first half of 1993, the mayor's management report asserts that New York City accounted for 32 percent of the overall drop in FBI Index Crimes, 29 percent of the drop in murders, and 44 percent of the drop in larceny/thefts.

The Mayor's office credits the New York Police Department's (NYPD's) "Compstat" system for much of the progress made in reducing crime. Compstat was introduced by Police Commissioner William Bratton, who had served as commissioner for the first 27 months (from January 1994 to April 1996) of Giuliani's first term as mayor. The Compstat system puts up-to-date crime data into the hands of NYPD managers at all levels and bolsters a department-wide process for precinct-level accountability in meeting the department's crime-reduction goals.

From *Crime & Delinquency*, vol. 45, no. 2, April 1999, pp. 171–187. Copyright © 1999 by Sage Publications. Reprinted by permission via Rightslink.

As described in Bratton's recent book, *Turnaround: How America's Top Cop Reversed the Crime Epidemic*, the Compstat system is built on four concepts: (1) accurate and timely intelligence, (2) rapid deployment of personnel and resources, (3) effective tactics, and (4) relentless follow-up and assessment. Compstat is the engine that drives "zero-tolerance" policing in New York City, and it is at the heart of the strategic organizational changes that Bratton introduced when he took command of the NYPD in 1994.

Bratton moved vigorously to transform the police department from top to bottom and to transfuse the department with a new mindset about what the police could and should do to attack the problem of crime and reduce its impact on the residents of the city. He directly confronted the common wisdom of many experts—and, perhaps, most New Yorkers—that the NYPD was too large, too rigid, too bureaucratic, and too parochial to be able to embrace the kinds of radical changes in policies and practices that would be required in a serious effort to win measurable reductions of the city's high crime rates. And he proved that they were wrong.

Zero-tolerance policing puts major emphasis on the kinds of "quality-of-life" issues that set the drumbeat rhythm for Giuliani's 1993 mayoral campaign. The "Squeegee Men" (beggars who accosted drivers in their cars to scrub their windshields and panhandle for cash), the petty drug dealers, the graffiti scribblers, and the prostitutes who ruled the sidewalks in certain high-crime neighborhoods all were targeted in candidate Giuliani's campaign promise to reclaim the streets of New York for law-abiding citizens.

Prior to his election, Giuliani's professional career had been spent in law enforcement. It is no coincidence that these types of disorderly persons and small-time criminals exactly fit the flesh-and-blood profile of the "broken windows" theory of policing. . . . The broken windows theory holds that if not firmly suppressed, disorderly behavior in public will frighten citizens and attract predatory criminals, thus leading to more serious crime problems.

Although "reclaiming the open spaces of New York" was but one of six specific crime strategies that Bratton designed and introduced to reshape the goals of the NYPD, it was moved quickly to the front of the line when city officials began to make the claim that the Giuliani administration's police reforms were *causing* the decreases in crime. Cracking down hard on the most visible symbols of urban disorder proved to be a powerful political tool for bolstering Giuliani's image as a highly effective mayor. The speed with which the city's crime statistics have fallen has been taken by many to prove that Wilson and Kelling are correct and that serious crime problems can be quelled by mounting a large-scale attack on petty crime and disorderly behavior through a broken windows, zero-tolerance strategy.

To at least some extent, rhetorical emphasis on the broken windows theory has served to obscure the truly phenomenal record that William Bratton set in managing organizational change within the NYPD. As chief executive officer of one of the world's largest police agencies, he introduced new management tools, techniques, and technology at lightning speed and moved quickly to decentralize authority. . . .

But Bratton's concept and style of police management has driven the NYPD a distinct and substantial distance apart from the community policing concepts that have been used to reshape and redirect police services in many other American cities. Moreover, some of these cities are closely rivaling the crime-reduction record set in New York City.

Ironically, Bratton has broad knowledge of and deep experience with community policing. He was a leading innovator in the development of the neighborhood policing concept while serving as a young officer in the Boston Police Department. He has often publicly expressed solid confidence in the basic tenets of the community policing movement—forging close working partnerships with the community, problem solving to address the causes of crime, and a fundamental commitment to crime prevention. . . .

An ambitious gun interdiction program was initiated during the [David] Dinkins administration [which preceded Giuliani] by Assistant Police Commissioner Jeremy Travis, who now heads the National Institute of Justice. This effort was spurred forward in 1993 by the Bureau of Alcohol, Tobacco, and Firearms—then under the leadership of Ronald Noble at the Department of Justice. The well-publicized 1993 interdiction campaign predated the Bratton/Giuliani gun strategy and involved capture of several large stores of weapons before they reached the hands of teenagers on New York City streets.

The early foundation for community policing in New York had been laid in the mid 1980s—during the [Ed] Koch administration—through a joint NYPD/Vera Institute of Justice pilot effort. Once the Safe Streets program was in place, Commissioner [Lee] Brown was able to design and build a citywide community policing program. Yet, in his book, *Turnaround,* Bratton abruptly dismissed this community-policing effort (already in place when he was named Police Commissioner) in three brief paragraphs.

In *Turnaround,* Bratton maintained that the program—although focused on the beat cop—had no real focus on crime, and he complained that the young officers assigned to community-policing beats were unprepared and ill equipped to handle the complex issues that underlie the crime problem in New York City. Moreover, he charged, even those few capable of winning significant results were never given the necessary authority to follow through under the NYPD's system of centralized decision making.

In a 1996 lecture sponsored by the Heritage Foundation, Bratton discussed the flaws that he perceives in the community policing initiatives of the early 1990s. He argued that community policing in New York was hampered by a lack of attention to those quality-of-life issues that cause widespread fear of crime among the public and by an unwieldy and highly centralized, over-specialized police bureaucracy. . . .

Once recruited by Mayor-elect Giuliani to serve as commissioner of the NYPD, Bratton used his prior experience combating subway crime as a springboard into a citywide campaign to aggressively apprehend the perpetrators of quality-of-life crimes on the streets. Bratton's managerial reforms were brilliantly innovative, using up-to-the-minute technology. But at the neighborhood level, his crime-fighting strategies were grounded in traditional law enforcement methods and in relentless crackdown campaigns to arrest and jail low-level drug offenders and other petty perpetrators. . . .

Bratton's crime-prevention concepts are more often cloaked in military campaign metaphors—" in New York City, we now know where the enemy is"—than in the public-health/epidemiological images now more common in community-focused prevention efforts elsewhere. And his quality-of-life law-enforcement style was hyperaggressive. In *Turnaround*, Bratton describes how his school truancy program grabbed so many school-age kids off the streets that "we had to set up 'catchment' areas in school auditoriums and gymnasiums." He retooled New York City's drug enforcement effort to target more muscle toward low- and middle-level dealers, and he lifted a longstanding police policy that discouraged drug enforcement arrests by patrol officers—freeing them to seek warrants, make narcotics arrests, and go after those they suspected of drug dealing for quality-of-life violations to sweep them off the streets and into the jails (Bratton 1998, p. 227).

Bratton attacked the legal restrictions that had impeded aggressive enforcement against those deemed disorderly. He "took the handcuffs off" the police department and unleashed patrol officers to stop and search citizens who were violating the most minor laws on the books (e.g., drinking a beer or urinating in public), to run warrant checks on them, or just to pull them in for questioning about criminal activity in their neighborhood. If, in the course of such an incident, a weapon was found and confiscated, Bratton asserts that it was lawful prevention of crime "before it happened."

If, as its keystone crime-prevention strategy, New York City has turned away from community policing and chosen instead a zero-tolerance campaign that is heavily reliant on traditional methods of law enforcement to eradicate quality-of-life problems, what negative consequences have resulted from this choice? And which New Yorkers have borne the brunt of these negative consequences?

Joel Berger—a prominent New York City civil rights attorney who represents alleged victims of police misconduct and abuse in New York City—reports that legal filings of new civil rights claims against the police for abusive conduct have increased by 75 percent in the city over the last four years. Berger says that the largest increase in new claims of this type occurred during the most recent fiscal year, indicating that the problem of police brutality is getting worse, not better.

Amnesty International has reported that police brutality and unjustifiable use of force is a widespread problem in New York City. There is a wealth of documentation to support the charge that police misconduct and abuse have increased under the Giuliani administration's zero-tolerance regime. The total number of citizen complaints filed annually with the Civilian Complaint Review Board (CCRB) increased more than 60 percent between 1992 and 1996, and Mark Green—the elected New York City public advocate—has charged that the police torture of Abner Louima in a precinct station house in the Borough of Brooklyn in the summer of 1997 was part of a larger "pattern of police abuse, brutality, and misconduct" in New York City that the Giuliani administration has failed to address. . . .

Complaints by citizens in New York City about police misconduct and abuse, and the response to these complaints by the New York City CCRB and the NYPD, have been the subject of hot debate between some resistant city officials and those who advocate for a more effective process to increase police account-ability for abuse of citizens. From the start, Mayor Giuliani resisted the effort to establish an independent CCRB. By the time it was set up, its budget had been slashed by 17 percent (about a million dollars) as compared with the police department-based civilian complaint unit it had replaced.

According to New York City Public Advocate Mark Green, recent CCRB complaint data suggest that the problem of police misconduct is disproportion-ately concentrated in New York City's high-crime minority neighborhoods. Nine out of 76 precincts account for more than 50 percent of the increase in CCRB complaints since 1992; 21 precincts account for more than 80 percent. Mark Green charges that those precincts with the highest incidence of misconduct "appear to have disproportionately higher percentages of African American and Latino residents." Norman Siegel—director of the New York Civil Liberties Union (NYCLU) and a harsh critic of the mayor on these issues—has presented data showing that three quarters of all CCRB complaints are filed by African Americans and Latinos. He reports that African Americans (who make up 29 percent of the city's population) filed 53 percent of all complaints in 1996.

Moreover, the vast majority of complaints filed with the CCRB are never substantiated, and the small portion that are substantiated usually do not result in proper disciplinary actions. In the first eight months of last year, only 8 percent of the 3,991 cases filed with the CCRB were substantiated. Further-more, Public Advocate Mark Green has complained that so few substantiated cases ever result in charges brought or disciplinary actions taken by the police department that the civilian complaint process is a sham.

This brief review of the downside *costs* that many New Yorkers argue have been incurred through the city's reliance on a highly aggressive, traditional law-enforcement style of policing begs the *benefits* question: Is there hard evi-dence that this strategy has been truly effective in reducing crime? How valid are the claims made by Mayor Giuliani that his police policies are responsible for the city's remarkable crime reduction record? . . .

Serious violent crime rates have been falling for the nation as a whole. The National Crime Victimization Survey crime-trends data (1973–1996) published by the Bureau of Justice Statistics indicate that rapes declined 60 percent from 1991 to 1996, whereas robberies began to decline more recently; robberies were down 17 percent from 1994 to 1996. Aggravated assaults declined by 27 percent from 1993 to 1996. The victimization data show that total violent crime was down 19 percent from 1994 to 1996. Data from the National Center for Health Statistics indicate that the nation's homicide rate fell by 10 percent from 1991 to 1995. Property crimes are also on the decline for the nation as a whole, accord-ing to the National Crime Victimization Survey. The rates reported for total property crime show a 25 percent decline from 1991 to 1996.

It has been argued by many that widespread innovations in police practices have made a major contribution to reducing crime—from the zero-tolerance campaign in New York City to community-policing strategies involving problem solving and police/community partnerships elsewhere. Yet, crime has fallen substantially in some locales where these reforms have not been embraced.

The huge increase in the incarceration rate resulting from mandatory minimum drug laws, "three strikes, you're out" laws, and other policy shifts producing longer prison terms are claimed by almost all proponents of these "get tough" approaches to be the force driving crime rates downward. But increased incarceration doesn't seem to explain many of the differences found when states are compared. New York City has experienced one of the sharpest declines in violent crime, but its jail population is down, and the New York state prison population growth rate slowed to less than one percent in 1997. The state's prison population growth rate has been relatively modest during the 1990s compared to states such as Texas and California. Crime rates were already beginning to fall before the state of Washington became the first to pass three-strikes legislation in 1993. Most states are enjoying declining crime rates regardless of whether they have such laws. . . .

If there is an ascendant theory among American criminologists, it may be simply stated: No single factor, cause, policy, or strategy has reduced the drop in crime rates.

A variety of structural changes in high-crime urban neighborhoods are cited by many experts as plausibly combining to produce declining crime rates. Many academic experts have long held that demographic factors are the most significant contributors to crime rates. Overall crime rates (as distinct from violent street crime) have been drifting downward for many years, as has alcohol consumption—a factor strongly associated with a broad range of criminal activity. America's healthy economy has produced low unemployment rates, another factor generally associated with lower crime rates.

Overall shifts in public attitudes regarding the problem of crime and increased public intolerance for various types of disorderly conduct that are believed to be criminogenic have stimulated moves toward the policing reforms and the "get tough" measures cited above, but they have also led to a raft of community organizing activities that may be paying off in reduced levels of crime. . . .

The binge of drug and/or gang-related violence in the 1980s left many dead, disabled, or in prison. Some argue that these causalities are now shaping marked shifts in values and attitudes among urban youth. Demand for crack cocaine has waned and—stimulated by tougher police enforcement against handguns—minor confrontations are said to be less likely to erupt into deadly shootouts. . . .

Recently, much social science research attention has turned to the declining homicide rates in many cities across the country. A team of researchers led by Pamela Lattimore (Lattimore, Trudeau, Riley, Leiter, and Edwards 1997) at the National Institute of Justice has discovered a strong correlation between cocaine use levels within the urban criminal population and changes in homicide rates. Alfred Blumstein has studied handgun murders involving urban street youth. He has pointed out that the surge in this type of gun violence in the late 1980s has drawn attention away from the more long-term and steady trend of declining homicides for adults age 25 and older since 1980.

The surprising decline in homicides since 1991 is driven largely by the falling incidence of gun homicides among the younger group.

The decline in homicides among *older* Americans cited by Blumstein includes a steady decline in national rates of intimate-partner homicide over the past two decades. Laura Dugan has traced the effects of three significant social developments on this type of homicide: changes in patterns of domesticity (exposure reduction), in the status of women, and in increased provision of domestic violence resources. Her research highlights the importance of legal advocacy efforts to expand the effective use and enforcement of restraining orders, although these measures are shown to favorably affect homicide rates solely from married male victims. Susan Wilt (1998; Wilt, Illman, and Brody-Field 1997) has been tracking homicides in New York City using data from the public health system. She has found that homicides of female victims have fallen far more slowly since 1990 than the decline for male victims (a 20 percent decline for females compared to a 51 percent decline for males). Wilt was able to obtain data to classify homicides by type, and she found that over this period, intimate partner homicides of women have not declined in New York City.

Jeffrey Fagan is conducting an important study of homicides in New York City geared specifically to documenting the effects of criminal justice policies on this problem. Fagan, along with Franklin Zimring and June Kim, has just completed a report that examines homicide patterns in the city back to the 1950s and compares the recent decline with homicide patterns in other American cities. By tracking homicide trends by type since 1985, they have determined that patterns in New York City for gun and non-gun killings differ sharply. The trend data for non-gun homicides show a fairly steady decline through the whole period, whereas gun homicides doubled between 1985 and 1991, returning to the 1985 level by 1995.

Examining trends in drug use and demographics, Fagan et at. believed them to be important factors but could not say to what extent they have influenced the decline. . . . They posited that the NYPD gun strategy may be the most salient factor. At the same time, they cautioned that it is not possible to unequivocally establish the strength of these policing strategies relative to the other factors that are interacting with the shifts in police practices. Moreover, they warned that simple regression (i.e., the tendency of crime problems to shift continuously, up and down, drawing cyclical patterns over time) cannot yet be ruled out as the cause of the recent decline in gun homicides.

. . . Malcolm Gladwell, a writer for *The New Yorker* magazine, has carefully considered the phenomenon of dropping crime rates in New York City. He offers an interesting theory—drawn from the annals of public health—that provides some clues about how distinctly divergent factors in disparate locales might result in similar patterns of falling crime.

In his 1996 *The New Yorker* article, "The Tipping-Point," Gladwell defines this public health expression as "the point at which an ordinary and stable phenomenon—a low-level flu outbreak—can turn into a public health crisis." Applied to the phenomenon of crime, this epidemiological argument means that once crime reaches a certain level or critical point, it spreads in a "non-linear" fashion—that is, at some point in time a small incremental increase in criminal activity can fuel a dramatic upturn in crime rates. One example that Gladwell gives involves drive-by shootings in Los Angeles, which, after seven years of fluctuating up and down between 22 and 51, rose steadily from 57 in 1987 to 211 in 1992.

Happily, the tipping-point phenomenon may also apply in reverse. When the level of crime in a community reaches a tipping point, any strategy that can effect even a small decrease may be able to trigger dramatic drops in crime rates. But the tipping-point theory also implies layers of subtle complexity that must be carefully assessed in the development of crime control policies because when the level of crime is not at or near the tipping point, large investments in crime-fighting activities may yield very small effects if any.

. . . Expert opinion notwithstanding, suppose it is true that a new policing strategy can turn the tide of crime and produce a dramatic ebb in its volume? Is a New York City zero-tolerance campaign the only possible approach? Is it the best approach? What other options should be considered? Are there other theories about effective crime control that can help us answer these questions?

Tracey Meares (1998), a law professor at the University of Chicago, has been studying the role of community social organization in reducing crime. She points out that certain critical mediating factors can produce differential crime rates in communities with similar socioeconomic conditions. If stronger elements of social organization—cohesive friendship networks, shared cultural values, supervision of teens, participation in church groups, parent-teacher associations, community policing organizations, and so forth—are present in a given neighborhood, crime will be less common than in neighborhoods where these elements have eroded.

Meares has applied this framework to critique the efficacy of various law enforcement strategies—especially drug enforcement efforts—to enhance or hinder crime control in communities. She argues that whereas "get tough" measures that lead to lengthy incarceration of a large number of young drug offenders may offer a measure of short-term relief for law-abiding residents of a drug-ravaged community, in the long run, the negative consequences may wash out the short-term positives. This is because the deterrent effects of such a strategy are weak at best, whereas its damaging effects—disruption of family ties, stigmatizing barriers to labor market participation, increased levels of alienation and distrust—may prove criminogenic in themselves.

This may be especially true in African American communities, where the asymmetry of current drug-enforcement policies has exacerbated longstanding attitudes of distrust between residents and police that are grounded in both negative stereotypes and historical events. . . .

San Diego and New York City have enjoyed virtually equal reductions in rates of serious crime over the first half of the 1990s. From 1990 to 1995, a period when the NYPD gained a 39.5 percent increase in the number of sworn officers, New York City's reduction in crime was 37.4 percent, whereas San Diego's was 36.8 percent, but during this same period the increase in sworn officers on the San Diego police force *was only 6.2 percent.* According to San Diego police officials, this is a far more favorable "yield" in terms of crimes reduced per each additional officer.

San Diego's police executives began to experiment with a form of community policing—the Neighborhood Policing Philosophy as they term it—in the late 1980s. In 1993, they laid the groundwork for a department-wide restructuring process coupled with an effort to retrain the entire force in problem-oriented (as opposed to incident-based) policing methods. Two key concepts of neighborhood policing in San Diego—as described by San Diego Police Department (SDPD) officials—are that police and citizens share responsibility for identifying and solving crime problems and that law enforcement is one important tool for addressing crime, but it is not an end in itself.

The emphasis of the San Diego neighborhood-policing approach is on creating problem-solving partnerships and fostering connections between police and community for sharing information, working with citizens to address crime and disorder problems, and tapping other public and private agencies for resources to help solve them. The types of activities fostered by the neighborhood policing strategy in San Diego resemble many that are common elements of community policing elsewhere, such as the following:

- support for "neighborhood watch" and citizen patrol groups that look for suspicious activity, identify community problems, and work on crime prevention projects;
- use of civil remedies and strict building code enforcement to abate nuisance properties and close down "drug houses"; and
- collaboration with community organizations and local business groups to clean up, close down, or redesign specific locations and properties that repeatedly attract prostitution, drug, and gang problems.

The role of organized neighborhood volunteers in efforts to impact local crime problems—and thus national crime patterns—is too often overlooked or misunderstood. There are important differences between community *policing* and community *participation,* yet San Diego seems to be striving to integrate these distinct, semiautonomous crime prevention tools. The SDPD has recruited and trained a pool of more than 1,000 citizen volunteers who perform a broad array of crime prevention and victim assistance services.

The restructuring of police services in San Diego has involved a geographic consolidation of 68 existing patrol sectors and a reconfiguration of their boundaries to correspond to 99 distinct neighborhoods defined by community residents. Laptop computers equipped with mapping software are now being introduced to automate field reporting and to put up-to-date crime and calls-for-service data into the hands of patrol officers. . . .

Data from the New York State Department of Criminal Justice Services from 1993 through 1996 show that arrests in New York City rose by 23 percent across the board. Reflecting the broken windows, zero-tolerance policing strategy introduced by Bratton, misdemeanor arrests rose by 40 percent—led by drug arrests, which were increased by 97 percent over this period.

Arrest statistics provided by the SDPD for this same period show a marked contrast, reflecting the contrasting philosophy of neighborhood policing adopted in that city.

Table 1

Adult Arrests in New York City

	1993	1994	1995	1996
Total arrests	255,087	307,802	316,690	314,292
Total felony arrests	125,684	138,043	135,141	132,601
Felony drug arrests	39,298	44,442	43,698	45,312
Total misdemeanor arrests	129,403	169,759	181,549	181,691
Misdemeanor drug arrests	27,446	42,546	52,891	54,133
Misdemeanor DWI arrests	5,621	5,628	5,763	4,624
Other misdemeanor arrests	96,335	121,585	122,895	122,934

Note: DWI = driving while intoxicated.

Table 2

Adult Arrests in San Diego

	1993	1994	1995	1996
Total arrests	56,631	55,887	55,909	48,264
Total felony arrests	17,007	17,135	16,854	13,825
Felony drug arrests	5,808	6,432	6,685	5,034
Total misdemeanor arrests	39,624	38,752	39,055	34,439
Misdemeanor drug arrests	7,099	8,313	7,965	6,352
Misdemeanor DWI arrests	3,782	3,649	3,749	3,545
Other misdemeanor arrests	28,743	26,790	27,341	24,542

Note: DWI = driving while intoxicated.

Across the board, arrests have fallen in San Diego by 15 percent, whereas reductions for key indicators of crime (homicides and FBI Index Crimes) closely rival the crime reductions in New York City. Total complaints filed during this period with the SDPD regarding police misconduct fell from 522 in 1993 to 508 in 1996.

San Diego police executives are understandably pleased with the recent dramatic drop in crime in their city. However, they have been less inclined than their counterparts in New York City to estimate the extent to which these trends may be directly attributed to the department's neighborhood policing and community-involvement efforts.

. . . Zero-tolerance policing in New York City uses the Compstat system to direct hyperaggressive crime-control tactics toward high-crime "hot spots," and city officials have been quick to claim credit for a dramatic drop in crime. Yet, the sharp contrast in arrest patterns and citizen complaints between New York City and San Diego offers compelling evidence that cooperative police-community problem solving can provide effective crime control through more efficient and humane methods. Moreover, the San Diego strategy seems better designed to support and sustain vital elements of community social organization that can inhibit criminality and build safer neighborhoods over the long run.

Note

1. Whereas community policing engages neighborhood residents in identification of crime problems and in planning crime-control strategies, community participation entails residents becoming directly involved in crime prevention activities and in effecting structural solutions to the neighborhood problems that give rise to crime.

References

William Bratton. 1998. *Turnaround: How America's Top Cop Reversed the Crime Epidemic*. New York: Random House.

Lattimore, Pamela K., James Trudeau, K. Jack Riley, Jordan Leiter, and Steven Edwards. 1997. *Homicide in Eight U.S. Cities: Trends, Context, and Policy Implications*. Washington, DC: Department of Justice, National Institute of Justice.

Meares, Tracey. 1998. "Place and Crime." *Chicago-Kent Law Review* 73: 669.

Wilt, Susan. A. 1998. *Changes in Assault Injuries and Death Rates in New York City 1990–1995*. New York: Department of Public Health, Injury Prevention Program.

Wilt, Susan A., Susan M. Illman, and Maia BrodyField. 1997. *Female Homicide Victims in New York City 1990–1994*. New York: Department of Public Health, Injury Prevention Program.

POSTSCRIPT

Should the Police Enforce Zero-Tolerance Laws?

Implicit in the broken windows theory is the community's abandonment of the people's civic responsibility to maintain their neighborhoods. The role of police then becomes one of restoring order by driving out the newly ensconced criminal elements. Certainly this approach takes as central the importance of community (including the lack of community, which results in crime). Greene does not consider synthesizing the two perspectives. How might that be done?

Is it possible that zero tolerance/broken windows policing is functional in extremely high crime areas but only for a short amount of time (e.g., less than a year)? If so, would this help to reduce the likelihood of "hyperaggressive" policing's becoming routinized so that citizens' rights are increasingly ignored?

Some suggest that even if terrible abuse of police power is the price to be paid for aggressive policing, the trade-off is more than worth it. Dozens of police officers' lives and hundreds of citizens' lives are saved in a few short years. If such reductions in violent crimes could be achieved only if they were accompanied by a relatively small number of blatant police abuses, would the trade-off be worth it? Is it possible, as Greene and many others say, to achieve a reduction in crime through other policing tactics? Also, is a comparison of New York and San Diego on the basis that they both have populations over 100,000 a fair one?

A helpful report by Kelling is *"Broken Windows" and Police Discretion* (October 1999), published by the National Institute of Justice. Bratton's most comprehensive discussion and defense of his position is *Turnaround: How America's Top Cop Reversed the Crime Epidemic*, coauthored by P. Knobler (Random House, 1998). For a trenchant criticism of zero-tolerance polices, see S. Henry et al., "Broken Windows: Prevention Strategy or Cracked Policy?" *Critical Criminologist* (Fall 1997).

Another attack on Kelling is *Shattering "Broken Windows": An Analysis of San Francisco's Alternative Crime Policies* by D. Macallair and K. Taqi-Eddin (October 1999), published by the Justice Policy Institute. More neutral research is presented in "Problem-Oriented Policing in Public Housing," by L. Maerolle et al., *Justice Quarterly* (March 2000). For additional attacks on zero tolerance, see the articles other than Kelling and Bratton's in the summer 1998 edition of *The Journal of Criminal Law & Criminology*. An early debate between P. Ruffins, in "How the Big Apple Cut to the Core of Its Crime Problem," and former New York City mayor David N. Dinkins, in "Does Quality-of-Life Policing Diminish Quality of Life for People of Color?" can be found in the July 1997 issue of *Crisis*.

ISSUE 15

Should Marijuana Be Legalized?

YES: Ethan A. Nadelmann, from "An End to Marijuana Prohibition: The Drive to Legalize Picks Up," *National Review* (July 12, 2004)

NO: John P. Walters, from "No Surrender," *National Review* (September 27, 2004)

ISSUE SUMMARY

YES: Ethan A. Nadelmann, the founder and director of the Drug Policy Alliance, contends that contemporary marijuana laws are unique among American criminal laws because no other law is both enforced so widely and yet deemed unnecessary by such a substantial portion of the public. Enforcing marijuana laws also wastes tens of billions of taxpayer dollars annually.

NO: John P. Walters, director of the Office of National Drug Control Policy, argues that marijuana does the most social harm of any illegal drug.

Should people be free to smoke marijuana without fear of criminal sanctions? Or, does smoking marijuana harm society as a whole as well as the drug user? A recent study by the Sentencing Project, a Washington-based think tank, has concluded that the drug war in the United States has shifted significantly in the past decade from a focus on hard drugs to marijuana law enforcement. Is this focus on marijuana suppression an effective or efficient way to spend our tax dollars? Moreover, is it good social policy to use criminal punishment to try to prevent people from using marijuana? The answers to these questions defy an easy resolution; however, some things are very clear about marijuana usage in the United States.

First, large numbers of people are affected by the stringent enforcement of our nation's marijuana laws. A recent study found that approximately 700,000 people are arrested on marijuana charges each year, and 60,000 are confined to jails and prisons. Moreover, approximately 87 percent of marijuana arrests are for nothing more than simple possession of small quantities. (Drug Policy Alliance, "Warning: Marijuana Causes Drug Czar to Behave Irrationally, Act Paranoid and Waste Billions of Dollars," May 4, 2005, http://drugpolicy.org.) Second, the costs to taxpayers to enforce marijuana laws are considerable. The annual price tag for enforcing marijuana laws is approximately $10–15 billion.

Moreover, recent studies suggest that a large number of Americans appear to favor decriminalization of marijuana. One poll suggests that 72 percent of Americans believe that fines, not imprisonment, are appropriate sanctions for violating marijuana laws. Moreover, approximately 80 percent of the people surveyed supported medical marijuana use.

In his classic essay "On Liberty," nineteenth-century philosopher John Stuart Mill discussed the nature and limits of power that can be legitimately exercised by society over an individual. Stated Mill:

> [T]he sole end for which mankind are warranted, individually or collectively, in interfering with the liberty of action of any of their number is self-protection. That the only purpose for which power can rightfully be exercised over any member of a civilized community, against his will, is to prevent harm to others. His own good, either physical or moral, is not a sufficient warrant. He cannot rightfully be compelled to do so or forebear because it will be better for him to do so, because it will make him happier, because, in the opinions of others, to do so would be wise or even right.

Is the decision to use marijuana properly left to the realm of individual conscience? Or, is society merely trying to protect itself? The authors of the articles in this section have very different viewpoints on this issue.

Ethan A. Nadelmann, the founder and director of the Drug Policy Alliance, believes that "the criminalization of marijuana is costly, foolish, and destructive." For example, Alabama currently imprisons people convicted three times of simple marijuana possession for 15 years to life. Moreover, foreign-born residents can be deported, and a parent's marijuana use may be the basis for taking away his or her children or placing them in foster care. Observes Nadelmann: "No one has ever died from a marijuana overdose, which cannot be said of most other drugs."

John P. Walters, director of the Office of National Drug Control Policy, disputes Nadelmann's contentions and believes that our marijuana laws are an effective "safeguard." Moreover, he asserts that legalization would increase drug use, health care costs, and "further burden our education system." Walters contends as well that those who advocate for drug legalization will never be satisfied with a limited distribution of medical marijuana, or its sale in convenience stores. Rather, asserts Walters, "[t]heir goal is clearly identifiable: tolerated addiction."

So, which position is the correct one? Would the legalization of marijuana have dire consequences for society? Should society interfere with an individual's decision to smoke a joint in his or her living room at 10:00 PM on a Saturday night while eating a pepperoni pizza and watching a movie on television? What about persons undergoing medical treatment who believe that their conditions are somehow improved by smoking marijuana: Should they have access to legal marijuana without any fear of criminal prosecution?

YES

Ethan A. Nadelmann

An End to Marijuana Prohibition: The Drive to Legalize Picks Up

Never before have so many Americans supported decriminalizing and even legalizing marijuana. Seventy-two percent say that for simple marijuana possession, people should not be incarcerated but fined: the generally accepted definition of "decriminalization." Even more Americans support making marijuana legal for medical purposes. Support for broader legalization ranges between 25 and 42 percent, depending on how one asks the question. Two of every five Americans—according to a 2003 Zogby poll—say "the government should treat marijuana more or less the same way it treats alcohol: It should regulate it, control it, tax it, and only make it illegal for children."

Close to 100 million Americans—including more than half of those between the ages of 18 and 50—have tried marijuana at least once. Military and police recruiters often have no choice but to ignore past marijuana use by job seekers. The public apparently feels the same way about presidential and other political candidates. Al Gore, Bill Bradley, and John Kerry all say they smoked pot in days past. So did Bill Clinton, with his notorious caveat. George W. Bush won't deny he did. And ever more political, business, religious, intellectual, and other leaders plead guilty as well.

The debate over ending marijuana prohibition simmers just below the surface of mainstream politics, crossing ideological and partisan boundaries. Marijuana is no longer the symbol of Sixties rebellion and Seventies permissiveness, and it's not just liberals and libertarians who say it should be legal, as William F. Buckley Jr. has demonstrated better than anyone. As director of the country's leading drug-policy-reform organization, I've had countless conversations with police and prosecutors, judges and politicians, and hundreds of others who quietly agree that the criminalization of marijuana is costly, foolish, and destructive. What's most needed now is principled conservative leadership. Buckley has led the way, and New Mexico's former governor, Gary Johnson, spoke out courageously while in office. How about others?

A Systemic Overreaction

Marijuana prohibition is unique among American criminal laws. No other law is both enforced so widely and harshly and yet deemed unnecessary by such a substantial portion of the populace.

From *National Review*, July 12, 2004, pp. 28–33. Copyright © 2004 by Ethan Nadelmann. Reprinted by permission of the author. www.drugpolicy.org

Police make about 700,000 arrests per year for marijuana offenses. That's almost the same number as are arrested each year for cocaine, heroin, methamphetamine, Ecstasy, and all other illicit drugs combined. Roughly 600,000, or 87 percent, of marijuana arrests are for nothing more than possession of small amounts. Millions of Americans have never been arrested or convicted of any criminal offense except this. Enforcing marijuana laws costs an estimated $10–15 billion in direct costs alone.

Punishments range widely across the country, from modest fines to a few days in jail to many years in prison. Prosecutors often contend that no one goes to prison for simple possession—but tens, perhaps hundreds, of thousands of people on probation and parole are locked up each year because their urine tested positive for marijuana or because they were picked up in possession of a joint. Alabama currently locks up people convicted three times of marijuana *possession* for 15 years to life. There are probably—no firm estimates exist—100,000 Americans behind bars tonight for one marijuana offense or another. And even for those who don't lose their freedom, simply being arrested can be traumatic and costly. A parent's marijuana use can be the basis for taking away her children and putting them in foster care. Foreign-born residents of the U.S. can be deported for a marijuana offense no matter how long they have lived in this country, no matter if their children are U.S. citizens, and no matter how long they have been legally employed. More than half the states revoke or suspend driver's licenses of people arrested for marijuana possession even though they were not driving at the time of arrest. The federal Higher Education Act prohibits student loans to young people convicted of any drug offense; all other criminal offenders remain eligible.

This is clearly an overreaction on the part of government. No drug is perfectly safe, and every psychoactive drug can be used in ways that are problematic. The federal government has spent billions of dollars on advertisements and anti-drug programs that preach the dangers of marijuana—that it's a gateway drug, and addictive in its own right, and dramatically more potent than it used to be, and responsible for all sorts of physical and social diseases as well as international terrorism. But the government has yet to repudiate the 1988 finding of the Drug Enforcement Administration's own administrative law judge, Francis Young, who concluded after extensive testimony that "marijuana in its natural form is one of the safest therapeutically active substances known to man."

Is marijuana a gateway drug? Yes, insofar as most Americans try marijuana before they try other illicit drugs. But no, insofar as the vast majority of Americans who have tried marijuana have never gone on to try other illegal drugs, much less get in trouble with them, and most have never even gone on to become regular or problem marijuana users. Trying to reduce heroin addiction by preventing marijuana use, it's been said, is like trying to reduce motorcycle fatalities by cracking down on bicycle riding. If marijuana did not exist, there's little reason to believe that there would be less drug abuse in the U.S.; indeed, its role would most likely be filled by a more dangerous substance.

Is marijuana dramatically more potent today? There's certainly a greater variety of high-quality marijuana available today than 30 years ago. But anyone who smoked marijuana in the 1970s and 1980s can recall smoking pot that was just as strong as anything available today. What's more, one needs to take only a few puffs of higher-potency pot to get the desired effect, so there's less wear and tear on the lungs.

Is marijuana addictive? Yes, it can be, in that some people use it to excess, in ways that are problematic for themselves and those around them, and find it hard to stop. But marijuana may well be the least addictive and least damaging of all commonly used psychoactive drugs, including many that are now legal. Most people who smoke marijuana never become dependent. Withdrawal symptoms pale compared with those from other drugs. No one has ever died from a marijuana overdose, which cannot be said of most other drugs. Marijuana is not associated with violent behavior and only minimally with reckless sexual behavior. And even heavy marijuana smokers smoke only a fraction of what cigarette addicts smoke. Lung cancers involving only marijuana are rare.

The government's most recent claim is that marijuana abuse accounts for more people entering treatment than any other illegal drug. That shouldn't be surprising, given that tens of millions of Americans smoke marijuana while only a few million use all other illicit drugs. But the claim is spurious nonetheless. Few Americans who enter "treatment" for marijuana are addicted. Fewer than one in five people entering drug treatment for marijuana do so voluntarily. More than half were referred by the criminal-justice system. They go because they got caught with a joint or failed a drug test at school or work (typically for having smoked marijuana days ago, not for being impaired), or because they were caught by a law-enforcement officer—and attending a marijuana "treatment" program is what's required to avoid expulsion, dismissal, or incarceration. Many traditional drug-treatment programs shamelessly participate in this charade to preserve a profitable and captive client stream.

Even those who recoil at the "nanny state" telling adults what they can or cannot sell to one another often make an exception when it comes to marijuana—to "protect the kids." This is a bad joke, as any teenager will attest. The criminalization of marijuana for adults has not prevented young people from having better access to marijuana than anyone else. Even as marijuana's popularity has waxed and waned since the 1970s, one statistic has remained constant: More than 80 percent of high-school students report it's easy to get. Meanwhile, the government's exaggerations and outright dishonesty easily backfire. For every teen who refrains from trying marijuana because it's illegal (for adults), another is tempted by its status as "forbidden fruit." Many respond to the lies about marijuana by disbelieving warnings about more dangerous drugs. So much for protecting the kids by criminalizing the adults.

The Medical Dimension

The debate over medical marijuana obviously colors the broader debate over marijuana prohibition. Marijuana's medical efficacy is no longer in serious dispute. Its use as a medicine dates back thousands of years. Pharmaceuticals products containing marijuana's central ingredient, THC, are legally sold in the U.S., and more are emerging. Some people find the pill form satisfactory, and others consume it in teas or baked products. Most find smoking the easiest and most effective way to consume this unusual medicine, but non-smoking consumption methods, notably vaporizers, are emerging.

Federal law still prohibits medical marijuana. But every state ballot initiative to legalize medical marijuana has been approved, often by wide margins—in California, Washington, Oregon, Alaska, Colorado, Nevada, Maine, and Washington, D.C. State legislatures in Vermont, Hawaii, and Maryland have followed suit, and many others are now considering their own medical-marijuana bills—including New York, Connecticut, Rhode Island, and Illinois. Support is often bipartisan, with Republican governors like Gary Johnson and Maryland's Bob Ehrlich taking the lead. In New York's 2002 gubernatorial campaign, the conservative candidate of the Independence party, Tom Golisano, surprised everyone by campaigning heavily on this issue. The medical-marijuana bill now before the New York legislature is backed not just by leading Republicans but even by some Conservative party leaders.

The political battleground increasingly pits the White House—first under Clinton and now Bush—against everyone else. Majorities in virtually every state in the country would vote, if given the chance, to legalize medical marijuana. Even Congress is beginning to turn; last summer about two-thirds of House Democrats and a dozen Republicans voted in favor of an amendment co-sponsored by Republican Dana Rohrabacher to prohibit federal funding of any Justice Department crackdowns on medical marijuana in the states that had legalized it. (Many more Republicans privately expressed support, but were directed to vote against.) And federal courts have imposed limits on federal aggression: first in *Conant* v. *Walters*, which now protects the First Amendment rights of doctors and patients to discuss medical marijuana, and more recently in *Raich* v. *Ashcroft* and *Santa Cruz* v. *Ashcroft*, which determined that the federal government's power to regulate interstate commerce does not provide a basis for prohibiting medical-marijuana operations that are entirely local and non-commercial. (The Supreme Court let the *Conant* decision stand, but has yet to consider the others.)

State and local governments are increasingly involved in trying to regulate medical marijuana, notwithstanding the federal prohibition. California, Oregon, Hawaii, Alaska, Colorado, and Nevada have created confidential medical-marijuana patient registries, which protect bona fide patients and caregivers from arrest or prosecution. Some municipal governments are now trying to figure out how to regulate production and distribution. In California, where dozens of medical-marijuana programs now operate openly, with tacit approval by local authorities, some program directors are asking to be licensed and regulated. Many state and local authorities, including law enforcement, favor this but are intimidated by federal threats to arrest and prosecute them for violating federal law.

The drug czar and DEA spokespersons recite the mantra that "there is no such thing as medical marijuana," but the claim is so specious on its face that it clearly undermines federal credibility. The federal government currently provides marijuana—from its own production site in Mississippi—to a few patients who years ago were recognized by the courts as bona fide patients. No one wants to debate those who have used marijuana for medical purposes, be it Santa Cruz medical-marijuana hospice founder Valerie Corral or National Review's Richard Brookhiser. Even many federal officials quietly regret the assault on medical marijuana. When the DEA raided Corral's hospice in September 2002, one agent was heard to say, "Maybe I'm going to think about getting another job sometime soon."

The Broader Movement

The bigger battle, of course, concerns whether marijuana prohibition will ultimately go the way of alcohol Prohibition, replaced by a variety of state and local tax and regulatory policies with modest federal involvement. Dedicated prohibitionists see medical marijuana as the first step down a slippery slope to full legalization. The voters who approved the medical-marijuana ballot initiatives (as well as the wealthy men who helped fund the campaigns) were roughly divided between those who support broader legalization and those who don't, but united in seeing the criminalization and persecution of medical-marijuana patients as the most distasteful aspect of the war on marijuana. (This was a point that Buckley made forcefully in his columns about the plight of Peter McWilliams, who likely died because federal authorities effectively forbade him to use marijuana as medicine.)

The medical-marijuana effort has probably aided the broader anti-prohibitionist campaign in three ways. It helped transform the face of marijuana in the media, from the stereotypical rebel with long hair and tie-dyed shirt to an ordinary middle-aged American struggling with MS or cancer or AIDS. By winning first Proposition 215, the 1996 medical-marijuana ballot initiative in California, and then a string of similar victories in other states, the nascent drug-policy-reform movement demonstrated that it could win in the big leagues of American politics. And the emergence of successful models of medical-marijuana control is likely to boost public confidence in the possibilities and virtue of regulating non-medical use as well.

In this regard, the history of Dutch policy on cannabis (i.e., marijuana and hashish) is instructive. The "coffee shop" model in the Netherlands, where retail (but not wholesale) sale of cannabis is defacto legal, was not legislated into existence. It evolved in fits and starts following the decriminalization of cannabis by Parliament in 1976, as consumers, growers, and entrepreneurs negotiated and collaborated with local police, prosecutors, and other authorities to find an acceptable middle-ground policy. "Coffee shops" now operate throughout the country, subject to local regulations. Troublesome shops are shut down, and most are well integrated into local city cultures. Cannabis is no more popular than in the U.S. and other Western countries, notwithstanding the effective absence of criminal sanctions and controls. Parallel developments are now underway in other countries.

Like the Dutch decriminalization law in 1976, California's Prop 215 in 1996 initiated a dialogue over how best to implement the new law. The variety of outlets that have emerged—ranging from pharmacy-like stores to medical "coffee shops" to hospices, all of which provide marijuana only to people with a patient ID card or doctor's recommendation—play a key role as the most public symbol and manifestation of this dialogue. More such outlets will likely pop up around the country as other states legalize marijuana for medical purposes and then seek ways to regulate distribution and access. And the question will inevitably arise: If the emerging system is successful in controlling production and distribution of marijuana for those with a medical need, can it not also expand to provide for those without medical need?

Millions of Americans use marijuana not just "for fun" but because they find it useful for many of the same reasons that people drink alcohol or take pharmaceutical drugs. It's akin to the beer, glass of wine, or cocktail at the end of the workday, or the prescribed drug to alleviate depression or anxiety, or the sleeping pill, or the aid to sexual function and pleasure. More and more Americans are apt to describe some or all of their marijuana use as "medical" as the definition of that term evolves and broadens. Their anecdotal experiences are increasingly backed by new scientific research into marijuana's essential ingredients, the cannabinoids. Last year a subsidiary of *The Lancet*, Britain's leading medical journal, speculated whether marijuana might soon emerge as the "aspirin of the 21st century," providing a wide array of medical benefits at low cost to diverse populations.

Perhaps the expansion of the medical-control model provides the best answer—at least in the U.S.—to the question of how best to reduce the substantial costs and harms of marijuana prohibition without inviting significant increases in real drug abuse. It's analogous to the evolution of many pharmaceutical drugs from prescription to over-the-counter, but with stricter controls still in place. It's also an incrementalist approach to reform that can provide both the control and the reassurance that cautious politicians and voters desire.

In 1931, with public support for alcohol Prohibition rapidly waning, President Hoover released the report of the Wickersham Commission. The report included a devastating critique of Prohibition's failures and costly consequences, but the commissioners, apparently fearful of getting out too far ahead of public opinion, opposed repeal. Franklin P. Adams of the *New World* neatly summed up their findings:

> Prohibition is an awful flop.
>> We like it.
> It can't stop what it's meant to stop.
>> We like it.
> It's left a trail of graft and slime
> It don't prohibit worth a dime
> It's filled our land with vice and crime.
>> Nevertheless, we're for it.

Two years later, federal alcohol Prohibition was history.

What support there is for marijuana prohibition would likely end quickly absent the billions of dollars spent annually by federal and other governments to prop it up. All those anti-marijuana ads pretend to be about reducing drug abuse, but in fact their basic purpose is sustaining popular support for the war on marijuana. What's needed now are conservative politicians willing to say enough is enough: Tens of billions of taxpayer dollars down the drain each year. People losing their jobs, their property, and their freedom for nothing more than possessing a joint or growing a few marijuana plants. And all for what? To send a message? To keep pretending that we're protecting our children? Alcohol Prohibition made a lot more sense than marijuana prohibition does today—and it, too, was a disaster.

No Surrender

The prospect of a drug-control policy that includes regulated legalization has enticed intelligent commentators for years, no doubt because it offers, on the surface, a simple solution to a complex problem. Reasoned debate about the real consequences usually dampens enthusiasm, leaving many erstwhile proponents feeling mugged by reality; not so Ethan Nadelmann, whose version of marijuana legalization ("An End to Marijuana Prohibition," *NR*, July 12) fronts for a worldwide political movement, funded by billionaire George Soros, to embed the use of all drugs as acceptable policy. Unfortunately for Nadelmann, his is not a serious argument. Nor is it attached to the facts.

To take but one example, Nadelmann's article alleges the therapeutic value of smoked marijuana by claiming: "Marijuana's medical efficacy is no longer in serious dispute." But he never substantiates his sweeping claim. In fact, smoked marijuana, a Schedule I controlled substance (Schedule I is the government's most restrictive category), has no medical value and a high risk of abuse. The Food and Drug Administration notes that marijuana has not been approved for any indication, that scientific studies do not support claims of marijuana's usefulness as a medication, and that there is a lack of accepted safety standards for the use of smoked marijuana.

The FDA has also expressed concern that marijuana use may worsen the condition of those for whom it is prescribed. Legalization advocates such as Nadelmann simply ignore these facts and continue their promotion, the outcome of which will undermine drug-prevention and treatment efforts, and put genuinely sick patients at risk.

The legalization scheme is also unworkable. A government-sanctioned program to produce, distribute, and tax an addictive intoxicant creates more problems than it solves.

First, drug use would increase. No student of supply-and-demand curves can doubt that marijuana would become cheaper, more readily available, and more widespread than it currently is when all legal risk is removed and demand is increased by marketing.

Second, legalization will not eliminate marijuana use among young people any more than legalizing alcohol eliminated underage drinking. If you think we can tax marijuana to where it costs more than the average teenager can afford, think again. Marijuana is a plant that can be readily grown by

As seen in *National Review*, September 27, 2004, pp. 41–42. Copyright © 2004 by John P. Walters, Office of National Drug Control Policy. Reprinted by permission.

anyone. If law enforcement is unable to distinguish "legal" marijuana from illegal, growing marijuana at home becomes a low-cost (and low-risk) way to supply your neighborhood and friends. "Official marijuana" will not drive out the black market, nor will it eliminate the need for tough law enforcement. It will only make the task more difficult.

In debating legalization, the burden is to consider the costs and benefits both of keeping strict control over dangerous substances and of making them more accessible. The Soros position consistently overstates the benefits of legalizing marijuana and understates the risks. At the same time, drug promoters ignore the current benefits of criminalization while dramatically overstating the costs.

Government-sanctioned marijuana would be a bonanza for trial lawyers (the government may wake up to find that it has a liability for the stoned trucker who plows into a school bus). Health-care and employment-benefits costs will increase (there is plenty of evidence that drug-using employees are less productive, and less healthy), while more marijuana use will further burden out education system.

The truth is, there are laws against marijuana because marijuana is harmful. With every year that passes, medical research discovers greater dangers from smoking it, from links to serious mental illness to the risk of cancer, and even dangers from in utero exposure.

In fact, given the new levels of potency and the sheer prevalence of marijuana (the number of users contrasted with the number of those using cocaine or heroin), a case can be made that marijuana does the most social harm of any illegal drug. Marijuana is currently the leading cause of treatment need: Nearly two-thirds of those who meet the psychiatric criteria for needing substance-abuse treatment do so because of marijuana use. For youth, the harmful effects of marijuana use now exceed those of all other drugs combined. Remarkably, over 40 percent of youths who are current marijuana smokers meet the criteria for abuse or dependency. In several states, marijuana smoking exceeds tobacco smoking among young people, while marijuana has become more important than alcohol as a factor in treatment for teenagers.

Legalizers assert that the justice system arrests 700,000 marijuana users a year, suggesting that an oppressive system is persecuting the innocent. This charge is a fraud. Less than 1 percent of those in prison for drug violations are low-level marijuana offenders, and many of these have "pled down" to the marijuana violation in the face of other crimes. The vast majority of those in prison on drug convictions are true criminals involved in drug trafficking, repeat offenses, or violent crime.

The value of legal control is that it enables judicial discretion over offenders, diverting minor offenders who need it into treatment while retaining the authority to guard against the violent and incorrigible. Further, where the sanction and supervision of a court are present, the likelihood of recovery is greatly increased. Removing legal sanction endangers the public and fails to help the offender.

Proponents of legalization argue that because approximately half of the referrals for treatment are from the criminal-justice system, it is the law and not marijuana that is the problem. Yet nearly half of all referrals for alcohol treatment likewise derive from judicial intervention, and nobody argues that drunk drivers do not really have a substance-abuse problem, or that it is the courts that are creating the perception of alcoholism. Marijuana's role in emergency-room cases has tripled in the past decade. Yet no judge is sending people to emergency rooms. They are there because of the dangers of the drug, which have greatly increased because of soaring potency.

Legalization advocates suggest that youth will reduce their smoking because of this new potency. But when tobacco companies were accused of deliberately "spiking" their product with nicotine, no one saw this as a public-health gesture intended to reduce cigarette consumption. The deliberate effort to increase marijuana potency (and market it to younger initiates) should be seen for what it is—a steeply increased threat of addiction.

Proponents of legalization argue that the fact that 100 million Americans admit on surveys that they have tried marijuana in their lifetime demonstrates the public's acceptance of the drug. But the pertinent number tells a different story. There are approximately 15 million Americans, mostly young people, who report using marijuana on a monthly basis. That is, only about 6 percent of the population age twelve and over use marijuana on a regular basis.

To grasp the impact of legal control, contrast that figure with the number of current alcohol users (approximately 120 million). Regular alcohol use is eight times that of marijuana, and a large part of the difference is a function of laws against marijuana use. Under legalization, which would decrease the cost (now a little-noticed impediment to the young) and eliminate the legal risk, it is certain that the number of users would increase. Can anyone seriously argue that American democracy would be strengthened by more marijuana smoking?

The law itself is our safeguard, and it works. Far from being a hopeless battle, the drug-control tide is turning against marijuana. We have witnessed an 11 percent reduction in youth marijuana use over the last two years, while perceptions of risk have soared.

Make no mistake about what is going on here: Drug legalization is a worldwide movement, the goal of which is to make drug consumption—including heroin, cocaine, and methamphetamine—an acceptable practice. Using the discourse of rights without responsibilities, the effort strives to establish an entitlement to addictive substances. The impact will be devastating.

Drug legalizers will not be satisfied with a limited distribution of medical marijuana, nor will they stop at legal marijuana for sale in convenience stores. Their goal is clearly identifiable: tolerated addiction. It is a travesty to suggest, as Ethan Nadelmann has done, that it is consistent with conservative principles to abandon those who could be treated for their addiction, to create a situation in which government both condones and is the agent of drug distribution, and to place in the hands of the state the power to grant or not grant access to an addictive substance. This is not a conservative vision. But it is the goal of George Soros.

POSTSCRIPT

Should Marijuana Be Legalized?

Marijuana has been around for a long time. It was not until 1937 that the Marijuana Tax Act banned most recreational and medicinal uses of this popular drug in the United States. Since that time, there has been significant controversy about whether our marijuana laws are effective, or whether they are a bad social policy that should be abandoned in favor of a more enlightened approach to drug abuse.

According to a 1998 study by the Harvard School of Public Health, 78 percent of Americans believe that U.S. anti-drug efforts have failed. In addition, 94 percent believe that the United States has lost control of the illegal drug problem, and 58 percent maintain that the problem is getting worse. At the same time, only 14 percent favored drug legalization, while a majority favored more severe prison sentences. (See Robert J. Blendon and John T. Young, "The Public and the War on Illicit Drugs," *Journal of the American Medical Association* (March 18, 1998, p. 827). Please note that a more recent survey has found that 34 percent of Americans support making "the use of marijuana legal." See Colleen McMurray, "Medicinal Marijuana: Is It What the Doctor Ordered?" *The Gallup Poll Tuesday Briefing* (December 2003, p. 89).) These statistics are interesting for a number of reasons.

At first glance, the percentages seem somewhat schizophrenic—even though the vast majority of Americans believe that U.S. drug control policies have failed and that the problem of drug abuse is getting worse, only a small minority of respondents believe that drugs should be legalized. One source asserts that this apparent contradiction may suggest that:

> [P]ublic support for the 'drug war' is more about moral values or fears than rational public safety measures. The bureaucracies and businesses engaged in the 'drug war' have been successful in creating support that is independent of failure to achieve objectives and rational analysis and evaluation. (PUBLIC OPINION, "News Briefs," March–April 1998.)

Could the statement above actually be true? Is it possible that bureaucracies, such as U.S. law enforcement agencies, and businesses with ties to drug law enforcement may have an interest in continuing the war on drugs regardless of whether it is good for society? For a classic discussion of these issues, see: Howard S. Becker, *Outsiders: Studies in the Sociology of Deviance* (The Free Press, 1963); for a more recent treatment of these issues, see Jeffrey Reiman, *The Rich Get Richer and the Poor Get Prison: Ideology, Class and Criminal Justice*, 7th ed. (Allyn & Bacon, 2004); Robert J. MacCoun and Peter Reuter, Jr., *Drug War Heresies: Learning from Other Vices, Times and Places* (Cambridge University Press, 2001).

Additional informative resources include: Clare Wilson, "Miracle Weed," *New Scientist* (February 5–11, 2005); David T. Courtwright, "Drug Wars: Policy Hots and Historical Cools," *Bulletin of the History of Medicine* (Johns Hopkins University Press, Summer 2004); Bruce Bullington, "Drug Policy Reform and Its Detractors: The United States as the Elephant in the Closet," *Journal of Drug Issues* (Summer 2004); Michael M. O'Hear, "Federalism and Drug Control," *Vanderbilt Law Review* (April 2004); Sasha Abramsky, "The Drug War Goes Up in Smoke," *The Nation* (August 18–25, 2003); David Boyum and Mark A. R. Kleiman, "Breaking the Drug-Crime Link," *Public Interest* (Summer 2003); Alex Kreit, "The Future of Medical Marijuana: Should the States Grow Their Own?" *University of Pennsylvania Law Review* (May 2003); Vanessa Grigoriadis, "The Most Stoned Kids on the Most Stoned Day on the Most Stoned Campus on Earth," *Rolling Stone* (September 16, 2004).

ISSUE 16

Should Juries Be Able to Disregard the Law and Free "Guilty" Persons in Racially Charged Cases?

YES: Paul Butler, from "Racially Based Jury Nullification: Black Power in the Criminal Justice System," *Yale Law Journal* (December 1995)

NO: Randall Kennedy, from "After the Cheers," *The New Republic* (October 23, 1995)

ISSUE SUMMARY

YES: Paul Butler, an associate professor at the George Washington University Law School, argues that black jurors should acquit black defendants of certain crimes to make up for inequities in the criminal justice system.

NO: Randall Kennedy, a professor at the Harvard Law School, finds it tragic that black jurors would pronounce a murderer "not guilty" just to send a message to white people.

The man that is not prejudiced against a horse thief is not fit to sit on a jury in this town.

—George Bernard Shaw (1856–1950)

The jury system of justice in the United States is considered by many to be sacred. Some 200,000 criminal and civil trials are decided by approximately 2 million jurors each year. Although the vast majority of cases do not go to trial, the symbolic importance of jury trials is great.

In theory, during a trial, the judge decides on correct legal procedures and matters of legal interpretation, while juries decide, based on the evidence, the guilt or innocence of the defendant. Generally, a person accused of a felony (a serious crime) or a misdemeanor in which a sentence of six months or more is possible, could request a jury trial. In all but six states and in the federal courts, juries consist of 12 jurors. In most states, a conviction must be by unanimous decision. Judges can sometimes set aside guilty verdicts that they feel are unfair, but verdicts of not guilty can never be changed.

The jury system is not without its critics. Many have expressed concern that juries do not always consist of the defendant's peers. In many states, for example, women were not allowed to serve on juries until relatively recently. Blacks and other minorities were either directly blocked from serving or were kept off juries by the jury selection process itself. Furthermore, in most states jurors were drawn from voter registrations, which meant that the poor—for whom political elections are frequently not of great concern—were disproportionately underrepresented. In many states, attorneys could exclude blacks from serving on juries. But in *Batson v. Kentucky* (1986), the U.S. Supreme Court ruled that jurors could not be challenged solely on the basis of their race.

Jury nullification—in which a jury acquits a criminal defendant even though guilt has been proven—can be seen throughout U.S. history. Before the Revolutionary War, for example, some juries acquitted men who they felt were being treated unfairly by the British. Many northern juries refused to convict people accused of aiding runaway slaves. And juries have acquitted defendants because they felt that the police or prosecutors were bullying or unfairly treating them. Note that in these examples, the justification for nullification seems to be based on the juries' sense of justice, not on the guilt or innocence of the defendant.

However, not all historical instances of jury nullification are what would likely be considered noble reasons. For instance, until not long ago, very few whites accused of killing blacks were ever found guilty in many parts of the United States. None until the 1960s were ever sentenced to death for killing a black person. Few who participated in black lynchings were even charged with a crime, and the few who were always got off.

In the following selections, Paul Butler—despite jury nullification's checkered past—encourages jurors to acquit black defendants in many cases to remedy past and current discrimination in the criminal justice system. Randall Kennedy argues that the "need to convict a murderer" and the "need to protest the intolerability of official racism" must remain separate if either need is to be met. He maintains that promoting jury nullification as a legitimate way to right racial wrongs will only worsen the crime situation in black communities. As you read this debate consider what unanticipated consequences, both positive and negative, might arise if jury nullification is widely accepted.

YES

Paul Butler

Racially Based Jury Nullification: Black Power in the Criminal Justice System

In 1990 I was a Special Assistant United States Attorney in the District of Columbia. I prosecuted people accused of misdemeanor crimes, mainly the drug and gun cases that overwhelm the local courts of most American cities. As a federal prosecutor, I represented the United States of America and used that power to put people, mainly African-American men, in prison. I am also an African-American man. During that time, I made two discoveries that profoundly changed the way I viewed my work as a prosecutor and my responsibilities as a black person.

The first discovery occurred during a training session for new assistants conducted by experienced prosecutors. We rookies were informed that we would lose many of our cases, despite having persuaded a jury beyond a reasonable doubt that the defendant was guilty. We would lose because some black jurors would refuse to convict black defendants who they knew were guilty.

The second discovery was related to the first but was even more unsettling. It occurred during the trial of Marion Barry, then the second-term mayor of the District of Columbia. Barry was being prosecuted by my office for drug possession and perjury. I learned, to my surprise, that some of my fellow African-American prosecutors hoped that the mayor would be acquitted, despite the fact that he was obviously guilty of at least one of the charges—an FBI videotape plainly showed him smoking crack cocaine. These black prosecutors wanted their office to lose its case because they believed that the prosecution of Barry was racist.

There is an increasing perception that some African-American jurors vote to acquit black defendants for racial reasons, sometimes explained as the juror's desire not to send another black man to jail. There is considerable disagreement over whether it is appropriate for a black juror to do so. I now believe that, for pragmatic and political reasons, the black community is better off when some non-violent lawbreakers remain in the community rather than go to prison. The decision as to what kind of conduct by African Americans ought to be punished is better made by African Americans, based on their understanding of the costs and benefits to their community, than

From *Yale Law Journal*, vol. 105, December 1995. Copyright © 1995 by The Yale Law Journal. Reprinted by permission of The Yale Law Journal Company and William S. Hein Company.

by the traditional criminal justice process, which is controlled by white law-makers and white law enforcers. Legally, African-American jurors who sit in judgment of African-American accused persons have the power to make that decision. Considering the costs of law enforcement to the black community, and the failure of white lawmakers to come up with any solutions to black antisocial conduct other than incarceration, it is, in fact, the moral responsibility of black jurors to emancipate some guilty black outlaws.

⋅◈⋅

Why would a black juror vote to let a guilty person go free? Assuming the juror is a rational, self-interested actor, she must believe that she is better off with the defendant out of prison than in prison. But how could any rational person believe that about a criminal?

Imagine a country in which a third of the young male citizens are under the supervision of the criminal justice system—either awaiting trial, in prison, or on probation or parole. Imagine a country in which two-thirds of the men can anticipate being arrested before they reach age thirty. Imagine a country in which there are more young men in prison than in college.

The country imagined above is a police state. When we think of a police state, we think of a society whose fundamental problem lies not with the citizens of the state but rather with the form of government, and with the powerful elites in whose interest the state exists. Similarly, racial critics of American criminal justice locate the problem not with the black prisoners but with the state and its actors and beneficiaries.

The black community also bears very real costs by having so many African Americans, particularly males, incarcerated or otherwise involved in the criminal justice system. These costs are both social and economic, and they include the large percentage of black children who live in female-headed, single-parent households; a perceived dearth of men "eligible" for marriage; the lack of male role models for black children, especially boys; the absence of wealth in the black community; and the large unemployment rate among black men.

According to a recent *USA Today/CNN/Gallup* poll, 66 percent of blacks believe that the criminal justice system is racist and only 32 percent believe it is not racist. Interestingly, other polls suggest that blacks also tend to be more worried about crime than whites; this seems logical when one considers that blacks are more likely to be victims of crime. This enhanced concern, however, does not appear to translate to black support for tougher enforcement of criminal law. For example, substantially fewer blacks than whites support the death penalty, and many more blacks than whites were concerned with the potential racial consequences of the strict provisions of last year's crime bill. Along with significant evidence from popular culture, these polls suggest that a substantial portion of the African-American community sympathizes with racial critiques of the criminal justice system.

African-American jurors who endorse these critiques are in a unique position to act on their beliefs when they sit in judgment of a black defendant.

As jurors, they have the power to convict the accused person or to set him free. May the responsible exercise of that power include voting to free a black defendant who the juror believes is guilty? The answer is "yes," based on the legal doctrine known as jury nullification.

Jury nullification occurs when a jury acquits a defendant who it believes is guilty of the crime with which he is charged. In finding the defendant not guilty, the jury ignores the facts of the case and/or the judge's instructions regarding the law. Instead, the jury votes its conscience.

The prerogative of juries to nullify has been part of English and American law for centuries. There are well-known cases from the Revolutionary War era when American patriots were charged with political crimes by the British crown and acquitted by American juries. Black slaves who escaped to the North and were prosecuted for violation of the Fugitive Slave Law were freed by Northern juries with abolitionist sentiments. Some Southern juries refused to punish white violence against African Americans, especially black men accused of crimes against white women.

The Supreme Court has officially disapproved of jury nullification but has conceded that it has no power to prohibit jurors from engaging in it; the Bill of Rights does not allow verdicts of acquittal to be reversed, regardless of the reason for the acquittal. Criticism of nullification has centered on its potential for abuse. The criticism suggests that when twelve members of a jury vote their conscience instead of the law, they corrupt the rule of law and undermine the democratic principles that made the law.

There is no question that jury nullification is subversive of the rule of law. Nonetheless, most legal historians agree that it was morally appropriate in the cases of the white American revolutionaries and the runaway slaves. The issue, then, is whether African Americans today have the moral right to engage in this same subversion.

Most moral justifications of the obligation to obey the law are based on theories of "fair play." Citizens benefit from the rule of law; that is why it is just that they are burdened with the requirement to follow it. Yet most blacks are aware of countless historical examples in which African Americans were not afforded the benefit of the rule of law: think, for example, of the existence of slavery in a republic purportedly dedicated to the proposition that all men are created equal, or the law's support of state-sponsored segregation even after the Fourteenth Amendment guaranteed blacks equal protection. That the rule of law ultimately corrected some of the large holes in the American fabric is evidence more of its malleability than its goodness; the rule of law previously had justified the holes.

If the rule of law is a myth, or at least not valid for African Americans, the argument that jury nullification undermines it loses force. The black juror is simply another actor in the system, using her power to fashion a particular outcome. The juror's act of nullification—like the act of the citizen who dials 911 to report Ricky but not Bob, or the police officer who arrests Lisa but not Mary, or the prosecutor who charges Kwame but not Brad, or the judge who finds that Nancy was illegally entrapped but Verna was not—exposes the indeterminacy of law but does not in itself create it.

A similar argument can be made regarding the criticism that jury nullification is anti-democratic. This is precisely why many African Americans endorse
it; it is perhaps the only legal power black people have to escape the tyranny
of the majority. Black people have had to beg white decision makers for most
of the rights they have: the right not to be slaves, the right to vote, the right to
attend an integrated school. Now black people are begging white people to preserve programs that help black children to eat and black businesses to survive.
Jury nullification affords African Americans the power to determine justice for
themselves in individual cases, regardless of whether white people agree or even
understand.

◆

At this point, African Americans should ask themselves whether the operation of the criminal law system in the United States advances the interests of
black people. If it does not, the doctrine of jury nullification affords African-
American jurors the opportunity to exercise the authority of the law over some
African-American criminal defendants. In essence, black people can "opt out"
of American criminal law.

How far should they go—completely to anarchy, or is there someplace
between here and there that is safer than both? I propose the following:
African-American jurors should approach their work cognizant of its political
nature and of their prerogative to exercise their power in the best interests of
the black community. In every case, the juror should be guided by her view of
what is "just." (I have more faith, I should add, in the average black juror's idea
of justice than I do in the idea that is embodied in the "rule of law.")

In cases involving violent *malum in se* (inherently bad) crimes, such as
murder, rape, and assault, jurors should consider the case strictly on the evidence presented, and if they believe the accused person is guilty, they should
so vote. In cases involving non-violent, *malum prohibitum* (legally proscribed)
offenses, including "victimless" crimes such as narcotics possession, there should
be a presumption in favor of nullification. Finally, for non-violent, *malum in se*
crimes, such as theft or perjury, there need be no presumption in favor of nullification, but it ought to be an option the juror considers. A juror might vote for
acquittal, for example, when a poor woman steals from Tiffany's but not when
the same woman steals from her next-door neighbor.

How would a juror decide individual cases under my proposal? Easy cases
would include a defendant who has possessed crack cocaine and an abusive
husband who kills his wife. The former should be acquitted and the latter
should go to prison.

Difficult scenarios would include the drug dealer who operates in the
ghetto and the thief who burglarizes the home of a rich white family. Under
my proposal, nullification is presumed in the first case because drug distribution is a non-violent *malum prohibitum* offense. Is nullification morally justifi-
able here? It depends. There is no question that encouraging people to engage
in self-destructive behavior is evil; the question the juror should ask herself
is whether the remedy is less evil. (The juror should also remember that the

criminal law does not punish those ghetto drug dealers who cause the most injury: liquor store owners.)

As for the burglar who steals from the rich white family, the case is troubling, first of all, because the conduct is so clearly "wrong." Since it is a nonviolent *malum in se* crime, there is no presumption in favor of nullification, but it is an option for consideration. Here again, the facts of the case are relevant. For example, if the offense was committed to support a drug habit, I think there is a moral case to be made for nullification, at least until such time as access to drug-rehabilitation services are available to all.

Why would a juror be inclined to follow my proposal? There is no guarantee that she would. But when we perceive that black jurors are already nullifying on the basis of racial critiques (i.e., refusing to send another black man to jail), we recognize that these jurors are willing to use their power in a politically conscious manner. Further, it appears that some black jurors now excuse some conduct—like murder—that they should not excuse. My proposal provides a principled structure of the exercise of the black juror's vote. I am not encouraging anarchy; rather I am reminding black jurors of their privilege to serve a calling higher than law: justice.

I concede that the justice my proposal achieves is rough. It is as susceptible to human foibles as the jury system. But I am sufficiently optimistic that my proposal will be only an intermediate plan, a stopping point between the status quo and real justice. To get to that better, middle ground, I hope that this [selection] will encourage African Americans to use responsibly the power they already have.

Randall Kennedy

After the Cheers

The acquittal of O. J. Simpson brings to an end an extraordinary criminal trial that attracted, like a magnet, anxieties over crime, sex, race and the possibility of reaching truth and dispensing justice in an American courtroom. The verdict is difficult to interpret since juries are not required to give reasons for the conclusions they reach and since, even if jurors do articulate their reasons, there remains the problem of deciphering them and distinguishing expressed views from real bases of decision.

My own view is that the verdict represents a combination of three beliefs. One is that the prosecution simply failed to prove that O. J. Simpson was guilty beyond a reasonable doubt. Reasonable people could come to this conclusion. After all, police investigators displayed remarkable incompetence, the prosecution erred mightily—remember the gloves that did not fit!—and, of course, there was the despicable [police officer] Mark Fuhrman. Even with help given by several questionable judicial rulings before the trial and near the end, the prosecution did permit a reasonable juror to vote to acquit on the basis of the evidence presented. I disagree with that conclusion. But I do concede that it could be reached reasonably and in good faith.

If this belief is what prompted the decision of all twelve of the jurors who acquitted Simpson, their decision has little broader cultural significance than that reasonable jurors sometimes come to different conclusions than those which many observers favor. I doubt, though, that this belief was the only or even the dominant predicate for the acquittal. I say this based on what I have heard many people say and write about the evidence presented at the trial and also on the remarkably short time that the jury deliberated. If the jury was at all representative of the American public, particularly that sector of the public which leaned toward acquittal, it was probably influenced considerably by two other beliefs.

The first is characterized by an unreasonable suspicion of law enforcement authorities. This is the thinking of people who would have voted to acquit O. J. Simpson even in the absence of Mark Fuhrman's racism and the L.A. police department's incompetence and even in the face of evidence that was more incriminating than that which was produced at trial. There is a paranoid, conspiracy-minded sector of the population that would honestly though irrationally have rejected the state's argument virtually without

From *The New Republic*, October 23, 1995, pp. 14, 16–18. Copyright © 1995 by New Republic. Reprinted by permission.

regard to the evidence. One of the things that nourishes much of this community, particularly that part comprised of African Americans, is a vivid and bitter memory of wrongful convictions of innocent black men and wrongful acquittals of guilty white men. A key example of the former were the convictions of the Scottsboro Boys in the 1930s for allegedly raping two white women. Now it is widely believed that these young men were framed. A key example of the latter was the acquittal of the murderers of Emmett Till forty years ago. In the face of overwhelming evidence of guilt, an all-white jury in Summer, Mississippi, took an hour and seven minutes to acquit two white men who later acknowledged that they had killed Till for having whistled at the wife of one of them. Asked why the jury had taken an hour to deliberate, one of the jurors declared that it would not have taken so long if they hadn't paused for a drink of soda pop. Some readers may find it hard to believe that these despicable events of sixty and forty years ago influence the way that people now evaluate people and events. But just as some in the Balkans remember battles fought 600 years ago as if they happened yesterday, so too do many blacks recall with pained disgust the racially motivated miscarriages of justice that they have helplessly witnessed or been told about. That recollection, refreshed occasionally by more recent outrages, prompts them to regard prosecutions against black men—especially black men accused of attacking white women—with such an intense level of skepticism that they demand more than that which should convince most reasonable people of guilt beyond a reasonable doubt.

A third belief is that to which [defense lawyer] Johnnie Cochran appealed directly in his summation when he pleaded with jurors to help "police the police." This belief animates jury nullification. By nullification, I mean the act of voting for acquittal even though you know that, in terms of the rules laid down by the judge, the evidence warrants conviction. A nullifier votes to acquit not because of dissatisfaction with the evidence but because, in the phrase of choice nowadays, he wants "to send a message." In many locales, black people in particular want to send a message that they are way past tolerating anti-black racism practiced by police and that they are willing to voice their protest in a wide variety of ways, including jury nullification. Frustrated, angry and politically self-aware, some black citizens have decided to take their protest against racism in the criminal justice system to the vital and vulnerable innards of that system: the jury box.

In a certain way, the specter of this sort of jury nullification represents an advance in American race relations. Not too long ago, blacks' dissatisfactions with the criminal justice system could often be largely ignored without significant immediate consequence because whites, on a racial basis, excluded them from decisionmaking. Invisible in courthouses, except as defendants, blacks could safely be permitted to stew in their own resentments. Now, however, because of salutary reforms, blacks are much more active in the administration of criminal justice and thus much more able to influence it.

Notwithstanding this advance, however, the current state of affairs as revealed by the Simpson case is marked by several large and tragic failures. The first and most important is the failure on the part of responsible officials to clearly, publicly and wholeheartedly abjure racism of the sort that Mark Fuhrman displayed during his hateful career as a police officer. Fuhrman's prejudice and his ability to act on it likely had much to do with O. J. Simpson's acquittal. His bigotry provided a vivid basis for the argument that the police framed Simpson. His bigotry also provided an emotionally satisfying basis upon which to follow Cochran's invitation to "send a message" by voting to acquit. In other words, the state inflicted upon itself a grievous wound when its representatives failed to establish a rigorous, anti-racist personnel policy that might have obviated the problem that ultimately crippled the prosecution most. Perhaps more headway on this front will now be made; practicality and morality dictate a more vigorous push against racism in law enforcement circles.

A second failure has occurred within the ranks of those who cheered the acquittal. I have no objection to cheers based on the assumption that the jury system worked properly, that is, cheers based on an honest and reasonable perception that the acquittal has freed a man against whom there existed too little evidence for a conviction. I get the impression, though, that there are other sentiments being voiced in the celebrations of some observers, including feelings of racial solidarity, yearnings to engage in racial muscle-flexing and a peculiar urge to protect the hero status of a man whose standing within the black community rose precipitously by dint of being charged with murder.

The failure of those moved by these sentiments is two-fold. First, such feelings can only predominate by minimizing the stark fact that two people were brutally murdered and by resisting the claim that *whoever* committed that dastardly deed ought to be legally punished, regardless of his color and regardless of the racism of Mark Fuhrman and company. To subordinate the need to convict a murderer to the need to protest the intolerability of official racism is a moral mistake. Both could have been done and should have been done. Contrary to the logic of Johnnie Cochran's summation, neither jurors nor onlookers were trapped in a situation in which they had to choose one imperative over the other. Second, as a practical matter, it cannot be emphasized too frequently the extent to which the black community in particular needs vigorous, efficient, enthusiastic law enforcement. As bad as racist police misconduct is, it pales in comparison to the misery that criminals (most of whom are black) inflict upon black communities. After all, blacks are four times as likely as whites to be raped, three times as likely to be robbed, twice as likely to be assaulted and seven times as likely to be murdered.

The problem of criminality perpetrated by blacks is the one that many black political leaders appear to have trouble discussing thoroughly. A good many prefer condemning white racist police to focusing on ways to render life in black communities more secure against ordinary criminals. That Simpson allegedly killed two white people makes him in some eyes far easier to rally around than had he allegedly killed two black people. This difference in sympathy based on the race of victims is itself a profoundly destructive racialist impulse, one deeply rooted in our political culture. But there is yet another difficulty with this particular racialist response. Like so much else about the Simpson case, the racial demographics of those who were killed was atypical. Because the more typical scenario features black victims of murder, those who claim to speak on behalf of blacks' interests should be extremely wary of supporting anything that further depresses law enforcement's ability to apprehend and convict those who prey upon their neighbors.

The O. J. Simpson trial is obviously a complicated event that will take years to understand more fully and place into proper perspective. At this point, however, the result, like so much of the trial itself, leaves me—normally an optimist—overcome by a sense of profound gloom.

POSTSCRIPT

Should Juries Be Able to Disregard the Law and Free "Guilty" Persons in Racially Charged Cases?

Should jury nullification be used to reduce inequities? Can a jury's decision to acquit a guilty person be considered a form of discretion, comparable to a person's decision to dial or not to dial 911 in an emergency or a police officer's deciding whether or not to arrest a potential suspect? Butler says, "Jury nullification affords African Americans the power to determine justice . . . regardless of whether white people agree or even understand." Is this statement blatantly racist? One critic has suggested that Butler's discussion is actually a satire. Could this be true?

An interesting concept that neither Butler nor Kennedy consider is the possibility of victim, community, or police "nullification." In other words, if many felt that criminals who were minority members would be allowed to go free by sympathetic juries, the probability would be high that even fewer cases would get to trial than currently do: the police, victims' families, or even vigilantes might be driven to administer "neighborhood justice" in order to ensure that criminals are punished.

The acquittal of murder suspect O. J. Simpson on October 3, 1995, revived debate on jury nullification. A thoughtful discussion is J. Q. Wilson, "Reading Jurors' Minds," *Commentary* (February 1996). A radically different analysis is T. Morrison and C. Lacour, eds., *Birth of a Nation'Hood: Gaze, Script, and Spectacle in the O. J. Simpson Case* (Pantheon Books, 1997). For another example of Kennedy's thinking, see his *Race, Crime and the Law* (Vintage Books, 1998).

Among the many attackers of Butler's thinking is J. Rosen, in "The Bloods and the Crits," *The New Republic* (December 9, 1996); E. M. Brown, in "The Tower of Babel: Bridging the Divide Between Critical Race Theory and 'Mainstream' Civil Rights Scholarship," *Yale Law Journal* (November 1995); and A. Leipold, in "The Dangers of Race-Based Jury Nullification: A Response to Professor Butler," *UCLA Law Review* (October 1, 1996). Outstanding current sources include B. R. Boxill, *Blacks and Social Justice,* 3rd ed. (Rowman & Littlefield, 2000); *The Color of Justice: Race, Ethnicity, and Crime in America,* 2d ed., by S. Walker, C. Spohn, and M. DeLone (Wadsworth Thomson Learning, 2000); *No Equal Justice: Race and Class in the American Criminal Justice System* by D. Cole (New Press, 2000); *"Law Never Here": A Social History of African American Responses to Issues of Crime and Justice* by F. Y. Bailey (Praeger, 1999); *The Color of Crime* by K. K. Russell (New York University Press, 1998); and *African-American Males and the Law: Cases and Materials* by F. D. Weatherspoon (University Press of America, 1998).

Internet References . . .

National Center for the Analysis of Violent Crime (NCAVC)

The National Center for the Analysis of Violent Crime (NCAVC) is a nationwide data information center that collects, collates, and analyzes crimes of violence—specifically murder. A program of the FBI's National Center for the Analysis of Violent Crime, its mission is to aid cooperation, communication, and coordination among law enforcement agencies and to provide support for their efforts.

http://www.fbi.gov/hq/isd/cirg/ncavc.htm

Fully Informed Jury Association

The Fully Informed Jury Association (FIJA) is a nonpartisan public policy research and education organization located in Helena, Montana. FIJA focuses on issues involving the role of the jury in our justice system and the preservation of the full function of the jury as the final arbiter in our courts of law.

http://www.fija.org/

The U.S. Supreme Court, Crime, and the Justice System

In the field of criminal justice, forecasting is an important device that entails extrapolating from present trends and projecting solutions to organizational problems. Criminologists supply the needed data, including the rates, frequencies, and distributions of crime. Yet even if we indeed know who commits what crimes, where, when, how, and why with any real certainty, there is no guarantee that this knowledge will hold true a few years from now. Moreover, as debatable as current policy proposals are, what we should do in the future is even more so. Might one way to make a better future be for juries to help to reduce inequities? Will locking up repeat offenders for life prove to be the best public policy? Finally, over 50 years after the Holocaust and 25 years after the victories of the civil rights movement, widespread violations of human rights are once again assuming a prominent place both on the world scene and within criminal justice. The past becomes the future as crime control is once again debated, this time on an international scale and with human rights as the focus.

- Does the U.S. Constitution Protect the Right to Possess a Firearm?

- Is the Death Penalty an Unconstitutional Punishment for Juvenile Offenders?

- Does Confining Sex Offenders Indefinitely in Mental Hospitals After They Have Served Their Prison Sentences Violate the Constitution?

- Does an Imprisoned Individual Have a Constitutional Right to Access the State's Evidence for DNA Testing?

ISSUE 17

Does the U.S. Constitution Protect the Right to Possess a Firearm?

YES: Antonin E. Scalia, form Majority Opinion, *District of Columbia v. Heller*, 554 U.S. 570 (2008)

NO: John Paul Stevens, from Dissenting Opinion, *District of Columbia v. Heller*, 554 U.S. 570 (2008)

ISSUE SUMMARY

YES: Justice Antonin E. Scalia, writing for the U.S. Supreme Court in *District of Columbia v. Heller* (2008), held that a District of Columbia law making it a crime to carry an unregistered handgun and prohibiting the registration of handguns, but that authorizes the police chief to issue 1-year licenses, and requires residents to keep lawfully owned handguns unloaded and dissembled or bound by a trigger lock or similar device, violates the Second Amendment.

NO: Justice John Paul Stevens, dissenting in *District of Columbia v. Heller* (2008), asserted that neither the text of the Second Amendment nor the arguments advanced by its proponents evidenced the slightest interest in limiting any legislature's authority to regulate private civilian uses of firearms. Moreover, there is no indication that the Framers intended to enshrine the common-law right of self-defense in the constitution.

The Right to Bear Arms may well be one of the more controversial issues in this volume. Proponents of such a right, including powerful lobbying interests such as the National Rifle Association (NRA), believe that the right to bear arms is a fundamental one. Firearms ownership should be an individual right guaranteed by the Second Amendment to the U.S. Constitution. Opponents of an individual right to bear arms contend that the Second Amendment refers to the right of a citizen militia to possess guns and that states and the federal government may justifiably regulate the ownership of firearms. This controversy is further exacerbated by the text of the Second Amendment, which on its face is not entirely clear:

> A well regulated Militia, being necessary to the security of a free State, the right of the people to keep and bear Arms, shall not be infringed.

Does the wording of this amendment imply that only persons who are part of a "well regulated Militia" have a right to keep and bear arms? Or, does it imply that the "people" have a "right to keep and bear Arms," independent of their association with a militia? These are questions that have challenged U.S. courts throughout U.S. history.

In *United States v. Emerson*, 270 F.3d 203 (5th Cir. 2001), the U.S. Court of Appeals identified three different basic interpretations of the Second Amendment. First, the "Second Amendment does not apply to individuals; rather, it merely recognizes the right of a state to arm its militia."

Advocates of another model of the Second Amendment assert that it recognizes some limited individual rights. "However, this supposedly 'individual' right to bear arms can only be exercised by members of a functioning, organized state militia who bear the arms while and as a part of actively participating in the organized militia's activities." It applies only if the federal or state governments fail to provide the firearms necessary for such militia service. The Court also asserted that the only such organized and actively functioning militia is the National Guard. Moreover, "under this model, the Second Amendment poses no obstacle to the wholesale disarmament of the American people." This perspective on the Second Amendment is often termed "the collective rights model."

A third model emphasizes that the Second Amendment provides a right for individuals to keep and bear arms. This view has received considerable academic endorsement, "especially in the last two decades." The U.S. Court of Appeals agreed with this perspective and held that the Second Amendment to the U.S. Constitution guarantees individuals the right to keep and bear arms.

The U.S. Court of Appeals for the Ninth Circuit has a different view of the Second Amendment, however. *Silveira v. Lockyear*, 312 F.3d 1052 (9th Cir. 2002), presented a challenge to California's gun control laws that placed restrictions on the possession, use, and transfer of semiautomatic weapons, often called "assault weapons." The plaintiff asserted, among other things, that the Second Amendment conferred an individual right to own and possess firearms. The U.S. Court of Appeals held, however, that "[t]he Amendment protects the people's right to maintain an effective state militia, and does not establish an individual right to own or possess firearms for personal or other use."

Both of the decisions cited above considered an important, but somewhat cryptic, Supreme Court precedent interpreting the Second Amendment. In *United States v. Miller*, 307 U.S. 174 (1939), the defendant was charged with possessing and transporting in interstate commerce a sawed-off shotgun with a barrel less than 18 inches long, without having registered it and without having in his possession a stamp-affixed written order for it, as required by the National Firearms Act. At his trial in the U.S. District Court, Western District of Arkansas, the defendant alleged that the statute was an unconstitutional violation of the Tenth Amendment because it usurped states' "police power." The defendant further argued that the statute violated the Second Amendment to the U.S. Constitution. The U.S. District Court agreed and held that the National Firearms Act violated the Second Amendment.

On appeal, Justice James C. McReynolds, writing for the U.S. Supreme Court, quickly dismissed the defendant's Tenth Amendment claim. The defendant's Second Amendment claim was somewhat more compelling; how-ever, Justice McReynolds held:

> In the absence of any evidence tending to show that possession or use of a "shotgun having a barrel of less than eighteen inches in length" at this time has some reasonable relationship to the preservation or efficiency of a well regulated militia, we cannot say that the Second Amendment guarantees the right to keep and bear such an instrument.

Justice McReynolds also presented a detailed historical analysis of what the Framers of the Second Amendment considered a "militia" to be. He stated that the militia in colonial America comprised "all males physically capable of acting in concert for the common defense." Further, when these individuals were called for service they "were expected to appear bearing arms supplied by themselves and of the kind in common use at that time." Therefore, the Court held that because the Second Amendment did not protect an individual's right to own firearms, the National Firearms Act was a lawful exercise of Congressional authority.

In 2008, the U.S. Supreme Court considered the case excerpted in this section, *District of Columbia v. Heller*, 554 U.S. 570 (2008). In *Heller*, the Court was asked to reconsider *United States v. Miller*'s holding that the Second Amendment did not protect an individual's right to own firearms. The facts that gave rise to *Heller* are as follows: The District of Columbia had passed a law making it a crime to carry an unregistered handgun and prohibiting the registration of handguns, but that authorized the police chief to issue 1-year licenses, and required residents to keep lawfully owned handguns unloaded and dissembled or bound by a trigger lock or similar device. Heller, a D.C. special policeman, applied to register a handgun he wished to keep at home, but the city denied his application. He then filed suit in U.S. District Court to prevent the city from enforcing the ban on handgun registration, the licensing requirement insofar as it prohibits carrying an unlicensed firearm in the home, and the trigger-lock requirement insofar as it prohibits the use of functional firearms in the home. The District Court dismissed the suit, but the U.S. Court of Appeals (D.C. Cir.) reversed, holding that the Second Amendment protects an individual's right to possess firearms and that the city's total ban on handguns, as well as its requirement that firearms in the home be kept nonfunctional even when needed for self-defense, violated that right.

The U.S. Supreme Court granted certiorari and held that the Second Amendment protects an individual right to possess a firearm unconnected with service in a militia, and to use that weapon for traditionally lawful purposes, such as self-defense. Accordingly, Justice Antonin E. Scalia, writing for a five-to-four majority, concluded:

> We are aware of the problem of handgun violence in this country, and we take seriously the concerns raised by the many amici who believe that prohibition of handgun ownership is the solution. The Constitution leaves the District of Columbia a variety of tools for combating that problem, including some measures regulating handguns. But the

enshrinement of constitutional rights necessarily takes certain policy choices off the table. These include the absolute prohibition of handguns held and used for self-defense in the home. . . . It is not the role of this Court to pronounce the Second Amendment extinct.

In a compelling dissenting opinion, Justice John Paul Stevens took issue with the majority's conclusion. Stated Justice Stevens:

The court properly disclaims any interest in evaluating the wisdom of the specific policy choice challenged in this case, but it fails to pay heed to a far more important policy choice—the choice made by the Framers themselves. The Court would have us believe that over 200 years ago, the Framers made a choice to limit the tools available to elected officials wishing to regulate civilian uses of weapons, and to authorize this Court to use the common-law process of case-by-case judicial lawmaking to define the contours of acceptable gun control policy. Absent compelling evidence that is nowhere to be found in the Court's opinion, I could not possibly conclude that the Framers made such a choice.

Who presents the more compelling view of the rights guaranteed by the Second Amendment, Justice Scalia, or Justice Stevens? If you agree with Justice Scalia, what, if any limitations, would you allow society to place on firearms ownership? Moreover, as you read the excerpts from the opinions in this important case, consider whether society should be able to limit other aspects of firearms ownership, such as the possession of Teflon-coated bullets, which can penetrate the bulletproof vests worn by many police officers.

YES

Antonin E. Scalia

Majority Opinion, *District of Columbia v. Heller*

J ustice Scalia delivered the opinion of the Court.

We consider whether a District of Columbia prohibition on the possession of usable handguns in the home violates the Second Amendment to the Constitution.

I

The District of Columbia generally prohibits the possession of handguns. It is a crime to carry an unregistered firearm, and the registration of handguns is prohibited. See D. C. Code §§7-2501.01(12), 7-2502.01(a), 7-2502.02(a)(4) (2001). Wholly apart from that prohibition, no person may carry a handgun without a license, but the chief of police may issue licenses for 1-year periods. See §§22-4504(a), 22-4506. District of Columbia law also requires residents to keep their lawfully owned firearms, such as registered long guns, "unloaded and dissembled or bound by a trigger lock or similar device" unless they are located in a place of business or are being used for lawful recreational activities. See §7-2507.02.

Respondent Dick Heller is a D.C. special police officer authorized to carry a handgun while on duty at the Federal Judicial Center. He applied for a registration certificate for a handgun that he wished to keep at home, but the District refused. He thereafter filed a lawsuit in the Federal District Court for the District of Columbia seeking, on Second Amendment grounds, to enjoin the city from enforcing the bar on the registration of handguns, the licensing requirement insofar as it prohibits the carrying of a firearm in the home without a license, and the trigger-lock requirement insofar as it prohibits the use of "functional firearms within the home." App. 59a. The District Court dismissed respondent's complaint, see *Parker v. District of Columbia,* 311 F. Supp. 2d 103, 109 (2004). The Court of Appeals for the District of Columbia Circuit, construing his complaint as seeking the right to render a firearm operable and carry it about his home in that condition only when necessary for self-defense, reversed, see *Parker v. District of Columbia,* 478 F. 3d 370, 401 (2007). It held that the Second Amendment protects an individual right to possess firearms and that the city's total ban on handguns, as well as its requirement that firearms in the home be kept nonfunctional even when necessary for self-defense,

Supreme Court of the United States, June 26, 2008.

violated that right. See *id.*, at 395, 399–401. The Court of Appeals directed the District Court to enter summary judgment for respondent.

We granted certiorari. 552 U.S. ___ (2007).

II

We turn first to the meaning of the Second Amendment.

A

The Second Amendment provides: "A well regulated Militia, being necessary to the security of a free State, the right of the people to keep and bear Arms, shall not be infringed." In interpreting this text, we are guided by the principle that "[t]he Constitution was written to be understood by the voters; its words and phrases were used in their normal and ordinary as distinguished from technical meaning." *United States v. Sprague*, 282 U. S. 716, 731 (1931); see also *Gibbons v. Ogden*, 9 Wheat. 1, 188 (1824). Normal meaning may of course include an idiomatic meaning, but it excludes secret or technical meanings that would not have been known to ordinary citizens in the founding generation.

The two sides in this case have set out very different interpretations of the Amendment. Petitioners and today's dissenting Justices believe that it protects only the right to possess and carry a firearm in connection with militia service. See Brief for Petitioners 11-12; *post,* at 1 (Stevens, J., dissenting). Respondent argues that it protects an individual right to possess a firearm unconnected with service in a militia, and to use that arm for traditionally lawful purposes, such as self-defense within the home. See Brief for Respondent 2-4.

The Second Amendment is naturally divided into two parts: its prefatory clause and its operative clause. The former does not limit the latter grammatically, but rather announces a purpose. The Amendment could be rephrased, "Because a well regulated Militia is necessary to the security of a free State, the right of the people to keep and bear Arms shall not be infringed." See J. Tiffany, A Treatise on Government and Constitutional Law §585, p. 394 (1867); Brief for Professors of Linguistics and English as *Amici Curiae* 3 (hereinafter Linguists' Brief). Although this structure of the Second Amendment is unique in our Constitution, other legal documents of the founding era, particularly individual-rights provisions of state constitutions, commonly included a prefatory statement of purpose. See generally Volokh, The Commonplace Second Amendment, 73 N. Y. U. L. Rev. 793, 814–821 (1998).

Logic demands that there be a link between the stated purpose and the command. The Second Amendment would be nonsensical if it read, "A well regulated Militia, being necessary to the security of a free State, the right of the people to petition for redress of grievances shall not be infringed." That requirement of logical connection may cause a prefatory clause to resolve an ambiguity in the operative clause ("The separation of church and state being an important objective, the teachings of canons shall have no place in our jurisprudence." The preface makes clear that the operative clause refers not to canons of interpretation but to clergymen.) But apart from that clarifying function, a prefatory clause does not limit or expand the scope of the operative clause. See F. Dwarris, A General Treatise on Statutes, 268–269 (P. Potter ed. 1871) (hereinafter Dwarris); T. Sedgwick, The Interpretation and Construction of Statutory and Constitutional Law, 42-45 (2d ed. 1874). "It is nothing unusual in acts . . . for the enacting part to go beyond the preamble; the remedy often extends beyond the particular act or mischief which first suggested the necessity of the law." J. Bishop, Commentaries on Written Laws and Their Interpretation §51, p. 49 (1882) (quoting *Rex v. Marks*, 3 East, 157, 165 (K. B. 1802)). Therefore, while we will begin our textual analysis with the operative clause, we will return to the prefatory clause to ensure that our reading of the operative clause is consistent with the announced purpose.

1. Operative Clause.
a. "Right of the People." The first salient feature of the operative clause is that it codifies a "right of the people." The unamended Constitution and the Bill of Rights use the phrase "right of the people" two other times, in the First Amendment's Assembly-and-Petition Clause and in the Fourth Amendment's Searchand-Seizure Clause. The Ninth Amendment uses very similar terminology ("The enumeration in the Constitution, of certain rights, shall not be construed to deny or disparage others retained by the people"). All three of these instances unambiguously refer to individual rights, not "collective" rights, or rights that may be exercised only through participation in some corporate body.

Three provisions of the Constitution refer to "the people" in a context other than "rights"—the famous preamble ("We the people"), §2 of Article I (providing that "the people" will choose members of the House), and the Tenth Amendment (providing that those powers not given the Federal Government remain with "the States" or "the people"). Those provisions arguably refer to "the people" acting collectively—but they deal with the exercise or reservation of powers, not rights. Nowhere else in the Constitution does a "right" attributed to "the people" refer to anything other than an individual right.

What is more, in all six other provisions of the Constitution that mention "the people," the term unambiguously refers to all members of the political community, not an unspecified subset. As we said in *United States v. Verdugo-Urquidez*, 494 U. S. 259, 265 (1990):

> "'[T]he people' seems to have been a term of art employed in select parts of the Constitution. . . . [Its uses] sugges[t] that 'the people' protected by the Fourth Amendment, and by the First and Second Amendments, and to whom rights and powers are reserved in the Ninth and Tenth Amendments, refers to a class of persons who are part of a national community or who have otherwise developed sufficient connection with this country to be considered part of that community."

This contrasts markedly with the phrase "the militia" in the prefatory clause. As we will describe below, the "militia" in colonial America consisted of a subset of "the people"—those who were male, able bodied, and within a certain age range. Reading the Second Amendment as protecting only the right to "keep and bear Arms" in an organized militia therefore fits poorly with the operative clause's description of the holder of that right as "the people."

We start therefore with a strong presumption that the Second Amendment right is exercised individually and belongs to all Americans.

b. "Keep and bear Arms." We move now from the holder of the right—"the people"—to the substance of the right: "to keep and bear Arms."

Before addressing the verbs "keep" and "bear," we interpret their object: "Arms." The 18th-century meaning is no different from the meaning today. The 1773 edition of Samuel Johnson's dictionary defined "arms" as "weapons of offence, or armour of defence." 1 *Dictionary of the English Language* 107 (4th ed.) (hereinafter Johnson). Timothy Cunningham's important 1771 legal dictionary defined "arms" as "any thing that a man wears for his defence, or takes into his hands, or useth in wrath to cast at or strike another." 1 *A New and Complete Law Dictionary* (1771); see also N. Webster, American Dictionary of the English Language (1828) (reprinted 1989) (hereinafter Webster) (similar).

The term was applied, then as now, to weapons that were not specifically designed for military use and were not employed in a military capacity. For instance, Cunningham's legal dictionary gave as an example of usage: "Servants and labourers shall use bows and arrows on *Sundays,* &c. and not bear other arms." See also, e.g., An Act for the trial of Negroes, 1797 Del. Laws ch. XLIII, §6, p. 104, in *First Laws of the state of Delaware* 102, 104 (J. Cushing ed. 1981 (pt. 1)); see generally *State v. Duke,* 42Tex. 455, 458 (1874) (citing decisions of state courts construing "arms"). Although one founding-era thesaurus limited "arms" (as opposed to "weapons") to "instruments of offence *generally* made use of in war," even that source stated that all firearms constituted "arms." 1 J. Trusler, The Distinction Between Words Esteemed Synonymous in the English Language 37 (1794) (emphasis added).

Some have made the argument, bordering on the frivolous, that only those arms in existence in the 18th century are protected by the Second Amendment. We do not interpret constitutional rights that way. Just as the First Amendment protects modern forms of communications, e.g., *Reno v. American Civil Liberties Union,* 521 U. S. 844, 849 (1997), and the Fourth Amendment applies to modern forms of search, e.g., *Kyllo v. United States,* 533 U. S. 27, 35–36 (2001), the Second Amendment extends, prima facie, to all instruments that constitute bearable arms, even those that were not in existence at the time of the founding.

We turn to the phrases "keep arms" and "bear arms." Johnson defined "keep" as, most relevantly, "[t]o retain; not to lose," and "[t]o have in custody." Johnson 1095. Webster defined it as "[t]o hold; to retain in one's power or possession." No party has apprised us of an idiomatic meaning of "keep Arms." Thus, the most natural reading of "keep Arms" in the Second Amendment is to "have weapons."

The phrase "keep arms" was not prevalent in the written documents of the founding period that we have found, but there are a few examples, all of which favor viewing the right to "keep Arms" as an individual right unconnected with militia service. William Blackstone, for example, wrote that Catholics convicted of not attending service in the Church of England suffered certain penalties, one of which was that they were not permitted to "keep arms in their houses." 4 Commentaries on the Laws of England 55 (1769) (hereinafter Blackstone); see also 1 W. & M., c. 15, §4, in 3 Eng. Stat. at Large 422 (1689) ("[N]o Papist . . . shall or may have or keep in his House . . . any Arms . . ."); 1 Hawkins, Treatise on the Pleas of the Crown 26 (1771) (similar). Petitioners point to militia laws of the founding period that required militia members to "keep" arms in connection with militia service, and they conclude from this that the phrase "keep Arms" has a militia-related connotation. See Brief for Petitioners 16-17 (citing laws of Delaware, New Jersey, and Virginia). This is rather like saying that, since there are many statutes that authorize aggrieved employees to "file complaints" with federal agencies, the phrase "file complaints" has an employment-related connotation. "Keep arms" was simply a common way of referring to possessing arms, for militiamen and everyone else.

At the time of the founding, as now, to "bear" meant to "carry." See Johnson 161; Webster; T. Sheridan, A Complete Dictionary of the English Language (1796); 2 Oxford English Dictionary 20 (2d ed. 1989) (hereinafter Oxford). When used with "arms," however, the term has a meaning that refers to carrying for a particular purpose—confrontation. In *Muscarello v. United States,* 524 U. S. 125 (1998), in the course of analyzing the meaning of "carries a firearm" in a federal criminal statute, Justice Ginsburg wrote that "[s]urely a most familiar meaning is, as the Constitution's Second Amendment . . . indicate[s]: 'wear, bear, or carry . . . upon the person or in the clothing or in a pocket, for the purpose . . . of being armed and ready for offensive or defensive action in a case of conflict with another person.'" *Id.,* at 143 (dissenting opinion) (quoting *Black's Law Dictionary* 214 (6th ed. 1998)). We think that Justice Ginsburg accurately captured the natural meaning of "bear arms." Although the phrase implies that the carrying of the weapon is for the purpose of "offensive or defensive action," it in no way connotes participation in a structured military organization. . . .

c. Meaning of the Operative Clause. Putting all of these textual elements together, we find that they guarantee the individual right to possess and carry weapons in case of confrontation. This meaning is strongly confirmed by the historical background of the Second Amendment. We look to this because it has always been widely understood that the Second Amendment, like the First and Fourth Amendments, codified a *pre-existing* right. The very text of the Second Amendment implicitly recognizes the pre-existence of the right and declares only that it "shall not be infringed." As we said in *United States v. Cruikshank,* 92 U. S. 542, 553 (1876), "[t]his is not a right granted by the Constitution. Neither is it in any manner dependent upon that instrument for its existence. The Second amendment declares that it shall not be infringed. . . ."

There seems to us no doubt, on the basis of both text and history, that the Second Amendment conferred an individual right to keep and bear arms. Of course the right was not unlimited, just as the First Amendment's right of free speech was not, see, e.g., *United States v. Williams,* 553 U.S.___ (2008). Thus, we do not read the Second Amendment to protect the right of citizens to carry arms for *any sort* of confrontation, just as we do not read the First

Amendment to protect the right of citizens to speak for *any purpose*. Before turning to limitations upon the individual right, however, we must determine whether the prefatory clause of the Second Amendment comports with our interpretation of the operative clause.

2. Prefatory Clause.

The prefatory clause reads: "A well regulated Militia, being necessary to the security of a free State. . . ."

a. "Well-Regulated Militia." In *United States v. Miller*, 307 U. S. 174, 179 (1939), we explained that "the Militia comprised all males physically capable of acting in concert for the common defense." That definition comports with founding-era sources. See, e.g., Webster ("The militia of a country are the able bodied men organized into companies, regiments and brigades . . . and required by law to attend military exercises on certain days only, but at other times left to pursue their usual occupations"); *The Federalist* No. 46, pp. 329, 334 (B. Wright ed. 1961) (J. Madison) ("near half a million of citizens with arms in their hands"); Letter to Destutt de Tracy (Jan. 26, 1811), in *The Portable Thomas Jefferson* 520, 524 (M. Peterson ed. 1975) ("[T]he militia of the State, that is to say, of every man in it able to bear arms").

Petitioners take a seemingly narrower view of the militia, stating that "[m]ilitias are the state- and congressionally-regulated military forces described in the Militia Clauses (art. I, §8, cls. 15-16)." Brief for Petitioners 12. Although we agree with petitioners' interpretive assumption that "militia" means the same thing in Article I and the Second Amendment, we believe that petitioners identify the wrong thing, namely, the organized militia. Unlike armies and navies, which Congress is given the power to create ("to raise . . . Armies"; "to provide . . . a Navy," Art. I, §8, cls. 12-13), the militia is assumed by Article I already to be *in existence*. Congress is given the power to "provide for calling forth the militia," §8, cl. 15; and the power not to create, but to "organiz[e]" it—and not to organize "a" militia, which is what one would expect if the militia were to be a federal creation, but to organize "the" militia, connoting a body already in existence, *ibid.*, cl. 16. This is fully consistent with the ordinary definition of the militia as all able-bodied men. From that pool, Congress has plenary power to organize the units that will make up an effective fighting force. That is what Congress did in the first militia Act, which specified that "each and every free able-bodied white male citizen of the respective states, resident therein, who is or shall be of the age of eighteen years, and under the age of forty-five years (except as is herein after excepted) shall severally and respectively be enrolled in the militia." Act of May 8, 1792, 1 Stat. 271. To be sure, Congress need not conscript every able-bodied man into the militia, because nothing in Article I suggests that in exercising its power to organize, discipline, and arm the militia, Congress must focus upon the entire body. Although the militia consists of all able-bodied men, the federally organized militia may consist of a subset of them.

Finally, the adjective "well-regulated" implies nothing more than the imposition of proper discipline and training. See Johnson 1619 ("Regulate": "To adjust by rule or method"); Rawle 121–122; cf. Va. Declaration of Rights

§13 (1776), in 7 Thorpe 3812, 3814 (referring to "a well-regulated militia, composed of the body of the people, trained to arms").

b. "Security of a Free State." The phrase "security of a free state" meant "security of a free polity," not security of each of the several States as the dissent below argued, see 478 F. 3d, at 405, and n. 10. Joseph Story wrote in his treatise on the Constitution that "the word 'state' is used in various senses [and in] its most enlarged sense, it means the people composing a particular nation or community." 1 Story §208; see also 3 *id.*, §1890 (in reference to the Second Amendment's prefatory clause: "The militia is the natural defence of a free country"). It is true that the term "State" elsewhere in the Constitution refers to individual States, but the phrase "security of a free state" and close variations seem to have been terms of art in 18th-century political discourse, meaning a "free country" or free polity. See Volokh, "Necessary to the Security of a Free State," 83 *Notre Dame L. Rev.* 1, 5 (2007); see, e.g., 4 Blackstone 151 (1769); Brutus Essay III (Nov. 15, 1787), in *The Essential Antifederalist* 251, 253 (W. Allen & G. Lloyd eds., 2d ed. 2002). Moreover, the other instances of "state" in the Constitution are typically accompanied by modifiers making clear that the reference is to the several States—"each state," "several states," "any state," "that state," "particular states," "one state," "no state." And the presence of the term "foreign state" in Article I and Article III shows that the word "state" did not have a single meaning in the Constitution.

There are many reasons why the militia was thought to be "necessary to the security of a free state." See 3 Story §1890. First, of course, it is useful in repelling invasions and suppressing insurrections. Second, it renders large standing armies unnecessary—an argument that Alexander Hamilton made in favor of federal control over the militia. The Federalist No. 29, pp. 226, 227 (B. Wright ed. 1961) (A. Hamilton). Third, when the able-bodied men of a nation are trained in arms and organized, they are better able to resist tyranny.

3. Relationship between Prefatory Clause and Operative Clause

We reach the question, then: Does the preface fit with an operative clause that creates an individual right to keep and bear arms? It fits perfectly, once one knows the history that the founding generation knew and that we have described above. That history showed that the way tyrants had eliminated a militia consisting of all the able-bodied men was not by banning the militia but simply by taking away the people's arms, enabling a select militia or standing army to suppress political opponents. This is what had occurred in England that prompted codification of the right to have arms in the English Bill of Rights. . . .

It is therefore entirely sensible that the Second Amendment's prefatory clause announces the purpose for which the right was codified: to prevent elimination of the militia. The prefatory clause does not suggest that preserving the militia was the only reason Americans valued the ancient right; most undoubtedly thought it even more important for self-defense and hunting. But the threat that the new Federal Government would destroy the citizens' militia by taking away their arms was the reason that right—unlike some other English rights—was codified in a written Constitution. Justice Breyer's assertion that individual self-defense is merely a "subsidiary interest" of the right to keep and bear arms, see *post*, at 36, is profoundly mistaken. He bases that assertion solely upon the prologue—but that can only show that self-defense had little to do with the right's *codification*; it was the *central component* of the right itself.

Besides ignoring the historical reality that the Second Amendment was not intended to lay down a "novel principl[e]" but rather codified a right "inherited from our English ancestors," *Robertson v. Baldwin*, 165 U. S. 275, 281 (1897), petitioners' interpretation does not even achieve the narrower purpose that prompted codification of the right. If, as they believe, the Second Amendment right is no more than the right to keep and use weapons as a member of an organized militia, see *Brief for Petitioners* 8—if, that is, the *organized* militia is the sole institutional beneficiary of the Second Amendment's guarantee—it does not assure the existence of a "citizens' militia" as a safeguard against tyranny. For Congress retains plenary authority to organize the militia, which must include the authority to say who will belong to the organized force. That is why the first Militia Act's requirement that only whites enroll caused States to amend their militia laws to exclude free blacks. See Siegel, The Federal Government's Power to Enact Color-Conscious Laws, 92 *Nw. U. L. Rev.* 477, 521 (1998). Thus, if petitioners are correct, the Second Amendment protects citizens' right to use a gun in an organization from which Congress has plenary authority to exclude them. It guarantees a select militia of the sort the Stuart kings found useful, but not the people's militia that was the concern of the founding generation.

B

Our interpretation is confirmed by analogous arms-bearing rights in state constitutions that preceded and immediately followed adoption of the Second Amendment. Four States adopted analogues to the Federal Second Amendment in the period between independence and the ratification of the Bill of Rights. Two of them—Pennsylvania and Vermont—clearly adopted individual rights unconnected to militia service. Pennsylvania's Declaration of Rights of 1776 said: "That the people have a right to bear arms *for the defence of themselves*, and the state. . . ." §XIII, in 5 Thorpe 3082, 3083 (emphasis added). In 1777, Vermont adopted the identical provision, except for inconsequential differences in punctuation and capitalization. See Vt. Const., ch. 1, §15, in 6 *id.*, at 3741. . . .

We therefore believe that the most likely reading of all four of these pre-Second Amendment state constitutional provisions is that they secured an individual right to bear arms for defensive purposes. Other States did not include rights to bear arms in their pre-1789 constitutions—although in Virginia a Second Amendment analogue was proposed (unsuccessfully) by Thomas Jefferson. (It read: "No freeman shall ever be debarred the use of arms [within his own lands or tenements]." 1 The Papers of Thomas Jefferson 344 (J. Boyd ed. 1950)). . . .

The historical narrative that petitioners must endorse would thus treat the Federal Second Amendment as an odd outlier, protecting a right unknown in state constitutions or at English common law, based on little more than an overreading of the prefatory clause.

C

Justice Stevens relies on the drafting history of the Second Amendment—the various proposals in the state conventions and the debates in Congress. It is dubious to rely on such history to interpret a text that was widely understood to codify a pre-existing right, rather than to fashion a new one. But even assuming that this legislative history is relevant, Justice Stevens flatly misreads the historical record. . . .

D

1. Post-ratification Commentary

[I]mportant founding-era legal scholars interpreted the Second Amendment in published writings. All three understood it to protect an individual right unconnected with militia service. . . .

We have found only one early 19th-century commentator who clearly conditioned the right to keep and bear arms upon service in the militia—and he recognized that the prevailing view was to the contrary. "The provision of the constitution, declaring the right of the people to keep and bear arms, Etc. was probably intended to apply to the right of the people to bear arms for such [militia-related] purposes only, and not to prevent congress or the legislatures of the different states from enacting laws to prevent the citizens from always going armed. A different construction however has been given to it." B. Oliver, The Rights of an American Citizen 177 (1832). . . .

4. Post-Civil War Commentators

Every late 19th-century legal scholar that we have read interpreted the Second Amendment to secure an individual right unconnected with militia service. The most famous was the judge and professor Thomas Cooley, who wrote a massively popular 1868 Treatise on Constitutional Limitations. Concerning the Second Amendment it said:

> "Among the other defences to personal liberty should be mentioned the right of the people to keep and bear arms. . . . The alternative to a standing army is 'a well-regulated militia,' but this cannot exist unless the people are trained to bearing arms. How far it is in the power of the legislature to regulate this right, we shall not undertake to say, as happily there has been very little occasion to discuss that subject by the courts." *Id.,* at 350. . . .
>
> "[The purpose of the Second Amendment is] to secure a well-armed militia. . . . But a militia would be useless unless the citizens were enabled to exercise themselves in the use of warlike weapons. To preserve this privilege, and to secure to the people the ability to oppose themselves in military force against the usurpations of government, as well as against enemies from without, that government is forbidden by any law or proceeding to invade or destroy the right to keep and bear arms. . . . The clause is analogous to the one securing the freedom of speech and of

the press. Freedom, not license, is secured; the fair use, not the libellous abuse, is protected." J. Pomeroy, An Introduction to the Constitutional Law of the United States 152–153 (1868) (hereinafter Pomeroy). . . .

"The right to bear arms has always been the distinctive privilege of freemen. Aside from any necessity of self-protection to the person, it represents among all nations power coupled with the exercise of a certain jurisdiction. . . . [I]t was not necessary that the right to bear arms should be granted in the Constitution, for it had always existed." J. Ordronaux, Constitutional Legislation in the United States 241–242 (1891).

E

We now ask whether any of our precedents forecloses the conclusions we have reached about the meaning of the Second Amendment. . . .

Justice Stevens places overwhelming reliance upon this Court's decision in *United States v. Miller,* 307 U. S. 174 (1939). "[H]undreds of judges," we are told, "have relied on the view of the amendment we endorsed there," *post,* at 2, and "[e]ven if the textual and historical arguments on both side of the issue were evenly balanced, respect for the well-settled views of all of our predecessors on this Court, and for the rule of law itself . . . would prevent most jurists from endorsing such a dramatic upheaval in the law," *post,* at 4. And what is, according to Justice Stevens, the holding of *Miller* that demands such obeisance? That the Second Amendment "protects the right to keep and bear arms for certain military purposes, but that it does not curtail the legislature's power to regulate the nonmilitary use and ownership of weapons." *Post,* at 2.

Nothing so clearly demonstrates the weakness of Justice Stevens' case. *Miller* did not hold that and cannot possibly be read to have held that. The judgment in the case upheld against a Second Amendment challenge two men's federal convictions for transporting an unregistered short-barreled shotgun in interstate commerce, in violation of the National Firearms Act, 48 Stat. 1236. It is entirely clear that the Court's basis for saying that the Second Amendment did not apply was *not* that the defendants were "bear[ing] arms" not "for . . . military purposes" but for "nonmilitary use," *post,* at 2. Rather, it was that the *type of weapon at issue* was not eligible for Second Amendment protection: "In the absence of any evidence tending to show that the possession or use of a [short-barreled shotgun] at this time has some reasonable relationship to the preservation or efficiency of a well regulated militia, we cannot say that the Second Amendment guarantees the right to keep and bear *such an instrument."* 307 U. S., at 178 (emphasis added). "Certainly," the Court continued, "it is not within judicial notice that this weapon is any part of the ordinary military equipment or that its use could contribute to the common defense." *Ibid.* Beyond that, the opinion provided no explanation of the content of the right.

This holding is not only consistent with, but positively suggests, that the Second Amendment confers an individual right to keep and bear arms (though only arms that "have some reasonable relationship to the preservation or efficiency of a well regulated militia"). Had the Court believed that the Second Amendment protects only those serving in the militia, it would have been odd to examine the character of the weapon rather than simply note that the two crooks were not militiamen. Justice Stevens can say again and again that *Miller* did "not turn on the difference between muskets and sawed-off shotguns, it turned, rather, on the basic difference between the military and nonmilitary use and possession of guns," *post*, at 42–43, but the words of the opinion prove otherwise. The most Justice Stevens can plausibly claim for *Miller* is that it declined to decide the nature of the Second Amendment right, despite the Solicitor General's argument (made in the alternative) that the right was collective, see Brief for United States, O. T. 1938, No. 696, pp. 4–5. *Miller* stands only for the proposition that the Second Amendment right, whatever its nature, extends only to certain types of weapons. . . .

We may as well consider at this point (for we will have to consider eventually) *what* types of weapons *Miller* permits. Read in isolation, *Miller*'s phrase "part of ordinary military equipment" could mean that only those weapons useful in warfare are protected. That would be a startling reading of the opinion, since it would mean that the National Firearms Act's restrictions on machineguns (not challenged in *Miller*) might be unconstitutional, machineguns being useful in warfare in 1939. We think that *Miller*'s "ordinary military equipment" language must be read in tandem with what comes after: "[O]rdinarily when called for [militia] service [able-bodied] men were expected to appear bearing arms supplied by themselves and of the kind in common use at the time." 307 U. S., at 179. The traditional militia was formed from a pool of men bringing arms "in common use at the time" for lawful purposes like self-defense. "In the colonial and revolutionary war era, [small-arms] weapons used by militiamen and weapons used in defense of person and home were one and the same." *State v. Kessler*, 289 Ore. 359, 368, 614 P. 2d 94, 98 (1980) (citing G. Neumann, Swords and Blades of the American Revolution 6–15, 252–254 (1973)). Indeed, that is precisely the way in which the Second Amendment's operative clause furthers the purpose announced in its preface. We therefore read *Miller* to say only that the Second Amendment does not protect those weapons not typically possessed by law-abiding citizens for lawful purposes, such as short-barreled shotguns. That accords with the historical understanding of the scope of the right, see Part III, infra.

We conclude that nothing in our precedents forecloses our adoption of the original understanding of the Second Amendment. It should be unsurprising that such a significant matter has been for so long judicially unresolved. For most of our history, the Bill of Rights was not thought applicable to the States, and the Federal Government did not significantly regulate the possession of firearms by law-abiding citizens. Other provisions of the Bill of Rights have similarly remained unilluminated for lengthy periods. This Court first held a law to violate the First Amendment's guarantee of freedom of speech in 1931, almost 150 years after the Amendment was ratified, see *Near v. Minnesota ex rel. Olson*, 283 U.S. 697 (1931), and it was not until after World War II that we held a law invalid under the Establishment Clause, see *Illinois ex rel. McCollum v. Board of Ed. of School Dist. No. 71, Champaign Cty.*, 333 U. S. 203 (1948). Even a question as basic as the scope of proscribable libel was not addressed by this Court until 1964, nearly two centuries after the founding. See *New York Times Co. v. Sullivan*, 376 U. S. 254 (1964). It is demonstrably not true that, as Justice Stevens claims, *post,* at 41–42, "for most of our history, the invalidity of Second-Amendment-based objections to firearms regulations has been well settled and uncontroversial." For most of our history the question did not present itself.

III

Like most rights, the right secured by the Second Amendment is not unlimited. From Blackstone through the 19th-century cases, commentators and courts routinely explained that the right was not a right to keep and carry any weapon whatsoever in any manner whatsoever and for whatever purpose. See, e.g., *Sheldon,* in 5 Blume 346; Rawle 123; Pomeroy 152–153; Abbott 333. For example, the majority of the 19th-century courts to consider the question held that prohibitions on carrying concealed weapons were lawful under the Second Amendment or state analogues. See, e.g., *State v. Chandler,* 5 La. Ann., at 489–490; *Nunn v. State,* 1 Ga., at 251; see generally 2 Kent *340, n. 2; The American Students' Blackstone 84, n. 11 (G. Chase ed. 1884). Although we do not undertake an exhaustive historical analysis today of the full scope of the Second Amendment, nothing in our opinion should be taken to cast doubt on longstanding prohibitions on the possession of firearms by felons and the mentally ill, or laws forbidding the carrying of firearms in sensitive places such as schools and government buildings, or laws imposing conditions and qualifications on the commercial sale of arms.

We also recognize another important limitation on the right to keep and carry arms. *Miller* said, as we have explained, that the sorts of weapons protected were those "in common use at the time." 307 U.S., at 179. We think that limitation is fairly supported by the historical tradition of prohibiting the carrying of "dangerous and unusual weapons." . . .

IV

We turn finally to the law at issue here. As we have said, the law totally bans handgun possession in the home. It also requires that any lawful firearm in the home be disassembled or bound by a trigger lock at all times, rendering it inoperable.

As the quotations earlier in this opinion demonstrate, the inherent right of self-defense has been central to the Second Amendment right. The handgun ban amounts to a prohibition of an entire class of "arms" that is overwhelmingly chosen by American society for that lawful purpose. The prohibition extends, moreover, to the home, where the need for defense of self, family, and property is most acute. Under any of the standards of scrutiny that we have applied to enumerated constitutional rights, banning from the home "the most preferred firearm in the nation to 'keep' and use for protection of one's home and family," 478 F. 3d, at 400, would fail constitutional muster.

Few laws in the history of our Nation have come close to the severe restriction of the District's handgun ban. And some of those few have been struck down. In *Nunn v. State*, the Georgia Supreme Court struck down a prohibition on carrying pistols openly (even though it upheld a prohibition on carrying concealed weapons). See 1 Ga., at 251. In *Andrews v. State*, the Tennessee Supreme Court likewise held that a statute that forbade openly carrying a pistol "publicly or privately, without regard to time or place, or circumstances," 50 Tenn., at 187, violated the state constitutional provision (which the court equated with the Second Amendment). That was so even though the statute did not restrict the carrying of long guns. *Ibid.* See also *State v. Reid*, 1 Ala. 612, 616–617 (1840) ("A statute which, under the pretence of regulating, amounts to a destruction of the right, or which requires arms to be so borne as to render them wholly useless for the purpose of defence, would be clearly unconstitutional").

It is no answer to say, as petitioners do, that it is permissible to ban the possession of handguns so long as the possession of other firearms (i.e., long guns) is allowed. It is enough to note, as we have observed, that the American people have considered the handgun to be the quintessential self-defense weapon. There are many reasons that a citizen may prefer a handgun for home defense: It is easier to store in a location that is readily accessible in an emergency; it cannot easily be redirected or wrestled away by an attacker; it is easier to use for those without the upper-body strength to lift and aim a long gun; it can be pointed at a burglar with one hand while the other hand dials the police. Whatever the reason, handguns are the most popular weapon chosen by Americans for self-defense in the home, and a complete prohibition of their use is invalid.

We must also address the District's requirement (as applied to respondent's handgun) that firearms in the home be rendered and kept inoperable at all times. This makes it impossible for citizens to use them for the core lawful purpose of self-defense and is hence unconstitutional. The District argues that we should interpret this element of the statute to contain an exception for self-defense. See *Brief for Petitioners* 56–57. But we think that is precluded by the unequivocal text, and by the presence of certain other enumerated exceptions: "Except for law enforcement personnel . . ., each registrant shall keep any firearm in his possession unloaded and disassembled or bound by a trigger lock or similar device unless such firearm is kept at his place of business, or while being used for lawful recreational purposes within the District of Columbia." D. C. Code §7-2507.02. The nonexistence of a self-defense exception is also suggested by the D. C. Court of Appeals' statement that the statute forbids residents to use firearms to stop intruders, see *McIntosh v. Washington*, 395 A. 2d 744, 755–756 (1978). . . .

In sum, we hold that the District's ban on handgun possession in the home violates the Second Amendment, as does its prohibition against rendering any lawful firearm in the home operable for the purpose of immediate self-defense. Assuming that Heller is not disqualified from the exercise of Second Amendment rights, the District must permit him to register his handgun and must issue him a license to carry it in the home.

*   *   *

We are aware of the problem of handgun violence in this country, and we take seriously the concerns raised by the many *amici* who believe that prohibition of handgun ownership is a solution. The Constitution leaves the District of Columbia a variety of tools for combating that problem, including some measures regulating handguns, see *supra,* at 54–55, and n. 26. But the enshrinement of constitutional rights necessarily takes certain policy choices off the table. These include the absolute prohibition of handguns held and used for self-defense in the home. Undoubtedly some think that the Second Amendment is outmoded in a society where our standing army is the pride of our Nation, where well-trained police forces provide personal security, and where gun violence is a serious problem. That is perhaps debatable, but what is not debatable is that it is not the role of this Court to pronounce the Second Amendment extinct.

We affirm the judgment of the Court of Appeals.

It is so ordered.

John Paul Stevens  **NO**

Dissenting Opinion, *District of Columbia v. Heller*

Supreme Court of the United States
District of Columbia, *et al.*, Petitioners *v.* Dick Anthony Heller

Justice Stevens, **with whom** Justice Souter, Justice Ginsburg, **and** Justice Breyer **join, dissenting.**

The question presented by this case is not whether the Second Amendment protects a "collective right" or an "individual right." Surely it protects a right that can be enforced by individuals. But a conclusion that the Second Amendment protects an individual right does not tell us anything about the scope of that right.

Guns are used to hunt, for self-defense, to commit crimes, for sporting activities, and to perform military duties. The Second Amendment plainly does not protect the right to use a gun to rob a bank; it is equally clear that it *does* encompass the right to use weapons for certain military purposes. Whether it also protects the right to possess and use guns for nonmilitary purposes like hunting and personal self-defense is the question presented by this case. The text of the Amendment, its history, and our decision in *United States v. Miller,* 307 U. S. 174 (1939), provide a clear answer to that question.

The Second Amendment was adopted to protect the right of the people of each of the several States to maintain a well-regulated militia. It was a response to concerns raised during the ratification of the Constitution that the power of Congress to disarm the state militias and create a national standing army posed an intolerable threat to the sovereignty of the several States. Neither the text of the Amendment nor the arguments advanced by its proponents evidenced the slightest interest in limiting any legislature's authority to regulate private civilian uses of firearms. Specifically, there is no indication that the Framers of the Amendment intended to enshrine the common-law right of self-defense in the Constitution.

In 1934, Congress enacted the National Firearms Act, the first major federal firearms law. Upholding a conviction under that Act, this Court held that, "[i]n the absence of any evidence tending to show that possession or use of a 'shotgun having a barrel of less than eighteen inches in length' at this time has some reasonable relationship to the preservation or efficiency of a well regulated militia, we cannot say that the Second Amendment guarantees the right to keep and bear such

Supreme Court of the United States, June 26, 2008.

an instrument." *Miller,* 307 U.S., at 178. The view of the Amendment we took in *Miller*—that it protects the right to keep and bear arms for certain military purposes, but that it does not curtail the Legislature's power to regulate the nonmilitary use and ownership of weapons—is both the most natural reading of the Amendment's text and the interpretation most faithful to the history of its adoption.

Since our decision in *Miller,* hundreds of judges have relied on the view of the Amendment we endorsed there; we ourselves affirmed it in 1980. See *Lewis v. United States,* 445 U.S. 55, n. 8 (1980). No new evidence has surfaced since 1980 supporting the view that the Amendment was intended to curtail the power of Congress to regulate civilian use or misuse of weapons. Indeed, a review of the drafting history of the Amendment demonstrates that its Framers *rejected* proposals that would have broadened its coverage to include such uses.

The opinion the Court announces today fails to identify any new evidence supporting the view that the Amendment was intended to limit the power of Congress to regulate civilian uses of weapons. Unable to point to any such evidence, the Court stakes its holding on a strained and unpersuasive reading of the Amendment's text; significantly different provisions in the 1689 English Bill of Rights, and in various 19th-century State Constitutions; postenactment commentary that was available to the Court when it decided *Miller;* and, ultimately, a feeble attempt to distinguish *Miller* that places more emphasis on the Court's decisional process than on the reasoning in the opinion itself.

Even if the textual and historical arguments on both sides of the issue were evenly balanced, respect for the well-settled views of all of our predecessors on this Court, and for the rule of law itself, see *Mitchell v. W. T. Grant Co.,* 416 U. S. 600, 636 (1974) (Stewart, J., dissenting), would prevent most jurists from endorsing such a dramatic upheaval in the law. As Justice Cardozo observed years ago, the "labor of judges would be increased almost to the breaking point if every past decision could be reopened in every case, and one could not lay one's own course of bricks on the secure foundation of the courses laid by others who had gone before him." The Nature of the Judicial Process 149 (1921).

In this dissent I shall first explain why our decision in *Miller* was faithful to the text of the Second Amendment and the purposes revealed in its drafting history. I shall then comment on the postratification history of the Amendment, which makes abundantly clear that the Amendment should not be interpreted as limiting the authority of Congress to regulate the use or possession of firearms for purely civilian purposes.

I

The text of the Second Amendment is brief. It provides: "A well regulated Militia, being necessary to the security of a free State, the right of the people to keep and bear Arms, shall not be infringed."

Three portions of that text merit special focus: the introductory language defining the Amendment's purpose, the class of persons encompassed within its reach, and the unitary nature of the right that it protects.

"A well regulated Militia, being necessary to the security of a free State"

The preamble to the Second Amendment makes three important points. It identifies the preservation of the militia as the Amendment's purpose; it explains that the militia is necessary to the security of a free State; and it recognizes that the militia must be "well regulated." In all three respects it is comparable to provisions in several State Declarations of Rights that were adopted roughly contemporaneously with the Declaration of Independence. Those state provisions highlight the importance members of the founding generation attached to the maintenance of state militias; they also underscore the profound fear shared by many in that era of the dangers posed by standing armies. While the need for state militias has not been a matter of significant public interest for almost two centuries, that fact should not obscure the contemporary concerns that animated the Framers. . . .

"The right of the people."

. . . The Court overlooks the significance of the way the Framers used the phrase "the people" in these constitutional provisions. In the First Amendment, no words define the class of individuals entitled to speak, to publish, or to worship; in that Amendment it is only the right peaceably to assemble, and to petition the Government for a redress of grievances, that is described as a right of "the people." These rights contemplate collective action. While the right peaceably to assemble protects the individual rights of those persons participating in the assembly, its concern is with action engaged in by members of a group, rather than any single individual. Likewise, although the act of petitioning the Government is a right that can be exercised by individuals, it is primarily collective in nature. For if they are to be effective, petitions must involve groups of individuals acting in concert.

Similarly, the words "the people" in the Second Amendment refer back to the object announced in the Amendment's preamble. They remind us that it is the collective action of individuals having a duty to serve in the militia that the text directly protects and, perhaps more importantly, that the ultimate purpose of the Amendment was to protect the States' share of the divided sovereignty created by the Constitution. . . .

"To keep and bear Arms"

Although the Court's discussion of these words treats them as two "phrases"—as if they read "to keep" and "to bear"—they describe a unitary right: to possess arms if needed for military purposes and to use them in conjunction with military activities.

As a threshold matter, it is worth pausing to note an oddity in the Court's interpretation of "to keep and bear arms." Unlike the Court of Appeals, the Court does not read that phrase to create a right to possess arms for "lawful, private purposes." *Parker v. District of Columbia*, 478 F. 3d 370, 382 (CADC 2007). Instead, the Court limits the Amendment's protection to the right "to possess and carry weapons in case of confrontation." *Ante*, at 19. No party or *amicus* urged this interpretation; the Court appears to have fashioned it out of whole cloth. But although this novel limitation lacks support in the text of the Amendment, the Amendment's text *does* justify a different limitation: the "right to keep and bear arms" protects only a right to possess and use firearms in connection with service in a state-organized militia.

The term "bear arms" is a familiar idiom; when used unadorned by any additional words, its meaning is "to serve as a soldier, do military service, fight." 1 *Oxford English Dictionary* 634 (2d ed. 1989). It is derived from the Latin *arma ferre*, which, translated literally, means "to bear *[ferre]* war equipment *[arma]*." Brief for Professors of Linguistics and English as *Amici Curiae* 19. One 18th-century dictionary defined "arms" as "weapons of offence, or armour of defence," 1 S. Johnson, *A Dictionary of the English Language* (1755), and another contemporaneous source explained that "[b]y *arms,* we understand those instruments of offence generally made use of in war; such as firearms, swords, & c. By *weapons,* we more particularly mean instruments of other kinds (exclusive of fire-arms), made use of as offensive, on special occasions." 1 J. Trusler, The Distinction Between Words Esteemed Synonymous in the English Language 37 (1794). Had the Framers wished to expand the meaning of the phrase "bear arms" to encompass civilian possession and use, they could have done so by the addition of phrases such as "for the defense of themselves," as was done in the Pennsylvania and Vermont Declarations of Rights. The *unmodified* use of "bear arms," by contrast, refers most naturally to a military purpose, as evidenced by its use in literally dozens of contemporary texts. The absence of any reference to civilian uses of weapons tailors the text of the Amendment to the purpose identified in its preamble. But when discussing these words, the Court simply ignores the preamble. . . .

This reading is confirmed by the fact that the clause protects only one right, rather than two. It does not describe a right "to keep arms" and a separate right "to bear arms." Rather, the single right that it does describe is both a duty and a right to have arms available and ready for military service, and to use them for military purposes when necessary. Different language surely would have been used to protect nonmilitary use and possession of weapons from regulation if such an intent had played any role in the drafting of the Amendment.

*   *   *

When each word in the text is given full effect, the Amendment is most naturally read to secure to the people a right to use and possess arms in conjunction with service in a well-regulated militia. So far as appears, no more than that was contemplated by its drafters or is encompassed within its terms. Even if the meaning of the text were genuinely susceptible to more than one interpretation, the burden would remain on those advocating a departure from the purpose identified in the preamble and from settled law to come forward with persuasive new arguments or evidence. The textual analysis offered by respondent and embraced by the Court falls far short of sustaining that heavy burden. And the Court's emphatic reliance on the claim "that the Second Amendment . . . codified a *pre-existing* right," *ante,* at 19, is of course beside the point because the right to keep and bear arms for service in a state militia was also a pre-existing right.

Indeed, not a word in the constitutional text even arguably supports the Court's overwrought and novel description of the Second Amendment as "elevat[ing] above all other interests" "the right of law-abiding, responsible citizens to use arms in defense of hearth and home." *Ante*, at 63.

II

The proper allocation of military power in the new Nation was an issue of central concern for the Framers. The compromises they ultimately reached, reflected in Article I's Militia Clauses and the Second Amendment, represent quintessential examples of the Framers' "splitting the atom of sovereignty." . . .

Madison, charged with the task of assembling the proposals for amendments sent by the ratifying States, was the principal draftsman of the Second Amendment. He had before him, or at the very least would have been aware of, all of these proposed formulations. In addition, Madison had been a member, some years earlier, of the committee tasked with drafting the Virginia Declaration of Rights. That committee considered a proposal by Thomas Jefferson that would have included within the Virginia Declaration the following language: "No freeman shall ever be debarred the use of arms [within his own lands or tenements]." 1 Papers of Thomas Jefferson 363 (J. Boyd ed. 1950). . . .

With all of these sources upon which to draw, it is strikingly significant that Madison's first draft omitted any mention of nonmilitary use or possession of weapons. Rather, his original draft repeated the essence of the two proposed amendments sent by Virginia, combining the substance of the two provisions succinctly into one, which read: "The right of the people to keep and bear arms shall not be infringed; a well armed, and well regulated militia being the best security of a free country; but no person religiously scrupulous of bearing arms, shall be compelled to render military service in person." Cogan 169.

Madison's decision to model the Second Amendment on the distinctly military Virginia proposal is therefore revealing, since it is clear that he considered and rejected formulations that would have unambiguously protected civilian uses of firearms. When Madison prepared his first draft, and when that draft was debated and modified, it is reasonable to assume that all participants in the drafting process were fully aware of the other formulations that would have protected civilian use and possession of weapons and that their choice to craft the Amendment as they did represented a rejection of those alternative formulations.

Madison's initial inclusion of an exemption for conscientious objectors sheds revelatory light on the purpose of the Amendment. It confirms an intent to describe a duty as well as a right, and it unequivocally identifies the military character of both. The objections voiced to the conscientious-objector clause only confirm the central meaning of the text. Although records of the debate in the Senate, which is where the conscientious-objector clause was removed, do not survive, the arguments raised in the House illuminate the perceived problems with the clause: Specifically, there was concern that Congress "can declare who are those religiously scrupulous, and prevent them from bearing arms." The ultimate removal of the clause, therefore, only serves to confirm the purpose of the Amendment—to protect against congressional disarmament, by whatever means, of the States' militias. . . .

The history of the adoption of the Amendment thus describes an overriding concern about the potential threat to state sovereignty that a federal standing army would pose, and a desire to protect the States' militias as the means by which to guard against that danger. But state militias could not effectively check the prospect of a federal standing army so long as Congress retained the power to disarm them, and so a guarantee against such disarmament was needed. As we explained in *Miller:* "With obvious purpose to assure the continuation and render possible the effectiveness of such forces the declaration and guarantee of the Second Amendment were made. It must be interpreted and applied with that end in view." 307 U.S., at 178. The evidence plainly refutes the claim that the Amendment was motivated by the Framers' fears that Congress might act to regulate any civilian uses of weapons. And even if the historical record were genuinely ambiguous, the burden would remain on the parties advocating a change in the law to introduce facts or arguments "newly ascertained," *Vasquez,* 474 U.S., at 266; the Court is unable to identify any such facts or arguments.

III

Although it gives short shrift to the drafting history of the Second Amendment, the Court dwells at length on four other sources: the 17th-century English Bill of Rights; Blackstone's Commentaries on the Laws of England; postenactment commentary on the Second Amendment; and post-Civil War legislative history. All of these sources shed only indirect light on the question before us, and in any event offer little support for the Court's conclusion. . . .

Thus, for most of our history, the invalidity of Second-Amendment-based objections to firearms regulations has been well settled and uncontroversial. Indeed, the Second Amendment was not even mentioned in either full House of Congress during the legislative proceedings that led to the passage of the 1934 Act. Yet enforcement of that law produced the judicial decision that confirmed the status of the Amendment as limited in reach to military usage. After reviewing many of the same sources that are discussed at greater length by the Court today, the *Miller* Court unanimously concluded that the Second Amendment did not apply to the possession of a firearm that did not have "some reasonable relationship to the preservation or efficiency of a well regulated militia." 307 U.S., at 178.

The key to that decision did not, as the Court belatedly suggests, *ante,* at 49–51, turn on the difference between muskets and sawed-off shotguns; it turned, rather, on the basic difference between the military and nonmilitary use and possession of guns. Indeed, if the Second Amendment were not limited in its coverage to military uses of weapons, why should the Court in *Miller* have suggested that some weapons but not others were eligible for

Second Amendment protection? If use for self-defense were the relevant stand-ard, why did the Court not inquire into the suitability of a particular weapon for self-defense purposes? . . .

The Court is simply wrong when it intones that *Miller* contained *"not a word"* about the Amendment's history. *Ante,* at 52. The Court plainly looked to history to construe the term "Militia," and, on the best reading of *Miller,* the entire guarantee of the Second Amendment. After noting the original Consti-tution's grant of power to Congres and to the States over the militia, the Court explained:

> "With obvious purpose to assure the continuation and render possi-ble the effectiveness of such forces the declaration and guarantee of the Second Amendment were made. It must be interpreted and applied with that end in view."
>
> "The Militia which the States were expected to maintain and train is set in contrast with Troops which they were forbidden to keep without the consent of Congress. The sentiment of the time strongly disfavored standing armies; the common view was that adequate defense of country and laws could be secured through the Militia—civilians primarily, soldiers on occasion."
>
> "The signification attributed to the term Militia appears from the debates in the Convention, the history and legislation of Colonies and States, and the writings of approved commentators." *Miller,* 307 U.S., at 178–179.

The majority cannot seriously believe that the *Miller* Court did not consider any relevant evidence; the majority simply does not approve of the conclusion the *Miller* Court reached on that evidence. Standing alone, that is insufficient reason to disregard a unanimous opinion of this Court, upon which substantial reliance has been placed by legislators and citizens for nearly 70 years.

V

The Court concludes its opinion by declaring that it is not the proper role of this Court to change the meaning of rights "enshrine[d]" in the Constitution. *Ante,* at 64. But the right the Court announces was not "enshrined" in the Second Amendment by the Framers; it is the product of today's law-changing decision. The majority's exegesis has utterly failed to establish that as a matter of text or history, "the right of law-abiding, responsible citizens to use arms in defense of hearth and home" is "elevate[d] above all other interests" by the Second Amendment. *Ante,* at 64.

Until today, it has been understood that legislatures may regulate the civilian use and misuse of firearms so long as they do not interfere with the preservation of a well-regulated militia. The Court's announcement of a new constitutional right to own and use firearms for private purposes upsets that settled understanding, but leaves for future cases the formidable task of defin-ing the scope of permissible regulations. Today judicial craftsmen have con-fidently asserted that a policy choice that denies a "law-abiding, responsible citize[n]" the right to keep and use weapons in the home for self-defense is "off the table." *Ante,* at 64. Given the presumption that most citizens are law abiding, and the reality that the need to defend oneself may suddenly arise in a host of locations outside the home, I fear that the District's policy choice may well be just the first of an unknown number of dominoes to be knocked off the table.

I do not know whether today's decision will increase the labor of federal judges to the "breaking point" envisioned by Justice Cardozo, but it will surely give rise to a far more active judicial role in making vitally important national policy decisions than was envisioned at any time in the 18th, 19th, or 20th centuries.

The Court properly disclaims any interest in evaluating the wisdom of the specific policy choice challenged in this case, but it fails to pay heed to a far more important policy choice—the choice made by the Framers themselves. The Court would have us believe that over 200 years ago, the Framers made a choice to limit the tools available to elected officials wishing to regulate civilian uses of weapons, and to authorize this Court to use the common-law process of case-by-case judicial lawmaking to define the contours of acceptable gun control policy. Absent compelling evidence that is nowhere to be found in the Court's opinion, I could not possibly conclude that the Framers made such a choice.

For these reasons, I respectfully dissent.

POSTSCRIPT

Does the U.S. Constitution Protect the Right to Possess a Firearm?

This issue presents one of the more controversial debates considered in this volume. Many Americans love guns. In fact, recent studies have indicated that there are more than 200,000,000 guns owned privately in the United States. That is almost one gun for every 1.5 Americans. What explains this fascination with guns?

Some persons believe that America has a "gun culture." The image of the United States as a frontier nation with a history of gun usage for self-defense, the acquisition of food, and as a part of the cultural heritage of the wild west, is a compelling one. America's love affair with guns has come at a substantial cost, however.

Professor Franklin E. Zimring asserts that while guns are used in only about 4 percent of all crimes, and only about 20 percent of all violent crimes, they are involved in almost 70 percent of all criminal homicides. States Zimring: "If the problem is lethal violence, the market share for firearms is 70 percent. Guns alone account for twice as many criminal deaths as all other means of killing combined." (Zimring, Firearms, Violence, and the Potential Impact of Firearms Control (2004, p. 34)). In response to the question "Can gun control work?" Professor Zimring states:

> The answer to this general question is a highly qualified 'yes, but.' If and to the extent that regulation reduces the use of loaded guns in crimes it will save American lives. But reducing the share of violence with guns is not an easy task to achieve in urban environments with large inventories of available handguns. Most gun control efforts do not make measurable impacts on gun use, particularly low budget symbolic legislation. If Congress when creating what it called a 'gun-free school zone' by legislation did reduce firearms violence, the result would be on a par with that of the miracle of loaves and fishes. But New York City's effort to tightly enforce one of the nation's most restrictive handgun laws did apparently have a substantial payoff in reduced shootings that saved many lives.

Professor Lance K. Stell responds, however:

> Strict gun control, by effect if not intent, institutionalizes the natural predatory advantages of larger, stronger, violence-prone persons or gangs of such persons, and yet its proponents incur no liability to offset resulting risks. . . .
>
> Prohibiting competent, adult, non-felons to possess 'equalizers' also has distributional wealth effects not only between criminals and

the law-abiding, but also among the law-abiding. Strict gun control disproportionately increases the risks of violent victimization for less well-off law-abiding citizens who cannot take advantage of the privileged connections to officials that wealthier citizens take for granted.

As you can see, the gun control debate is not an easy one. Is it better to restrict the number of guns in the population, or to arm everyone in the interests of having a "fair fight?" These are difficult questions that seem unable to produce little compromise among even very rational proponents of the different viewpoints.

Moreover, the gun control debate appears to be raging within the U.S. Supreme Court as well. The Court's five-to-four decision in *District of Columbia v. Heller* appears to reflect the cultural divide in the nation as a whole.

It seems important to recognize, however, that *Heller* does not appear to have opened the floodgates to unrestricted private firearms ownership. Justice Scalia stated, "[W]e do not read the Second Amendment to protect the right of citizens to carry arms for any sort of confrontation just as we do not read the First Amendment to protect the right of citizens to speak for any purpose." He continued:

[T]he right [to bear arms is] not a right to keep and carry any weapon whatsoever in any manner whatsoever and for whatever purpose. . . [N]othing in our opinion should be taken to cast doubt on longstanding prohibitions on the possession of firearms by felons and the mentally ill, or laws forbidding the carrying of firearms in sensitive places such as schools and government building, or laws imposing conditions and qualification on the commercial sale of firearms.

Therefore, it appears that *Heller* will not mean that Americans will witness persons sauntering down Main Street with high-powered assault rifles, such as AK-47s, sawed-off shotguns, or fully automatic weapons, anytime soon. Stated Justice Scalia in *Heller*, "[W]e therefore read *Miller* to say only that the Second Amendment does not protect those weapons not typically possessed by law-abiding citizens for lawful purposes, such as short-barreled shotguns." Moreover, it seems to indicate as well that governments will continue to be able to impose meaningful "time, place, and manner," restrictions on firearms possession. For example, laws prohibiting firearms possession in places such as bars and taverns, where alcohol is sold, are likely to continue to be upheld by U.S. Courts. However, now that the Supreme Court has recognized an individual right to possess firearms under the Second Amendment, where do we go from here?

Another case was decided recently by the U.S. Supreme Court that may have further implications for the development of a Constitutional Right to Bear Arms. In 2010, *McDonald v. City of Chicago*, 561 U.S. ___ (2010), presented a challenge to the city of Chicago's gun control law. Specifically, the plaintiff challenged the following aspects of the city's law: (1) its prohibition on the registration of handguns; (2) its requirement for gun registration before they can be purchased by Chicago residents; (3) the city's requirement for the re-registration of guns on an annual basis, along with the payment of an annual fee; and (4) the city's declaration that if the registration lapses on any gun, it may never be registered again.

An important distinction between *District of Columbia v. Heller* and *McDonald v. City of Chicago* is that the former case involved a federal jurisdiction, the District of Columbia, whereas the latter one originated in the state of Illinois. The distinction is crucial because the *Heller* Court's recognition of an individual right to bear arms under the Second Amendment had not yet been applied to the state and local governments, which were free to continue to maintain restrictive firearms laws.

In *McDonald*, however, the plaintiff argued that the Second Amendment's Right to Bear Arms should be applied to the states, or "incorporated," through the Due Process Clause of the Fourteenth Amendment. Essentially, the plaintiff argued that the right to bear arms is "implicit in the concept of ordered liberty," and is thus a "fundamental" right that the states, or municipalities, may not deny. Writing for the Court, Justice Samuel Alito agreed. He stated that the Fourteenth Amendment's Due Process Clause guaranteed the right of individuals to keep and bear arms for self-defense because the Constitution's Framers believed that those rights were "necessary to the Nation's system of ordered liberty." Thus, states and municipalities across the United States may not prohibit firearms possession for self-defense within their jurisdictions.

The issues discussed in this section present a great many challenging questions. Additional resources to pursue further study in this area include Kathleen M. Sullivan and Gerald Gunther, *Constitutional Law* (Foundation Press, 15th ed., 2004); Laurence H. Tribe, *American Constitutional Law* (Foundation Press, 2nd ed., 1988); Alpheus Thomas Mason and Donald Grier Stephenson, Jr., *American Constitutional Law* (Pearson Prentice Hall, 15th ed., 2009; 14th ed., 2005); Bernard Schwartz, *A History of the Supreme Court* (Oxford University Press, 1993); Kermit L. Hall, Paul Finkelman, and James Ely, Jr., *American Legal History: Cases and Materials* (Oxford University Press, 3rd ed., 2005); Kermit L. Hall, *The Oxford Companion to the Supreme Court of the United States* (Oxford University Press, 1992); Walter F. Murphy, James E. Flemming, Sotirios A. Barber, and Stephen Macedo, *American Constitutional Interpretation* (Foundation Press, 3rd ed., 2003); David M. O'Brien, *Constitutional Law and Politics: Struggles for Power and Government Accountability* (W.W. Norton & Company, 6th ed., 2005); Craig R. Ducat, *Constitutional Interpretation* (Wadsworth, 9th ed., 2009); John H. Garvey, T. Alexander Aleinikoff, and Daniel A. Farber, *Modern Constitutional Theory: A Reader* (Thompson West, 5th ed., 2004). See also: Cramer and Olson, "What Did 'Bear Arms' Mean in the Second Amendment?" *Geo. J. L. & Pub. Pol.* (vol. 6, 2008, p. 511); Cramer, Johnson, and Mocsary, "This Right is Not Allowed by Governments That Are Afraid of the People: The Public Meaning of the Second Amendment," *Geo. Mason L. Rev.* (vol. 17, 2010, p. 823); Henigan, "The Second Amendment and the Right to Bear Arms After *D.C. v. Heller:* The Heller Paradox," *U.C.L.A. L. Rev.* (vol. 823, 2009, p. 1171); Zimring, "Firearms, Violence, and the Potential Impact of Firearms Control," *J. L. Med. & Ethics* (vol. 32, 2004, p. 1); Stell, "The Production of Criminal Violence in America: Is Strict Gun Control the Solution?" *J. L. Med. & Ethics* (vol. 32, 2004, p. 1); Tushnet, "*Heller* and the New Originalism," *Ohio St. L.J.* (vol. 69, 2008, p. 609).

ISSUE 18

Is the Death Penalty an Unconstitutional Punishment for Juvenile Offenders?

YES: Anthony M. Kennedy, from Majority Opinion, *Roper v. Simmons,* U.S. Supreme Court (2005)

NO: Antonin E. Scalia, from Dissenting Opinion, *Roper v. Simmons,* U.S. Supreme Court (2005)

ISSUE SUMMARY

YES: Associate Justice Anthony M. Kennedy, writing for the Court, asserts that the death penalty is an unacceptable punishment for juveniles who commit murder because it constitutes cruel and unusual punishment in violation of the Eighth and Fourteenth Amendments.

NO: Associate Justice Antonin E. Scalia, dissenting in the same case, argues that there is no clear social consensus that would favor abolishing the death penalty in these cases and that in doing so the Court's majority is usurping the powers of state legislatures.

Perhaps the single-most controversial issue concerning U.S. justice system policy is the use of the death penalty. A significant percentage of Americans appear to support capital punishment. A 2005 ABC News/Washington Post Poll showed that approximately 65 percent of adults surveyed nationwide favor the death penalty, while 29 percent oppose it, and 6 percent remain unsure. But, as pollsters know, how they ask the death penalty question has a great deal to do with the responses they receive. A 2005 CBS News Poll asked: "What do you think should be the penalty for persons convicted of murder: the death penalty, life in prison with no chance of parole, or a long prison sentence with a chance of parole?" Thirty-nine percent of the respondents selected the death penalty, 39 percent chose life in prison with no chance of parole, 6 percent indicated a long prison sentence with a chance of parole, and 3 percent were unsure.

 What these polls show is that while death penalty proponents are quick to point to polls showing that a majority of Americans support capital punishment, the reality is that many people are somewhat ambivalent about it. When penal alternatives to capital punishment are offered, support for the death penalty is much more equivocal.

But, how do Americans feel about executing juvenile offenders? A significant majority clearly do not support it. A 2001 University of Chicago study found that while 62 percent of those surveyed supported the death penalty, only 34 percent supported it for juvenile offenders. A 2002 Gallup Poll showed similar results: While 72 percent of Americans supported the death penalty, only 26 percent supported it for juvenile offenders.

What are the arguments on both sides of the juvenile death penalty debate? One argument favoring the juvenile death penalty is that if the offender is old enough to commit a heinous crime, he or she is old enough to pay the consequences. Another related argument is based on the doctrine of "just deserts"—the offender should receive the death penalty because the act that he or she committed deserves to be punished by death. Likewise, by virtue of committing a violent murder, the juvenile offender has demonstrated that he or she is "unfit" to live and that society is justified in applying the punishment of death.

On the other side, juvenile death penalty opponents note that children have less cognitive capacity than adults. That is why our legal system assumes that children who commit crimes are less responsible for their offenses than mature adults. Accordingly, scientific research appears to indicate that the portions of the human brain that control thinking and impulsiveness are not developed until a person reaches his or her early twenties. Moreover, a strong case can be made that executing offenders for crimes committed as juveniles is simply barbaric and, according to Justice Anthony M. Kennedy's majority opinion in *Roper v. Simmons*, places the United States in the same category with the Democratic Republic of Congo, Iran, Nigeria, Pakistan, Saudi Arabia, and Yemen as the only countries that execute juvenile offenders.

So, should the death penalty be an unacceptable punishment for juvenile offenders? The Supreme Court justices who authored the majority and dissenting opinions in *Roper v. Simmons* have very different views of this controversy. Justice Kennedy, writing for the Court, asserted that persons should not be eligible for the death penalty if they committed their crimes as juveniles. Justice Antonin E. Scalia, however, believed that decisions about whether to execute juveniles should be left to state legislatures.

In Your Opinion . . .

- Based on what you know about the death penalty, should society be permitted to execute persons who committed murder as juveniles?
- Is the death penalty a barbaric practice that is inconsistent with American values and ideals?
- Is there a less drastic alternative method of punishing juvenile murderers?

YES

Anthony M. Kennedy

Majority Opinion, *Roper v. Simmons*

J ustice Kennedy delivered the opinion of the Court.

This case requires us to address, for the second time in a decade and a half, whether it is permissible under the Eighth and Fourteenth Amendments to the Constitution of the United States to execute a juvenile offender who was older than 15 but younger than 18 when he committed a capital crime. In *Stanford v. Kentucky*, 492 U.S. 361, 106 L. Ed. 2d 306, 109 S. Ct. 2969 (1989), a divided Court rejected the proposition that the Constitution bars capital punishment for juvenile offenders in this age group. We reconsider the question. . . .

I

The Eighth Amendment provides: "Excessive bail shall not be required, nor excessive fines imposed, nor cruel and unusual punishments inflicted." The provision is applicable to the States through the Fourteenth Amendment. As the Court explained in *Atkins*, the Eighth Amendment guarantees individuals the right not to be subjected to excessive sanctions. The right flows from the basic "'precept of justice that punishment for crime should be graduated and proportioned to [the] offense.'" By protecting even those convicted of heinous crimes, the Eighth Amendment reaffirms the duty of the government to respect the dignity of all persons.

The prohibition against "cruel and unusual punishments," like other expansive language in the Constitution, must be interpreted according to its text, by considering history, tradition, and precedent, and with due regard for its purpose and function in the constitutional design. To implement this framework we have established the propriety and affirmed the necessity of referring to "the evolving standards of decency that mark the progress of a maturing society" to determine which punishments are so disproportionate as to be cruel and unusual.

In *Thompson v. Oklahoma*, a plurality of the Court determined that our standards of decency do not permit the execution of any offender under the age of 16 at the time of the crime. The plurality opinion explained that no death penalty State that had given express consideration to a minimum age for the death penalty had set the age lower than 16. The plurality also observed that "[t]he conclusion that it would offend civilized standards of decency to execute a person who was less than 16 years old at the time of his or her

Supreme Court of the United States, March 1, 2005.

offense is consistent with the views that have been expressed by respected professional organizations, by other nations that share our Anglo-American heritage, and by the leading members of the Western European community." The opinion further noted that juries imposed the death penalty on offenders under 16 with exceeding rarity; the last execution of an offender for a crime committed under the age of 16 had been carried out in 1948, 40 years prior.

Bringing its independent judgment to bear on the permissibility of the death penalty for a 15-year-old offender, the *Thompson* plurality stressed that "[t]he reasons why juveniles are not trusted with the privileges and responsibilities of an adult also explain why their irresponsible conduct is not as morally reprehensible as that of an adult." According to the plurality, the lesser culpability of offenders under 16 made the death penalty inappropriate as a form of retribution, while the low likelihood that offenders under 16 engaged in "the kind of cost-benefit analysis that attaches any weight to the possibility of execution" made the death penalty ineffective as a means of deterrence. With Justice O'Connor concurring in the judgment on narrower grounds, the Court set aside the death sentence that had been imposed on the 15-year-old offender.

The next year, in *Stanford v. Kentucky*, the Court, over a dissenting opinion joined by four justices, referred to contemporary standards of decency in this country and concluded the Eighth and Fourteenth Amendments did not proscribe the execution of juvenile offenders over 15 but under 18. The Court noted that 22 of the 37 death penalty States permitted the death penalty for 16-year-old offenders, and, among these 37 States, 25 permitted it for 17-year-old offenders. These numbers, in the Court's view, indicated there was no national consensus "sufficient to label a particular punishment cruel and unusual." A plurality of the Court also "emphatically reject[ed]" the suggestion that the Court should bring its own judgment to bear on the acceptability of the juvenile death penalty.

The same day the Court decided *Stanford*, it held that the Eighth Amendment did not mandate a categorical exemption from the death penalty for the mentally retarded. In reaching this conclusion it stressed that only two States had enacted laws banning the imposition of the death penalty on a mentally retarded person convicted of a capital offense. According to the Court, "the two state statutes prohibiting execution of the mentally retarded, even when added to the 14 States that have rejected capital punishment completely, [did] not provide sufficient evidence at present of a national consensus."

Three Terms ago the subject was reconsidered in *Atkins*. We held that standards of decency have evolved since *Penry* and now demonstrate that the execution of the mentally retarded is cruel and unusual punishment. The Court noted objective indicia of society's standards, as expressed in legislative enactments and state practice with respect to executions of the mentally retarded. When *Atkins* was decided only a minority of States permitted the practice, and even in those States it was rare. On the basis of these indicia the Court determined that executing mentally retarded offenders "has become truly unusual, and it is fair to say that a national consensus has developed against it." . . .

Just as the *Atkins* Court reconsidered the issue decided in *Penry*, we now reconsider the issue decided in *Stanford*. The beginning point is a review of objective indicia of consensus, as expressed in particular by the enactments of legislatures that have addressed the question. This data gives us essential instruction. We then must determine, in the exercise of our own independent judgment, whether the death penalty is a disproportionate punishment for juveniles.

II

A

The evidence of national consensus against the death penalty for juveniles is similar, and in some respects parallel, to the evidence *Atkins* held sufficient to demonstrate a national consensus against the death penalty for the mentally retarded. When *Atkins* was decided, 30 States prohibited the death penalty for the mentally retarded. This number comprised 12 that had abandoned the death penalty altogether, and 18 that maintained it but excluded the mentally retarded from its reach. By a similar calculation in this case, 30 States prohibit the juvenile death penalty, comprising 12 that have rejected the death penalty altogether and 18 that maintain it but, by express provision or judicial interpretation, exclude juveniles from its reach. *Atkins* emphasized that even in the 20 States without formal prohibition, the practice of executing the mentally retarded was infrequent. Since *Penry*, only five States had executed offenders known to have an IQ under 70. In the present case, too, even in the 20 States without a formal prohibition on executing juveniles, the practice is infrequent. Since *Stanford*, six States have executed prisoners for crimes committed as juveniles. In the past 10 years, only three have done so: Oklahoma, Texas, and Virginia. In December 2003, the Governor of Kentucky decided to spare the life of Kevin Stanford and commuted his sentence to one of life imprisonment without parole, with the declaration that "'[w]e ought not be executing people who, legally, were children.'" By this act the Governor ensured Kentucky would not add itself to the list of States that have executed juveniles within the last 10 years even by the execution of the very defendant whose death sentence the Court had upheld in *Stanford v. Kentucky*.

There is, to be sure, at least one difference between the evidence of consensus in *Atkins* and in this case. Impressive in *Atkins* was the rate of abolition of the death penalty for the mentally retarded. Sixteen States that permitted the execution of the mentally retarded at the time of *Penry* had prohibited the practice by the time we heard *Atkins*. By contrast, the rate of change in reducing the incidence of the juvenile death penalty, or in taking specific steps to abolish it, has been slower. Five States that allowed the juvenile death penalty at the time of *Stanford* have abandoned it in the intervening 15 years—four through legislative enactments and one through judicial decision.

Though less dramatic than the change from *Penry* to *Atkins* ("telling," to borrow the word *Atkins* used to describe this difference), we still consider the change from *Stanford* to this case to be significant. As noted in *Atkins*, with respect to the States that had abandoned the death penalty for the mentally retarded since *Penry*, "[i]t is not so much the number of these States that is significant, but the consistency of the direction of change." In particular we found it significant that, in the wake of *Penry*, no State that had already prohibited the execution of the mentally retarded had passed legislation to reinstate the penalty. The number of States that have abandoned capital punishment for juvenile offenders since *Stanford* is smaller than the number of States that abandoned capital punishment for the mentally retarded after *Penry*; yet we think the same consistency of direction of change has been demonstrated. Since *Stanford*, no State that previously prohibited capital punishment for juveniles has reinstated it. This fact, coupled with the trend toward abolition of the juvenile death penalty, carries special force in light of the general popularity of anticrime legislation, and in light of the particular trend in recent years toward cracking down on juvenile crime in other respects. Any difference between this case and *Atkins* with respect to the pace of abolition is thus counterbalanced by the consistent direction of the change. . . .

As in *Atkins*, the objective indicia of consensus in this case—the rejection of the juvenile death penalty in the majority of States; the infrequency of its use even where it remains on the books; and the consistency in the trend toward abolition of the practice—provide sufficient evidence that today our society views juveniles, in the words *Atkins* used respecting the mentally retarded, as "categorically less culpable than the average criminal."

B

A majority of States have rejected the imposition of the death penalty on juvenile offenders under 18, and we now hold this is required by the Eighth Amendment.

Because the death penalty is the most severe punishment, the Eighth Amendment applies to it with special force. Capital punishment must be limited to those offenders who commit "a narrow category of the most serious crimes" and whose extreme culpability makes them "the most deserving of execution." This principle is implemented throughout the capital sentencing process. States must give narrow and precise definition to the aggravating factors that can result in a capital sentence. In any capital case a defendant has wide latitude to raise as a mitigating factor "any aspect of [his or her] character or record and any of the circumstances of the offense that the defendant proffers as a basis for a sentence less than death." There are a number of crimes that beyond question are severe in absolute terms, yet the death penalty may not be imposed for their commission. The death penalty may not be imposed on certain classes of offenders, such as juveniles under 16, the insane, and the mentally retarded, no matter how heinous the crime. These rules vindicate the underlying principle that the death penalty is reserved for a narrow category of crimes and offenders.

Three general differences between juveniles under 18 and adults demonstrate that juvenile offenders cannot with reliability be classified among the worst offenders. First, as any parent knows and as the scientific and sociological studies respondent and his *amici* cite tend to confirm, "[a] lack of maturity and an underdeveloped sense of responsibility are found in youth more often than in adults and are more understandable among the young. These qualities often result in impetuous and ill-considered actions and decisions." It has been noted that "adolescents are overrepresented statistically in virtually every category of reckless behavior." In recognition of the comparative immaturity and irresponsibility of juveniles, almost every State prohibits those under 18 years of age from voting, serving on juries, or marrying without parental consent.

The second area of difference is that juveniles are more vulnerable or susceptible to negative influences and outside pressures, including peer pressure. ("[Y]outh is more than a chronological fact. It is a time and condition of life when a person may be most susceptible to influence and to psychological damage"). This is explained in part by the prevailing circumstance that juveniles have less control, or less experience with control, over their own environment.

The third broad difference is that the character of a juvenile is not as well formed as that of an adult. The personality traits of juveniles are more transitory, less fixed.

These differences render suspect any conclusion that a juvenile falls among the worst offenders. The susceptibility of juveniles to immature and irresponsible behavior means "their irresponsible conduct is not as morally reprehensible as that of an adult." Their own vulnerability and comparative lack of control over their immediate surroundings mean juveniles have a greater claim than adults to be forgiven for failing to escape negative influences in their whole environment. The reality that juveniles still struggle to define their identity means it is less supportable to conclude that even a heinous crime committed by a juvenile is evidence of irretrievably depraved character. From a moral standpoint it would be misguided to equate the failings of a minor with those of an adult, for a greater possibility exists that a minor's character deficiencies will be reformed. Indeed, "[t]he relevance of youth as a mitigating factor derives from the fact that the signature qualities of youth are transient; as individuals mature, the impetuousness and recklessness that may dominate in younger years can subside."

Once the diminished culpability of juveniles is recognized, it is evident that the penological justifications for the death penalty apply to them with lesser force than to adults. We have held there are two distinct social purposes served by the death penalty: "'retribution and deterrence of capital crimes by prospective offenders.'" As for retribution, we remarked in *Atkins* that "[i]f the culpability of the average murderer is insufficient to justify the most extreme sanction available to the State, the lesser culpability of the mentally retarded offender surely does not merit that form of retribution." The same conclusions follow from the lesser culpability of the juvenile offender. Whether viewed as an attempt to express the community's moral outrage or as an attempt to right the balance for the wrong to the victim, the case for retribution is not as strong with a minor as with an adult. Retribution is not proportional if the law's most severe penalty is imposed on one whose culpability or blameworthiness is diminished, to a substantial degree, by reason of youth and immaturity.

As for deterrence, it is unclear whether the death penalty has a significant or even measurable deterrent effect on juveniles, as counsel for the petitioner acknowledged at oral argument. In general we leave to legislatures the assessment of the efficacy of various criminal penalty schemes. Here, however, the absence of evidence of deterrent effect is of special concern because the same characteristics that render juveniles less culpable than adults suggest as well that juveniles will be less susceptible to deterrence. In particular, as the plurality observed in *Thompson*, "[t]he likelihood that the teenage offender has made the kind of cost-benefit analysis that attaches any weight to the possibility of execution is so remote as to be virtually nonexistent." To the extent the juvenile death penalty might have residual deterrent effect, it is worth noting that the punishment of life imprisonment without the possibility of parole is itself a severe sanction, in particular for a young person.

In concluding that neither retribution nor deterrence provides adequate justification for imposing the death penalty on juvenile offenders, we cannot deny or overlook the brutal crimes too many juvenile offenders have committed. Certainly it can be argued, although we by no means concede the point, that a rare case might arise in which a juvenile offender has sufficient psychological maturity, and at the same time demonstrates sufficient depravity, to merit a sentence of death. Indeed, this possibility is the linchpin of one contention pressed by petitioner and his *amici*. They assert that even assuming the truth of the observations we have made about juveniles' diminished culpability in general, jurors nonetheless should be allowed to consider mitigating arguments related to youth on a case-by-case basis, and in some cases to impose the death penalty if justified. A central feature of death penalty sentencing is a particular assessment of the circumstances of the crime and the characteristics of the offender. The system is designed to consider both aggravating and mitigating circumstances, including youth, in every case. Given this Court's own insistence on individualized consideration, petitioner maintains that it is both arbitrary and unnecessary to adopt a categorical rule barring imposition of the death penalty on any offender under 18 years of age.

We disagree. The differences between juvenile and adult offenders are too marked and well understood to risk allowing a youthful person to receive the death penalty despite insufficient culpability. An unacceptable likelihood exists that the brutality or cold-blooded nature of any particular crime would overpower mitigating arguments based on youth as a matter of course, even where the juvenile offender's objective immaturity, vulnerability, and lack of true depravity should require a sentence less severe than death. In some cases a defendant's youth may even be counted against him. In this very case, as we noted above, the prosecutor argued Simmons' youth was aggravating rather than mitigating. While this sort of overreaching could be corrected by a particular rule to ensure that the mitigating force of youth is not overlooked, that would not address our larger concerns.

It is difficult even for expert psychologists to differentiate between the juvenile offender whose crime reflects unfortunate yet transient immaturity, and the rare juvenile offender whose crime reflects irreparable corruption. As we understand it, this difficulty underlies the rule forbidding psychiatrists from diagnosing any patient under 18 as having antisocial personality disorder, a disorder also referred to as psychopathy or sociopathy, and which is characterized by callousness, cynicism, and contempt for the feelings, rights, and suffering of others. If trained psychiatrists with the advantage of clinical testing and observation refrain, despite diagnostic expertise, from assessing any juvenile under 18 as having antisocial personality disorder, we conclude that States should refrain from asking jurors to issue a far graver condemnation—that a juvenile offender merits the death penalty. When a juvenile offender commits a heinous crime, the State can exact forfeiture of some of the most basic liberties, but the State cannot extinguish his life and his potential to attain a mature understanding of his own humanity.

Drawing the line at 18 years of age is subject, of course, to the objections always raised against categorical rules. The qualities that distinguish juveniles from adults do not disappear when an individual turns 18. By the same token, some under 18 have already attained a level of maturity some adults will never reach. For the reasons we have discussed, however, a line must be drawn. The plurality opinion in *Thompson* drew the line at 16. In the intervening years the *Thompson* plurality's conclusion that offenders under 16 may not be executed has not been challenged. The logic of *Thompson* extends to those who are under 18. The age of 18 is the point where society draws the line for many purposes between childhood and adulthood. It is, we conclude, the age at which the line for death eligibility ought to rest. . . .

III

Our determination that the death penalty is disproportionate punishment for offenders under 18 finds confirmation in the stark reality that the United States is the only country in the world that continues to give official sanction to the juvenile death penalty. This reality does not become controlling, for the task of interpreting the Eighth Amendment remains our responsibility. Yet at least from the time of the Court's decision in *Trop*, the Court has referred to the laws of other countries and to international authorities as instructive for its interpretation of the Eighth Amendment's prohibition of "cruel and unusual punishments." . . .

As respondent and a number of *amici* emphasize, Article 37 of the United Nations Convention on the Rights of the Child, which every country in the world has ratified save for the United States and Somalia, contains an express prohibition on capital punishment for crimes committed by juveniles under 18. No ratifying country has entered a reservation to the provision prohibiting the execution of juvenile offenders. Parallel prohibitions are contained in other significant international covenants.

Respondent and his *amici* have submitted, and petitioner does not contest, that only seven countries other than the United States have executed juvenile offenders since 1990: Iran, Pakistan, Saudi Arabia, Yemen, Nigeria, the Democratic Republic of Congo, and China. Since then each of these countries has either abolished capital punishment for juveniles or made public disavowal of the practice. Brief for Respondent 49–50. In sum, it is fair to say that the United States now stands alone in a world that has turned its face against the juvenile death penalty.

Though the international covenants prohibiting the juvenile death penalty are of more recent date, it is instructive to note that the United Kingdom abolished the juvenile death penalty before these covenants came into being. The United Kingdom's experience bears particular relevance here in light of the historic ties between our countries and in light of the Eighth Amendment's own origins. The Amendment was modeled on a parallel provision in the English Declaration of Rights of 1689, which provided: "[E]xcessive Bail ought not to be required nor excessive Fines imposed; nor cruel and unusual Punishments inflicted." As of now, the United Kingdom has abolished the death penalty in its entirety; but, decades before it took this step, it recognized the disproportionate nature of the juvenile death penalty; and it abolished that penalty as a separate matter.

It is proper that we acknowledge the overwhelming weight of international opinion against the juvenile death penalty, resting in large part on the understanding that the instability and emotional imbalance of young people may often be a factor in the crime. The opinion of the world community, while not controlling our outcome, does provide respected and significant confirmation for our own conclusions.

Over time, from one generation to the next, the Constitution has come to earn the high respect and even, as Madison dared to hope, the veneration of the American people. The document sets forth, and rests upon, innovative principles original to the American experience, such as federalism; a proven balance in political mechanisms through separation of powers; specific guarantees for the accused in criminal cases; and broad provisions to secure individual freedom and preserve human dignity. These doctrines and guarantees are central to the American experience and remain essential to our present-day self-definition and national identity. Not the least of the reasons we honor the Constitution, then, is because we know it to be our own. It does not lessen our fidelity to the Constitution or our pride in its origins to acknowledge that the express affirmation of certain fundamental rights by other nations and peoples simply underscores the centrality of those same rights within our own heritage of freedom. . . .

Antonin E. Scalia  **NO**

Dissenting Opinion, *Roper v. Simmons*

J ustice Scalia, with whom the Chief Justice and Justice Thomas join, dissenting.

In urging approval of a Constitution that gave life-tenured judges the power to nullify laws enacted by the people's representatives, Alexander Hamilton assured the citizens of New York that there was little risk in this, since "[t]he judiciary . . . ha[s] neither FORCE nor WILL but merely judgment." But Hamilton had in mind a traditional judiciary, "bound down by strict rules and precedents which serve to define and point out their duty in every particular case that comes before them." Bound down, indeed. What a mockery today's opinion makes of Hamilton's expectation, announcing the Court's conclusion that the meaning of our Constitution has changed over the past 15 years—not, mind you, that this Court's decision 15 years ago was *wrong*, but that the Constitution *has changed*. The Court reaches this implausible result by purporting to advert, not to the original meaning of the Eighth Amendment, but to "the evolving standards of decency," of our national society. It then finds, on the flimsiest of grounds, that a national consensus which could not be perceived in our people's laws barely 15 years ago now solidly exists. Worse still, the Court says in so many words that what our people's laws say about the issue does not, in the last analysis, matter: "[I]n the end our own judgment will be brought to bear on the question of the acceptability of the death penalty under the Eighth Amendment." The Court thus proclaims itself sole arbiter of our Nation's moral standards—and in the course of discharging that awesome responsibility purports to take guidance from the views of foreign courts and legislatures. Because I do not believe that the meaning of our Eighth Amendment, any more than the meaning of other provisions of our Constitution, should be determined by the subjective views of five Members of this Court and like-minded foreigners, I dissent.

I

In determining that capital punishment of offenders who committed murder before age 18 is "cruel and unusual" under the Eighth Amendment, the Court first considers, in accordance with our modern (though in my view mistaken) jurisprudence, whether there is a "national consensus," that laws allowing such executions contravene our modern "standards of decency." We have held that this determination should be based on "objective indicia that reflect the

Supreme Court of the United States, March 1, 2005.

public attitude toward a given sanction"—namely, "statutes passed by society's elected representatives." As in *Atkins v. Virginia,* the Court dutifully recites this test and claims halfheartedly that a national consensus has emerged since our decision in *Stanford,* because 18 States—or 47% of States that permit capital punishment—now have legislation prohibiting the execution of offenders under 18, and because all of four States have adopted such legislation since *Stanford.*

Words have no meaning if the views of less than 50% of death penalty States can constitute a national consensus. Our previous cases have required overwhelming opposition to a challenged practice, generally over a long period of time. In *Coker v. Georgia,* a plurality concluded the Eighth Amendment prohibited capital punishment for rape of an adult woman where only one jurisdiction authorized such punishment. The plurality also observed that "[a]t no time in the last 50 years ha[d] a majority of States authorized death as a punishment for rape." In *Ford v. Wainwright,* we held execution of the insane unconstitutional, tracing the roots of this prohibition to the common law and noting that "no State in the union permits the execution of the insane." In *Enmund v. Florida,* we invalidated capital punishment imposed for participation in a robbery in which an accomplice committed murder, because 78% of all death penalty States prohibited this punishment. Even there we expressed some hesitation, because the legislative judgment was "neither 'wholly unanimous among state legislatures,' . . . nor as compelling as the legislative judgments considered in *Coker.*" By contrast, agreement among 42% of death penalty States in *Stanford,* which the Court appears to believe was correctly decided at the time, was insufficient to show a national consensus.

In an attempt to keep afloat its implausible assertion of national consensus, the Court throws overboard a proposition well established in our Eighth Amendment jurisprudence. "It should be observed," the Court says, "that the *Stanford* Court should have considered those States that had abandoned the death penalty altogether as part of the consensus against the juvenile death penalty . . .; a State's decision to bar the death penalty altogether of necessity demonstrates a judgment that the death penalty is inappropriate for all offenders, including juveniles." The insinuation that the Court's new method of counting contradicts only "the *Stanford* Court" is misleading. *None* of our cases dealing with an alleged constitutional limitation upon the death penalty has counted, as States supporting a consensus in favor of that limitation, States that have eliminated the death penalty entirely. And with good reason. Consulting States that bar the death penalty concerning the necessity of making an exception to the penalty for offenders under 18 is rather like including old-order Amishmen in a consumer-preference poll on the electric car. Of *course* they don't like it, but that sheds no light whatever on the point at issue. That 12 States favor *no* executions says something about consensus against the death penalty, but nothing—absolutely nothing—about consensus that offenders under 18 deserve special immunity from such a penalty. In repealing the death penalty, those 12 States considered *none* of the factors that the Court puts forth as determinative of the issue before us today—lower culpability of the young, inherent recklessness, lack of capacity for considered judgment, etc. What might be relevant, perhaps, is how many of those States permit 16- and 17-year-old offenders to be treated as adults with respect to noncapital offenses. (They all do; indeed, some even *require* that juveniles as young as 14 be tried as adults if they are charged with murder.) The attempt by the Court to turn its remarkable minority consensus into a faux majority by counting Amishmen is an act of nomological desperation.

Recognizing that its national-consensus argument was weak compared with our earlier cases, the *Atkins* Court found additional support in the fact that 16 States had prohibited execution of mentally retarded individuals since *Penry v. Lynaugh*. Indeed, the *Atkins* Court distinguished *Stanford* on that very ground, explaining that "[a]lthough we decided *Stanford* on the same day as *Penry*, apparently *only two* state legislatures have raised the threshold age for imposition of the death penalty." Now, the Court says a legislative change in four States is "significant" enough to trigger a constitutional prohibition. It is amazing to think that this subtle shift in numbers can take the issue entirely off the table for legislative debate.

I also doubt whether many of the legislators who voted to change the laws in those four States would have done so if they had known their decision would (by the pronouncement of this Court) be rendered irreversible. After all, legislative support for capital punishment, in any form, has surged and ebbed throughout our Nation's history. As Justice O'Connor has explained:

> "The history of the death penalty instructs that there is danger in inferring a settled societal consensus from statistics like those relied on in this case. In 1846, Michigan became the first State to abolish the death penalty. . . . In succeeding decades, other American States continued the trend towards abolition. . . . Later, and particularly after World War II, there ensued a steady and dramatic decline in executions. . . . In the 1950s and 1960s, more States abolished or radically restricted capital punishment, and executions ceased completely for several years beginning in 1968. . . .
>
> "In 1972, when this Court heard arguments on the constitutionality of the death penalty, such statistics might have suggested that the practice had become a relic, implicitly rejected by a new societal consensus. . . . We now know that any inference of a societal consensus rejecting the death penalty would have been mistaken. But had this Court then declared the existence of such a consensus, and outlawed capital punishment, legislatures would very likely not have been able to revive it. The mistaken premise of the decision would have been frozen into constitutional law, making it difficult to refute and even more difficult to reject."

Relying on such narrow margins is especially inappropriate in light of the fact that a number of legislatures and voters have expressly affirmed their support for capital punishment of 16- and 17-year-old offenders since *Stanford*. Though the Court is correct that no State has lowered its death penalty age, both the Missouri and Virginia Legislatures—which, at the time of *Stanford*, had no minimum age requirement—expressly established 16 as the minimum. The people of Arizona and Florida have done the same by ballot initiative. Thus, even States that have not executed an under-18 offender in recent years unquestionably favor the possibility of capital punishment in some circumstances.

The Court's reliance on the infrequency of executions, for under-18 murderers, credits an argument that this Court considered and explicitly rejected in *Stanford*. That infrequency is explained, we accurately said, both by "the undisputed fact that a far smaller percentage of capital crimes are committed by persons under 18 than over 18," and by the fact that juries are required at sentencing to consider the offender's youth as a mitigating factor. Thus, "it is not only possible, but overwhelmingly probable, that the very considerations which induce [respondent] and [his] supporters to believe that death should *never* be imposed on offenders under 18 cause prosecutors and juries to believe that it should *rarely* be imposed."

It is, furthermore, unclear that executions of the relevant age group have decreased since we decided *Stanford*. Between 1990 and 2003, 123 of 3,599 death sentences, or 3.4%, were given to individuals who committed crimes before reaching age 18. By contrast, only 2.1% of those sentenced to death between 1982 and 1988 committed the crimes when they were under 18. As for actual executions of under-18 offenders, they constituted 2.4% of the total executions since 1973. In *Stanford*, we noted that only 2% of the executions between 1642 and 1986 were of under-18 offenders and found that lower number did not demonstrate a national consensus against the penalty. Thus, the numbers of under-18 offenders subjected to the death penalty, though low compared with adults, have either held steady or slightly increased since *Stanford*. These statistics in no way support the action the Court takes today.

II

Of course, the real force driving today's decision is not the actions of four state legislatures, but the Court's "own judgment" that murderers younger than 18 can never be as morally culpable as older counterparts. The Court claims that this usurpation of the role of moral arbiter is simply a "retur[n] to the rul[e] established in decisions predating *Stanford*." That supposed rule—which is reflected solely in dicta and never once in a *holding* that purports to supplant the consensus of the American people with the justices' views—was repudiated in *Stanford* for the very good reason that it has no foundation in law or logic. If the Eighth Amendment set forth an ordinary rule of law, it would indeed be the role of this Court to say what the law is. But the Court having pronounced that the Eighth Amendment is an ever-changing reflection of "the evolving standards of decency" of our society, it makes no sense for the justices then to *prescribe* those standards rather than discern them from the practices of our people. On the evolving-standards hypothesis, the only legitimate function of this Court is to identify a moral consensus of the American people. By what conceivable warrant can nine lawyers presume to be the authoritative conscience of the Nation?

The reason for insistence on legislative primacy is obvious and fundamental: "'[I]n a democratic society legislatures, not courts, are constituted to respond to the will and consequently the moral values of the people.'" For a similar reason we have, in our determination of society's moral standards, consulted the practices of sentencing juries: Juries "'maintain a link between contemporary community values and the penal system'" that this Court cannot claim for itself.

Today's opinion provides a perfect example of why judges are ill equipped to make the type of legislative judgments the Court insists on making here. To support its opinion that States should be prohibited from imposing the death penalty on anyone who committed murder before age 18, the Court looks to scientific and sociological studies, picking and choosing those that support its position. It never explains why those particular studies are methodologically sound; none was ever entered into evidence or tested in an adversarial proceeding. As the Chief Justice has explained:

> "[M]ethodological and other errors can affect the reliability and validity of estimates about the opinions and attitudes of a population derived from various sampling techniques. Everything from variations in the survey methodology, such as the choice of the target population, the sampling design used, the questions asked, and the statistical analyses used to interpret the data can skew the results."

In other words, all the Court has done today, to borrow from another context, is to look over the heads of the crowd and pick out its friends.

We need not look far to find studies contradicting the Court's conclusions. As petitioner points out, the American Psychological Association (APA), which claims in this case that scientific evidence shows persons under 18 lack the ability to take moral responsibility for their decisions, has previously taken precisely the opposite position before this very Court. In its brief in *Hodgson v. Minnesota,* the APA found a "rich body of research" showing that juveniles are mature enough to decide whether to obtain an abortion without parental involvement. The APA brief, citing psychology treatises and studies too numerous to list here, asserted: "[B]y middle adolescence (age 14–15) young people develop abilities similar to adults in reasoning about moral dilemmas, understanding social rules and laws, [and] reasoning about interpersonal relationships and interpersonal problems." Given the nuances of scientific methodology and conflicting views, courts—which can only consider the limited evidence on the record before them—are ill equipped to determine which view of science is the right one. Legislatures "are better qualified to weigh and 'evaluate the results of statistical studies in terms of their own local conditions and with a flexibility of approach that is not available to the courts.'"

Even putting aside questions of methodology, the studies cited by the Court offer scant support for a categorical prohibition of the death penalty for murderers under 18. At most, these studies conclude that, *on average,* or *in most cases,* persons under 18 are unable to take moral responsibility for their actions. Not one of the cited studies opines that all individuals under 18 are unable to appreciate the nature of their crimes.

Moreover, the cited studies describe only adolescents who engage in risky or antisocial behavior, as many young people do. Murder, however, is more than just risky or antisocial behavior. It is entirely consistent to believe that young people often act impetuously and lack judgment, but, at the same time, to believe that those who commit premeditated murder are—at least sometimes—just as culpable as adults. Christopher Simmons, who was only seven months shy of his 18th birthday when he murdered Shirley Crook, described to his friends *beforehand*—"[i]n chilling, callous terms," as the Court puts it—the murder he planned to commit. He then broke into the home of an innocent woman, bound her with duct tape and electrical wire, and threw her off a bridge alive and conscious. In their *amici* brief, the States of Alabama, Delaware, Oklahoma, Texas, Utah, and Virginia offer additional examples of murders committed by individuals under 18 that involve truly monstrous acts. In Alabama, two 17-year-olds, one 16-year-old, and one 19-year-old picked up a female hitchhiker, threw bottles at her, and kicked and stomped her for approximately 30 minutes until she died. They then sexually assaulted her lifeless body and, when they were finished, threw her body off a cliff. They later returned to the crime scene to mutilate her corpse. Other examples in the brief are equally shocking. Though these cases are assuredly the exception rather than the rule, the studies the Court cites in no way justify a constitutional imperative that prevents legislatures and juries from treating exceptional cases in an exceptional way—by determining that some murders are not just the acts of happy-go-lucky teenagers, but heinous crimes deserving of death.

That "almost every State prohibits those under 18 years of age from voting, serving on juries, or marrying without parental consent," is patently irrelevant—and is yet another resurrection of an argument that this Court gave a decent burial in *Stanford*. (What kind of Equal Justice under Law is it that—without so much as a "Sorry about that"—gives as the basis for sparing one person from execution arguments *explicitly rejected* in refusing to spare another?) As we explained in *Stanford*, it is "absurd to think that one must be mature enough to drive carefully, to drink responsibly, or to vote intelligently, in order to be mature enough to understand that murdering another human being is profoundly wrong, and to conform one's conduct to that most minimal of all civilized standards." Serving on a jury or entering into marriage also involve decisions far more sophisticated than the simple decision not to take another's life.

Moreover, the age statutes the Court lists "set the appropriate ages for the operation of a system that makes its determinations in gross, and that does not conduct individualized maturity tests." The criminal justice system, by contrast, provides for individualized consideration of each defendant. In capital cases, this Court requires the sentencer to make an individualized determination, which includes weighing aggravating factors and mitigating factors, such as youth. In other contexts where individualized consideration is provided, we have recognized that at least some minors will be mature enough to make difficult decisions that involve moral considerations. For instance, we have struck down abortion statutes that do not allow minors deemed mature by courts to bypass parental notification provisions. It is hard to see why this context should be any different. Whether to obtain an abortion is surely a much more complex decision for a young person than whether to kill an innocent person in cold blood.

The Court concludes, however, that juries cannot be trusted with the delicate task of weighing a defendant's youth along with the other mitigating and aggravating factors of his crime. This startling conclusion undermines the very foundations of our capital sentencing system, which entrusts juries with "mak[ing] the difficult and uniquely human judgments that defy codification and that 'buil[d] discretion, equity, and flexibility into a legal system.'" The Court says that juries will be unable to appreciate the significance of a defendant's youth when faced with details of a brutal crime. This assertion is based on no evidence; to the contrary, the Court itself acknowledges that the execution of under-18 offenders is "infrequent" even in the States "without a formal prohibition on executing juveniles," suggesting that juries take seriously their responsibility to weigh youth as a mitigating factor.

Nor does the Court suggest a stopping point for its reasoning. If juries cannot make appropriate determinations in cases involving murderers under 18, in what other kinds of cases will the Court find jurors deficient? We have already held that no jury may consider whether a mentally deficient defendant can receive the death penalty, irrespective of his crime. Why not take other mitigating factors, such as considerations of childhood abuse or poverty, away from juries as well? Surely jurors "overpower[ed]" by "the brutality or cold-blooded nature" of a crime, could not adequately weigh these mitigating factors either.

The Court's contention that the goals of retribution and deterrence are not served by executing murderers under 18 is also transparently false. The argument that "[r]etribution is not proportional if the law's most severe penalty is imposed on one whose culpability or blameworthiness is diminished," is simply an extension of the earlier, false generalization that youth *always* defeats culpability. The Court claims that "juveniles will be less susceptible to deterrence," because "'[t]he likelihood that the teenage offender has made the kind of cost-benefit analysis that attaches any weight to the possibility of execution is so remote as to be virtually nonexistent.'" The Court unsurprisingly finds no support for this astounding proposition, save its own case law. The facts of this very case show the proposition to be false. Before committing the crime, Simmons encouraged his friends to join him by assuring them that they could "get away with it" because they were minors. This fact may have influenced the jury's decision to impose capital punishment despite Simmons' age. Because the Court refuses to entertain the possibility that its own unsubstantiated generalization about juveniles could be wrong, it ignores this evidence entirely.

III

Though the views of our own citizens are essentially irrelevant to the Court's decision today, the views of other countries and the so-called international community take center stage.

The Court begins by noting that "Article 37 of the United Nations Convention on the Rights of the Child, which every country in the world has ratified *save for the United States* and Somalia, contains an express prohibition on capital punishment for crimes committed by juveniles under 18." . . .

Unless the Court has added to its arsenal the power to join and ratify treaties on behalf of the United States, I cannot see how this evidence favors, rather than refutes, its position. That the Senate and the President—those actors our Constitution empowers to enter into treaties, see Art. II, § 2—have declined to join and ratify treaties prohibiting execution of under-18 offenders can only suggest that *our country* has either not reached a national consensus on the question, or has reached a consensus contrary to what the Court announces. That the reservation to the ICCPR was made in 1992 does not suggest otherwise, since the reservation still remains in place today. It is also worth noting that, in addition to barring the execution of under-18 offenders, the United Nations Convention on the Rights of the Child prohibits punishing them with life in prison without the possibility of release. If we are truly going to get in line with the international community, then the Court's reassurance that the death penalty is really not needed, since "the punishment of life imprisonment without the possibility of parole is itself a severe sanction," gives little comfort.

It is interesting that whereas the Court is not content to accept what the States of our Federal Union *say*, but insists on inquiring into what they *do* (specifically, whether they in fact *apply* the juvenile death penalty that their laws allow), the Court is quite willing to believe that every foreign nation—of whatever tyrannical political makeup and with however subservient or incompetent a court system—in fact *adheres* to a rule of no death penalty for offenders under 18. Nor does the Court inquire into how many of the countries that have the death penalty, but have forsworn (on paper at least) imposing that penalty on offenders under 18, have what no State of this country can constitutionally have: a *mandatory* death penalty for certain crimes, with no possibility of mitigation by the sentencing authority, for youth or any other reason. I suspect it is most of them. To forbid the death penalty for juveniles under such a system may be a good idea, but it says nothing about our system, in which the sentencing authority, typically a jury, always can, and almost always does, withhold the death penalty from an under-18 offender except, after considering all the circumstances, in the rare cases where it is warranted. The foreign authorities, in other words, do not even speak to the issue before us here.

More fundamentally, however, the basic premise of the Court's argument—that American law should conform to the laws of the rest of the world—ought to be rejected out of hand. In fact the Court itself does not believe it. In many significant respects the laws of most other countries differ from our law—including not only such explicit provisions of our Constitution as the right to jury trial and grand jury indictment, but even many interpretations of the Constitution prescribed by this Court itself. . . .

The Court has been oblivious to the views of other countries when deciding how to interpret our Constitution's requirement that "Congress shall make no law respecting an establishment of religion. . . ." Most other countries—including those committed to religious neutrality—do not insist on the degree of separation between church and state that this Court requires. . . .

And let us not forget the Court's abortion jurisprudence, which makes us one of only six countries that allow abortion on demand until the point of viability. . . .

The Court's special reliance on the laws of the United Kingdom is perhaps the most indefensible part of its opinion. It is of course true that we share a common history with the United Kingdom, and that we often consult English sources when asked to discern the meaning of a constitutional text written against the backdrop of 18th-century English law and legal thought. If we applied that approach today, our task would be an easy one. . . . It is beyond comprehension why we should look, for that purpose, to a country that has developed, in the centuries since the Revolutionary War—and with increasing speed since the United Kingdom's recent submission to the jurisprudence of European courts dominated by continental jurists—a legal, political, and social culture quite different from our own. If we took the Court's directive seriously, we would also consider relaxing our double jeopardy prohibition, since the British Law Commission recently published a report that would significantly extend the rights of the prosecution to appeal cases where an acquittal was the result of a judge's ruling that was legally incorrect. . . .

The Court should either profess its willingness to reconsider all these matters in light of the views of foreigners, or else it should cease putting forth foreigners' views as part of the *reasoned basis* of its decisions. To invoke alien law when it agrees with one's own thinking, and ignore it otherwise, is not reasoned decisionmaking, but sophistry.

The Court responds that "[i]t does not lessen our fidelity to the Constitution or our pride in its origins to acknowledge that the express affirmation of certain fundamental rights by other nations and peoples simply underscores the centrality of those same rights within our own heritage of freedom." To begin with, I do not believe that approval by "other nations and peoples" should buttress our commitment to American principles any more than (what should logically follow) disapproval by "other nations and peoples" should weaken that commitment. More importantly, however, the Court's statement flatly misdescribes what is going on here. Foreign sources are cited today, *not* to underscore our "fidelity" to the Constitution, our "pride in its origins," and "our own [American] heritage." To the contrary, they are cited *to set aside* the centuries-old American practice—a practice still engaged in by a large majority of the relevant States—of letting a jury of 12 citizens decide whether, in the particular case, youth should be the basis for withholding the death penalty. What these foreign sources "affirm," rather than repudiate, is the justices' own notion of how the world ought to be, and their diktat that it shall be so henceforth in America. The Court's parting attempt to downplay the significance of its extensive discussion of foreign law is unconvincing. "Acknowledgment" of foreign approval has no place in the legal opinion of this Court *unless it is part of the basis for the Court's judgment*—which is surely what it parades as today.

IV

To add insult to injury, the Court affirms the Missouri Supreme Court without even admonishing that court for its flagrant disregard of our precedent in *Stanford*. Until today, we have always held that "it is this Court's prerogative alone to overrule one of its precedents." That has been true even where "'changes in judicial doctrine' ha[ve] significantly undermined" our prior holding, and even where our prior holding "appears to rest on reasons rejected in some other line of decisions." Today, however, the Court silently approves a state-court decision that blatantly rejected controlling precedent.

One must admit that the Missouri Supreme Court's action, and this Court's indulgent reaction, are, in a way, understandable. In a system based upon constitutional and statutory text democratically adopted, the concept of "law" ordinarily signifies that particular words have a fixed meaning. Such law does not change, and this Court's pronouncement of it therefore remains authoritative until (confessing our prior error) we overrule. The Court has purported to make of the Eighth Amendment, however, a mirror of the passing and changing sentiment of American society regarding penology. The lower courts can look into that mirror as well as we can; and what we saw 15 years ago bears no necessary relationship to what they see today. Since they are not looking at the same text, but at a different scene, why should our earlier decision control their judgment?

However sound philosophically, this is no way to run a legal system. We must disregard the new reality that, to the extent our Eighth Amendment decisions constitute something more than a show of hands on the current justices' current personal views about penology, they purport to be nothing more than a snapshot of American public opinion at a particular point in time (with the timeframes now shortened to a mere 15 years). We must treat these decisions just as though they represented *real* law, *real* prescriptions democratically adopted by the American people, as conclusively (rather than sequentially) construed by this Court. Allowing lower courts to reinterpret the Eighth Amendment whenever they decide enough time has passed for a new snapshot leaves this Court's decisions without any force—especially since the "evolution" of our Eighth Amendment is no longer determined by objective criteria. To allow lower courts to behave as we do, "updating" the Eighth Amendment as needed, destroys stability and makes our case law an unreliable basis for the designing of laws by citizens and their representatives, and for action by public officials. The result will be to crown arbitrariness with chaos.

POSTSCRIPT

Is the Death Penalty an Unconstitutional Punishment for Juvenile Offenders?

The opinion poll results we examined in the introduction to this issue provided some very interesting information. First, support for the death penalty when the alternative of sentencing someone to a life term in prison without the possibility of parole was provided was equivocal—as many Americans supported the imprisonment option as favored the death penalty. Second, only a small number of Americans support using the death penalty for criminals who committed their crimes as juveniles. This would seem to support Justice Anthony M. Kennedy's position that the "evolving standards of decency that mark the progress of a maturing society" would counsel against imposition of the death penalty for juveniles.

Moreover, the United States was the only Western nation that still permitted individuals to be executed for the crimes they committed as juveniles. Although this factor did not appear to be the sole motivation for the Court's decision in *Roper v. Simmons,* that fact did seem to influence some of the justices. Justice Kennedy noted this fact:

> Article 37 of the United Nations Convention on the Rights of the Child, which every country in the world has ratified save for the United States and Somalia, contains an express prohibition on capital punishment for crimes committed by juveniles under 18. . . . [O]nly seven countries other than the United States have executed juvenile offenders since 1990: Iran, Pakistan, Saudi Arabia, Yemen, Nigeria, the Democratic Republic of Congo, and China. Since then each of these countries has either abolished capital punishment for juveniles or made public disavowal of the practice.

Do you think that the justice system policies of other nations should influence penal practices in the United States? If the United States is out of step with the world community, should we not search consciences to determine if we have made a serious mistake?

Another significant issue surrounding the use of capital punishment that has become prominent in recent years is the fact that our justice system has made mistakes in the past. A 2002 study conducted by Columbia Law School Professor James Liebman concluded that "aggressive death sentencing is a magnet for serious error." Liebman's study, which tried to answer the question of why so many mistakes happen in death penalty cases, found that 68 percent of all death verdicts reviewed from 1973 to 1995 were reversed by courts.

Of these reversals, 82 percent resulted in less severe sentences, and 9 percent of these individuals were found not guilty. Moreover, Liebman observes that since the death penalty was reinstituted in the United States in 1973, 99 death row inmates have been found innocent and released.

These data indicate that our justice system makes mistakes. If a convicted offender is sentenced to prison and it later becomes clear that he or she did not commit the crime, society can release the individual and provide appropriate compensation. If we have executed the accused, however, there is no way to rectify the mistake. The finality of the death penalty thus makes it unlike any other type of sentence in our justice system. This fact may make this punishment even more questionable in cases involving juvenile offenders.

There are many additional resources that shed light on the issues considered in this section. See: Mary Ann Mason, "The U.S. and the International Children's Rights Crusade: Leader or Laggard," *Journal of Social History*, vol. 38, no. 4 (2005); Robert H. Bork, "Travesty Time, Again," *National Review*, vol. 57, no. 5 (2005); Kenneth Anderson, "Foreign Law and the U.S. Constitution," *Policy Review*, vol. 131 (2005); Jeffrey Fagan and Valerie West, "The Decline of the Juvenile Death Penalty: Scientific Evidence of Evolving Norms," *Journal of Criminal Law & Criminology*, vol. 95, no. 2 (2005); James Liebman, Andrew Gelman, Alexander Kiss, and Valerie West, "A Broken System: The Persistent Pattern of Reversals of Death Penalty Cases," *Journal of Empirical Legal Studies*, vol. 1, no. 209 (2004); James D. Unnever and Francis Cullen, "Executing the Innocent and Support for Capital Punishment: Implications for Public Policy," *Criminology & Public Policy*, vol. 4, no. 1 (2005); Lucy C. Ferguson, "The Implications of Developmental Cognitive Research on 'Evolving Standards of Decency' and the Imposition of the Death Penalty on Juveniles," *American University Law Review*, vol. 54, no. 2 (2004); Donna M. Bishop, "Injustice and Irrationality in Contemporary Youth Policy," *Criminology & Public Policy*, vol. 3, no. 4 (2004); Scott Vollum, Dennis R. Longmire, and Jacqueline Buffinton-Vollum, "Confidence in the Death Penalty and Support for Its Use: Exploring the Value-Expressive Dimension of Death Penalty Attitudes," *Justice Quarterly*, vol. 21, no. 3 (2004); and Michael E. Antonio, Benjamin D. Fleury-Steiner, Valerie P. Hans, and William J. Bowers, "Capital Jurors as the Litmus Test of Community Conscience for the Juvenile Death Penalty," *Judicature*, vol. 87, no. 6 (2004).

ISSUE 19

Does Confining Sex Offenders Indefinitely in Mental Hospitals After They Have Served Their Prison Sentences Violate the Constitution?

YES: Stephen Breyer, from "Dissenting Opinion," *Kansas v. Hendricks,* U.S. Supreme Court (1997)

NO: Clarence Thomas, from "Opinion," *Kansas v. Hendricks,* U.S. Supreme Court (1997)

ISSUE SUMMARY

YES: Associate Justice Stephen Breyer asserts that if a state's law attempts to inflict additional punishment on an offender after he has served a prison sentence, it will violate the federal Constitution.

NO: Associate Justice Clarence Thomas, writing for the Court, contends that post-imprisonment civil confinement laws do not violate the Constitution.

Imagine for a moment that you are a criminal who has been sentenced to a term of incarceration in a state prison and that you have almost completed your sentence. One month before you are to be released, you learn that the state alleges that you pose a continuing threat to society and will initiate a civil commitment proceeding designed to confine you indefinitely in a state mental hospital. How would you react? Would you attempt to challenge the state's authority to keep you confined beyond your original prison term? Which legal theories would you use?

One possible legal theory is that the potential commitment is a violation of the Fifth Amendment's double jeopardy clause. The Supreme Court has held that the double jeopardy protection extends not only to two trials for the same offense but also to two punishments for the same crime. Would it seem like a "slam dunk" argument that a mandatory confinement in a mental institution after someone has served their full prison sentence for the same crime violates the double jeopardy clause? Don't bet on it.

Kansas v. Hendricks, 521 U.S. 346 (1997) presented similar facts. Shortly before he was to be released from a Kansas prison to a halfway house from his sentence for taking indecent liberties with two adolescents, Hendricks was found by a jury to be a sexually violent predator. During the trial, he agreed with the state physician's diagnosis that he suffered from pedophilia. The trial judge ordered Hendricks, under the Kansas Sexually Violent Predator Act, committed to a mental institution for an indefinite period, although the continuing necessity of his confinement was subject to an annual review by the Court. On appeal, the Kansas Supreme Court held that the commitment violated Hendricks' Fourteenth Amendment due process rights.

The Court also held that a confinement in a state mental institution after the completion of an offender's original prison sentence does not violate the Fifth Amendment's double jeopardy clause because that provision prohibits only a second *punishment* for the same offense. Stated Thomas: "The State may take measures to restrict the freedom of the dangerously mentally ill. This is a legitimate nonpunitive governmental objective and has been historically so regarded."

Are you persuaded by the Court's reasoning? Justice Thomas contends that Hendricks' indefinite incarceration, after he had completed his state prison sentence for the *same offenses,* did not violate the double jeopardy clause. As a number of commentators have pointed out, the line between punishment and indefinite commitment to a mental institution may be a difficult one to identify.

Justice Stephen Breyer's dissenting opinion disagrees with the majority's holding that Hendricks' later confinement in a state mental institution did not constitute punishment. Stated Justice Breyer: "The statutory provisions before us do amount to punishment primarily because, as I have said, the legislature did not tailor the statute to fit the nonpunitive civil aim of treatment, which it concedes exists in Hendricks' case."

What is your view of this issue? Is it fundamentally fair to apply to a convict a statute passed after they had committed their offense? Moreover, does society have a right to protect itself from dangerous sexual predators by keeping them confined? The available evidence in this area suggests that many pedophiles have long careers involving numerous child-victims. Must we wait for someone like Hendricks to commit another pedophilic incident before we can incapacitate him? These difficult issues may be the real foundation of this decision. It is sometimes said that "hard cases make bad law." This may be a case where we like the results of the decision, even though the legal reasoning supporting the decision is less than completely persuasive. As a member of the U.S. Supreme Court, how would you decide this case?

YES

Stephen Breyer

Dissenting Opinion

I agree with the majority that the Kansas Act's "definition of 'mental abnormality" satisfies the "substantive" requirements of the Due Process Clause. Kansas, however, concedes that Hendricks' condition is treatable; yet the Act did not provide Hendricks (or others like him) with any treatment until after his release date from prison and only inadequate treatment thereafter. These, and certain other special features of the Act convince me that it was not simply an effort to commit Hendricks civilly, but rather an effort to inflict further punishment upon him. The *Ex Post Facto* Clause therefore prohibits the Act's application to Hendricks, who committed his crimes prior to its enactment.

I

I begin with the area of agreement. This Court has held that the civil commitment of a "mentally ill" and "dangerous" person does not automatically violate the Due Process Clause provided that the commitment takes place pursuant to proper procedures and evidentiary standards. The Kansas Supreme Court, however, held that the Due Process Clause forbids application of the Act to Hendricks for "substantive" reasons, *i.e.*, irrespective of the procedures or evidentiary standards used. The Court reasoned that Kansas had not satisfied the "mentally ill" requirement of the Due Process Clause because Hendricks was not "mentally ill." Moreover, Kansas had not satisfied what the Court believed was an additional "substantive due process" requirement, namely the provision of treatment. I shall consider each of these matters briefly.

A

In my view, the Due Process Clause permits Kansas to classify Hendricks as a mentally ill and dangerous person for civil commitment purposes. I agree with the majority that the Constitution gives States a degree of leeway in making this kind of determination. But, because I do not subscribe to all of its reasoning, I shall set forth three sets of circumstances that, taken together, convince me that Kansas has acted within the limits that the Due Process Clause substantively sets.

First, the psychiatric profession itself classifies the kind of problem from which Hendricks suffers as a serious mental disorder. But the very presence and vigor of this debate is important. The Constitution permits a State to follow one reasonable professional view, while rejecting another. The psychiatric debate, therefore, helps to inform the law by setting the bounds of what is

Supreme Court of the United States, 521 U.S. 346, 1997.

reasonable, but it cannot here decide just how States must write their laws within those bounds.

Second, Hendricks' abnormality does not consist simply of a long course of antisocial behavior, but rather it includes a specific, serious, and highly unusual inability to control his actions. (For example, Hendricks testified that, when he gets "stressed out," he cannot "control the urge" to molest children.) The law traditionally has considered this kind of abnormality akin to insanity for purposes of confinement. Indeed, the notion of an "irresistible impulse" often has helped to shape criminal law's insanity defense and to inform the related recommendations of legal experts as they seek to translate the insights of mental health professionals into workable legal rules.

Third, Hendricks' mental abnormality also makes him dangerous. Hendricks "has been convicted of . . . a sexually violent offense," and a jury found that he "suffers from a mental abnormality . . . which makes" him "likely to engage" in similar "acts of sexual violence" in the future. The evidence at trial favored the State. Dr. Befort, for example, explained why Hendricks was likely to commit further acts of sexual violence if released. And Hendricks' own testimony about what happens when he gets "stressed out" confirmed Dr. Befort's diagnosis.

Because (1) many mental health professionals consider pedophilia a serious mental disorder; and (2) Hendricks suffers from a classic case of irresistible impulse, namely he is so afflicted with pedophilia that he cannot "control the urge" to molest children; and (3) his pedophilia presents a serious danger to those children; I believe that Kansas can classify Hendricks as "mentally ill" and "dangerous" as this Court used those terms in *Foucha*.

The Kansas Supreme Court's contrary conclusion rested primarily upon that Court's view that Hendricks would not qualify for civil commitment under Kansas own state civil commitment statute. The issue before us, however, is one of constitutional interpretation. The Constitution does not require Kansas to write all of its civil commitment rules in a single statute or forbid it to write two separate statutes each covering somewhat different classes of committable individuals. Moreover, Hendricks apparently falls outside the scope of the Kansas general civil commitment statute because that statute permits confinement only of those who "lack capacity to make an informed decision concerning treatment." The statute does not tell us why it imposes this requirement. Capacity to make an informed decision about treatment is not always or obviously incompatible with severe mental illness. Neither Hendricks nor his *amici* point to a uniform body of professional opinion that says as much, and we have not found any. Consequently, the boundaries of the federal Constitution and those of Kansas' general civil commitment statute are not congruent.

B

The Kansas Supreme Court also held that the Due Process Clause requires a State to provide treatment to those whom it civilly confines (as "mentally ill" and "dangerous"). It found that Kansas did not provide Hendricks with significant treatment. And it concluded that Hendricks' confinement violated the Due Process Clause for this reason as well.

This case does not require us to consider whether the Due Process Clause *always* requires treatment—whether, for example, it would forbid civil confinement of an *untreatable* mentally ill, dangerous person. To the contrary, Kansas argues that pedophilia is an "abnormality" or "illness" that can be treated. Two groups of mental health professionals agree. Indeed, no one argues the contrary. Hence the legal question before us is whether the Clause forbids Hendricks' confinement unless Kansas provides him with treatment *that it concedes is available.*

Nor does anyone argue that Kansas somehow could have violated the Due Process Clause's *treatment* concerns had it provided Hendricks with the treatment that is potentially available (and I do not see how any such argument could succeed). Rather, the basic substantive due process treatment question is whether that Clause requires Kansas to provide treatment that it concedes is potentially available to a person whom it concedes is treatable. This same question is at the heart of my discussion of whether Hendricks' confinement violates the Constitution's *Ex Post Facto* Clause. For that reason, I shall not consider the substantive due process treatment question separately, but instead shall simply turn to the *Ex Post Facto* Clause discussion.

II

Kansas' 1994 Act violates the Federal Constitution's prohibition of "any . . . *ex post facto* Law" if it "inflicts" upon Hendricks "a greater punishment" than did the law "annexed to" his "crimes" when he "committed" those crimes in 1984. The majority agrees that the Clause "forbids the application of any *new punitive measure* to a crime already consummated." But it finds the Act is not "punitive." With respect to that basic question, I disagree with the majority.

Certain resemblances between the Act's "civil commitment" and traditional criminal punishments are obvious. Like criminal imprisonment, the Act's civil commitment amounts to "secure" confinement, and "incarceration against one's will." In addition, a basic objective of the Act is incapacitation, which, as Blackstone said in describing an objective of criminal law, is to "deprive the party injuring of the power to do future mischief."

Moreover, the Act, like criminal punishment, imposes its confinement (or sanction) only upon an individual who has previously committed a criminal offense. And the Act imposes that confinement through the use of persons (county prosecutors), procedural guarantees (trial by jury, assistance of counsel, psychiatric evaluations), and standards ("beyond a reasonable doubt") traditionally associated with the criminal law.

These obvious resemblances by themselves, however, are not legally sufficient to transform what the Act calls "civil commitment" into a criminal punishment. Civil commitment of dangerous, mentally ill individuals by its very nature involves confinement and incapacitation. Yet "civil commitment," from a constitutional perspective, nonetheless remains civil. Nor does the fact that criminal behavior triggers the Act make the critical difference. The Act's insistence upon a prior crime, by screening out those whose past behavior does not concretely demonstrate the existence of a mental problem or potential future danger, may serve an important noncriminal evidentiary purpose. Neither is the presence of criminal law-type procedures determinative. Those procedures can serve an important purpose that in this context one might consider noncriminal, namely helping to prevent judgmental mistakes that would wrongly deprive a person of important liberty.

If these obvious similarities cannot by themselves prove that Kansas' "civil commitment" statute is criminal, neither can the word "civil" written into the statute, by itself prove the contrary. This Court has said that only the "clearest proof" could establish that a law the legislature called "civil," was, in reality a "punitive" measure. But the Court has also reiterated that a "civil label is not always dispositive"; it has said that in close cases the label is "not of paramount importance"; and it has looked behind a "civil" label fairly often.

In this circumstance, with important features of the Act pointing in opposite directions, I would place particular importance upon those features that would likely distinguish between a basically punitive and a basically non-punitive purpose. And I note that the Court, in an earlier civil commitment case, looked primarily to the law's concern for treatment as an important distinguishing feature. I do not believe that *Allen* means that a particular law's lack of concern for treatment, by itself, is enough to make an incapacitative law punitive. But, for reasons I will point out, when a State believes that treatment does exist, and then couples that admission with a legislatively required delay of such treatment until a person is at the end of his jail term (so that further incapacitation is therefore necessary), such a legislative scheme begins to look punitive.

In *Allen*, the Court considered whether, for Fifth Amendment purposes, proceedings under an Illinois statute were civil or "criminal." The Illinois statute, rather like the Kansas statute here, authorized the confinement of persons who were sexually dangerous, who had committed at least one prior sexual assault, and who suffered from a "mental disorder." The *Allen* Court, looking behind the statute's "civil commitment" label, found the statute civil—in important part because the State had "provided for the treatment of those it commits" (also referring to facts that the State had "disavowed any interest in punishment" and that it had "established a system under which committed persons may be released after the briefest time in confinement").

In reaching this conclusion, the Court noted that the State Supreme Court had found the proceedings "essentially civil" because the statute's aim was to provide "treatment, not punishment." It observed that the State had "a statutory obligation to provide 'care and treatment . . . designed to effect recovery" in a "facility set aside to provide psychiatric care." And it referred to the State's purpose as one of "*treating* rather than punishing sexually dangerous persons."

The *Allen* Court's focus upon treatment, as a kind of touchstone helping to distinguish civil from punitive purposes, is not surprising, for one would expect a nonpunitive statutory scheme to confine, not simply in order to protect, but also in order to cure. That is to say, one would expect a nonpunitively motivated legislature that confines *because of* a dangerous mental abnormality to seek to help the individual himself overcome that abnormality (at least insofar as professional treatment for the abnormality exists and is potentially helpful, as Kansas, supported by some groups of mental health professionals, argues is the case here). Conversely, a statutory scheme that provides confinement that does not reasonably fit a practically available, medically oriented treatment objective, more likely reflects a primarily punitive legislative purpose.

Several important treatment-related factors—factors of a kind that led the five-member *Allen* majority to conclude that the Illinois' legislature's purpose was primarily civil, not punitive—in this case suggest precisely the opposite. First, the State Supreme Court here, unlike the state Court in *Allen,* has held that treatment is not a significant objective of the Act. The Kansas Court wrote that the Act's purpose is "segregation of sexually violent offenders," with "treatment" a matter that was "incidental at best." By way of contrast, in *Allen* the Illinois Court had written that "treatment, not punishment" was "the aim of the statute."

We have generally given considerable weight to the findings of state and lower federal Courts regarding the intent or purpose underlying state officials' actions, although the level of deference given to such findings varies with the circumstances, and is not always as conclusive as a state Court's construction of one of its statutes. For example, *Allen*'s dissenters, as well as its majority, considered the state Court's characterization of the state law's purpose an important factor in determining the constitutionality of that statute.

The record provides support for the Kansas Court's conclusion. The Court found that, as of the time of Hendricks' commitment, the State had not funded treatment, it had not entered into treatment contracts, and it had little, if any, qualified treatment staff. Indeed, were we to follow the majority's invitation to look beyond the record in this case, an invitation with which we disagree, it would reveal that Hendricks, according to the commitment program's own director, was receiving "essentially no treatment."

It is therefore not surprising that some of the Act's official supporters had seen in it an opportunity permanently to confine dangerous sex offenders. Others thought that effective treatment did not exist—a view, by the way, that the State of Kansas, supported by groups of informed mental health professionals, here strongly denies.

The Kansas Court acknowledged the existence of "provisions of the Act for treatment" (although it called them "somewhat disingenuous"). Nor did the Court deny that Kansas could later increase the amount of treatment it provided. But the Kansas Supreme Court could, and did, use the Act's language, history, and initial implementation to help it characterize the Act's primary purposes.

Second, the Kansas statute insofar as it applies to previously convicted offenders, such as Hendricks, commits, confines, and treats those offenders *after* they have served virtually their entire criminal sentence. That time-related circumstance seems deliberate. The Act explicitly defers diagnosis, evaluation, and commitment proceedings until a few weeks prior to the "anticipated release" of a previously convicted offender from prison. But why, one might ask, does the Act not commit and require treatment of sex offenders sooner, say soon after they begin to serve their sentences?

An Act that simply seeks confinement, of course, would not need to begin civil commitment proceedings sooner. Such an Act would have to begin proceedings only when an offender's prison term ends, threatening his release from the confinement that imprisonment assures. But it is difficult to see why rational legislators who seek treatment would write the Act in this way—providing treatment years after the criminal act that indicated its necessity. And it is particularly difficult to see why legislators who specifically wrote into the statute a finding that "prognosis for rehabilitating . . . in a prison setting is poor" would leave an offender in that setting for months or years before beginning treatment. This is to say, the timing provisions of the statute confirm the Kansas Supreme Court's view that treatment was not a particularly important legislative objective.

I recognize one possible counter-argument. A State, wanting both to punish Hendricks (say, for deterrence purposes) and also to treat him, might argue that it should be permitted to postpone treatment until after punishment in order to make certain that the punishment in fact occurs. But any such reasoning is out of place here. Much of the treatment that Kansas offered here (called "ward milieu" and "group therapy") can be given at the same time as, and in the same place where, Hendricks serves his punishment. The evidence adduced at the state habeas proceeding, were we to assume it properly before the Court, see *infra,* at 20–21, supports this conclusion as well. Hence, assuming arguendo that it would be otherwise permissible, Kansas need not postpone treatment in order to make certain that sex offenders serve their full terms of imprisonment, *i.e.,* to make certain that they receive the entire punishment that Kansas criminal law provides. To the contrary, the statement in the Act itself, that the Act aims to respond to special "long term" "treatment needs," suggests that treatment should begin during imprisonment. It also suggests that, were those long-term treatment needs (rather than further punishment) Kansas' primary aim, the State would require that treatment begin soon after conviction, not 10 or more years later.

Third, the statute, at least as of the time Kansas applied it to Hendricks, did not require the committing authority to consider the possibility of using less restrictive alternatives, such as postrelease supervision, halfway houses, or other methods that *amici* supporting Kansas here have mentioned. The laws of many other States require such consideration. This Court has said that a failure to consider, or to use, "alternative and less harsh methods" to achieve a nonpunitive objective can help to show that legislature's "purpose . . . was to punish." And one can draw a similar conclusion here. Legislation that seeks to help the individual offender as well as to protect the public would avoid significantly greater restriction of an individual's liberty than public safety requires. Legislation that seeks almost exclusively to incapacitate the individual through confinement, however, would not necessarily concern itself with potentially less restrictive forms of incapacitation. I would reemphasize that this is not a case in which the State claims there is no treatment potentially available. Rather, Kansas and supporting *amici* argue that pedophilia is treatable.

Fourth, the laws of other States confirm, through comparison, that Kansas' "civil commitment" objectives do not require the statutory features that indicate a punitive purpose. I have found 17 States with laws that seek to protect the public from mentally abnormal, sexually dangerous individuals through civil commitment or other mandatory treatment programs. Ten of those statutes, unlike the Kansas statute, begin treatment of an offender soon after he has been apprehended and charged with a serious sex offense. Only seven, like Kansas, delay "civil" commitment (and treatment) until the offender has served his criminal sentence (and this figure includes the Acts of Minnesota and New Jersey, both of which generally do not delay treatment). Of these seven, however, six (unlike Kansas) require consideration of less restrictive alternatives. Only one State other than Kansas, namely Iowa, both delay civil commitment (and consequent treatment) and do not explicitly consider less restrictive alternatives. But the law of that State applies prospectively only, thereby avoiding *ex post facto* problems. Thus the practical experience of other States, as revealed by their statutes, confirms what the Kansas Supreme Court's finding, the timing of the civil commitment proceeding, and the failure to consider less restrictive alternatives, themselves suggest, namely, that for *Ex Post Facto* Clause purposes, the purpose of the Kansas Act (as applied to previously convicted offenders) has a punitive, rather than a purely civil, purpose.

Kansas points to several cases as support for a contrary conclusion. It points to *Allen*—which is, as we have seen, a case in which the Court concluded that Illinois' "civil commitment" proceedings were not criminal. I have explained in detail, however, how the statute here differs from that in *Allen,* and why *Allen's* reasoning leads to a different conclusion in this litigation.

Kansas also points to *Addington v. Texas,* where the Court held that the Constitution does not require application of criminal law's "beyond a reasonable doubt" standard in a civil commitment proceeding. Nothing I say here would change the reach or holding of *Addington* in any way. That is, a State is free to commit those who are dangerous and mentally ill in order to treat them. Nor does my decision preclude a State from deciding that a certain subset of people are mentally ill, dangerous, and untreatable, and that confinement of this subset is therefore necessary (again, assuming that all the procedural safeguards of *Addington* are in place). But when a State decides offenders can be treated and confines an offender to provide that treatment, but then refuses to provide it, the refusal to treat while a person is fully incapacitated begins to look punitive.

The majority suggests that this is the very case I say it is not, namely a case of a mentally ill person who is *untreatable.* And it quotes a long excerpt from the Kansas Supreme Court's opinion in support. That Court, however, did not find that Hendricks was untreat*able*; it found that he was untreat*ed*—quite a different matter. Had the Kansas Supreme Court thought that Hendricks, or others like him, are untreatable, it could not have written the words that follow that excerpt, adopting by reference the words of another Court opinion:

> "The statute forecloses the possibility that offenders will be evaluated and treated until after they have been punished. . . . Setting aside the question of whether a prison term exacerbates or minimizes the mental condition of a sex offender, it plainly delays the treatment that must constitutionally accompany commitment pursuant to the Statute. The

failure of the Statute to provide for examination or treatment prior to the completion of the punishment phase strongly suggests that treatment is of secondary, rather than primary, concern."

This quotation, and the rest of the opinion, make clear that the Court is finding it objectionable that the Statute, among other things, has not provided adequate treatment to one who, all parties here concede, *can* be treated. . . .

. . . We have found no evidence in the record to support the conclusion that Kansas was in fact providing the treatment that all parties agree that it could provide. Thus, even had the Kansas Supreme Court considered the majority's new evidence—which it did not—it is not likely to have changed its characterization of the Act's treatment provisions as "somewhat disingenuous."

Regardless, the Kansas Supreme Court did so characterize the Act's treatment provisions and did find that treatment was "at best" an "incidental" objective. Thus, the circumstances here are different from *Allen,* where the Illinois Supreme Court explicitly found that the statute's aim was to provide treatment, not punishment. There is no evidence in the record that contradicts the finding of the Kansas Court. Thus, *Allen's* approach—its reliance on the State Court—if followed here would mean the Act as applied to *Leroy Hendricks* (as opposed to others who may have received treatment or who were sentenced after the effective date of the Act), is punitive.

Finally, Kansas points to *United States v. Salerno,* a case in which this Court held preventive detention of a dangerous accused person pending trial constitutionally permissible. *Salerno,* however, involved the brief detention of that person, after a finding of "probable cause" that he had committed a crime that would justify further imprisonment, and only pending a speedy judicial determination of guilt or innocence. This Court, in *Foucha,* emphasized the fact that the confinement at issue in *Salerno* was "strictly limited in duration." 504 U.S. at 82. It described that "pretrial detention of arrestees" as "one of those carefully limited exceptions permitted by the Due Process Clause." And it held that *Salerno* did not authorize the indefinite detention, on grounds of dangerousness, of "insanity acquittees who are not mentally ill but who do not prove they would not be dangerous to others." Whatever *Salerno's* "due process" implications may be, it does not focus upon, nor control, the question at issue here, the question of "punishment" for purposes of the *Ex Post Facto* Clause.

One other case warrants mention. In *Kennedy v. Mendoza-Martinez,* this Court listed seven factors that helped it determine whether a particular statute was primarily punitive for purposes of applying the Fifth and Sixth Amendments. Those factors include whether a sanction involves an affirmative restraint, how history has regarded it, whether it applies to behavior already a crime, the need for a finding of scienter, its relationship to a traditional aim of punishment, the presence of a nonpunitive alternative purpose, and whether it is excessive in relation to that purpose. This Court has said that these seven factors are "neither exhaustive nor dispositive," but nonetheless "helpful." *Ward,* 448 U.S. at 249. Paraphrasing them here, I believe the Act before us involves an affirmative restraint historically regarded as punishment; imposed upon behavior already a crime after a finding of scienter; which restraint, namely confinement, serves a traditional aim of punishment, does not primarily serve an alternative purpose (such as treatment) and is excessive in relation to any alternative purpose assigned.

This is to say that each of the factors the Court mentioned in *Martinez-Mendoza* on balance argues here in favor of a constitutional characterization as "punishment." It is not to say that I have found "a single 'formula' for identifying those legislative changes that have a sufficient effect on substantive crimes or punishments to fall within the constitutional prohibition." We have not previously done so, and I do not do so here. Rather, I have pointed to those features of the Act itself, in the context of this litigation, that lead me to conclude, in light of our precedent, that the added confinement the Act imposes upon Hendricks is basically punitive. This analysis, rooted in the facts surrounding Kansas' failure to treat Hendricks, cannot answer the question whether the Kansas Act, as it now stands, and in light of its current implementation, is punitive towards people other than he. And I do not attempt to do so here.

III

To find that the confinement the Act imposes upon Hendricks is "punishment" is to find a violation of the *Ex Post Facto* Clause. Kansas does not deny that the 1994 Act changed the legal consequences that attached to Hendricks earlier crimes, and in a way that significantly "disadvantaged the offender."

To find a violation of that Clause here, however, is not to hold that the Clause prevents Kansas, or other States, from enacting dangerous sexual offender statutes. A statute that operates prospectively, for example, does not offend the *Ex Post Facto* Clause. Neither does it offend the *Ex Post Facto* Clause for a State to sentence offenders to the fully authorized sentence, to seek consecutive, rather than concurrent, sentences, or to invoke recidivism statutes to lengthen imprisonment. Moreover, a statute that operates retroactively, like Kansas' statute, nonetheless does not offend the Clause *if the confinement that it imposes is not punishment*—if, that is to say, the legislature does not simply add a later criminal punishment to an earlier one.

The statutory provisions before us do amount to punishment primarily because, as I have said, the legislature did not tailor the statute to fit the nonpunitive civil aim of treatment, which it concedes exists in Hendricks' case. The Clause in these circumstances does not stand as an obstacle to achieving important protections for the public's safety; rather it provides an assurance that, where so significant a restriction of an individual's basic freedoms is at issue, a State cannot cut corners. Rather, the legislature must hew to the Constitution's liberty-protecting line.

Opinion

J USTICE THOMAS delivered the opinion of the Court.

In 1994, Kansas enacted the Sexually Violent Predator Act, which establishes procedures for the civil commitment of persons who, due to a "mental abnormality" or a "personality disorder," are likely to engage in "predatory acts of sexual violence." The State invoked the Act for the first time to commit Leroy Hendricks, an inmate who had a long history of sexually molesting children, and who was scheduled for release from prison shortly after the Act became law. Hendricks challenged his commitment on, *inter alia*, "substantive" due process, double jeopardy, and *ex post facto* grounds. The Kansas Supreme Court invalidated the Act, holding that its precommitment condition of a "mental abnormality" did not satisfy what the Court perceived to be the "substantive" due process requirement that involuntary civil commitment must be predicated on a finding of "mental illness." The State of Kansas petitioned for certiorari.

I

A

The Kansas Legislature enacted the Sexually Violent Predator Act (Act) in 1994 to grapple with the problem of managing repeat sexual offenders. Although Kansas already had a statute addressing the involuntary commitment of those defined as "mentally ill," the legislature determined that existing civil commitment procedures were inadequate to confront the risks presented by "sexually violent predators." In the Act's preamble, the legislature explained:

> "[A] small but extremely dangerous group of sexually violent predators exist who do not have a mental disease or defect that renders them appropriate for involuntary treatment pursuant to the [general involuntary civil commitment statute]. . . . In contrast to persons appropriate for civil commitment under the [general involuntary civil commitment statute], sexually violent predators generally have anti-social personality features which are unamenable to existing mental illness treatment modalities and those features render them likely to engage in sexually violent behavior. The legislature further finds that sexually violent predators' likelihood of engaging in repeat acts of predatory sexual violence is high. The existing involuntary commitment procedure . . . is

Supreme Court of the United States, 521 U.S. 346, 1997.

inadequate to address the risk these sexually violent predators pose to society. The legislature further finds that the prognosis for rehabilitating sexually violent predators in a prison setting is poor, the treatment needs of this population are very long term and the treatment modalities for this population are very different than the traditional treatment modalities for people appropriate for commitment under the [general involuntary civil commitment statute]."

As a result, the Legislature found it necessary to establish "a civil commitment procedure for the long-term care and treatment of the sexually violent predator." The Act defined a "sexually violent predator" as:

"any person who has been convicted of or charged with a sexually violent offense and who suffers from a mental abnormality or personality disorder which makes the person likely to engage in the predatory acts of sexual violence."

A "mental abnormality" was defined, in turn, as a "congenital or acquired condition affecting the emotional or volitional capacity which predisposes the person to commit sexually violent offenses in a degree constituting such person a menace to the health and safety of others."

As originally structured, the Act's civil commitment procedures pertained to: (1) a presently confined person who, like Hendricks, "has been convicted of a sexually violent offense" and is scheduled for release; (2) a person who has been "charged with a sexually violent offense" but has been found incompetent to stand trial; (3) a person who has been found "not guilty by reason of insanity of a sexually violent offense"; and (4) a person found "not guilty" of a sexually violent offense because of a mental disease or defect.

The initial version of the Act, as applied to a currently confined person such as Hendricks, was designed to initiate a specific series of procedures. The custodial agency was required to notify the local prosecutor 60 days before the anticipated release of a person who might have met the Act's criteria. The prosecutor was then obligated, within 45 days, to decide whether to file a petition in state Court seeking the person's involuntary commitment. If such a petition were filed, the Court was to determine whether "probable cause" existed to support a finding that the person was a "sexually violent predator" and thus eligible for civil commitment. Upon such a determination, transfer of the individual to a secure facility for professional evaluation would occur. After that evaluation, a trial would be held to determine beyond a reasonable doubt whether the individual was a sexually violent predator. If that determination were made, the person would then be transferred to the custody of the Secretary of Social and Rehabilitation Services (Secretary) for "control, care and treatment until such time as the person's mental abnormality or personality disorder has so changed that the person is safe to be at large."

In addition to placing the burden of proof upon the State, the Act afforded the individual a number of other procedural safeguards. In the case of an indigent person, the State was required to provide, at public expense, the assistance of counsel and an examination by mental health care professionals. The individual also received the right to present and cross-examine witnesses, and the opportunity to review documentary evidence presented by the State.

Once an individual was confined, the Act required that "the involuntary detention or commitment . . . shall conform to constitutional requirements for care and treatment." Confined persons were afforded three different avenues of review: First, the committing Court was obligated to conduct an annual review to determine whether continued detention was warranted. Second, the Secretary was permitted, at any time, to decide that the confined individual's condition had so changed that release was appropriate, and could then authorize the person to petition for release. Finally, even without the Secretary's permission, the confined person could at any time file a release petition. If the Court found that the State could no longer satisfy its burden under the initial commitment standard, the individual would be freed from confinement.

B

In 1984, Hendricks was convicted of taking "indecent liberties" with two 13-year-old boys. After serving nearly 10 years of his sentence, he was slated for release to a halfway house. Shortly before his scheduled release, however, the State filed a petition in state Court seeking Hendricks' civil confinement as a sexually violent predator. On August 19, 1994, Hendricks appeared before the Court with counsel and moved to dismiss the petition on the grounds that the Act violated various federal constitutional provisions. Although the Court reserved ruling on the Act's constitutionality, it concluded that there was probable cause to support a finding that Hendricks was a sexually violent predator, and therefore ordered that he be evaluated at the Larned State Security Hospital.

Hendricks subsequently requested a jury trial to determine whether he qualified as a sexually violent predator. During that trial, Hendricks' own testimony revealed a chilling history of repeated child sexual molestation and abuse, beginning in 1955 when he exposed his genitals to two young girls. At that time, he pleaded guilty to indecent exposure. Then, in 1957, he was convicted of lewdness involving a young girl and received a brief jail sentence. In 1960, he molested two young boys while he worked for a carnival. After serving two years in prison for that offense, he was paroled, only to be rearrested for molesting a 7-year-old girl. Attempts were made to treat him for his sexual deviance, and in 1965 he was considered "safe to be at large," and was discharged from a state psychiatric hospital.

Shortly thereafter, however, Hendricks sexually assaulted another young boy and girl—he performed oral sex on the 8-year-old girl and fondled the 11-year-old boy. He was again imprisoned in 1967, but refused to participate in a sex offender treatment program, and thus remained incarcerated until his parole in 1972. Diagnosed as a pedophile, Hendricks entered into, but then abandoned, a treatment program. He testified that despite having received professional help for his pedophilia, he continued to harbor sexual desires for children. Indeed, soon after his 1972 parole, Hendricks began to abuse his own stepdaughter and stepson. He forced the children to engage in sexual activity with him over a period of approximately four years. Then, as noted above, Hendricks was convicted of "taking indecent liberties" with two adolescent boys after he attempted to fondle them. As a result of that conviction, he was once again imprisoned, and was serving that sentence when he reached his conditional release date in September 1994.

Hendricks admitted that he had repeatedly abused children whenever he was not confined. He explained that when he "gets stressed out," he "can't control the urge" to molest children. Although Hendricks recognized that his behavior harms children, and he hoped he would not sexually molest children again, he stated that the only sure way he could keep from sexually abusing children in the future was "to die." Hendricks readily agreed with the state physician's diagnosis that he suffers from pedophilia and that he is not cured of the condition; indeed, he told the physician that "treatment is bull—." The jury unanimously found beyond a reasonable doubt that Hendricks was a sexually violent predator. The trial Court subsequently determined, as a matter of state law, that pedophilia qualifies as a "mental abnormality" as defined by the Act, and thus ordered Hendricks committed to the Secretary's custody.

Hendricks appealed, claiming, among other things, that application of the Act to him violated the Federal Constitution's Due Process, Double Jeopardy, and *Ex Post Facto* Clauses. The Kansas Supreme Court accepted Hendricks' due process claim. The Court declared that in order to commit a person involuntarily in a civil proceeding, a State is required by "substantive" due process to prove by clear and convincing evidence that the person is both (1) mentally ill, and (2) a danger to himself or to others. The Court then determined that the Act's definition of "mental abnormality" did not satisfy what it perceived to be this Court's "mental illness" requirement in the civil commitment context. As a result, the Court held that "the Act violates Hendricks' substantive due process rights."

The majority did not address Hendricks' *ex post facto* or double jeopardy claims. The dissent, however, considered each of Hendricks' constitutional arguments and rejected them.

II

A

Kansas argues that the Act's definition of "mental abnormality" satisfies "substantive" due process requirements. We agree. Although freedom from physical restraint "has always been at the core of the liberty protected by the Due Process Clause from arbitrary governmental action," that liberty interest is not absolute. The Court has recognized that an individual's constitutionally protected interest in avoiding physical restraint may be overridden even in the civil context:

> "The liberty secured by the Constitution of the United States to every person within its jurisdiction does not import an absolute right in each person to be, at all times and in all circumstances, wholly free from restraint. There are manifold restraints to which every person is

necessarily subject for the common good. On any other basis organized society could not exist with safety to its members."

Accordingly, States have in certain narrow circumstances provided for the forcible civil detainment of people who are unable to control their behavior and who thereby pose a danger to the public health and safety. We have consistently upheld such involuntary commitment statutes provided the confinement takes place pursuant to proper procedures and evidentiary standards. It thus cannot be said that the involuntary civil confinement of a limited subclass of dangerous persons is contrary to our understanding of ordered liberty.

The challenged Act unambiguously requires a finding of dangerousness either to one's self or to others as a prerequisite to involuntary confinement. Commitment proceedings can be initiated only when a person "has been convicted of or charged with a sexually violent offense," and "suffers from a mental abnormality or personality disorder which makes the person likely to engage in the predatory acts of sexual violence." The statute thus requires proof of more than a mere predisposition to violence; rather, it requires evidence of past sexually violent behavior and a present mental condition that creates a likelihood of such conduct in the future if the person is not incapacitated. As we have recognized, "previous instances of violent behavior are an important indicator of future violent tendencies." A finding of dangerousness, standing alone, is ordinarily not a sufficient ground upon which to justify indefinite involuntary commitment. We have sustained civil commitment statutes when they have coupled proof of dangerousness with the proof of some additional factor, such as a "mental illness" or "mental abnormality." These added statutory requirements serve to limit involuntary civil confinement to those who suffer from a volitional impairment rendering them dangerous beyond their control. The Kansas Act is plainly of a kind with these other civil commitment statutes: It requires a finding of future dangerousness, and then links that finding to the existence of a "mental abnormality" or "personality disorder" that makes it difficult, if not impossible, for the person to control his dangerous behavior. The precommitment requirement of a "mental abnormality" or "personality disorder" is consistent with the requirements of these other statutes that we have upheld in that it narrows the class of persons eligible for confinement to those who are unable to control their dangerousness.

Hendricks nonetheless argues that our earlier cases dictate a finding of "mental illness" as a prerequisite for civil commitment. He then asserts that a "mental abnormality" is *not* equivalent to a "mental illness" because it is a term coined by the Kansas Legislature, rather than by the psychiatric community. Contrary to Hendricks' assertion, the term "mental illness" is devoid of any talismanic significance. Not only do "psychiatrists disagree widely and frequently on what constitutes mental illness," but the Court itself has used a variety of expressions to describe the mental condition of those properly subject to civil confinement.

To the extent that the civil commitment statutes we have considered set forth criteria relating to an individual's inability to control his dangerousness, the Kansas Act sets forth comparable criteria and Hendricks' condition doubtless satisfies those criteria. The mental health professionals who evaluated Hendricks diagnosed him as suffering from pedophilia, a condition the psychiatric profession itself classifies as a serious mental disorder. Hendricks even conceded that, when he becomes "stressed out," he cannot "control the urge" to molest children. This admitted lack of volitional control, coupled with a prediction of future dangerousness, adequately distinguishes Hendricks from other dangerous persons who are perhaps more properly dealt with exclusively through criminal proceedings. Hendricks' diagnosis as a pedophile, which qualifies as a "mental abnormality" under the Act, thus plainly suffices for due process purposes.

B

We granted Hendricks' cross-petition to determine whether the Act violates the Constitution's double jeopardy prohibition or its ban on *ex post facto* lawmaking. The thrust of Hendricks' argument is that the Act establishes criminal proceedings; hence confinement under it necessarily constitutes punishment. He contends that where, as here, newly enacted "punishment" is predicated upon past conduct for which he has already been convicted and forced to serve a prison sentence, the Constitution's Double Jeopardy and *Ex Post Facto* Clauses are violated. We are unpersuaded by Hendricks' argument that Kansas has established criminal proceedings.

The categorization of a particular proceeding as civil or criminal "is first of all a question of statutory construction." We must initially ascertain whether the legislature meant the statute to establish "civil" proceedings. If so, we ordinarily defer to the legislature's stated intent. Here, Kansas' objective to create a civil proceeding is evidenced by its placement of the Sexually Violent Predator Act within the Kansas probate code, instead of the criminal code, as well as its description of the Act as creating a *"civil commitment procedure."* Nothing on the face of the statute suggests that the legislature sought to create anything other than a civil commitment scheme designed to protect the public from harm.

Although we recognize that a "civil label is not always dispositive," we will reject the legislature's manifest intent only where a party challenging the statute provides "the clearest proof" that "the statutory scheme [is] so punitive either in purpose or effect as to negate [the State's] intention" to deem it "civil." In those limited circumstances, we will consider the statute to have established criminal proceedings for constitutional purposes. Hendricks, however, has failed to satisfy this heavy burden.

As a threshold matter, commitment under the Act does not implicate either of the two primary objectives of criminal punishment: retribution or deterrence. The Act's purpose is not retributive because it does not affix culpability for prior criminal conduct. Instead, such conduct is used solely for evidentiary purposes, either to demonstrate that a "mental abnormality" exists or to support a finding of future dangerousness. We have previously concluded that an Illinois statute was nonpunitive even though it was triggered by the commission of a sexual assault, explaining that evidence of the prior criminal conduct was "received not to punish past misdeeds, but primarily to show the accused's mental condition and to predict future behavior." In addition, the Kansas Act does not make a criminal conviction a prerequisite for commitment—persons absolved of criminal responsibility may nonetheless be subject to confinement under the Act. An absence of the necessary criminal responsibility suggests that the State is not seeking retribution for a past misdeed. Thus, the fact that the Act may be "tied to criminal activity" is "insufficient to render the statute punitive."

Moreover, unlike a criminal statute, no finding of scienter is required to commit an individual who is found to be a sexually violent predator; instead, the commitment determination is made based on a "mental abnormality" or "personality disorder" rather than on one's criminal intent. The existence of a scienter requirement is customarily an important element in distinguishing criminal from civil statutes. The absence of such a requirement here is evidence that confinement under the statute is not intended to be retributive.

Nor can it be said that the legislature intended the Act to function as a deterrent. Those persons committed under the Act are, by definition, suffering from a "mental abnormality" or a "personality disorder" that prevents them from exercising adequate control over their behavior. Such persons are therefore unlikely to be deterred by the threat of confinement. And the conditions surrounding that confinement do not suggest a punitive purpose on the State's part. The State has represented that an individual confined under the Act is not subject to the more restrictive conditions placed on state prisoners, but instead experiences essentially the same conditions as any involuntarily committed patient in the state mental institution. Because none of the parties argues that people institutionalized under the Kansas general civil commitment statute are subject to punitive conditions, even though they may be involuntarily confined, it is difficult to conclude that persons confined under this Act are being "punished."

Although the civil commitment scheme at issue here does involve an affirmative restraint, "the mere fact that a person is detained does not inexorably lead to the conclusion that the government has imposed punishment." The State may take measures to restrict the freedom of the dangerously mentally ill. This is a legitimate nonpunitive governmental objective and has been historically so regarded. The Court has, in fact, cited the confinement of "mentally unstable individuals who present a danger to the public" as one classic example of nonpunitive detention. If detention for the purpose of protecting the community from harm *necessarily* constituted punishment, then all involuntary civil commitments would have to be considered punishment. But we have never so held.

Hendricks focuses on his confinement's potentially indefinite duration as evidence of the State's punitive intent. That focus, however, is misplaced. Far from any punitive objective, the confinement's duration is instead linked to the stated purposes of the commitment, namely, to hold the person until his mental abnormality no longer causes him to be a threat to others. If, at any time, the confined person is adjudged "safe to be at large," he is statutorily entitled to immediate release.

Furthermore, commitment under the Act is only *potentially* indefinite. The maximum amount of time an individual can be incapacitated pursuant to a single judicial proceeding is one year. If Kansas seeks to continue the detention beyond that year, a Court must once again determine beyond a reasonable doubt that the detainee satisfies the same standards as required for the initial confinement. This requirement again demonstrates that Kansas does not intend an individual committed pursuant to the Act to remain confined any longer than he suffers from a mental abnormality rendering him unable to control his dangerousness.

Hendricks next contends that the State's use of procedural safeguards traditionally found in criminal trials makes the proceedings here criminal rather than civil. In *Allen,* we confronted a similar argument. There, the petitioner "placed great reliance on the fact that proceedings under the Act are accompanied by procedural safeguards usually found in criminal trials" to argue that the proceedings were civil in name only. We rejected that argument, however, explaining that the State's decision "to provide some of the safeguards applicable in criminal trials cannot itself turn these proceedings into criminal prosecutions." The numerous procedural and evidentiary protections afforded here demonstrate that the Kansas Legislature has taken great care to confine only a narrow class of particularly dangerous individuals, and then only after meeting the strictest procedural standards. That Kansas chose to afford such procedural protections does not transform a civil commitment proceeding into a criminal prosecution.

Finally, Hendricks argues that the Act is necessarily punitive because it fails to offer any legitimate "treatment." Without such treatment, Hendricks asserts, confinement under the Act amounts to little more than disguised punishment. Hendricks' argument assumes that treatment for his condition is available, but that the State has failed (or refused) to provide it. The Kansas Supreme Court, however, apparently rejected this assumption, explaining:

> "It is clear that the overriding concern of the legislature is to continue the segregation of sexually violent offenders from the public. Treatment with the goal of reintegrating them into society is incidental, at best. The record reflects that treatment for sexually violent predators is all but nonexistent. The legislature concedes that sexually violent predators are not amenable to treatment under [the existing Kansas involuntary commitment statute]. If there is nothing to treat under [that statute], then there is no mental illness. In that light, the provisions of the Act for treatment appear somewhat disingenuous."

It is possible to read this passage as a determination that Hendricks' condition was *untreatable* under the existing Kansas civil commitment statute, and thus the Act's sole purpose was incapacitation. Absent a treatable mental illness, the Kansas Court concluded, Hendricks could not be detained against his will.

Accepting the Kansas Court's apparent determination that treatment is not possible for this category of individuals does not obligate us to adopt its legal conclusions. We have already observed that, under the appropriate circumstances and when accompanied by proper procedures, incapacitation may be a legitimate end of the civil law. Accordingly, the Kansas Court's determination that the Act's "overriding concern" was the continued "segrega-tion of sexually violent offenders" is consistent with our conclusion that the Act establishes civil proceedings, especially when that concern is coupled with the State's ancillary goal of providing treatment to those offenders, if such is possible. While we have upheld state civil commitment statutes that aim both to incapacitate and to treat, see *Allen, supra,* we have never held that the Con-stitution prevents a State from civilly detaining those for whom no treatment is available, but who nevertheless pose a danger to others. A State could hardly be seen as furthering a "punitive" purpose by involuntarily confining persons afflicted with an untreatable, highly contagious disease. Similarly, it would be of little value to require treatment as a precondition for civil confinement of the dangerously insane when no acceptable treatment existed. To conclude otherwise would obligate a State to release certain confined individuals who were both mentally ill and dangerous simply because they could not be suc-cessfully treated for their afflictions. . . .

Although the treatment program initially offered Hendricks may have seemed somewhat meager, it must be remembered that he was the first per-son committed under the Act. That the State did not have all of its treatment procedures in place is thus not surprising. What is significant, however, is that Hendricks was placed under the supervision of the Kansas Department of Health and Social and Rehabilitative Services, housed in a unit segregated from the general prison population and operated not by employees of the Depart-ment of Corrections, but by other trained individuals. And, before this Court, Kansas declared "absolutely" that persons committed under the Act are now receiving in the neighborhood of "31.5 hours of treatment per week."

Where the State has "disavowed any punitive intent"; limited confine-ment to a small segment of particularly dangerous individuals; provided strict procedural safeguards; directed that confined persons be segregated from the general prison population and afforded the same status as others who have been civilly committed; recommended treatment if such is possible; and per-mitted immediate release upon a showing that the individual is no longer dangerous or mentally impaired, we cannot say that it acted with punitive intent. We therefore hold that the Act does not establish criminal proceedings and that involuntary confinement pursuant to the Act is not punitive. Our conclusion that the Act is nonpunitive thus removes an essential prerequisite for both Hendricks' double jeopardy and *ex post facto* claims.

1

The Double Jeopardy Clause provides: "Nor shall any person be subject for the same offence to be twice put in jeopardy of life or limb." Although generally understood to preclude a second prosecution for the same offense, the Court has also interpreted this prohibition to prevent the State from "punishing twice, or attempting a second time to punish criminally, for the same offense." Hendricks argues that, as applied to him, the Act violates double jeopardy principles because his confinement under the Act, imposed after a conviction and a term of incarceration, amounted to both a second prosecution and a second punishment for the same offense. We disagree.

Because we have determined that the Kansas Act is civil in nature, initiation of its commitment proceedings does not constitute a second prosecution. Moreover, as commitment under the Act is not tantamount to "punishment," Hendricks' involuntary detention does not violate the Double Jeopardy Clause, even though that confinement may follow a prison term. Indeed, in *Baxstrom v. Herold,* we expressly recognized that civil commitment could follow the expiration of a prison term without offending double jeopardy principles. We reasoned that "there is no conceivable basis for distinguishing the commitment of a person who is nearing the end of a penal term from all other civil commitments." If an individual otherwise meets the requirements for involuntary civil commitment, the State is under no obligation to release that individual simply because the detention would follow a period of incarceration. . . .

2

Hendricks' *ex post facto* claim is similarly flawed. The *Ex Post Facto* Clause, which "forbids the application of any new punitive measure to a crime already consummated," has been interpreted to pertain exclusively to penal statutes. As we have previously determined, the Act does not impose punishment; thus, its application does not raise *ex post facto* concerns. Moreover, the Act clearly does not have retroactive effect. Rather, the Act permits involuntary confinement based upon a determination that the person *currently* both suffers from a "mental abnormality" or "personality disorder" and is likely to pose a future danger to the public. To the extent that past behavior is taken into account, it is used, as noted above, solely for evidentiary purposes. Because the Act does not criminalize conduct legal before its enactment, nor deprive Hendricks of any defense that was available to him at the time of his crimes, the Act does not violate the *Ex Post Facto* Clause.

III

We hold that the Kansas Sexually Violent Predator Act comports with due process requirements and neither runs afoul of double jeopardy principles nor constitutes an exercise in impermissible *ex post facto* lawmaking. Accordingly, the judgment of the Kansas Supreme Court is reversed.

POSTSCRIPT

Does Confining Sex Offenders Indefinitely in Mental Hospitals After They Have Served Their Prison Sentences Violate the Constitution?

The readings in this section were excerpts from the U.S. Supreme Court's decision in *Kansas v. Hendricks*. If you were a member of the Court, would you have joined the majority opinion, or would you have joined Justice Breyer's dissent? Do you agree with Justice Breyer's assertion that the Kansas Sexually Violent Predator Act is an unconstitutional *ex post facto* law as applied in this case?

Moreover, are you convinced by Justice Thomas' contention that committing someone to confinement in a state mental institution after they have completed their prison sentence does not constitute *punishment?* Rather, according to the Court, confining someone in this manner is therapeutic *treatment*. Therefore, the Fifth Amendment's double jeopardy clause does not bar the additional confinement. Is the distinction that the Court has drawn between punishment and treatment a matter of form triumphing over substance? Is this a case where you agree with the result—dangerous pedophiles should not be allowed to prey on our children, but disagree with how the court reached their conclusion?

Please recall the debate presented in Issue 12 about whether to castrate serious sex offenders. What if a state were to pass a law providing that after receiving a complete psychiatric examination, a certified pedophile about to be released from prison could have the choice of undergoing physical castration in lieu of an indefinite commitment to a mental institution? What constitutional issues would you raise as the attorney for the sex offender faced with this difficult choice?

Another interesting issue concerns the sex offender's Sixth Amendment right to counsel. Suppose that as an attorney you were appointed by a court to represent someone like Leroy Hendricks in a proceeding to determine whether he would be indefinitely confined to a mental hospital following the completion of his sentence. Would you accept the case? The Rules of Professional Responsibility that govern the conduct of attorneys provide that if you accept the case, you must defend the offender's interest to the best of your ability. The Rules provide as well that if you cannot do so, you must refuse to take the case. What would you do?

The issue considered in this section is a challenging one. Fortunately there are additional resources that add substantially to the discussion of these matters. See American Psychiatric Association, *Dangerous Sex Offenders: A Task Force Report of the American Psychiatric Association* (American Psychiatric Press, 1999); Lisa L. Sample and Timothy M. Bray, "Are Sex Offenders Dangerous?" *Criminology & Public Policy* (vol. 3, no. 1, 2003); Holly A. Miller, Amy E. Amenta, and Mary Alice Conroy, "Sexually Violent Predator Evaluations: Empirical Evidence, Strategies for Professionals, and Research Directions," *Law & Human Behavior* (vol. 29, no. 1, 2005); Leam A. Craig, Kevin D. Browne, Ian Stringer, and Anthony Beech, "Limitations in Actuarial Risk Assessment of Sexual Offenders: A Methodological Note," *The British Journal of Forensic Practice* (vol. 6, no. 1, 2004); Wanda D. Beyer Kendall and Monit Cheung, "Sexually Violent Predators and Civil Commitment Laws," *Journal of Child Sexual Abuse* (vol. 13, no. 2, 2004).

Additional resources include Ron Langevin, Suzanne Cumoe, Paul Federoff, and Renee Bennett, et al., "Lifetime Sex Offender Recidivism: A 25-Year Follow-Up Study," *Canadian Journal of Criminology and Criminal Justice* (vol. 46, no. 5, 2004); Kyron Huigens, "Dignity and Desert in Punishment Theory," *Harvard Journal of Law and Public Policy* (vol. 27, no. 1, 2003); Patricia E. Erickson, "The Legal Standard of Volitional Impairment: An Analysis of Substantive Due Process and the United States Supreme Court's Decision in *Kansas v. Hendricks*," *Journal of Criminal Justice* (vol. 30, no. 1, 2002); and Eric S. Janus, "Sex Predator Commitment Laws: Constitutional but Unwise," *Psychiatric Annals* (vol. 30, no. 6, 2000).

ISSUE 20

Does an Imprisoned Individual Have a Constitutional Right to Access the State's Evidence for DNA Testing?

YES: **John Paul Stevens**, from "Dissenting Opinion," *District Attorney's Office v. Osborne*, 557 U.S. ____ (2009).

NO: **John Roberts**, from "Majority Opinion," *District Attorney's Office v. Osborne*, 557 U.S. ____ (2009).

ISSUE SUMMARY

YES: Justice John Paul Stevens, in a dissenting opinion in *District Attorney's Office for the Third Judicial District v. Osborne* (2009), contends that a fundamental responsibility to ensure that "justice" has been served requires a state to provide a defendant with postconviction access to DNA evidence. Because it could conclusively establish whether an accused had committed the crime in the first place, this right should be protected by the Fourteenth Amendment's Due Process Clause.

NO: Chief Justice John Roberts, writing for the majority, in *District Attorney's Office for the Third Judicial District v. Osborne* (2009), held that the U.S. Constitution's Due Process Clause provides no right to postconviction access to DNA evidence because it would take the development of rules and procedures in criminal cases out of the hands of state legislatures and courts.

$\mathbf{T}$he U.S. Constitution requires that in criminal prosecutions, a defendant's guilt must be proven "beyond a reasonable doubt." In practical terms, this means that the prosecution must demonstrate that the accused has committed the charged offense and that there is unlikely to be a plausible alternative explanation. Moreover, in *In re Winship*, 397 U.S. 358 (1970), the Supreme Court held that the prosecution is required to present evidence to prove each element of the charged crime beyond a reasonable doubt.

One of the more compelling types of evidence that is sometimes produced in either criminal or civil cases involves the use of DNA sequencing.

DNA evidence may be used in a number of different ways. The Human Genome Project lists several examples:

- To identify potential suspects whose DNA may match evidence left at crime scenes
- To exonerate persons wrongly accused of crimes
- To identify crime and catastrophe victims
- To establish paternity and other family relationships
- To identify endangered and protected species as an aid to wildlife officials (could be used for prosecuting poachers)
- To detect bacteria and other organisms that may pollute air, water, soil, and food
- To match organ donors with recipients in transplant programs (http://www.gneomics.energy.gov)

According to the Human Genome Project, scientists seeking to identify a particular individual will scan 13 different DNA regions, termed *loci*, which vary from person to person and can be used to create someone's unique DNA profile. States scientist Daniel Drell:

DNA identification can be quite effective if used intelligently. . . . [Y]ou can look for matches (based on sequence or on numbers of small repeating units of DNA sequence) at many different locations on a person's genome; one or two (even three) aren't enough to be confident that the suspect is the right one, but thirteen sites are used. A match at all thirteen is rare enough that you (or a prosecutor or a jury) can be very confident ('beyond a reasonable doubt') that the right person is accused. (http://www.genomics.energy.gov)

Therefore, because there is virtually no chance that two persons will have identical DNA profiles, it becomes very powerful evidence in cases where the identity of a perpetrator is an issue.

In addition, an important federal law, the DNA Identification Act of 1994, mandated the development of a national DNA data bank administered by the Federal Bureau of Investigation (42 U.S.C. Section 14135a). The acronym for this database is CODIS, the Combined DNA Index System, which uses two different indexes to produce leads when biological evidence is recovered from a crime scene. The Convicted Offender Index contains DNA profiles of felony sex offenders as well as other violent criminals. The Forensic Index contains DNA profiles found from crime scene evidence. Federal, state, and local law enforcement officers take DNA samples from biological evidence left at crime scenes that have no suspect and compare it to DNA samples in the CODIS systems. If a match is found, the CODIS database can be used to identify the perpetrator. (*Id.*)

All 50 states authorize the collection and analysis of DNA samples from convicted state offenders and enter the profiles into CODIS. Several states also authorize the collection of DNA samples from all individuals they arrest. (Federal Register, vol. 73, no. 238/Wednesday, December 10, 2008)

For example, the state of California mandates DNA collection from persons in the following circumstances:

> (a) Any person (adult or juvenile) who is newly convicted/adjudicated of a felony offense, or who is newly convicted/adjudicated of a misdemeanor or infraction offense but has a prior felony of record; . . . (b) Any person (adult or juvenile) currently in custody or on probation, parole, or any other supervised release after conviction for any felony offense; . . . (c) Any person (adult or juvenile) currently on probation or any other supervised release for any offense with a prior felony . . . of record. (Cal. Pen. Code, Sections 295, 296, 296.1)

Currently, California has collected approximately 1,337,105 offender profiles and 33,673 forensic samples, and has 12,777 *investigations aided*, which is the primary measuring criterion used to assess the effectiveness of CODIS. (http://www.fbi.gov/about-us/lab/codis/ndis-statistics)

To illustrate just how comprehensive the CODIS national database has become, as of March, 2011, the National DNA Index (NDIS) contained more than 9,535,059 offender profiles and 366,762 forensic profiles. It has produced more than 141,000 "hits" assisting in more than 135,000 investigations.

As scholars and commentators from across the political spectrum have observed, one of the most compelling uses of DNA evidence is to exonerate persons who have been wrongly convicted. Once someone has been convicted of a crime, however, should they have a federal constitutional right to have DNA evidence reevaluated if it was not available during their original trial? Or, should the states be free to develop their own protections for those who may have been wrongly convicted?

In formulating your response to these questions, it is important to keep in mind that these cases involve a request for *postconviction* relief by a defendant who has already had a full and fair trial in a state court. One of the principal modes of challenging a conviction after an offender has exhausted his or her appeals in state courts is termed a *habeas corpus lawsuit,* a civil proceeding in federal court, which asserts that a prisoner is being held unlawfully due to an error in the state proceedings (42 U.S.C. Section 1983). Although a comprehensive discussion of these issues is beyond the scope of this initiative, it is safe to say that the U.S. Congress and the federal courts have seemed determined in recent years to stem the tide of federal habeas corpus lawsuits filed by state prison inmates. So, once a defendant has exhausted his or her appeals in state court, should the U.S. Supreme Court recognize a special constitutional right for postconviction review of DNA evidence, due to its exceptional ability to ensure that "justice has been served" by exonerating the wrongly accused?

The questions presented above are compelling ones. Justice John Paul Stevens, dissenting in *District Attorney's Office v. Osborne*, 557 U.S. ____ (2009), asserts that the U.S. Constitution should recognize such a right. Stevens summarizes the issues posed in this case as follows:

The State of Alaska possesses physical evidence that, if tested, will conclusively establish whether [Osborne] committed rape and attempted murder. If he did, justice has been served by his conviction and sentence. If not, Osborne has needlessly spent decades behind bars while the true culprit has not been brought to justice. The DNA test Osborne seeks is a simple one, its cost modest, and its results uniquely precise. Yet for reasons the State has been unable or unwilling to articulate, it refuses to allow Osborne to test the evidence at his own expense and to thereby ascertain the truth once and for all.

Justice Stevens' opinion also emphasizes that a criminal conviction does not eliminate the constitutional liberty interests of convicted persons, "including the fundamental liberty of freedom from [wrongful] physical restraint." Justice Stevens concludes that "there is no reason to deny access to the evidence and there are many reasons to provide it, not least of which is a fundamental concern in ensuring that justice has been done in this case."

Chief Justice John Roberts disagrees, however. He states that Osborne has proposed "the recognition of a freestanding and far-reaching constitutional right of access to [DNA] evidence." Justice Roberts believes that such an "approach would take the development of rules and procedures in this area out of the hands of legislatures and state courts shaping policy in a focused manner and turn it over to federal courts applying the broad parameters of the Due Process Clause."

Who presents the more compelling argument: Justice Stevens or Chief Justice Roberts? Despite the fact that the states have a strong interest in the administration of their own justice systems, do you believe that the unique accuracy of DNA evidence and its potential for acquitting the wrongly convicted justify the development of a special federal constitutional right designed to vindicate these interests? Consider Chief Justice Roberts's assertion that the justice system, "like any human endeavor, cannot be perfect." Should properly collected and analyzed DNA evidence constitute an exception to that rule? Finally, would you agree with the famous and authoritative British jurist William Blackstone's assertion that it is "better that ten guilty persons escape than one innocent suffer?" (William Blackstone, *Commentaries* [vol. 4, p. 358]). Do you believe that the majority opinion in *District Attorney's Office v. Osborne* is consistent with Blackstone's famous aphorism?

YES

John Paul Stevens

Dissenting Opinion, *District Attorney's Office v. Osborne*

Justice Stevens, with whom Justice Ginsburg and Justice Breyer join, and with whom Justice Souter joins as to Part I, dissenting.

The State of Alaska possesses physical evidence that, if tested, will conclusively establish whether respondent William Osborne committed rape and attempted murder. If he did, justice has been served by his conviction and sentence. If not, Osborne has needlessly spent decades behind bars while the true culprit has not been brought to justice. The DNA test Osborne seeks is a simple one, its cost modest, and its results uniquely precise. Yet for reasons the State has been unable or unwilling to articulate, it refuses to allow Osborne to test the evidence at his own expense and to thereby ascertain the truth once and for all.

On two equally problematic grounds, the Court today blesses the State's arbitrary denial of the evidence Osborne seeks. First, while acknowledging that Osborne may have a due process right to access the evidence under Alaska's postconviction procedures, the Court concludes that Osborne has not yet availed himself of all possible avenues for relief in state court. As both a legal and factual matter, that conclusion is highly suspect. More troubling still, based on a fundamental mischaracterization of the right to liberty that Osborne seeks to vindicate, the Court refuses to acknowledge "in the circumstances of this case" any right to access the evidence that is grounded in the Due Process Clause itself. Because I am convinced that Osborne has a constitutional right of access to the evidence he wishes to test and that, on the facts of this case, he has made a sufficient showing of entitlement to that evidence, I would affirm the decision of the Court of Appeals.

I

The Fourteenth Amendment provides that "[n]o State shall . . . deprive any person of life, liberty, or property, without due process of law." §1. Our cases have frequently recognized that protected liberty interests may arise "from the Constitution itself, by reason of guarantees implicit in the word 'liberty,' . . . or it may arise from an expectation or interest created by state laws or policies." . . . Osborne contends that he possesses a right to access DNA evidence arising from both these sources.

Supreme Court of the United States, 129 S.Ct 2308, June 19, 2009.

Osborne first anchors his due process right in Alaska Stat. §12.72.010(4) (2008). Under that provision, a person who has been "convicted of, or sentenced for, a crime may institute a proceeding for post-conviction relief if the person claims... that there exists evidence of material facts, not previously presented and heard by the court, that requires vacation of the conviction or sentence in the interest of justice." . . . Osborne asserts that exculpatory DNA test results obtained using state-of-the-art Short Tandem Repeat (STR) and Mitochondrial (mtDNA) analysis would qualify as newly discovered evidence entitling him to relief under the state statute. The problem is that the newly discovered evidence he wishes to present cannot be generated unless he is first able to access the State's evidence—something he cannot do without the State's consent or a court order.

Although States are under no obligation to provide mechanisms for post-conviction relief, when they choose to do so, the procedures they employ must comport with the demands of the Due Process Clause . . . by providing litigants with fair opportunity to assert their state-created rights. Osborne contends that by denying him an opportunity to access the physical evidence, the State has denied him meaningful access to state postconviction relief, thereby violating his right to due process.

Although the majority readily agrees that Osborne has a protected liberty interest in demonstrating his innocence with new evidence under Alaska Stat. §12.72.010(4) . . . it rejects the Ninth Circuit's conclusion that Osborne is constitutionally entitled to access the State's evidence. The Court concludes that the adequacy of the process afforded to Osborne must be assessed under the standard set forth . . . Under that standard, Alaska's procedures for bringing a claim under §12.72.010(4) will not be found to violate due process unless they "'offen[d] some principle of justice so rooted in the traditions and conscience of our people as to be ranked as fundamental,' or 'transgres[s] any recognized principle of fundamental fairness in operation.'" . . . After conducting a cursory review of the relevant statutory text, the Court concludes that Alaska's procedures are constitutional on their face.

While I agree that the statute is not facially deficient, the state courts' application of §12.72.010(4) raises serious questions whether the State's procedures are fundamentally unfair in their operation. As an initial matter, it is not clear that Alaskan courts ordinarily permit litigants to utilize the state postconviction statute to obtain new evidence in the form of DNA tests. . . .

Of even greater concern is the manner in which the state courts applied §12.72.010(4) to the facts of this case. In determining that Osborne was not entitled to relief under the postconviction statute, the Alaska Court of Appeals concluded that the DNA testing Osborne wished to obtain could not qualify as "newly discovered" because it was available at the time of trial. . . . In his arguments before the state trial court and his briefs to the Alaska Court of Appeals, however, Osborne had plainly requested STR DNA testing, a form of DNA testing not yet in use at the time of his trial. . . . The state appellate court's conclusion that the requested testing had been available at the time of trial was therefore clearly erroneous. Given these facts, the majority's assertion that

Osborne "attempt[ed] to sidestep state process" by failing "to use the process provided to him by the State" is unwarranted. . . .

The same holds true with respect to the majority's suggestion that the Alaska Constitution might provide additional protections to Osborne above and beyond those afforded under afforded under §12.72.010(4). In Osborne's state postconviction proceedings, the Alaska Court of Appeals held out the possibility that even when evidence does not meet the requirements of §12.72.010(4), the State Constitution might offer relief to a defendant who is able to make certain threshold showings. . . . On remand from that decision, however, the state trial court denied Osborne relief on the ground that he failed to show that (1) his conviction rested primarily on eyewitness identification; (2) there was a demonstrable doubt concerning his identity as the perpetrator; and (3) scientific testing would like be conclusive on this issue. . . .

Osborne made full use of available state procedures in his efforts to secure access to evidence for DNA testing so that he might avail himself of the postconviction relief afforded by the State of Alaska. He was rebuffed at every turn. The manner in which the Alaska courts applied state law in this case leaves me in grave doubt about the adequacy of the procedural protections afforded to litigants under Alaska Stat. §12.72.010(4), and provides strong reason to doubt the majority's flippant assertion that if Osborne were "simply [to] see[k] the DNA through the State's discovery procedures, he might well get it." . . . However, even if the Court were correct in its assumption that Osborne might be given the evidence he seeks were he to present his claim in state court a second time, there should be no need for him to do so.

II

Wholly apart from his state-created interest in obtaining postconviction relief under Alaska Stat. §12.72.010(4), Osborne asserts a right to access the State's evidence that derives from the Due Process Clause itself. Whether framed as a "substantive liberty interest . . . protected through a procedural due process right" to have evidence made available for testing, or as a substantive due process right to be free of arbitrary government action, . . . the result is the same: On the record now before us, Osborne has established his entitlement to test the State's evidence.

The liberty protected by the Due Process Clause is not a creation of the Bill of Rights. Indeed, our Nation has long recognized that the liberty safeguarded by the Constitution has far deeper roots. See Declaration of Independence ¶2 (holding it self-evident that "all men are . . . endowed by their Creator with certain unalienable Rights," among which are "Life, Liberty, and the pursuit of Happiness.") . . . The "most elemental" of the liberties protected by the Due Process Clause is "the interest in being free from physical detention by one's own government." . . .

Although a valid criminal conviction justifies punitive detention, it does not entirely eliminate the liberty interests of convicted persons. For while a prisoner's "rights may be diminished by the needs and exigencies of the institutional environment[,[. . . [t]here is no iron curtain drawn between the

Constitution and the prisons of this country." . . . Our cases have recognized protected interests in a variety of postconviction contexts, extending substantive constitutional protections to state prisoners on the premise that the Due Process Clause of the Fourteenth Amendment requires States to respect certain fundamental liberties in the postconviction context. . . . It is therefore far too late in the day to question the basic proposition that convicted persons such as Osborne retain a constitutionally protected measure of interest in liberty, including the fundamental liberty of freedom from physical restraint.

Recognition of this right draws strength from the fact that 46 States and the Federal Government have passed statutes providing access to evidence for DNA testing, and 3 additional states (including Alaska) provide similar access through court-made rules alone, . . . These legislative developments are consistent with recent trends in legal ethics recognizing that prosecutors are obliged to disclose all forms of exculpatory evidence that come into their possession following conviction. . . . The fact that nearly all the States have now recognized some postconviction right to DNA evidence makes it more, not less, appropriate to recognize a limited federal right to such evidence in cases where litigants are unfairly barred from obtaining relief in state court.

Insofar as it is process Osborne seeks, he is surely entitled to less than "the full panoply of rights," that would be due [10] a criminal defendant prior to conviction. . . . That does not mean, however, that our pretrial due process cases have no relevance in the postconviction context. In *Brady* v. *Maryland*, 373 U.S. 83, 87 (1963), we held that the State violates due process when it suppresses "evidence favorable to an accused" that is "material either to guilt or to punishment, irrespective of the good faith or bad faith of the prosecution." Although *Brady* does not directly provide for a postconviction right to such evidence, the concerns with fundamental fairness that motivated our decision in that case are equally present when convicted persons such as Osborne seek access to dispositive DNA evidence following conviction.

Recent scientific advances in DNA analysis have made "it literally possible to confirm guilt or innocence beyond any question whatsoever, at least in some categories of cases." . . . As the Court recognizes today, the powerful new evidence that modern DNA testing can provide is "unlike anything known before." . . . Discussing these important forensic developments in his often-cited opinion in Harvey, Judge Luttig explained that although "no one would contend that fairness, in the constitutional sense, requires a post-conviction right of access or a right to disclosure anything approaching in scope that which is required pretrial," in cases "where the government holds previously produced forensic evidence, the testing of which concededly could prove beyond any doubt that the defendant did not commit the crime for which he was convicted, the very same principle of elemental fairness that dictates pre-trial production of all potentially exculpatory evidence dictates post-trial production of this infinitely narrower category of evidence." . . . It does so "out of recognition of the same systemic interests in fairness and ultimate truth." . . .

If the right Osborne seeks to vindicate is framed as purely substantive, the proper result is no less clear. "The touchstone of due process is protection of the individual against arbitrary action of government.". . . When government action is so lacking in justification that it "can properly be characterized as arbitrary, or conscience shocking, in a constitutional sense," . . . violates the Due Process Clause. In my view, the State's refusal to provide Osborne with access to evidence for DNA testing qualifies as arbitrary.

Throughout the course of state and federal litigation, the State has failed to provide any concrete reason for denying Osborne the DNA testing he seeks, and none is apparent. Because Osborne has offered to pay for the tests, cost is not a factor. And as the State now concedes, there is no reason to doubt that such testing would provide conclusive confirmation of Osborne's guilt or revelation of his innocence. In the courts below, the State refused to provide an explanation for its refusal to permit testing of the evidence, . . . and in this Court, its explanation has been, at best, unclear. Insofar as the State has articulated any reason at all, it appears to be a generalized interest in protecting the finality of the judgment of conviction from any possible future attacks. . . .

While we have long recognized that States have an interest in securing the finality of their judgments, . . . finality is not a stand-alone value that trumps a State's overriding interest in ensuring that justice is done in its courts and secured to its citizens. Indeed, when absolute proof of innocence is readily at hand, a State should not shrink from the possibility that error may have occurred. Rather, our system of justice is strengthened by "recogniz[ing] the need for, and imperative of, a safety valve in those rare instances where objective proof that the convicted actually did not commit the offense later becomes available through the progress of science.". . . DNA evidence has led to an extraordinary series of exonerations, not only in cases where the trial evidence was weak, but also in cases where the convicted parties confessed their guilt and where the trial evidence against them appeared overwhelming. The examples provided by amici of the power of DNA testing serve to convince me that the fact of conviction is not sufficient to justify a State's refusal to perform a test that will conclusively establish innocence or guilt.

This conclusion draws strength from the powerful state interests that offset the State's purported interest in finality *per se.* When a person is convicted for a crime he did not commit, the true culprit escapes punishment. DNA testing may lead to his identification. . . . Crime victims, the law enforcement profession, and society at large share a strong interest in identifying and apprehending the actual perpetrators of vicious crimes, such as the rape and attempted murder that gave rise to this case.

The arbitrariness of the State's conduct is highlighted by comparison to the private interests it denies. It seems to me obvious that if a wrongly convicted person were to produce proof of his actual innocence, no state interest would be sufficient to justify his continued punitive detention. If such proof can be readily obtained without imposing a significant burden on the State, a refusal to provide access to such evidence is wholly unjustified.

In sum, an individual's interest in his physical liberty is one of constitutional significance. That interest would be vindicated by providing postconviction access to DNA evidence, as would the State's interest in ensuring that it punishes the true perpetrator of a crime. In this case, the State has suggested no countervailing interest that justifies its refusal to allow Osborne to test the

evidence in its possession and has not provided any other nonarbitrary explanation for its conduct. Consequently, I am left to conclude that the State's
failure to provide Osborne access to the evidence constitutes arbitrary action
that offends basic principles of due process. . . .

III

. . . Before our decision in *Powell* v. *Alabama,* 287 U. S. 45 (1932), state law alone
governed the manner in which counsel was appointed for indigent defendants.
"Efforts to impose a minimum federal standard for the right to counsel in state
courts routinely met the same refrain: 'in the face of these widely varying state
procedures', this Court refused to impose the dictates of 'due process' onto the
states and 'hold invalid all procedure not reaching that standard.'" . . . When at
last this Court recognized the Sixth Amendment right to counsel for all indigent
criminal defendants in *Gideon* v. *Wainwright,* 372 U. S. 335 (1963), our decision
did not impede the ability of States to tailor their appointment processes to local
needs, nor did it unnecessarily interfere with their sovereignty. It did, however,
ensure that criminal defendants were provided with the counsel to which they
were constitutionally entitled. In the same way, a decision to recognize a limited
right of postconviction access to DNA testing would not prevent the States from
creating procedures by which litigants request and obtain such access; it would
merely ensure that States do so in a manner that is nonarbitrary. . . .

IV

Osborne has demonstrated a constitutionally protected right to due process
which the State of Alaska thus far has not vindicated and which this Court is
both empowered and obliged to safeguard. On the record before us, there is no
reason to deny access to the evidence and there are many reasons to provide it,
not least of which is a fundamental concern in ensuring that justice has been
done in this case. I would affirm the judgment of the Court of Appeals, and
respectfully dissent from the Court's refusal to do so.

 **NO**

Majority Opinion, *District Attorney's Office v. Osborne*

Chief Justice Roberts delivered the opinion of the Court.

DNA testing has an unparalleled ability both to exonerate the wrongly convicted and to identify the guilty. It has the potential to significantly improve both the criminal justice system and police investigative practices. The Federal Government and the States have recognized this, and have developed special approaches to ensure that this evidentiary tool can be effectively incorporated into established criminal procedure—usually but not always through legislation.

Against this prompt and considered response, the respondent, William Osborne, proposes a different approach: the recognition of a freestanding and far-reaching constitutional right of access to this new type of evidence. The nature of what he seeks is confirmed by his decision to file this lawsuit in federal court under 42 U. S. C. §1983, not within the state criminal justice system. This approach would take the development of rules and procedures in this area out of the hands of legislatures and state courts shaping policy in a focused manner and turn it over to federal courts applying the broad parameters of the Due Process Clause. There is no reason to constitutionalize the issue in this way. Because the decision below would do just that, we reverse.

I

A

This lawsuit arose out of a violent crime committed 16 years ago, which has resulted in a long string of litigation in the state and federal courts. On the evening of March 22, 1993, two men driving through Anchorage, Alaska, solicited sex from a female prostitute, K. G. She agreed to perform fellatio on both men for $100 and got in their car. The three spent some time looking for a place to stop and ended up in a deserted area near Earthquake Park. When K. G. demanded payment in advance, the two men pulled out a gun and forced her to perform fellatio on the driver while the passenger penetrated her vaginally, using a blue condom she had brought. The passenger then ordered K. G. out of the car and told her to lie face-down in the snow. Fearing for her life, she refused, and the two men choked her and beat her with the gun. When K. G. tried to flee, the passenger beat her with a wooden axe handle and shot her in

Supreme Court of the United States, 129 S.Ct 2308, June 18, 2009.

the head while she lay on the ground. They kicked some snow on top of her and left her for dead. 521 F. 3d 1118, 1122 (CA9 2008) (case below); *Osborne* v. *State,* 163 P. 3d 973, 975–976 (Alaska App. 2007) (*Osborne II*); App. 27, 42–44.

K. G. did not die; the bullet had only grazed her head. Once the two men left, she found her way back to the road, and flagged down a passing car to take her home. Ultimately, she received medical care and spoke to the police. At the scene of the crime, the police recovered a spent shell casing, the axe handle, some of K. G.'s clothing stained with blood, and the blue condom. . . .

Six days later, two military police officers at Fort Richardson pulled over Dexter Jackson for flashing his headlights at another vehicle. In his car they discovered a gun (which matched the shell casing), as well as several items K. G. had been carrying the night of the attack. . . . The car also matched the description K. G. had given to the police. Jackson admitted that he had been the driver during the rape and assault, and told the police that William Osborne had been his passenger. . . . Other evidence also implicated Osborne. K. G. picked out his photograph (with some uncertainty) and at trial she identified Osborne as her attacker. Other witnesses testified that shortly before the crime, Osborne had called Jackson from an arcade, and then driven off with him. An axe handle similar to the one at the scene of the crime was found in Osborne's room on the military base where he lived.

The State also performed DQ Alpha testing on sperm found in the blue condom. DQ Alpha testing is a relatively inexact form of DNA testing that can clear some wrongly accused individuals, but generally cannot narrow the perpetrator down to less than 5% of the population. . . . The semen found on the condom had a genotype that matched a blood sample taken from Osborne, but not ones from Jackson, K. G., or a third suspect named James Hunter. Osborne is black, and approximately 16% of black individuals have such a genotype. App. 117–119. In other words, the testing ruled out Jackson and Hunter as possible sources of the semen, and also ruled out over 80% of other black individuals. The State also examined some pubic hairs found at the scene of the crime, which were not susceptible to DQ Alpha testing, but which state witnesses attested to be similar to Osborne's. . . .

B

Osborne and Jackson were convicted by an Alaska jury of kidnaping, assault, and sexual assault. They were acquitted of an additional count of sexual assault and of attempted murder. Finding it "'nearly miraculous'" that K. G. had survived, the trial judge sentenced Osborne to 26 years in prison, with 5 suspended. *Id.,* at 128a. His conviction and sentence were affirmed on appeal. *Id.,* at 113a–130a.

Osborne then sought postconviction relief in Alaska state court. He claimed that he had asked his attorney, Sidney Billingslea, to seek more discriminating restriction-fragment-length-polymorphism (RFLP) DNA testing during trial, and argued that she was constitutionally ineffective for not doing so. Billingslea testified that after investigation, she had concluded that further testing would do more harm than good. She planned to mount a defense of mistaken identity, and thought that the imprecision of the DQ Alpha test gave her "Very good numbers in a mistaken identity, cross-racial identification case, where the victim was in the dark and had bad eyesight'. "

Osborne I, 110 P. 3d, at 990. Because she believed Osborne was guilty, "'insisting on a more advanced . . . DNA test would have served to prove that Osborne committed the alleged crimes.'" *Ibid.* The Alaska Court of Appeals concluded that Billingslea's decision had been strategic and rejected Osborne's claim. *Id.*, at 991–992.

In this proceeding, Osborne also sought the DNA testing that Billingslea had failed to perform, relying on an Alaska postconviction statute, Alaska Stat. §12.72 (2008), and the State and Federal Constitutions. In two decisions, the Alaska Court of Appeals concluded that Osborne had no right to the RFLP test. According to the court, §12.72 "apparently" did not apply to DNA testing that had been available at trial.[1] *Osborne I*, 110 P. 3d, at 992–993. The court found no basis in our precedents for recognizing a federal constitutional right to DNA evidence. *Id.*, at 993. After a remand for further findings, the Alaska Court of Appeals concluded that Osborne could not claim a state constitutional right either, because the other evidence of his guilt was too strong and RFLP testing was not likely to be conclusive. *Osborne II*, 163 P. 3d, at 979–981. Two of the three judges wrote separately to say that "[i]f Osborne could show that he were in fact innocent, it would be unconscionable to punish him," and that doing so might violate the Alaska Constitution. *Id.*, at 984–985 (Mannheimer, J., concurring).

The court relied heavily on the fact that Osborne had confessed to some of his crimes in a 2004 application for parole—in which it is a crime to lie. *Id.*, at 978–979, 981 (majority opinion) (citing Alaska Stat. §11.56.210 (2002)). In this statement, Osborne acknowledged forcing K. G. to have sex at gunpoint, as well as beating her and covering her with snow. *Id.*, at 977–978, n. 11. He repeated this confession before the parole board. Despite this acceptance of responsibility, the board did not grant him discretionary parole. App. to Pet. for Cert. 8a. In 2007, he was released on mandatory parole, but he has since been rearrested for another offense, and the State has petitioned to revoke this parole. Brief for Petitioners 7, n. 3.

Meanwhile, Osborne had also been active in federal court, suing state officials under 42 U. S. C. §1983. He claimed that the Due Process Clause and other constitutional provisions gave him a constitutional right to access the DNA evidence for what is known as short-tandemrepeat (STR) testing (at his own expense). App. 24. This form of testing is more discriminating than the DQ Alpha or RFLP methods available at the time of Osborne's trial. The District Court first dismissed the claim under *Heck* v. *Humphrey,* 512 U. S. 477 (1994), holding it "inescapable" that Osborne sought to "set the stage" for an attack on his conviction, and therefore "must proceed through a writ of habeas corpus." App. 207 (internal quotation marks omitted). The United States Court of Appeals for the Ninth Circuit reversed, concluding that §1983 was the proper vehicle for Osborne's claims, while "express[ing] no opinion as to whether Osborne ha[d] been deprived of a federally protected right." 423 F. 3d, at 1056. . . .

We granted certiorari to decide whether Osborne's claims could be pursued using §1983, and whether he has a right under the Due Process Clause to obtain postconviction access to the State's evidence for DNA testing. . . . We now reverse on the latter ground.

II

Modern DNA testing can provide powerful new evidence unlike anything known before. Since its first use in criminal investigations in the mid-1980s, there have been several major advances in DNA technology, culminating in STR technology. It is now often possible to determine whether a biological tissue matches a suspect with near certainty. While of course many criminal trials proceed without any forensic and scientific testing at all, there is no technology comparable to DNA testing for matching tissues when such evidence is at issue. Postconviction DNA Testing 1–2; Future of Forensic DNA Testing 13-14. DNA testing has exonerated wrongly convicted people, and has confirmed the convictions of many others.

At the same time, DNA testing alone does not always resolve a case. Where there is enough other incriminating evidence and an explanation for the DNA result, science alone cannot prove a prisoner innocent. See *House* v. *Bell*, 547 U. S. 518, 540–548 (2006). The availability of technologies not available at trial cannot mean that every criminal conviction, or even every criminal conviction involving biological evidence, is suddenly in doubt. The dilemma is how to harness DNA's power to prove innocence without unnecessarily overthrowing the established system of criminal justice.

That task belongs primarily to the legislature. "[T]he States are currently engaged in serious, thoughtful examinations," *Washington* v. *Glucksberg*, 521 U. S. 702, 719 (1997), of how to ensure the fair and effective use of this testing within the existing criminal justice framework. Forty-six States have already enacted statutes dealing specifically with access to DNA evidence. . . . The Federal Government has also passed the Innocence Protection Act of 2004, §411, 118 Stat. 2278, codified in part at 18 U. S. C. §3600, which allows federal prisoners to move for court-ordered DNA testing under certain specified conditions. That Act also grants money to States that enact comparable statutes . . . and as a consequence has served as a model for some state legislation. At oral argument, Osborne agreed that the federal statute is a model for how States ought to handle the issue. . . .

These laws recognize the value of DNA evidence but also the need for certain conditions on access to the State's evidence. A requirement of demonstrating materiality is common, . . . but it is not the only one. The federal statute, for example, requires a sworn statement that the applicant is innocent. . . . This requirement is replicated in several state statutes. . . . States also impose a range of diligence requirements. Several require the requested testing to "have been technologically impossible at trial." . . . Others deny testing to those who declined testing at trial for tactical reasons. . . .

Alaska is one of a handful of States yet to enact legislation specifically addressing the issue of evidence requested for DNA testing. But that does not mean that such evidence is unavailable for those seeking to prove their inno-cence. Instead, Alaska courts are addressing how to apply existing laws for discovery and postconviction relief to this novel technology. . . . The same is true with respect to other States that do not have DNA-specific statutes. . . .

First, access to evidence is available under Alaska law for those who seek to subject it to newly available DNA testing that will prove them to be actually innocent. Under the State's general postconviction relief statute, a prisoner may challenge his conviction when "there exists evidence of material facts, not previously presented and heard by the court, that requires vacation of the conviction or sentence in the interest of justice." . . . Such a claim is exempt from otherwise applicable time limits if "newly discovered evidence," pursued with due diligence, "establishes by clear and convincing evidence that the applicant is innocent." . . .

Both parties agree that under these provisions of [Alaska Law] "a defend-ant is entitled to post-conviction relief if the defendant presents newly dis-covered evidence that establishes by clear and convincing evidence that the defendant is innocent." . . . If such a claim is brought, state law permits general discovery. . . . Alaska courts have explained that these procedures are available to request DNA evidence for newly available testing to establish actual inno-cence. . . .

In addition to this statutory procedure, the Alaska Court of Appeals has invoked a widely accepted three-part test to govern additional rights to DNA access under the State Constitution. . . . Drawing on the experience with DNA evidence of State Supreme Courts around the country, the Court of Appeals explained that it was "reluctant to hold that Alaska law offers no remedy to defendants who could prove their factual innocence." . . . It was "prepared to hold, however, that a defendant who seeks post-conviction DNA testing . . . must show (1) that the conviction rested primarily on eyewitness identification evidence, (2) that there was a demonstrable doubt concerning the defendant's identification as the perpetrator, and (3) that scientific testing would likely be conclusive on this issue.". . . Thus, the Alaska courts have suggested that even those who do not get discovery under the State's criminal rules have available to them a safety valve under the State Constitution.

This is the background against which the Federal Court of Appeals ordered the State to turn over the DNA evidence in its possession, and it is our starting point in analyzing Osborne's constitutional claims. . . .

IV

A

"No State shall . . . deprive any person of life, liberty, or property, without due process of law." U. S. Const., Amdt. 14, §1; accord Amdt. 5. This Clause imposes procedural limitations on a State's power to take away protected entitlements. . . . Osborne argues that access to the State's evidence is a "process" needed to vindicate his right to prove himself innocent and get out of jail. Process is not an end in itself, so a necessary premise of this argument is that he has an entitlement (what our precedents call a "liberty interest") to prove his innocence even after a fair trial has proved otherwise. We must first examine this asserted liberty interest to determine what process (if any) is due. . . .

In identifying his potential liberty interest, Osborne first attempts to rely on the Governor's constitutional authority to "grant pardons, commutations, and reprieves." Alaska Const., Art. Ill, §21. That claim can be readily disposed of. We have held that noncapital defendants do not have a liberty interest in traditional state executive clemency, to which no particular claimant is *entitled* as a matter of state law. . . . Osborne therefore cannot challenge the constitutionality of any procedures available to vindicate an interest in state clemency.

Osborne does, however, have a liberty interest in demonstrating his innocence with new evidence under state law. As explained, Alaska law provides that those who use "newly discovered evidence" to "establis[h] by clear and convincing evidence that [they are] innocent" may obtain "vacation of [their] conviction or sentence in the interest of justice." . . . This "state-created right can, in some circumstances, beget yet other rights to procedures essential to the realization of the parent right." . . .

The Court of Appeals went too far, however, in concluding that the Due Process Clause requires that certain familiar preconviction trial rights be extended to protect Osborne's postconviction liberty interest. . . .

A criminal defendant proved guilty after a fair trial does not have the same liberty interests as a free man. At trial, the defendant is presumed innocent and may demand that the government prove its case beyond reasonable doubt. But "[o]nce a defendant has been afforded a fair trial and convicted of the offense for which he was charged, the presumption of innocence disappears." . . . "Given a valid conviction, the criminal defendant has been constitutionally deprived of his liberty." . . .

The State accordingly has more flexibility in deciding what procedures are needed in the context of postconviction relief. "[W]hen a State chooses to offer help to those seeking relief from convictions," due process does not "dictat[e] the exact form such assistance must assume." . . . Osborne's right to due process is not parallel to a trial right, but rather must be analyzed in light of the fact that he has already been found guilty at a fair trial, and has only a limited interest in postconviction relief. . . .

Instead, the question is whether consideration of Osborne's claim within the framework of the State's procedures for postconviction relief "offends some principle of justice so rooted in the traditions and conscience of our people as to be ranked as fundamental," or "transgresses any recognized principle of fundamental fairness in operation." . . . Federal courts may upset a State's postconviction relief procedures only if they are fundamentally inadequate to vindicate the substantive rights provided.

We see nothing inadequate about the procedures Alaska has provided to vindicate its state right to postconviction relief in general, and nothing inadequate about how those procedures apply to those who seek access to DNA evidence. Alaska provides a substantive right to be released on a sufficiently compelling showing of new evidence that establishes innocence. It exempts such claims from otherwise applicable time limits. The State provides for discovery in postconviction proceedings, and has—through judicial decision—specified that this discovery procedure is available to those seeking access to DNA evidence. . . . These procedures are not without limits. The evidence must indeed be newly available to qualify under Alaska's statute, must have been diligently pursued, and must also be sufficiently material. These procedures are similar to those provided for DNA evidence by federal law and the law of other States, . . . and they are not inconsistent with the "traditions and conscience of our people" or with "any recognized principle of fundamental fairness." . . .

And there is more. While the Alaska courts have not had occasion to conclusively decide the question, the Alaska Court of Appeals has suggested that the State Constitution provides an additional right of access to DNA. In expressing its "reluctan[ce] to hold that Alaska law offers no remedy" to those who belatedly seek DNA testing, and in invoking the three-part test used by other state courts, the court indicated that in an appropriate case the State Constitution may provide a failsafe even for those who cannot satisfy the statutory requirements under general postconviction procedures. . . .

To the degree there is some uncertainty in the details of Alaska's newly developing procedures for obtaining postconviction access to DNA, we can hardly fault the State for that. Osborne has brought this §1983 action without ever using these procedures in filing a state or federal habeas claim relying on actual innocence. In other words, he has not tried to use the process provided to him by the State or attempted to vindicate the liberty interest that is now the centerpiece of his claim. When Osborne *did* request DNA testing in state court, he sought RFLP testing that had been available at trial, not the STR testing he now seeks, and the state court relied on that fact in denying him testing under Alaska law. . . .

His attempt to sidestep state process through a new federal lawsuit puts Osborne in a very awkward position. If he simply seeks the DNA through the State's discovery procedures, he might well get it. If he does not, it may be for a perfectly adequate reason, just as the federal statute and all state statutes impose conditions and limits on access to DNA evidence. It is difficult to criticize the State's procedures when Osborne has not invoked them. This is not to say that Osborne must exhaust state-law remedies. . . . But it is Osborne's burden to demonstrate the inadequacy of the state-law procedures available to him in state postconviction relief. . . . These procedures are adequate on their face, and without trying them, Osborne can hardly complain that they do not work in practice.

As a fallback, Osborne also obliquely relies on an asserted federal constitutional right to be released upon proof of "actual innocence." Whether such a federal right exists is an open question. We have struggled with it over the years, in some cases assuming, *arguendo*, that it exists while also noting the difficult questions such a right would pose and the high standard any claimant would have to meet. . . . In this case too we can assume without deciding that such a claim exists, because even if so there is no due process problem. . . .

B

The Court of Appeals below relied only on procedural due process, but Osborne seeks to defend the judgment on the basis of substantive due process as well. He asks that we recognize a freestanding right to DNA evidence untethered from the liberty interests he hopes to vindicate with it. We reject the invitation and conclude, in the circumstances of this case, that there is no such substantive due process right. "As a general matter, the Court has always been reluctant to expand the concept of substantive due process because guideposts for responsible decisionmaking in this unchartered area are scarce and open-ended." . . . Osborne seeks access to state evidence so that he can apply new DNA-testing technology that might prove him innocent. There is no long history of such a right, and "[t]he mere novelty of such a claim is reason enough to doubt that 'substantive due process' sustains it." . . .

And there are further reasons to doubt. The elected governments of the States are actively confronting the challenges DNA technology poses to our criminal justice systems and our traditional notions of finality, as well as the opportunities it affords. To suddenly constitutionalize this area would short-circuit what looks to be a prompt and considered legislative response. . . . In the past decade, 44 States and the Federal Government have followed suit, reflecting the increased availability of DNA testing. As noted, Alaska itself is considering such legislation. . . . "By extending constitutional protection to an asserted right or liberty interest, we, to a great extent, place the matter outside the arena of public debate and legislative action. We must therefore exercise the utmost care whenever we are asked to break new ground in this field." . . . "[J]udicial imposition of a categorical remedy . . . might pretermit other responsible solutions being considered in Congress and state legislatures." . . . If we extended substantive due process to this area, we would cast these statutes into constitutional doubt and be forced to take over the issue of DNA access ourselves. We are reluctant to enlist the Federal Judiciary in creating a new constitutional code of rules for handling DNA.

Establishing a freestanding right to access DNA evidence for testing would force us to act as policymakers, and our substantive-due-process rulemaking authority would not only have to cover the right of access but a myriad of other issues. We would soon have to decide if there is a constitutional obligation to preserve forensic evidence that might later be tested. . . . If so, for how long? Would it be different for different types of evidence? Would the State also have some obligation to gather such evidence in the first place? How much, and when? No doubt there would be a miscellany of other minor directives. . . .

In this case, the evidence has already been gathered and preserved, but if we extend substantive due process to this area, these questions would be before us in short order, and it is hard to imagine what tools federal courts would use to answer them. At the end of the day, there is no reason to suppose that their answers to these questions would be any better than those of state courts and legislatures, and good reason to suspect the opposite. . . .

* * *

DNA evidence will undoubtedly lead to changes in the criminal justice system. It has done so already. The question is whether further change will primarily be made by legislative revision and judicial interpretation of the existing system, or whether the Federal Judiciary must leap ahead—revising (or even discarding) the system by creating a new constitutional right and taking over responsibility for refining it.

Federal courts should not presume that state criminal procedures will be inadequate to deal with technological change. The criminal justice system has historically accommodated new types of evidence, and is a time-tested means of carrying out society's interest in convicting the guilty while respecting individual rights. That system, like any human endeavor, cannot be perfect. DNA evidence shows that it has not been. But there is no basis for Osborne's approach of assuming that because DNA has shown that these procedures are not flawless, DNA evidence must be treated as categorically outside the process, rather than within it. That is precisely what his §1983 suit seeks to do, and that is the contention we reject.

The judgment of the Court of Appeals is reversed, and the case is remanded for further proceedings consistent with this opinion.

It is so ordered.

Note

1. It is not clear whether the Alaska Court of Appeals was correct that Osborne sought *only* forms of DNA testing that had been available at trial, compare *Osborne I, supra*, at 992, 995, with 521 F. 3d 1118, 1123, n. 2 (CA9 2008), but it resolved the case on that basis.

POSTSCRIPT

Does an Imprisoned Individual Have a Constitutional Right to Access the State's Evidence for DNA Testing?

This is a difficult issue. On one hand, Chief Justice Roberts contends that the states play an important role in the formation of justice system policy that the federal courts should respect. Conversely, it is difficult to imagine how our justice system can live with the realization that innocent persons may be confined for crimes they did not commit, when it is relatively simple to prove the matter conclusively with DNA evidence. It is also important to note that DNA evidence, as compelling as it may be in various cases, may not be infallible. Perhaps the most celebrated case in recent years that has used DNA evidence was the O. J. Simpson murder trial. It appears as though the Simpson jury concluded that the DNA evidence in that case carried little or no weight due to improper collection methods and sloppy laboratory analysis of the evidence.

One factor that may influence the debate about the use of DNA evidence is the extent to which DNA evidence has already been used to exonerate innocent persons who have been incarcerated. The *Innocence Project* is an organization that has worked tirelessly to free wrongfully convicted persons since its founding in 1992 at Yeshiva University by Barry C. Sheck and Peter Neufeld. The nonprofit clinic's stated mission is to "exonerate wrongfully convicted people through DNA testing and [to] reform the criminal justice system to prevent future injustice." Most of the project's clients are indigent and have exhausted all of the traditional legal avenues for relief. The project emphasizes that DNA evidence has "provided scientific proof that our system convicts and sentences innocent people—and that wrongful convictions are not isolated or rare events."

To this point, the Innocence Project has determined the following:

- Seventeen people had been sentenced to death before DNA proved their innocence and led to their release.
- The average sentence served by those who have been exonerated by DNA evidence has been 13 years.
- About 70 percent of those exonerated by DNA testing are members of minority groups.
- In almost 40 percent of DNA exoneration cases, the actual perpetrator has been identified by DNA testing.
- Exonerations have won in 34 states and Washington, D.C. (http://www.innocenceproject.org)

Thus, it is clear that while the U.S. justice system often does an effective job of balancing important social interests in attaining justice for the victims of crime and the individual rights of suspected criminals, it sometimes makes mistakes. Given this fact and the unprecedented ability of DNA evidence to conclusively establish a person's guilt or innocence, the question then becomes, "What approach should the justice system take in these cases?"

If you agree with Chief Justice John Roberts's assertion that the "task of establishing rules to harness DNA's power to prove innocence without unnecessarily overthrowing the established criminal justice system belongs primarily to the [state] legislature[s]," do you think that the cause of "justice" has been served by the majority's holding in *Osborne*? Further, do you agree with Chief Justice Roberts's statement that "[t]he elected governments of the States are actively confronting the challenges DNA technology poses to our criminal justice systems and our traditional notions of finality, as well as the opportunities it affords. To suddenly constitutionalize this area would short-circuit what looks to be a prompt and considered legislative response." Would the Supreme Court's intervention in this area force the Court to "act as policymakers," or is it more important to ensure that justice has been done and free those who are wrongfully accused? As Justice Stevens' opinion emphasizes, do you feel that Osborne "demonstrated a constitutionally protected right to due process which the State of Alaska thus far has not vindicated and which this Court is both empowered and obliged to safeguard"?

These are contentious issues. Fortunately, there are numerous additional resources to consult for further discussion of these important matters, including Kathleen M. Sullivan and Gerald Gunther, *Constitutional Law* (Foundation Press, 15th ed., 2004); Laurence H. Tribe, *American Constitutional Law* (Foundation Press, 2nd ed., 1988); Simon J. Walsh, *Forensic DNA Evidence Interpretation* (CBC Press, 2004); Ron C. Michaelis, *A Litigator's Guide to DNA: From the Laboratory to the Courtroom* (Academic Press, 2008); John M. Butler, *Forensic DNA Typing: Biology, Technology and Genetics of STR Markers* (Academic Press, 2005); Jay D. Aronson, *Genetic Awareness: Science, Law, and Controversy* (Rutgers University Press, 2007); and David H. Kaye, *The Double Helix and the Law of Evidence* (Harvard University Press, 2010). See also Millard, "*District Attorney's Office for the Third Judicial District v. Osborne*: Leaving Prisoners' Access to DNA Evidence in Limbo?" *U. Maryland L.R.* (vol. 69, 2010, p. 4); Comment, "Due Process—Postconviction Access to DNA Evidence," *Harv. L. Rev.* (vol. 123, 2009, p. 222); Cooley, "Advancing DNA Technology and Evolving Standards of Decency," *Charleston L. Rev.* (vol. 4, 2009, p. 582); Hoeffel, "The Roberts Court's Failed Innocence Project," *Chic. Kent L. Rev.* (2010); Roach, "The Role of Innocence Commissions: Discovery, Systematic Reform, or Both?" *Chic. Kent L. Rev.* (2010); and Thornton, "A Second Comment on *Skinner v. Switzer*," *Am. Crim. L. Rev.* (2010).

Internet References . . .

Recording Industry Association of America (RIAA)

Web site for the trade organization that supports and promotes the major music labels.

www.riaa.com

Recording Industry v. The People

Popular blogger Ray Beckerman regularly posts updated links to court documents involving pending litigation.

www.recordingindustryvspeople.blogspot.com

All Things Considered

Link to a 5-minute audio clip from NPR's "All Things Considered" news program, discussing the U.S. Supreme Court's decision in the *Florence v. Board of Chosen Freeholders of County of Burlington* case.

http://goo.gl/TzlW2

Bonus Issues

*T*he debates considered in this unit are on the cutting-edge of crime, criminology, and the U.S. justice system. Both issues will be hotly debated by students and teachers as well as contemporary justice system practitioners. The first debate considers an issue that is highly relevant to modern, Internet-savvy readers: Is it wrong to download music and other copyrighted material from the Internet without paying for it? The second issue, which was considered by the U.S. Supreme Court only a few weeks ago, concerns the propriety of conducting jailhouse strip searches of persons arrested for minor offenses.

- Should It Be a Crime to Download Copyrighted Music from the Internet?
- Should It Be Lawful for the Police to Conduct Jailhouse Strip Searches of Persons Arrested for Minor Offenses?

ISSUE 21

Should It Be a Crime to Download Copyrighted Music from the Internet?

YES: **Barry Shrum**, from "The Magical Ring of Gyges: Why Illegal Downloading Is so Rampant in the Age of Cyberspace," *Law on the Row* (2011)

NO: **Janis Ian**, from "The Internet Debacle—An Alternative View," *Performing Songwriter Magazine* (May 2002)

ISSUE SUMMARY

YES: Attorney Barry Shrum argues that downloading music illegally from the Internet is wrong morally and should be considered a crime because it fails to pay creative individuals for their intellectual property. Moreover, because approximately 95 percent of the music downloaded from the Internet is done so illegally, the problem is a very compelling one.

NO: Noted recording artist and songwriter Janis Ian, in contrast, believes that there is no evidence to support the proposition that material available for free online downloading is harming anyone, especially the artists who produce it. In fact, free downloading may actually benefit the majority of artists because it allows them potentially to reach millions of new listeners, who may later purchase CDs, and attend their live concerts.

At a recent faculty luncheon, a discussion began about downloading music and other copyrighted materials from the Internet. Although several of those present indicated a belief that it was happening with "some frequency," no one expressed a serious concern. The issue intrigued me, so after lunch, I decided to ask my students the following question in an introductory-level course: Have you, within the past year, downloaded music from the Internet that you knew was copyright protected? A resounding 92 percent of the students indicated that they had done so. Although the poll taken in my class was an admittedly unscientific one, there is no apparent reason to think that the results would be significantly different at other public universities. I then asked two follow-up questions: (1) Do you think it is wrong? (2) Should downloading music in this manner be considered a crime?

Students' answers to these queries were quite interesting. Although most indicated a belief that it was "wrong" to download copyrighted music from the Internet, a significant majority (approximately 76 percent) believed that it should not be considered a "crime." When asked to explain this apparent contradiction, the students provided a number of different reasons. Several suggested that the "wrong," if any, involved in downloading copyrighted music was so insubstantial that it did not constitute a crime. Another suggested that all materials placed on the Internet should be considered a part of the "public domain," which should not receive any copyright protection. Still another held the opinion that because the recording industry in the United States has been engaged in an egregious pattern of "ripping off" those who purchase CDs and other forms of music, consumers were justified in taking private action to attempt to recover some of the excessive profits generated by the recording industry in the past.

Another student's justification for downloading copyrighted music was a more philosophical one: *Stealing* involves taking someone's property in a permanent way that does not allow them to use it any more. Simply *copying* material from the Internet does not deny a writer the ability to use the original work for whatever purpose he or she wishes.

One student, however, stated unequivocally that downloading copyrighted music from the Internet is a crime because it involves an intentional act that deprives the recording artist and the record companies of compensation for their intellectual property. She also asked: "How would you like it if instead of buying this book, I had photocopied it on my laser printer for less than two cents per page? What's the difference between doing that and illegally downloading someone's music?" I had to admit that this was a very difficult question indeed. Following our discussion, it was quite clear that most of my students were very ambivalent about the issue of downloading copyrighted material from the Internet.

The U.S. justice system has demonstrated a similar ambivalence toward these difficult issues. It seems apparent as well that U.S. law has not yet evolved to deal effectively with the problem. As one commentator has suggested, illegally downloading music is a movement "into another dimension of crime—a dimension not only of cops and robbers, but of technology and guile. It's the middle ground between privacy and exposure; suspicion and surveillance; and security and panic. You're moving into [a world] created on the next frontier of crime: The ever-evolving world of Cyber Crime." (*The Cyber Sleuth*, Monday, January 19, 2009).

One approach to dealing with the issue of illegal downloading that has been used by the American legal system is to apply currently existing federal "copyright" laws. Under these laws, "copyright infringement" is defined as the act of exercising, without legal authorization, the rights granted to a copyright owner (Section 106 of the U.S. Copyright Act, Title 17 of the United States Code (U.S.C.)). According to a recent summary of copyright laws published by the University of North Carolina Wilmington, these rights include reproducing or distributing a copyrighted work, and/or downloading or uploading substantial parts of a copyrighted work. (UNCW.edu/www.dmca.html).

The potential penalties for copyright infringement include both criminal and civil sanctions. A person found liable for civil copyright infringement may be ordered to pay either actual damages or damages of not less than $750 or more than $30,000 per work infringed. For intentional infringement, a court may award up to $150,000 per work infringed. In addition, willful infringement may also result in criminal penalties, including imprisonment of up to 5 years in prison and/or fines of up to $250,000 per offense (UNCW.edu/www .dmca.html).

Criminal prosecutions for illegal downloading are highly uncommon. One recent U.S. district court case has held that under U.S. federal law, downloading music from the Internet does not constitute a "public performance" for which a performance royalty fee is due. (See *United States v. ASCAP,* 485 F. Supp. 2d 438 (SDNY 2007).) The U.S. Supreme Court has declined to review it, so the original ruling stands (*ASCAP v. United States,* No. 10-1337). Some commentators have asserted that *ASCAP* means that downloading copyrighted music from the Internet is not a crime. (See *Reuters,* Monday, October 3, 2011.)

Civil lawsuits, often supported and/or funded by the Recording Industry Association of America (RIAA), however, are much more common. According to the Cable News Network (CNN), in June 2009, a federal jury found a 32-year-old Minnesota woman guilty of illegally downloading music from the Internet and fined her $80,000 per song. The total fine was $1.9 million, even though the cost to lawfully download the music would have been only 99 cents per song! (CNN, June 18, 2009).

Likewise, in February 2004, a 12-year-old girl, Briana LaHara, was the first of 261 defendants to settle a civil lawsuit brought by the RIAA. The child (or her parents) agreed to pay $2,000, or approximately $2.00 per song she had shared on a file-sharing Web site (CNN, February 18, 2004).

These cases illustrate that illegally downloading music and other copyrighted materials from the Internet can have serious consequences, even though these actions are deemed to be relatively harmless by many people, especially students. The essential question, however, remains whether the actions are morally wrong, and if they should constitute crimes.

Attorney Barry Shrum, who lives and works in Nashville, Tennessee, and represents many popular songwriters and recording artists, contends that illegally downloading music from the Internet is morally wrong and should be considered a crime because it fails to provide compensation to those who have produced creative works. Shrum observes that 95 percent of the music downloaded from the Internet is taken illegally. He states: "Imagine how our society would react if one out of four people in retail malls were carrying out stolen merchandise on a daily basis, or if 95 percent of the product leaving the mall was stolen." The problem, according to Shrum, is that "the fear of being punished or getting caught is eliminated in the evanescent world of Cyberspace." Shrum concludes that even though most "people would not even think about walking up on stage after a singer/songwriter in a nightclub takes a break and stealing his guitar, . . . that very same person doesn't think twice of taking that same singer/songwriter's song from the Internet."

Shrum also points out that "very real people" are "being affected" by illegal downloading, "and the effect is devastating." He observes that some of his clients "are songwriters who are no longer creating art because they are forced to take odd jobs to support their families." He concludes, however, that while there will always be people who will choose to steal because they are covered by a cloak of anonymity, "there will always be people" who embrace the idea of "giving to every man his own."

Songwriter Janis Ian, in contrast, does not believe that downloading copyrighted music from the Internet should be considered a crime. Rather, Ms. Ian believes that much of the tempest surrounding the issue has been generated by the commercial music industry to create the impression that Internet downloads have harmed the recording industry. States Ian: "[t]he music industry had *exactly* the same response to the advent of reel-to-reel home tape recorders, cassettes, DATs, minidiscs, VHS, BETA, music videos ('Why buy the record when you can tape it?'), MTV, and a host of other technological advances designed to make the consumer's life easier and better." Ian continues:

> If you think about it, the music industry should be rejoicing at this new technological advance! Here's a new fool-proof way to deliver music to millions who might otherwise never purchase a CD in a store. The cross-marketing opportunities are unbelievable. It's instantaneous, costs are minimal, shipping non-existent . . . a staggering vehicle for higher earnings and lower costs. Instead, they're running around like chickens with their heads cut off, bleeding on everyone and making no sense.

Do you agree with Barry Shrum or Janis Ian? Is downloading copyrighted music from the Internet simply another form of stealing, or does it have significant benefits for everyone involved? The authors of the YES and NO selections provide very different answers to this difficult question.

YES

Barry Shrum

The Magical Ring of Gyges: Why Illegal Downloading Is So Rampant in the Age of Cyberspace

In 2010, NBC Universal hired a company called Envisional to study counterfeiting activity over the Internet. The results of this study—despite the fact that it is industry funded—are literally astonishing: 24% of all global Internet traffic involves digital theft! Stated another way, one in every four people surfing the Internet are stealing intellectual property, i.e., illegally downloading either copyrighted or trademarked materials. According to the International Federation of the Phonographic Industry, 95% of the music downloaded from the Internet is downloaded illegally! Imagine how our society would react if one out of every four people in retail malls were carrying out stolen merchandise on a daily basis, or if 95% of the product leaving the mall was stolen. It would be chaos.

Now consider whether these people who so quickly download a song or a movie on the Internet without paying for it would also walk up to an artist selling their painting in the park and steal one of their paintings. I firmly believe the answer to that question is a resounding no! But why? What is different about the world wide web, i.e. cyberspace, that gives these consumers the feeling that they are entitled to download music and movies through mechanisms like BitTorrent without compensating those who created such product? What are these people thinking?

I think the answer can be found in the writings of Plato. In the second book of his Republic, Plato's student, Glaucon, poses the illustration of the "Ring of Gyges." In the story, Gyges is a shepherd who finds a magical ring in a chasm created by a lightning storm. The ring gives him a cloak of invisibility. Using his newfound power, Gyges seduces the Queen of Lydia, murders the King, and takes the throne, gaining power, wealth and fame. In the Republic, Glaucon argues that given a similar opportunity, any person, whether or not they were previously just or unjust, would use the power to commit as many crimes as necessary to get what they want [Book II, 359d]. Glaucon was responding to Socrates' refutation of arguments put forth by Thrasymachus in Book I of the Republic, i.e., that "justice is nothing but the advantage of the stronger" [Book I, 338c].

I believe Glaucon's experiment in thought informs us as to why someone who would not normally steal a tangible object in the physical world is nonetheless more than willing to download music or movies, intangible objects, on the Internet for free: because the fear of being punished or getting caught is eliminated in the evanescent world of Cyberspace. The Internet, like Gyges' ring, confers upon its users a seeming cloak of invisibility as it were. As one astute commentator surmised in response to an interview with Alice in Chain's lead singer, Sean Kinney, "The real reason people steal music is that they CAN and very easily." That this is a truth is evident from the plethora of "how to" guides on the Internet, teaching people "How not to get caught." There you have it in a nutshell. All of the commentary about how the record industry has been thieves and how the RIAA unjustly goes after the defenseless people, these are mere justifications for actions people otherwise know in their hearts are wrong.

It's important to read Plato's response to his student to understand fully, as Plato did not agree with Glaucon. Plato's argument in the remaining portion of the Republic is that the just man would not be tempted by this cloak of invisibility to commit crimes. Rather, the just man understands that crime itself makes a person unhappy and that he is better off to remain just. I frequently discuss this issue with my college students at Belmont University when teaching a course on Copyright Law. One of my students made the following observation, which confirms Plato's conclusion. She said:

> I do not follow the rules because I am scared of the RIAA busting me for illegal downloading. I follow the rules because I have respect for the people who wrote and recorded the songs, and even more, because I want to work in the music industry.

Another relevant opinion is offered in the excellent blog article found on arbiteronline entitled "Illegal downloading: The real cost of 'free' music." In that article, a student at Boise State, Ammon Roberts, is quoted as saying:

> "I don't do it because I don't feel it's right. If I were making the music, I'd be upset if people were downloading it for free."

For these two students, following the rules is not about whether or not they'll be caught, it's about doing the right thing. It's about honoring, i.e. compensating, the people who created the music. This illustrates Plato's point precisely: a just person understands that even with a cloak of invisibility, doing the right thing makes a person happy or, in the words of Roberts, makes the person "feel right."

The Internet is also very much the Land of Oz. In addition to this cloak of invisibility endowed on us by the Internet, it also deceives us with illusions of anonymity—not so much that the user is anonymous, as that's merely another form of invisibility—but in the sense that it's difficult to know who's behind the curtain. As Trent Reznor said in an interview, "there is a perception that you don't pay for music when your hear it . . . on MySpace." Because of its sheer vastness and its mysteriousness, Cyberspace gives people false perceptions that their actions on the Internet do not affect real people. This, in turn, creates an illusion that "resistance is futile." Everyone is doing it, so I can too. In other words, Cyberspace alters our reality in that it makes the real people behind the music an amorphous, anonymous entity. The result is that it's much easier to steal from an amorphous, anonymous entity—the man behind the curtain—than it is from a struggling songwriter, particularly when all your friends are doing it.

I truly believe that most of the people who are illegally downloading music from the Internet have no idea who they are affecting or how widespread the effect is. Most of these people would not even think about walking up on stage after a singer/songwriter in a nightclub takes a break and stealing his guitar, but that very same person doesn't think twice of taking that same singer/songwriter's song from the Internet. They wouldn't steal the filmmaker's camera, but downloading the movie doesn't phase their consciousness. In fact, many who contribute to the dialog would argue that these two thefts are not analogous. But one analysis conducted by the Institute for Policy Innovation states otherwise. The report indicated that music piracy causes $12.5 billion of economic losses every year. It further concluded that 71,060 U.S. jobs are lost, with a total loss of $2.7 billion in workers' earnings. Such reports abound throughout the industry, yet many of the people guilty of illegal download continue to view these reports as industry-driven and, therefore, skewed. Take this comment by anti-copyright blogger Michael Arrington as an example:

> Eventually the reality of the Internet will force the laws to change, too. One way or another the music labels will eventually surrender, and recorded music will be free. Until it is, I refuse to feel guilty for downloading and sharing music. Every time I listen to a song, or share it with a friend, I'm doing the labels a favor. One that eventually I should be paid for. Until that day comes, don't even think about trying to tell me that I'm doing something ethically wrong when it's considered quite legal, with the labels' blessing, in China.

But what this illusion of anonymity, and such misguided opinions, miss is the fact that very real people—not amorphous masses—are being affected. And the effect is devastating. I have clients who are songwriters who are no longer creating art because they are forced to take odd jobs to support their families. The performance royalties they used to receive from ASCAP, BMI or SESAC are down by half or more from a few years ago. Their mechanical royalty checks are virtually non-existent. They simply cannot afford to create simply for the sake of creation. And now, working sometimes two jobs, they don't have the time to create. What will become of the art of songwriting if Mr. Arrington has his way and all recorded music is free? I believe we will not have the quality of music in this country that we have enjoyed throughout the last millennium. In this instance, I do not believe that "resistance is futile."

Now, getting back to Plato and the Ring of Gyges: in answer to Glaucon, Plato would say that the root of all trouble is unlimited desire. How true is that in this world of Cyberspace, in this world of rampant illegal downloading.

The wheels really fell off the wagon when the RIAA sued Diamond Multimedia, bringing the MP3 into society's field of view. Then, Napster exploded and almost everyone found that almost every song they ever loved was available for free. It's as if they were Harrison Ford and discovered the treasure room in an unknown, ancient tomb: everything your heart desires is within your grasp. It's yours for the taking. With its cloak of invisibility and its illusion of anonymity, what the Internet has done, in short, is to return the power—*i.e.,* the control—back to the people. Everyone is now a creater, a publisher, and distributor. No one needs the conglomerates anymore—the people have the power. But, as Lord Acton said, beware: "Power tends to corrupt, and absolute power corrupts absolutely." With power, therefore, comes responsibility. Unfortunately for the music industry, the power is currently being abused and will, ultimately, mean the end of the recording industry as it existed through the 20th century unless the creators regain that power.

So what does this mean for those of us who have chosen to make our living in the world of creation? Does it mean the end of our industry? Does it mean an end to copyright law as it exists? If we examine the origins of copyright—i.e., the protection of an original idea expressed in a tangible format—as passed down to us from our forefathers, we find a concept on which we can continue to build. In the now famous Radiohead experiment in which Reznor and crew allowed consumers to pay what and only if they wanted to, 18% of the consumers chose to do so! That to me, is an encouraging statistic, and one that confirms a belief in the viability of creating art. At least one in five people, even with the cloak of anonymity provided by the Ring of Gyges of this era, *i.e.,* Cyberspace, choose to pay the creators for their creation. Take that Glaucon! Take that Arrington! What does that say for our society? It says that there are people who still chose to do the right thing, even when the tide of conformity rises above their heads.

The bottom line is that it really doesn't matter what laws are passed by society, there will always be a certain percentage of people who will chose to steal, take and plunder, whether it be because they are more powerful or because they are cloaked with invisibility or shielded by anonymity. But—and here is the important thing—there will also always be a segment of society that recognizes the idea that Thomas Hobbes first advanced hundreds of years ago, i.e., the idea of "giving to every man his own." If a man bakes a loaf of bread, is it not his right to trade that to the artist for whose painting he wishes to barter? This idea was later incorporated by our Forefathers into Article I, Section 8, Clause 8 of the U.S. Constitution, which gives Congress the authority "[to] promote the progress of science and useful arts, by securing for limited times to Authors and Inventors the exclusive rights to their respective Writings and Discoveries." Without this Constitutional right, a creator has no hope of protecting his or her property against plunder. And as long as a segment of society believes this proposition to be beneficial to society as a whole, it will hopefully continue to motivate creators to create, and so profit from their creations, despite the efforts of those who choose to destroy it under a cloak of invisibility and unjustly take for themselves the kingdom of Lydia.

Quotations from *Republic* are taken from the W.H.D. Rouse translation, *Great Dialogues of Plato,* Mentor Books, 1956.

Janis Ian

The Internet Debacle—An Alternative View

"The Internet, and downloading, are here to stay . . . Anyone who thinks otherwise should prepare themselves to end up on the slagheap of history."

(Janis Ian during a live European radio interview, September 1998)

When I research an article, I normally send 30 or so emails to friends and acquaintances asking for opinions and anecdotes. I usually receive 10–20 in reply. But not so on this subject!

I sent 36 emails requesting opinions and facts on free music downloading from the Net. I stated that I planned to adopt the viewpoint of devil's advocate: free Internet downloads are good for the music industry and its artists.

I've received, to date, over 300 replies, every single one from someone legitimately "in the music business."

What's more interesting than the emails are the phone calls. I don't know anyone at NARAS (home of the Grammy Awards), and I know Hilary Rosen (head of the Recording Industry Association of America, or RIAA) only vaguely. Yet within 24 hours of sending my original email, I'd received two messages from Rosen and four from NARAS requesting that I call to "discuss the article."

Huh. Didn't know I was that widely read.

Ms. Rosen, to be fair, stressed that she was only interested in presenting RIAA's side of the issue, and was kind enough to send me a fair amount of statistics and documentation, including a number of focus group studies RIAA had run on the matter.

However, the problem with focus groups is the same problem anthropologists have when studying peoples in the field—the moment the anthropologist's presence is known, everything changes. Hundreds of scientific studies have shown that any experimental group *wants to please the examiner*. For focus groups, this is particularly true. Coffee and donuts are the least of the pay-offs.

The NARAS people were a bit more pushy. They told me downloads were "destroying sales," "ruining the music industry," and "costing *you* money."

Costing *me* money? I don't pretend to be an expert on intellectual property law, but I do know one thing. If a music industry executive claims I should agree with their agenda because it will make me more money, I put my hand on my wallet . . . and check it after they leave, just to make sure nothing's missing.

Am I suspicious of all this hysteria? You bet. Do I think the issue has been badly handled? Absolutely. Am I concerned about losing friends, opportunities, my 10th Grammy nomination by publishing this article? Yeah. I am. But sometimes things are just *wrong*, and when they're *that* wrong, they have to be addressed.

The premise of all this ballyhoo is that the industry (and its artists) [is] being harmed by free downloading.

Nonsense. Let's take it from my personal experience. My site (www .janisian.com) gets an average of 75,000 hits a year. Not bad for someone whose last hit record was in 1975. When Napster was running full-tilt, we received about 100 hits a month from people who'd downloaded *Society's Child* or *At Seventeen* for free, then decided they wanted more information. Of those 100 people (and these are only the ones who let us know how they'd found the site), 15 bought CDs. Not huge sales, right? No record company is interested in 180 extra sales a year. But . . . that translates into $2700, which is a lot of money in my book. And that doesn't include the ones who bought the CDs in stores, or who came to my shows.

Or take author Mercedes Lackey, who occupies entire shelves in stores and libraries. As she said herself: "For the past ten years, my three "Arrows" books, which were published by DAW about 15 years ago, have been generating a nice, steady royalty check per pay-period each. A reasonable amount, for fifteen-year-old books. However . . . I just got the first half of my DAW royalties . . . And suddenly, out of nowhere, each Arrows book has paid me three times the normal amount! . . . And the only change during that pay-period was that I had Eric put the first of my books on the Free Library. There's an increase in all of the books on that statement, actually, and what it looks like is what I'd expect to happen if a steady line of people who'd never read my stuff encountered it on the Free Library—a certain percentage of them liked it, and started to work through my backlist, beginning with the earliest books published. The really interesting thing is, of course, that these aren't Baen books, they're DAW—another publisher—so it's 'name loyalty' rather than 'brand loyalty.' I'll tell you what, I'm sold. Free works." I've found that to be true myself; every time we make a few songs available on my website, sales of all the CDs go up. A lot.

And I don't know about you, but as an artist with an in-print record catalogue that dates back to 1965, I'd be *thrilled* to see sales on my old catalogue rise.

Now, RIAA and NARAS, as well as most of the entrenched music industry, are arguing that free downloads hurt sales. (More than hurt—they're saying it's destroying the industry.)

Alas, the music industry needs no outside help to destroy itself. We're doing a very adequate job of that on our own, thank you.

Here are a few statements from the RIAA's website:

1. "Analysts report that just one of the many peer-to-peer systems in operation is responsible for over 1.8 billion unauthorized downloads per month." (Hilary B. Rosen letter to the Honorable Rick Boucher, Congressman, February 28, 2002)
2. "Sales of blank CD-R discs have . . . grown nearly 2 ½ times in the last two years . . . if just half the blank discs sold in 2001 were used to copy music, the number of burned CDs worldwide is about the same as the number of CDs sold at retail." (Hilary B. Rosen letter to the Honorable Rick Boucher, Congressman, February 28, 2002)
3. "Music sales are already suffering from the impact . . . in the United States, sales decreased by more than 10% in 2001." (Hilary B. Rosen letter to the Honorable Rick Boucher, Congressman, February 28, 2002)
4. "In a recent survey of music consumers, 23% . . . said they are not buying more music because they are downloading or copying their music for free." (Hilary B. Rosen letter to the Honorable Rick Boucher, Congressman, February 28, 2002)

Let's take these points one by one, but before that, let me remind you of something: the music industry had *exactly* the same response to the advent of reel-to-reel home tape recorders, cassettes, DATs, minidiscs, VHS, BETA, music videos ("Why buy the record when you can tape it?"), MTV, and a host of other technological advances designed to make the consumer's life easier and better. I know, because I was there.

The only reason they didn't react that way publicly to the advent of CDs was because *they believed CDs were uncopyable.* I was told this personally by a former head of Sony marketing, when they asked me to license *Between the Lines* in CD format, at a reduced royalty rate. ("Because it's a brand new technology.")

1. Who's to say that any of those people would have bought the CDs if the songs weren't available for free? I can't find a single study on this, one where a reputable surveyor such as Gallup actually asks people that question. I think no one's run one because everyone is afraid of the truth—most of the downloads are people who want to try an artist out, or who can't find the music in print.

   And if a percentage of that 1.8 billion is because people are downloading a current hit by Britney or In Sync, who's to say it really hurt their sales? Soft statistics are easily manipulated. How many of those people went out and bought an album that had been over-played at radio for months, just because they downloaded a portion of it?
2. Sales of blank CDs have grown? You bet. I bought a new Vaio in December (ironically enough, made by Sony), and now back up all my files onto CD. I go through 7–15 CDs a week that way, or about 500 a year. Most new PCs come with XP, which makes backing up to CD painless; how many people are doing what I'm doing? Additionally, when I buy a new CD, I make a copy for my car, a copy for

upstairs, and a copy for my partner. That's three blank discs per CD. So I alone account for around 750 blank CDs yearly.

3. I'm sure the sales decrease had nothing to do with the economy's decrease, or a steady downward spiral in the music industry, or the garbage being pushed by record companies. Aren't you? There were *32,000 new titles* released in this country in 2001, and that's not including reissues, DIY's, or smaller labels that don't report to SoundScan. Our "Unreleased" series, which we haven't bothered SoundScanning, sold 6,000+ copies last year. A conservative estimate would place the number of "newly available" CDs per year at 100,000. That's an awful lot of releases for an industry that's being destroyed. And to make matters worse, we hear music everywhere, whether we want to or not; stores, amusement parks, highway rest stops. The original concept of Muzak (to be played in elevators so quietly that its soothing effect would be subliminal) has run amok. Why buy records when you can learn the entire Top 40 just by going shopping for groceries?

4. Which music consumers? College kids who can't afford to buy 10 new CDs a month, but want to hear their favorite groups? When I bought my nephews a new Backstreet Boys CD, I asked why they hadn't downloaded it instead. They patiently explained to their senile aunt that the download wouldn't give them the cool artwork, and more important, the video they could see only on the CD.

Realistically, why do most people download music? *To hear new music, or records that have been deleted and are no longer available for purchase.* Not to avoid paying $5 at the local used CD store, or taping it off the radio, but to hear music they can't find anywhere else. Face it—most people can't afford to spend $15.99 to experiment. That's why listening booths (which labels fought against, too) are such a success.

You can't hear new music on radio these days; I live in Nashville, "Music City USA," and we have exactly one station willing to play a non-top-40 format. On a clear day, I can even tune it in. The situation's not much better in Los Angeles or New York. College stations are sometimes bolder, but their wattage is so low that most of us can't get them.

One other major point: in the hysteria of the moment, everyone is forgetting the main way an artist becomes successful—*exposure*. Without exposure, no one comes to shows, no one buys CDs, no one enables you to earn a living doing what you love. Again, from my personal experience: in 37 years as a recording artist, I've created 25+ albums for major labels, and I've *never once* received a royalty check that didn't show I owed *them* money. So I make the bulk of my living from live touring, playing for 80–1500 people a night, doing my own show. I spend hours each week doing press, writing articles, making sure my website tour information is up to date. Why? Because all of that gives me exposure to an audience that might not come otherwise. So when someone writes and tells me they came to my show because they'd downloaded a song and gotten curious, I am thrilled!

Who gets hurt by free downloads? Save a handful of super-successes like Celine Dion, none of us. We only get helped.

But not to hear Congress tell it. Senator Fritz Hollings, chairman of the Senate Commerce Committee studying this, said "When Congress sits idly by in the face of these [file-sharing] activities, we essentially sanction the Internet as a haven for thievery," then went on to charge "over 10 million people" with stealing. [Steven Levy, Newsweek 3/11/02]. That's what we think of consumers — they're thieves, out to get something for nothing.

Baloney. Most consumers have no problem paying for entertainment. One has only to look at the success of Fictionwise.com and the few other websites offering books and music at reasonable prices to understand that. If the music industry had a shred of sense, they'd have addressed this problem seven years ago, when people like Michael Camp were trying to obtain legitimate licenses for music online. Instead, the industry-wide attitude was *"It'll go away."* That's the same attitude CBS Records had about rock 'n' roll when Mitch Miller was head of A&R. (And you wondered why they passed on The Beatles and The Rolling Stones.)

I don't blame the RIAA for Holling's attitude. They are, after all, the *Recording Industry* Association of America, formed so the labels would have a lobbying group in Washington. (In other words, they're permitted to make contributions to politicians and their parties.) But given that our industry's success is based on communication, the industry response to the Internet has been abysmal. Statements like the one above do nothing to help the cause.

Of course, communication has always been the artist's job, not the executive's. That's why it's so scary when people like current NARAS president Michael Greene begin using shows like the Grammy Awards to drive their point home.

Grammy viewership hit a six-year low in 2002. Personally, I found the program so scintillating that it made me long for Rob Lowe dancing with Snow White, which at least was so bad that it was entertaining. Moves like the ridiculous Elton John–Eminem duet did little to make people want to watch again the next year. And we're not going to go into the Los Angeles Times' Pulitzer Prize-winning series on Greene and NARAS, where they pointed out that MusiCares has spent less than 10% of its revenue on disbursing emergency funds for people in the music industry (its primary purpose), or that Greene recorded his own album, pitched it to record executives while discussing Grammy business, then negotiated a $250,000 contract with Mercury Records for it (later withdrawn after the public flap). Or that NARAS quietly paid out at least $650,000 to settle a sexual harassment suit against him, a portion of which the non-profit Academy paid. Or that he's paid two million dollars a year, along with "perks" like his million-dollar country club membership and Mercedes. (Though it does make one wonder when he last entered a record store and bought something with his own hard-earned money.)

Let's just note that in his speech he told the viewing audience that NARAS and RIAA were, in large part, taking their stance to protect artists. He hired three teenagers to spend a couple of days doing nothing but downloading, and they managed to download "6,000 songs." Come on. For free "front-row seats" at the Grammys and an appearance on national TV, I'd download twice that amount! But . . . who's got time to download that many songs? Does Greene really think people out there are spending twelve hours a day downloading our music? If they are, they must be starving to death, because they're not making a living or going to school. How many of us can afford a T-1 line?

This sort of thing is indicative of the way statistics and information are being tossed around. It's dreadful to think that consumers are being asked to take responsibility for the industry's problems, which have been around far longer than the Internet. It's even worse to think that the consumer is being told they are charged with protecting us, the artists, when our own industry squanders the dollars we earn on waste and personal vendettas.

Greene went on to say that "Many of the nominees here tonight, especially the new, less-established artists, are in immediate danger of being marginalized out of our business." Right. Any "new" artist who manages to make the Grammys has millions of dollars in record company money behind them, The "real" new artists aren't people you're going to see on national TV, or hear on most radio. They're people you'll hear because someone gave you a disc, or they opened at a show you attended, or were lucky enough to be featured on NPR or another program still open to playing records that aren't already hits.

As to artists being "marginalized out of our business," the only people being marginalized out are the employees of our Enron-minded record companies, who are being fired in droves because the higher-ups are incompetent.

And it's difficult to convince an educated audience that artists and record labels are about to go down the drain because they, the consumer, are downloading music. Particularly when they're paying $50–$125 apiece for concert tickets, and $15.99 for a new CD they know costs less than a couple of dollars to manufacture and distribute.

I suspect Greene thinks of downloaders as the equivalent of an old-style television drug dealer, lurking next to playgrounds, wearing big coats and whipping them open for wide-eyed children, who then purchase black market CDs at generous prices.

What's the new industry byword? *Encryption.* They're going to make sure no one can copy CDs, even for themselves, or download them for free. Brilliant, except that it flouts previous court decisions about blank cassettes, blank videotapes, etc. And it pisses people off.

How many of you know that many car makers are now manufacturing all their CD players to also play DVDs? or that part of the encryption record companies are using doesn't allow your store-bought CD to be played on a DVD player, because that's the same technology as your computer? And if you've had trouble playing your own self-recorded copy of *O Brother Where Art Thou* in the car, it's because of this lunacy.

The industry's answer is to put on the label: "This audio CD is protected against unauthorized copying. It is designed to play in standard audio CD players and computers running Windows O/S; however, playback problems may be experienced. If you experience such problems, return this disc for a refund."

Now I ask you. After three or four experiences like that, *shlepping* to the store to buy it, than *shlepping* back to return it (and you still don't have your music), who's going to bother buying CDs?

The industry has been complaining for years about the stranglehold the middle-man has on their dollars, yet they wish to do nothing to offend those middle-men. (BMG has a strict policy for artists buying their own CDs to sell at concerts—$11 per CD. They know very well that most of us lose money if we have to pay that much; the point is to keep the big record stores happy by ensuring sales go to them. What actually happens is no sales to us *or* the stores.) NARAS and RIAA are moaning about the little mom & pop stores being shoved out of business; no one worked harder to shove them out than our own industry, which greeted every new Tower or mega-music store with glee, and offered steep discounts to Target and WalMart et al for stocking CDs. The Internet has zero to do with store closings and lowered sales.

And for those of us with major label contracts who *want* some of our music available for free downloading . . . well, the record companies own our masters, our outtakes, even our demos, and they won't allow it. Furthermore, they own our *voices* for the duration of the contract, so we can't even post a live track for downloading!

If you think about it, the music industry should be rejoicing at this new technological advance! Here's a fool-proof way to deliver music to millions who might otherwise never purchase a CD in a store. The cross-marketing opportunities are unbelievable. It's instantaneous, costs are minimal, shipping non-existant . . . a staggering vehicle for higher earnings and lower costs. Instead, they're running around like chickens with their heads cut off, bleeding on everyone and making no sense. . . .

I have no objection to Greene et al trying to protect the record labels, who are the ones fomenting this hysteria. RIAA is funded by them. NARAS is supported by them. *However, I object violently to the pretense that they are in any way doing this for our benefit.* If they really wanted to do something for the great majority of artists, who eke out a living against all odds, they could tackle some of the real issues facing us:

- The normal industry contract is for seven albums, with no end date, which would be considered at best indentured servitude (and at worst slavery) in any other business. In fact, it would be illegal.
- A label can shelve your project, then extend your contract by one more album because what you turned in was "commercially or artistically unacceptable." They alone determine that criteria.
- Singer-songwriters have to accept the "Controlled Composition Clause" (which dictates that they'll be paid only 75% of the rates set by Congress in publishing royalties) for any major or subsidiary label recording contract, or lose the contract. Simply put, the clause demanded by the labels provides that a) if you write your own songs, you will only be paid 3/4 of what Congress has told the record companies they must pay you, and b) if you co-write, you will use your "best efforts" to ensure that other songwriters accept the 75% rate as well. If they refuse, you must agree to make up the difference out of your share.
- Congressionally set writer/publisher royalties have risen from their 1960s high (2 cents per side) to a munificent 8 cents.

NO / Janis Ian

- Many of us began in the 50s and 60s; our records are still in release, and we're still being paid royalty rates of 2% (if anything) on them.
- If we're not songwriters, and not hugely successful commercially (as in platinum-plus), we don't make a dime off our recordings. Recording industry accounting procedures are right up there with films.
- Worse yet, when records go out-of-print, we don't get them back! We can't even take them to another company. Careers have been deliberately killed in this manner, with the record company refusing to release product or allow the artist to take it somewhere else.
- And because a record label "owns" your voice for the duration of the contract, you can't go somewhere else and re-record those same songs they turned down.
- And because of the re-record provision, even after your contract is over, you can't record those songs for someone else for years, and sometimes decades.
- Last but not least, America is the only country I am aware of that pays no live performance royalties to songwriters. In Europe, Japan, Australia, when you finish a show, you turn your set list in to the promoter, who files it with the appropriate organization, and then pays a small royalty per song to the writer. It costs the singer nothing, the rates are based on venue size, and it ensures that writers whose songs no longer get airplay, but are still performed widely, can continue receiving the benefit from those songs.

Additionally, we should be speaking up, and Congress should be listening. At this point they're only hearing from multi-platinum acts. What about someone like Ani Difranco, one of the most trusted voices in college entertainment today? What about those of us who live most of our lives outside the big corporate system, and who might have very different views on the subject?

There is *zero* evidence that material available for free online downloading is financially harming anyone. In fact, most of the hard evidence is to the contrary.

Greene and the RIAA are correct in one thing—these are times of great change in our industry. But at a time when there are arguably only four record labels left in America (Sony, AOL/Time/Warner, Universal, BMG—and where is the RICO act when we need it?) . . . when entire *genres* are glorifying the gangster mentality and losing their biggest voices to violence . . . when executives change positions as often as Zsa Zsa Gabor changed clothes, and "A&R" has become a euphemism for "Absent & Redundant". . . well, we have other things to worry about.

It's absurd for us, as artists, to sanction—or countenance—the shutting down of something like this. It's sheer stupidity to rejoice at the Napster decision. Short-sighted, and ignorant.

Free exposure is practically a thing of the past for entertainers. Getting your record played at radio costs more money than most of us dream of ever earning. Free downloading gives a chance to every do-it-yourselfer out there. Every act that can't get signed to a major label, for whatever reason, can reach literally millions of new listeners, enticing them to buy the CD and come to the concerts. Where else can a new act, or one that doesn't have a label deal, get that kind of exposure?

Please note that I am *not* advocating indiscriminate downloading without the artist's permission. I am *not* saying copyrights are meaningless. I am objecting to the RIAA spin that they are doing this to protect "the artists", and make us more money. I am annoyed that so many records I once owned are out of print, and the only place I could find them was Napster. Most of all, I'd like to see an end to the hysteria that causes a group like RIAA to spend over 45 million dollars in 2001 lobbying "on our behalf", when every record company out there is complaining that they have no money.

We'll turn into Microsoft if we're not careful, folks, insisting that any household wanting an extra copy for the car, the kids, or the portable CD player, has to go out and "license" multiple copies.

As artists, we have the ear of the masses. We have the trust of the masses. By speaking out in our concerts and in the press, we can do a great deal to dampen this hysteria, and put the blame for the sad state of our industry right back where it belongs—in the laps of record companies, radio programmers, and our own apparent inability to organize ourselves in order to better our own lives—and those of our fans. If we don't take the reins, no one will.

POSTSCRIPT

Should It Be a Crime to Download Copyrighted Music from the Internet?

This is a difficult issue. On one hand, basic justice seems to demand that persons should be compensated for what they have produced. On the other hand, since its inception the Internet has been widely viewed as a "wide open," "everything goes," "marketplace of ideas," and a venue where persons possess a measure of freedom from all forms of traditional regulation and constraint. The issue posed in this debate places these competing value systems in direct competition.

One way to analyze the issue may be to analyze it within the context of our current definitions of crime. A legal definition of crime states that it is any conduct that violates the legal code. If this definition is used, it seems clear that downloading copyrighted music from the Internet should be considered a crime because it violates traditional copyright law. The problem with this type of definition of crime, however, is that it does not consider the morality of the conduct itself and how the law is created. That task was left to the legislative body that created the definition in the first place. If they had failed to do an honest and effective job of balancing the competing interests impacted by the law, society would have left with a statute that will be widely viewed as unfair and lack popular support. For example, if it could be shown that an organization such as the RIAA had, through its contributions to Congress and lobbying efforts on behalf of the recording industry, influenced the passage of laws being used to sanction downloading protected materials from the Internet, is it really a surprise that so many people appear to view these laws as unfair and disregard them?

An alternative way to define crime was proposed by a late nineteenth-century Italian criminologist, Raffaele Garofalo, who proposed a natural definition. From this perspective, a crime is any conduct that violates normal human sentiments of pity, or probity. Conduct that violated the sentiment of pity would include actions that harmed other persons or animals without justification. Actions that violated the sentiment of probity would include activities that violate the private property rights of others. From this perspective, illegally downloading copyrighted materials from the Internet may well qualify as a crime because it may infringe on the private property rights of the writer.

Still another perspective on the definition of crimes was developed by the celebrated utilitarian philosopher and social critic, Jeremy Bentham. The doctrine of social utility asserts that the guiding principle of all social policies should be whatever constitutes the "greatest good for the greatest number" of people.

From this perspective, does it really make sense to criminalize downloading copyrighted materials from the Internet when so many people appear to believe that their own "good" is maximized by engaging in this behavior? Of course, it can be argued convincingly that many people in society simply do not understand what is truly "good" for themselves and consequently, society must do it for them.

A final perspective on defining crimes has been developed by a wide number of Marxist or conflict criminologists. Speaking generally, these individuals question the fundamental legitimacy of the existing social order that creates the definitions of crimes in the first place. Marxists also believe that these definitions are created to benefit the wealthy in society at the expense of ordinary people and point out the apparent inconsistencies in the application of our system of criminal laws. For example, Marxist criminologists have pointed to the injustice of jailing a hungry person who steals food from a grocery store, whereas those persons who caused the latest catastrophic Wall Street banking collapse are free to return to their happy country club lifestyles. From the Marxist perspective, the widespread support for downloading copyrighted music from the Internet would simply be a collective response by most members of society to a system that permits exploitation and oppression of the powerless by the wealthy. From a Marxist perspective, in a capitalist society, such a response is justified and should be expected from those who have become alienated from traditional society.

Which of the preceding definitions of crime best fits the act of downloading copyrighted materials from the Internet? Although a full discussion of the benefits and limitations of each of these approaches is beyond the scope of the present initiative, any good introductory criminology textbook will provide an effective discussion of these issues.

After reading the YES and NO selections, do you believe that downloading copyrighted materials from Internet should be considered a crime? If you have downloaded protected materials in the past, will you continue to do so? Hopefully, the authors of the YES and NO selections have caused you to think more carefully about these issues, regardless of your final conclusion.

There are numerous additional resources to consult for further discussion of these important matters, including: Sue Titus Reid, *Crime and Criminology*, 13th ed. (Oxford University Press, 2011); Franklin P. Williams and Marilyn McShane, *Criminological Theory*, 5th ed. (Pearson, 2010); Larry Siegel, *Criminology* (Wadsworth, 2013); Thomas J. Bernard, Jeffrey B. Snipes, and Alexander L. Gould, *Vold's Theoretical Criminology*, 6th ed. (Oxford University Press, 2009); See also: Slane, "Democracy, Social Space and the Internet," 57 U. Toronto L.J. 1 (2007); Dean Hendrix, "Peer to Peer (P2P) Knowledge, Use, and Attitudes of Academic Librarians," *Libraries and the Academy* (vol. 7, no. 2, 2007); Tim Brooks, "Only in America: The Unique Status of Sound Recordings Under U.S. Copyright Law and How It Threatens Our Audio Heritage," *American Music* (vol. 27, no. 2, 2009); Tim Brooks, "Copyright and Historical Sound Recordings: Recent Efforts to Change U.S. Law," *Technology and Culture* (vol. 65, 2009); Evgeny Morazoo, "Whither Internet Control?," *Journal of Democracy* (vol. 22, no. 2, 2010); Steve Cisler, "Pirates of the Pacific Rim," *Leonardo* (vol. 39, no. 4, 2006); Sarah Leonard, "Into the Ether," *Dissent* (vol. 58, no. 4, 2011).

ISSUE 22

Should It Be Lawful for the Police to Conduct Jailhouse Strip Searches of Persons Arrested for Minor Offenses?

YES: Anthony M. Kennedy, from "Majority Opinion," *Florence v. Board of Chosen Freeholders of County of Burington*, 566 U.S. ___ (2012)

NO: Stephen Breyer, from "Dissenting Opinion," *Florence v. Board of Chosen Freeholder of County of Burlington*, 556 U.S. ___ (2012)

ISSUE SUMMARY

YES: U.S. Supreme Court Associate Justice Anthony M. Kennedy asserts that police officers and correctional officials must be permitted to develop reasonable search policies to detect and deter the possession of contraband within their facilities. Moreover, exempting people arrested for minor offenses from such searches may put the police at greater risk and result in more contraband being brought into jails.

NO: Associate Justice Stephen Breyer, in contrast, believes that because strip searches involve close observation of the private areas of the body, they constitute a serious invasion of personal privacy and may not be justified in cases involving minor offenses.

Personal privacy is a fundamental value of most Americans. The topic considered in this issue is strip searches of those arrested for crimes and taken to jail. It would be hard to imagine any practice that would violate an American conception of personal privacy more than a strip search during which one's clothing is removed and private bodily areas are examined to determine if they conceal weapons or possible contraband. People may have a tendency to believe that strip searches are directed by law enforcement agents only against "serious bad guys," who commit heinous crimes. As the Supreme Court's recent decision in *Florence v. Board of Chosen Freeholders of County of Burlington*, 566 U.S. ___ (2012), illustrates, however, that is not always the case.

For example, several months ago, in a case that mirrors *Florence*, one of my former clients was stopped by the police for a nonserious traffic violation, a broken tail light lens. The same individual had been stopped by the police and ticketed for speeding a few months earlier. She had pled guilty by mail to the speeding charge, sent in the requisite fine of approximately $160.00, and thought nothing more about the incident, that is, until she was stopped for the broken tail light. After examining her driver's license and auto registration, the officer told her that an arrest warrant had been issued due to her nonpayment of the earlier speeding ticket. (The clerk of the court who had accepted the guilty plea had neglected to record the $160.00 payment.)

This individual was placed under arrest and transported to the county jail by the police officer. Fortunately, this incident occurred during normal weekday business hours and the officer involved used common sense and checked quickly with the court that had issued the arrest warrant about my former client's contention that she had paid the earlier speeding fine. Within a few minutes, the officer was able to verify that she was telling the truth and discharged her from the county jail.

What would have happened, however, if the same incident had occurred on a weekend, or a holiday? In that case, it is highly probable that the officer would not have been able to contact court personnel who could verify the clerical recording error. In these circumstances, it is very likely that my client would have been placed in jail until she could "make bail," or until the police could contact the court that issued the arrest warrant to ascertain that there had been an error.

Under the U.S. Supreme Court's ruling in *Florence v. Board of Chosen Freeholders of County of Burlington*, 566 U.S. ___ (2012), it would appear that the police and/or correctional officials at the jail would have been justified in conducting a full strip search of my client. Such a search is highly intrusive and would involve the removal of all clothing and a visual inspection of highly personal areas and body cavities. One should note, however, at the time of my client's arrest, most police and corrections agencies would have had a policy in place that requires that a person of the same gender as the arrested individual actually conduct the strip search.

Prior to *Florence*, many law enforcement agencies had strip search policies that provided for this type of invasive search procedure only in specified serious cases. For example, if an individual was being charged with a serious crime, possession of illegal drugs, or whenever officers had a reasonable suspicion to believe that the alleged offender could possess a weapon or illegal contraband. After *Florence*, law enforcement agencies would appear to be free to adopt a blanket rule that would permit anyone who is arrested for a crime to be strip searched if they are going to be held in a local jail. Although most reasonable persons would be likely to support such a rule for *convicted* offenders being taken to prison, or those serving their sentence in a local jail, it was significant that the Supreme Court held that even those who had not yet been convicted of any offense could be subjected to this type of intrusive search.

The U.S. Supreme Court's rationale for permitting strip searches and body cavity inspections of those who had been charged with a crime and taken to jail, but who had not yet been convicted, was first developed in *Bell v. Wolfish*, 441 U.S. 520 (1979). In that case, *pretrial detainees* in a newly constructed jail, the Metropolitan Correctional Center in Washington, DC, challenged several of the jail's policies in the U.S. federal court. One of the challenged policies required a strip search and body-cavity inspection of all persons awaiting trial at the jail. The Supreme Court held that because the Fourth Amendment prohibits only "unreasonable searches," the jail's practices were subject to a "reasonableness test," which "is not capable of precise definition or mechanical application." The Court observed: "In each case, it requires a balancing of the need for the particular search against the invasion of personal rights that the search entails." Chief Justice Rehnquist continued:

> We do not underestimate the degree to which these searches may invade the personal privacy of inmates. Nor do we doubt . . . that, on occasion, a security guard may conduct the search in an abusive fashion. Such abuse cannot be condoned. The searches must be conducted in a reasonable manner . . . But here we deal with the question whether visual body cavity inspections can *ever* be conducted on less than probable cause. Balancing the significant and legitimate security interests of the institution against the privacy interests of the inmates, we conclude that they can.

> (441 U.S. 520, 560)

The Supreme Court's decision in *Florence v. Board of Chosen Freeholders of County of Burlington* expanded the principle laid down in *Bell v. Wolfish*. In *Florence*, an individual was arrested during a traffic stop by a police officer who had checked a statewide computer database and found a warrant for the motorist's arrest for failing to appear at a hearing to enforce a fine. Like my unfortunate client discussed previously, he was initially detained at a county jail, but released once it was determined that he had paid the fine. At the jail, the unfortunate motorist, like all detainees, had to shower with a delousing agent and was checked for scars, marks, gang tattoos, and contraband as he undressed. He also had to open his mouth, lift his tongue, hold out his arms, turn around, and lift his genitals.

The arrested motorist filed a federal Civil Rights lawsuit under 42 U.S.C. Section 1983, against the government entities that ran the jails and the officers who conducted the searches, arguing that persons arrested for minor offenses cannot be subjected to invasive searches unless jail officials have reason to suspect concealment of weapons, drugs, or other contraband. The U.S. District Court agreed, but the Third Circuit U.S. Court of Appeals reversed. The U.S. Supreme Court granted certiorari and in a five-to-four decision affirmed the decision of the Court of Appeals.

Justice Kennedy, writing for the Court, stated that "correctional officials must be permitted to devise reasonable search policies to detect and deter the possession of contraband in their facilities." Moreover, stated Kennedy, "[t]he danger of [new detainees] introducing lice or contagious infections . . . is well-documented . . . [and] it may be difficult to identify and treat these problems until detainees remove their clothes for a visual inspection." Justice Kennedy also rejected the motorist's argument that those detained for non-serious offenses should not be subjected to invasive searches unless there is reasonable suspicion to believe that he or she possesses contraband or may be concealing a weapon. Stated Kennedy: "[T]he seriousness of an offense is a poor predictor of who has contraband and it would be difficult in practice to determine whether individuals fall within the proposed exemption. People detained for minor offenses can turn out to be the most devious and dangerous criminals."

Justice Stephen Breyer, dissenting, took issue with the majority's opinion. Justice Breyer stated:

> In my view, a search of an individual arrested for a minor offense that does not involve drugs or violence—say a traffic offense, a regulatory offense, an essentially civil matter, or any other such misdemeanor—is an 'unreasonable search' forbidden by the Fourth Amendment, unless prison authorities have reasonable suspicion to believe that the individual possesses drugs or other contraband.

At first glance, do you agree with Justice Kennedy, or Justice Breyer? Do you think that a "reasonable suspicion" requirement for conducting a strip and body cavity search of a person being admitted to a jail would be a practical standard? The authors of the opinions presented in the YES and NO selections have very different perspectives on this issue.

YES

Anthony M. Kennedy

Majority Opinion

Correctional officials have a legitimate interest, indeed a responsibility, to ensure that jails are not made less secure by reason of what new detainees may carry in on their bodies. Facility personnel, other inmates, and the new detainee himself or herself may be in danger if these threats are introduced into the jail population. This case presents the question of what rules, or limitations, the Constitution imposes on searches of arrested persons who are to be held in jail while their cases are being processed. The term "jail" is used here in a broad sense to include prisons and other detention facilities. The specific measures being challenged will be described in more detail; but, in broad terms, the controversy concerns whether every detainee who will be admitted to the general population may be required to undergo a close visual inspection while undressed.

The case turns in part on the extent to which this Court has sufficient expertise and information in the record to mandate, under the Constitution, the specific restrictions and limitations sought by those who challenge the visual search procedures at issue. In addressing this type of constitutional claim courts must defer to the judgment of correctional officials unless the record contains substantial evidence showing their policies are an unnecessary or unjustified response to problems of jail security. That necessary showing has not been made in this case.

I

In 1998, seven years before the incidents at issue, petitioner Albert Florence was arrested after fleeing from police officers in Essex County, New Jersey. He was charged with obstruction of justice and use of a deadly weapon. Petitioner entered a plea of guilty to two lesser offenses and was sentenced to pay a fine in monthly installments. In 2003, after he fell behind on his payments and failed to appear at an enforcement hearing, a bench warrant was issued for his arrest. He paid the outstanding balance less than a week later; but, for some unexplained reason, the warrant remained in a statewide computer database.

Two years later, in Burlington County, New Jersey, petitioner and his wife were stopped in their automobile by a state trooper. Based on the outstanding warrant in the computer system, the officer arrested petitioner and took him to the Burlington County Detention Center. He was held there for six days and then was transferred to the Essex County Correctional Facility. It is not the

Kennedy, Anthony M. From United States Supreme Court, 2012.

arrest or confinement but the search process at each jail that gives rise to the claims before the Court.

Burlington County jail procedures required every arrestee to shower with a delousing agent. Officers would check arrestees for scars, marks, gang tattoos, and contraband as they disrobed. Petitioner claims he was also instructed to open his mouth, lift his tongue, hold out his arms, turn around, and lift his genitals. (It is not clear whether this last step was part of the normal practice.) Petitioner shared a cell with at least one other person and interacted with other inmates following his admission to the jail.

The Essex County Correctional Facility, where petitioner was taken after six days, is the largest county jail in New Jersey. It admits more than 25,000 inmates each year and houses about 1,000 gang members at any given time. When petitioner was transferred there, all arriving detainees passed through a metal detector and waited in a group holding cell for a more thorough search. When they left the holding cell, they were instructed to remove their clothing while an officer looked for body markings, wounds, and contraband. Apparently without touching the detainees, an officer looked at their ears, nose, mouth, hair, scalp, fingers, hands, arms, armpits, and other body openings. This policy applied regardless of the circumstances of the arrest, the suspected offense, or the detainee's behavior, demeanor, or criminal history. Petitioner alleges he was required to lift his genitals, turn around, and cough in a squatting position as part of the process. After a mandatory shower, during which his clothes were inspected, petitioner was admitted to the facility. He was released the next day, when the charges against him were dismissed.

Petitioner sued the governmental entities that operated the jails, one of the wardens, and certain other defendants. The suit was commenced in the United States District Court for the District of New Jersey. Seeking relief under 42 U. S. C. § 1983 for violations of his Fourth and Fourteenth Amendment rights, petitioner maintained that persons arrested for a minor offense could not be required to remove their clothing and expose the most private areas of their bodies to close visual inspection as a routine part of the intake the process. Rather, he contented officials could conduct this kind of search only if they had reason to suspect to particular inmate of concealing a weapon, drugs, or other contraband. . . .

After discovery, the court granted petitioner's motion for summary judgment on the unlawful search claim. It concluded that any policy of "strip searching" nonindictable offenders without reasonable suspicion violated the Fourth Amendment. A divided panel of the United States Court of Appeals for the Third Circuit reversed, holding that the procedures described by the District Court struck a reasonable balance between inmate privacy and the security needs of the two jails. The case proceeds on the understanding that the officers searched detainees prior to their admission to the general population, as the Court of Appeals seems to have assumed. Petitioner has not argued this factual premise is incorrect.

The opinions in earlier proceedings, the briefs on file, and some cases of this Court refer to a "strip search." The term is imprecise. It may refer simply to the instruction to remove clothing while an officer observes from a distance of, say, five feet or more; it may mean a visual inspection from a closer, more uncomfortable distance; it may include directing detainees to shake their heads or to run their hands through their hair to dislodge what might be hidden there; or it may involve instructions to raise arms, to display foot insteps, to expose the back of the ears, to move or spread the buttocks or genital areas, or to cough in a squatting position. In the instant case, the term does not include any touching of unclothed areas by the inspecting officer. There are no allegations that the detainees here were touched in any way as part of the searches.

The Federal Courts of Appeals have come to differing conclusions as to whether the Fourth Amendment requires correctional officials to exempt some detainees who will be admitted to a jail's general population from the searches here at issue. This Court granted certiorari to address the question. 563 U.S. — (2011).

II

The difficulties of operating a detention center must not be underestimated by the courts. Jail (in the stricter sense of the term, excluding prison facilities) admit more than 13 million inmates a year. The largest facilities process hundreds of people every day; smaller jails may be crowded on weekend nights, after a large police operation, or because of detainees arriving from other jurisdictions. Maintaining safety and order at these institutions requires the expertise of correctional officials, who must have substantial discretion to devise reasonable solutions to the problems they face. The Court has confirmed the importance of deference to correctional officials and explained that a regulation impinging on an inmate's constitutional rights must be upheld "if it is reasonably related to legitimate penological interests."

. . .

The Court's opinion in *Bell* v. *Wolfish,* 441 U. S. 520 (1979), is the starting point for understanding how this framework applies to Fourth Amendment challenges. That case addressed a rule requiring pretrial detainees in any correctional facility run by the Federal Bureau of Prisons "to expose their body cavities for visual inspection as a part of a strip search conducted after every contact visit with a person from outside the institution." Inmates at the federal Metropolitan Correctional Center in New York City argued there was no security justification for these searches. Officers searched guests before they entered the visiting room, and the inmates were under constant surveillance during the visit. There had been but one instance in which an inmate attempted to sneak contraband back into the facility. The Court nonetheless upheld the search policy. It deferred to the judgment of correctional officials that the inspections served not only to discover but also to deter the smuggling of weapons, drugs, and other prohibited items inside. The Court explained that there is no mechanical way to determine whether intrusions on an inmate's privacy are reasonable. The need for a particular search must be balanced against the resulting invasion of personal rights.

Policies designed to keep contraband out of jails and prisons have been upheld in cases decided since *Bell.* In *Block* v. *Rutherford,* 468 U. S. 576 (1984), for example, the Court concluded that the Los Angeles County Jail could ban all contact visits because of the threat they posed:

> "They open the institution to the introduction of drugs, weapons, and other contraband. Visitors can easily conceal guns, knives, drugs, or other contraband in countless ways and pass them to an inmate unnoticed by even the most vigilant observers. And these items can readily be slipped from the clothing of an innocent child, or transferred by other visitors permitted close contact with inmates."

There were "many justifications" for imposing a general ban rather than trying to carve out exceptions for certain detainees. Among other problems, it would be "a difficult if not impossible task" to identify "inmates who have propensities for violence, escape, or drug smuggling." This was made "even more difficult by the brevity of detention and the constantly changing nature of the inmate population."

The Court has also recognized that deterring the possession of contraband depends in part on the ability to conduct searches without predictable exceptions. In *Hudson* v. *Palmer,* 468 U. S. 517 (1984), it addressed the question of whether prison officials could perform random searches of inmate lockers and cells even without reason to suspect a particular individual of concealing a prohibited item. The Court upheld the constitutionality of the practice, recognizing that "[f]or one to advocate that prison searches must be conducted only pursuant to an enunciated general policy or when suspicion is directed at a particular inmate is to ignore the realities of prison operation." Inmates would adapt to any pattern or loopholes they discovered in the search protocol and then undermine the security of the institution.

These cases establish that correctional officials must be permitted to devise reasonable search policies to detect and deter the possession of contraband in their facilities. ("[Maintaining institutional security and preserving internal order and discipline are essential goals that may require limitation or retraction of retained constitutional rights of both convicted prisoners and pretrial detainees"). The task of determining whether a policy is reasonably related to legitimate security interests is "peculiarly within the province and professional expertise of corrections officials." This Court has repeated the admonition that, "in the absence of substantial evidence in the record to indicate that the officials have exaggerated their response to these considerations courts should ordinarily defer to their expert judgment in such matters."

In many jails officials seek to improve security by requiring some kind of strip search of everyone who is to be detained. These procedures have been used in different places throughout the country, from Cranston, Rhode Island, to Sapulpa, Oklahoma, to Idaho Falls, Idaho.

Persons arrested for minor offenses may be among the detainees processed at these facilities. This is, in part, a consequence of the exercise of state authority that was the subject of *Atwater* v. *Lago Vista,* 532 U. S. 318 (2001).

Atwater addressed the perhaps more fundamental question of who may be deprived of liberty and taken to jail in the first place. The case involved a woman who was arrested after a police officer noticed neither she nor her children were wearing their seatbelts. The arrestee argued the Fourth Amendment prohibited her custodial arrest without a warrant when an offense could not result in jail time and there was no compelling need for immediate detention. The Court held that a Fourth Amendment restriction on this power would put officers in an "almost impossible spot." Their ability to arrest a suspect would depend in some cases on the precise weight of drugs in his pocket, whether he was a repeat offender, and the scope of what counted as a compelling need to detain someone. The Court rejected the proposition that the Fourth Amendment barred custodial arrests in a set of these cases as a matter of constitutional law. It ruled, based on established principles, that officers may make an arrest based upon probable cause to believe the person has committed a criminal offense in their presence. The Court stated that "a responsible Fourth Amendment balance is not well served by standards requiring sensitive, case-by-case determinations of government need, lest every discretionary judgment in the field be converted into an occasion for constitutional review."

Atwater did not address whether the Constitution imposes special restrictions on the searches of offenders suspected of committing minor offenses once they are taken to jail. Some Federal Courts of Appeals have held that corrections officials may not conduct a strip search of these detainees, even if no touching is involved, absent reasonable suspicion of concealed contraband. . . .

III

The question here is whether undoubted security imperatives involved in jail supervision override the assertion that some detainees must be exempt from the more invasive search procedures at issue absent reasonable suspicion of a concealed weapon or other contraband. The Court has held that deference must be given to the officials in charge of the jail unless there is "substantial evidence" demonstrating their response to the situation is exaggerated. Petitioner has not met this standard, and the record provides full justifications for the procedures used.

A

Correctional officials have a significant interest in conducting a thorough search as a standard part of the intake process. The admission of inmates creates numerous risks for facility staff, for the existing detainee population, and for a new detainee himself or herself. The danger of introducing lice or contagious infections, for example, is well documented. The Federal Bureau of Prisons recommends that staff screen new detainees for these conditions. Persons just arrested may have wounds or other injuries requiring immediate medical attention. It may be difficult to identify and treat these problems until detainees remove their clothes for a visual inspection.

Jails and prisons also face grave threats posed by the increasing number of gang members who go through the intake process. The groups recruit new members by force, engage in assaults against staff, and give other inmates a reason to arm themselves. Fights among feuding gangs can be deadly, and the officers who must maintain order are put in harm's way. These considerations provide a reasonable basis to justify a visual inspection for certain tattoos and other signs of gang affiliation as part of the intake process. The identification and isolation of gang members before they are admitted protects everyone in the facility.

Detecting contraband concealed by new detainees, furthermore, is a most serious responsibility. Weapons, drugs, and alcohol all disrupt the safe operation of a jail. Correctional officers have had to confront arrestees concealing knives, scissors, razor blades, glass shards, and other prohibited items on their person, including in their body cavities. . . . They have also found crack, heroin, and marijuana. The use of drugs can embolden inmates in aggression toward officers or each other; and, even apart from their use, the trade in these substances can lead to violent confrontations.

There are many other kinds of contraband. The textbook definition of the term covers any unauthorized item. . . . Contraband obviously includes drugs or weapons, but it can also be money, cigarettes, or even some types of clothing. Everyday items can undermine security if introduced into a detention facility:

> "Lighters and matches are fire and arson risks or potential weapons. Cell phones are used to orchestrate violence and criminality both within and without jailhouse walls. Pills and medications enhance suicide risks. Chewing gum can block locking devices; hair pins can open handcuffs; wigs can conceal drugs and weapons."

Something as simple as an overlooked pen can pose a significant danger. Inmates commit more than 10,000 assaults on correctional staff every year and many more among themselves.

Contraband creates additional problems because scarce items, including currency, have value in a jail's culture and underground economy. Correctional officials inform us "[t]he competition . . . for such goods begets violence, extortion, and disorder." Gangs exacerbate the problem. They "orchestrate thefts, commit assaults, and approach inmates in packs to take the contraband from the weak." This puts the entire facility, including detainees being held for a brief term for a minor offense, at risk. Gangs do coerce inmates who have access to the outside world, such as people serving their time on the weekends, to sneak things into the jail. . . . These inmates, who might be thought to pose the least risk, have been caught smuggling prohibited items into jail. Concealing contraband often takes little time and effort. It might be done as an officer approaches a suspect's car or during a brief commotion in a group holding cell. Something small might be tucked or taped under an armpit, behind an ear, between the buttocks, in the instep of a foot, or inside the mouth or some other body cavity.

It is not surprising that correctional officials have sought to perform thorough searches at intake for disease, gang affiliation, and contraband. Jails are often crowded, unsanitary, and dangerous places. There is a substantial interest in preventing any new inmate, either of his own will or as a result of coercion, from putting all who live or work at these institutions at even greater risk when he is admitted to the general population.

B

Petitioner acknowledges that correctional officials must be allowed to conduct an effective search during the intake process and that this will require at least some detainees to lift their genitals or cough in a squatting position. These procedures, similar to the ones upheld in *Bell*, are designed to uncover contraband that can go undetected by a patdown, metal detector, and other less invasive searches. Petitioner maintains there is little benefit to conducting these more invasive steps on a new detainee who has not been arrested for a serious crime or for any offense involving a weapon or drugs. In his view these detainees should be exempt from this process unless they give officers a particular reason to suspect them of hiding contraband. It is reasonable, however, for correctional officials to conclude this standard would be unworkable. The record provides evidence that the seriousness of an offense is a poor predictor of who has contraband and that it would be difficult in practice to determine whether individual detainees fall within the proposed exemption.

1

People detained for minor offenses can turn out to be the most devious and dangerous criminals. Hours after the Oklahoma City bombing, Timothy McVeigh was stopped by a state trooper who noticed he was driving without a license plate. Police stopped serial killer Joel Rifkin for the same reason. One of the terrorists involved in the September 11 attacks was stopped and ticketed for speeding just two days before hijacking Flight 93. Reasonable correctional officials could conclude these uncertainties mean they must conduct the same thorough search of everyone who will be admitted to their facilities.

Experience shows that people arrested for minor offenses have tried to smuggle prohibited items into jail, sometimes by using their rectal cavities or genitals for the concealment. They may have some of the same incentives as a serious criminal to hide contraband. A detainee might risk carrying cash, cigarettes, or a penknife to survive in jail. Others may make a quick decision to hide unlawful substances to avoid getting in more trouble at the time of their arrest. This record has concrete examples. Officers at the Atlantic County Correctional Facility, for example, discovered that a man arrested for driving under the influence had "2 dime bags of weed, 1 pack of rolling papers, 20 matches, and 5 sleeping pills" taped under his scrotum. A person booked on a misdemeanor charge of disorderly conduct in Washington State managed to hide a lighter, tobacco, tattoo needles, and other prohibited items in his rectal cavity. San Francisco officials have discovered contraband hidden in body cavities of people arrested for trespassing, public nuisance, and shoplifting. There have been similar incidents at jails throughout the country.

Even if people arrested for a minor offense do not themselves wish to introduce contraband into a jail, they may be coerced into doing so by others. . . . This could happen any time detainees are held in the same area, including in a van on the way to the station or in the holding cell of the jail. If, for example, a person arrested and detained for unpaid traffic citations is not subject to the same search as others, this will be well known to other detainees with jail experience. A hardened criminal or gang member can, in just a few minutes, approach the person and coerce him into hiding the fruits of a crime, a weapon, or some other contraband. As an expert in this case explained, "the interaction and mingling between misdemeanants and felons will only increase the amount of contraband in the facility if the jail can only conduct admission searches on felons." Exempting people arrested for minor offenses from a standard search protocol thus may put them at greater risk and result in more contraband being brought into the detention facility. This is a substantial reason not to mandate the exception petitioner seeks as a matter of constitutional law.

2

It also may be difficult, as a practical matter, to classify inmates by their current and prior offenses before the intake search. Jails can be even more dangerous than prisons because officials there know so little about the people they admit at the outset. An arrestee may be carrying a false ID or lie about his identity. The officers who conduct an initial search often do not have access to criminal history records. . . . Petitioner's rap sheet is an example. It did not reflect his previous arrest for possession of a deadly weapon. In the absence of reliable information it would be illogical to require officers to assume the arrestees in front of them do not pose a risk of smuggling something into the facility.

The laborious administration of prisons would become less effective, and likely less fair and evenhanded, were the practical problems inevitable from the rules suggested by petitioner to be imposed as a constitutional mandate. Even if they had accurate information about a detainee's current and prior arrests, officers, under petitioner's proposed regime, would encounter serious implementation difficulties. They would be required, in a few minutes, to determine whether any of the underlying offenses [was] serious enough to authorize the more invasive search protocol. Other possible classifications based on characteristics of individual detainees also might prove to be unworkable or even give rise to charges of discriminatory application. Most officers would not be well equipped to make any of these legal determinations during the pressures of the intake process. ("[T]he Court's approach will necessitate a case-by-case evaluation of the seriousness of particular crimes, a difficult task for which officers and courts are poorly equipped"). To avoid liability, officers might be inclined not to conduct a thorough search in any close case, thus creating unnecessary risk for the entire jail population. . . .

Individual jurisdictions can of course choose "to impose more restrictive safeguards through statutes limiting warrantless arrests for minor offenders."

. . . Officers who interact with those suspected of violating the law have an "essential interest in readily administrable rules. The officials in charge of the jails in this case urge the Court to reject any complicated constitutional scheme requiring them to conduct less thorough inspections of some detainees based on their behavior, suspected offense, criminal history, and other factors. They offer significant reasons why the Constitution must not prevent them from conducting the same search on any suspected offender who will be admitted to the general population in their facilities. The restrictions suggested by petitioner would limit the intrusion on the privacy of some detainees but at the risk of increased danger to everyone in the facility, including the less serious offenders themselves.

IV

This case does not require the Court to rule on the types of searches that would be reasonable in instances where, for example, a detainee will be held without assignment to the general jail population and without substantial contact with other detainees. . . . The accommodations provided in these situations may diminish the need to conduct some aspects of the searches at issue . . . The circumstances before the Court, however, do not present the opportunity to consider a narrow exception [that] might restrict whether an arrestee whose detention has not yet been reviewed by a magistrate or other judicial officer, and who can be held in available facilities removed from the general population, may be subjected to the types of searches at issue here.

Petitioner's *amici* raise concerns about instances of officers engaging in intentional humiliation and other abusive practices. ("[I]ntentional harassment of even the most hardened criminals cannot be tolerated by a civilized society"). There also may be legitimate concerns about the invasiveness of searches that involve the touching of detainees. These issues are not implicated on the facts of this case, however, and it is unnecessary to consider them here.

V

Even assuming all the facts in favor of petitioner, the search procedures at the Burlington County Detention Center and the Essex County Correctional Facility struck a reasonable balance between inmate privacy and the needs of the institutions. The Fourth and Fourteenth Amendments do not require adoption of the framework of rules petitioner proposes.

The judgment of the Court of Appeals for the Third Circuit is affirmed.

It is so ordered.

Dissenting Opinion

The petition for certiorari asks us to decide "[w]hether the Fourth Amendment permits a . . . suspicionless strip search of every individual arrested for any minor offense . . . ." This question is phrased more broadly than what is at issue. The case is limited to strip searches of those arrestees entering a jail's general population. And the kind of strip search in question involves more than undressing and taking a shower (even if guards monitor the shower area for threatened disorder). Rather, the searches here involve close observation of the private areas of a person's body and for that reason constitute a far more serious invasion of that person's privacy.

The visually invasive kind of strip search at issue here is not unique. A similar practice is well described in *Dodge* v. *County of Orange,* 282 F. Supp. 2d 41 (SONY 2003). In that New York case, the "strip search" (as described in a relevant prison manual) involved:

> "a visual inspection of the inmate's naked body. This should include the inmate opening his mouth and moving his tongue up and down and from side to side, removing any dentures, running his hands through his hair, allowing his ears to be visually examined, lifting his arms to expose his arm pits, lifting his feet to examine the sole, spreading and/ or lifting his testicles to expose the area behind them and bending over and/or spreading the cheeks of his buttocks to expose his anus. For females, the procedures are similar except females must in addition, squat to expose the vagina."

Because the *Dodge* court obtained considerable empirical information about the need for such a search in respect to minor offenders, and because the searches alleged in this case do not differ significantly, I shall use the succinct *Dodge* description as a template for the kind of strip search to which the Question Presented refers. . . .

In my view, such a search of an individual arrested for a minor offense that does not involve drugs or violence—say a traffic offense, a regulatory offense, an essentially civil matter, or any other such misdemeanor—is an "unreasonable searc[h]" forbidden by the Fourth Amendment, unless prison authorities have reasonable suspicion to believe that the individual possesses drugs or other contraband. And I dissent from the Court's contrary determination.

Breyer, Stephen. Supreme Court of the United States.

I

Those confined in prison retain basic constitutional rights. *Bell* v. *Wolfish*, 441 U. S. 520, 545 (1979). . . . The constitutional right at issue here is the Fourth Amendment right to be free of "unreasonable searches and seizures." And, as the Court notes, the applicable standard is the Fourth Amendment balancing inquiry announced regarding prison inmates in *Bell* v. *Wolfish, supra.* The Court said:

> "The test of reasonableness under the Fourth Amendment is not capable of precise definition or mechanical application. In each case it requires a balancing of the need for the particular search against the invasion of personal rights that the search entails. Courts must consider the scope of the particular intrusion, the manner in which it is conducted, the justification for initiating it, and the place in which it is conducted."

I have described in general terms, the place, scope and manner of "the particular intrusion." I now explain why I believe that the "invasion of personal rights" here is very serious and lacks need or justification—at least as to the category of minor offenders at issue.

II

A strip search that involves a stranger peering without consent at a naked individual, and in particular at the most private portions of that person's body, is a serious invasion of privacy. We have recently said, in respect to a schoolchild (and a less intrusive search), that the "meaning of such a search, and the degradation its subject may reasonably feel, place a search that intrusive in a category of its own demanding its own specific suspicions." The Courts of Appeals have more directly described the privacy interests at stake, writing, for example, that practices similar to those at issue here are "demeaning, dehumanizing, undignified, humiliating, terrifying, unpleasant, embarrassing, [and] repulsive, signifying degradation and submission." ("[A]ll courts" have recognized the "severe if not gross interference with a person's privacy" that accompany visual body cavity searches). Even when carried out in a respectful manner, and even absent any physical touching, such searches are inherently harmful, humiliating, and degrading. And the harm to privacy interests would seem particularly acute where the person searched may well have no expectation of being subject to such a search, say, because she had simply received a traffic ticket for failing to buckle a seatbelt, because he had not previously paid a civil fine, or because she had been arrested for a minor trespass.

In *Atwater* v. *Logo Vista*, 532 U. S. 318, 323–324 (2001), for example, police arrested a mother driving with her two children because their seat belts were not buckled. This Court held that the Constitution did not forbid an arrest for a minor seatbelt offense. But, in doing so, it pointed out that the woman was held for only an hour (before being taken to a magistrate and released on bond) and that the search—she had to remove her shoes, jewelry, and the contents of her pockets,—was not "'unusually harmful to [her] privacy or . . . physical interests.'" Would this Court have upheld the arrest had the magistrate not been immediately available, had the police housed her overnight in the jail, and had they subjected her to a search of the kind at issue here?

The petitioner, Albert W. Florence, states that his present arrest grew out of an (erroneous) report that he had failed to pay a minor civil fine previously assessed because he had hindered a prosecution (by fleeing police officers in his automobile). He alleges that he was held for six days in jail before being taken to a magistrate and that he was subjected to two strip searches of the kind in question.

Amicus briefs present other instances in which individuals arrested for minor offenses have been subjected to the humiliations of a visual strip search. They include a nun, a Sister of Divine Providence for 50 years, who was arrested for trespassing during an antiwar demonstration. They include women who were strip-searched during periods of lactation or menstruation. . . . They include victims of sexual violence. . . . They include individuals detained for such infractions as driving with a noisy muffler, driving with an inoperable headlight, failing to use a turn signal, or riding a bicycle without an audible bell. . . . They include persons who perhaps should never have been placed in the general jail population in the first place. . . .

I need not go on. I doubt that we seriously disagree about the nature of the strip search or about the serious affront to human dignity and to individual privacy that it presents. The basic question before us is whether such a search is nonetheless justified when an individual arrested for a minor offense is involuntarily placed in the general jail or prison population.

III

The majority, like the respondents, argues that strip searches are needed (1) to detect injuries or diseases, such as lice, that might spread in confinement, (2) to identify gang tattoos, which might reflect a need for special housing to avoid violence, and (3) to detect contraband, including drugs, guns, knives, and even pens or chewing gum, which might prove harmful or dangerous in prison. In evaluating this argument, I, like the majority, recognize: that managing a jail or prison is an "inordinately difficult undertaking," that prison regulations that interfere with important constitutional interests are generally valid as long as they are "reasonably related to legitimate penological interests," that finding injuries and preventing the spread of disease, minimizing the threat of gang violence, and detecting contraband are "legitimate penological interests," and that we normally defer to the expertise of jail and prison administrators in such matters.

Nonetheless, the "particular" invasion of interests must be "reasonably related" to the justifying "penological interest" and the need must not be "exaggerated." It is at this point that I must part company with the majority. I have found no convincing reason indicating that, in the absence of reasonable suspicion, involuntary strip searches of those arrested for minor offenses are necessary in order to further the penal interests mentioned. And there are strong reasons to believe they are not justified.

The lack of justification is fairly obvious with respect to the first two penological interests advanced. The searches already employed at Essex and Burlington include: (a) pat-frisking all inmates; (b) making inmates go through metal detectors (including the Body Orifice Screening System (BOSS) chair used at Essex County Correctional Facility that identifies metal hidden within the body); (c) making inmates shower and use particular delousing agents or bathing supplies; and (d) searching inmates' clothing. In addition, petitioner concedes that detainees could be lawfully subject to being viewed in their undergarments by jail officers or during showering (for security purposes). ("Showering in the presence of officers is not something that requires reasonable suspicion"). No one here has offered any reason, example, or empirical evidence suggesting the inadequacy of such practices for detecting injuries, diseases, or tattoos. In particular, there is no connection between the genital lift and the "squat and cough" that Florence was allegedly subjected to and health or gang concerns.

The lack of justification for such a strip search is less obvious but no less real in respect to the third interest, namely that of detecting contraband. The information demonstrating the lack of justification is of three kinds. First, there are empirically based conclusions reached in specific cases. The New York Federal District Court, to which I have referred, conducted a study of 23,000 persons admitted to the Orange County correctional facility between 1999 and 2003. These 23,000 persons underwent a strip search of the kind described. Of these 23,000 persons, the court wrote, "the County encountered three incidents of drugs recovered from an inmate's anal cavity and two incidents of drugs falling from an inmate's underwear during the course of a strip search." The court added that in four of these five instances there may have been "reasonable suspicion" to search, leaving only one instance in 23,000 in which the strip search policy "arguably" detected additional contraband. The study is imperfect, for search standards changed during the time it was conducted. But the large number of inmates, the small number of "incidents," and the District Court's own conclusions make the study probative though not conclusive.

Similarly, in *Shain* v. *Ellison*, 273 F. 3d 56, 60 (CA2 2001), the court received data produced by the county jail showing that authorities conducted body-cavity strip searches, similar to those at issue here, of 75,000 new inmates over a period of five years. In 16 instances the searches led to the discovery of contraband. The record further showed that 13 of these 16 pieces of contraband would have been detected in a patdown or a search of shoes and outer-clothing. In the three instances in which contraband was found on the detainee's body or in a body cavity, there was a drug or felony history that would have justified a strip search on individualized reasonable suspicion.

Second, there is the plethora of recommendations of professional bodies, such as correctional associations, that have studied and thoughtfully considered the matter. The American Correctional Association (ACA)—an association that informs our view of "what is obtainable and what is acceptable in corrections philosophy,"—has promulgated a standard that forbids suspicionless strip searches. And it has done so after consultation with the American Jail Association, National Sheriffs Association, National Institute of Corrections of the Department of Justice, and Federal Bureau of Prisons. A standard desk reference for general information about sound correctional practices advises against suspicionless strip searches.

Moreover, many correctional facilities apply a reasonable suspicion standard before strip searching inmates entering the general jail population, including the U. S. Marshals Service, the Immigration and Customs Service, and the Bureau of Indian Affairs. The Federal Bureau of Prisons (BOP) itself forbids suspicionless strip searches for minor offenders, though it houses separately (and does not admit to the general jail population) a person who does not consent to such a search.

Third, there is general experience in areas where the law has forbidden here-relevant suspicionless searches. Laws in at least 10 States prohibit suspicionless strip searches. . . .

At the same time at least seven Courts of Appeals have considered the question and have required reasonable suspicion that an arrestee is concealing weapons or contraband before a strip search of one arrested for a minor offense can take place. Respondents have not presented convincing grounds to believe that administration of these legal standards has increased the smuggling of contraband into prison.

Indeed, neither the majority's opinion nor the briefs set forth any clear example of an instance in which contraband was smuggled into the general jail population during intake that could not have been discovered if the jail was employing a reasonable suspicion standard. The majority does cite general examples from Atlantic County and Washington State where contraband has been recovered in correctional facilities from inmates arrested for driving under the influence and disorderly conduct. Similarly, the majority refers to information, provided by San Francisco jail authorities, stating that they have found handcuff keys, syringes, crack pipes, drugs, and knives during body-cavity searches, including during searches of minor offenders, including a man arrested for illegally lodging (drugs), and a woman arrested for prostitution and public nuisance ("bindles of crack cocaine"). And associated statistics indicate that the policy of conducting visual cavity searches of *all* those admitted to the general population in San Francisco may account for the discovery of contraband in approximately 15 instances per year.

But neither San Francisco nor the respondents tell us *whether reasonable suspicion was present or absent* in *any* of the 15 instances. Nor is there any showing by the majority that the few unclear examples of contraband recovered in Atlantic County, Washington State, or anywhere else could not have been discovered through a policy that required reasonable suspicion for strip searches. And without some such indication, I am left without an example of any instance in which contraband was found on an individual through an inspection of their private parts or body cavities which could not have been found under a policy requiring reasonable suspicion. Hence, at a minimum these examples, including San Francisco's statistics, do not provide a significant counterweight to those presented in *Dodge* and *Shain*.

Nor do I find the majority's lack of examples surprising. After all, those arrested for minor offenses are often stopped and arrested unexpectedly. And they consequently will have had little opportunity to hide things in their body cavities. Thus, the widespread advocacy by prison experts and the widespread application in many States and federal circuits of "reasonable suspicion" requirements indicates an ability to apply such standards in practice without unduly interfering with the legitimate penal interest in preventing the smuggling of contraband.

The majority is left with the word of prison officials in support of its contrary proposition. And though that word is important, it cannot be sufficient.

The majority also relies upon *Bell*, 441 U. S. 520, itself. In that case, the Court considered a prison policy requiring a strip search of *all* detainees after "contact visits" with unimprisoned visitors. The Court found that policy justified. Contrary to the majority's suggestion, that case does not provide precedent for the proposition that the word of prison officials (accompanied by a "single instance" of empirical example) is sufficient to support a strip search policy. The majority correctly points out that there was but "one instance" in which the policy had led to the discovery of an effort to smuggle contraband. But the Court understood that the prison had been open only four months. And the Court was also presented with other examples where inmates attempted to smuggle contraband during contact visits. . . .

The *Bell* Court had no occasion to focus upon those arrested for minor crimes, prior to a judicial officer's determination that they should be committed to prison. I share JUSTICE ALITO's intuition that the calculus may be different in such cases, given that "[m]ost of those arrested for minor offenses are not dangerous, and most are released from custody prior to or at the time of their initial appearance before a magistrate." As he notes, this case does not address, and "reserves judgment on," whether it is always reasonable "to strip search an arrestee before the arrestee's detention has been reviewed by a judicial officer." In my view, it is highly questionable that officials would be justified, for instance, in admitting to the dangerous world of the general jail population and subjecting to a strip search someone with no criminal background arrested for jaywalking or another similarly minor crime. Indeed, that consideration likely underlies why the Federal Government and many States segregate such individuals even when admitted to jail, and several jurisdictions provide that such individuals be released without detention in the ordinary case.

In an appropriate case, therefore, it remains open for the Court to consider whether it would be reasonable to admit an arrestee for a minor offense to the general jail population, and to subject her to the "humiliation of a strip search," prior to any review by a judicial officer.

. . .

For the reasons set forth, I cannot find justification for the strip search policy at issue here—a policy that would subject those arrested for minor offenses to serious invasions of their personal privacy. I consequently dissent.

POSTSCRIPT

Should It Be Lawful for the Police to Conduct Jailhouse Strip Searches of Persons Arrested for Minor Offenses?

This is a challenging issue. On one hand, as Associate Justice Kennedy asserts, police officers and correctional officials must be accorded some latitude to develop jailhouse policies that will ensure the safety of inmates and the staff. Moreover, the presence of contraband and illegal substances inside correctional facilities are a real and significant problem. As the Supreme Court observed in *Bell v. Wolfish*, the need to maintain order and security will clearly justify some intrusion on the individual Fourth Amendment rights of those individuals confined within these institutions. The question is: How far should this principle extend?

In *Florence, Bell v. Wolfish,* and many other Fourth Amendment cases over the last half-century, the Supreme Court has often utilized a "balancing test," to weigh the various interests at stake. Although a detailed treatment of this very interesting subject is beyond the scope of the present initiative, such a test most often balances an individual's privacy rights under the Fourth Amendment against a purported governmental interest in restricting those rights for some compelling reason.

For example, in the well-known case of *Michigan v. Sitz,* 496 U.S. 444 (1990), the Supreme Court, using "balancing" methodology, sanctioned the use of sobriety checkpoints designed to catch intoxicated drivers, even though there was no reasonable suspicion or probable cause to believe that persons stopped at those checkpoints were operating under the influence of alcohol. They reached this conclusion by balancing the relatively "minor" intrusion on individual privacy of motorists traveling on public highways who are stopped at these checkpoints with the compelling public/governmental interest in combatting drunken driving. Cast in this manner, is it surprising that the individual privacy interest was sacrificed to the public interest in stopping those driving while intoxicated (DWI) on our nation's highways?

Cases such as *Sitz,* however, have led some legal scholars to conclude that the Supreme Court's use of "balancing" analysis is designed to arrive at a preordained conclusion in Fourth Amendment cases: That individual privacy interests must give way to more important government interests in virtually all cases involving issues such as motor vehicle stops, jailhouse searches, searches for evidence of crimes or contraband (especially in illegal drug cases), and various other practices implicating privacy rights. In fact, some years ago, Professor

Silas Wasserstrom, an expert in Fourth Amendment law, who had conducted a detailed analysis of these issues wrote an article titled "The Incredible Shrinking Fourth Amendment," which implied that the Supreme Court's balancing methodology was simply a form of *conservative judicial activism* designed to narrow the scope of individual rights in Fourth Amendment cases.

Regardless of one's position on whether "balancing methodology" is a legitimate form of legal analysis, it is clear that the Supreme Court has narrowed the scope of individual Fourth Amendment rights in recent years. Is it a good thing that the Supreme Court in various Fourth Amendment cases has made it easier for law enforcement officers to apprehend those who have committed crimes? To paraphrase the renowned Supreme Court Justice Benjamin Cardozo, Should the criminal go free because the constable has blundered? Or, is it preferable to require police officers to comply with the constraints imposed by due process and individual privacy rights, even if it means that a factually guilty person must be set free? These are difficult questions.

The Supreme Court's decision in *Florence* signals that a majority of the present Supreme Court is likely to tilt the Fourth Amendment balancing test toward the side of governmental interests in the administration of justice, rather than vindicating individual privacy rights. Whether or not this is seen as a positive development is likely to depend on one's personal values and political orientation.

Justice Anthony Kennedy, writing the majority in *Florence*, clearly adopted a position that favored governmental interests in the administration of justice. Stated Justice Kennedy:

> Detecting contraband concealed by new detainees . . . is a most serious responsibility. Weapons, drugs, and alcohol all disrupt the safe operation of a jail. Correctional officers have had to confront arrestees concealing knives, scissors, razorblades, glass shards, and other prohibited items on their person, including in their body cavities.

Justice Breyer and the Dissenting Justices, in contrast, would have struck the Fourth Amendment balance in favor of the individual privacy interests of those who stand accused of noserious crimes. According to Justice Breyer:

> [S]uch a search of an individual arrested for a minor offense that does not involve drugs or violence—say a traffic offense, a regulatory offense, an essentially civil matter, or any other such misdemeanor—is an "unreasonable search" forbidden by the Fourth Amendment, unless prison authorities have reasonable suspicion to believe that the individual possesses drugs or other contraband.

After reading the case excerpts presented in this section, do you agree with Justice Kennedy's Majority opinion, or Justice Breyer and the Dissenting Justices? Whatever your opinion is in this case, additional reading in this area is readily available. See Kathleen M. Sullivan and Gerald Gunther, *Constitutional Law*, 15th ed. (Foundation Press, 2004); Laurence H. Tribe, *American*

Constitutional LawI, 2nd ed. (Foundation Press, 1988); Rolando V. del Carmen, *Criminal Procedure: Law and Practice,* 8th ed. (Academic Press, 2009); Thomas J. Hickey, *Criminal Procedure* (McGraw Hill, 2001); Yale A. Kamisar, Wayne R. LaFave, Jerold H. Israel, and Nancy J. King, *Modern Criminal Procedure,* 12th ed. (West Publishing, 2008). See also: Silas J. Wasserstrom, "The Incredible Shrinking Fourth Amendment,"*American Criminal Law Review.* (vol. 21, 1984); Akhil Reed Amar, "Fourth Amendment First Principles," *Harvard Law Review* (vol. 107, no. 4, 1994); Ivan Elandn "Bush's War and the State of Civil Liberties," *Mediterranean Quarterly* (vol. 14, no. 4, 2003); Jodie Michelle Lawston, "Women, the Criminal Justice System, and Incarceration: Processes of Power, Silence and Resistance," *NWSA Journal* (vol. 20, no. 2, 2008).

Contributors to This Volume

EDITOR

THOMAS J. HICKEY is the dean of the School of Liberal Arts and Sciences and a professor of government at the State University of New York (SUNY Cobleskill). He received his bachelor's degree from Providence College, MA and PhD degrees from Sam Houston State University. He also received a law degree from the University of Oregon, School of Law. His areas of expertise include criminology and law. He is the author of two books, *Criminal Procedure* (McGraw-Hill, Inc., 2001, 1998) and *Stand: Legal Issues* (Coursewise, 1999) as well as many journal articles. In addition, he is a licensed attorney who specializes in the areas of labor law and tort litigation. Professor Hickey may be reached by e-mail at hickeytj@cobleskill.edu.

AUTHORS

Anthony A. D'Amato is the Leighton Professor of Law at Northwestern University School of Law where he teaches courses in international law, international human rights, jurisprudence, and justice. He is the author of over 20 books and 110 articles.

KEVIN M. BEAVER is an assistant professor in the College of Criminology and Criminal Justice at Florida State University. He has published more than 50 articles and more than 15 book chapters and has authored seven books including *Biosocial Criminology: A Primer* (2009).

WILLIAM J. BRATTON, currently president of Carco Group, Inc., began his career as a police officer in Boston, Massachusetts, in 1970 and rose to superintendent of police by 1980. He was appointed Boston police commissioner in 1993 and police commissioner of New York City in 1994.

STEPHEN BREYER is an associate justice of the U.S. Supreme Court. He received an AB from Stanford University, a BA from Magdalen College, Oxford, and an LLB from Harvard Law School. He served as a law clerk to Justice Arthur Goldberg of the Supreme Court of the United States during the 1964 term. Prior to being appointed as a judge of the United States Court of Appeals for the First Circuit, he was a professor at Harvard Law School. From 1990 to 1994, he served as chief judge for the First Circuit Court of Appeals. President Clinton nominated him as an associate Justice of the Supreme Court in 1994.

PAUL BUTLER is an associate professor of law at the George Washington University Law School. He also served in the Justice Department's Public Integrity Section for several years.

Wayne H. Calabrese served as Consultant of The GEO Group, Inc. since January 3, 2011. Mr. Calabrese served as President of The GEO Group, Inc. (Formerly, Wackenhut Corrections Corp.) from January 1997 to December 31, 2010 and served as its Chief Operating Officer from January 1996 to December 31, 2010.

EMILE DURKHEIM (1858–1917) was a French sociologist and one of the founders and leading figures of modern sociology. He was a professor of philosophy at the University of Bordeaux.

BARRY C. FELD is the Centennial Professor of Law at the University of Minnesota Law School, where he has been teaching since 1972, and the author of *Readings in Juvenile Justice Administration* (Oxford University Press, 1999).

CHRIS L. GIBSON is an assistant professor in the Department of Criminology, Law, and Society at the University of Florida. He also serves on the editorial board of the *American Journal of Criminal Justice*.

JUDITH A. GREENE is a senior fellow of the Institute on Criminal Justice at the University of Minnesota Law School.

Rodney J. Henningsen is a Professor Emeritus in the department of Criminal Justice at Sam Houston State University.

GREGORY L. HERSHBERGER is a former regional director for the North Central Region of the Federal Bureau of Prisons. He is a former warden of ADX Florence, as well as other FBP institutions.

JANIS IAN is a songwriter, musician, and author. She began performing as a teenager in the mid-sixties and in 1975 she won a Grammy Award for her song "At Seventeen." She is an outspoken critic of the Recording Industry Association of America (RIAA).

W. WESLEY JOHNSON is currently associate dean in the College of Criminal Justice at Sam Houston State University and holds the rank of professor. He received his PhD in criminology from Florida State University. He has published extensively in the areas of corrections, crime and the media, and contemporary drug policy.

GEORGE L. KELLING is a professor in the School of Criminal Justice at Rutgers University and a professor emeritus in the College of Criminal Justice at Northeastern University. He is coauthor, with Catherine M. Coles, of *Fixing Broken Windows: Restoring Order in American Cities* (Free Press, 1996).

ANTHONY M. KENNEDY is an associate justice of the U.S. Supreme Court. He received his LLB from Harvard Law School in 1961 and worked for law firms in San Francisco and Sacramento, California, until he was nominated by President Gerald Ford to the U.S. Court of Appeals for the Ninth Circuit in 1975. He was nominated by President Ronald Reagan to the Supreme Court in 1988.

RANDALL KENNEDY is a professor of law at Harvard Law School and the author of *Race, Crime and the Law* (Vintage Books, 1998).

MICHAEL J. LYNCH is a professor in the Department of Criminology at the University of South Florida. He has published extensively in the area of environmental crime, race and justice, and criminological theory. His most recent book, coauthored with Ronald G. Burns, is titled *The Sourcebook on Environmental Crime* (LFB Publishers, 2004). Professor Lynch has also served as division chair for the Critical Criminology section of the American Society of Criminology.

Sean Maddan is the Chair of the Criminology Department at the University of Tampa. He has published extensively in the area of criminal justice system policy formulation and specializes in the advancement of criminological theory, refining both research methods and statistical applications and applying them to the responses of the criminal justice system to crime in society.

ELISA MASSIMINO is Washington director of Human Rights First. She is the organization's chief advocacy strategist, an expert on a range of international human rights issues, and a national authority on U.S. compliance with human rights law. She holds philosophy degrees from Trinity University (BA, 1982) and Johns Hophins (MA, 1984), and a JD from the University of Michigan School of Law. She has taught international human rights law at the University of Virginia School of Law and teaches refugee and asylum law at the George Washington University School of Law.

EUGENE H. METHVIN is the senior editor for *Reader's Digest*. He has reported on the American criminal justice system for more than 40 years.

J. MITCHELL MILLER is chair of the Department of Criminal Justice at the University of Texas at San Antonio. He has authored or coauthored several textbooks on criminal justice and also served as editor of two journals (*Journal of Crime and Justice; Journal of Criminal Justice Education*).

ANDREW A. MOHER received his BA from the University of Michigan (2002) and his JD from the Thomas Jefferson School of Law (2005). He is now a practicing attorney.

DANIEL PATRICK MOYNIHAN is a former senior U.S. senator (D) from New York (1976–2001). He has held academic appointments at Cornell University, Syracuse University, and Harvard University.

ETHAN A. NADELMANN is a highly respected critic of U.S. and international drug control policies. He received his BA, JD, and PhD degrees in political science from Harvard University as well as a masters degree in international relations from the London School of Economics. In 1994, with the support of George Soros, he founded the Lindesmith Center, a leading drug policy institute. He serves presently as director of the Lindesmith Center–Drug Policy Foundation. Nadelmann's works have been published in *Science*, *Rolling Stone, National Review, The Public Interest, Daedalus*, and various other publications.

ADRIAN RAINE is the Robert Grandford Wright Professor in the Department of Psychology, University of Southern California. He received his bachelor's degree in experimental psychology from Oxford University in 1977, and his DPhil in psychology from York University in England in 1982. After working as a prison psychologist, he became a university professor, and in 1999, he was named the Robert Grandford Wright Professor of Psychology at the University of Southern California. Dr. Raine's research has focused on the biosocial bases of violent behavior. He is a prolific writer, who has published numerous books and over 100 professional journal articles.

JEFFREY H. REIMAN is the William Fraser McDowell Professor of Philosophy at American University in Washington, DC, and the author of *Justice and Modern Moral Philosophy* (Yale University Press, 1992).

JOHN ROBERTS is the current chief justice of the U.S. Supreme Court. He received an AB from Harvard College in 1976 and a JD from Harvard Law School in 1979. He served as a law clerk for former U.S. Supreme Court chief justice William H. Rehnquist during the 1980 term, and in various other legal capacities until his appointment to the U.S. Court of Appeals for the District of Columbia Circuit in 2003. President George W. Bush nominated him as chief justice in 2005.

DIANA E. H. RUSSELL is a writer and activist engaged in research on sexual violence against women and girls. She has written numerous books and articles on rape, incest, and pornography, including *The Secret Trauma* (Basic Books, 1987), which won the C. Wright Mills award.

ANTONIN E. SCALIA is an associate justice of the U.S. Supreme Court. He taught law at the University of Virginia, the American Enterprise Institute, Georgetown University, and the University of Chicago before being nominated to the U.S. Court of Appeals by President Ronald Reagan in 1982. He served in that capacity until he was nominated by Reagan to the Supreme Court in 1986.

VINCENT SCHIRALDI is founder and executive director of the Center on Juvenile and Criminal Justice and director of the Justice Policy Institute, a think tank in San Francisco and Washington, DC, that analyzes crime policy.

DAVID SHICHOR is a professor in the Department of Criminal Justice at California State University, San Bernardino.

BARRY SHRUM is an entertainment attorney located on the famous Music Row in Nashville, Tennessee. He has many years of litigation experience in the areas of music law and publishing as well as copyright law and infringement.

JEFF SINDEN, managing editor of the *Human Rights Tribune*, is a staunch opponent of prison privatization and was formerly a research associate at Human Rights Internet.

LANCE K. STELL received his MA and PhD degrees from the University of Michigan. He is currently the Charles A. Dana Professor and director of Medical Humanities in the Department of Philosophy at Davidson College. He holds a faculty appointment in the Department of Internal Medicine at Carolinas Medical Center, a teaching hospital in Charlotte. Dr. Stell also serves as a consultant to hospitals and professional medical associations.

JOHN PAUL STEVENS is an associate justice of the U.S. Supreme Court. He worked in law firms in Chicago, Illinois, for 20 years before being nominated by President Richard Nixon to the U.S. Court of Appeals in 1970. He served in that capacity until he was nominated to the Supreme Court by President Gerald Ford in 1975.

Jared Taylor is the President of the New Century Foundation and is an author and commentator on race in U.S. politics. He is also the editor of *American Renaissance* magazine. His works include *Paved with Good Intentions: The Failure of Race Relations in Contemporary America* (Carol & Graf, 1992).

CLARENCE THOMAS is an associate justice of the U.S. Supreme Court. A former judge on the U.S. Court of Appeals for the District of Columbia, he was nominated by President George H. W. Bush to the Supreme Court in 1991. He received his JD from the Yale University School of Law in 1974.

KARI A. VANDERZYL is a graduate of the Northern Illinois University School of Law and is a licensed attorney in the State of Illinois.

ERNEST VAN DEN HAAG is a retired professor of jurisprudence and public policy. He has contributed more than 200 articles to magazines and sociology journals in the United States, England, France, and Italy, and he is the author of *Punishing Criminals: Concerning a Very Old and Painful Question* (Basic Books, 1978).

DAVID VON DREHLE is an art editor for *The Washington Post.* His publications include *Among the Lowest of the Dead* (Times Books, 1995).

JEFFERY T. WALKER is a professor in the Department of Criminal Justice at the University of Arkansas Little Rock.

JOHN P. WALTERS, the nation's "drug czar," became the director of the Office of National Drug Control Policy (ONDCP) in 2001. He controls all aspects of federal drug initiatives. Walters was formerly chief of staff for William Bennett, the former drug czar and conservative commentator, and has been responsible for the government's various anti-drug programs. He has also presided over a dramatic increase in federal spending for drug control programs. His drug control strategy has emphasized demand reduction and market disruption. Walters, who holds a BA from Michigan State University and an MA from the University of Toronto, has taught political science at Michigan State University and at Boston College.

GLAYDE WHITNEY, the late professor of psychology and neuroscience at Florida State University, taught behavior genetics and the history of science. He was also past-president of the Behavior Genetics Association.

LAWRENCE WRIGHT is a graduate of Tulane University and the American University in Cairo, where he taught English and received an MA in applied linguistics in 1969. He has worked for *Texas Monthly* and *Rolling Stone.* He has written several books, with his most recent being a history of al-Qaeda (Knopf, 2006). Wright is coauthor of *The Seige,* which starred Denzel Washington, Bruce Willis, and Annette Benning. He has won the New York University Olive Branch Award for international reporting as well as the Overseas Press Club's Ed Cunningham Award for best magazine reporting.

JASON ZIEDENBERG is a policy analyst with the Justice Policy Institute.

FRANKLIN E. ZIMRING is the William F. Simon Professor of Law and director of the Earl Warren Legal Institute at the University of California at Berkeley. His many publications include *American Youth Violence* (Oxford University Press, 2000).